ULTIMATE
RUSSIAN

BEGINNER–INTERMEDIATE

LIVING LANGUAGE®

ULTIMATE
RUSSIAN

BEGINNER–INTERMEDIATE

WRITTEN BY NANCY NOVAK
EDITED BY ANA STOJANOVIĆ, M.A.

ACKNOWLEDGMENTS

Thanks to the Living Language team: Tom Russell, Elizabeth Bennett, Christopher Warnasch, Zviezdana Verzich, Suzanne McQuade, Amelia Muqaddam, Denise De Gennaro, Linda Schmidt, John Whitman, Alison Skrabek, Helen Kilcullen, Heather Lanigan, Fabrizio La Rocca, Guido Caroti, and Sophie Chin. Special thanks to Sergei Mihailov, Galina Samoukova, Alla Akishina, Serafima Radivilova, Frank Miller, and Richard Schupbach for essential comments and suggestions. Огромное спасибо to Yehuda and Pamela Frumkin, and special thanks to Gary Cohen, Carol Novak, and the Portland RC community for help beyond measure.

In memory of Frederick Johnson, a wise colleague and friend, and Russian teacher par excellence.

CONTENTS

Contents

INTRODUCTION

Living Language® *Ultimate Russian* is a practical and enjoyable way to learn Russian. The complete course consists of this text and eight hours of recordings. You can, however, use the text on its own if you already know how to pronounce Russian.

With *Ultimate Russian,* you will speak Russian from the start. Each lesson begins with a dialogue about a common situation that you are likely to experience at home or abroad. You'll learn the most common and useful expressions for everyday conversation.

Key grammatical structures introduced in the dialogue are clearly explained in a separate section. The lessons build on one another. The material you've already studied is "recycled," or used again, in later lessons, as you learn new words, phrases, and grammatical forms. This method helps you increase your language skills gradually while reinforcing and perfecting the material learned previously. In addition, notes on relevant cultural topics will add to your understanding of Russian and Russian-speaking people.

COURSE MATERIALS

The Manual

Living Language® *Ultimate Russian* consists of forty lessons, eight review sections and four reading sections. The review sections appear after every five lessons, and the reading sections after every ten.

Read and study each lesson (урóк) before listening to the recordings. Or, try listening to the recorded dialogue first to see how much you understand without the help of reading the text or looking at the translations. This is an excellent way to test and practice comprehension.

Диалóг (Dialogue): Each lesson begins with a dialogue presenting a realistic situation in a Russian locale. The dialogue is followed by a translation in colloquial English. Note that while there are many regional dialects and accents, we will be using standard Russian grammar and vocabulary throughout the course.

Произношéние (Pronunciation): In lessons 1–10, you will learn the correct pronunciation of vowels, consonants, and consonant combinations, as well as intonation patterns. The Pronunciation chart in the beginning will get you started.

Грамма́тика и словоупотребле́ние (Grammar and Usage): This section explains the major grammatical points covered in the lesson. The heading of each topic corresponds to its listing in the Table of Contents.

Слова́рь (Vocabulary): In this section you can review the words and expressions from the dialogue and learn additional vocabulary. As the vocabulary is arranged in alphabetical order according to the Russian alphabet, you will find it very helpful to memorize the order of the Russian letters as shown in the Alphabet and Sounds Chart on page 5.

Ру́сская культу́ра (Russian Culture): These notes put the language and topic of each dialogue in their cultural context. Cultural awareness will enrich your understanding of Russian and your ability to communicate effectively.

Упражне́ния (Exercises): These exercises test your mastery of each lesson's essential grammatical structures and vocabulary. You can check your answers in the **Ключ к упражне́ниям** (Answer Key) section in the back of the book.

Прове́рка (Review): Review sections appear after every five lessons. Similar to the exercises in format, they integrate material from all the lessons you have studied up to that point, with particular emphasis on the five lessons just completed.

Текст для чте́ния (Reading): The four reading passages are not translated in order to give you an opportunity to practice your comprehension. However, the material covered in the previous lessons, along with the vocabulary notes that accompany each reading, will enable you to infer the meaning, just as you would when reading a newspaper abroad.

Приложе́ния (Appendixes): There are three appendixes: a Grammar Summary; Verb Charts; and a section on Letter Writing.

Слова́рь (Glossary): Be sure to make use of the two-way glossary in the back of the manual, where you can check the meaning and connotation of new words. As a general rule, however, try not to translate word for word from English to Russian or vice versa—especially with idioms.

Index: The manual ends with an Index of the grammar points discussed in the course.

The Appendix, Glossary, and Index make this manual an excellent resource for future reference and study.

RECORDINGS (SETS A & B)

This course provides you with eight hours of audio practice, divided into two sets. The first set is designed for use with the text, while the second set is designed for review and practice without the manual. By listening to and imitating the native speakers on the recordings, you'll improve your pronunciation and comprehension while learning new phrases and structures.

RECORDINGS FOR USE WITH THE MANUAL (SET A)

This set of recordings gives you four hours of audio practice, all in Russian, with translations in the manual.

All the dialogues, pronunciation sections, and vocabulary sections are featured on these recordings. The words and expressions that are recorded appear in ***bold-faced italic type*** in your manual.

First, you will hear native Russian speakers read the complete dialogue at normal conversational speed without interruption; then you'll have a chance to listen a second time and repeat each phrase in the pauses provided.

Next, listen carefully to learn the sounds from the pronunciation sections. By repeating after the native speakers, you will gradually master the sounds.

Finally, the vocabulary words from each lesson will also be modeled by the native speakers for you to repeat in the pauses provided.

After studying each lesson and practicing with Set A, you can go on to the second set of recordings (Set B), which you can use on the go— while driving, exercising, or even while doing housework.

RECORDINGS FOR USE ON THE GO (SET B)

The On the Go recordings give you four hours of audio practice in Russian and English. Because they are bilingual, Set B recordings may be used without the manual, anywhere it's convenient to learn. The forty lessons on Set B correspond to those in the text. A bilingual instructor leads you through the four sections of each lesson:

The first section presents the most important phrases from the original dialogue. You will first hear the abridged dialogue at normal conversational speed. You'll then hear it again, phrase by phrase, with English translations and pauses for you to repeat after the native Russian speakers.

In the second section you'll explore the lesson's most important grammatical structures. After a quick review of the rules, you can practice with illustrative phrases and sentences. You'll also have a chance to review and practice important words and phrases related to the topic at hand.

The exercises in the last section integrate what you've learned and help you generate sentences in Russian on your own. You'll take part in brief conversations, respond to questions, transform sentences, and occasionally translate from English into Russian and vice versa. After you respond, you'll hear the correct answer from a native speaker.

The interactive approach on this set of recordings will teach you to speak, understand, and think in Russian.

As the Russian saying goes, **Хороша́ верёвка дли́нная, а речь коро́ткая.** (A good rope is long; a good speech—short.) So, let's begin!

THE RUSSIAN ALPHABET
AND SOUNDS

PRINTED LETTER	SCRIPT LETTER	SOUND	SOUND IN ENGLISH WORD	EXAMPLE
А а	*Аа*	ah	*father*	а (*a*)
Б б	*Бб*	b	*boy*	ба́бушка (*BAbooshka*)
В в	*Вв*	v	*voice*	во́дка (*VODka*)
Г г	*Гг*	g	*go*	гром (*grom*)
Д д	*Дg*	d	*day*	да (*dah*)
Е е	*Ее*	yeh	*yet*	есть (*yest'*)
Ё ё	*Ёё*	yo	*yoke*	ёлка (*YOLka*)
Ж ж	*Жж*	zh	*measure*	жена́ (*zheNAH*)
З з	*Зз*	z	*zero*	зада́ча (*zaDAcha*)
И и	*Ии*	ee	*feel*	и (*ee*)
Й й	*Йй*	y	*yes, boy*	Ой! (*Oy!*) трамва́й (*tramVAI*)
К к	*Кк*	k	*kit*	ка́ша (*KAsha*)
Л л	*Лл*	l	*lamp*	ла́мпа (*LAMpa*)
М м	*Мм*	m	*map*	ма́ма (*MAma*)
Н н	*Нн*	n	*now*	нос (*nos*)
О о	*Оо*	oh	*bought*	он (*on*)
П п	*Пп*	p	*pan*	пол (*pol*)
Р р	*Рр*	rr (rolled)		рот (*rot*)
С с	*Сс*	s	*see*	стол (*stol*)
Т т	*Тт*	t	*top*	там (*tam*)
У у	*Уу*	oo	*boot*	уро́к (*ooROK*)
Ф ф	*Фф*	f	*fun*	фа́брика (*FAbrika*)
Х х	*Хх*	kh	*Bach*	хо́бби (*KHOBbee*)
Ц ц	*Цц*	ts	*cats*	центр (*tsentr*)
Ч ч	*Чч*	ch	*chair*	чай (*chai*)
Ш ш	*Шш*	sh	*she*	шко́ла (*SHKOla*)
Щ щ	*Щщ*	shch	*fresh cheese*	щи (*shchee*)
Ъ ъ	*ъ*	hard sign		отьéзд (*ot"EZD*)
Ы ы	*ыы*	iy	(no equivalent)	ты (*ty*) вы (*vy*)
Ь ь	*ь*	soft sign		мать (*mat'*) пальто́ (*pal'TO*)
Э э	*Ээ*	eh	*pet*	э́то (*Eto*)
Ю ю	*Юю*	yoo	*unite*	ю́бка (*YOOBka*) люблю́ (*lyooBLYOO*)
Я я	*Яя*	yah	*yacht*	я (*yah*)

Note: As you learn Russian, and especially as you go through the first chapter, it is *essential* that you pronounce everything out loud. This is the only way to learn the alphabet and be able to understand what you read: by hearing the correspondences between English and Russian and thus connecting the letters with the correct sounds.

INTONATION PATTERNS ИК 1–5

ИК 1 is for simple statements. It starts at mid-level then drops down on the stressed syllable of the stressed word.

Это *мо́*дем.   Очень прия́тно.

ИК 2 is for greetings and questions with question words. The stress is on the beginning of the sentence or greeting and falls from there.

*Что э́*то?   *Здра́вст*вуйте!

ИК 3 is for yes/no questions and requests. It starts at mid-level, rises in the middle, then returns to mid-level or falls.

Он *до́*ма?   Извини́те, пожа́луйста.

With questions with **есть** or **Вы не зна́ете** … ?, the rise in pitch is sharper and goes up much higher. Answers with **есть** also drop lower than usual.

Ты не *зна́*ешь, где по́чта?   У вас *есть* автосе́рвис? —Да, *есть*.

ИК 4 is for tag questions with **А**. It starts at mid-tone, and gradually rises on the last syllable if it is accented, or it dips slightly on the accented syllable then rises.

Я иду́ на по́чту. А *ты*?   Хорошо́. А у теб*я́*?   Я зна́ю. А *Са́*ша?

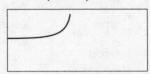

ИК 5 is for exclamations with **как** or **какой**. It begins on a rising note, and continues high until it drops down on the last accented syllable.

Кака́я маши́на!   Как хорошо́!

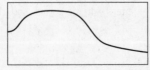

УРОК 1

ЗНАКОМСТВО. Getting acquainted.

А. ДИАЛОГ (Dialogue)

На вы́ставке америка́нской компью́терной те́хники.

АНЯ: Элеонора! Здра́вствуйте!

ЭЛЕОНОРА: До́брое у́тро, Аня! Как ва́ши дела́?

АНЯ: Хорошо́, спаси́бо. А как вы?

ЭЛЕОНОРА: То́же хорошо́. Пошли́?

АНЯ: Да.

У сте́нда на вы́ставке.

ПЕТЯ: Вот.

АНЯ: Что э́то?

ПЕТЯ: Брошю́ра.

АНЯ: Пе́тя! Приве́т! Что ты здесь де́лаешь?

ПЕТЯ: Рабо́таю. А ты?

АНЯ: Я ищу́ факс-мо́дем.

ЭЛЕОНОРА: О, вот хоро́ший но́тбук компью́тер!

АНЯ: Это ИБМ?

ПЕТЯ: Нет, э́то не ИБМ, э́то Макинто́ш.

АНЯ: Пе́тя, э́то Элеонора Джо́нсон. Элеонора—
программи́ст из Чика́го.

ПЕТЯ: Так мы колле́ги!

ЭЛЕОНОРА: Да.

ПЕТЯ: Очень прия́тно. Рома́нов, Пётр Ива́нович.

ЭЛЕОНОРА: Очень прия́тно.

АНЯ: Ну, нам порá идти.

ПЕТЯ: Ну лáдно, Аня, покá! До свидáния, Элеонора!

ЭЛЕОНОРА: До свидáния!

At an American computer show.

ANYA: Eleanor! Hello!

ELEANOR: Good morning, Anya! How are you?

ANYA: Fine, thank you. And you?

ELEANOR: Fine, also. Shall we go?

ANYA: Yes.

At a booth at the exhibit.

PETYA: Here you go.

ANYA: What's this?

PETYA: A brochure.

ANYA: Petya! Hi! What are you doing here?

PETYA: Working. And you?

ANYA: I'm looking for a modem.

ELEANOR: Oh, here's a good laptop!

ANYA: Is it an IBM?

PETYA: No, it's not an IBM; it's a Macintosh.

ANYA: Petya, this is Eleanor Johnson. Eleanor's a programmer from Chicago.

PETYA: So, we're colleagues!

ELEANOR: Yes.

PETYA: Nice to meet you. I'm Pyotr Ivanovich Romanov.

ELEANOR: Nice to meet you.

ANYA: Well, we must be going.

Пéрвый урóк

PETYA: OK, Anya. See you! Goodbye, Eleanor!

ELEANOR: Goodbye!

B. ПРОИЗНОШЕНИЕ (Pronunciation)

In Russian, every letter is generally pronounced, except for the soft sign ь (and the hard sign ъ, which occurs infrequently). Russian vowels frequently mutate, appear, or disappear, while the consonants change less often. This is helpful to keep in mind as you try to read the following words which are probably familiar to you.

Горбачёв	*Ельцин*	*да*	*нет*
до свида́ния	*борщ*	*Бори́с*	*Ната́ша*

1. THE CONSONANTS б, з, к, м, AND т

Cognates are words that sound alike and have similar meanings in two different languages. They are a good way of becoming familiar with the sounds of a new language. All of the cognates in this section begin with the consonants б, з, к, м, and т, which are easy letters to learn as they look and sound like the corresponding English letters: b, z, k, m, and t.

би́знес	*компа́кт-ди́ск*	*ма́ркетинг*	*такси́*
метро́	*те́ннис*	*банк*	*зо́на*

Cognates are also helpful when becoming familiar with the Cyrillic alphabet. Sounding out cognates is a very good way to associate Russian sounds with letters.

Бо́стон	*Калифо́рния*	*Ки́ев*	*Тайм*
Москва́	*Толсто́й*	*Михаи́л Бары́шников*	

2. УДАРЕНИЕ (STRESS)

In Russian there is usually only one stressed syllable per word. Since there are no simple rules governing stress, the best way to learn this important part of the language is to let your ear do it for you. To make it easier, throughout this manual, stress will be indicated with an accent mark (´) over the vowel that is the core of the stressed syllable. Words of only one syllable will not be marked, as that syllable is always stressed. Also, note that the letter ё is simply an accented e. Finally, words beginning with stressed, capitalized vowels will not be marked, so stress the first syllable of any unmarked, two-syllable capitalized words, e.g. **Аня**.

компью́тер   *такси́*   *код*   *тётя*

3. ИНТОНАЦИЯ (INTONATION)

Russian intonation is quite different from that of American English. Russians often comment that Americans speak in monotone voices without emotion, while Americans perceive regular Russian speech as complaining or argumentative. One reason for this difference is the greater vigor used when speaking Russian.

In order to learn to speak Russian fluently, Americans must open their mouths much wider than they are used to, and exaggerate the highs and lows of their pitch. It is often helpful, when first learning Russian, to speak with an exaggerated Russian accent. Though this may feel very overdone, it is often just the right amount of added expression.

These fluctuations in pitch are known as intonation. Just as each word has a stress pattern, each sentence has an intonation pattern. It is very important to use the appropriate intonation patterns to avoid misunderstandings and ensure that you have not asked a question when you meant to make a statement, or vice versa.

There are five intonation patterns in Russian, commonly referred to as **ИК** (*Ee Kah*) 1–5. **ИК** stands for **Интонацио́нная Констру́кция**, meaning "Intonation Structure." We will describe two of them here. **ИК** 1 is used for simple statements. The intonation starts at mid-level and drops at the stressed syllable of the main word.

Да.   **Н<u>ет</u>**.   *Вот <u>факс</u>.*   *Это <u>при́нтер</u>.*

ИК 2 is used with greetings and question words (who, what, where, when, why, and how). The stress is on the beginning of the sentence—the question word or greeting—and drops from there.

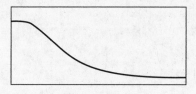

Здра́вствуйте!   *До́брый день!*   *Что э́то?*

C. ГРАММАТИКА И СЛОВОУПОТРЕБЛЕНИЕ
(Grammar and Usage)

1. THE ABSENCE OF "TO BE" IN THE PRESENT TENSE

The present tense forms of the verb "to be" are not used in Russian. Instead, they are understood from context. In sentences that equate a subject and its description, the understood verb is usually indicated in writing with a dash.

Элинор—программи́ст.
Eleanor's a programmer. (Lit. Eleanor a programmer.)

Компью́тер—ИБМ?
Is the computer an IBM? (Lit. The computer an IBM?)

With words such as **э́то** (this/that/it is) or **вот** (here is/there is), or if the subject is a pronoun, the dash is omitted.

Это компью́тер.
That's a computer.

Вот Ива́н.
Here's Ivan.

Вы тури́ст?
Are you a tourist?

2. ARTICLES

Unlike in English, there are no articles (a, an, the) in Russian. They are implied from context and must be added in accordingly when translating from Russian to English.

First Lesson   11

Вот мо́дем.

Here's [a] modem.

Это Интерне́т.

This is [the] Internet.

Вот при́нтер.

Here is [a/the] printer.

3. PERSONAL PRONOUNS

The personal pronouns in Russian are:

	SINGULAR	PLURAL	
I	я	мы	we
you (familiar)	ты	вы	you (plural, polite singular)
he	он		
she	она́	они́	they
it	оно́		

Note that **я** (I) is not capitalized unless it begins a sentence. The pronouns **он** (he) and **она́** (she) mean "it" when they refer to a thing.

Она́ программи́ст.

She is a programmer.

Где факс-мо́дем? —Вот он.

Where's the modem? —There it is.

Они́ здесь.

They are here.

Мы из Чика́го.

We're from Chicago.

Note that there are two forms of the pronoun "you" in Russian. **Ты** (informal "you") is used to address close friends, family members, long-time acquaintances, children, and pets. **Вы** (formal "you") is used to address adults you are meeting for the first time or don't know well and to show respect to an older person, a colleague, or a superior. When in doubt, it is better to use **вы** and err on the side of formality. A safe rule of thumb is never to use **ты** with adults unless someone addresses you that way first. With children and pets, however, always use **ты**. In the dialogue **Пе́тя** and **Аня** use **ты** with each other because they are long-time acquaintances.

Что ты здесь и́щешь?
What are you (informal) looking for here?

А ты?
And you (informal)?

However, **Пе́тя** addresses Eleanor with **вы** because he's just been introduced to her, and **Аня** uses **вы** with Eleanor because she does not know her well.

А как вы?
And how are you?

In addition, **вы** is the plural "you" and is always used when addressing two or more people, regardless of their status, age, or relationship to you.

Что вы и́щете? —Мы и́щем мо́дем.
What are you (plural) looking for? —We're looking for a modem.

4. SIMPLE NEGATION

The Russian equivalent of "not" is **не**. It immediately precedes the part of the sentence it is negating.

Это Ка́тя.
This is Katya.

Это не Ка́тя.
This is not Katya.

Макси́м—бизнесме́н.
Maksim is a businessman.

Макси́м не бизнесме́н.
Maksim is not a businessman.

Они́ из Чика́го.
They are from Chicago.

Они́ не из Чика́го.
They are not from Chicago.

5. ASKING AND ANSWERING QUESTIONS

English yes/no questions and Russian **да/нет** questions are similar. Answers with **да** often omit the subject and consist only of the word that was questioned, while answers with **нет** generally repeat the subject.

Элеонора—турист? —Да, турист./ Нет, она программист.
Is Eleanor a tourist? —Yes, she is./ No, she's a programmer.

Это Катя? —Да, Катя./ Нет, это Аня.
Is this Katya? —Yes, it is./ No, it's Anya.

Это принтер? —Да, принтер./ Нет, это скэннер.
Is this a printer? —Yes, it is./ No, it's a scanner.

Two useful question words in Russian are **кто** (who), and **что** (what). You can respond to both using **это** (this/that is). Use the **ИК** 2 intonation pattern when asking questions beginning with **кто** or **что**.

Кто это? —Это Элеонора Джонсон.
Who is this? —This is Eleanor Johnson.

Что это? —Это брошюра.
What is this? —It's a brochure.

Кто это? —Это я.
Who is it? —It's me.

D. СЛОВАРЬ (Vocabulary)

а	and; but
американский	American (adjective)
брошюра	brochure
в	in; at; to
Вот ...	Here is/are . . .
да	yes
До свидания!	Goodbye!
Доброе утро.	Good morning.
Добрый день.	Good afternoon.
здесь	here
Здравствуйте!	Hello! (polite)
из	from

ищу́; и́щешь	I am looking for; you (familiar) are looking for
Как ва́ши дела́?	How are you (polite)?
колле́га	colleague
компью́тер	computer
кто	who
ла́дно	O.K.
Нам пора́ идти́.	It's time for us to go.; We must be going.
не	not
нет	no
Ну, ...	Well, . . .
о́чень	very
Очень прия́тно.	Nice to meet you.
пожа́луйста	please; you're welcome
Пока́!	See you! (informal)
Приве́т!	Hi!
при́нтер	printer
программи́ст	programmer
спаси́бо	thank you
так	so
те́хника	technology
то́же	also
факс-мо́дем	modem
хорошо́	good; well
что	what
э́то	this; that; it is

РУССКАЯ КУЛЬТУРА
(Russian Culture)

Learning the "unspoken language" of a culture is often as important as learning to speak, as many a politician or diplomat has discovered to his or her dismay. Cultural faux-pas can be very amusing, but they can be downright insulting, as well.

Russians and Americans differ significantly in the amount of personal space required for comfort. Americans require more personal space. Russians are used to living in very close quarters and traveling on overcrowded public transportation. As a people, Russians tend to be warm, emotional, and passionate. Therefore, when talking with someone, even a business associate, Russians tend to stand very close. If their American friend or colleague steps back to re-establish his or her comfort level, the Russian will often step closer again. The

Russian may thus get the impression that the American is unfriendly or doesn't feel comfortable. Russians also tend to be more physical. Russian women frequently walk arm in arm, and Russian men often put their arms over each other's shoulders. Friends and family members of both sexes often kiss each other in the European way, a few times back and forth on either cheek, and usually with great enthusiasm.

УПРАЖНЕНИЯ (Exercises)

A. **Переведи́те слова́ на англи́йский. Произнеси́те с ру́сским акце́нтом.**
(Translate the words into English. Pronounce them out loud using a Russian accent.)

1. карате́
2. зигза́г
3. кооперати́в
4. Ташке́нт
5. Массачу́сетс

6. боксёр
7. банки́р
8. То́кио
9. Мари́на
10. Кана́да

B. **Переведи́те э́ти предложе́ния на англи́йский.** (Translate these sentences into English.)

1. Это Аня.
2. Вот факс-мо́дем.
3. Джим—тури́ст.
4. Мы из Сан-Франци́ско.
5. Это Макинто́ш?

C. **Как обрати́ться к э́тим лю́дям: на ты и́ли на вы?**
(How would you address these people: with ты or with вы?)

1. your Russian teacher
2. a five year old girl
3. a sales clerk
4. your good friend
5. your friend's grandmother
6. your grandmother

7. someone (your age) on the street
8. your new next-door neighbor
9. a fifteen year old boy
10. your dog

D. Подбери́те утверди́тельные предложе́ния к отрица́тельным предложе́ниям. (Match the sentences with their opposites.)

ОБРАЗЕЦ: 1. Она́ из Чика́го   g. Она́ <u>не</u> из Чика́го
             2. Это Сан-Франци́ско?   h. Нет, э́то Нью-Йо́рк.

1. Это при́нтер.   a. Он не здесь.
2. Я тури́ст.   b. Нет, э́то он.
3. Он здесь.   c. Я не тури́ст.
4. Это Ка́тя.   d. Нет, он бизнесме́н.
5. Он тури́ст.   e. Это не Ка́тя.
6. Это она́?   f. Нет, э́то скэ́ннер.
                         g. Она́ не из Чикаго.
                         h. Нет, э́то Нью-Йорк.

E. Поста́вьте вопро́сы по-ру́сски к предложе́ниям. (Ask the appropriate questions in Russian.)

ОБРАЗЕЦ: 1. Это мо́дем.—А что э́то?
             2. Это тури́ст.—А кто э́то?

1. Это Ка́тя. К
2. Это она́. К
3. Это при́нтер. Ч
4. Это программи́ст из Чика́го. К
5. Это факс. Ч

УРОК 2

В АЭРОПОРТУ. At the airport.

A. ДИАЛОГ (Dialogue)

На тамо́жне.

ТАМОЖЕННИК: *Ваш па́спорт.*

ВИКИ: *Вот, пожа́луйста.*

ТАМОЖЕННИК: *Вы америка́нка?*

ВИКИ: *Да.*

ТАМОЖЕННИК: *Где вы живёте в СНГ¹?*

ВИКИ: *В Москве́, у мои́х друзе́й.*

ТАМОЖЕННИК: *Поня́тно. Что у вас в чемода́не?*

ВИКИ: *Журна́лы, кни́ги, оде́жда. Ещё у меня́ фотоаппара́т и но́тбук компью́тер.*

ТАМОЖЕННИК: *Хорошо́. Это всё. Проходи́те, пожа́луйста.*

Ма́ша встреча́ет Ви́ки.

МАША: *С прие́здом, Ви́ки!*

ВИКИ: *Здра́вствуй, Ма́ша!*

МАША: *Ну, как ты?*

ВИКИ: *Хорошо́. А ты?*

МАША: *То́же ничего́.*

ВИКИ: *А где Ви́тя?*

МАША: *Он нас ждёт до́ма. Ну, пое́хали!*

ВИКИ: *Пое́хали!*

---

1. In English: the CIS, or the Commonwealth of Independent States, i.e., the former Soviet Union.

At customs.

CUSTOMS OFFICIAL: Your passport.

VICKI: Here it is.

CUSTOMS OFFICIAL: You're an American?

VICKI: Yes.

CUSTOMS OFFICIAL: Where are you staying in the CIS?

VICKI: In Moscow, with friends.

CUSTOMS OFFICIAL: I see. What's in the suitcase?

VICKI: Magazines, books, clothes. And I have a camera and a lap-top computer.

CUSTOMS OFFICIAL: O.K. That's all. Go ahead, please.

Masha greets Vicki.

MASHA: Welcome, Vicki!

VICKI: Hi, Masha!

MASHA: So, how are you?

VICKI: Fine. And you?

MASHA: Also O.K.

VICKI: And where's Vitya?

MASHA: He's waiting for us at home. So, let's go!

VICKI: Let's go!

B. ПРОИЗНОШЕНИЕ (Pronunciation)

1. THE STRESSED VOWELS o, a, AND ы

The Russian vowel sounds that cause English speakers the most difficulty are the accented vowels **o** and **a** (which look the same as "o" and "a" in English, but are pronounced very differently) and the accented vowel **ы**, which has no equivalent in English.[2] Stressed **a** is always pronounced like "a" in "father." The closest equivalent in English to stressed **o** is "o" in "coffee" when spoken with a strong New York accent.

вот	*о́чень*	*да*	*А́ня*	*ты*	*мы*

2. THE UNSTRESSED VOWELS o, a, я, AND e

As in English, unstressed vowels in Russian tend to be lessened in length and emphasis (e.g., compare the letters "o" and "a" in "photograph" and "photography"). This is called vowel reduction. In Russian, unstressed **a** and **o** are both pronounced "uh." However, if unstressed **o** appears just before the stressed syllable, it is pronounced "ah." Unstressed **я** and **e** are pronounced "i," as in the word "hit," unless they appear in the last syllable, in which case they are pronounced as if stressed.

в Москве́	*на тамо́жне*	*хорошо́*
Ма́ша	*смо́трят*	*Ви́тя*

3. THE VOWELS и, у, ю, AND э

The vowels **и** (*ee*), **у** (*oo*), **ю** (*yoo*) and **э** (*eh*) are pronounced the same whether stressed or unstressed.

из/и́ли	*ну/уро́к*	*юг/бюро́*	*э́то/эта́ж*

C. ГРАММАТИКА И СЛОВОУПОТРЕБЛЕНИЕ
(Grammar and Usage)

1. FORMAL VERSUS INFORMAL SPEECH

Once you've determined whether you should address someone as **вы** or **ты**, you must use the appropriate formal or informal forms for greeting, parting, or asking questions.

---

2. Try a sound halfway between *oo* and *ee*, but pronounced back in the throat.

	PLURAL OR FORMAL (WITH вы)	INFORMAL (WITH ты)
Hello! Hi!	Здра́вствуйте!	Здра́вствуй! Приве́т!
What is your name?	Как вас зову́т?	Как тебя́ зову́т?
How are you?	Как вы пожива́ете?	Как ты?
How are things?	Как ва́ши дела́?	Как дела́?
Where do you live?	Где вы живёте?	Где ты живёшь?
Do you have . . . ?	У вас есть ... ?	У тебя́ есть ... ?
Nice to meet you.	Очень прия́тно (познако́миться с ва́ми).	Очень прия́тно.
Goodbye! See you!	До свида́ния!	Пока́! Счастли́во!

2. THE "UMBRELLA" SPELLING RULE

This three-part rule will be invaluable to you when learning the grammatical endings of Russian words.

RULE 1. The vowels ы, ю, and я change to и, у, and а, respectively, after ж, к, г, х, ч, ш, or щ.

жить	ру́сский	ха́та	чу́до	ищу́	кни́га	Ма́ша
to live	Russian	hut	miracle	(I) look for	book	Masha

RULE 2. ю and я change to у and а respectively after ц.

отца́	отцу́	отцы́	цирк
father's	to the father	fathers	circus

RULE 3. Unstressed о changes to е after ж, ц, ч, ш, or щ.

с му́жем	яйцо́	с ключо́м	большо́е	пи́шущее
with the husband	egg	with a key	big	writing

This rule is especially useful to remember when forming noun plurals or adding endings of any kind.

3. THE GENDER OF NOUNS

Every noun in Russian has grammatical gender, regardless of whether it refers to a person, animal, object, or abstract concept. Russian nouns can be feminine, masculine, or neuter. Feminine nouns usually end in -а or -я.

Second Lesson

вы́ставка	деклара́ция	кни́га	ру́чка	тамо́жня
exhibit	declaration	book	pen	customs

Masculine nouns usually end in a consonant. This is commonly referred to as having a zero-ending.

факс-мо́дем	при́нтер	бизнесме́н	тури́ст	уро́к
fax-modem	printer	businessman	tourist	lesson

Some common words denoting a male person do not follow the usual pattern, in that they have feminine endings yet are still considered masculine nouns.

мужчи́на	дя́дя	де́душка	Ми́ша[3]
man	uncle	grandfather	Misha

Nouns ending in -ь can be either masculine or feminine and must be learned on a case-by-case basis. Nouns ending in a husher sound (ж, ш, щ, у) and -ь can be only feminine.

Masculine:	день	портфе́ль	Feminine:	вещь	тетра́дь
	day	briefcase		thing	notebook

Neuter nouns usually end in -o or -e. However, most foreign nouns are considered neuter, so this group also includes some cognates that end in -и or another vowel.

у́тро	ра́дио	упражне́ние	такси́	произноше́ние
morning	radio	exercise	taxi	pronunciation

Note that some grammatically masculine nouns can refer to people of either gender, especially with traditionally male professions.

до́ктор	профе́ссор	программи́ст	строи́тель	учёный
doctor	professor	programmer	construction worker	scientist

In some cases, there is a gender-specific form of a noun for a profession or nationality. The masculine forms of such nouns often end in -ец, -ен, or -ин. The feminine equivalent is formed by adding -ница, -ка, -шица, or -ша to the masculine form as a suffix. While the feminine forms **студентка** and **туристка** exist, **студе́нт** and **тури́ст** are also used often to refer to women.

---

3. And most other male diminutives.

продаве́ц/продавщи́ца	бизнесме́н/бизнесме́нка	учи́тель/учи́тельница
salesperson	businessman/businesswoman	teacher

актёр/актри́са	америка́нец/америка́нка	англича́нин/англича́нка
actor/actress	American	Englishman/Englishwoman

In the vocabulary, noun gender will only be marked when it is not obvious from the ending.

4. NOUN PLURALS

To form the plural of nouns, simply drop the final vowel, -ь, or -й (if there is one) from the singular form and add the appropriate plural ending. The regular plural ending for masculine and feminine nouns is -ы, and for neuter nouns it's -a. Note that neuter nouns frequently shift stress in the plural.

	SINGULAR	PLURAL
FEMININE	-a	-ы
	-я/-ь	-и
MASCULINE	consonant	-ы
	-ь/-й	-и
NEUTER	-o	-a
	-e	-я

Remember to apply Spelling Rule #1 with the plural ending -ы: after -г, -ж, -к, -х, -ч, -ш, or -щ, the plural ending will be -и.

	SINGULAR	PLURAL	
car	маши́на	маши́ны	cars
book	кни́га	кни́ги	books
aunt	тётя	тёти	aunts
night	ночь	но́чи	nights
magazine	журна́л	журна́лы	magazines
lesson	уро́к	уро́ки	lessons
museum	музе́й	музе́и	museums
driver	води́тель	води́тели	drivers
letter	письмо́	пи́сьма	letters

The best way to learn which plural endings go with which nouns is to let your ear learn them for you by practicing with the tapes.

5. "TO HAVE"

The concept of possession, or having something, is expressed quite differently in Russian. In order to say, "I have," Russian uses the structure **у + меня́ + есть**, which translates literally as "by me there is . . . "

	SINGULAR	PLURAL	
I have	у меня́ есть	у нас есть	we have
you (familiar) have	у тебя́ есть	у вас есть	you (plural or polite
he/it has	у него́ есть		singular) have
she/it has	у неё есть	у них есть	they have

У тебя́ есть фотоаппара́т? —Да, у меня́ есть фотоаппара́т.

Do you have a camera? —Yes, I have a camera.

У вас есть бага́ж? —Да, есть.

Do you have luggage? —Yes, I do.

"Do you have . . . ?" is **У + вас/тебя + есть ... ?** Есть is only used when the existence of something is being emphasized, not when a quality or location is in question. **У вас есть . . . ?** can also be translated as "Is there a . . . ?", as in **У вас есть туалет?** (Is there a restroom?).

D. СЛОВА́РЬ (Vocabulary)

америка́нец	American (male)
америка́нка	American (female)
аэропо́рт	airport
бага́ж	baggage, luggage
ви́за	visa
живёте; живёшь	you (plural/formal) live; you (fam.) live
Вы́леты	Departures (air)
Где ... ?	Where (is) . . . ?
деклара́ция	declaration
до́ма	at home
журна́л	magazine
Здра́вствуй!	Hi!
Как вас зову́т?	What is your name? (formal/plural)
Как тебя́ зову́т?	What is your name? (familiar)
Как вы поживае́те?	How are you? (formal/plural)
Как дела́?	How are things? (familiar)
кни́га	book

Второ́й уро́к

ме́сто	seat; place
Ничего́.	O.K./Fine. (response to **Как дела́**?); nothing
но́мер ре́йса	flight number
носи́льщик	porter
оде́жда	clothing
па́спорт	passport
Пое́хали!	Let's go! (only when driving)
Поня́тно.	I see.; Understood.
Прилёт (sg.)	Arrivals (air)
Проходи́те.	Go ahead.; Pass along.
Регистра́ция	Check-in
самолёт	airplane
СНГ	C.I.S. (Commonwealth of Independent States)
С прие́здом!	Welcome! (for people arriving from afar)
Спра́вки	Information
тамо́жня	customs
тамо́женник	customs official
теле́жка	baggage cart
У вас есть ... ?	Do you have . . . ? (formal/plural)
У тебя́ есть ... ?	Do you have . . . ? (familiar)
У меня́ есть ...	I have . . .
фотоаппара́т	camera
чемода́н	suitcase
Это всё.	That's all.

РУССКАЯ КУЛЬТУРА
(Russian Culture)

The most common way to travel to Russia is by air to Moscow's Sheremyetevo International Airport (**Шереме́тьево-2**), or St. Petersburg's Pulkovo International Airport (**Пу́лково-2**). **Шереме́тьево-2** is now a fairly typical international airport, though customs officials are known to be somewhat abrupt, and porters, luggage carts, and information tend to be a little harder to find than in some other countries that have had service economies for a longer time.

Upon entering Russia, you will need to fill out an immigration card and pass through immigration and customs. The only things that might cause a problem are Russian currency in a noticeable amount, or any item in amounts clearly in excess of what one person could need. You will probably have to fill out a declaration of all expensive items and any hard currency you are bringing in, which you need to turn in when you leave the country. Although it is no longer mandatory to keep records of every single transaction made in Russia, it is a good idea to bring receipts for any expensive items you're bringing in with you, and to keep the receipts of any expensive items you purchase while in Russia, in order to avoid paying excessive duties.

Due to the vastness of the country and the often poor or non-existent roads in many areas, air travel is still the most common means of transportation within Russia. **Аэрофло́т** (Aeroflot), the national airline, handles domestic air travel with regular flights all over the former Soviet Union. When planning travel within the former Soviet Union, it is a good idea to allow an entire day to get to your destination even if the flight is not that long. There are frequent delays, and getting on and off the flight often takes longer than you might expect. In general, when traveling in Russia, be sure to bring a good supply of patience with you! As the Russian saying goes, **Ти́ше е́дешь, да́льше бу́дешь.** (The more quietly you go, the farther you'll get.)

УПРАЖНЕ́НИЯ (Exercises)

A. **Подбери́те вопро́сы и́ли приве́тствия к сле́дующим ситуа́циям.**
   (Match the questions or greetings with the situations.)

1. Ask your boss how things are.
2. Ask your friend, **Петя**, where he lives.
3. Say hello to your friend's grandmother.
4. Ask your teacher how she is.
5. Ask a little girl her name.
6. Say hi to your friend.

a. Где ты живёшь?
b. Здра́вствуйте!
c. Как дела́?
d. Как вы пожива́ете?
e. Приве́т!
f. Как ва́ши дела́?
g. Как тебя́ зову́т?
h. До свида́ния!

B. **Напиши́те род ка́ждого сло́ва: мужско́го, же́нского или сре́днего.**
   (Write the gender for each word: masculine, feminine, or neuter.)

1. ви́за
2. бага́ж
3. у́тро
4. самолёт
5. ме́сто

6. тамо́жня
7. деклара́ция
8. аэропо́рт
9. оде́жда
10. чемода́н

C. Подберите множественное число. Помните правила орфографии и отнимайте окончания до того, как добавить новые окончания.
(Give the plurals. Remember the spelling rules, and remove endings before adding new ones.)

1. виза
2. компьютер
3. носильщик
4. актриса
5. место

6. дядя
7. строитель
8. упражнение
9. компания
10. продавщица

D. Подберите слова по-русски, подходящие по значению к английским.
(Match the Russian words with the English meanings.)

1. У тебя есть паспорт?
2. Да, есть.
3. У меня есть виза.
4. У вас есть место?
5. Да, у меня есть чемодан.

a. I have a visa.
b. Do you have a seat?
c. Yes, I have a suitcase.
d. Do you have a passport?
e. Yes, I do./Yes, there is.
f. Do you have a customs declaration?

УРОК 3

В ГОСТИНИЦЕ. At a hotel.

А. ДИАЛОГ (Dialogue)

Муж и жена́ у сто́йки регистра́ции.

ФРЭНК: *Здра́вствуйте! У меня́ зака́зан но́мер на имя Ха́рви.*

РЕГИСТРАТОР: *До́брый ве́чер. Отку́да вы?*

ДЖЕЙН: *Мы из США.*

РЕГИСТРАТОР: *Вы прие́хали как тури́сты?*

ФРЭНК: *Нет, я рабо́таю—мы в командиро́вке. А наш но́мер?*

РЕГИСТРАТОР: *Да, да. Всему́ своё вре́мя. Так ... когда́ вы уезжа́ете?*

ДЖЕЙН: *Че́рез неде́лю.*

РЕГИСТРАТОР: *Хорошо́. Да́йте, пожа́луйста, паспорта́ и ви́зы. Вы в но́мере 501.*

ДЖЕЙН: *Пожа́луйста. А когда́ за́втрак?*

РЕГИСТРАТОР: *В семь часо́в.*

ФРЭНК: *Тогда́ разбуди́те нас, пожа́луйста, в шесть часо́в.*

С дежу́рной по этажу́.

ДЖЕЙН: *Извини́те. Бу́дьте добры́, ключ от но́мера 501?*

ДЕЖУРНАЯ: *Да, пожа́луйста.*

ФРЭНК: *А у вас есть пра́чечная?*

ДЕЖУРНАЯ: *Коне́чно!*

ФРЭНК: *Отли́чно. Ну, спаси́бо.*

ДЕЖУРНАЯ: *Споко́йной но́чи!*

A husband and wife at a hotel reception desk.

FRANK: Hello. I have a reservation under the name of Harvey.

DESK CLERK: Good evening. Where are you from?

JANE: We're from the U.S.

DESK CLERK: Are you on vacation?

FRANK: No, I'm working—we're on a business trip. And our room?

DESK CLERK: Yes, yes. All in good time. So . . . when are you leaving?

JANE: In a week.

DESK CLERK: O.K. Please give me your passports and visas. You're in room No. 501.

JANE: Here you go. And when is breakfast?

DESK CLERK: At seven o'clock.

FRANK: Then please wake us at six.

With the woman on duty [on the fifth floor].

JANE: Excuse me. The key for Room No. 501, please.

WOMAN ON DUTY: Yes, here you go.

FRANK: And is there a laundry service?

WOMAN ON DUTY: Of course!

FRANK: Great. Well, thank you.

WOMAN ON DUTY: Good night!

B. ПРОИЗНОШЕНИЕ (Pronunciation)

1. INTONATION PATTERN ИК 3

The ИК 3 intonation pattern is used with yes/no questions. It starts at mid-level, rises on the stressed syllable of the word in question, then returns to mid-level or drops down.

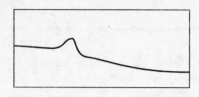

Вы в о́тпуске?

Are you on vacation?

Вы америка́нец?

Are you an American?

When used for questions with **есть**, the rise in pitch is much sharper, and goes up very high. The affirmative answer, as with other declarative sentences, is of course in **ИК** 1, but it drops lower than regular **ИК** 1 utterances.

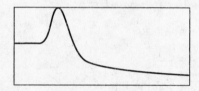

У вас есть пра́чечная? —Да, есть.

Is there a laundry service? —Yes, there is.

У тебя́ есть магнитофо́н? —Есть.

Do you have a tape-recorder? —Yes, I do.

ИК 3 is also used with requests.

Да́йте, пожа́луйста, паспорта́ и ви́зы.

Give me your passports and visas, please.

Разбуди́те меня́, пожа́луйста, в шесть часо́в.

Wake me at six, please.

2. SOFT AND HARD VOWELS

Russian vowels are either soft or hard.

	HARD	SOFT	
ah	а	я	*yah*
eh	э	е	*yeh*
oh	о	ё	*yo*
oo	у	ю	*yoo*
iy	ы	и	*ee*

All of the soft vowels, except for и, begin with a "y" sound. The hard vowels sound much like their soft counterparts without the initial "y" sound. The presence or lack of the "y" sound does not apply to ы/и, but they are still technically considered a hard/soft pair. The following examples illustrate the hard/soft contrast.

а/я　　　　*Ольга/Оля*　　　*э́то/его́*　　　　*эта́ж/есть*

Фрэнк/нет　　*карате́/мо́ре*　　*Ольга/ёлка*　　*уро́к/живёт*

уро́к/юри́ст　*всему́/неде́лю*　*вы/Ви́тя*　　　*до́брый/кни́ги*

3. THE CONSONANTS д, г, л, н, AND ф

Although they may look quite different, the Russian letters д, г, л, н, and ф sound very similar to the English letters d, g, l, n, and f, respectively.

диало́г　　　*гость*　　　*лифт*　　　　*неде́ля*　　　*Фрэнк*

The letter г is usually pronounced "g" (as in "girl"). However, when it appears at the end of a word between "о" and "о" or between "е" and "о", it is usually pronounced "v" (as in "visit") instead. An important exception to this rule is мно́го (many), in which the г is pronounced "g" even though it appears between о and о, e.g., *MNOga*.

его́　　　　　*ничего́*　　　*сего́дня*

C. ГРАММАТИКА И СЛОВОУПОТРЕБЛЕНИЕ
(Grammar and Usage)

1. INTRODUCTION TO VERB CONJUGATION

Verb conjugation is the process of changing a verb to reflect its subject and tense. In English there is little variation between the different forms of a single tense (e.g. I eat, you eat, he/she eats, we eat, they eat). In contrast, Russian verb conjugations are said to be "rich" because the forms change based on person and number.

Я рабо́таю.
I'm working.

Фрэнк рабо́тает.
Frank works.

Фрэнк и Джейн рабо́тают.
Frank and Jane are working.

Regular Russian verbs fall into one of two groups, known as Conjugation I and Conjugation II. The endings within each group are the same for all regular verbs. Also, each verb has a stem which remains the same in all the forms. Always learn the stem of a new verb first, then add the correct endings. The stem for the verb above is **рабо́та+**, and it is a regular Conjugation I verb.

2. THE PRESENT TENSE OF CONJUGATION I VERBS

Conjugation I verbs usually end in -**ать** or -**ять** in the infinitive [1] form. To form the present tense, simply drop the infinitive ending, -**ть** (or -**ти** or -**чь**), and replace it with the appropriate personal ending. The personal endings are -**ю,** -**ешь** and -**ет** for the singular forms, and -**ем**, -**ете** and -**ют** for the plural forms. For example, **де́лать ›› де́ла+ ю ›› де́лаю.** Following is a sample Conjugation I verb:

---

1. The infinitive is the unconjugated form of a verb, e.g., to be.

де́лать: to do

I do	я де́лаю	мы де́лаем	we do
you (familiar) do	ты де́лаешь	вы де́лаете	you (plural, or
			polite singular) do
he/she does	он/она́ де́лает	они́ де́лают	they do

stem: **де́ла+**

Что вы здесь де́лаете? —Я рабо́таю.

What are you doing here? —I'm working.

Что де́лает Аня? —Ничего́.

What is Anya doing? —Nothing.

Что они́ де́лают ве́чером?

What do they do in the evening?

The stress in a conjugated form is on the same syllable as in the infinitive for regular verbs. In **де́лать**, for example, it remains on the first syllable in every form. Other common Conjugation I verbs include: **понима́ть** (to understand), **знать** (to know), **за́втракать** (to eat breakfast), and **обе́дать** (to eat lunch).

Мы по́здно за́втракаем, и мы не обе́даем.

We eat breakfast late, and we don't eat lunch.

Вы понима́ете по-ру́сски? —Нет, я по-ру́сски не понима́ю.

Do you understand Russian? —No, I don't understand Russian.

Ты не зна́ешь? —Нет, я не зна́ю.

You don't know? —No, I don't.

Note that the Russian present tense can be translated into English in three ways:

Я рабо́таю.

I work./I am working./I do work.

3. CARDINAL NUMBERS 0–10

Here are the cardinal numbers from 0 to 10 in Russian.

0	*ноль*		4	*четы́ре*
1	*оди́н* (masculine)		5	*пять*
	одна́ (feminine)		6	*шесть*
	одно́ (neuter)		7	*семь*
2	*два* (masculine, neuter)		8	*во́семь*
	две (feminine)		9	*де́вять*
3	*три*		10	*де́сять*

Когда́ вы за́втракаете? —В во́семь часо́в.
When do you eat breakfast? —At eight o'clock.

У тебя́ есть четы́ре до́ллара?
Do you have four dollars?

Notice that the numbers 1 and 2 have different gender forms that must agree with the nouns to which they refer. When counting, however, only the masculine form of 2 is used, and 1 has the special form раз: раз, два, три ... (one, two, three . . .). оди́н can also be used to mean "alone," as in Мы здесь одни́ (we are alone here).

У вас есть две мину́ты?
Do you have two minutes?

Пожа́луйста, оди́н апельси́н и одно́ я́блоко.
One orange and one apple, please.

4. IRREGULAR NOUN PLURALS

There are a number of noun plurals that do not follow the regular plural formation rules but are nevertheless grouped by type. Which plurals fall in which group must simply be memorized.

a. Neuter nouns

Neuter nouns that end in -мя form their plural by dropping the -я, and adding -ена́. For example, и́мя (first name) >> имена́.

Дми́трий, Ната́ша и Кири́лл—ру́сские имена́.
Dmitrii, Natasha, and Kirill are Russian names.

Тре́тий уро́к

Хоро́шие бы́ли времена́!
Those were the good old days!

b. Masculine nouns

The plural of quite a few common masculine nouns ends in a stressed -**a**, or -**я**. For example, **дом** (house) >> **дома́** (houses), **учи́тель** (teacher) >> **учителя́** (teachers).

Да́йте, пожа́луйста, паспорта́ и ви́зы.
Give me your passports and visas, please.

Учителя́ обе́дают в рестора́не.
The teachers are eating lunch in the restaurant.

Most masculine nouns that end in -**ок, -ек**, or -**ец** lose the final vowel when the plural ending is added, e.g. **носо́к** (sock) >> **носки́** (socks). This is called a "fleeting vowel."

Мы америка́нцы.
We're Americans.

Чулки́ и носки́ вон там.
The socks and stockings are over there.

c. Foreign words

The singular and plural forms of many nouns of foreign origin are the same. These include:

кино́	кафе́	пальто́	бюро́	ра́дио	такси́
cinema	cafe	overcoat	office	radio	taxi

Где все такси́?
Where are all the taxis?

Вот пальто́.
Here are the overcoats.

The formation of noun plurals can be confusing, so give your ear a chance to learn them for you by practicing with the tape. When adding any kind of noun endings, remember to:

1. Remove the old ending before adding a new one.
2. Add a hard ending (beginning with **а, о, у, ы**), unless the stem ends in **-ь, -й**, or a soft vowel (**е, ё, и, ю, я**).
3. Always follow the umbrella spelling rules.

D. СЛОВАРЬ (Vocabulary)

администра́тор	manager
Бу́дьте добры́ ...	Would you be so kind . . .
в семь часо́в	at seven o'clock
в командиро́вке	on a business trip
в о́тпуске	on vacation (from work only)
Всему́ своё вре́мя.	All in good time.
вы уезжа́ете	you (plural/formal) are leaving
гости́ница	hotel
дежу́рная	woman on duty
де́лать (де́лаю, де́лаешь, де́лают)	to do
До́брый ве́чер.	Good evening.
жена́	wife
за́втрак	breakfast
за́втракать (за́втракаю, за́втракаешь, за́втракают)	to eat breakfast
зака́зан но́мер	reserved room
знать (зна́ю, зна́ешь, зна́ют)	to know
Извини́те, пожа́луйста ...	Excuse me, please . . .
ка́рточка го́стя	hotel pass (lit. visitor's card)
ключ	key
когда́	when
коне́чно	of course
лифт	elevator
муж	husband
на и́мя ...	under the name of . . .
обе́дать (обе́даю, обе́даешь, обе́дают)	to eat lunch
Отку́да вы?	Where are you from?
Отли́чно.	Great.; Excellent.
понима́ть (понима́ю, понима́ешь, понима́ют)	to understand
пра́чечная	laundry room
рабо́тать (рабо́таю, рабо́таешь, рабо́тают)	to work
Разбуди́те меня́, пожа́луйста, (в ...)	Please wake me (at . . .)

регистра́тор	hotel desk-clerk
рестора́н	restaurant
США	the U.S.A.
сто́йка регистра́ции	hotel reception desk
Споко́йной но́чи!	Good night!
тогда́	then; in that case; at that time
че́рез неде́лю	in a week
эта́ж	(numbered) floor

РУССКАЯ КУЛЬТУРА
(Russian Culture)

Although the range of accommodation choices is now greater than ever (including staying with friends, bed and breakfasts, homestays, and private hotels), most visitors to Russia stay in a fairly large hotel. When you check into a hotel, the clerk will ask for your passport and visa in order to register you with the local authorities. It will usually be returned to you either that day or the next.

In Russian hotels you will need to turn in your key every time you leave your room, either at the front desk or to the **дежу́рная** on your floor. You will then be given a **ка́рточка го́стя,** or hotel pass, to carry with you instead of the key. The **дежу́рная** is the woman "on duty," who is there to answer questions, hold keys, make sure everything is in order, and who often runs a **самова́р** (an urn of hot water with a little pot of concentrated tea on top) where glasses of tea can sometimes be had for the asking. Finally, the best and most modern hotels in Moscow or St. Petersburg now have direct international dialing, but it is more economical to purchase a credit card.

УПРАЖНЕНИЯ (Exercises)

A. Впиши́те пра́вильные оконча́ния глаго́лов. (Fill in the blanks with the correct endings of the verbs.)

1. Когда́ вы за́втрака_____ ? —Я за́втрака_____ в 9 часо́в.
2. Они́ не зна_____? —Нет, они́ не зна́_____ .
3. Джейн понима́_____ по-ру́сски? —Да, она́ по-ру́сски понима́_____ .

4. Когда́ мы обе́да_____ ? —Я не зна_____ .
5. Что он здесь де́ла_____ ? —Он тури́ст.

B. **Напиши́те сле́дующие ци́фры по-ру́сски. Не забу́дьте о ро́де.** (Write the following numbers in Russian. Don't forget about gender.)

ОБРАЗЕ́Ц: У тебя́ есть 1 мину́та?   1 = одна́

1. Вы в но́мере 10.   10 =
2. Да, у меня́ 1 брат.   1 =
3. Вот авто́бус № 9.   9 =
4. У тебя́ есть 6 до́лларов?   6 =
5. Там ско́лько до́лларов? о.   0 =

C. **Подбери́те мно́жественное число́. По́мните пра́вила орфогра́фии и отними́те ста́рые оконча́ния до того́, как доба́вить но́вые оконча́ния.** (Give the plurals. Remember the spelling rules, and remove old endings before adding new ones.)

1. па́спорт   6. кафе́
2. учи́тель   7. вре́мя
3. ключ   8. ви́за
4. носо́к   9. но́мер
5. америка́нец   10. пирожо́к

УРОК 4

ОБМЕН ДЕНЕГ. Exchanging money.

A. ДИАЛОГ (Dialogue)

В ба́нке «Москва».

ДЖЕЙСОН: *Кака́я о́чередь!*

ЖЕНЩИНА: *Да, мы ждём уже́ полчаса́, а они́ закрыва́ют на обе́д че́рез мину́ту.*

ДЖЕЙСОН: *Вы не зна́ете, где я могу́ обменя́ть де́ньги?*

ЖЕНЩИНА: *Или на по́чте, йли в ба́нке «Кооперати́в» вон там.*

В ба́нке «Кооперати́в».

ДЖЕЙСОН: *Поменя́йте, пожа́луйста, валю́ту.*

КАССИРША: *Ско́лько?*

ДЖЕЙСОН: *Два́дцать до́лларов.*

КАССИРША: *Подпиши́те чек, пожа́луйста.*

ДЖЕЙСОН: (подпи́сывает) *Так ...*

КАССИРША: *Ваш па́спорт, пожа́луйста ... и вот рубли́.*

ДЖЕЙСОН: *Спаси́бо. Вы не зна́ете, где я могу́ откры́ть че́ковый счёт?*

КАССИРША: *Поговори́те с заве́дующим о но́вом счёте.*

ДЖЕЙСОН: *А где он?*

КАССИРША: *В кабине́те напра́во.*

At the "Moscow" Bank.

JASON: What a line!

WOMAN: Yes, we've been waiting for half an hour already, and they close for lunch in a minute.

JASON: Would you happen to know where I could exchange money?

WOMAN: Either at the post office, or at the Cooperative Bank over there.

At the Cooperative Bank.

JASON: I'd like to exchange some money, please.

TELLER: How much?

JASON: Twenty dollars.

TELLER: Sign the check, please.

JASON: (signing) Okay . . .

TELLER: Your passport, please . . . and here are the rubles.

JASON: Thank you. Would you happen to know where I could open a checking account?

TELLER: You should speak with the manager about a new account.

JASON: And where is he?

TELLER: In the office on the right.

B. ПРОИЗНОШЕНИЕ (Pronunciation)

1. THE SOFT SIGN (ь)

The letter ь has no equivalent in English. It is silent, but has a big effect on pronunciation by softening the consonant that immediately precedes it. Compare:

мат; мать *дар; дверь* *пол; апре́ль*

Англия; де́ньги *рад; тетра́дь*

When forming plurals or otherwise changing word endings, it is important to remember that ь plus a hard vowel equals the corresponding soft vowel. Therefore, if you add a hard vowel ending to a word that ends with **ь**, the ending combines with **ь** and changes to its soft counterpart.

дверь + ы = **двéри**   учи́тель + а = **учителя́**

2. INTONATION OF «ВЫ НЕ ЗНАЕТЕ ... ?»

The intonation of questions beginning with **Вы не зна́ете** . . . ? (Would you happen to know?) is like that of questions with **есть**: they use the **ИК** 3 intonation pattern, but go up higher, with a sharper rise in pitch.

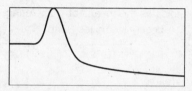

Вы не зна́ете, где меня́ют валю́ту?
Would you happen to know where I can change some money?

Вы не зна́ете, когда́ мы за́втракаем?
Would you happen to know when we have breakfast?

C. ГРАММАТИКА И СЛОВОУПОТРЕБЛЕНИЕ
(Grammar and Usage)

1. AN INTRODUCTION TO CASES

Cases are used to describe a noun's role in a sentence. In English, cases are apparent only in personal pronouns. Compare: "I"—nominative (the subject or agent of an action) and "me"—accusative (the object of an action or of a preposition). In general, however, English nouns do not change to reflect case, and word order is used to clarify the functions of words. Russian, on the other hand, has an explicit case system, i.e. nouns, and the adjectives that describe them, have different endings in each case. Changing the endings to reflect case is known as declension. There are six cases in Russian.

CASE	PRIMARY MEANING AND FUNCTION
Nominative	denotes the subject or agent of an action
Accusative	denotes the direct object of an action
Prepositional	used with prepositions, especially to show location (also called locative case)
Genitive	shows possession (of); used with amounts, numbers, and negative verbs
Dative	denotes the indirect object of an action
Instrumental	indicates the means of completing an action; generally implies "with"

Ве́ра чита́ет.

Vera (nominative) is reading.

Ве́ра чита́ет кни́гу.

Vera is reading the book (accusative).

Ве́ра чита́ет в библиоте́ке.

Vera is reading in the library (prepositional).

Я чита́ю кни́гу Ве́ры.

I'm reading Vera's (genitive) book. (Lit. the book of Vera)

Ве́ра чита́ет о Москве́.

Vera is reading about Moscow (prepositional).

Ве́ра мне даёт кни́гу.

Vera is giving the book to me (dative).

Ве́ра пи́шет письмо́ ру́чкой.

Vera is writing a letter with a pen (instrumental).

One result of the rich case system in Russian is that word order is relatively free. In English, for example, "Vera listens to Masha," is quite different from "Masha listens to Vera," but the only way to tell who is the subject and who the object is by word order. In Russian, however, the subject and object are identified by word endings. Thus, the following two sentences have the same meaning.

Ве́ра слу́шает Ма́шу.　　　　Ма́шу слу́шает Ве́ра.
Vera listens to Masha.　　　　Vera listens to Masha.

In both sentences, **Ве́ра** is the subject and **Ма́шу** (i.e. **Ма́ша** with the accusative case ending) is the object, even though the word order has changed.

Determining the proper case will generally be easy, i.e. directly based on a word's function. However, certain prepositions and verbs require certain cases. These special correspondences must simply be memorized. Keep in mind that using cases correctly takes a great deal of practice. As a beginning student of Russian, try to keep the cases in mind, but don't let fear of mistakes prevent you from speaking. You will generally be understood even if your case endings are incorrect.

2. THE NOMINATIVE CASE

The nominative case is used to answer the questions **Кто?** (Who?) and **Что?** (What?) and is applied to the subject of the sentence. You have already learned the nominative case of personal pronouns in **Уро́к** 1 (i.e. the subject pronouns), and you already know the nominative case endings for nouns (see **Уро́к** 2).

Они́ за́втракают, а я чита́ю.
They're eating breakfast, and I'm reading.

Кто гуля́ет? —Дже́йсон гуля́ет.
Who's taking a walk? —Jason (nominative) is taking a walk.

Что здесь? —Здесь банк.
What's here? —The bank (nominative) is here.

Что хорошо́? —Это хорошо́.
What's good? —This (nominative) is good.

Кто до́ктор? —Она́ до́ктор.
Who's a doctor? —She (nominative) is a doctor.

The nominative case is also used for nouns that are equated with the subject by the understood verb "to be." For example, in the phrase "he is a tourist," "tourist" is in the nominative case.

Он тури́ст.

He (nominative) is a tourist (nominative).

Это банк.

This (nominative) is a bank (nominative).

The nominative case is also known as the "base" case: the nominative case endings are the ones with which you start before changing the ending of a noun, pronoun, or adjective into another case. Nouns and adjectives are listed in the nominative case in any dictionary, and in this manual.

3. THE PREPOSITIONAL (LOCATIVE) CASE

The prepositional case gets its name from the fact that it is never used without a preposition. It most often follows the prepositions **в** (in/at) and **на** (on/at) to express location and answers the question **Где?** (Where?). For the prepositional case of most nouns, simply drop the final vowel, if there is one, and add **-е**. For example, по́чта >> по́чт + е » по́чте.

Где он? —В кабине́те напра́во.

Where is he? —In the office on the right.

Дже́йсон на по́чте? —Нет, он в ба́нке.

Is Jason at the post office? —No, he's at the bank.

В чемода́не кни́ги и оде́жда.

In the suitcase are books and clothing.

For feminine or neuter nouns ending in **-ия, -ие**, or **-ь** in the nominative, drop the final letter and replace it with **-и**. For masculine nouns ending in **-й** or **-ь**, replace the final letter with **-е**. Remember that foreign words generally do not decline, i.e. they do not change endings in the prepositional or any other case.

Пе́тя ещё в зда́нии? (nominative: зда́ние)

Is Petya still in the building?

Па́па уже́ на пе́нсии. (nominative: пе́нсия)

Papa is already retired (on pension).

Где Ма́ша, в кино́? —Нет, она́ в музе́е. (nominative: кино́, музе́й)
Where's Masha, at the movies? —No, she's at the museum.

Джейсон ждёт в о́череди. (nominative: о́чередь)
Jason's waiting in line.

Both the prepositions **в** and **на** can mean "at." **В** also means "in" and **на** also means "on." Russian usage of "in" and "at" is similar to English. You are always *in* (**в**) cities and countries. Often, however, there is no obvious reason for the use of **в** rather than **на**, and you must simply memorize the phrase. So, for example, it is **в ба́нке** (at a bank), **в о́череди** (in line), and **в гости́нице** (at a hotel), but **на по́чте** (at the post office), **на рабо́те** (at work), and **на столе́** (on the table).

Джейсон в о́тпуске в Москве́. Он меня́ет валю́ту в ба́нке.
Jason's on vacation in Moscow. He is exchanging money (currency) at the bank.

Де́ньги в се́йфе.
The money is in the safe.

In addition to expressing location, the prepositional case is used with verbs such as **говори́ть** (to speak), **ду́мать** (to think), **знать** (to know), **чита́ть** (to read), or **писа́ть** (to write), following the preposition **о** (about). It answers the questions **О ком?** (About whom?) and **О чём?** (About what?). Note that **о** becomes **об** before another vowel and **обо** before different forms of **Я** (I) and **всё** (everything).

Поговори́те с заве́дующим о счёте. (nominative: счёт)
You can speak with the manager about an account.

Она́ зна́ет о пробле́ме. (nominative: пробле́ма)
She knows about the problem.

4. THE PREPOSITIONAL CASE OF PERSONAL PRONOUNS

Pronouns in the prepositional case generally answer the question **О ком?** They must also be used after any preposition requiring the prepositional case.

	SINGULAR	PLURAL	
about me	обо мне́	о нас	about us
about you (familiar)	о тебе́	о вас	about you (plural, or polite singular)
about him/her	о нём/ней	о них	about them

Что ты ду́маешь о ней?
What do you think about her?

Что вы пи́шете о нас?
What are you writing about us?

Портфе́ль на столе́, и письмо́ в нём.
The briefcase is on the table, and the letter is in it.

With **мне, всё,** and **все о** becomes **обо,** and it remains unstressed.

Они́ зна́ют обо мне́/обо всём/обо всех.
They know about me/about everything/about everybody.

5. EITHER/OR

The concept of either/or is expressed by repeating the word **и́ли** (or) before the items in question. There is no separate word meaning "either."

Дже́йсон и́ли на по́чте, и́ли в ба́нке.
Jason's either at the post office or at the bank.

Ве́ра и́ли меня́ет валю́ту, и́ли открыва́ет счёт.
Vera's either exchanging money (currency) or opening an account.

Он и́ли тури́ст, и́ли бизнесме́н.
He's either a tourist or a businessman.

6. CARDINAL NUMBERS 11–20

Here are the Russian cardinal numbers from 11 to 25.

11	оди́ннадцать	13	трина́дцать
12	двена́дцать	14	четы́рнадцать

15	пятна́дцать	21	два́дцать оди́н
16	шестна́дцать	22	два́дцать два
17	семна́дцать	23	два́дцать три
18	восемна́дцать	24	два́дцать четы́ре
19	девятна́дцать	25	два́дцать пять
20	два́дцать		

Когда́ вы обе́даете? —В четы́рнадцать часо́в.

When do you eat lunch? —At 2 p.m. (lit. 14 o'clock) [1]

У тебя́ есть два́дцать пять до́лларов?

Do you have twenty-five dollars?

D. СЛОВА́РЬ (Vocabulary)

банк	bank
валю́та	foreign currency
вон там	over there
Вы не зна́ете ... ?	You wouldn't happen to know . . . ?
де́ньги	money
депози́тный счёт	savings account
ду́мать (ду́маю, ду́маешь, ду́мают)	to think
ещё	still; yet; else
ждать (жду, ждёшь, ждут)	to wait
же́нщина	woman
жить (живу́, живёшь, живу́т)	to live
заве́дующий	manager
закрыва́ть (закрыва́ю, закрыва́ешь, закрыва́ют)	to close
на обе́д	for lunch
и́ли	or
и́ли ... и́ли ...	either . . . or . . .
Кака́я о́чередь!	What a line!
кабине́т	office
касси́рша	teller (female)
меня́ть (меня́ю, меня́ешь, меня́ют)	to exchange (money)
могу́	I can; I am able to
на пе́нсии	retired (lit. on pension)
напра́во	on the right
но́вый	new

1. Russians use the twenty–four hour clock for anything that happens at an officially scheduled time. For more on telling time in Russian, see Уро́к 11 and Уро́к 12.

о (об, обо)	about
открыва́ть (открыва́ю, открыва́ешь, открыва́ют)	to open
откры́ть	to open
о́чередь	f. line; turn
Подпиши́те, пожа́луйста.	Please sign.
полчаса́	half-hour
Поменя́йте, пожа́луйста, валюту.	I'd like to exchange some money, please.
по́чта	post office
рабо́та	work
рубль	(m.) ruble
ско́лько	how much; how many
счёт	account; bill
уже́	already; yet
чек	check
чеко́вый счёт	checking account
че́рез мину́ту	in a minute
чита́ть (чита́ю, чита́ешь, чита́ют)	to read

РУССКАЯ КУЛЬТУРА
(Russian Culture)

In Russia money can be exchanged at central post offices, large banks, international hotels, airports, or any major points of entry. Banks are generally open in the morning and afternoon, but check when the lunch break is if you plan to change money at a certain time. You might be asked to produce your passport as well as your customs declaration when you change money. You may have opportunities to exchange money or goods on the black market, but be advised that this is illegal.

In an effort to stabilize the economy and stop inflation, hard currency is becoming less accepted by official, legitimate businesses. However, some transactions, both domestic and international, are still made with dollars or other hard currency instead of rubles. For this purpose, you should bring clean, crisp bills in smaller denominations. Many businesses accept a variety of credit cards but it's a good idea to check first. Foreigners may open checking and savings accounts in Russian banks.

УПРАЖНЕНИЯ (Exercises)

A. **Отве́тьте на вопро́сы.** (Answer the questions.)

1. Which case had you learned before this lesson? N
2. Which case is used for subjects? N
3. Which case can answer the question **Где?** N
4. In which case would "boy" be if this sentence were in Russian: "The girl hit the boy."? A
5. Which case is used only with prepositions? P
6. Do you conjugate or decline a verb? C

B. **Поста́вьте сло́во в ско́бках в предло́жный паде́ж.** (Put the word in parentheses into the prepositional case.)

1. Где Пе́тя? —Он на _собрании_. (собра́ние)
2. Са́ша в _Москве́_. (Москва́)
3. Портфе́ль на _столе_. (стол)
4. Они́ сейча́с в _парке_. (парк)
5. Где свитера́? —Они́ в _чемодане_. (чемода́н)
6. Где па́па? —Он в _Париже_. (Пари́ж)
7. Где вы живёте? —В _Цинцинате_. (Цинцинна́ти)
8. Где гости́ница? В _Петербурге_? (Санкт-Петербу́рг)
9. Где сейча́с ма́ма? —Она́ на _работе_. (рабо́та)
10. Что он де́лает в _институте_? (институ́т)

C. **Подбери́те пра́вильный предло́г: в и́ли на.** (Give the correct preposition: в or на.)

1. Бары́шников _в_ США.
2. Она́ не рабо́тает. Она́ уже́ _не_ пе́нсии.
3. Что он де́лает _на_ по́чте?
4. У вас есть счёт _в_ ба́нке «Коопера́тив»?
5. Где вы живёте _в_ СНГ? — _в_ гости́нице «Метроттол» _в_ Москве́.

D. **Поста́вьте сло́во в ско́бках в предло́жный паде́ж.** (Put the word in parentheses into the prepositional case.)

1. Что он ду́мает о _проблеме_ ? (пробле́ма)
2. Студе́нт мно́го зна́ет об _Антарктике_ . (Анта́рктика)
3. Я пишу́ письмо́ о _России_ . (Росси́я)
4. Кто зна́ет о _собрании_ ? (собра́ние)
5. Они́ ничего́ не зна́ют о _тебе_ . (ты)

УРОК 5

НА РАБОТЕ. At work.

А. ДИАЛОГ (Dialogue)

В учреждéнии в понедéльник ýтром.

НАЧАЛЬНИК: *Где все?*

СЕКРЕТАРША: *Дóброе ýтро, Дмѝтрий Сергéевич! Как вы поживáете?*

НАЧАЛЬНИК: *Так себé. А где Мáша?*

СЕКРЕТАРША: *Её ребёнок заболéл.*

НАЧАЛЬНИК: *Как всегдá. А Грѝша?*

СЕКРЕТАРША: *Он зáвтракает.*

НАЧАЛЬНИК: *Зáвтракает! А Михаѝл Семёнович?*

СЕКРЕТАРША: *Он опáздывает.*

НАЧАЛЬНИК: *Это не учреждéние, а цирк! А что дéлают Лáра и Оля?*

СЕКРЕТАРША: *Лáра дéлает фотокóпии, а Оля посылáет факс.*

НАЧАЛЬНИК: *Молодцы̀! А где Пéтя? Газéту читáет?*

СЕКРЕТАРША: *Нет, нет! Он ... он в туалéте.*

НАЧАЛЬНИК: *Это безобрáзие! Гáля, напишѝте объявлéние: Во втóрник собрáние. Явка обязáтельна.*

На собрáнии.

НАЧАЛЬНИК: *С этого момéнта, вы отдыхáете, читáете газéты, слýшаете рáдио—*

СЕКРЕТАРША: *Но мы ...*

НАЧАЛЬНИК: *... и зáвтракаете дóма; на рабóте вы рабóтаете!! Ясно?!*

СЕКРЕТАРША: *Ясно!*

At the office on Monday morning.

BOSS: Where is everyone?

SECRETARY: Good morning, Dmitri Sergeevich! How are you?

BOSS: So so. Well, where's Masha?

SECRETARY: Her child is sick.

BOSS: As always. And Grisha?

SECRETARY: He's having breakfast.

BOSS: He's having breakfast! And Mikhail Semyonovich?

SECRETARY: He's late.

BOSS: This isn't an office, it's a circus! And what are Lara and Olya doing?

SECRETARY: Lara's making photocopies, and Olya's sending a fax.

BOSS: Good for them! And where's Petya? Reading the paper?

SECRETARY: No, no! He's . . . he's in the restroom.

BOSS: This is outrageous behavior! Galya, post a notice: There's a meeting on Tuesday. Attendance is mandatory.

At the meeting.

BOSS: From now on, you relax, read the paper, listen to the radio—

SECRETARY: But we . . .

BOSS: . . . and eat breakfast at home; at work, you work!! Is that clear?

SECRETARY: Yes, it's clear!

B. ПРОИЗНОШЕНИЕ (Pronunciation)

1. CONSONANT DEVOICING

Like their English counterparts, Russian consonants tend to come in voiced/voiceless pairs. Voiced consonants cause vibration of the vocal cords, while voiceless consonants do not. For example, "d" and "t" are produced in the same place in the mouth; the only difference is that "d" is voiced and "t" is voiceless. The voiced/voiceless pairs in Russian are:[1]

VOICED	б	в	г	д	ж	з
VOICELESS	п	ф	к	т	ш	с

Compare:

бар/пар   *зуб/суп*   *гид/кит*

When a voiced and a voiceless consonant (or vice versa) come in immediate succession, the first changes its voicing to match the second. Thus, when a voiced consonant immediately precedes a voiceless consonant, the voiced consonant is pronounced like its voiceless counterpart.

все   *вто́рник*   *Пора́ идти́.*

When a voiceless consonant immediately precedes б, г, д, ж, or з, it is pronounced like its voiced counterpart. Note that prepositions, e.g. в (in, at) and с (with), are pronounced as part of the words that follow them.

отдыха́ете   *с друзья́ми*   *про́сьба*   *экза́мен*

Word-final voiced consonants are devoiced in pronunciation.

раз   *Рома́нов*   *хлеб*

2. CONSONANT CLUSTERS

Clusters of three or more consonants are often simplified into forms that are easier to pronounce—especially in very common words. This is achieved either by devoicing or by dropping one or more letters altogether.

Здра́вствуйте!   *Сча́стливо!*

Some consonant clusters are easy to say and so do not require simplification. These clusters are pronounced just as written:

С прие́здом!   *беспла́тно*

---

1. Of the remaining unpaired consonants, л, м, н, р are voiced, and х, ч, щ, ц are voiceless.

3. THE CONSONANTS в, п, р, AND с

The letters **в, п, р,** and **с** sound similar to the English letters v, p, r, and s, respectively.

ви́за   *па́спорт*   *рестора́н*   *Са́ша*

C. ГРАММАТИКА И СЛОВОУПОТРЕБЛЕНИЕ (Grammar and Usage)

1. THE VERBS ЖИТЬ (TO LIVE) AND ПИСАТЬ (TO WRITE)

These two common verbs have irregular stems. Their endings are regular, although they are formed with -**у**, rather than -**ю**, and in the case of **жить**, with -**ё** rather than -**е**. Notice the stress pattern of **писа́ть**[2]: the infinitive stress pattern (stress on the ending) is retained only in the **я** form: **пишу́**. In all the other forms the stress falls on the stem.

ЖИТЬ: TO LIVE

I live	я живу́	мы живём	we live
you (fam.) live	ты живёшь	вы живёте	you (pl., or pol.) live
he/she lives	он/она́ живёт	они́ живу́т	they live

stem: жив+

ПИСА́ТЬ: TO WRITE

I write	я пишу́	мы пи́шем	we write
you (fam.) write	ты пи́шешь	вы пи́шете	you (pl. or pol.) write
he/she writes	он/она́ пи́шет	они́ пи́шут	they write

stem: пиш+

Где ты живёшь? —Я живу́ в США.

Where do you live? —I live in the USA.

---

2. Be careful: if you stress this infinitive incorrectly, i.e. on the first syllable, it has a completely different and vulgar meaning. (The conjugated forms are not a problem, as it is conjugated differently.)

Что вы пи́шете? —Я пишу́ статьи́.

What are you writing? —I'm writing articles.

Оле́г и Ва́ня пи́шут письмо́.

Oleg and Vanya are writing a letter.

2. THE ACCUSATIVE CASE AND DIRECT OBJECTS

The accusative case is used for direct objects (the things acted on by the subject), the destination of a movement (e.g. I go home), and the passage of time. In this chapter, we will focus on the accusative used with direct objects. To form the accusative of a singular feminine noun, remove the final -а or -я and replace it with -у or -ю, respectively. For example, газе́та >> газе́ту, статья́ >> статью́.

Га́ля слу́шает му́зыку, а я чита́ю кни́гу.

Galya is listening to music, and I'm reading a book.

Пе́тя чита́ет статью́.

Petya is reading the article.

Ла́ра де́лает фотоко́пии, а Аня посыла́ет фа́ксы.

Lara is making photocopies, and Anya is sending faxes.

Га́ля пи́шет объявле́ние, а я пишу́ письмо́.

Galya's writing the notice, and I'm writing a letter.

Nouns that end in -ь have the same endings in the accusative as in the nominative.[3]

Кто де́лает за́пись?

Who's making the recording?

Note that some Russian verbs take a direct object, while their English counterparts take an indirect object (i.e., one preceded by a preposition). It is best to try to remember these on a case-by-case basis, as they arise.

Ма́ма слу́шает Аню.

Mama listens to Anya.

3. Except for masculine, animate (living) nouns ending in -ь, e.g. учи́тель. See Уро́к 7 for the accusative endings of those nouns.

3. THE DAYS OF THE WEEK

The days of the week are not capitalized in Russian, unless they begin a sentence. The week begins on Monday and ends on Sunday.

понеде́льник	Monday	Includes the word **неде́ля** (week) because it begins the week
вто́рник	Tuesday	From **второ́й** (second) because it's the second day
среда́	Wednesday	From **сре́дний** (middle) because it's the middle day of the work week
четве́рг	Thursday	From **четвёртый** (fourth) because it's the fourth day
пя́тница	Friday	From **пя́тый** (fifth) because it's the fifth day
суббо́та	Saturday	Sabbath
воскресе́нье	Sunday	Resurrection

When speaking about the current day, use the nominative alone. To express "on Monday," "on Tuesday," et cetera, use **в** plus the day in the accusative case. Notice that **в** becomes **во** when it precedes **вто́рник**.

Сла́ва Бо́гу сего́дня—пя́тница!
Thank God today's Friday!

В учрежде́нии в понеде́льник у́тром.
At the office on Monday morning.

Во вто́рник собра́ние.
There's a meeting on Tuesday.

4. THE CONJUNCTION а

The conjunction **а** means "and" or "but," depending on how it is used in the sentence. It compares or mildly contrasts the information following it with the information preceding it.

When used with **не** (not) it means "but."

Это не учрежде́ние, а цирк!
This isn't an office—it's a circus! (This is not an office, but a circus!)

Гáля пи́шет не объявлéние, а письмó.

Galya's writing a letter, not a notice.

Это не Кáтя, а Аня.

This isn't Katya—it's Anya.

When used to introduce or ask about a contrasting situation, it means "and."

А э́то что?

And what is this?

Я живу́ в Калифóрнии. А вы?

I live in California. And you?

5. PATRONYMICS AND LAST NAMES

Middle names and words such as "Mrs.," "Mr.," and "Miss" do not exist in Russian, and last names are used less frequently. Instead, the patronymic (**óтчество**), derived from the father's first name, is used for formal address and to establish lineage. For example, if your father is **Михáил,** your patronymic would be **Михáйлович**, if you are male, or **Михáйловна**, if you are female. The suffix **-ович** means "son of," and **-овна** means "daughter of." Every Russian has a patronymic as their official second name. From their 20s on, they will be addressed in formal situations by their full **и́мя** (first name) and their **óтчество**. You should use the **и́мя-óтчество** with anyone you would address as **вы**. With someone you would address as **ты** you may use just their **и́мя**.

Дóброе у́тро, Дми́трий Сергéевич.[4] Как вы поживáете?

Good morning, Dmitriy Sergeevich. How are you?

А где Михаи́л Семёнович?

And where's Mikhail Semyonovich?

Вот Натáлья Петрóвна. Онá учи́тельница.

Here's Natalya Petrovna. She's a teacher.

---

4. **-ович** is spelled **-евич** (**-евна,** for a female) if the father's first name ends in **-й,** such as **Сергéй.**

The last name (**фами́лия**) also differs according to sex; a male **фами́лия** ends in a consonant, e.g. **Рома́нов**, but the female version ends in -**а,** e.g. **Рома́нова**. The plural form ends in -**ы**, e.g. **Рома́новы**. Women often keep their maiden names when they marry.

D. СЛОВА́РЬ (Vocabulary)

безобра́зие	outrageous behavior
все	all; everyone
газе́та	newspaper
гуля́ть (гуля́ю, гуля́ешь, гуля́ют)	to walk, to go out
журна́л	magazine
и́мя	first name
как всегда́	as always
Молодцы́!	Good for you! (plural)
на за́втрак	for breakfast
нача́льник	boss
обе́д	lunch
объявле́ние	announcement, notice
опа́здывать (опа́здываю, опа́здываешь, опа́здывают)	to be late
отдыха́ть (отдыха́ю, отдыха́ешь, отдыха́ют)	to relax, to rest
о́тчество	patronymic
печа́тать (на маши́нке)	to type
писа́ть (пишу́, пи́шешь, пи́шут)	to write
письмо́	letter
посыла́ть (посыла́ю, посыла́ешь, посыла́ют)	to send
с э́того моме́нта	from now on
секрета́рша	secretary (female)
слу́жащий	employee
слу́шать (слу́шаю, слу́шаешь, слу́шают)	to listen to
собра́ние	meeting
статья́	article
Так себе́.	So so. (answers the question **Как дела́**?)
тетра́дь	f. notebook
у́жин	dinner

у́жинать (у́жинаю, у́жинаешь, у́жинают)	to eat dinner
у́тром	in the morning
учрежде́ние	office
фотоко́пия	photocopy
Я́вка обяза́тельна.	Attendance is mandatory.
я́сно	clear

РУССКАЯ КУЛЬТУРА
(Russian Culture)

The dialogue in this chapter touches on what still is a pressing problem in Russian society: the lack of motivation to work. This situation is largely a holdover from Soviet times, summed up by the saying that "they [the government] pretend to pay us and we pretend to work."

With the legacy of work as something to endure rather than a way to grow and better oneself, one of the first and most difficult tasks of the new Russian entrepreneurs after glasnost was to change people's attitudes towards work. They needed to find motivated, independent, creative employees, or else find a way to get the current employees involved and interested in the new system of free enterprise. Not surprisingly, such complete changes in thinking come about slowly.

Russia has been caught between the conflicting pulls of its Eastern roots and Westernization for a few centuries. Therefore, even if Russia develops a more Western social and economic system, business as usual as we know it in the United States will probably never exist there. Instead of our emphasis on punctuality, order, and efficient, businesslike relationships, Russian business will probably always be somewhat more relaxed and less orderly, and with more emphasis on personal relationships.

УПРАЖНЕНИЯ (Exercises)

A. Подбери́те слова́ по-ру́сски, подходя́щие к слова́м по-англи́йски. (Match the Russian words with the English words.)

1. отдыха́ть   a. (we) are listening
2. опа́здывают   b. живёте
3. you (plural/formal) live   c. (they) live

4. (we) are reading *f*
5. слу́шать ра́дио *g*
6. слу́шаем *a*
7. писа́ть *k*
8. пишу́ письмо́ *d*
9. гуля́ешь *j*
10. (she) is eating dinner *h*

d. (I) am writing a letter
e. to rest
f. чита́ем
g. to listen to the radio
h. у́жинает
i. (they) are late
j. (you familiar) stroll/walk
k. to write

B. **Поста́вьте сло́во в ско́бках в вини́тельный паде́ж.** (Put the word in parentheses into the accusative case.)

1. Пе́тя зна́ет __Машу__ . (Ма́ша)
2. Я чита́ю __тетрадть__ . (тетра́дь)
3. Вы пи́шете __статью__ . (статья́)
4. Де́ти слу́шают __музыку__ . (му́зыка)
5. Я пишу́ __письмо__ . (пи́сьма)
6. Да́йте, пожа́луйста, __декларацию__ . (деклара́ция)
7. Па́па слу́шает __джаз__ . (джаз)
8. Подпиши́те __чеки__ , пожа́луйста. (че́ки)
9. Ба́бушка слу́шает __радио__ . (ра́дио)
10. Поменя́йте, пожа́луйста, __валюту__ . (валю́та)

C. **Отве́тьте на вопро́сы по-ру́сски.** (Answer the questions in Russian.)

1. Which day comes from the number four? четверг
2. понедельник is the first day of the week.
3. Translate into Russian: Today is Saturday. Сегодня суббота
4. Translate into Russian: on Wednesday. В среду
5. Complete this sentence: Сла́ва Бо́гу сего́дня — __пятница__!

D. **Переведи́те на англи́йский.** (Translate into English.)

1. Я бизнесме́н. А вы?
2. Это не Элинор, а Аня.
3. Это компью́тер. —А что э́то?
4. Да, э́то Пу́тин. А э́то кто?
5. Это не Кли́нтон, а Буш.

E. **Отве́тьте на вопро́сы.** (Answer the questions.)

1. What would **Ива́н**'s daughter **Ольга**'s **и́мя-о́тчество** be?
2. What is **Дми́трий Алексе́евич**'s father's first name?
3. **Ни́на**'s father's name is **Никола́й Я́ковлевич Петро́в**. What is her patronymic?
4. What is **Ни́на**'s full name, including her last name?
5. **Макси́м**'s father's full name is **Алекса́ндр Льво́вич Ники́тин**. What is his full name?

ПЕРВАЯ ПРОВЕРКА (First Review)

A. Обведи́те кружка́ми, и́ли горизонта́льно и́ли вертика́льно, э́ти слова́ по-ру́сски. (Circle these words in Russian, either horizontally or vertically.)

1. at home
2. what
3. there
4. when
5. where
6. over there
7. who
8. here
9. in the morning
10. how

о	п	у	ц	с	я	х	т	э	в
ч	я	м	ё	г	з	ы	ч	т	о
л	к	й	к	а	к	ж	д	ь	н
ж	в	о	т	б	о	з	ё	ш	т
у	т	р	о	м	г	д	о	м	а
п	а	з	и	г	д	е	и	х	м
ъ	м	ю	ч	л	а	с	щ	а	в
р	с	ф	я	ю	н	ь	о	п	у

B. Поста́вьте слова́ в ну́жную фо́рму (измени́те оконча́ния, е́сли ну́жно).
(Put into the correct form; change endings if necessary.)

1. Они́ всегда́ опа́здыва_ют_ .
2. Ма́ма сего́дня отдыха́_ет_ .
3. Где он рабо́та_ет_ ? —Он на пе́нсии.
4. Она́ ничего́ не зна́_ет_ .
5. Вы ра́но ужина́_ете_ ? —Да, мы ра́но ужина́_ем_ .
6. Вы гуля́_ете_ ? —Да, мы гуля́_ем_ .
7. Она́ чита́_ет_ _журнал_ . (журна́л)
8. Я ищ_у_ _тетрадь_ . (тетра́дь)
9. Де́ти слу́ша_ют_ _музыку_ . (му́зыка)
10. Поменя́йте, пожа́луйста, _валюту_ . (валю́та)
11. Подпиши́те _чеки_ , пожа́луйста. (че́ки)
12. Студе́нт мно́го зна́ет об _Антарктике_ . (Анта́рктика)
13. Да́йте, пожа́луйста, _декларацию_ . (деклара́ция)
14. Я пишу́ _статью_ о _России_ . (статья́, Росси́я)
15. Где Пе́тя? —Он на _собрании_ . (собра́ние)
16. Где вы живёте? —В _Гонолулу_ . (Гонолу́лу)
17. Где гости́ница? В _Петербурге_ . (Санкт-Петербу́рг)
18. Где сейча́с ма́ма? —Она́ на _работе_ . (рабо́та)
19. Заве́дующий зна́ет о _счёте_ . (счёт)
20. Па́па слу́шает _Аню_ . (Аня)

C. **Переведи́те на англи́йский.** (Translate into English.)

1. Ольга гуля́ет в па́рке.
2. Да, у меня́ есть магнитофо́н.
3. У тебя́ есть маши́на?
4. Где сигаре́ты?
5. Кто живёт в кварти́ре № 13?
6. Это не учрежде́ние, а цирк!
7. Я чита́ю журна́л «Тайм.»
8. Ми́ша сейча́с обе́дает.
9. Сла́ва Бо́гу сего́дня—пя́тница!
10. Письмо́ на столе́.
11. У вас есть рестора́н?
12. Споко́йной но́чи!
13. Где банк?
14. Они́ рабо́тают в институ́те?
15. Она́ в командиро́вке в Пари́же.

D. **Переведи́те на ру́сский.** (Translate into Russian.)

1. Americans read magazines and newspapers.
2. Do you (familiar) have a passport? —Yes, I do.
3. The books are in the suitcase.
4. Here are the keys!
5. Are they students? —No, they are not students.

УРОК 6

СНЯТИЕ КВАРТИРЫ. Renting an apartment.

___

A. ДИАЛОГ

В институ́те.

ДЖОН: Пе́тя, ты не зна́ешь, как мо́жно снять кварти́ру?

ПЕТЯ: Посмотри́ в газе́те, и́ли вон там, на стене́. Гмм ... ско́лько ко́мнат ты и́щешь?

ДЖОН: Две ко́мнаты.

ПЕТЯ: С ме́белью?

ДЖОН: Да.

ПЕТЯ: Моя́ тётя сдаёт кварти́ру за 550 до́лларов в ме́сяц. Хо́чешь её посмотре́ть?

ДЖОН: Да, коне́чно, хочу́!

В кварти́ре, с тётей Пе́ти.

МАРИНА АЛЕКСАНДРОВНА: На ско́лько вре́мени вы хоти́те снять кварти́ру?

ДЖОН: На шесть ме́сяцев. Это прия́тные ко́мнаты. А где ва́нная?

МАРИНА АЛЕКСАНДРОВНА: Вон там.

ДЖОН: О, это дива́н-крова́ть?

МАРИНА АЛЕКСАНДРОВНА: Да. Она́ о́чень удо́бная. А вот электропл́итка и холоди́льник.

ПЕТЯ: Кварти́ра ую́тная, да? И э́тот райо́н безопа́сный, и метро́ бли́зко.

ДЖОН: Хорошо́, е́сли вы согла́сны, Мари́на Алекса́ндровна, я её сниму́.

МАРИНА АЛЕКСАНДРОВНА: Отли́чно! Я согла́сна!

At the Institute.

JOHN: Petya, do you know how I can find an apartment to rent?

PETYA: Look in the newspaper, or over there, on the wall [bulletin board]. Hmm . . . how many rooms are you looking for?

JOHN: Two rooms.

PETYA: Furnished?

JOHN: Yes.

PETYA: My aunt has an apartment for rent for 550 dollars a month. Would you like to see it?

JOHN: Yes, I would!

At the apartment, with Petya's aunt.

MARINA ALEKSANDROVNA: How long do you want to rent the apartment for?

JOHN: For six months. These are nice rooms. And where is the bathroom?

MARINA ALEKSANDROVNA: Over there.

JOHN: Oh, is this a sofa-bed?

MARINA ALEKSANDROVNA: Yes. It's very comfortable. And here's the hot plate and the refrigerator.

PETYA: The apartment is cozy, isn't it? And this area is safe, and the metro is nearby.

JOHN: Okay, if you agree, Marina Aleksandrovna, I'll take it.

MARINA ALEKSANDROVNA: Excellent! I agree!

B. ПРОИЗНОШЕНИЕ

1. THE CONSONANTS ш AND щ

The difference between ш and щ is often subtle to American ears, as there are no exact English equivalents for these Russian letters. However, ш is similar to

<u>sh</u>, and **щ** is pronounced as a palatalized, soft **ш**, similar to <u>shsh</u> (as in "wi<u>sh</u> <u>ship</u>").

и́щешь	*шесть*	*щётка*	*хорошо́*
you look for	six	toothbrush	good

2. THE HARD SIGN ъ

Unlike the soft sign (**ь**), the hard sign (**ъ**) rarely occurs in modern Russian. However, it appears in some very common words. The hard sign acts as a pause between two sounds. It never begins a word.

объе́кт	*объявле́ние*	*съёмщик*	*отъе́зд*
object	posted notice	tenant	departure

C. ГРАММАТИКА И СЛОВОУПОТРЕБЛЕНИЕ

1. AN INTRODUCTION TO ADJECTIVES

Russian adjectives agree with the nouns they describe in gender, number, and case. They answer the question **Како́й?** (Which?; What kind of?), and have three possible endings: basic (hard), soft, and stressed (also soft). Adjectives take hard endings, unless the last letter of their stem requires a soft ending according to the umbrella spelling rules. Some adjectives are not affected by the umbrella spelling rules, but require soft endings anyway. They are known as "soft adjectives," and will be marked as such in the manual. Following are the regular adjective endings:

	SINGULAR MASCULINE	SINGULAR FEMININE	SINGULAR NEUTER	PLURAL
BASIC (HARD)	-ый	-ая	-ое	-ые
SOFT	-ий	-ая/-яя	-ее	-ие
STRESSED (SOFT)	-о́й	-а́я	-о́е	-ые

Кварти́<u>ра</u> уютн<u>ая</u>, да? И э́тот райо́<u>н</u> безопа́с<u>ный</u>.
The apartment is cozy, isn't it? And this area is safe.

Письм<u>о́</u> о́чень хоро́ш<u>ее</u>.—Как<u>о́е</u> письм<u>о́</u>?
The letter is very good.—Which letter?

Это прия́тные ко́мнаты.

These are nice rooms.

Ковёр хоро́ший и кре́сло краси́вое.

The carpet is good, and the armchair is beautiful.

Како́й телеви́зор вы хоти́те? —Большо́й америка́нский телеви́зор!

What kind of television do you want? —A big, American television!

It is helpful to learn common adjectives as opposite pairs.

хоро́ший/плохо́й	большо́й/ма́ленький	жа́ркий/холо́дный
good/bad	big/small	hot/cold

но́вый/ста́рый	молодо́й/ста́рый	коро́ткий/дли́нный
new/old	young/old	short/long

As in English, the negative form of many adjectives is formed by simply adding the prefix **не-** (meaning "not" or "un-").

прия́тный/неприя́тный	ва́жный/нева́жный	дорого́й/недорого́й
pleasant/unpleasant	important/ unimportant	expensive/ inexpensive

The adjective endings you have learned so far have been for the nominative case. You will learn the adjective endings for the other cases in upcoming lessons. The "base" form of any adjective is the nominative masculine singular. This is the form you will find listed in dictionaries and glossaries.

2. SHORT-FORM ADJECTIVES

In addition to the forms you have just learned, most Russian adjectives also have a short form, which may only be used with verbs like "to be." The short-form adjective endings are:

	SINGULAR	PLURAL
MASCULINE	(consonant)	
FEMININE	-а	-ы
NEUTER	-о	

Short-form adjectives are generally used to describe a temporary condition, while the long-form adjectives describe a permanent condition. Compare these two sentences:

Я за́нята сего́дня.

I'm busy today.

Он о́чень занято́й члове́к.

He's a very busy person.

Following are some common short-form adjectives.

	SICK	OPEN	CLOSED	BUSY	READY	GLAD
я/ты/он	бо́лен	откры́т	закры́т	за́нят	гото́в	рад
я/ты/она́	больна́	откры́та	закры́та	за́нята	гото́ва	ра́да
оно́	больно́	откры́то	закры́то	за́нято	гото́во	ра́до
мы/вы/они́	больны́	откры́ты	закры́ты	за́няты	гото́вы	ра́ды

Мари́на Алекса́ндровна, вы согла́сны? —Да, я согла́сна.

Marina Aleksandrovna, do you agree? —Yes, I agree (lit. I'm in agreement).

Джон согла́сен и Пе́тя о́чень рад.

John agrees, and Petya is very glad.

Мы гото́вы!

We're ready!

Кафе́ сего́дня закры́то.

The cafe is closed today.

Де́ти больны́ сего́дня.

The children are sick today.

Note that **бо́лен** and **согла́сен** have a fleeting **е** in the masculine form only. This is true for all short-form adjectives ending in -**ен**.

3. THE VERB "TO WANT"

Хоте́ть (to want) is an irregular verb that does not fall in either conjugation group and must simply be memorized. Notice that the singular forms take Conjugation I endings, and have a stem ending in -**ч**, while the plural forms take Conjugation II endings, and have a stem ending in -**т**.

хоте́ть: to want

I want	я хочу́	мы хоти́м	we want
you (fam.) want	ты хо́чешь	вы хоти́те	you (pl./pol.) want
he/she wants	он/она́ хо́чет	они́ хотя́т	they want

singular stem: хоч+
plural stem: хот+

As in English, **хоте́ть** can be followed either by an infinitive or by a noun.

Хо́чешь посмотре́ть кварти́ру? —Да, коне́чно хочу́!

Do you want to see the apartment? —Yes, of course I want to!

На ско́лько вре́мени вы хоти́те снять кварти́ру?

How long do you want to rent the apartment for?

Они́ хотя́т большо́й америка́нский телеви́зор.

They want a big, American television.

4. CARDINAL NUMBERS 30–1,000

Here are the Russian cardinal numbers from 30 to 100 and 100 to 1,000.

30	три́дцать	200	две́сти
31	три́дцать оди́н	300	три́ста
40	со́рок	400	четы́реста
50	пятьдеся́т	500	пятьсо́т
60	шестьдеся́т	600	шестьсо́т
70	се́мьдесят	700	семьсо́т
80	во́семьдесят	800	восемьсо́т
90	девяно́сто	900	девятьсо́т
100	сто	1000	ты́сяча

Single digit numbers (1–9) are added just as in 31 above.

Моя́ тётя сдаёт кварти́ру за пятьсо́т пятьдеся́т до́лларов в ме́сяц.

My aunt rents out an apartment for five hundred and fifty dollars a month.

Хаба́ровск шестьсо́т киломе́тров к се́веру от Владивосто́ка.

Khabarovsk is six hundred kilometers to the north of Vladivostok.

Сто девяносто пять человек ждут квартиры в городе.

One hundred ninety-five people are waiting for apartments in the city.

Сколько с меня? —1.940[1] рублей, пожалуйста.

How much do I owe you? —1,940 rubles, please.

D. СЛОВАРЬ

безопасный	safe, secure
близко	near
ванная	bathroom
горячий	hot (to touch)
диван-кровать	sofa-bed
дорогой (не-)	expensive (in-)
жаркий	hot (climate or weather)
за	for
задаток	deposit
здание	building
искать (ищу, ищешь, ищут)	to look for
квартира	apartment
квартплата	rent (for an apartment only)
ковёр	carpet, rug
кресло	armchair
кухня	kitchen
маленький	small
меблированный (не-)	furnished (un-)
месяц	month
метро	subway, metro
На сколько времени ... ?	For how long . . . ?
на шесть месяцев	for six months
найти	to find
отлично	excellent
плита	stove
плохой	bad
приятный (не-)	pleasant (un-)
район	area, region
сдать	to rent out
сколько	how much; how many
снимать квартиру	to rent (occupy) an apartment
спальня	bedroom

1. Notice that Russian numbers are written with a period or a space where a comma is used in English.

Шестой урок

согла́сен/-на/-ны	to be in agreement
стена́	wall
телеви́зор	television set
тётя	aunt
ую́тный	cozy, comfortable
холоди́льник	refrigerator
холо́дный	cold
хоро́ший	good
хоте́ть (хочу́, хо́чешь, хо́чет, хоти́м, хоти́те, хотя́т)	to want (irregular)
электропли́тка	hot plate

РУССКАЯ КУЛЬТУРА

When looking for an apartment or room to rent in Russia, it is important to understand that space is at a premium. The only Russian houses are those out in the countryside, and they are often owned by city-dwellers for use as да́чи (summer homes). In the cities there are mostly one- or two-bedroom apartments, or sometimes, коммуна́лки (communal apartments) with one shared kitchen and bathroom for a number of families. These tend to be quite crowded, although they may be in older, more attractive buildings than the newer, separate apartments. The apartments that may be available will likely be away from the center in newer buildings, so it is important to make sure they are near a bus or metro line, and that they have some shops and services nearby.

It is helpful to know that when Russians count rooms, they do not include the bathroom, kitchen, or entryway. Apartments are measured in square meters. The words for living room (гости́ная) and dining room (столо́вая) are usually used to describe Western homes, as most Russian apartments are too small to allow the luxury of separate rooms for separate activities. The main room is usually called the больша́я ко́мната (the big room) and is used for eating, entertaining, and often sleeping. If the bedroom is separate, it is called the спа́льня (bedroom), and it is usually very small. The sink and bathtub are usually in one room (ва́нная), and the toilet is in another (туале́т).

Apartments or rooms for rent are advertised in the newspapers, on bulletin boards at universities, and in various other public places. The best way to find one, however, is to ask Russian colleagues and acquaintances if they know of anyone who is looking for someone to rent all or part of an apartment. Along with the more casual manner of locating apartments, rental arrangements tend to charge a finder's fee. Renters are usually asked for a month's rent in advance.

УПРАЖНЕНИЯ

A. Измени́те прилага́тельные в ско́бках, что́бы они́ согласова́лись с существи́тельными в предложе́ниях. (Change the adjectives in parentheses to agree with the nouns in the sentences.)

1. Как ко́мнаты? Они́ _плохая_. (плохо́й)
2. Как крова́ть? Крова́ть _хорошая_. (хоро́ший)
3. Райо́н _безопасный_. (безопа́сный)
4. Она́ чита́ет _интресное_ письмо́. (интере́сный)
5. Сту́лья о́чень _неудобноая_. (неудо́бный)

B. Запо́лните про́пуски пра́вильными фо́рмами глаго́ла «хоте́ть». (Fill in the blanks with the correct form of the verb **хоте́ть**.)

1. Я _хочу_ слу́шать му́зыку.
2. Что ты _хочешь_, Ми́ша?
3. Роди́тели _хочет_ жить в Евро́пе.
4. Мы _хотим_ но́вый телеви́зор.
5. А что вы _хотите_, Михаи́л Семёнович?

C. Ка́ждая фра́за включа́ет ци́фру. Напиши́те ци́фру.
   (Every phrase contains a number. Write the number.)

1. шестьсо́т пятьдеся́т до́лларов в ме́сяц _650_
2. на три́дцать дней _30_
3. со́рок пять мину́т от Москвы́ _45_
4. три́ста се́мьдесят пять киломе́тров от Ки́ева _375_
5. девяно́сто челове́к в ко́мнате _90_

D. **Запо́лните про́пуски пра́вильными оконча́ниями кра́тких прилага́тельных и переведи́те предложе́ния.** (Fill in the blanks with the correct endings of the short adjectives, and translate the sentences.)

1. Джон: Если Мари́на Алекса́ндровна согла́с*ена* , я согла́с*ен* .
2. Пе́тя о́чень рад*а* .
3. Кварти́ра гото́в*а* ?
4. Окно́ закры́т*о* .
5. Они́ всегда́ за́нят*ы* .

УРОК 7

РАЗГОВОР О ДОМЕ И СЕМЬЕ. Talking about home and family.

А. ДИАЛОГ

В поезде, у Красноярского вокзала.

МАЙКЛ: *Так, вы живёте в Красноярске?*

ПАССАЖИР: *Нет. Я живу на Дальнем Востоке.*

МАЙКЛ: *Неужели? В каком городе?*

ПАССАЖИР: *В Хабаровске, к северу от Владивостока. А вы?*

МАЙКЛ: *Я тоже живу на востоке: в Бостоне, на восточном берегу США.*

ПАССАЖИР: *О, вы американец! Как вы хорошо говорите по-русски!*

МАЙКЛ: *Спасибо. Я люблю говорить по-русски.*

ПАССАЖИР: *Здорово! А вы не скучаете по семье?*

МАЙКЛ: *Да, очень. Хотите посмотреть их фотографию?*

ПАССАЖИР: *Да, с удовольствием!*

МАЙКЛ: *Вот мой родители и мой брат.*

ПАССАЖИР: *Ваш брат очень похож на вас.*

МАЙКЛ: *Верно. А это наш дом.*

ПАССАЖИР: *Какой красивый дом! Сколько человек в вашей семье?*

МАЙКЛ: *Родители, я и мой брат. А у вас есть семья?*

ПАССАЖИР: *Нет, я не замужем. Но вот моя мама и —*

ПРОВОДНИК: *Билеты, пожалуйста!*

————

On the train, near Krasnoyarsk Station.

MICHAEL: You live in Krasnoyarsk?

PASSENGER: No. I live in the Far East.

MICHAEL: Really? In which city?

PASSENGER: In Khabarovsk, to the north of Vladivostok. And you?

MICHAEL: I also live in the east: in Boston, on the East coast of the United States.

PASSENGER: Oh, you're an American! You speak Russian so well!

MICHAEL: Thank you. I love speaking Russian.

PASSENGER: That's great! But don't you miss your family?

MICHAEL: Very much. Would you like to see a picture of them?

PASSENGER: Yes, gladly.

MICHAEL: Here are my parents and my brother.

PASSENGER: Your brother looks a lot like you.

MICHAEL: That's true. And here's our house.

PASSENGER: What a beautiful house! How many people are there in your family?

MICHAEL: My parents, me, and my brother. And do you have a family of your own?

PASSENGER: No, I'm not married. But here's my mother and—

CONDUCTOR: Tickets, please!

B. ПРОИЗНОШЕНИЕ

1. THE CONSONANTS ж, х, ц, AND ч

The Russian letters **ж, х, ц,** and **ч** have no direct English equivalents. However, **х** is similar to *h,* **ц** is similar to *ts,* **ч** is like *ch,* and **ж** is pronounced approximately *zh.*

Ха́баровск	*учи́ть*	*то́же*	*америка́нец*
о́чень	*цирк*	*хорошо́*	*живу́*

2. EXCLAMATIONS WITH ИК 5

Exclamations that begin with **Как** or **Какой** (What a ...!) have the intonation pattern **ИК 5**, which begins on a rising note, and continues with a high tone until dropping down on the last accented syllable. This final syllable is often heavily stressed, creating two intonational centers; one on the first word and one on the last word.

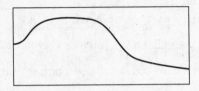

Как вы хорошо говорйте по-русски!
How well you speak Russian!

Какой дом!
What a house!

Какая красйвая река!
What a beautiful river!

3. THE SOFT л

One of the most challenging Russian sounds for an English speaker is the soft л, which occurs when л is followed by a ь or by a soft vowel. Try pronouncing the English letters "l" followed by "y" (as in "yet") in very rapid succession or simultaneously. It is similar to the "lli" in "million."

ско<u>ль</u>ко   *люб<u>лю</u>*   *О<u>ль</u>га*

C. ГРАММАТИКА И СЛОВОУПОТРЕБЛЕНИЕ

1. THE PRESENT TENSE OF CONJUGATION II VERBS

To form the present tense of Conjugation II verbs, simply drop the infinitive ending -ть and replace it with the appropriate personal ending: -ю/-у, -ишь, and -ит for the singular forms, and -им, -ите and -ят/-ат for the plural forms.

говори́ть: to speak

I speak	я говорю́	мы говори́м	we speak
you (fam.) speak	ты говори́шь	вы говори́те	you (pl./pol.) speak
he/she speaks	он/она́ говори́т	они́ говоря́т	they speak

stem: говор+

Как хорошо́ вы говори́те по-ру́сски!
How well you speak Russian!

Они́ говоря́т об Аме́рике.
They're talking about America.

Other common Conjugation II verbs include: **учи́ть** (to learn; to study) and **люби́ть** (to love). **Люби́ть** has an extra **л** in the first person singular form[1] (**я люблю́**) but is otherwise regular. **Учи́ть** is also regular, but because its stem ends in **ч-**, the umbrella spelling rules apply. As is common with Conjugation II verbs, both verbs retain the infinitive stress only in the **я** form, and have first syllable stress in all the other forms.

Я люблю́ говори́ть по-ру́сски.
I love to speak Russian.

Майкл лю́бит э́ту соба́ку.
Michael loves that dog.

Они́ у́чат исто́рию.
They are studying history.

Knowing the first person singular (**я**), the second person singular (**ты**), and the third person plural (**они́**) forms of any verb will allow you to determine the remaining forms, i.e. whether the verb is irregular, and if so, in what way. These three forms will always be listed in parentheses following the infinitive in this manual. The infinitive is usually the form that tells you to which conjugation group a verb belongs: most verbs ending in -**ать**/-**ять** are Conjugation I verbs, and most verbs ending in -**ить** are Conjugation II verbs.

---

1. See **Уро́к** 27 for other such verbs.

2. POSSESSIVE ADJECTIVES AND PRONOUNS (SPECIAL MODIFIERS)

For each personal pronoun (I, you, etc.) there is a corresponding possessive adjective (my, your, etc.) and pronoun (mine, yours, etc.) that answers the question **Чей?** (Whose?).[2] In Russian, possessive adjectives and pronouns, also known as "special modifiers," have the same form. They agree in gender, number, and case with the nouns they modify. Following are the nominative forms.

	MASCULINE	FEMININE	NEUTER	PLURAL
Whose?	Чей?	Чья?	Чьё?	Чьи?
my/mine	мой	моя́	моё	мои́
your/yours (fam.)	твой	твоя́	твоё	твои
his, its	его́	его́	его́	его́
her/hers	её	её	её	её
our/ours	наш	на́ша	на́ше	на́ши
your/yours (pl./pol.)	ваш	ва́ша	ва́ше	ва́ши
their/theirs	их	их	их	их
one's own	свой	своя́	своё	свой

The third person forms—**его́, её,** and **их**—never change, regardless of gender, number, or case. The stems of the first and second person forms are also constant.

Вот мои́ роди́тели и мой брат. —А э́то ва́ша соба́ка?
Here are my parents and my brother. —And is this your dog?

Чьё э́то ме́сто—Его́. (Это его́ ме́сто.)
Whose seat is this? —His. (It's his seat.)

Чей э́тот дом? —Наш. (Это наш дом.)
Whose house is this? —Ours. (This is our house.)

Это не моё де́ло, а твоё.
It's not my problem, it's yours. (lit. It's not my affair, but yours.)

In Russian there are two words for each third person possessive modifier: **его́, её, их** (someone else's) and **свой** (his/her/their own). **Свой** is used when the modifier and the subject noun refer to the same person.

2. Please see the Appendix for a complete chart of the possessive special modifiers, listed by case.

Седьмо́й уро́к

Майкл лю́бит свою́ соба́ку.

Michael loves his (own) dog.

Майкл лю́бит его́ соба́ку.

Michael loves his (someone else's) dog.

When using one possessive modifier to describe several nouns of different genders in conversation, use a plural modifier.

Это мой брат. Это моя́ сестра́. ›› Это мои́ брат и сестра́.

This is my brother. This is my sister. >> This is my brother and sister.

When ownership is obvious from context, it is preferable not to use a special modifier at all—especially if the noun modified is a family member, a piece of clothing, or a part of the body.

До́ктор мо́ет ру́ки.

The doctor is washing (his/her) hands.

Я отвезла́ Са́шу к ма́ме.

I took Sasha to (my) mother's.

Тебе́ нра́вится но́вое пальто́.

You like (your) new coat.

3. DEMONSTRATIVE ADJECTIVES (SPECIAL MODIFIERS)

You already know the invariable demonstrative pronoun **э́то** (this/that is; these/those are), as in **э́то парк** (that's a park) or **э́то Аня** (this is Anya). Demonstrative adjectives (this, these; that, those) on the other hand, must always modify a noun and agree with it in gender, number, and case. They are also known as special modifiers. The nominative endings are just like those of the short-form adjectives. Following are the nominative forms of the demonstrative adjective **э́тот** (this/these).

	SINGULAR	PLURAL
MASCULINE	э́тот	
FEMININE	э́та	э́ти
NEUTER	э́то	

Эти лю́ди мои́ роди́тели.
These people are my parents.

Эта фотогра́фия хоро́шая.
This photograph is good.

Это ме́сто за́нято.
This seat is taken.

4. THE PREPOSITIONAL CASE OF ADJECTIVES AND SPECIAL MODIFIERS

a. Adjectives

Adjectives agree with the nouns they modify not only in gender and number, but in case as well. The basic adjective ending is hard, but some adjective stems require soft endings. Following are the prepositional case endings for adjectives:

	HARD	SOFT
MASCULINE/NEUTER	-ом	-ем
FEMININE	-ой	-ей

To form the prepositional case of adjectives, simply replace the nominative ending with the appropriate prepositional ending. For example, **америка́нская вы́ставка >> на америка́нской вы́ставке.**

Я живу́ на Да́льнем[3] восто́ке. (nominative: Да́льний восто́к)
I live in the Far East.

Я живу́ на восто́чном берегу́[4] США. (nominative: восто́чный бе́рег)
I live on the East Coast of the U.S.

Джон живёт в прия́тной кварти́ре. (nominative: прия́тная кварти́ра)
John's living in a nice apartment.

3. Like many adjectives whose stem ends in н-, да́льний has a soft ending.
4. Some masculine nouns take the prepositional ending -у rather than -е (see Уро́к 29).

Седьмо́й уро́к

b. Special Modifiers

The prepositional case endings for special modifiers are identical to the prepositional endings for adjectives. Notice, however, that the demonstrative adjectives always take the hard endings (-ом or -ой), and possessive adjectives always take the soft endings (-ем or -ей). This is true across all cases. Remember that the third person possessive adjectives (**его́, её,** and **их**) never change.

	DEMONSTRATIVES	POSSESSIVES
MASCULINE/NEUTER	э́том	моём, твоём, его, её, своём, на́шем, ва́шем, их
FEMININE	э́той	мое́й, твое́й, его, её, свое́й, на́шей, ва́шей, их

Ско́лько челове́к в ва́шей семье́? (nominative: ва́ша семья́)
How many people are there in your family?

В его́ семье́ четы́ре челове́ка. (nominative: его́ семья́)
There are four people in his family.

Она́ хо́чет кварти́ру в э́том зда́нии. (nominative: э́то зда́ние)
She wants an apartment in that building.

5. THE ACCUSATIVE CASE OF NOUNS AND PRONOUNS

Nouns and pronouns in the accusative case answer the question **Кого́?** (Whom?) or **Что** (What?). They are used as the direct object of an action. You already know the accusative endings for feminine, neuter, and inanimate masculine nouns from **Уро́к** 5. The accusative ending for most masculine, animate nouns is -а (or -я if the noun ends in -ь or -й). Remember that some nouns referring to men, especially nicknames, end in -а in the nominative (e.g. **Ми́ша**), and are considered to be grammatically feminine.

	NOMINATIVE	ACCUSATIVE
MASCULINE INANIMATE	consonant/-ь/-й	no change
MASCULINE ANIMATE	consonant	-а
	-ь/-й	-я
FEMININE	-а	-у
	-я/-ь	-ю/no change
NEUTER	-о/-е	-о/-е

Он ждёт Ма́йкла на вокза́ле.

He's waiting for Michael at the train station.

Студе́нт понима́ет учи́теля.

The student understands the teacher.

Она́ лю́бит Ми́шу.

She loves Misha.

Following are the personal pronouns in the accusative case.

	SINGULAR	PLURAL	
me	меня́	нас	us
you (fam.)	тебя́	вас	you (pl./pol. sing.)
him/her/it	его́/её/его́	их	them

Как вас зову́т? —Меня́ зову́т Майкл.

What is your name? —My name is Michael.

Где он его́ ждёт? —На платфо́рме №5.

Where is he waiting for him? —On platform No. 5.

Я тебя́ люблю́.

I love you.

6. FAMILY AND RELATIONSHIP WORDS

a. Masculine nouns

The noun **оте́ц** (father) has a fleeting **e** which disappears in all declined and plural forms: **отцы́, отца́, отцу́,** etc. The plural form of some common masculine nouns ends in -ья, e.g. **муж >> мужья́.** Notice that the plurals for **друг, муж,** and **сын** are stressed on the last syllable. Some masculine nouns are simply irregular in the plural: **ребёнок** (child) >> **де́ти, челове́к** (person) >> **лю́ди.**

Пе́тя и Ми́ша—бра́тья.

Petya and Misha are brothers.

У тебя́ есть друзья́ в Уика́го?

Do you have friends in Chicago?

Седьмо́й уро́к

Турге́нев написа́л кни́гу «Отцы́ и де́ти».

Turgenev wrote the book *Fathers and Sons*.

Что лю́ди де́лают?

What are the people doing?

Их сыновья́ живу́т в Ташке́нте.

Their sons live in Tashkent.

b. Feminine nouns

Some common feminine nouns change in unexpected ways: жена́ (wife) >> жёны, сестра́ (sister) >> сёстры, мать (mother) >> ма́тери, дочь (daughter) >> до́чери.

Аня и Ма́ша—сёстры.

Anya and Masha are sisters.

Ма́тери и до́чери понима́ют друг дру́га.

Mothers and daughters understand each other.

7. ПОХОЖ (SIMILAR) AND THE ACCUSATIVE

The short-form adjective похо́ж/похо́жа/похо́жи, meaning "similar," is always followed by на and the accusative case.

Ваш брат похо́ж на вас.

Your brother looks like (lit. is similar to) you.

Мои́ сёстры похо́жи на ма́му и на меня́.

My sisters are similar to Mom and me.

D. СЛОВАРЬ

бе́рег	shore; coast
✗*биле́т*	ticket
✗*брат*	brother
ваго́н	car
Ве́рно!	That's true!, That's right!
✗*вокза́л*	train station
восто́к	east

восто́чный	eastern
го́род	city
говори́ть (говорю́, говори́шь, говоря́т)	to speak
дом	house; home
друг	friend
жена́т	married (only for men)
здо́рово	wonderful, great
како́й	which; what kind of
киломе́тр	kilometer
краси́вый	beautiful
люби́ть (люблю́, лю́бишь, лю́бят)	to love
мать	mother
ме́сто	seat, place
Неуже́ли?	Really?
оте́ц	father
пассажи́р	passenger
платфо́рма	platform
по-англи́йски	(in) English
по-ру́сски	(in) Russian
по́езд	train
подру́га	female friend; girlfriend
пое́здка	trip
похо́ж/-а/-и (на + accusative)	similar
ребёнок	child
роди́тели	parents
ру́сский	Russian
с удово́льствием	with pleasure; gladly
се́вер	north
семья́	family (spouse and children)
сестра́	sister
скуча́ть (скуча́ю, скуча́ешь, скуча́ют)	to miss: to yearn for; to be bored
учи́ть (учу́, у́чишь, у́чат)	to study; to learn
фотогра́фия	photograph
челове́к	person
э́тот/э́та/э́то/э́ти	this/these; that/those

РУ́ССКАЯ КУЛЬТУ́РА

Traveling by train is a very pleasant way to get around Russia. The CIS rail network is the largest and most heavily used in the world. There are four classes: first (св) with two cushioned berths to a compartment, second (купе́йный ваго́н) with four cushioned berths per compartment, and third (плацка́ртный ваго́н) with open compartments. Third class is rarely sold to foreigners. When on the train you must use the bathrooms at either end of the car, and you may end up sharing your compartment with someone of the opposite sex. Most trains have dining cars, but it's customary to bring food and drink along for anything longer than a day trip. It's usually possible to get tea, drinks, and snacks from the attendant.

The busiest train route is between Moscow and St. Petersburg, which is normally an eight-hour, overnight trip, but only takes about four hours on the fastest trains. The longest route, and probably the most quintessentially Russian, is the famed Trans-Siberian Railway (**Транссиби́рская магистра́ль**). This route takes approximately six days to cross Russia. There are brief stops for fifteen minutes or less at certain stations, but the experience primarily consists of watching the **тайга́**, the dense forest which covers a great deal of Siberia, and the towns, cities, and villages go by, while drinking tea, eating the plentiful, always available meals, and chatting with people on the train.

УПРАЖНЕНИЯ

A. **Отве́тьте на вопро́сы одни́м сло́вом, употреби́те слова́ в ско́бках по образцу́.** (Answer the questions with one word, using the words in parentheses.)

1. Чья э́та кни́га? (он)
2. Чьё э́то зда́ние? (они́)
3. Чьи э́ти джи́нсы? (я)
4. Чей э́тот журна́л? (ты)
5. Чья э́та маши́на? (мы)
6. Чей э́тот диск? (вы)

B. **Поста́вьте прилага́тельные в ско́бках в ну́жную фо́рму и запо́лните про́пуски.** (Put the adjectives in the parentheses into the correct form and fill in the blanks.)

1. В _____ ко́мнате ты живёшь? —В _____ ко́мнате. (како́й/э́тот)
2. Где Ма́ша? —В _____ ко́мнате. (мой)

3. Где вы живёте? —На _____ восто́ке. (Да́льний)

4. Где ты живёшь? —На _____ бе́регу США. (восто́чный)

5. Майкл в _____ по́езде? (э́тот)

C. Запо́лните про́пуски пра́вильными оконча́ниями глаго́лов. (Fill in the blanks with the correct endings of the verbs.)

1. Вы уч_____ ру́сский язы́к? —Да, я уч_____ ру́сский язы́к.

2. Кого́ ты люб_____? —Я люб_____ па́пу.

3. Они́ хорошо́ говор_____ по-ру́сски? —Да, о́чень хорошо́.

4. Они́ уч_____ матема́тику? —Нет, они́ уч_____ филосо́фию.

5. Вы уч_____ исто́рию? —Да, мы уч_____ исто́рию.

D. Запо́лните про́пуски пра́вильными фо́рмами слов в ско́бках. (Fill in the blanks with the correct form of the words in parentheses.)

1. Его́ сестра́ о́чень _____ на _____ . (похо́ж/вы)

2. Ми́ша, ты _____ на _____ . (похо́ж/Серге́й)

3. Кто _____ на _____ ? (похо́ж/Пе́тя)

4. Мои́ бра́тья _____ на _____ . (похо́ж/ты)

5. Студе́нты _____ _____ . (люби́ть/учи́тель)

УРОК 8

НА КОНЦЕРТЕ. At a concert.

А. ДИАЛОГ

В фойе́ зал филармо́нии.

ФИ́МА: *Где Анто́н?*

СО́НЯ: *Не зна́ю. А биле́ты у него́!*

ФИ́МА: *Не беспоко́йся. Я уве́рен, что он придёт.*

СО́НЯ: *Пожа́луйста, позвони́ ему́ на вся́кий слу́чай.*

ФИ́МА: *Ла́дно, но у меня́ нет ме́лочи для телефо́на-автома́та.*

СО́НЯ: *Вот. У меня́ есть.*

Фи́ма звони́т Анто́ну и возвраща́ется.

ФИ́МА: *Яко́в Семёнович не зна́ет, где Анто́н.*

СО́НЯ: *Ах! Вот и он!*

АНТО́Н: *Прости́те, ребя́та!*

СО́НЯ: *Почему́ ты так опа́здываешь?*

АНТО́Н: *Потому́ что я перепу́тал день.*

ФИ́МА: *Ничего́. Пошли́!*

В за́ле.

СО́НЯ: *Како́е пе́рвое произведе́ние?*

ФИ́МА: *Симфо́ния Шостако́вича.*

АНТО́Н: *Мой люби́мый композитор!*

СО́НЯ: *Да? А я предпочита́ю Мо́царта, осо́бенно его́ му́зыку из о́перы «Волше́бная фле́йта.»*

ФИМА: *А мой любимый композитор, наверно—Прокофьев.*

СОНЯ: *Тссс! Вот дирижёр.*

In the foyer at the symphony.

FIMA: Where's Anton?

SONYA: I don't know. And he has the tickets!

FIMA: Don't worry. I'm sure he's coming.

SONYA: Please, call him just in case.

FIMA: Okay, but I don't have any change for the pay phone.

SONYA: Here. I have some.

Fima calls Anton and returns.

FIMA: Yakov Semyonovich doesn't know where Anton is.

SONYA: Oh! Here he is!

ANTON: Sorry, guys!

SONYA: Why are you so late?

ANTON: Because I mixed up the day.

FIMA: That's okay. Let's go in.

In the concert hall.

SONYA: Which piece is first?

FIMA: A Shostakovich symphony.

ANTON: My favorite composer!

SONYA: Really? I prefer Mozart, especially his music from the opera "The Magic Flute."

FIMA: Prokofiev is probably my favorite composer.

SONYA: Shh! Here's the conductor.

B. ПРОИЗНОШЕНИЕ

1. QUESTIONS WITH ИК 4

The most common use of this intonation pattern is with questions beginning with the word **a**. **ИК 4** is similar to the way questions such as "And you?" or "And Jennifer?" are pronounced in English. **ИК** 4 questions start at mid-tone and gradually rise on the last syllable if it is accented, or dip slightly on the accented syllable and then rise.

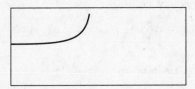

Нормáльно. А у тебя́?
Fine. And you?

Я предпочитáю óперу. А вы?
I prefer opera. And you?

2. PRONUNCIATION OF COMPLEX SENTENCES

In Russian complex sentences, dependent clauses beginning with question words or with **что** (that) are always preceded by a comma. However, this comma does not indicate a pause or change in rhythm.

Я увéрена, что он придёт.
I'm sure that he's coming.

Яков Семёнович не знáет, где он.
Yakov Semyonovich doesn't know where he is.

C. ГРАММАТИКА И СЛОВОУПОТРЕБЛЕНИЕ

1. THE GENITIVE CASE

The genitive case is primarily used to indicate possession, much like the English 's or the preposition "of." The genitive case answers the questions **Кого**? (Of whom?) and **Чего**? (Of what?). To form the genitive of any noun, simply remove any final vowels, -ь, or -й from the nominative form, and add the appropriate genitive ending. Note that the masculine and neuter endings are the same as those of accusative masculine animate nouns.

MASCULINE/NEUTER	FEMININE
-а -я (to replace -ь, -й, or -е)	-ы -и (to replace -ь, -я, or follow an umbrella letter)

Я предпочита́ю му́зыку Мо́царта. (Nominative: Мо́царт)
I prefer Mozart's music.

Кто компози́тор э́того произведе́ния? (Nominative: произведе́ние)
Who's the composer of the piece?

Вот Ма́лый зал филармо́нии. (Nominative: филармо́ния)
Here's the Lesser Symphony Hall (the lesser hall of the symphony).

Я люблю́ балла́ды Була́та Окуджа́вы. (Nominative: Була́т Окуджа́ва)
I love Bulat Okudzhava's ballads.

Она́ а́втор кни́ги о смы́сле жи́зни. (Nominative: кни́га, жизнь)
She's the author of a book about the meaning of life.

Certain prepositions also require the genitive case. These include: **для** (for the purpose/sake of), **без** (without), and those meaning "from" (**из, от, с**).

Я предпочита́ю его́ му́зыку для бале́та.
I prefer his music for the ballet.

Он музыка́нт из Москвы́.

He's a musician from Moscow.

Они́ говоря́т по-ру́сски без акце́нта.

They speak Russian fluently. (Literally, without accent)

2. THE GENITIVE CASE OF PERSONAL PRONOUNS

Personal pronouns in the genitive have the same form as in the accusative (Уро́к 7), except that the third person forms begin with н- after a preposition.

	SINGULAR	PLURAL	
me	меня́	нас	us
you (fam.)	тебя́	вас	you (pl./pol.)
him/her	(н)его́/ (н)её	(н)их	them

Pronouns in the genitive case are most commonly used following the preposition у to express possession. In Уро́к 2, you were introduced to the formula У меня́ есть as an equivalent for "I have." In this formula, меня́ is in the genitive case, and you can substitute any noun or pronoun in the genitive in its stead. Remember that есть is used only when the very existence or possession of an object is emphasized, in answer to the question У кого́ … ? (Who has … ?).

У тебя́ есть биле́ты? —Да, у меня́ есть биле́ты.

Do you have tickets? —Yes, I have tickets.

У Со́ни есть ме́лочь.

Sonya has some change.

У них есть места́?

Do they have seats?

When a quality or the location of the object possessed is emphasized or questioned, есть is omitted.

Где биле́ты? —Биле́ты у него́ до́ма.

Where are the tickets? —He has the tickets at home.

У кого́ биле́ты? У Анто́на? —Нет, они́ у меня́.

Who has the tickets? Anton? —No, *I* have them.

У нас хоро́шие места́.

We have *good* seats.

3. НЕТ WITH THE GENITIVE CASE

Нет plus the genitive case is used to indicate absence, or nonexistence. It is the opposite of **есть**. The object or person whose existence or presence is being negated must be in the genitive case.

У меня́ нет ме́лочи.

I don't have any change. (lit. By me there is no change.)

В програ́мме нет Мо́царта.

There's no Mozart in the program.

Анто́н до́ма? —Нет, его́ не́ту.[1] (Нет, Анто́на нет до́ма.)

Is Anton home? —No, he's not. (No, Anton's not home.)

4. COMPLEX SENTENCES

In Russian, as in English, question words can be used to introduce a dependent clause.[2] In Russian, however, a comma is required before the question word.

Где Анто́н? —Я не зна́ю, где он.

Where's Anton? —I don't know where he is.

Ты не зна́ешь, когда́ переры́в?

Do you happen to know when the intermission is?

Како́й бале́т? —Я не зна́ю, како́й бале́т.

Which ballet? —I don't know which ballet (it is).

---

1. **Не́ту** has the same meaning as **нет**, but it is used only in informal style and conversation.
2. Dependent clauses are thoughts that cannot stand alone as sentences.

Что э́то? —Мы не зна́ем, что э́то.

What is it? —We don't know what it is.

Я не понима́ю, почему́ он там живёт.

I don't understand why he lives there.

The word **что** can mean "that" as well as "what." In English "that" can be omitted from a complex sentence, but in Russian it is always required.

Я уве́рен, что он придёт.

I'm sure (that) he's coming.

Я наде́юсь, что он по́мнит о конце́рте.

I hope (that) he remembers about the concert.

The phrase **потому́ что** (because) behaves just like the phrases above.

Анто́н опа́здывает, потому́ что он перепу́тал день.

Anton is late because he mixed up the day.

5. COMMANDS AND REQUESTS

You may have noticed that commands and requests, also known as imperatives, sometimes end in **-те** and sometimes do not. Those that end in **-те** are the polite or plural forms, used with people you would address with **вы.** The informal imperative, used with people you would address with **ты,** is formed by simply dropping the **-те** from the polite form.

Извини́те за опозда́ние!

Excuse me for being late!

Прости́те, ребя́та!

Sorry (lit. Forgive), guys!

Пожа́луйста, позвони́.

Please call.

D. СЛОВАРЬ

антра́кт	intermission
бале́т	ballet
Вот и он!	There he is!
дирижёр	conductor
для	for the purpose/sake of
Его́ не́ту.	He's not here. (colloquial)
зал	hall
исполне́ние	performance (musical)
ка́сса	ticket window
композитор	composer
конце́рт	concert
люби́мый	favorite
ме́лочь	f. (small) change
музыка́нт	musician
на вся́кий слу́чай	just in case
наве́рно	probably
Не беспоко́йся.	Don't worry.
норма́льно	fine (lit. normally)
орке́стр	orchestra
осо́бенно	especially
о́пера	opera
перепу́тывать (перепу́тываю, перепу́тываешь, перепу́тывают)	to mix up, confuse, muddle
потому́ что	because
почему́	why
Пошли́!	Let's go!
предпочита́ть (предпочита́ю, предпочита́ешь, предпочита́ют)	to prefer
програ́мма	program
произведе́ние	work, production
Прости́те!	Sorry!; Forgive me!
ребя́та	guys (always plural)
ряд	row
симфо́ния	symphony
телефо́н-автома́т	pay phone
уве́рен/-а/-ы	sure
филармо́ния	philharmonic (noun)
фойе́	foyer

РУССКАЯ КУЛЬТУРА

A trip to Russia cannot be complete without experiencing its rich arts heritage at one of the many excellent theaters. Moscow is home to the **Большо́й теа́тр**, the **МХАТ** (Moscow Art Theater), co-founded by **Станисла́вский**, and the avant-garde **Тага́нка** theater. In St. Petersburg you can go to an opera or ballet at the **Марии́нский** Theater (also known as the **Ки́ров** Theater), a classical music concert at the **Большо́й** and **Ма́лый зал филармо́нии** (the Greater and Lesser Halls), or a drama at the **Большо́й драмати́ческий теа́тр (БДТ)** or the **Пу́шкинский** (Pushkin) theater.

Russia's tremendous legacy to the world of classical music and ballet includes pieces such as *The Nutcracker Suite*, *Scheherezade*, *The Fire Bird*, and *Swan Lake*, composers such as **Проко́фьев, Чайко́вский, Ри́мский-Ко́рсаков, Страви́нский, Рахма́нинов,** and **Шостако́вич**, and unparalleled dancers such as **Анна Па́влова, Ва́цлав Нижи́нский, Рудо́льф Нури́ев, Ма́я Плисе́цкая,** and **Михаи́л Бары́шников**. Also worthy of mention are the Moscow Virtuosos, a string orchestra, and the **Анса́мбль Моисе́ева**, a folk dance troupe. Russia's legacy to the dramatic arts is no less remarkable with the many works of the famous playwright **Анто́н Че́хов**, as well as plays written by **Алекса́ндр Пу́шкин, Никола́й Го́голь,** and **Ива́н Турге́нев.**

УПРАЖНЕНИЯ

A. **Запо́лните про́пуски роди́тельным падежо́м слов в ско́бках и переведи́те.** (Fill in the blanks with the genitive case of the words in parentheses and translate.)

1. кни́га _____ (Фи́ма)
2. програ́мма _____ (Анто́н)
3. но́мер _____ (ме́сто)
4. дирижёр _____ (орке́стр)
5. композитор _____ (вещь)
6. му́зыка для _____ (исполне́ние)
7. биле́т _____ (Со́ня)
8. балла́да _____ (Була́т Окуджа́ва)
9. жена́ _____ (Яков Семёнович)
10. письмо́ для _____ (Серге́й)

B. **Запо́лните про́пуски пра́вильными фо́рмами слов в ско́бках.** (Fill in the blanks with the correct form of the words in parentheses.)

1. У _____ есть биле́ты. (он)
2. У _____ есть телефо́н? (вы)
3. У _____ хоро́шие места́? —Да, хоро́шие. (они́)
4. У _____ есть програ́мма? —Да, у _____ есть програ́мма. (вы/мы)
5. У _____ есть ме́лочь? —У _____ есть ме́лочь. (кто/она́)

C. **Отве́тьте отрица́тельно на вопро́сы.** (Answer the questions negatively.)

1. У Со́ни есть ме́лочь?
2. У Анто́на есть ме́сто?
3. У тебя́ есть симфо́ния Мо́царта?
4. Анто́н до́ма?
5. Биле́ты у неё?

D. **Переведи́те на англи́йский.** (Translate into English.)

1. Я не зна́ю, где ма́ма.
2. Он ду́мает, что она́ на конце́рте.
3. Вы не зна́ете, когда́ антра́кт?
4. Я уве́рена, что Шостако́вич ру́сский.
5. Они́ не зна́ют, что э́то.

E. **Подбери́те соотве́тствующие ру́сские предложе́ния к англи́йским значе́ниям.** (Match the Russian sentences with the appropriate English translations.)

1. Ой, извини́!   a. Listen, guys!
2. Говори́ по-ру́сски!   b. Go ahead, please.
3. Пожа́луйста, позвони́.   c. Excuse me!
4. Слу́шай, па́па!   d. Oh, excuse me! (informal)
5. Прости́те!   e. Give me your passport please.
6. Слу́шайте, ребя́та!   f. Speak Russian! (informal)
7. Дай ме́лочь.   g. Listen, Papa!
8. Да́йте паспо́рт, пожа́луйста.   h. Please repeat that slowly.
9. Проходи́те, пожа́луйста.   i. Rest, rest!
10. Повтори́те ме́дленно, пожа́луйста.   j. Please call. (informal)
     k. Give me some change.

УРОК 9

ПРОКАТ АВТОМОБИЛЯ, ЗАПРАВКА БЕНЗИНОМ.

Renting a car; getting gas.

А. ДИАЛОГ

На пу́нкте прока́та автомоби́лей в Ки́еве.

ЛЭРРИ: *До́брый день. Я хочу́ взять напрока́т ма́ленькую, недорогу́ю маши́ну на неде́лю.*

ПРОДАВЩИЦА: *Вот прейскура́нт. Цена́ включа́ет страхо́вку и неограни́ченный километра́ж. Мо́жет быть, вы хоти́те Ла́ду?*

ЛЭРРИ: *Хорошо́. Вы принима́ете креди́тные ка́рточки?*

ПРОДАВЩИЦА: *Да. А ваш маршру́т?*

ЛЭРРИ: *Из Ки́ева в Москву́. Мо́жно там верну́ть маши́ну?*

ПРОДАВЩИЦА: *Коне́чно. Так ... Да́йте, пожа́луйста, ваш па́спорт и води́тельские права́.*

На запра́вочной ста́нции по доро́ге.

ЛЭРРИ: *Со́рок ли́тров се́мьдесят второ́го и прове́рьте, пожа́луйста, аккумуля́тор.*

ЗАПРАВЩИК: *Здесь самообслу́живание—мы то́лько продаём бензи́н.*

ЛЭРРИ: *Поня́тно. А где автосе́рвис?*

ЗАПРАВЩИК: *Вон там.*

ЛЭРРИ: *Эта доро́га идёт к шоссе́ №60?*

ЗАПРАВЩИК: *Куда́ же вы е́дете?*

ЛЭРРИ: *В Москву́.*

ЗАПРАВЩИК: *Вы не так е́дете. Сде́лайте разворо́т, пото́м сра́зу поезжа́йте нале́во, и э́та доро́га продолжа́ется пря́мо до шоссе́.*

ЛЭРРИ: *Спаси́бо большо́е.*

At the car rental agency in Kiev.

LARRY: Hello. I want to rent a small, inexpensive car for a week.

CLERK: Here's the price list. The price includes insurance and unlimited mileage. Perhaps you would like a Lada?

LARRY: Fine. Do you take credit cards?

CLERK: Yes. And your route?

LARRY: From Kiev to Moscow. Can I return the car there?

CLERK: Of course. So . . . Give me your passport and driver's license, please.

At a gas station along the way.

LARRY: Forty liters of 72, and please check the battery.

ATTENDANT: It's self-service here—we only sell gas.

LARRY: I see. And where's a service station?

ATTENDANT: Over there.

LARRY: Does this road go to Highway No. 60?

ATTENDANT: *Where* are you going?

LARRY: To Moscow.

ATTENDANT: You're going the wrong way. Make a U-turn, go left immediately, and that road continues straight to the highway.

LARRY: Thanks a lot.

B. ПРОИЗНОШЕНИЕ

1. DOUBLE LETTERS

Since Russian is mostly phonetic (every letter is pronounced), double letters are usually found only in foreign words. Such letters are pronounced as one long letter.

аккумуля́тор　　　　　*грамма́тика*　　　　　*пассажи́р*

2. INTONATION OF NEW OR QUESTIONED INFORMATION

When asking or answering a question, the stress falls on the new or questioned information, which is generally found at the end of the sentence. In conversation this information is not always at the end, but it will still be stressed wherever it is.

Куда́ вы е́дете? —Я е́ду в Москву́.
Where are you going? —I'm going to Moscow.

Эта доро́га идёт к шоссе́ №6о? —Нет, она́ идёт к це́нтру.
Does this road go to Highway 60? —No, it goes downtown.

Ни́на в шко́ле? —Да, в шко́ле.
Nina's in school? —Yes, (she's) in school.

C. ГРАММАТИКА И СЛОВОУПОТРЕБЛЕНИЕ

1. TWO VERBS OF MOTION: ИДТИ AND ЕХАТЬ

The verb "to go" is expressed in Russian by a group of verbs called the verbs of motion. The verb you use depends on a number of distinctions. In this lesson, we will concentrate on the manner of going. Two basic verbs of motion are **идти́** (to go under one's own power) and **е́хать** (to go in a vehicle, i.e. not under one's own power). They are regular Conjugation I verbs, but have irregular infinitives.[1] **Е́хать** also has an irregular imperative form.

идти́: to go (on foot)

I go	я иду́	мы идём	we go
you (fam.) go	ты идёшь	вы идёте	you (pl./pol.) go
he/she goes	он/она́ идёт	они́ иду́т	they go

stem: ид+
imperative: Иди́ (те)!

---

1. This is common in Russian since the infinitive is usually the most irregular Russian verb form.

е́хать: to go (by vehicle)

I go	я е́ду	мы е́дем	we go
you (fam.) go	ты е́дешь	вы е́дете	you (pl./pol.) go
he/she goes	он/она́ е́дет	они́ е́дут	they go

stem: е́д+
imperative: **Поезжа́й**(те)!

Вы не так е́дете.
You're going the wrong way.

Поезжа́йте вперёд!
Go forward!

Иди́ сюда́!
Come here!

Эта доро́га идёт к шоссе́ №60?
Does this road go to Highway No. 60?

Куда́ Анна идёт? —Она́ идёт сюда́.
Where's Anna going? —She's coming over here.

Ехать and **идти́** can be translated as either "go" or "come" when referring to an action currently being observed. Notice also that **идти́,** like the English verb "to go," can be used in a figurative sense to mean forward movement or direction with an object such as a road, or with time, films, rain and snow, etc. To specify the mode of transportation, use **пешко́м** (on foot) with **идти**, or else **е́хать на** + a vehicle in the prepositional.

Вы е́дете в университе́т на метро́ и́ли на авто́бусе?
Are you going to the university by subway or by bus?

Мы идём домо́й пешко́м, а он е́дет на маши́не.
We're going home on foot, and he's going by car.

Они́ е́дут в теа́тр на такси́, потому́ что идёт снег.
They're going to the theater by taxi because it's snowing.

2. ГДЕ VERSUS КУДА (LOCATION VERSUS DIRECTION)

Verbs of motion refer to movement in a direction, and they must be used with the words куда́ (to where), сюда́ (to here), and туда́ (to there) instead of the location words где (where), здесь (here), and там (there). Compare:

Куда́ вы е́дете? —В Ки́ев.
Where are you going? —To Kiev.

Где вы живёте? —В Ки́еве.
Where do you live? —In Kiev.

Куда́ они́ иду́т? —Они́ иду́т домо́й.
Where are they going?
—They're going home.

Где они́? —Они́ до́ма.
Where are they?
—They're at home.

Он е́дет туда́? —Нет, он е́дет сюда́.
Is he going there?
—No, he's coming here.

Он там? —Нет, он здесь.
Is he there?
—No, he's here.

Notice that где, здесь, and там are always used with an understood form of the verb "to be" or a verb expressing a state of being. Also, they are only used with the nominative or prepositional cases. Куда́, сюда́, and туда́, on the other hand, are always used with a verb of motion, (i.e. one expressing movement in some direction) and are only used with the accusative case. Here are some more contrasting examples:

А я сейча́с <u>где</u>? —<u>В</u> дере́вне Во́лково.
And where am I? —In the village of Volkovo.

<u>Куда́</u> вы е́дете? —<u>В</u> дере́вню Во́лково.
Where are you going? —To the village of Volkovo.

<u>Где</u> ста́нция техобслу́живания? —Вон <u>там</u>.
Where is an auto repair shop? —Over there.

<u>Куда́</u> он е́дет? —<u>Туда́</u>, <u>на</u> ста́нцию техобслу́живания.
Where is he going? —There, to the auto repair shop.

3. THE ACCUSATIVE OVER TIME AND SPACE

Another usage of the accusative case is to express movement through space or in time. It answers the questions Куда́?, Когда́?, or Как до́лго? (For how long?). For example, in the phrases **в Ки́ев** (to Kiev) and **в сре́ду** (on Wednesday), **Ки́ев** and **среда́** are both in the accusative case. Remember that **на** is used with some places, e.g., **на конце́рте/ конце́рт,** and **в** with others, e.g. **в музе́е/музе́й.**[2]

Я е́ду в автосе́рвис и пото́м в Ки́ев.
> I'm going to the service station and then to Kiev.

Дочь идёт в шко́лу, а мать е́дет на рабо́ту.
> The daughter is going to school, and the mother is going to work.

Верни́тесь сюда́ в сре́ду.
> Come back on Wednesday.

Я хочу́ взять напрока́т маши́ну на неде́лю.
> I want to rent a car for a week.

4. THE ACCUSATIVE CASE OF ADJECTIVES AND SPECIAL MODIFIERS

The accusative form of adjectives is obtained by replacing the nominative endings with the appropriate accusative endings.

	NOMINATIVE SINGULAR	ACCUSATIVE SINGULAR	ACCUSATIVE PLURAL
MASC. INANIMATE	-ый	-ый	-ые
	-ий/-ой	-ий/-ой	-ие
FEMININE	-ая	-ую	-ые
	-яя	-юю	-ие
NEUTER	-ое	-ое	-ые
	-ее	-ее	-ие

Notice that the neuter, masculine inanimate, and plural accusative forms are the same as the nominative.

Я хочу́ взять напрока́т ма́ленькую, недорогу́ю маши́ну.
> I want to rent a small, inexpensive car. (base forms: **ма́ленький, недорого́й; маши́на**)

2. See **Уро́к** 4 (The Prepositional Case) for more examples of **в** versus **на**.

Вы принима́ете креди́тные ка́рточки?

Do you accept credit cards? (base forms: **креди́тный**; **ка́рточка**)

Я ищу́ ста́рую ка́рту страны́ и но́вый план го́рода.

I'm looking for an old map of the country and a new map of the city.
(base forms: **ста́рый, но́вый**; **ка́рта, план**)

The accusative case of the special modifiers follows:

	NOMINATIVE SINGULAR	ACCUSATIVE SINGULAR	PLURAL
MASC. INANIMATE	мой, твой, наш, ваш э́тот	мой, твой, наш, ваш э́тот	
FEMININE	моя́, твоя́, на́ша, ва́ша э́та	мою́, твою́, на́шу, ва́шу э́ту	мои́, твои́, на́ши, ва́ши э́ти
NEUTER	моё, твоё, на́ше, ва́ше э́то	моё, твоё, на́ше, ва́ше э́то	

Notice that masculine inanimate, neuter, and plural special modifiers are also identical in the accusative and the nominative. As always, **его́, её,** and **их** do not change.

Да́йте, пожа́луйста, ва́шу ви́зу и па́спорт. (base forms: ваш; ви́за)

Give me your visa and passport, please.

Слу́шай твою́ учи́тельницу! (base forms: твой; учи́тельница)

Listen to your teacher!

Посмотри́ его́ но́вый велосипе́д! (base forms: его́; велосипе́д)

Take a look at his new bicycle!

Ты чита́ешь э́ту кни́гу и́ли э́тот журна́л? (base forms: э́тот; кни́га; журна́л)

Are you reading this book or this magazine?

5. REFLEXIVE VERBS

Verbs that end in -**ся** (from **себя́**, meaning "self") are reflexive— they are used to describe actions that the subject performs on itself. Reflexive verbs are more common in Russian than in English, with the result that a verb is often reflexive in Russian, but its English counterpart is not. Reflexive verbs are conjugated just like regular verbs, but -**ся** is always attached on the end. The -**ся** ending should not be taken into account while conjugating. If a verb ends in a vowel, the -ся ending is spelled -сь. For example, the они form of возвраща́ться (to return) is formed as follows: возвраща́ть + ся >> возвраща́ют + ся >> возвраща́ются.

возвраща́ться: to return

I return	я возвраща́юсь	мы возвраща́емся	we return
you (fam.) return	ты возвраща́ешься	вы возвраща́етесь	you (pl./pol.) return
he/she returns	он/она́ возвраща́ется	они́ возвраща́ются	they return

stem: возвраща́ + ся
imperative: Возвраща́й(те)ся!

Эта доро́га продолжа́ется пря́мо до шоссе́.
That road continues straight to the highway.

И не возвраща́йся!
And don't come back!

Я возвраща́юсь домо́й.
I'm going back home.

Other common verbs ending with -ся include: называ́ться (to be called), находи́ться (to be located), сади́ться (to sit down), and начина́ться (to begin).

Как называ́ется дере́вня? И где она́ нахо́дится?
What's the name of the village? And where is it located?

Дя́дя, ты здесь сиди́шь?—Нет-нет. Сади́сь, сади́сь.
Uncle, are you sitting here? —No. Sit down, sit down.

Конце́рт начина́ется в во́семь часо́в.
The concert begins at 8 p.m.

6. EMPHASIS WITH ЖЕ

The particle же is not a word in itself but adds emphasis to any word it follows. It often translates to "_____ on earth . . . ?" Notice that it is never stressed but pronounced as part of the word it follows.

Куда́ же вы е́дете?

Where are you going?

А где же Анто́н?

And where on earth is Anton?

Кто же э́то?

Who on earth is that?

Возвраща́йся домо́й сра́зу же!

Go (return) home this instant!

D. СЛОВА́РЬ

автомоби́ль	automobile
автосе́рвис	service station
аккумуля́тор	battery
бензи́н	gas (petrol)
включа́ть (включа́ю, включа́ешь, включа́ют)	to include
води́тельские права́	driver's license
возвраща́ться (возвраща́юсь, возвраща́ешься, возвраща́ются)	to return
взять напрока́т	to rent (a car)
движе́ние	traffic (lit. movement)
дере́вня	village; countryside
до	until; (up) to; before
доро́га	road; way
е́хать (е́ду, е́дешь, е́дут)	to go (ride, drive)
же	emphatic particle
запра́вочная ста́нция	gas station
идти́ (иду́, идёшь, иду́т)	to go (by one's own power)
креди́тная ка́рточка	credit card
куда́	(to) where
литр	liter
маршру́т	route
маши́на	car; machine
находи́ться (нахожу́сь, нахо́дишься, нахо́дятся)	to be located
начина́ться (начина́юсь, начина́ешься, начина́ются)	to begin

не так	the wrong way (only with direction)
№ (но́мер)	number
перехо́д	pedestrian underpass
по доро́ге	on the way (only for people)
пото́м	then, after that
прейскура́нт	price list
принима́ть (принима́ю, принима́ешь, принима́ют)	to accept; to take (medicine; a shower)
про́бка	cork; traffic jam (colloquial)
Прове́рьте, пожа́луйста ...	Please check . . .
продолжа́ется	it continues
пря́мо	straight (direction)
разворо́т	U-turn
самообслу́живание	self-service
светофо́р	traffic light
Спаси́бо большо́е!	Thank you very much!
сра́зу	immediately
страна́	country
страхо́вка	insurance
сюда́	(to) here
туда́	(to) there
цена́	price
шоссе́	highway

РУССКАЯ КУЛЬТУРА

In order to drive in the CIS, you must have an international driver's license and visas for any country you plan to visit. Car rental agencies will often get the visas for you. If you plan to travel there by car, you should consult a recent guidebook (preferably one that gives international and Russian road signs) as well as someone who has driven in the CIS fairly recently. You should also be prepared for the attitude of Russian drivers that driving is a game with few if any rules, and of Russian pedestrians, who will cross wherever and whenever they can. If you see someone standing by the roadside with an arm raised, they are hitchhiking (**голосова́ние, автосто́п**), a common practice in outlying areas as well as in the cities. If you need to hitch a ride for any reason, although this is inadvisable in cities, be prepared to pay the driver.

Gas stations can be few and far between on the highway, so plan accordingly. There are three types of gas: 72 octane, 93 octane, and diesel, none of which are unleaded. Sometimes you can buy oil and other such things at a gas station, but for anything else, look for a service station or repair shop. For help while on the road, including directions, repairs, and to report an accident, find a **ГИПДД**, or **гайшник** (traffic officer or inspector from the former name **ГАИ**). They are located at posts in cities or along the highways, or are patrolling by car or motorcycle. **ГИПДД** issues **штрафы** (fines) for jay-walking while **ДПС** regulates traffic.

УПРАЖНЕНИЯ

A. **Запо́лните про́пуски пра́вильными фо́рмами глаго́лов «идти́» и́ли «е́хать».** (Fill in the blanks with the correct form of the verbs **идти́** or **е́хать**.)

1. Лэ́рри _____ в Москву́.
2. Ты _____ в шко́лу пешко́м и́ли _____ на авто́бусе?
3. _____ пря́мо к шоссе́. —Спаси́бо большо́е!
4. Са́шка, _____ сюда́!
5. Эта доро́га _____ в Ки́ев?

B. **Подбери́те вопро́сы и отве́ты. Да́йте са́мый лу́чший отве́т на ка́ждый вопро́с.** (Match the questions and the answers. Give the best answer to each question.)

1. Когда́ ты е́дешь в Новосиби́рск?
2. Куда́ ты е́дешь в четве́рг?
3. Как вы е́дете?
4. Куда́ ты идёшь?
5. Где они́ живу́т?
6. Куда́ они́ е́дут?
7. Где они́?
8. Вы е́дете в Петербу́рг в воскресе́нье?
9. Они́ е́дут туда́?
10. Я сейча́с где?

a. Вы в дере́вне Во́лково.
b. Они́ е́дут в Москву́.
c. Я е́ду в Новосиби́рск.
d. В Большо́й Теа́тр.
e. Они́ до́ма.
f. Нет, они́ е́дут на рабо́ту.
g. На такси́.
h. В четве́рг.
i. Я иду́ домо́й.
j. Да, в воскресе́нье.
k. Они́ живу́т в Москве́.

C. Поста́вьте прилага́тельные в ско́бках в вини́тельный паде́ж и заполните про́пуски. (Put the adjectives in parentheses into the accusative case and fill in the blanks.)

1. Дай _____ _____ ка́рту райо́на. (твой/ста́рый)
2. Да́йте, пожа́луйста, _____ план го́рода. (недорого́й)
3. Смотри́те _____ _____ телеви́зор. (наш/но́вый)
4. Я люблю́ чита́ть _____ _____ _____ кни́ги.
   (э́тот/класси́ческий/ру́сский)
5. Она́ хо́чет _____ _____ пла́тье? (мой/ста́рый)

D. Заполните про́пуски пра́вильными оконча́ниями глаго́лов.
(Fill in the blanks with the correct endings of the verbs.)

1. Лэ́рри, ты туда́ возвраща_____ в суббо́ту.
2. Мы сад _____ вон туда́.
3. Фильм называ_____ «Дерсу́ Узала́» и он о Сиби́ри.
4. Аня и Са́ша, возвраща_____ домо́й сра́зу же!
5. Про́бка до́лго продолжа_____ .

УРОК 10

НА ПОЧТЕ. At the post office.

A. ДИАЛОГ

В кафете́рии университе́та.

ЖАН-ФРАНСУА: *Эй, Макси́м! Я иду́ на главпочта́мт посыла́ть посы́лку домо́й. Ты не зна́ешь, где он?*

МАКСИМ: *Зна́ю! Перейди́ че́рез у́лицу, и по́чта нахо́дится нале́во. Спроси́, где междунаро́дное окно́.*

ЖАН-ФРАНСУА: *Спаси́бо. Извини́, но я спешу́. Пока́!*

На Главпочта́мте, у окна́.

ЖАН-ФРАНСУА: *Здесь мо́жно посла́ть посы́лки и откры́тки?*

РАБОТНИК ПОЧТЫ: *Да, мо́жно. А что у вас?*

ЖАН-ФРАНСУА: *Я хочу́ посла́ть э́ту посы́лку в Пари́ж.*

РАБОТНИК ПОЧТЫ: *Кому́?*

ЖАН-ФРАНСУА: *Вот напи́сана фами́лия и а́дрес.*

РАБОТНИК ПОЧТЫ: *Хорошо́. Что внутри́?*

ЖАН-ФРАНСУА: *Я посыла́ю пода́рки мое́й семье́ — оди́н плато́к, две игру́шки.*

РАБОТНИК ПОЧТЫ: *Так ... паке́т ве́сит 2,3 килогра́мма. Авиапо́чтой?*

ЖАН-ФРАНСУА: *Нет, обы́чной. А э́ти откры́тки авиапо́чтой.*

РАБОТНИК ПОЧТЫ: *Вот ва́ши ма́рки.*

ЖАН-ФРАНСУА: *Спаси́бо. А когда́ дойдёт посы́лка?*

РАБОТНИК ПОЧТЫ: *Че́рез четы́ре дня. Что-нибу́дь ещё?*

ЖАН-ФРАНСУА: *Да. Где мо́жно отпра́вить телегра́мму?*

РАБОТНИК ПОЧТЫ: *Обрати́тесь в о́кна 5–8.*

At the university cafeteria.

JEAN-FRANCOIS: Hey, Maksim! I'm on my way to the main post office to send a package home. Would you happen to know where it is?

MAKSIM: Yes. Cross the street, and the post office is on the left. Ask where the international window is.

JEAN-FRANCOIS: Thanks. Sorry, but I'm in a hurry. See you!

At a window at the Main Post Office.

JEAN-FRANCOIS: Can I mail packages and postcards here?

POSTAL EMPLOYEE: Yes, you can. What do you have?

JEAN-FRANCOIS: I want to send this package to Paris.

POSTAL EMPLOYEE: To whom?

JEAN-FRANCOIS: Here's the last name and address.

POSTAL EMPLOYEE: Good. What's inside?

JEAN-FRANCOIS: I'm sending presents to my family: one shawl, two toys.

POSTAL EMPLOYEE: Okay ... the package weighs 2.3 kilos. Air mail?

JEAN-FRANCOIS: No, regular. But these postcards are air mail.

POSTAL EMPLOYEE: Here are your stamps.

JEAN-FRANCOIS: Thank you. And when will the package arrive?

POSTAL EMPLOYEE: In four days. Anything else?

JEAN-FRANCOIS: Yes. Where can I send a telegram?

POSTAL EMPLOYEE: You'll have to go to windows 5–8 for that.

B. ПРОИЗНОШЕНИЕ

1. THE CONSONANT й

The English equivalent of **й** would be "y" because, like y, it lengthens any vowel it follows. This is particularly noticeable with the vowels **a**, **o**, and **e**.

окно́; домо́й   *да; май*   *семье́; мое́й*

Like ь, й combines with any following hard vowel to form a soft vowel.

музе́й + ы = *музе́и*   май + а = *ма́я*   трамва́й + у = *трамва́ю*

2. THE SOFT р

Like the soft л, the soft р can be challenging for an English speaker. Р is soft-ened when followed by a ь or by a soft vowel. Again, try pronouncing *r* and *y* simultaneously. Remember that the Russian р is always trilled, or rolled, whether hard or soft. Following are some contrasting soft р/hard р pairs.

пря́мо/пра́вда   *дере́вня/рэ́кет*   *октя́брь/бра́т*

C. ГРАММАТИКА И СЛОВОУПОТРЕБЛЕНИЕ

1. THE DATIVE CASE (INDIRECT OBJECTS)

a. Singular Nouns

The dative case generally answers the question **Кому́?** (To/For whom?) or **Чему́?** (To/For what?). It roughly corresponds to the indirect object in English. To obtain the dative case, simply replace the nominative ending with the ap-propriate dative ending. The dative case endings for singular nouns are:

	HARD	SOFT
MASCULINE	-у	-ю
NEUTER	-у	-ю
FEMININE	-е/-и	-е

Notice that the feminine endings are the same as in the prepositional.

Я посыла́ю платки́ жене́ и ма́тери.
I'm sending shawls to my wife and my mother.

Я посыла́ю игру́шку сы́ну.

I'm sending a toy to my son.

Ты пи́шешь письмо́ Ни́не и Макси́му?

Are you writing a letter to Nina and Maksim?

b. Adjectives and Special Modifiers

The singular dative endings for all adjectives and special modifiers are:

	HARD	SOFT
MASCULINE/NEUTER	-ому	-ему
FEMININE	-ой	-ей

Notice that they are the same as in the prepositional.

Я посыла́ю пода́рки мое́й семье́.

I'm sending presents to my family.

Кому́ он пи́шет письмо́? —Хоро́шему дру́гу.

To whom is he writing a letter? —To a good friend.

Она́ чита́ет кни́гу э́тому ма́ленькому ма́льчику.

She's reading a book to this little boy.

2. THE ACCUSATIVE WITH ЧЕРЕЗ

Че́рез, a preposition meaning "through" or "across," is always followed by a noun in the accusative. It is used to describe passage through space or time.

Перейди́ че́рез у́лицу и пото́м че́рез Кра́сную пло́щадь.

Go across the street and then across Red Square.

Посы́лка дойдёт че́рез неде́лю.

The package will arrive in a week.

По́чта открыва́ется че́рез мину́ту.

The post office is opening in a minute.

3. THE GENITIVE AFTER THE PREPOSITIONS У, ДО, AND ОТ

In addition to its general usage indicating possession, the genitive can be used to describe the origin or onset of an action (following **от**), the destination or end-limit of an action (following **до**), and location (following **у**).

Посы́лка идёт от четырёх дней до неде́ли.
The package will arrive in four days to a week.

На Главпочта́мте у окна́.
At a window of the Main Post Office.

От Ки́ева до Москвы́ Ля́рри е́дет на маши́не.
Larry is going by car from Kiev to Moscow.

От (from) and **до** (until, up to) are often used together to mean "from . . . to . . . ," describing an area in space or an interval in time.

4. THE GENITIVE WITH NUMBERS 2–4

The numbers 2 to 4, or compound numerals ending in those numbers (e.g. 32, 63), are always followed by the genitive singular. Remember the special feminine form for 2: **две.**

Паке́т ве́сит 2,3 килогра́мма. (килогра́мм ≫ килогра́мма)
The package weighs 2.3 kilos.

Я посыла́ю две игру́шки. (игру́шка ≫ игру́шки)
I'm sending two toys.

Заня́тие ещё продолжа́ется 24 мину́ты. (мину́та ≫ мину́ты)
The class is continuing for another 24 minutes.

Here are some nouns commonly used with numbers:

4 го́да, 23 ме́сяца, 52 неде́ли, 33 дня, 4 часа́, 3 мину́ты, 2 (две) секу́нды
4 years, 23 months, 52 weeks, 33 days, 4 hours, 3 minutes, 2 seconds

54 рубля́, 2 (две) копе́йки, 83 до́ллара, 92 це́нта
54 rubles, 2 kopecks, 83 dollars, 92 cents

5. POSSIBILITY AND PERMISSION: МО́ЖНО AND НЕЛЬЗЯ́

Мо́жно (it is possible with a perfective verb/permitted with an imperfective verb) is used frequently in Russian. It is an impersonal expression, as there is no stated subject other than the implied "it," and is usually followed by an infinitive[1]. As with **есть**, questions asked with **мо́жно** may be answered with the word itself—**Да, мо́жно.** (Yes, it is possible/permitted.)—or with **нет, нельзя́** (no, it is impossible/not permitted). **Нельзя́** is the opposite of **мо́жно** and is also usually followed by an infinitive.

Здесь мо́жно посла́ть посы́лки и откры́тки? —Да, мо́жно.
Can I mail packages and postcards here? ——Yes, you can.

Где мо́жно отпра́вить телегра́мму?
Where can I send a telegram?

Здесь мо́жно кури́ть? —Нет, нельзя́.
Is smoking allowed here? ——No, it isn't (allowed).

Мо́жно can be used alone when the context is obvious. For example, if a person is pointing to an empty seat, **Мо́жно?** implies "May I sit here?"

6. FEMININE NOUNS ENDING IN -ь

Feminine nouns that end in **-ь** do not change endings in the accusative case, but in the genitive, prepositional, and dative cases the **-ь** becomes **-и**, e.g. **жизнь** (life) >> **жи́зни, вещь** (thing) >> **ве́щи, часть** (part) >> **ча́сти. Дочь** and **мать** follow a similar rule, where the **-ь** becomes **-ери** rather than **-и**[2]: **дочь** >> **до́чери.**

Жан-Франсуа́ хо́чет посла́ть пода́рок <u>до́чери</u>.
Jean-Francois wants to send a present to his daughter.

Кто компози́тор этой <u>ве́щи</u>? —Джордж Ви́нстон.
Who's the composer of this piece? ——George Winston.

---

1. See Уро́к 26 for more on using the correct infinitives with **мо́жно** and **нельзя́**.
2. До́чери and ма́тери are also the nominative plural forms.

Моя жена́ пи́шет письмо́ <u>мое́й ма́тери</u> о <u>на́шей жи́зни</u>.

My wife is writing a letter to my mother about our life.

7. CAPITALIZATION

Fewer words are capitalized in Russian than in English. In Russian the days of the week, the months, the words **ма́ма** and **па́па**, and any nouns derived from proper names, e.g. **москви́ч** (Muscovite) are not capitalized, unless they begin a sentence. Also, only the first word in titles of books, films, etc., is capitalized.

У нас собра́ние в пе́рвую пя́тницу в октябре́.

We have a meeting on the first Friday in October.

Его́ па́па слу́шает переда́чу «Москва́ и москвичи́.»

His father is listening to the program "Moscow and Muscovites."

The words **ма́ма** and **па́па** can be used to refer to someone else's mother and father as well as to one's own.

D. СЛОВАРЬ

авиапо́чта	air mail
а́дрес	address
Вам на́до ...	You need to . . .
ве́сить (ве́шу, ве́сишь, ве́сят)	to weigh (followed by weight)
внутри́	inside (a container); indoors
вход	entrance
год	year
дочь	f. daughter
жизнь	f. life
и́ндекс	zip code
килогра́мм	kilogram (1,000 grams, or 2.2 pounds)
конве́рт	envelope
кури́ть (курю́, ку́ришь, ку́рят)	to smoke
ма́рка	stamp
междунаро́дный	international
ме́сяц	month
мину́та	minute
мо́жно	it is possible/permitted
нале́во	to the left; on the left

неде́ля	week
нельзя́	it is impossible/forbidden
обы́чная по́чта	regular mail
окно́	window
откры́тка	postcard (from **откры́ть,** to open)
отправля́ть (отправля́ю, отправля́ешь, отправля́ют)	to send
пода́рок	present, gift
посыла́ть (посыла́ю, посыла́ешь, посыла́ют)	to send
посы́лка	package (from **посыла́ть,** to send)
по́чта	post office
почтальо́н	mail-carrier
почто́вый я́щик	mailbox
секу́нда	second (1/60th of a minute)
спеши́ть (спешу́, спеши́шь, спеша́т)	to hurry
сын	son
телегра́мма	telegram
у́лица	street
фами́лия	last name
че́рез	through; across; in
что́-нибудь	anything

РУССКАЯ КУЛЬТУРА

At Russian post offices you can not only send and receive mail and packages and buy money orders, but you can also make long distance calls and send telegrams. Sometimes there is also a small bank where people can pay utility bills and receive pension payments. International packages, including those to former Soviet republics, can only be sent from a **междунаро́дный** (international) or **гла́вный** (main) **почта́мт** (post office). International packages and letters can either be sent by air or surface mail. A package weighing under one kilogram is a **бандеро́ль,** and one weighing from one to eight kilograms is a **посы́лка.** Since the contents of packages must be inspected before mailing, do not seal or wrap them. They will be wrapped for you.

Anything that is not explicitly meant to be mailed (i.e., has the words **куда́** and **кому́,** lines for the address, and a place for the **и́ндекс**) must be put in a **конве́рт** (envelope). This includes any postcards that do not have the required address form on the right-hand side. Since the reliability of the postal system is variable, letters and packages are often sent registered to ensure arrival. Telegrams and telexes are a common way to send information, especially if it is urgent, and faxes and electronic mail (электро́нная по́чта) are widely used in business. FedEx, UPS or DHL are also available in Russia. Another common method of sending mail to Russia is to send packages or letters with people traveling. Sending money through the mail is ill-advised, but wire transfers and Western Union are common.

УПРАЖНЕ́НИЯ

A. Поста́вьте слова́ в ско́бках в да́тельный паде́ж и запо́лните про́пуски. (Put the words in the parentheses into the dative case and fill in the blanks.)

1. Жан-Франсуа́ посыла́ет пода́рки _____ и _____ . (жена́, мать)
2. Ни́на хо́чет посла́ть игру́шки _____ и _____ . (дочь, сын)
3. Мы ча́сто пи́шем пи́сьма _____ _____ в Аме́рике. (наш друг)
4. Пожа́луйста, чита́йте кни́гу _____ _____ _____ _____ .
   (э́та хоро́шая ма́ленькая де́вочка)
5. Я пишу́ откры́тку _____ _____ _____ . (моя́ ру́сская подру́га)

B. Поста́вьте слова́ в ско́бках в пра́вильный паде́ж и запо́лните про́пуски. (Put the words in the parentheses into the correct case and fill in the blanks.)

1. Я пишу́ письмо́ _____ _____ о _____ _____ . (моя́ мать, на́ша жизнь)
2. Я уве́рена, что Шостако́вич а́втор _____ _____ . (э́та вещь)
3. Мои́ друзья́ живу́т у _____ . (парк)
4. Мо́жно е́хать от _____ до _____ на по́езде? (Владивосто́к, Москва́)
5. У нас обе́д че́рез _____ . (час)
6. У нас ещё оди́н день до _____ . (выходны́е)
7. Главпочта́мт закрыва́ется че́рез _____ . (мину́та)
8. У меня́ сего́дня собра́ние до _____ . (обе́д)
9. Слу́шай _____ _____ ! (э́та часть)
10. Он е́дет на тролле́йбусе до _____ и пото́м на метро́ до _____ . (музе́й, це́нтр)

C. **Подберите соответствующие русские предложения к английским значениям.** (Match the Russian sentences with the English meanings.)

1. Можно смотреть телевизор? —Да, можно.
2. Нельзя ехать туда?
3. Можно прочитать твоё письмо?
4. Почему нельзя слушать радио?
5. (В кафе) Можно? —Да, пожалуйста.
6. Здесь нельзя отправить эту посылку.
7. Можно позвонить домой?
8. Нельзя учить русский язык в школе.
9. Где можно взять напрокат машину?
10. Нельзя опаздывать на занятие.

a. Why can't you listen to the radio?
b. It's impossible to mail that package here.
c. Can I call home?
d. Where can I rent a car?
e. Is listening to the radio allowed here?
f. (In a cafe) May I? —Yes, go ahead.
g. It's impossible to study Russian in school.
h. May I watch T.V.? —Yes, you may.
i. Being late to class is not allowed.
j. It's impossible to drive there?
k. May I read your letter?

D. **Заполните пропуски правильными формами слов в скобках.** (Fill in the blanks with the correct form of the words in parentheses.)

1. 2 _____ = 24 _____ (год, месяц)
2. 1 _____ = 52 _____ (год, неделя)
3. Через 4 _____ и 23 _____ . (день, час)
4. Молодец! У тебя 3 _____ 2 _____ ! (минута, секунда)
5. 4 _____ 2 _____ , пожалуйста. (рубль, копейка)

ВТОРАЯ ПРОВЕРКА (Second Review)

A. Запо́лните про́пуски. (Fill in the blanks.)

1. Как_____ больш_____ окно́!
2. Как_____ интере́сн_____ письмо́!
3. Как_____ краси́в_____ маши́на!
4. Как_____ хоро́ш_____ челове́к!
5. Ребя́та, вы гото́в_____? —Да, мы гото́в_____.
6. Михаи́л Семёнович, вы согла́сн_____? —Да, я согла́с_____.
7. Эт_____ ма́леньк_____ де́вочка о́чень похо́ж_____ на тво_____ мать.
8. Ч_____ э́то чемода́ны? Ваш_____? —Да, наш_____.
9. В как_____ го́роде он живёт? —Во Владивосто́ке, на Да́льн_____ восто́ке.
10. Она́ посыла́ет эт_____ ста́р_____ игру́шку их нов_____ ру́сск_____ дру́гу.

B. Поста́вьте слова́ в ско́бках в ну́жную фо́рму и запо́лните про́пуски.
(Put the words in parentheses into the correct form and fill in the blanks.)

1. А что вы хоти́те? —Я хочу́ _____ че́ки. (поменя́ть)
2. Они́ _____ _____ ру́сский язы́к. —Да, я _____. Они́ ка́ждый день _____ но́вые слова́. (люби́ть/учи́ть/знать/учи́ть)
3. Моя́ ру́сская подру́га ча́сто _____: «Я тебя́ _____.» Но я её не _____. (говори́ть/люби́ть/понима́ть)
4. Ты _____ домо́й? —Да, я _____ домо́й. (возвраща́ться)
5. Заня́тие _____ ещё 22 мину́ты. (продолжа́ться)

C. Переведи́те слова́ в ско́бках и запо́лните про́пуски. По́мните ра́зницу ме́жду глаго́лами «е́хать» и «идти́» и ме́жду вы- и ты-фо́рмами императи́вов. (Translate the word in parentheses, and fill in the blanks. Remember the difference between the verbs идти́ and е́хать, and between the вы and ты forms of the imperative.)

ОБРАЗЕ́Ц: Са́ша, где ты? Иди́ сюда́! (Come)
Sasha, where are you? Come here!

1. _____ ваш па́спорт и _____, пожа́луйста. (Give (me)/go ahead)
2. _____, ма́ма! (Listen)
3. Де́ти, _____ домо́й сра́зу же! (return (go back))

4. Ты _____ на рабо́ту пешко́м? —Нет, я _____ на метро́. (go/go)

5. Куда́ _____ э́та доро́га? —Она́ _____ в Москву́. (go/goes)

D. **Переведи́те с ру́сского на англи́йский и́ли с англи́йского на ру́сский.**
(Translate from Russian to English or from English to Russian.)

1. Ира о́чень ра́да, потому́ что за́втра начина́ется уике́нд.

2. Мы не зна́ем, чьё это ме́сто. —Ои, э́то моё ме́сто!

3. Позови́те, пожа́луйста, Пе́тю. —Вы не туда́ попа́ли.

4. Мы не принима́ем э́ту креди́тную ка́рточку. Что вы бу́дете де́лать?

5. Ми́ша и Ма́ша, иди́те сюда́ сейча́с (now) же!

6. Olya, give me a pen, please. —I don't have a pen. Maybe Sasha has a pen.

7. Katya is sure that Papa's going back (returning) there in three hours.

8. I'm writing a letter to our new friend in Russia.

9. Excuse me, would you (polite) happen to know where I can rent a car?

10. We have a big meeting on the first Sunday of the month.

ТЕКСТ ДЛЯ ЧТЕНИЯ (Reading)

Now you're ready to practice your reading skills! You have been reading the dialogues, of course, but the four **текст для чтения** sections offer you the chance to practice reading as you would read a newspaper article or essay abroad. First, read through each passage without referring to the accompanying vocabulary notes. Try to understand the main idea of the text, inferring the meanings of new words from context and making use of any English cognates. Don't worry if a passage seems long or if you don't know each word; you can go back and reread it, checking the vocabulary notes to learn the exact meaning of new words and phrases.

ГЕОГРАФИЯ

Россия—огромная[1] страна, самая[2] большая в мире[3]. Там 10 времянных поясов[4], от Балтийского моря[5] до Тихого океана[6]. Когда в Москве пять часов—во Владивостоке уже двенадцать. На Крайнем[7] Севере, в Сибири, климат арктический, а совсем на юге[8]—субтропический. Температура зимой[9] в Москве и в Миннеаполисе похожа. На Крайнем севере, например[10] в Якутске, вечная мерзлота[11]. Далеко[12] на севере находятся города-порты: Мурманск и Архангельск. В Мурманске климат неприятный: там холодно и сыро[13]. Порт в Архангельске замерзает[14] зимой, а в Мурманске не замерзает, потому что там проходит Гольфстрим. Поэтому[15] Мурманск для России—очень важный порт. На крайнем севере России находится тундра, к югу от тундры начинается тайга.

Уральские горы[16] разделяют[17] Россию на две части[18]—запад[19] и восток. На запад от них—Европа, а на восток—Азия. На западе находятся самые большие города в СНГ: Москва и Санкт Петербург, и самые важные реки[20]: Волга, Дон и Днепр. Самые длинные реки в России—в Сибири. Это—Обь, Енисей, Иртыш, Амур и Лена. В Сибири есть город Иркутск и озеро[21] Байкал, самое глубокое[22] озеро в мире. В Сибири зима очень длинная, холодная, а лето[23] короткое, но жаркое.

СЛОВАРЬ

1. огромный	enormous
2. самый	the most; the (adj.)-est

3. мир	world/peace
4. временны́е пояса́ / пояса́ вре́мени	time zones
5. Балти́йское мо́ре	Baltic Sea
6. Ти́хий океа́н	Pacific Ocean
7. кра́йний	extreme
8. юг	south
9. зима́ (зимо́й)	winter (in the winter)
10. наприме́р	for example
11. ве́чная мерзлота́	permafrost
12. далеко́	far
13. сы́ро	damp
14. замерза́ть (замерза́ю, замерза́ешь, замерза́ют)	to freeze
15. поэ́тому	therefore
16. гора́ (го́ры)	mountain (mountains)
17. разделя́ть (разделя́ю, разделя́ешь, разделя́ют)	to divide
18. часть	f. part
19. за́пад	west
20. река́	river
21. о́зеро	lake
22. глубо́кий	deep
23. ле́то	summer

УРОК 11

ПОХОД В КИНО. Going to a movie.

А. ДИАЛОГ

По телефо́ну.

КАТЯ: Слу́шаю.

ВАЛЕРА: Это Ира?

КАТЯ: Нет. Одну́ мину́точку.

ИРА: Алло́, Вале́ра?

ВАЛЕРА: Да, э́то я. Приве́т! Слу́шай, Ирочка! Ты смотре́ла фильм «Манхэ́ттен»?

ИРА: Нет, никогда́. О чём фильм?

ВАЛЕРА: Поня́тия не име́ю, но Ву́ди Аллен—режиссёр и игра́ет гла́вную роль.

ИРА: О, он мне о́чень нра́вится! Фильм дубли́рованный?

ВАЛЕРА: Нет, он с субти́трами. Пойдём сего́дня ве́чером!

ИРА: Договори́лись! Где он идёт?

ВАЛЕРА: В кинотеа́тре «Росси́я».

ИРА: О, да, я была́ там. Во ско́лько начина́ется фильм?

ВАЛЕРА: Есть два сеа́нса, оди́н в шесть и друго́й в де́вять.

ИРА: Мне всё равно́. В де́вять?

ВАЛЕРА: Ла́дно. До встре́чи!

В кинотеа́тре.

ИРА: Приве́т! Ско́лько сейча́с вре́мени? Я не опозда́ла?

ВАЛЕРА: Нет. Сейча́с 8.30. Фильм начина́ется че́рез полчаса́.

ИРА: *Отли́чно. Ты не зна́ешь, как до́лго идёт фильм?*

ВАЛЕРА: *Два часа́ без переры́ва.*

On the telephone.

KATYA: Hello.

VALERA: Is this Ira?

KATYA: No. Just a minute.

IRA: Hello, Valera?

VALERA: Yes, it's me. Hi! Listen, Ira. Have you seen the movie "Manhattan"?

IRA: No, never. What's it about?

VALERA: I have no idea, but Woody Allen is the director and plays the lead.

IRA: Oh, I really like him! Is it dubbed?

VALERA: No, it's subtitled. Let's go see it tonight!

IRA: Alright! Where's it playing?

VALERA: At the Russia Theater.

IRA: Oh, yes, I've been there. What time does the movie start?

VALERA: There are two shows, one at six and another at nine.

IRA: It doesn't matter to me. At nine?

VALERA: Okay. See you then!

At the movie theater.

IRA: Hi! What time is it? Am I late?

VALERA: No. It's 8:30 now. The movie starts in half an hour.

IRA: Great. Do you happen to know how long the movie is?

VALERA: Two hours, without an intermission.

B. ГРАММАТИКА И СЛОВОУПОТРЕБЛЕНИЕ

1. THE PAST TENSE

The Russian past tense is probably the easiest tense to form. Depending on context, it can be translated into English as "I did," "I was doing," "I have done," or "I used to do." The past tense verb agrees in gender and number with its subject. Simply replace the infinitive -ть ending with -л for the masculine form, -ла for the feminine form, -ло for the neuter form, and -ли for the plural form. For example, де́лать >> де́ла + л >> де́лал. Following is a sample verb in the past tense.

быть: to be

	SINGULAR	PLURAL
MASCULINE	был	
FEMININE	была́	бы́ли
NEUTER	бы́ло	

Я вчера́ был в кино́.
I was at the movies yesterday. (the speaker is male)

Что они́ де́лали вчера́ ве́чером? —Они́ слу́шали переда́чу конце́рта.
What did they do last night? —They listened to a broadcast of the concert.

Аня, ты смотре́ла фильм «Манхэ́ттен»? —Нет, никогда́.
Anya, have you seen the movie "Manhattan"? —No, never.

Когда́ мы жи́ли в Москве́, мы ча́сто смотре́ли америка́нские фи́льмы.
When we lived in Moscow, we often used to watch American movies.

Reflexive verbs are conjugated the same way, but they retain the -ся suffix in all verb forms. Remember that -ся is spelled -сь after vowels. In the past tense, therefore, -сь is used for all but the masculine forms.

Договори́лись!
Agreed! (literally, We have agreed!)

Фильм начина́лся в шесть.

The movie began at six.

2. THE DATIVE CASE OF PERSONAL PRONOUNS

Pronouns in the dative case generally represent indirect objects. They answer the question **Кому́?** (To/For whom?).

to me	мне	нам	to us
to you (fam.)	тебе́	вам	to you (pl./pol.)
to him/to her	ему́/ей	им	to them

Мне всё равно́.

It's all the same to me.

Ира, тебе́ звоно́к.

Ira, the call is for you.

Напиши́те нам письмо́!

Write us a letter!

Certain verbs and expressions require the dative case (and therefore dative pronouns). Some will be obvious from the translations, as in the above examples, but those that are not must simply be memorized. Some common verbs requiring the dative include: **помога́ть** (to help), **дать** (to give), and **сказа́ть** (to tell, say).

Да́йте мне, пожа́луйста, оди́н биле́т.

Please give me one ticket.

Он им помога́ет учи́ть ру́сский язы́к.

He's helping them learn Russian.

Скажи́те мне, когда́ начина́ется фильм?

Tell me, when does the movie start?

3. EXPRESSING "TO LIKE"

The Russian verb **нра́виться** is used quite differently from its English counterpart, "to like." The subject in English becomes an indirect object (dative) in

Russian, and the object in English—that which is liked— becomes the subject (nominative) in Russian. It might be helpful to translate **нра́виться** as "to be pleasing to."

Ву́ди Аллен мне о́чень нра́вится!
I like Woody Allen very much! (literally, Woody Allen is very pleasing to me.)

Коне́чно, ты Анто́ну нра́вишься!
Of course Anton likes you! (literally, you are pleasing to Anton.)

Ей нра́вилась э́та кни́га?
Did she use to like that book? (literally, Was that book pleasing to her?)

Нра́виться is a regular Conjugation II verb, but note that it is most often used in the third person. If the object or person liked is singular, use the third person singular form **нра́вится**; if the object or person liked is plural, use the third person plural form, **нра́вятся**.

Со́не не нра́вится му́зыка Була́та Окуджа́вы.
Sonya doesn't like Bulat Okudzhava's music.

Тебе́ нра́вятся америка́нские фи́льмы?
Do you like American movies?

4. TELLING TIME

To ask the time in Russian, use the expression:

Ско́лько сейча́с вре́мени?
What time is it (now)?

To tell the time, state the current hour plus the number of minutes elapsed. One o'clock is expressed simply as **час**.

Ско́лько сейча́с вре́мени? —Сейча́с час.
What time is it? —It's one o'clock.

Сейча́с во́семь (часо́в) три́дцать (мину́т).
It's now eight (hours) - thirty (minutes).

Сейча́с четы́ре (часа́) пятьдеся́т три (мину́ты).
It's now four (hours) - fifty-three (minutes).

Remember that different numbers require different cases. This also applies to nouns reflecting units of time, e.g. hours and minutes. Remember, too, that **два** has the feminine form **две**, e.g. **две мину́ты**.

NUMBERS ENDING IN:	WITH HOURS/MINUTES	EXAMPLES
1	час, мину́та	одна́ мину́та
2, 3, 4	часа́, мину́ты	три часа́
5–9, 0	часо́в, мину́т	семь часо́в пять мину́т

Ско́лько сейча́с вре́мени? —Сейча́с два часа́ со́рок мину́т.
What time is it? —It's two (hours) - forty (minutes).

Где ты был? Я тебя́ жду уже́ со́рок две мину́ты!
Where've you been? I've been waiting for you for forty-two minutes!

To ask at what time an event takes place, use **во ско́лько** (at what time). To respond, use the preposition **в** followed by the time.

Во ско́лько начина́ется фильм? —Фильм начина́ется в де́вять.
What time (when) does the movie begin? —The movie starts at nine.

Во ско́лько она́ идёт на рабо́ту? —В шесть часо́в.
What time (when) does she go to work? —At six o'clock.

The 24-hour clock is used in official schedules and time tables, but generally not in conversation. If it is necessary to specify a.m. or p.m. in conversation, use **утра́** or **ве́чера,** respectively.

«По́езд на Псков: 19.00, 7.00» зна́чит, что оди́н по́езд отхо́дит в семь часо́в ве́чера, а друго́й в семь часо́в утра́.
"Train to Pskov: 19:00, 7:00" means that one train leaves at 7 p.m. and the other at 7 a.m.

Following are some expressions for the time of day:

у́тро	morning (from dawn to noon)
у́тром	in the morning

Оди́ннадцатый уро́к

день	afternoon, day (from noon to 5, or daylight hours)
днём	in the afternoon, during the day
ве́чер	evening (from 6 p.m. to 11 p.m. or midnight)
ве́чером	in the evening
ночь	night (from 12 a.m. to dawn)
но́чью	at night

They are often used together with the adverbs вчера́ (yesterday), сего́дня (today), and за́втра (tomorrow). For example, tonight is **сего́дня ве́чером.**

Пойдём за́втра днём!
Let's go tomorrow afternoon!

А что ты де́лала вчера́ ве́чером?
And what were you doing last night?

Споко́йной но́чи!
Good night!

Note that Russians use a period instead of a colon to separate hours from minutes (e.g., 8.30 as opposed to 8:30).

C. СЛОВАРЬ

Алло́?	Hello? (only on the telephone)
без (чего́/кого́)	without (someone/something)
быть	to be (I.) [1]
ве́чер	evening
ве́чером	in the evening
Во ско́лько ... ?	At what time . . . ?
вчера́	yesterday
гла́вный	main; central
днём	in the afternoon
Договори́лись!	Agreed!
До встре́чи!	Until then! (lit. Until meeting!)
до́лго	long; for a long time (not in present)
дубли́рованный	dubbed
за́втра	tomorrow
и́мени	named after
кино́ (кинотеа́тр)	cinema; movie theater

1. Verbs that are not obviously Conjugation I or Conjugation II will be marked as follows: (I.) or (II.).

Мне всё равнó.	I don't care.; It's all the same to me.
никогдá	never
ночь	night
нóчью	at night
нрáвиться (нрáвится, нрáвятся) (комý)	to like, to be pleasing (to someone)
Однý минýточку.	Just a minute.
по телефóну	on the telephone
Пойдём!	Let's go!
Поня́тия не имéю.	I have no idea.
похóд	going (process of); hike (noun)
режиссёр	director (film or play)
роль	role
сеáнс	scheduled showing
Скóлько врéмени? —Сейчáс ...	What time is it? —It's . . .
Слýшаю	Hello? (lit. I'm listening.)
смотрéть (смотрю́, смóтришь, смóтрят)	to watch, to look at (I.)
с субти́трами	subtitled; with subtitles
ýтро	morning
ýтром	in the morning
фильм	film; movie

РУССКАЯ КУЛЬТУРА

When entering a row in the theater in Russia, be sure to face the people sitting in the row rather than the screen, as to do otherwise is considered quite rude. Also, be aware that, like many European films, most Russian films tend to be longer and slower-moving than American films.

Following **глáсность**, the Russian film industry experienced a rebirth. Many of these new films depict life during the Soviet years and offer a great way to learn about Russian and Soviet history, in particular about the Stalin years. Most notable are: *The Inner Circle* (1991), **Покая́ние** (*Repentance*, 1987) and the Oscar-winning *Burnt by the Sun* (1994). Other popular **глáсность** films include: **Чýчело** (*Scarecrow*, 1985), about a girl in a small country town, and **Мáленькая Вéра** (*Little Vera*, 1988), about a young woman in the provinces. Among the easiest Russian films for American audiences to appreciate are probably **Ребрó Адáма** (*Adam's Rib*, 1992), about three generations of women living in a small apartment and a thriller **Брат** (*Brother,* 1997).

УПРАЖНЕНИЯ

A. **Поста́вьте глаго́лы в ско́бках в проше́дшее вре́мя и запо́лните про́пуски.** (Put the verbs in the parentheses into the past tense, and fill in the blanks.)

1. Аня, что ты _____ де́лать вчера́ у́тром? —Я _____ гуля́ть в па́рке. (хоте́ть)
2. Но мы _____ в па́рке сего́дня у́тром! (гуля́ть)
3. Па́па _____ и _____ ру́сскую класси́ческую му́зыку. (отдыха́ть/слу́шать)
4. Что он _____ вчера́ ве́чером? —Он _____ кни́гу. (де́лать/чита́ть)
5. О чём они́ _____ ? —О поли́тике. (говори́ть)

B. **Переведи́те на ру́сский язы́к.** (Translate into Russian.)

1. A park used to be (located) there.
2. What was he reading about yesterday?
3. Where did they use to live?
4. Have you been at this movie theater? —No, never.
5. What did you do/were you doing this morning? —We were relaxing at home.

C. **Поста́вьте местоиме́ния в ско́бках в да́тельный паде́ж и запо́лните про́пуски.** (Put the pronouns in parentheses into the dative case, and fill in the blanks.)

1. _____ всё равно́, где она́ живёт. (она́)
2. Пиши́ _____ ! (мы)
3. _____ ты пи́шешь? —Я _____ пишу́. (кто/они́)
4. Этот режиссёр _____ нра́вится? —Да, о́чень. (ты)
5. Ты хо́чешь смотре́ть фильм и́ли нет? —_____ всё равно́. (я)

D. **Подбери́те соотве́тствующие ру́сские предложе́ния к англи́йским значе́ниям. Употреби́те оди́н отве́т два ра́за.** (Match the Russian sentences with the English meanings. Use one answer twice.)

1. When/at what time?
2. 17.20
3. this morning
4. At 2 o'clock.

a. за́втра днём
b. Сейча́с 2 часа́.
c. 5:20 p.m.
d. It's 1:00.

5. **сего́дня но́чью**
6. It's 2 o'clock.
7. **вчера́ ве́чером**
8. What time is it?
9. **пять часо́в два́дцать мину́т ве́чера**
10. tomorrow afternoon

e. yesterday evening/last night
f. **Ско́лько вре́мени?**
g. **сего́дня у́тром**
h. tonight
i. **Во ско́лько?**
j. **В 2 часа́.**

УРОК 12

ПОКУПКА БИЛЕТА НА ПОЕЗД. Buying a train ticket.

А. ДИАЛОГ

У билéтной кáссы вокзáла.

РИТА: *Скажи́те, пожáлуйста, когдá отхóдит пóезд на Псков?*

КАССИР: *Есть два пóезда: оди́н в полвосьмóго утрá и другóй в полвосьмóго вéчера.*

РИТА: *Тогдá я хочý заказáть три билéта на ночнóй пóезд в купéйном вагóне.*

КАССИР: *Тудá и обрáтно и́ли в оди́н конéц?*

РИТА: *Тудá и обрáтно.*

КАССИР: *Три взрóслых?*

РИТА: *Нет, с нáми éдет нáша дóчка.*

КАССИР: *На какóе числó?*

РИТА: *Желáтельно тудá на вторóе апрéля и обрáтно на пéрвое мáя.*

КАССИР: *Так. У вас закáзаны три мéста в спáльном вагóне—однó ни́жнее для вáшей дéвочки и два вéрхних.*

РИТА: *Отли́чно. Нýжно дéлать пересáдку? И во скóлько пóезд прихóдит в Псков?*

КАССИР: *В семь часóв утрá. Нет, у вас нет пересáдки. Вы бывáли в Пскóве?*

РИТА: *Да, там живýт рóдственники моегó мýжа. Мы кáждую веснý éздим тудá и бывáем у них в гостя́х мéсяц.*

КАССИР: *Да? Псков—мой роднóй гóрод. Я óчень скучáю по немý. Ну, счастли́вого пути́!*

At the train station ticket-window.

Twelfth Lesson

RITA: Could you please tell me when the train for Pskov leaves?

TICKET CLERK: There are two trains: one at 7:30 A.M. and the other at 7:30 P.M.

RITA: Then I'd like to reserve three second-class tickets for the overnight train.

TICKET CLERK: Round-trip or one-way?

RITA: Round-trip.

TICKET CLERK: Three adults?

RITA: No, our little daughter is going with us.

TICKET CLERK: For what date?

RITA: Preferably leaving on April 2nd and returning on May 1st.

TICKET CLERK: Okay. You have three reserved berths in the sleeping car, one lower berth for your little girl and two upper berths.

RITA: Great. Do we have to change trains? And at what time does the train arrive in Pskov?

TICKET CLERK: At 7 A.M., and no, you don't have to change trains. Have you been to Pskov?

RITA: Yes, my husband's relatives live there. We go there every spring and visit them for a month.

TICKET CLERK: Really? Pskov is my native city. I miss it a lot. Well, have a great trip!

В. ГРАММАТИКА И СЛОВОУПОТРЕБЛЕНИЕ

1. UNI- VERSUS MULTI-DIRECTIONAL VERBS OF MOTION

The verbs **идти** (to go on foot) and **éхать** (to go by vehicle; see **Урок 9**) are known as unidirectional verbs of motion because they refer to movement in one direction or towards a specific destination, i.e. a one-way trip with no implication of returning. Each unidirectional verb of motion has a multidirectional counterpart: a verb used to describe motion in many directions without a specific destination, or to indicate a round trip, or repeated motion. **Ходить** is the multidirectional counterpart of **идти**.

ходить: to go (to go and return)

I go	**хожу́**	**хо́дим**	we go
you (fam.) go	**хо́дишь**	**хо́дите**	you (pl./pol.) go
he/she goes	**хо́дит**	**хо́дят**	they go

stem: **хо́д+**
imperative: **Ходи́(те)!**

Са́ша ходи́ла в шко́лу. Она́ сейча́с до́ма.
Sasha went to school. She's home now.

Я хожу́ на рабо́ту пешко́м.
I go to (and from) work on foot.

Е́здить is the multidirectional counterpart of **е́хать**.

е́здить: to go (go and return) by vehicle

I go	**е́зжу**	**е́здим**	we go
you (fam.) go	**е́здишь**	**е́здите**	you (pl./pol.) go
he/she goes	**е́здит**	**е́здят**	they go

stem: **е́зд+**
imperative: none

На́ша до́чка е́здит с на́ми.
Our little daughter rides with us.

Где ты была́? —Я е́здила в Москву́.
Where were you? — I went to Moscow (and returned).

Like **идти́**, **ходи́ть** does not necessarily refer to walking. In order to specify "walking," **пешко́м** (on foot) must be added. Otherwise, **ходи́ть** is often used to mean "to go" when it is a local activity and the means of going are not specified, e.g. "to go to the movies." **Е́здить**, on the other hand, like **е́хать**, can only mean "to go by vehicle."

Мы лю́бим ходи́ть в кино́.
We love going to the movies.

Он е́дет на рабо́ту?
He's on his way (driving) to work?

Я ча́сто е́зжу на велосипе́де в па́рке.

I often go bike-riding (ride on a bike) in the park.

2. THE SINGULAR GENITIVE AND ACCUSATIVE CASE OF ADJECTIVES

a. The genitive forms

Adjectives in the genitive case answer the question **Како́го?/Како́й?** (Of what kind?/Which?). The genitive case of masculine and neuter adjectives is formed by replacing the nominative ending with **-ого** or **-его**. For example, **восьмо́й** ≫ **восьмо́го, хоро́шее** ≫ **хоро́шего**. The genitive of feminine adjectives is formed by replacing the nominative ending with **-ой** or **-ей** (just like the prepositional and dative). For example, **но́вая** ≫ **но́вой, си́няя** ≫ **си́ней**.

	HARD	SOFT
MASCULINE/NEUTER	-ого	-его
FEMININE	-ой	-ей

Есть два по́езда: оди́н в <u>полвосьмо́го</u>[1] утра́ и друго́й в <u>полвосьмо́го</u> ве́чера.

There are two trains: one at 7:30 a.m. and the other at 7:30 p.m.

У <u>биле́тной</u> ка́ссы на вокза́ле.

At the ticket window at the train station.

Чайко́вский—компози́тор <u>класси́ческой</u> му́зыки.

Tchaikovskiy is a composer of classical music.

b. The accusative forms

Remember that masculine *inanimate* and all neuter adjectives in the accusative case are identical to adjectives in the nominative case.[2] Masculine *animate* adjectives in the accusative, however, are identical to masculine and neuter adjectives in the genitive case.

---

1. For an explanation of why 7:30 is an adjective in the genitive case, see section 4 in this lesson.
2. For more on feminine adjectives in the accusative, see **Уро́к 9**.

Двена́дцатый уро́к

	NOMINATIVE	ACCUSATIVE
MASCULINE INANIMATE	-ый/-ий/-о́й	-ый/-ий/-о́й
MASCULINE ANIMATE	-ый/-ий/-о́й	-ого/-его
NEUTER	-ое/-ее	-ое/-ее
FEMININE	-ая/-яя	-ую/-юю

The adjectives in the following sentences are all in the accusative case.

Жела́тельно туда́ на <u>второ́е</u> апре́ля и обра́тно на <u>пе́рвое</u> ма́я.
Preferably leaving on April 2nd and returning on May 1st.

Я хочу́ заказа́ть три биле́та на <u>ночно́й</u> по́езд.
I'd like to reserve three tickets for the overnight train.

Я люблю́ э́тот <u>ста́рый</u> фильм. —Да, и я та́кже люблю́ э́того <u>ста́рого</u> актёра.
I love that old film. —Yes, and I love that old actor, too.

3. THE SINGULAR GENITIVE AND ACCUSATIVE CASE OF SPECIAL MODIFIERS

Possessive adjectives in the genitive case answer the question **Чьего́?** (Whose?), and are formed like soft-stem adjectives: the masculine and neuter ending is -его, and the feminine ending is -ей. As always, the third person forms remain unchanged.

	SINGULAR		PLURAL		
	MASC./NEUTER	FEMININE	MASC./NEUTER	FEMININE	
(of) my	моего́	мое́й	на́шего	на́шей	(of) our
(of) your (fam.)	твоего́	твое́й	ва́шего	ва́шей	(of) your (pl./pol.)
(of) his, her	его́/своего́	её/свое́й	их	их	(of) their

Ро́дственники <u>моего́</u> му́жа живу́т там.
My husband's relatives live there.

А одно́ ни́жнее ме́сто для <u>ва́шей</u> де́вочки?
And one lower berth for your little girl?

У <u>её</u> окна́ краси́вое де́рево.

By her window is a beautiful tree.

Demonstrative adjectives in the genitive answer the question **Како́го/ Како́й?** (Of which?) and have hard adjective endings, i.e. **э́тот/э́то » э́того, э́та »** **э́той**.

	NOMINATIVE	ACCUSATIVE
MASCULINE INANIMATE	-consonant	-consonant
MASCULINE ANIMATE	-consonant	-ого/-его
NEUTER	-о/-е	-о/-е
FEMININE	-а/-я	-у/-ю

Я знал э́ту семью́, но я не зна́ю э́того ма́льчика.

I used to know that family, but I don't know that boy.

In future lessons, adjectives and special modifiers will be treated together.

4. THE MONTHS AND THE DATE

The months of the year in Russian are not capitalized, unless they begin a sentence.

янва́рь	January	**ию́ль**	July
февра́ль	February	**а́вгуст**	August
март	March	**сентя́брь**	September
апре́ль	April	**октя́брь**	October
май	May	**ноя́брь**	November
ию́нь	June	**дека́брь**	December

Май—мой люби́мый ме́сяц.

May is my favorite month.

To indicate that something was, is, or will be occurring during a specific month, the month is introduced by the preposition **в** and is in the prepositional case.

Мы всегда́ быва́ем у них в гостя́х в апре́ле.

We always visit them in April.

День рожде́ния мое́й сестры́ в ма́рте.
My sister's birthday is in March.

When providing a specific date, the number given is an ordinal number.[3] It is expressed in the nominative if it answers the question, **Како́е число́?** (What's the date?) or **Како́е сего́дня число́?** (What's today's date?), and in the accusative if it answers the question **На како́е число́?** (For what date?). It is in the genitive, however, if it answer the questions **Когда́?** (When?) or **Како́го числа́?** (On what date?). The month itself, however, is always in the genitive.

На како́е число́? —Туда́ на второ́е апре́ля и обра́тно на пе́рвое ма́я.
For what date? — Leaving on the 2nd of April and returning on the 1st of May.

Како́е сего́дня число́? —Двена́дцатое января́.
What's today's date? —The twelfth of January.

Како́го числа́ твой день рожде́ния? —Пя́того ию́ня.
When is your birthday? —On the fifth of June.

Когда́ вы е́здили в Москву́? —Шесто́го сентября́.
When (on what date) did you go to Moscow? —On September sixth.

If the date includes the day of the week, the day is in the accusative case.

Наш отъе́зд—в понеде́льник, второ́го апре́ля.
Our departure is on Monday, April 2nd.

5. MORE ON TELLING TIME (WITH GENITIVE)

The genitive case is often used in telling time. The Russian expression for "a quarter to/of" is **без че́тверти** (literally, without a quarter) + the coming hour in the nominative. The expression for "half past" is **пол** + an ordinal number in the genitive, literally "half of" the following hour. **Пол** is is short for **полови́на** (half).

3. You're already familiar with the ordinal numbers from 1–12, if you've been reading the footers at the bottom of each even page. For more on ordinal numbers, see **Уро́к** 20.

Один по́езд в полвосьмо́го утра́ и друго́й в полвосьмо́го ве́чера.
One train is at 7:30 A.M., and the other is at 7:30 P.M.

Ско́лько сейча́с вре́мени? — Сейча́с без че́тверти де́вять.
What time is it (now)? — It's quarter of nine.

As mentioned in the previous chapter, you can also express time by stating the current hour plus the number of minutes in the appropriate case. Don't forget to use **утра́** (A.M.) or **ве́чера** (P.M.) when necessary.

Ско́лько сейча́с вре́мени? — Сейча́с 8.45 (во́семь со́рок-пять).
What time is it? — It's eight forty-five.

По́езд отхо́дит в 7.30 (семь три́дцать) ве́чера.
The train leaves at seven-thirty in the evening.

6. THE INSTRUMENTAL CASE OF PERSONAL PRONOUNS

The instrumental case is often used following the preposition **с** (with, accompanied by). Pronouns in the instrumental answer the question **С кем?** (With whom?). **С** becomes **со** before **мной: со мной**, and the third person forms begin with **н-** when they follow **с: с ним, с ней, с ни́ми**.

(with) me	**мной**	**на́ми**	(with) us
(with) you (fam.)	**тобо́й**	**ва́ми**	(with) you (pl./pol.)
(with) him	**(н)им**	**(н)и́ми**	(with) them
(with) her	**(н)ей**		

На́ша до́чка е́дет с на́ми.
Our little daughter is going (there and back) with us.

Мы до́лго разгова́ривали с ни́ми.
We talked with them for a long time.

Что с тобо́й сего́дня? —Со мной ничего́. А что?
What's with you today? — Nothing's with me. Why?

7. PERSONAL PRONOUNS WITH PREPOSITIONS

Whenever third person pronouns are immediately preceded by a preposition, an initial **н-** is added. Thus you say **у него́/у неё/у них** (genitive), **о нём/о** ней/о них (prepositional), к нему́/к ней/к ним (dative), and с ним/с ней/с ни́ми (instrumental). However, this rule does not apply to the possessive special modifiers его́ (his/its), её (her/its), and их (their).

Псков—мой родно́й го́род. Я о́чень скуча́ю по нему́.

Pskov is my native city. I miss it a lot.

Ни́жнее ме́сто у их до́чки.

Their daughter has the lower berth.

The prepositions с, к, and о change before first person singular pronouns beginning with мн-. С and к become со and ко, and о becomes обо.

Да, она́ ча́сто е́здит со мной.

Yes, she often goes with me.

Что они́ говори́ли обо мне́?

What were they saying about me?

C. СЛОВА́РЬ

бы́ть в гостя́х	to be visiting
в оди́н коне́ц	one-way (lit. to one end)
ве́рхний	high; higher
велосипе́д	bicycle
взро́слый	grown-up, adult
всегда́	always
де́рево	tree
до́чка	daughter, the diminutive form
друго́й	other; the other
е́здить (е́зжу, е́здишь, е́здят)	to go by vehicle
жела́тельно	preferably
зака́зан/-а/-о/-ы	reserved
заказа́ть (закажу́, зака́жешь, зака́жут)	to reserve, to order
Како́го числа́? (Когда́?)	On what date? (When?)
Како́е сего́дня число́?	What's today's date?
ка́сса	(cash) register
ни́жний	low; lower
ночно́й	night (adjective)
ну́жно	is needed, necessary

отходи́ть (отхожу́, отхо́дишь, отхо́дят)	to depart (multidirectional)
отъе́зд	departure
парк	park
переса́дка	transfer (noun; with transportation only)
полови́на (пол)	half
ро́дственник	relative
родно́й	native (adjective)
с/со (чем/кем); (чего́/кого́)	with, accompanied by (someone/thing); from (someone/thing)
с кем	with whom
с чем	with what
скуча́ть по (чему́/кому́)	to miss (someone/thing)
спа́льный ваго́н	sleeping car
Счастли́вого пути́!	Have a good trip!
тогда́	at that time; then; in that case
туда́ и обра́тно	roundtrip (lit. to there and back)
ходи́ть (хожу́, хо́дишь, хо́дят)	to go (multidirectional)
центр	(the) center; downtown
ча́сто	often

РУ́ССКАЯ КУЛЬТУ́РА

Russia was a largely agrarian society until the mid-twentieth century. Spending time in the country is often a way to temporarily return to what Russians view as the less rushed and less complicated time of their parents and grandparents. Russians also passionately identify with the place where they were born and grew up.

It is common for Russians to visit relatives for an extended period, especially if the relatives live in the country. Families are closer and have stronger bonds with each other and the family as a whole than the average American family. There is less privacy and private ownership of things, space, and personal time. Russians are more dependent on their families for emotional and material support, and adult children often live with their parents until they marry. A lack of available apartments and/or money often means that many do not move out even then, but simply add the new spouse to the family. Those who don't marry generally continue to live with their parents, eventually caring for them in their old age. Institutions such as nursing homes seem still hard to accept for the average Russian.

УПРАЖНЕНИЯ

A. Подбери́те соотве́тствующие предложе́ния в коло́нке А к коло́нке Б.
(Match the sentences in column A with the phrases in column B.)

A	B
1. Са́ша лю́бит <u>to walk</u>, когда́ идёт дождь.	a. They are going to school.
2. Мы е́здили в Ки́ев.	b. е́ду
3. Они́ иду́т в шко́лу.	c. ходи́ть
4. Я <u>go</u> (every day) на рабо́ту на метро́.	d. We went to Kiev.
5. Я <u>am going</u> (today) на рабо́ту на метро́.	e. е́зжу
	f. Мы не в Ки́еве.

B. Поста́вьте слова́ в ско́бках в пра́вильный паде́ж и запо́лните про́пуски. (Put the words in parentheses into the correct case, and fill in the blanks.)

1. Како́го числа́? —_____ апре́ля. (пе́рвый)
2. По́езд отхо́дит от _____ го́рода в пять часо́в вечера́. (ста́рый)
3. Како́е сего́дня число́? —_____ апре́ля. (пе́рвый)
4. Родстве́нники _____ му́жа живу́т в Пско́ве. (её)
5. Это ме́сто _____ до́чки. (мой)
6. Ско́лько сейча́с вре́мени? —Сейча́с пол_____ . (девя́тый)
7. Я зна́ю мужчи́ну с _____ восто́ка. (Да́льний)
8. Кто режиссёр _____ _____ фи́льма? (э́тот, прекра́сный)
9. Кто а́втор _____ _____ кни́ги? (твой, люби́мый)
10. У меня́ пода́рок для _____ сы́на. (их)

C. Поста́вьте местоиме́ния в ско́бках в твори́тельный паде́ж и запо́лните про́пуски. (Put the pronouns in parentheses into the instrumental case, and fill in the blanks.)

1. Ва́ля, пойдём со _____ ! (я)
2. Мы жи́ли с _____ в Петербу́рге. (они́)
3. Лёня, что с _____ ? (ты)
4. Чита́й письмо́ с _____ , ла́дно? (она́)
5. Я не зна́ю, что с _____ сего́дня! (он)

D. Переведи́те англи́йские слова́ и оборо́ты на ру́сский язы́к.
   (Translate the English words or phrases into Russian.)

1. Он хо́чет говори́ть с ва́ми. <u>With me</u>?
2. Па́па рабо́тает <u>with him</u>.
3. Они́ говоря́т <u>about her</u> кварти́ре.
4. Ребёнок идёт <u>towards her</u>.
5. Что ты зна́ешь <u>about me</u>?

УРОК 13

СИМПТОМЫ И ЛЕКАРСТВО. Symptoms and medicine.

А. ДИАЛОГ

В аптеке.

НЭНСИ: Чхи! Ап-чхи!

ФАРМАЦЕВТ: Такая сильная простуда!

НЭНСИ: Да, йли это может быть грипп. Кхе! кхе!

ФАРМАЦЕВТ: У вас и кашель и насморк.

НЭНСИ: Да. Мне ничего не хочется делать, кроме как лежать в постели.

ФАРМАЦЕВТ: У вас есть сенная лихорадка?

НЭНСИ: По-моему, нет.

ФАРМАЦЕВТ: Голова у вас болит?

НЭНСИ: Да. И у меня небольшой жар и расстройство желудка.

ФАРМАЦЕВТ: Тогда вот хорошее лекарство без аспирина и без рецепта. Принимайте по одной таблетке, три раза в день вместе с едой.

НЭНСИ: Отлично. А у вас есть капли от кашля?

ФАРМАЦЕВТ: Да, вот. Вы должны отдыхать, пить тёплое питьё, и нужно поставить банки. Скоро вы будете чувствовать себя гораздо лучше.

НЭНСИ: Что такое банки?

ФАРМАЦЕВТ: Банки—старое русское народное лечение.

НЭНСИ: Интересно. Наверно, моя соседка всё знает об этом. Спасибо большое!

ФАРМАЦЕВТ: Пожалуйста. Выздоравливайте!

At a pharmacy.

NANCY: Choo! Ah-choo!

PHARMACIST: Such a bad cold!

NANCY: Yes, or maybe it's the flu. Cough! Cough!

PHARMACIST: And you have a cough and a runny nose.

NANCY: Yes. I don't feel like doing anything except lying in bed.

PHARMACIST: Do you get hayfever?

NANCY: No.

PHARMACIST: Does your head hurt?

NANCY: Yes. And I have a slight fever and an upset stomach.

PHARMACIST: Then here's a good, non-prescription medicine without aspirin. Take one tablet three times a day, with food.

NANCY: Great. And do you have any cough drops?

PHARMACIST: Yes, here you go. You should rest, drink hot liquids, and use banki. In a few days you'll feel much better.

NANCY: What are banki?

PHARMACIST: Banki are an old Russian folk remedy.

NANCY: Interesting. My neighbor probably knows all about them. Thank you very much!

PHARMACIST: You're welcome. Get better soon!

B. ГРАММАТИКА И СЛОВОУПОТРЕБЛЕНИЕ

1. THE FUTURE TENSE WITH БЫТЬ

The Russian future tense corresponds to the English simple future (I will live) and future continuous tenses (I will be living). It is formed with the future tense of the verb **быть** (to be) and the infinitive of the main verb, e.g. **я бу́ду жить**

(I will live/I will be living). Following is the conjugation of **быть** in the future tense.

быть: to be

I will be	**бу́ду**	**бу́дем**	we will be
you (fam.) will be	**бу́дешь**	**бу́дете**	you (pl./pol.) will be
he/she will be	**бу́дет**	**бу́дут**	they will be

stem: **буд+**
imperative: **Бу́дь(те)!**

Ско́ро вы бу́дете чу́вствовать себя́ гора́здо лу́чше.
Soon you'll be feeling much better.

Как мы бу́дем знать, когда́ ему́ дать лека́рство?
How will we know when to give him the medicine?

Во ско́лько магази́н бу́дет закрыва́ться на э́той неде́ле?
What time will the store be closing this week?

To express the future tense of "to be," conjugate **быть** in the future tense but do not repeat it as an infinitive.

Когда́ ты бу́дешь в Пско́ве? —Я бу́ду там че́рез ме́сяц.
When will you be in Pskov? —I'll be there in a month.

2. THE INSTRUMENTAL CASE OF SINGULAR NOUNS

To form the instrumental case of singular nouns, replace **-ь, -й**, or any vowels with **-ом or -ем** for masculine or neuter nouns. For feminine nouns, replace any vowels with **-ой** or **-ей**, or add **-ю** onto any nouns ending in **-ь**[1]. For example, **друг » дру́гом, ма́ма » ма́мой**.

	HARD	SOFT
MASCULINE/NEUTER	**-ом**	**-ем**
FEMININE	**-ой**	**-ей**
		-ь » -ью

1. **Дочь, мать,** and **путь** are exceptions: **дочь » до́черью, мать » ма́терью, путь » путём**.

Remember that the instrumental is most often used following the preposition **с**, in which case it answers the questions **С кем?** (With whom?) or **С чем?** (With what?).

Принима́йте по одно́й табле́тке, три ра́за в день вме́сте с едо́й.
Take one tablet three times a day, with food.

Я люблю́ пить ко́фе с молоко́м.
I love to drink coffee with milk.

С кем она́ говори́т? —С дя́дей Ди́мой и тётей Ната́шей.
Who is she talking with? —With Uncle Dima and Aunt Natasha.

С plus the instrumental is used in many common idiomatic expressions of good wishes or congratulations.

С днём[2] рожде́ния!
Happy birthday! (literally, With the day of birth!)

С больши́м успе́хом!
Congratulations (on your accomplishment)! (literally, With a big success!)

С пра́здником!
Happy holiday! (literally, With the holiday!)

3. EXPRESSING OBLIGATION WITH ДОЛЖЕН

The Russian word **до́лжен** (should, must, had better) is a short form adjective (**до́лжен/должна́ /должно́/должны́**) and must always agree in gender and number with the subject of the sentence. It is always followed by an infinitive. **До́лжен** is used often in Russian conversation.

Вы должны́ отдыха́ть и пить тёплое питьё.
You should rest and drink hot liquids.

Она́ сего́дня не должна́ идти́ в шко́лу—она́ больна́!
She mustn't go to school today—she's sick!

2. The noun **день** has a fleeting vowel, so the ending is added onto the stem **дн+**.

Я про́сто не зна́ю. —Тогда́ ты до́лжен ещё поду́мать об э́том.

I just don't know. —Then you'd better think about it a little more.

4. DOUBLE NEGATIVES

You have already learned that **не** expresses general negation.

Я не зна́ю, что де́лать.

I don't know what to do.

Не can also be used in conjunction with other negative words to express a more specific negation. These negative words consist of the emphatic particle **ни-** (meaning "no" or "not") plus a question word in the appropriate case. They are always immediately followed by **не**. When used with a preposition, the preposition splits the negative word and is placed between **ни** and the question word. Note that double negation, which is unacceptable in English, is correct in Russian.

a. **ничто́** (nothing)

Although **ничто́** is the nominative form of "nothing," it is not often used. **Ничего́**, the more common form, is actually the genitive form.

Мне ничего́ не хо́чется де́лать. У меня́ си́льно боли́т голова́, а ничего́ не помога́ет!

I don't feel like doing anything. I have such a headache, and nothing's helping!

О чём вы говори́те? —Мы ни о чём не говори́м.

What are you talking about? —We're not talking about anything.

Ни с че́м не на́до принима́ть э́то лека́рство.

It's not necessary to take this medicine with anything.

b. **никто́** (no one)

Никто́ не́ был у Ма́ши, когда́ она́ была́ больна́.

No one visited Masha when she was sick.

Я никого́ не зна́ю в апте́ке.
I don't know anyone at the pharmacy.

Они́ ещё никому́ не сказа́ли о ребёнке.
They haven't told anyone about the baby yet.

c. **никако́й** (no kind of)

Како́е лека́рство вы принима́ете? —Я никако́го лека́рства не принима́ю.
What kind of medicine are you taking? —I'm not taking any kind of medicine.

Кака́я у вас боль? —У меня никако́й боли нет.
What kind of pain do you have? —I don't have any (kind of) pain.

d. **нигде́** (nowhere), **никуда́** (to nowhere)

Она́ на пе́нсии. Она́ нигде́ не рабо́тает.
She's retired. She doesn't work anywhere.

Они́ никуда́ не иду́т. Ва́ня бо́лен.
They're not going anywhere. Vanya is sick.

e. **никогда́** (never)

Он иногда́ пло́хо себя́ чу́вствует, но он никогда́ не хо́дит к врачу́.
He sometimes feels sick, but he never goes to the doctor.

Ира никогда́ не смотре́ла фильм «Манхэ́ттен».
Ira's never seen the movie "Manhattan."

5. ONOMATOPOEIAS

Onomatopoeias are words whose sound reflects their meaning. Here are some common Russian onomatopoetic expressions. Note that they are not capitalized.

ап-чхи́!	Ah-choo!	**мур, мур.**	Purr, purr.
кхе-кхе!	Cough! Cough!	**и-го-го́!**	Neighhh!
ха-ха-ха́! хи-хи-хи́!	Ha ha! Hee-hee!	**му, му!**	Moo!

бах! (бац!)	Bang!	мя́у!	Meow!
скрип!	Cre-e-ak!	ква-ква!	Croak! Croak!
дзынь!	Br-r-ing!	гав-гав!	Bow-wow!
брысь!	Scat! (cats)	кукареку́!	Cock-a-doodle-doo!
кыш!	Shoo! (birds, etc.)	ж-ж-ж!	Bzzz!

C. СЛОВАРЬ

аллерги́я	allergy
апте́ка	pharmacy
аспири́н	aspirin
ба́нки	cupping-glasses (old Russian remedy)
боле́знь	f. illness
быть (бу́ду, бу́дешь, бу́дут)	to be (future tense only) (I.)
Выздора́вливай(те)!	Get better!
гора́здо	much
грипп	flu
до́лжен/-на́/-ны́	should; must; obligated to
еда́	food
жар	fever
ка́пли от ка́шля	cough drops
ка́шель	cough (noun)
кро́ме как	besides, other than, except
лежа́ть (лежу́, лежи́шь, лежа́т)	to lay, lie (II.)
лека́рство	medicine
лече́ние	remedy; cure
лу́чше	better
Мне хо́чется ... (+ infinitive)	I feel like . . . (verb + -ing)
на́сморк	runny nose
наро́дный	folk (adjective)
нигде́	nowhere
никако́й	no one
никто́	no one
пить (пью, пьёшь, пьют)	to drink (I.)
питьё	drink (noun)
поста́вить (поста́влю, поста́вишь, поста́вят)	to put
посте́ль	f. bed; bed-clothes
принима́ть (принима́ю, принима́ешь, принима́ют)	to take (medicine; shower); to accept
просту́да	cold
раз	time (once, twice, etc.); one (counting)

расстро́йство желу́дка	upset stomach
реце́пт	prescription
себя́	self
си́льный	strong; bad (illness)
сосе́д/сосе́дка	neighbor (m./f.)
тёплый	warm; hot (for drinks)
табле́тка	pill, tablet
У меня́ боли́т голова́.	I have a headache.
фармаце́вт	pharmacist
Что тако́е_____?	What is _____ ?
чу́вствовать себя́	to feel (a feeling)

РУССКАЯ КУЛЬТУРА

Pharmacies in Russia differ from those in the United States, and their function far surpasses that of a mere drugstore. Russian pharmacists often recommend medicine, a course of treatment, and even make diagnoses, and people frequently first consult a pharmacist when they are ill. Furthermore, there is a much greater reliance on over-the-counter medicines, self-treatment, and herbal remedies, and a trend away from modern medicine. This is probably due to a general distrust of modern drugs and the state of the medical profession in general—patients' rights are much less protected in Russia than in the United States, and malpractice suits are rare. Medicinal plants and herbal remedies make up about a third of any Russian pharmacy, and treatments such as homeopathy and osteopathy, and even faith-healing, have become quite popular.

Many traditional Russian folk remedies date back to the old days when folk-healing was widespread, and people went to healers to be treated with herbs or exorcised of devils or evil influences. The most common of these include **горчи́чники** (mustard plasters) on the back or chest; onion, garlic, or radish with honey; black tea or various herbal teas; **ба́нки** (cupping glasses) in which the air is burned with a match to create a vacuum and then the cupping glasses are placed on the chest or back. By increasing circulation, this relieves congestion, colds, flus, or coughs; and vodka, as an anesthetic or for massage. Some of these remedies, such as **ба́нки**, are often part of a Russian doctor's training, and are used in hospitals, as well.

УПРАЖНЕНИЯ

A. Поста́вьте предложе́ния в бу́дущее вре́мя. (Put the sentences into the future tense.)

1. Я принима́ю по две табле́тки раз в день.
2. Ма́ма и па́па е́здят на рабо́ту в шесть часо́в.
3. Мы живём в Петербу́рге.
4. Ты хо́дишь домо́й пешко́м?
5. Вы говори́те по-англи́йски.

B. Поста́вьте слова́ в ско́бках в твори́тельный паде́ж и запо́лните про́пуски. (Put the words in parentheses into the instrumental case, and fill in the blanks.)

1. Дава́й пойдём в кино́. —С _____ ! (удово́льствие)
2. Она́ живёт с _____ ? (друг)
3. С кем ты е́здишь на велосипе́де? —С _____ . (муж)
4. Вы принима́ете лека́рство с _____ ? (еда́)
5. Я говорю́ с _____ . Она́ хо́чет поздра́вить тебе́ с _____ рожде́ния. (тётя Ма́ша, день)

C. Переведи́те англи́йские слова́ соотве́тствующей фо́рмой сло́ва «до́лжен», и пото́м подбери́те сове́ты из коло́нки А к фра́зам из коло́нки Б. (Translate the English words into the correct form of до́лжен, and then match the advice in column A with the sentences in column B.)

A	B
1. Она́ shouldn't идти́ в шко́лу.	a. Он не понима́ет по-ру́сски.
2. Вы should отдыха́ть и пить тёплое питьё.	b. Како́й прекра́сный фильм!
3. Мы shouldn't говори́ть по-ру́сски.	c. Она́ больна́.
4. Пе́тя, ты have to посмотре́ть э́тот фильм!	d. У него́ серьёзная боле́знь.
5. Он had better принима́ть лека́рство.	e. У вас просту́да.
	f. Они́ ничего́ не зна́ют о поли́тике

D. **Отве́тьте на вопро́сы отрица́тельно и переведи́те отве́ты на англи́йский.** (Answer the questions negatively, then translate the answers into English.)

1. Куда́ и с кем вы е́дете?
2. Кого́ ты там зна́ешь?
3. Когда́ ты жила́ в Москве́?
4. Что ду́мает фармаце́вт об э́том?
5. О чём ты говори́шь?

УРОК 14

СОБСТВЕННОЕ ОПИСАНИЕ. Describing oneself.

А. ДИАЛОГ

По телефо́ну.

ВЛАДИК: До́брый ве́чер. Позови́те, пожа́луйста, Ната́лью Ивано́ву.

ЖЕНЩИНА: Вы не туда́ попа́ли.

ВЛАДИК: Ой, извини́те!

Вла́дик ещё раз набира́ет но́мер.

НАТАША: (Дзын-н-нь!) Алло́?

ВЛАДИК: Ната́лья Ивано́ва?

НАТАША: Да?

ВЛАДИК: Здра́вствуйте! Это говори́т Влади́мир Попо́в, друг Ма́рка. Марк мне сказа́л, что вы то́же увлека́етесь те́ннисом. Пра́вда?

НАТАША: Да, пра́вда. Но он мне сказа́л, что вы обы́чно выи́грываете!

ВЛАДИК: Нет-нет, он шу́тит. Ну, мы должны́ ско́ро встре́титься и поигра́ть.

НАТАША: Да, с больши́м удово́льствием. Вы мо́жете в суббо́ту? Я свобо́дна в э́тот день.

ВЛАДИК: Прекра́сно! На стадио́не в три часа́?

НАТАША: Хорошо́. А как мы друг дру́га узна́ем?

ВЛАДИК: Ну, я блонди́н высо́кого ро́ста с бородо́й. На мне бу́дут очки́, джи́нсы, чёрные кроссо́вки и кра́сная ку́ртка. А вы?

НАТАША: У меня́ коро́ткие ры́жие во́лосы и ка́рие глаза́. Я сре́днего ро́ста, и на мне бу́дут си́нее пальто́ и зелёная шля́па.

ВЛАДИК: Ну, тогда́ до суббо́ты!

On the telephone.

VLADIK: Good evening. Could I please speak with Natalya Ivanova?

WOMAN: You have the wrong number.

VLADIK: Oh, I'm sorry!

Vladik dials the number again.

NATASHA: *(Br-r-ing!)* Hello?

VLADIK: Natalya Ivanova?

NATASHA: Yes?

VLADIK: Hello! This is Vladimir Popov speaking, Mark's friend. Mark said that you also love tennis. Is that right?

NATASHA: Yes, that's right. But he told me that you usually win!

VLADIK: No, no, he's kidding. So, we should meet soon and play.

NATASHA: Yes, I'd love to. How about Saturday? I'm free that day.

VLADIK: Great! At the stadium at three o'clock?

NATASHA: Fine. And how will we recognize each other?

VLADIK: Well, I'll be the tall blonde with the beard. I'll be wearing glasses, jeans, black sneakers, and a red jacket. And you?

NATASHA: I have short, red hair and brown eyes. I'm of medium height, and I'll be wearing a dark blue coat and a green hat.

VLADIK: Until Saturday then!

В. ГРАММАТИКА И СЛОВОУПОТРЕБЛЕНИЕ

1. DESCRIPTION OF COLOR AND HEIGHT (WITH GENITIVE)

a. Color
Colors are adjectives, and, therefore, agree in gender, number, and case with the nouns they modify. Following are the most common:

кра́сный	red	ро́зовый	pink
жёлтый	yellow	бе́лый	white
зелёный	green	чёрный	black
си́ний	dark blue	кори́чневый	brown
голубо́й	light blue	се́рый	grey
ора́нжевый	orange	золото́й	gold
фиоле́товый	purple	сере́бряный	silver

Фиоле́товый—мой люби́мый цвет.

Purple is my favorite color.

На Ната́ше бу́дут си́нее пальто́ и зелёная шля́па.

Natasha will be wearing a dark blue coat and a green hat.

When giving a single word response to the question **Како́го цве́та?** (What color is it/are they?), the color should take the masculine singular genitive form because it refers to the word **цвет**.[1] However, if the answer begins with "It's ...," the color is in the nominative, and agrees in gender and number with the noun it modifies.

Како́го цве́та ва́ша маши́на? — Кра́сного.

What color is your car? — Red.

Како́го цве́та ва́ша маши́на? — Она́ кра́сная.

What color is your car?— It's red.

There are some special words used to describe hair color. Eye color is described with regular color adjectives, except for brown eyes, which are referred to as **ка́рие**. Note that "hazel" eyes are referred to as **светлока́рие** (light-brown).

рыжие	red hair
кашта́новые	chestnut hair
ру́сые	dark blond/light brown hair
седы́е	gray hair
тёмные	dark brown hair (literally, dark)
све́тлые	blond hair (literally, light)
лы́сый	bald

1. Be careful not to confuse the nouns **цвето́к** (flower) and **цвет** (color). They sound similar (in fact, the same word was originally used for both) but they have different meanings and different nominative plural forms; all oblique plurals are the same.

Note also the nouns **брюне́т(ка)** and **блонди́н(ка)**, meaning "brunette" (m./f.) and "blond" (m./f.), respectively.

У меня́ коро́ткие ры́жие во́лосы и ка́рие глаза́.
I have short red hair and brown eyes.

Я блонди́н с бородо́й, и у меня́ голубы́е глаза́.
I'm a blond with a beard, and I have blue eyes.

b. Height
The question **Како́го ро́ста?** (How tall is/are [someone]?) literally translates as "Of what height?" Therefore, the response is in the genitive[2]: **ма́ленького ро́ста** (short), **сре́днего ро́ста** (of medium height), or **высо́кого ро́ста** (tall).

Я сре́днего ро́ста, и на мне бу́дет си́нее пальто́.
I'm of average height, and I'll be wearing a dark blue coat.

Он како́го ро́ста? —Он о́чень ма́ленького ро́ста.
How tall is he? —He's very short.

2. A VERSUS И AND HO

The conjunctions **а**, **и**, and **но** lie on a continuum between "and" and "but," with **и** and **но** at opposite ends and **а** in the middle. **А** and **но** are always preceded by commas (unless they begin a sentence), while **и** is not, unless it joins clauses with different subjects.

As you learned in **Уро́к** 5, the conjunction **а** can be translated as "and" or "but" (but rather) and is used to show a comparison or contrast. It can compare two mutually exclusive items or it can be used to introduce or ask about a contrasting situation.

У Ната́ши не све́тлые во́лосы, а ры́жие.
Natasha's hair isn't blond, <u>but</u> red.

Я высо́кого ро́ста. А вы?
I'm tall. <u>And</u> you?

А can also be used to make *different* comments about the same or two *different* subjects, implying some sort of comparison.

---

2. Or the answer may be a person's height, given in centimeters, e.g. 175 cm. (see **Уро́к** 32).

Он ма́ленького ро́ста и по́лный, а она́ высо́кого ро́ста и худа́я.

He's short and fat, <u>but</u> she's tall and thin.

Я говорю́ по-ру́сски и по-англи́йски, а он то́лько говори́т по-англи́йски.

I speak Russian and English, <u>but</u> he only speaks English.

a. A versus и

The conjunction и also translates as "and," but it acts as a grammatical plus sign and joins words, phrases, or clauses that are equal in some way.

На мне бу́дут си́нее пальто́ и зелёная шля́па.

I'll have on a dark blue coat <u>and</u> a green hat.

Я блонди́нка сре́днего ро́ста и у меня́ се́рые глаза́.

I'm a blond of average height, <u>and</u> I have grey eyes.

И is also used to make the *same* comment about two *different* subjects.

Ната́лья ры́жая и ты ры́жий.

Natalya's a redhead, <u>and</u> you're a redhead.

Она́ увлека́ется те́ннисом, и он то́же увлека́ется те́ннисом.

She loves tennis, <u>and</u> he loves tennis, too.

And it can be used to show that the information in the second clause is a logical result of the first clause.

Вла́дик мно́го игра́ет в те́ннис, и он стро́йный.

Vladik plays tennis a lot, <u>and</u> he's slender.

Псков—мой родно́й го́род, и я скуча́ю по нему́.

Pskov is my native city, <u>and</u> I miss it.

Unlike **а**, и cannot be used to contrast two elements or to introduce a contrasting situation. Again, **а** is used when making *different* comments about *different* subjects, while и is used to make the *same* comment about *different* subjects. Compare:

Она́ за́мужем, а он разведён.

She's married, <u>but</u> he's divorced.

Она́ не за́мужем и он не жена́т.
She's not married, and he's not married.

b. **А** versus **но**
The primary difference between the conjunctions **а** and **но** (but, however) is that **а** is mainly used to make comparisons while **но** is never used this way. **Но** is used to restrict or qualify the information in the previous clause.

Поня́тия не име́ю, но Ву́ди Алле́н—режиссёр.
I don't have any idea, but Woody Allen is the director.

Я по-ру́сски говорю́, но не чита́ю и не пишу́.
I speak Russian, but I don't read or write it.

Но can also introduce information that is somehow unexpected, or is not a logical consequence of the information in the previous clause.

Да, пра́вда. Но он мне сказа́л, что вы обы́чно выи́грываете!
Yes, that's right. But he told me that you usually win!

Я увлека́юсь те́ннисом, но я пло́хо игра́ю.
I'm fascinated with tennis, but I don't play well.

3. THE INSTRUMENTAL CASE OF ADJECTIVES AND SPECIAL MODIFIERS

Masculine and neuter adjectives with soft stems in the nominative end in **-им** in the instrumental, e.g. **хоро́ший/хоро́шее ≫ хоро́шим,** and those with hard stems in the nominative end in **-ым** in the instrumental, e.g. **но́вый/но́вое ≫ но́вым**. Feminine adjectives are the same in the instrumental as in the prepositional, genitive, and dative: they end in **-ой** or **-ей,** according to the spelling rules, e.g. **си́няя ≫ си́ней, но́вая ≫ но́вой**.

	HARD	SOFT
MASCULINE/NEUTER	-ым	-им
FEMININE	-ой	-ей

С больши́м удово́льствием.
With great pleasure.

Я то́лько что познако́мился с мое́й но́вой сосе́дкой. Она́ о́чень симпати́чная.

I just met my new neighbor. She's very nice.

Feminine possessive special modifiers have a soft instrumental ending, **-ей**, and demonstrative special modifiers have a hard ending, **-ой**. The masculine and neuter special modifiers all end in **-им** in the instrumental. As always, the third person plural possessive adjectives **его́**, **её**, and **их** do not change.

Я хочу́ познако́миться с э́тим челове́ком.

I want to meet this person.

Они́ там живу́т с её ста́рым отцо́м.

They live there with her old father.

4. VERBS THAT REQUIRE THE INSTRUMENTAL CASE

Certain verbs require that their objects be in the instrumental case. These include: **интересова́ться** (to be interested in), **занима́ться** (to study; to be occupied with), and **увлека́ться** (to be fascinated with), as well as all verbs commonly used with the preposition **с** (as **с** itself requires the instrumental), such as **познако́миться с** (to be acquainted with).

Марк мне сказа́л, что вы то́же увлека́етесь те́ннисом.

Mark told me that you also love (are fascinated with) tennis.

Я познако́милась с ним на сва́дьбе мое́й подру́ги.

I met him at my friend's wedding.

Он ра́ньше интересова́лся исто́рией, а тепе́рь он занима́ется фи́зикой.

He was interested in history before, but now he's taken up physics.

5. EACH OTHER (ДРУГ ДРУГА)

When **друг дру́га** (each other, one another) changes according to case, only the second word declines. If it is used with a preposition, the preposition is placed between the two parts.

А как мы друг дру́га узна́ем?

And how will we recognize one another?

Они познакомились друг с другом через объявление в газете.

They met each other through the personals in the paper.

6. NOUNS USED ONLY IN THE PLURAL OR SINGULAR

Certain nouns are always plural and do not have a singular form. Some of these are only used in the plural in English as well, but many are not.

деньги	money	брюки	pants
очки	glasses	джинсы	jeans
родители	parents	волосы	hair
часы	watch	усы	mustache

На мне будут очки, джинсы, чёрные кроссовки и красная куртка.

I'll be wearing glasses, jeans, black sneakers and a red jacket.

У меня русые волосы.

I have light brown hair.

Conversely, there are certain non-count nouns that can only be used in the singular, e.g. **обувь** (footware). These nouns are generally the same ones as in English.

Где молоко? — На столе.

Where's the milk? — On the table.

C. СЛОВАРЬ

белый	white
борода	beard
волосы	hair
встретиться	to meet
встреча	meeting; appointment
Вы не туда попали.	You have the wrong number.
выигрывать (выигрываю, выигрываешь, выигрывают)	to win
высокого роста	tall
глаз(а)	eye(s)
голубой	light blue
Давайте ...	Let's . . .
длинный	long (length only)

друг дру́га	each other; one another
жёлтый	yellow
занима́ться (занима́юсь, занима́ешься, занима́ются) (чем)	to study; to be involved with (something)
зелёный	green
игра́ть (игра́ю, игра́ешь, игра́ют)	to play
интересова́ться (чем)	to be interested in (something)
Како́го ро́ста?	How tall (is someone)?
Како́го цве́та?	What color is it?
коро́ткий	short (length only)
кра́сный	red
кроссо́вки	sneakers; running shoes
ку́ртка	short jacket
ма́ленького ро́ста	short (lit. of small height)
на мне (бу́дет/бу́дут) ...	I'll have on; I'll be wearing . . .
очки́	glasses
Позови́те, пожа́луйста, ...	May I please speak with . . . ?
по́лный	fat (people only)
ра́ньше	before; formerly (opp. of **тепе́рь**)
разведён/-а́/-ы́	divorced
ре́дко	rarely
све́тлый	light; blonde
свобо́ден/на/но/ны	free
си́ний	dark blue
симпати́чный	nice, likeable
сре́днего ро́ста	of medium height
стадио́н	stadium
стро́йный	slender; with a good figure
тёмный	dark; brunette
те́ннис	tennis
увлека́ться (увлека́юсь, увлека́ешься, увлека́ются) (чем/кем)	to be interested in (someone/thing) to go in for (something)
усы́	mustache
ходи́ть на свида́ния	to go on dates
худо́й	skinny
чёрный	black
шути́ть (шучу́, шу́тишь, шу́тят)	to joke
Это говори́т_____ .	This is _____ speaking.

РУССКАЯ КУЛЬТУРА

Social interaction and dating in Russia is in many ways different than in the West. Teenage girls and boys usually spend time in mixed groups as friends rather than couples, and they do not start pairing off seriously until university-age. Even then, their form of dating is often within groups, and the emphasis is more on friendships than on being part of a couple. There is no precise word in Russian for "dating," "boyfriend," or "girlfriend." The terms **подру́га** (female friend usually of a female), **друг** (friend, either male or female, but usually male), and **па́рень** (fellow), pronounced with a certain intonation, are understood to refer to a romantic interest. There are also some colloquial expressions such as **ма́льчик** (little boy) and **де́вочка** (little girl), and newly borrowed English words, such as **бойфренд** and **герлфренд**, but these are not widely used.

In Russia, relationships outside of marriage are generally not recognized, and the status of any such relationships is largely unspoken. Russians generally don't live together unless they are married (more often due to a lack of living space than a strict moral code). There are, therefore, no terms signifying long-term, unmarried relationships, such as "going out with somebody," "seeing someone," "being a couple," or "live-in partner." Although Russians are very romantic and emotional, they do not tend to speak about their intimate, romantic relationships. Of course, all this is even more true of homosexual relationships, which are not recognized or publicly accepted.

Recent economic and political changes have had a strong social impact as well. There are more places, such as clubs and cafes, for single and homosexual people to meet, and some papers now have **ли́чные коло́нки** (personal columns) to help single and homosexual people get together.

УПРАЖНЕНИЯ

A. **Подбери́те соотве́тствующие предложе́ния о диало́ге в коло́нке А к коло́нке Б.** (Match the sentences about the dialogue in column A to those in column B.)

	A		B
1.	Како́го цве́та кроссо́вки Вла́дика?	a.	Я не зна́ю.
2.	Ната́ша седа́я?	b.	Она́ кра́сная. (or: Кра́сного.)
3.	Како́го ро́ста Вла́дик, сре́днего?	c.	Нет, она́ ры́жая.
4.	У него́ голубы́е глаза́?	d.	Оно́ си́нее. (or: Си́него.)
5.	Како́го цве́та пальто́ Ната́ши?	e.	Нет, он высо́кого ро́ста.
		f.	Да, они́ ка́рие.
		g.	Они́ чёрные. (or: Чёрного.)

B. Запо́лните про́пуски сою́зами «и», «а», «но». (Fill in the blanks with the conjunctions **и, а,** or **но.**)

1. Я живу́ здесь, _____ он живёт там.
2. Я здесь живу́, _____ я здесь никого́ не зна́ю.
3. Ната́ша _____ Вла́дик игра́ют в те́ннис, _____ Марк нет.
4. Он высо́кого ро́ста, _____ не игра́ет в баскетбо́л.
5. У Вла́дика не ру́сые во́лосы, _____ све́тлые.

C. Поста́вьте слова́ в ско́бках в твори́тельный паде́ж, доба́вьте предло́г «с», е́сли ну́жно, и запо́лните про́пуски. (Put the words in parentheses into the instrumental, add **с** if necessary, and fill in the blanks.)

1. Вы познако́мились _____ в университе́те? (ва́ша жена́)
2. Я ра́ньше интересова́лась _____ . (америка́нская исто́рия)
3. _____ ты тепе́рь увлека́ешься? —_____ . (како́й спорт, скалола́зание (rock-climbing))
4. Я сего́дня познако́мился _____ . (но́вый секрета́рь)
5. _____ он занима́ется? —_____ . (Что, медици́на)

D. Запо́лните про́пуски ну́жной фо́рмой словосочета́ния «друг дру́га». (Fill in the blanks with the correct form of **друг дру́га.**)

1. Они́ не понима́ют _____ .
2. Мы ча́сто ду́маем _____ .
3. Вы зна́ете _____ ?
4. —Да, мы жи́ли _____ !
5. —А как вы познако́мились _____ ?

УРОК 15

ОБРАЗОВАНИЕ И РАСПИСАНИЯ. Education and schedules.

А. ДИАЛОГ

В общежи́тии университе́та.

ЖЕНЯ: Ско́лько лет, ско́лько зим! Что но́вого, стари́к?

ИЛЬЯ: Ничего́ осо́бенного. Как идёт твоя́ диссерта́ция?

ЖЕНЯ: Она́ сво́дит меня́ с ума́!

ИЛЬЯ: Ты ещё собира́ешься зако́нчить аспиранту́ру в ию́не?

ЖЕНЯ: Ду́маю, что да! А что ты де́лаешь?

ИЛЬЯ: Я то́же мно́го занима́юсь. Но мой грант ко́нчился.

ЖЕНЯ: Жаль.

ИЛЬЯ: Да. Тепе́рь я рабо́таю по вто́рникам и четверга́м в медлаборато́рии.

ЖЕНЯ: Ну и как?

ИЛЬЯ: Рабо́та интере́сная, но остаётся ме́ньше вре́мени для заня́тий.

ЖЕНЯ: Поня́тно. А как твоя́ семья́?

ИЛЬЯ: Норма́льно, спаси́бо. Ва́ля уже́ у́чится в университе́те!

ЖЕНЯ: Неуже́ли?! Я по́мню, как она́ учи́лась чита́ть!

ИЛЬЯ: Да, я зна́ю. Слу́шай, мне пора́ на рабо́ту. Дава́й поговори́м за́втра.

ЖЕНЯ: За́втра у нас пра́здник. Я пое́ду домо́й.

ИЛЬЯ: Хорошо́, позвони́ мне.

ЖЕНЯ: Ла́дно. Счастли́во!

In a university dormitory.

ZHENYA: Long time no see! What's new, old man?

ILYA: Nothing much. How's your dissertation going?

ZHENYA: It's driving me crazy!

ILYA: Are you still planning to graduate in June?

ZHENYA: I think so! And what are you doing?

ILYA: I'm studying hard, too. But my grant's finished.

ZHENYA: That's too bad.

ILYA: Yeah. Now I'm working at a medical lab on Tuesdays and Thursdays.

ZHENYA: And how's that?

ILYA: The work is interesting, but it leaves less time to study.

ZHENYA: I understand. And how's your family?

ILYA: Fine, thanks. Valya's in college already!

ZHENYA: Really?! I remember when she was learning to read!

ILYA: Yes, I know. Listen, I have to go to work. Let's talk tomorrow.

ZHENYA: Tomorrow's a holiday. I'm going home.

ILYA: Okay then, give me a call.

ZHENYA: Okay. Bye!

B. ГРАММАТИКА И СЛОВОУПОТРЕБЛЕНИЕ

1. THE DATIVE CASE OF PLURAL NOUNS

Dative plural noun endings are the same for all genders: the hard ending is -ам, and the soft ending is -ям. As always, remember to remove any vowels or the letters -й and -ь before adding these endings.

	HARD	SOFT
MASCULINE FEMININE NEUTER	-ам	-ям

Ты зна́ешь отве́ты к упражне́ниям?

Do you know the answers to the exercises?

Я пишу́ пи́сьма друзья́м.

I'm writing letters to friends.

In addition to answering the questions **Кому́?** (To whom?) and **Чему́?** (To what?), the dative plural is also commonly used with the days of the week, following the preposition **по**, to indicate that something happens repeatedly on the same day.

Тепе́рь я рабо́таю в медлаборато́рии по вто́рникам и четверга́м.

Now I work at a medical lab on Tuesdays and Thursdays.

У меня́ выходны́е дни по пя́тницам и воскресе́ньям.

I have my days off on Fridays and Sundays.

2. GREETINGS AND GOOD WISHES

The genitive is used in many common idiomatic expressions in Russian. It appears in:

informal greetings and remarks;

Что но́вого? —Ничего́ осо́бенного.

What's new? —Nothing much.

Ничего́ стра́шного.

It's no big deal.

expressions of good wishes[1], especially when parting;

Всего́ хоро́шего! Всего́ до́брого!

All the best!

Всего́ наилу́чшего!

All the very best!

---

1. See **Уро́к** 13 for similar uses of the instrumental, e.g. **С пра́здником!** (Happy holiday!)

Счастливого пути!
Have a great trip!

Успеха!
Good luck! (literally, Success!)

Приятного аппетита!
Bon appetit!

До скорого!
See you soon!

3. VERBS OF STUDYING, LEARNING, AND TEACHING

The Russian verb **учить** means both "to teach" and "to learn," which is often confusing for English speakers. When it is used to mean "to learn" or "to memorize," it is generally followed by a noun in the accusative case.

Валя учит уроки каждый день.
Valya does her homework (literally, learns [her] lessons) every day.

Детям не очень трудно учить песни.
It's not difficult for children to learn (memorize) songs.

When **учить** means "to teach," the person taught is in the accusative case, and the subject taught is in the dative. **Учить** is generally used in reference to elementary and secondary education, but may also be used by adults when referring to acquisition of a specific skill.

Моя русская подруга учит меня русскому языку.
My Russian girlfriend is teaching me Russian.

Учительница учит детей читать.
The teacher is teaching the children to read.

The verbs **учиться**, **изучать**, and **заниматься** all mean "to study" and are most often used in reference to higher education. **Учиться** is generally used without reference to a specific subject to mean "to go to school; to be a student." However, when it does refer to a specific subject, the subject is in the dative case.

Ва́ля уже́ у́чится в университе́те!
Valya is already in college!

Она́ у́чится языка́м.
She's studying languages (with no indication of how seriously).

Учи́ться may also be followed by an infinitive, in which case it has the meaning of "to learn how to do something."

Я по́мню, когда́ она́ учи́лась чита́ть!
I remember when she was learning to read!

Я, наконе́ц, учу́сь води́ть маши́ну.
I am finally learning to drive.

Изуча́ть is used when a subject is being studied in depth or a course of study is being pursued on an advanced academic level. The subject studied is in the accusative case.

Илья́ изуча́ет медици́ну.
Iliya is pursuing medicine.

Она́ изуча́ет англи́йский язы́к.
She's studying the English language (in depth, probably to the exclusion of other studies).

Занима́ться means "to be occupied with" when it refers to a particular subject or activity, which is then in the instrumental. When speaking about school, however, it is used without a complement (i.e. a subject or activity) and means simply "to study; to do homework." Compare:

Я то́же мно́го занима́юсь.
I also study hard.

Она́ занима́ется спо́ртом.
She's involved with ("into") sports.

Преподава́ть (to teach, to instruct) is generally used to speak about university students or adults. The person being taught is in the dative case, and the subject taught is in the accusative.

Он преподаёт студе́нтам америка́нскую литерату́ру.
He teaches the students American literature.

Я преподава́ла бизнесме́нам ру́сский язы́к.
I used to teach Russian to businessmen.

4. ADVERBS OF PLACE, TIME, AND FREQUENCY

Like English adverbs, Russian adverbs modify verbs, adjectives, or other adverbs. They answer the questions **Где?/Куда́?** (Where?), **Когда́?** (When?), **Как?** (How?), or **Как ча́сто?** (How often?), and they have a wide variety of forms. Russian adverbs usually precede any verbs they modify. However, they may be placed after a verb for emphasis, or because they provide new information. Following are some of the most common adverbs of place, most of which you have already encountered.

здесь/сюда́	here; in this place	до́ма/домо́й	at home/homewards
там/туда́	there	бли́зко/ря́дом	near; nearby
тут	here (colloquial)	(не)далеко́	(not) far
вон там	over there	внутри́	inside; indoors

Я пойду́ домо́й.
I'm going home.

Его́ общежи́тие нахо́дится недалеко́ отсю́да.
His dorm is located not far from here.

Following are some of the most common adverbs of time and frequency, many of which you already know.

за́втра	tomorrow	пото́м	then; after that
сего́дня	today	сра́зу	immediately
вчера́	yesterday	до́лго	for a long time
ско́ро	soon	всё вре́мя	all the time
давно́	a long time ago	иногда́	sometimes
неда́вно	recently	всегда́	always

ра́ньше	formerly; before	ре́дко	rarely
тепе́рь	now; nowadays	обы́чно	usually
сейча́с	right now	никогда́	never
тогда́	then; at that time	ча́сто	often

Дава́й за́втра поговори́м.
Let's talk tomorrow.

Илья́ ча́сто занима́ется всю ночь, а Же́ня совсе́м ре́дко занима́ется.
Iliya often studies all night, but Zhenya rarely studies at all.

5. УЖЕ VERSUS ЕЩЁ

Two Russian adverbs that are often confused with each other are **уже** (already, yet) and **ещё** (still, yet). While English has three separate words for "still," "yet," and "already," Russian combines them into these two. Here are two rules that should make the distinction easier: Whenever it is possible to use "already" in English, use **уже́** in Russian. Whenever it is possible to use "still" in English, use **ещё** in Russian.

Ва́ля уже́ у́чится в университе́те!
Valya's already in college!

Ты ещё собира́ешься ко́нчить в ию́не?
Are you still planning on graduating in June?

По́езд уже́ здесь? —К сча́стью, ещё нет.
Is the train here already (yet)? —Fortunately, not yet.

Они́ уже́ гото́вы? —Ещё нет!
Are they ready yet? —Not yet!

C. СЛОВАРЬ

аспира́нт	graduate student
Всего́ наилу́чшего!	All the very best!
всегда́	always
выходно́й день	day off
грант	grant
давно́	a long time ago

диссерта́ция	dissertation
До ско́рого!	See you soon!
до́лго	for a long time
дома́шнее зада́ние	homework
Ду́маю, что да.	I think so.
Жаль.	That's too bad.; I'm sorry.
заня́тия	studies
изуча́ть (изуча́ю, изуча́ешь, изуча́ют)	to study (a subject) in depth
иногда́	sometimes
к сча́стью	fortunately
ка́ждый	every; each
ко́нчить (ко́нчу, ко́нчишь, ко́нчат) (что)	to graduate, to finish (something)
ме́ньше	less
медици́на	medicine (study or practice of)
на у́лице	outdoors; outside; in the street
неда́вно	recently
Ничего́ осо́бенного.	Nothing much.
Ничего́ стра́шного.	No big deal.; It's nothing.
Ну и как?	And how is/was it?
общежи́тие	dormitory
обы́чно	usually
по (+ dative plural day of week)	on (day of week)
пра́здник	holiday
преподава́ть (преподаю́, преподаёшь, преподаю́т)	to teach (college/adults)
расписа́ние	schedule
своди́ть (кого́) *с ума́*	to drive (someone) crazy (lit. out of the mind)
Ско́лько лет, ско́лько зим!	Long time no see!
собира́ться (собира́юсь, собира́ешься,собира́ются)	to plan to
стари́к	old man
стипе́ндия	stipend, scholarship
тепе́рь	now (opp. of before); nowadays
университе́т	university
Успе́ха!	Good luck!
учи́ться (учу́сь, у́чишься, у́чатся)	to go to school, to learn how
Что но́вого?	What's new?
э́то зна́чит	that/it means

РУССКАЯ КУЛЬТУРА

Education and scholars have always been respected and supported in Russia. Under communism, education was free. Because governmental support has since diminished or disappeared, many schools in the CIS now charge tuition in some form. Although there has been a great deal of educational reform, traditional Russian education still emphasizes a centralized curriculum, rote learning, oral exams, and public commendation or censure.

Russian children go to **де́тский сад** (kindergarten) from ages three to six. Then they attend **шко́ла** (school), as **шко́льники** (pupils), from grades 1–9. Throughout this period they remain with the same group of classmates. They are graded on a five-point system from **пятёрка** (5), or excellent, to **дво́йка** (2), or unsatisfactory (a failing grade of 1 is rarely given). After ninth grade, they can find work, go to a vocational school (**ССУЗ**), or attend high school, from which they graduate after the eleventh grade with an **аттеста́т зре́лости** (high school diploma). After high school they may apply to a **ВУЗ** (**вы́сшее уче́бное заведе́ние**—institution of higher learning): either an **университе́т** (university), or an **институ́т** (more specialized, but also a general term for "college"). Students are accepted into a certain major and are paid a **стипе́ндия** (stipend) until, after five or six years, they receive their **дипло́м** (diploma). The **университе́т** is generally more competitive than the **институ́т**, but both require students to pass very difficult entrance exams.

УПРАЖНЕНИЯ

A. **Поста́вьте сушестви́тельные в ско́бках в да́тельный паде́ж и запо́лните про́пуски.** (Put the nouns in parentheses into the dative case and fill in the blanks.)

1. Когда́ ты рабо́таешь в лаборато́рии? —По _____ .
   (понеде́льники)
2. Профе́ссор преподаёт _____ фи́зику. (студе́нты)
3. Учи́тельницы пи́шут пи́сьма _____ . (роди́тели)

4. Я посыла́ю посы́лку _____ . (де́ти)
5. Мы обы́чно отдыха́ем по _____ . (воскресе́нья)

B. Подбери́те соотве́тствующие ру́сские предложе́ния к англи́йским
значе́ниям. У одного́ предложе́ния два значе́ния. (Match the Russian
sentences with the English meanings. One sentence has two meanings.)

1. Nothing much.
2. All the best!
3. Ничего́ стра́шного.
4. All the very best!
5. Что но́вого?

a. Всего́ наилу́чшего!
b. До ско́рого!
c. It's no big deal.
d. Всего́ до́брого!
e. Have a good trip!
f. Всего́ хоро́шего!
g. Ничего́ осо́бенного.
h. What's new?

C. Переведи́те глаго́лы в ско́бках и запо́лните про́пуски. (Translate the
verbs in parentheses and fill in the blanks.)

1. Она́ _____ их ру́сскому языку́. (is teaching)
2. Я _____ моё дома́шнее зада́ние. (doing)
3. Я _____ в америка́нском ко́лледже. (am a student)
4. Он _____ ру́сскую литерату́ру. (was studying in
   depth)
5. Вчера́ ве́чером я _____ до утра́. (studied)
6. Она́ _____ студе́нтам ру́сский язы́к. (teaches)
7. Я мно́го _____ . (study)
8. Он _____ в университе́те. (is a student)
9. Мы _____ ру́сский язы́к. (study in depth)
10. Ты до́лжен _____ э́ти слова́ сего́дня. (learn/memorize)

D. Отве́тьте на вопро́сы о диало́ге наре́чием. (Answer the questions about
the dialogue with an adverb.)

1. Как ча́сто Илья́ рабо́тает в медлаборато́рии, ре́дко и́ли
   ча́сто?
2. Когда́ сестра́ Ильи́ учи́лась чита́ть, давно́ и́ли неда́вно?
3. Когда́ Илья́ хоте́л поговори́ть с Же́ней?
4. Куда́ пое́дет Же́ня на пра́здник?
5. Когда́ Илья́ сказа́л Же́не ему́ позвони́ть?

E. **Запо́лните про́пуски наре́чиами «уже́» и́ли «ещё».** (Fill in the blanks with the adverbs **уже́** or **ещё**.)

1. Я _____ ко́нчил институ́т в ию́не.
2. Же́ня _____ у́чится в университе́те. Он собира́ется ко́нчить в ию́не.
3. Они́ _____ здесь? —Нет, я не зна́ю, где они́.
4. Мне не нра́вится моя́ рабо́та, но я _____ там рабо́таю.
5. Жаль, что твоя́ стипе́ндия _____ ко́нчилась.

ТРЕТЬЯ ПРОВЕРКА (Third Review)

A. Восстанови́те диало́г в логи́ческий поря́док.
(Put the lines of the dialogue into a logical order.)

HINT: **Алло́**! is the first line of dialogue 1, and **Хорошо́. До встре́чи**! is the last line of dialogue 2.

1. Же́нщина: m. (Алло́?)
2. Вале́ра:
3. Же́нщина:
4. Вале́ра:
5. Же́нщина:

Вале́ра ещё раз набира́ет но́мер.

6. Ми́ша:
7. Вале́ра:
8. Ми́ша:
9. Пе́тя:
10. Вале́ра:
11. Пе́тя:
12. Вале́ра:
13. Пе́тя:
14. Вале́ра:

a. Вы не туда́ попа́ли!
b. О, приве́т!
c. Слу́шаю.
d. Алло́. Кто э́то?
e. Хорошо́. До встре́чи!
f. Нет, одну́ мину́точку.
g. Ой, извини́те!
h. Здра́вствуйте. Позови́те, пожа́луйста, Петра́ Попо́ва.
i. Это я, Вале́ра.
j. Ничего́.
k. Это Пе́тя?
l. В де́вять.
m. Алло́?
n. Пе́тя, во ско́лько начина́ется фильм?

B. Поста́вьте снача́ла предложе́ния в проше́дшее вре́мя, а пото́м в бу́дущее вре́мя. (First put the sentences into the past tense, then into the future tense.)

1. Фильм начина́ется в семь.
2. Они́ в Пско́ве.
3. Что вы де́лаете ве́чером?
4. Я (feminine) хожу́ в кино́ ка́ждую неде́лю.
5. Как она́ чу́вствует себя́?

C. Отве́тьте на вопро́сы коро́ткими отве́тами. (Answer the questions with short answers.)

ОБРАЗЕЦ: У Вла́дика есть борода́? —Да, есть.
Does Vladik have a beard? —Yes, he does.

1. Како́й фильм бу́дут смотре́ть Ира и Вале́ра, и где он идёт?
2. Во ско́лько начина́ется фильм?
3. Ско́лько часо́в идёт фильм?
4. Ско́лько биле́тов Ри́та хо́чет заказа́ть, на како́й по́езд и в како́й ваго́н?
5. Когда́ (час и день) отхо́дит её по́езд?
6. Для кого́ э́тот го́род-родно́й?
7. Что Нэнси должна́ де́лать?
8. Ско́лько табле́ток она́ бу́дет принима́ть, и ско́лько раз в день?
9. Когда́ Же́ня собира́ется ко́нчить институ́т?
10. Как идёт его́ диссерта́ция?

D. **Переведи́те на ру́сский.** (Translate into Russian.)

1. People usually like going to the movies.
2. Who likes to play tennis? —Natasha's fascinated with tennis.
3. What time is it? —It's one o'clock. —And what time do you need to go? —At 9:30 p.m.
4. What day is it? —It's June first. —And when (on what day) will your exam be? —On June fourth.
5. What color will the flower be? —Yellow.
6. With whom do you (formal) live? —With my husband and our little daughter.
7. We've already been (gone and come back by vehicle) to your (familiar) favorite place.
8. They write to each other, but not very often (rarely).
9. How will we recognize each other? —I'm tall, I have light brown hair and glasses, and I'll have on a big, orange hat.
10. Happy Birthday!
11. Ow! My head hurts!
12. Do you (familiar) often teach your Russian friend English words?
13. She shouldn't go anywhere today.
14. What subject (**предме́т**) did she used to teach at the university? —Russian literature.

УРОК 16

В РЕСТОРАНЕ. At a restaurant.

А. ДИАЛОГ

Ужин с друзьями.

ЛЁНЯ: Здесь так мно́го наро́да! И я так го́лоден!

ЛЮСЯ: Да, рестора́н о́чень популя́рный, а мест ма́ло.

ЛИНДА: Отли́чно, вот свобо́дный стол. Каки́е здесь фи́рменные блю́да?

ЛЁНЯ: Хозя́ева—грузи́ны и узбе́ки. Поэ́тому национа́льные блю́да о́чень хоро́шие.

ЛИНДА: Зна́чит, здесь говоря́т и по-грузи́нски и по-узбе́кски?

ЛЁНЯ: Наве́рно, а та́кже по-ру́сски.

ОФИЦИАНТ: Сто́лик на трои́х?

ЛЮСЯ: Да.

ОФИЦИАНТ: Сади́тесь сюда́, пожа́луйста. Вот меню́ ... Что вы зака́зываете?

ЛЁНЯ: Гмм ... ры́ба у вас све́жая?

ОФИЦИАНТ: Да, но о́страя.

ЛЁНЯ: Хорошо́, я её возьму́, и на заку́ску чебуре́ки. Ты вы́брала, Ли́нда?

ЛИНДА: Почти́. Как по-англи́йски «бара́нина»?

ЛЮСЯ: По-мо́ему «lamb.»

ЛИНДА: О, я не ем мя́со. Что у вас для вегетариа́нцев?

ОФИЦИАНТ: Есть хачапу́ри и ры́бный суп, уха́.

ЛИНДА: Ла́дно.

ЛЮСЯ: А я возьму́ харчо́ и пото́м шашлы́к.

ОФИЦИАНТ: А что вы бу́дете пить?

ЛЁНЯ: Минера́льную во́ду и одну́ буты́лочку сухо́го бе́лого вина́.

Че́рез не́которое вре́мя.

ЛЁНЯ: Молодо́й челове́к! Принеси́те, пожа́луйста, ча́ю и ча́шку ко́фе.

ОФИЦИА́НТ: А сла́дкое?

ЛЮ́СЯ: Спаси́бо, нет. То́лько счёт. Всё бы́ло о́чень вку́сно!

Dinner with friends.

LYONYA: It's so crowded here! And I'm so hungry!

LYUSYA: Yes, the restaurant's very popular, and there aren't many places to sit.

LINDA: Oh, good, there's a free table. What are the specialties here?

LYONYA: The owners are Georgian and Uzbek. So, the ethnic dishes are good.

LINDA: So they speak both Georgian and Uzbek here?

LYONYA: Probably, and Russian, too.

WAITRESS: A table for three?

LYUSYA: Yes.

WAITRESS: Sit here, please. Here are the menus . . . What would you like?

LYONYA: Hmm . . . is your fish fresh?

WAITRESS: Yes, but spicy.

LYONYA: Okay, I'll have that, and the meat pastries for starters. Have you decided, Linda?

LINDA: Almost. What is "бара́нина" in English?

LYUSYA: "Lamb," I think.

LINDA: Oh, I don't eat meat. What do you have for vegetarians?

WAITRESS: There's khachapuri and the fish soup, ookhah.

LINDA: Alright.

LYUSYA: And I'll have the lamb soup and then the shish kebab.

WAITRESS: And what would you like to drink?

LYONYA: Mineral water, and a bottle of dry, white wine.

Later.

LYONYA: Waiter! Could we please have some tea and a cup of coffee?

WAITRESS: And dessert?

LYUSYA: No, thank you. Just the bill. Everything was delicious!

B. ГРАММАТИКА И СЛОВОУПОТРЕБЛЕНИЕ

1. QUANTIFIERS

Quantifiers answer the question **Ско́лько?** (How much/How many?) and they generally precede the word they modify. When used with nouns, the noun must be in the genitive case. Notice that in Russian there is no difference between "much" and "many."

мно́го	much, many, a lot
ма́ло	not much, few, a little
немно́го, немно́жко	a little, few
чуть-чу́ть	a little bit (informal)
не́сколько	several, a few (only with count nouns)

Здесь так мно́го наро́да! —И так ма́ло мест!
There are so many people here! — And so few places!

Он мно́го занима́ется. Он хоро́ший студе́нт.
He studies a lot. He's a good student.

Хо́чешь попро́бовать мой суп? —Да, чуть-чу́ть.
Do you want to try my soup? — Yes, just a little.

Не́сколько and ско́лько are followed by plural nouns in the genitive.

Я зна́ю не́сколько вегетариа́нцев в Росси́и. —А ско́лько лет ты вегетериа́нка?
> I know several vegetarians in Russia. — And how many years have you been a vegetarian?

2. THE GENITIVE AND ACCUSATIVE CASE OF PLURAL NOUNS

a. Genitive Plural Endings

To form the genitive of plural nouns, drop -ь, -й or any vowels from the nominative singular form, and add the appropriate genitive plural endings. Note that feminine and neuter plural nouns have the same basic ending in the genitive. Masculine and feminine nouns ending in -ь also have the same ending. As always, the umbrella rule will help you determine whether to use soft or hard endings. The endings are:

	NOMINATIVE ENDS IN	GENITIVE
MASCULINE	consonant	-ов/-ев
	-ь/-ж/-ш/-ч/-щ	-éй
FEMININE	-а	(zero ending)
	-я (-ия)	-ь (-ий)
	-ь	-éй
NEUTER	-о	(zero ending)
	-е (-ие)	-ей (-ий)

Здесь так мно́го госте́й! —И ма́ло мест. (nominative: гость, ме́сто)
> There are so many people (guests) here! — And so few places.

Что у вас для вегетариа́нцев[1]? (nominative: вегетариа́нец)
> What do you have for vegetarians?

Не име́й сто рубле́й, име́й сто друзе́й. (nominative: рубль, друзья́)
> Better to have a lot of friends than to have a lot of money.

Ско́лько этаже́й в э́том зда́нии? (nominative: эта́ж)
> How many floors are there in this building?

---

1. Like many words ending in -ец, вегетариа́нец has a fleeting е; вегетариа́нец » вегетариа́нцев.

Notice that neuter and feminine nouns ending in -о and -а in the nominative singular take a "zero-ending" in the genitive plural. In other words, the final vowel is simply dropped without being replaced.[2] For example, кни́га » книг, сло́во » слов. For nouns ending in -е or -я in the nominative, remove the final vowel and add -ь if the remaining final letter is a consonant, or -й if the final letter is -и. For example, неде́ля » неде́ль, упражне́ние » упражне́ний.

Я учи́лась гото́вить мно́го грузи́нских блюд. (nominative singular: **блю́до**)
I learned to prepare many Georgian dishes.

Ско́лько неде́ль вы бы́ли в Петербу́рге? (nominative singular: **неде́ля**)
How many weeks were you in Petersburg?

b. Accusative Plural Endings

Inanimate nouns have the same plural endings in the accusative as in the nominative. Animate nouns have the same plural endings in the accusative as in the genitive. The basic accusative endings are:

	ACCUSATIVE INANIMATE	ACCUSATIVE ANIMATE
MASCULINE	-ы/-и	-ов/-ев/-е́й
FEMININE	-ы/-и	zero ending/-ь (-ий)/-е́й
NEUTER	-а/-я	zero ending/-ей (-ий)

Я зна́ю официа́нтов и официа́нток в э́том кафе́. Я ча́сто обе́даю здесь. (nominative: **официа́нт, официа́нтка**)
I know the waiters and waitresses at this cafe. I often eat lunch here.

Ты зна́ешь рестора́ны в э́том райо́не? (nominative: **рестора́н**)
Do you know the restaurants in this area?

c. Irregular Genitive Noun Plural Endings

Some common nouns have irregular genitive plural forms. The most common include: **раз** (time; once, twice), **год** (year), **челове́к** (person), **ребёнок** (child), **де́ньги** (money), and **грамм** (gram). Note that if a noun has an irregular nominative plural ending, it will probably have an irregular genitive plural ending also.

---

2. For any nouns in which this results in two consonants together, add **о** or **е** back into the final syllable, e.g. **письмо́ » пи́сем, окно́ » о́кон.**

Ско́лько <u>раз</u> вы здесь е́ли? (nominative: **раз)**
How many times have you eaten here?

Пять <u>челове́к</u> уже́ ждут стол. (nominative: **челове́к)**
Five people are already waiting for a table.

Ско́лько у вас <u>дете́й</u>? (nominative: **де́ти)**
How many children do you have?

Я жила́ не́сколько <u>лет</u> в Ташке́нте. (nominative: **год)**
I lived in Tashkent for a few years.

Э́то сли́шком мно́го <u>де́нег</u>. —Нет, э́то включа́ет чаевы́е. (nominative: **де́ньги)**
That's too much money. — No, it includes the tip.

Note that **челове́к** is used instead of **лю́ди** after numbers and after **не́сколько**.

3. LANGUAGES AND NATIONALITIES (ПО-РУ́ССКИ VERSUS РУ́ССКИЙ)

По-ру́сски (in Russian) is an adverb of manner, answering the question **Как?** (How?; In what manner?), and it always modifies a verb. It is generally used when referring to language skills because you are describing *how* you speak, read, or write. **Ру́сский** (Russian), on the other hand, is an adjective, used to describe a noun. It is used when referring to a language in a general way, and the noun **язы́к** (language) is often understood.

Я говорю́ по-ру́сски.
I speak Russian (literally, in the Russian manner).

Я зна́ю ру́сский язы́к.
I know Russian (literally, the Russian language).

This adverb/adjective distinction is true for all languages and nationalities. Notice that the adverbs begin with **по-** and end in **-и**.

Я чита́ю, пишу́ и понима́ю по-францу́зски.
I read, write, and understand French. (literally, in the French manner)

Здесь говоря́т по-грузи́нски и по-узбе́кски? —Да, а та́кже по-ру́сски.

Do they speak Georgian and Uzbek here? —Yes, and Russian, too.
(literally, in the Georgian/Uzbek/Russian manner)

Как по-англи́йски бара́нина?

What is **бара́нина** in English (literally, in the English manner)?

However, to speak about studying a language, you must say:

Ви́ки у́чит неме́цкий и италья́нский языки́.

Vicki's learning German and Italian.

Он зна́ет кита́йский язы́к.

I know Chinese.

Note that nationality can be expressed in two ways: with an adjective, as in the English "She's German," or with a noun, as in "the Germans." The nouns often end in -ка (feminine) or -ец (masculine) in the singular. Unlike in English, none of the adverbs, adjectives, or nouns referring to nationality or language are capitalized, unless they begin a sentence.

Хозя́ева—грузи́ны и узбе́ки, то есть она́ грузи́нка, а он у́збек.

The owners are Georgian and Uzbek, that is, she's a Georgian and he's an Uzbek.

Я америка́нка и он то́же америка́нец.

I'm an American, and he's American, too.

Я япо́нка, а она́ ру́сская.

I'm Japanese, and she's Russian.

4. И ... И ... (BOTH ... AND ...)

The structure и ... и ... means "both . . . and . . ." It is also a milder form of "not only . . . but also . . ." and can be used with verbs, adverbs, adjectives or nouns.

Sixteenth Lesson   185

Хозя́ева—грузи́ны и узбе́ки. — Зна́чит, здесь говоря́т и по-грузи́нски и по-узбе́кски?

The owners are Georgian and Uzbek. — So they speak both Georgian and Uzbek here?

Принеси́те, пожа́луйста, и ви́лку, и ло́жку.

Could I please have both a fork and a spoon?

Я здесь и живу́, и рабо́таю.

I both work and live here.

Еда́ была́ и вку́сная, и дешёвая.

The meal was not only tasty but also cheap.

5. SOME OF (THE PARTITIVE GENITIVE)

To express the notion "some (of)," the partitive genitive form of the noun is used. While for most nouns, this is just the regular genitive ending, some common, masculine, food-related nouns take the special, partitive genitive ending **-y or -ю**. These include:

мёду	some honey	сы́ру	some cheese
са́хару	some sugar	ча́ю	some tea
су́пу	some soup	шокола́ду	some chocolate
со́ку	some juice		

Принеси́те, пожа́луйста, ча́ю и са́хару. (nominative: чай, са́хар)

Please bring us some tea and some sugar.

Да́йте, пожа́луйста, хле́ба и сы́ру. (nominative: хлеб, сыр)

Please give me some bread and some cheese.

Хо́чешь ры́бы и́ли мя́са? (nominative: ры́ба, мя́со)

Do you want some fish or some meat?

6. THE VERB ЕСТЬ (TO EAT)

The conjugation of this verb is completely irregular, although in its plural forms it takes Conjugation II endings. Be careful not to confuse the infinitive **есть** with the form in **У вас есть** ...? (Do you have . . . ?).

Шестна́дцатый уро́к

есть: to eat

I eat	я ем	мы еди́м	we eat
you (fam.) eat	ты ешь	вы еди́те	you (pl./pol.) eat
he/she eats	он/она́ ест	они́ едя́т	they eat

plural stem: ед+
imperative: Ешь(те)!

О, я не ем мя́со. —А ты что, ешь то́лько о́вощи?!
Oh, I don't eat meat. — What do you eat then, only vegetables?!

Са́шка, сейча́с же ешь! С дру́гом мо́жно игра́ть по́сле обе́да.
Sashka, eat now. You can play with your friend after lunch.

C. СЛОВАРЬ

блю́до	dish (food)
буты́лка	bottle
вегетариа́нец (-ка)	vegetarian (noun) (m./f.)
ви́лка	fork
вино́	wine
вку́сный, вку́сно	tasty; good (food)
вы́брать	to choose
го́лоден/на́/ны	hungry
горчи́ца	mustard
еда́	meal
есть (ем, ешь, ест, еди́м, еди́те, едя́т)	to eat (irregular)
и ... и ...	both . . . and . . .
Как по-(language) _____ ?	How do you say _____ in (language)?
кафе́	cafe
ко́фе	coffee
ку́рица	chicken
ло́жка	spoon
мя́со	meat
ма́ло	not much; few; a little
меню́	menu
минера́льная вода́	mineral water
мно́го	much; many; a lot
на пе́рвое	for starters (lit. for the first)
на сла́дкое	for dessert (lit. for the sweet)

наро́д	(the) people
национа́льный	national; ethnic
немно́го/немно́жко	a little
не́сколько (+ genitive plural)	several; a few
нож	knife
о́вощи	vegetables
о́стрый	spicy; hot
официа́нт(ка)	waiter/waitress
пе́рец	pepper
по-мо́ему	I think; in my opinion
по́рция	portion
почти́	almost
Принеси́те, пожа́луйста, ...	Please bring . . .
рестора́н	restaurant
ры́ба	fish
све́жий	fresh
свобо́дный	free; unoccupied
сла́дкий	sweet
соль	f. salt
сто́лик на одного́/двои́х/трои́х	a table for one/two/three
суп	soup
сухо́й	dry
счёт	bill, check, account
фи́рменные блю́да	specialties (of the house)
фру́кты	fruit
хлеб	bread
чуть-чу́ть	a little bit
Я возьму́ ...	I'll have . . .
язы́к	language; tongue

РУССКАЯ КУЛЬТУРА

The best Russian food is still probably to be found at the home of a good cook. Russians do not eat out often, especially for **у́жин** (supper). When they do, it is generally a big, celebratory occasion including many people and much preparation and planning, and it usually takes place at a **рестора́н** (restaurant) where they know someone, to ensure better service and food. The focus tends to be more on a good time with good friends, and less on the food itself. The meal usually lasts the entire evening and often includes live music, dancing, and many toasts.

Although Russians tend to eat at home, there are still a number of choices for eating out. If you're on the run, you can try one of the bistros (**вистро́**) and cafés (**кафе́**), which might serve **пельме́ни** (meat dumplings with sour-cream), **блины́** (crepes), or **чай** (tea) and snacks, or you can stop at a street cart for some **пирожки́** (pastries with meat and vegetables), **шашлы́к** (shish-kebab), **моро́женое** (ice cream), or **по́нчики** (doughnuts). On your hotel floor or on the street you may see a **буфе́т** (small snack bar) selling **чай, ко́фе, бутербро́ды** (bread with cheese or meat), **круты́е я́йца** (hard-boiled eggs), and **фру́кты** (fruit) or **пече́нье** (biscuits), as well as wine (**вино́**), beer (**пи́во**), and vodka (**во́дка**). There are also western-style fast-food restaurants, such as **пицце́рия** (pizzerias), and, in major cities, **Макдо́налдс** (McDonald's). For lighter fare, try coffee shops (**кофе́йня**) such as a **конди́терская** (cake shop). For a full meal, a restaurant or cafe offers good food and service, but at higher prices.

УПРАЖНЕНИЯ

A. Подбери́те соотве́тствующие ру́сские слова́ к англи́йским значе́ниям. У не́которых слов два значе́ния. (Match the Russian words with the English meanings. Some words have two meanings.)

1. Я <u>немно́го</u> понима́ю по-ру́сски.
2. У него́ <u>ма́ло</u> друзе́й.
3. У него́ <u>мно́го</u> друзе́й.
4. <u>Ско́лько</u> челове́к там живу́т?
   —Там живу́т <u>не́сколько</u> челове́к.
5. Она́ <u>мно́го</u> ест.
6. Хо́чешь попро́бовать? —То́лько <u>чуть-чу́ть</u>.
7. Я <u>не́сколько</u> раз ему́ звони́л, но его́ нет.
8. <u>Ско́лько</u> вре́мени у тебя́?
9. У меня́ <u>мно́го</u> вре́мени.
10. У меня́ <u>ма́ло</u> вре́мени.

a. a lot
b. a little bit
c. a little
d. much
e. How much
f. little
g. few
h. not much
i. several
j. many
k. How many, a few

B. Поста́вьте сушестви́тельные в ско́бках в вини́тельный паде́ж мно́жественного числа́ и запо́лните про́пуски. (Put the nouns in parentheses into the genitive plural and fill in the blanks.)

1. Сейча́с де́сять _____ утра́. (час)
2. Ско́лько _____ в год вы у́жинаете в рестора́не? Ка́ждый шесть _____. (раз, ме́сяц)
3. Я здесь живу́ уже́ пять _____ . (год)
4. Че́рез ско́лько _____ вы уезжа́ете? (неде́ля)
5. Че́рез пятна́дцать _____ . (мину́та)
6. В э́той кварти́ре ма́ло _____ . (окно́)
7. Там есть мно́го _____ . (зда́ние)
8. Не име́й сто _____ , а име́й сто _____ . (рубль, друг)
9. Вот не́сколько _____ от неё. (письмо́)
10. Ско́лько _____ вам ну́жно? (ме́сто)

C. Подбери́те ру́сские предложе́ния, соотве́тствующие англи́йским значе́ниям. (Match the Russian sentences with the English meanings.)

1. Я учу́ ру́сский язы́к.
2. Я и чита́ю и пишу́ по-кита́йски.
3. Они́ понима́ют по-неме́цки.
4. Я зна́ю неме́цкий язы́к.
5. Я говорю́ по-францу́зски.
6. Я говорю́ по-англи́йски.
7. Я не понима́ю по-грузи́нски.
8. Япо́нский язы́к—краси́вый язы́к.
9. Ты чита́ешь по-италья́нски?
10. Он япо́нец.

a. I speak English.
b. I speak Russian.
c. He's Japanese.
d. I study Russian.
e. Japanese is a beautiful language.
f. I don't understand Georgian.
g. I both read and write (in) Chinese.
h. Do you read Italian?
i. I know German.
j. I speak French.
k. They understand German.

D. **Запо́лните про́пуски раздели́тельной роди́тельной фо́рмой существи́тельных.** (Fill in the blanks with the partitive genitive form of the nouns in parentheses.)

Принеси́те, пожа́луйста,

1. _____ . (ка́ша [porridge] и мёд)
2. _____ . (сок)
3. _____ . (ко́фе и са́хар)
4. _____ . (суп и хлеб)
5. _____ . (вино́)

E. **Запо́лните про́пуски пра́вильными оконча́ниями глаго́ла «есть».** (Fill in the blanks with the correct endings of the verb **есть**.)

1. Я не _____ мя́со и ку́рицу. Я вегетериа́нец.
2. А почему́ ты не _____ ку́рицу?
3. Мы лю́бим _____ грузи́нские блю́да.
4. Мы _____ шашлы́к.
5. Лю́ся и Лёня _____ мя́со, а Ли́нда _____ ры́бу.

УРОК 17

НОВОСТИ ПО ТЕЛЕВИЗОРУ. The news on television.

___

А. ДИАЛОГ

Дóма вéчером.

ДЕДУШКА: По телевúзору сейчáс идýт вечéрние нóвости. Давáй посмóтрим.

ВНУК: Хорошó, давáй. *(включáет телевúзор)*

ДИКТОР: В заключéние, в Чернóбыле ещё высóкий ýровень радиáции. Мнóгие там сúльно страдáют от рáка, и э́та ситуáция, навéрно, бýдет продолжáться ещё мнóго лет.

ДЕДУШКА: А правúтельству всё равнó!

ВНУК: Я не соглáсен с тобóй. Нынешнее правúтельство всячески пытáется решúть проблéмы прóшлого, но емý никтó не помогáет.

ДИКТОР: А сейчáс, прогнóз погóды ...

ДЕДУШКА: Минýточку, я её не слышу. Что они сказáли?

ВНУК: Они сказáли, что зáвтра весь день бýдет óблачно и прохлáдно.

ДЕДУШКА: Замечáтельно!

ВНУК: Почемý?

ДЕДУШКА: Потомý что зáвтра я хочý пойтú на рынок, а там лéтом всегдá так жáрко.

ВНУК: Прáвда, на рынке прия́тно тóлько óсенью úли веснóй.

ДЕДУШКА: Ну, ужé пóздно. Мне порá спать! А тебé?

ВНУК: Нет, я бýду смотрéть специáльную передáчу об окружáющей средé.

ДЕДУШКА: Ах, юность! Стóлько энéргии! Не забýдь выключить свет. Спокóйной нóчи!

At home in the evening.

GRANDFATHER: The evening news is on TV now. Let's watch it.

GRANDSON: Alright. *(turns on the TV)*

NEWSCASTER: To conclude, at Chernobyl there is still a high level of radiation. Many are suffering badly from cancer, and this situation will probably continue for many years.

GRANDFATHER: And the government doesn't care!

GRANDSON: I don't agree with you. The present government is really trying to solve the problems from the past, but no one is helping them.

NEWSCASTER: And now, for the weather . . .

GRANDFATHER: Just a minute, I can't hear. What did they say?

GRANDSON: They said that it'll be cloudy and cool all day tomorrow.

GRANDFATHER: Wonderful!

GRANDSON: Why?

GRANDFATHER: Because I want to go to the outdoor market tomorrow, and it's always so hot there in the summer.

GRANDSON: True, the market's only pleasant in the spring or fall.

GRANDFATHER: Well, it's late. Time for me to go to bed. What about you?

GRANDSON: No, I'm going to watch a special program on the environment.

GRANDFATHER: Ah, youth! So energetic! Don't forget to turn off the lights. Good night!

B. ГРАММАТИКА И СЛОВОУПОТРЕБЛЕНИЕ

1. ADVERBS OF MANNER

Adverbs of manner are the ones we think of most often as adverbs, those ending in -ly in English, e.g. quickly, happily. In Russian, these adverbs usually end in **-o**, and they answer the question **Как?** (How? In what manner?). These adverbs are often formed from adjectives, by replacing the nominative adjective ending with **-o** (see **Уро́к** 6). Remember that the adverbs of language you learned in the previous lesson, e.g. **по-ру́сски**, are also considered adverbs of manner.

хорошо́	well	пло́хо	poorly
бы́стро	quickly	ме́дленно	slowly
ти́хо	quietly	гро́мко	loudly
си́льно	badly, strongly		

Мно́гие там си́льно страда́ют от ра́ка.
Many are suffering badly from cancer there.

Повтори́те ме́дленно, пожа́луйста.
Please repeat that slowly.

Вы хорошо́ спи́те но́чью? —Нет, я о́чень пло́хо сплю.
Do you sleep well at night? —No, I sleep very poorly.

Note that adverbs of manner often look exactly the same as short-form neuter adjectives (see **Уро́к** 6). However, you can tell them apart by context, as adjectives and adverbs have different functions.

Бы́ло хорошо́.
It was fine.

Она́ хорошо́ говори́т по-ру́сски.
She speaks Russian well.

Это замеча́тельно! Бу́дет о́блачно и прохла́дно весь день за́втра.
That's wonderful! It'll be cloudy and cool all day tomorrow.

2. IMPERSONAL EXPRESSIONS

An impersonal expression is one where the subject is not explicitly stated. In English, we use indefinite subjects such as "there," "it," or a general "you." These "subjectless sentences" are much more common in Russian than in English, and they are expressed much as they sound: with an understood subject and a neuter verb or adjective. Short-form adjectives, neuter to agree with the neuter subject, are often part of such expressions.

Ну, уже́ по́здно.

Well, it's late.

Здесь хо́лодно.

It's cold here.

В Черно́быле есть радиа́ция.

There is radiation in Chernobyl.

If the expression refers to a specific person, that person is in the dative case and sometimes performs the function of subject when the sentence is translated into English. Compare the following impersonal constructions, noting whether they have stated or understood subjects.

Пора́ спать!

Time to go to bed!

Мне пора́ спать!

It's time for me to go to bed!

Всё равно́.

It doesn't matter. (literally, It's all the same.)

А прави́тельству всё равно́!

And the government doesn't care! (literally, It's all the same to the government.)

3. REPORTED SPEECH

Reported, or indirect, speech is one instance where Russian is easier than English. In English, we often change tenses when reporting what someone said ("I am watching the news," John said. >> John said that he was watching the news.), but in Russian the tense of the actual statement does not change, whether quoted directly or reported. Compare:

Они́ сказа́ли: «Бу́дет о́блачно и прохла́дно весь день за́втра.»

They said: "It will be cloudy and cool all day tomorrow."

Они́ сказа́ли, что бу́дет о́блачно и прохла́дно весь день за́втра.

They said that it would be cloudy and cool all day tomorrow.

Она́ сказа́ла: «Я смотрю́ э́ту переда́чу.»

She said: "I'm watching this program."

Она́ сказа́ла, что она́ смо́трит э́ту переда́чу.

She said that she was watching this program.

4. "ONE" AND "ALL"

The special modifiers **весь** (all) and **оди́н** (one; some) agree in gender, number, and case with the nouns they modify. You learned the different forms of **оди́н** in the nominative singular in **Уро́к** 3 (Cardinal Numbers 0–10), and you have seen **весь** in a number of common expressions.

Всё равно́, что идёт дождь. Мы до́ма весь день.

It doesn't matter that it's been raining. We've been at home all day.

Весь is translated differently depending on context. When used alone, the nominative neuter form **всё** means "everything." Following are the singular forms of **весь** and **оди́н** in all the genders and cases. Don't try to memorize all the forms now. You'll pick them up gradually as you continue your study of Russian.

	MASCULINE	FEMININE	NEUTER	MASCULINE	FEMININE	NEUTER
NOMINATIVE	весь	вся	всё	оди́н	одна́	одно́
ACCUSATIVE	весь/всего́	всю	всё	оди́н/одного́	одну́	одно́
GENITIVE	всего́	всей	всего́	одного́	одно́й	одного́
PREPOSITIONAL	всём	всей	всём	одно́м	одно́й	одно́м
DATIVE	всему́	всей	всему́	одному́	одно́й	одному́
INSTRUMENTAL	всем	всей	всем	одни́м	одно́й	одни́м

Бу́дет о́блачно и прохла́дно весь день за́втра.

It'll be cloudy and cool all day tomorrow.

А прави́тельству всё равно́!

It's all the same to the government!

Почему́ все говоря́т так ти́хо?

Why is everyone (literally, all) speaking so quietly?

Всего́ хоро́шего!

All the best!

Семна́дцатый уро́к

У нас то́лько оди́н стол, одно́ кресло́ и одна́ ла́мпа.

We only have one table, one armchair, and one lamp.

Одному́ челове́ку не понра́вилосб на да́че.

One person didn't like it at the docks.

Notice that **все**, the plural[1] of **весь**, when used alone means "everyone."

5. TO TRY (ПЫТА́ТЬСЯ VERSUS СТАРА́ТЬСЯ VERSUS ПОПРО́БОВАТЬ)

There are several ways to say "to try" in Russian. **Попро́бовать** refers to tasting something, or trying something for the first time; **стара́ться** indicates an effort to do something difficult; and **пыта́ться** means "to endeavor, to attempt" and is generally used in a formal or official context.

Я о́чень стара́юсь говори́ть по-ру́сски, но мне о́чень тру́дно.

I'm really trying to speak Russian, but it's hard for me.

Хо́чешь попро́бовать мой суп? —Да, чуть-чу́ть.

Do you want to try my soup? —Yes, just a little.

Прави́тельство пыта́ется реши́ть пробле́мы про́шлого.

The government is trying to solve the problems from the past.

6. THE SEASONS

The seasons (**времена́ го́да**) in Russian are:

зима́	winter	зимо́й	in the winter
весна́	spring	весно́й	in the spring
ле́то	summer	ле́том	in the summer
о́сень	fall	о́сенью	in the fall

Зима́-хоро́шее вре́мя го́да на Кавка́зе.

The winter is a good time of year in the Caucasus.

Осень-моё люби́мое вре́мя го́да.

Autumn is my favorite time of year (season).

---

1. For a chart of the plural case endings of **весь** and **оди́н**, please see the Appendix.

На ры́нке прия́тно то́лько о́сенью и́ли весно́й.

The market's only pleasant in the spring or fall.

Там всегда́ ле́том так жа́рко.

It's always so hot there in the summer.

C. СЛОВАРЬ

бы́ло/не́ было	(it/there) was/wasn't
ве́черний (ве́черняя, ве́чернее)	evening (soft adjective)
весна́	spring
весь/вся/всё/все	all
включа́ть (включа́ю, включа́ешь, включа́ют)	to turn (something) on
внук	grandson
вре́мя го́да	time of year; season
всё (always singular)	everything
все (always plural)	everyone
вся́чески	in every way possible
выключа́ть (выключа́ю, выключа́ешь, выключа́ют)	to turn (something) off
де́душка	grandfather
заключе́ние	conclusion
зима́	winter
ле́то	summer
ме́дленно	slow(ly)
но́вости	news; the news
о́блачный	cloudy
о́сень	f. autumn
окружа́ющая среда́	the environment
переда́ча	program; broadcast
по́здно	late
помога́ть (помога́ю, помога́ешь, помога́ют) (кому́)	to help (someone)
после́дствие	consequence; after-effect
прави́тельство	government
про́шлый	past
прогно́з пого́ды	weather forecast
прохла́дный	cool
пыта́ться (пыта́юсь, пыта́ешься, пыта́ются)	to try, to attempt, to endeavor
радиа́ция	radiation

рак	cancer; crab
решáть (решáю, решáешь, решáют)	to decide, to solve, to settle
свет	light (noun)
сúльно	strong(ly); very
ситуáция	situation
сказáть (скажý, скáжешь, скáжут) (комý)	to say, to tell (someone)
слы́шать (слы́шу, слы́шишь, слы́шат)	to hear (II)
спать (сплю, спишь, спят)	to sleep (II)
специáльный	special
старáться (старáюсь, старáешься, старáются)	to try, to make an effort
стóлько (чегó)	so much (of something)
страдáть (страдáю, страдáешь, страдáют)	to suffer
такóй	such (a); so
телевúзор	television
температýра	temperature
тúхо	quietly; quiet
ýровень	m. level
холóдный	cold
энéргия	energy

РУССКАЯ КУЛЬТУРА

Virtually everyone in Russia has a TV and radio of some kind, and in many families one or the other is on all the time, often at high volume. The main national television station **Остáнкино**, also known as **пéрвая прогрáмма** (first channel), is broadcast from Moscow throughout Russia and most of the former republics. The second channel is general interest for Russians, the third is educational, the fourth is the St. Petersburg channel, and there are local channels for other areas. With the right equipment, it is also possible to receive BBC and CNN. Television today reflects the continuing imbalances and upheavals in Russia. All latest technology is available now, with **видеоплéйеры**, or **вúдики** (VCRs), DVDs, and **видеокáмеры** (camcorders), and many apartment buildings in large cities now have building antennas to receive cable programs. While a wide variety of programming is now available, much of it is of poor quality, such as Mexican soap operas, B-grade American movies, and government-run news.

The situation with radio is somewhat better. There are two different means of receiving radio programs. With one system, in which you tune into **кана́лы** (stations) on different wavelengths such as FM, AM, or shortwave with a **приёмник** (receiver), it is possible to receive BBC, Radio Liberty, or Voice of America. The other system is less sophisticated. It is a centralized radio system, essentially a speaker wired to a central location ("cable" radio). There are two main radio stations on this system: **Ра́дио Росси́и** (Radio Russia), the Russian news and general interest station, which broadcasts news every hour and has a news review every evening, and **Мая́к** (Lighthouse), devoted primarily to a wide variety of music. The other stations are regional, or are broadcast by interest groups.

УПРАЖНЕНИЯ

A. **Каки́е подчёркнутые слова́—наре́чия, а каки́е—кра́ткие прилага́тельные?** (Which underlined words are adverbs, and which are short-form adjectives?)

1. Как идёт твоя́ диссерта́ция? —Непло́хо, спаси́бо.
2. Она́ ра́да, что мы здесь.
3. Он сли́шком ти́хо говори́т. Я его́ не понима́ю.
4. Всё бы́ло гото́во?
5. Я прекра́сно игра́ю в тенни́с.

B. **Переведи́те на англи́йский.** (Translate into English.)

1. Пора́ идти́.
2. Нам я́сно, что ей всё равно́.
3. Вре́мя есть.
4. Де́душке всё равно́.
5. Макси́му жа́рко, а им хо́лодно.

C. Переведи́те предложе́ния в ко́свенную речь по образцу́.
(Put the sentences into indirect speech.)

1. Де́душка: Сейча́с иду́т вече́рние но́вости.
2. Ди́ктор: Эта ситуа́ция бу́дет продолжа́ться ещё мно́го лет.
3. Де́душка: Я хочу́ пойти́ на ры́нок.
4. Лю́ся: Всё бы́ло о́чень вку́сно!
5. Внук: Я бу́ду смотре́ть специа́льную переда́чу.

D. Поста́вьте слова́ в ско́бках в ну́жную фо́рму и запо́лните про́пуски.
(Put the words in parentheses into the correct form, and fill in the blanks.)

1. У меня́ есть _____ , что ну́жно. (весь)
2. _____ говоря́т, что ско́ро у нас бу́дет плоха́я пого́да.
3. Принеси́те, пожа́луйста, _____ пи́во и _____ стака́н вина́. (оди́н, оди́н)
4. Я _____ _____ у́тро чита́ла кни́гу. (весь, э́тот)
5. _____ _____ лю́ди живу́т в _____ кварти́ре? (весь, э́тот, оди́н)

E. Подбери́те соотве́тствующие слова́ в коло́нке Б к про́пускам в коло́нке А. (Match the words in column B to the blanks in column A.)

A	B
1. _____ в Росси́и о́чень холо́дная (cold).	a. Ле́том
2. Шко́ла начина́ется _____ .	b. зимо́й
3. _____ — хоро́шее вре́мя го́да для того чтобы ходи́ть на пляж.	c. весно́й
4. Но́вый год _____ .	d. о́сенью
5. _____ ру́сские шко́льники в шко́лу не хо́дят.	e. Ле́то
	f. Зима́

УРОК 18

ПЛАНИРОВАНИЕ ПОЕЗДКИ. Planning a trip.

А. ДИАЛОГ

В туристи́ческом аге́нстве.

ГЭРИ: *До́брое у́тро. Я хочу́ пое́хать на неде́лю в како́е-нибу́дь краси́вое ме́сто.*

АГЕНТ: *Ну, е́сли вы хоти́те купа́ться и загора́ть, я рекоменду́ю Крым. Там замеча́тельные пля́жи и тёплое мо́ре.*

ГЭРИ: *Мне ску́чно про́сто лежа́ть на со́лнце. Интере́сно, мо́жете ли вы порекомендова́ть что-нибу́дь ещё? Наприме́р о́тдых в гора́х?*

АГЕНТ: *Не хоти́те ли пое́хать на Кавка́з? В Кавка́зских гора́х мо́жно ката́ться на лы́жах, и там то́лько что вы́пало мно́го сне́га.*

ГЭРИ: *Вот тепе́рь вы говори́те де́ло! А как там с жильём?*

АГЕНТ: *Мо́жно останови́ться в гости́нице на неско́льких ра́зных горнолы́жных куро́ртах: Чеге́т, Дамба́й, Терска́л йли Гудау́ри.*

ГЭРИ: *А как туда́ дое́хать?*

АГЕНТ: *Самолётом и по́том авто́бусом.*

ГЭРИ: *Нет ли друго́го ви́да тра́нспорта, как наприме́р по́езд?*

АГЕНТ: *Это сли́шком далеко́ отсю́да. У вас не бу́дет доста́точно вре́мени.*

ГЭРИ: *Поня́тно. Ла́дно, я верну́сь по́сле обе́да заказа́ть биле́ты.*

АГЕНТ: *Хорошо́, тогда́ мы всё организу́ем. До свида́ния.*

At a travel agency.

GARY: Good morning. I'd like to go somewhere beautiful for a week.

TRAVEL AGENT: Well, if you want to swim and get a tan, I recommend the Crimea. There are wonderful beaches there and a warm sea.

GARY: It's hard for me to just lie there in the sun. Can you recommend anywhere else? For example, somewhere in the mountains?

TRAVEL AGENT: Perhaps you'd like to go to the Caucasus? You can go skiing in the Caucasian mountains, and they just got a lot of snow.

GARY: Now you're talking! What kinds of accomodations are there?

TRAVEL AGENT: There are several different ski resorts where you can stay: Cheget, Dambai, Terskal, or Gudauri.

GARY: And how do I get there?

TRAVEL AGENT: By plane and then by bus.

GARY: There's no other way to get there, like the train?

TRAVEL AGENT: It's too far from here. You won't have enough time.

GARY: I see. Okay, I'll be back this afternoon to order tickets.

TRAVEL AGENT: Fine, we'll arrange everything then. Goodbye.

B. ГРАММАТИКА И СЛОВОУПОТРЕБЛЕНИЕ

1. PREPOSITIONAL PLURAL ENDINGS

The prepositional plural endings for nouns, adjectives, and special modifiers are the same across all genders. All prepositional plural forms are derived from the nominative plural forms. For nouns, simply replace the endings with **-ax or -ях**. For adjectives, replace **-e** with **-x**. For special modifiers, simply add **-x**. As always, the third person forms **его, её,** and **их** do not change.

	NOMINATIVE	PREPOSITIONAL	EXAMPLE
NOUNS	-ы	-ах	го́ры ›› гора́х
	-а	-ах	пи́сьма ›› пи́сьмах
	(г/к/ж/х/ч/ш/щ+) -и	-ах	ве́щи ›› веща́х
	-и	-ях	неде́ли ›› неде́лях
	-я	-ях	зда́ния ›› зда́ниях
ADJECTIVES	-ые	-ых	но́вые ›› но́вых
	-ие	-их	больши́е ›› больши́х
SPECIAL MODIFIERS	-и	-их	мои́ ›› мои́х э́ти ›› э́тих
	-е	-ех	все ›› всех

В Кавка́зских гора́х мо́жно ката́ться на лы́жах.

You can ski in the Caucasian mountains.

Америка́нцы не зна́ют о на́ших со́лнечных, краси́вых пля́жах?

Don't Americans know about our beautiful, sunny beaches?

Во всех э́тих места́х на́до быть осторо́жным.

In all these places you have to be careful.

2. ЕСЛИ VERSUS ЛИ

Если and **ли** can both be translated into English as "if," but they are used quite differently. **Ли** is used in dependent clauses whenever "whether" can be used in English. To use **ли**, move the word or phrase under question to the beginning of the dependent clause, followed by **ли**, then the rest of the clause.

Интере́сно, мо́жете ли вы порекоменова́ть что-нибу́дь ещё?

I wonder if (whether) you <u>can</u> recommend anyplace else?

Я не зна́ю, живёт ли она́ в Москве́.

I don't know if (whether) she <u>lives</u> in Moscow.

Я не зна́ю, в Москве́ ли жила́ она́ и́ли в Петербу́рге.

I don't know if (whether) she lived <u>in Moscow</u> or in St. Petersburg.

Ли can also be used to make polite suggestions. It translates into English roughly as "Wouldn't you like/Perhaps you'd like to ...?" but not as "if" or "whether."

Не хоти́те ли вы пое́хать на Кавка́з?

Perhaps you'd like to go to the Caucasus?

In contrast, **е́сли** (if, in case, in the event that) is used whenever "whether" cannot be substituted for "if" in English. It is always the first word in the dependent clause.

Е́сли вы хоти́те купа́ться и загора́ть, вы должны́ пое́хать в Крым.

If you want to swim and get a tan, you should go to the Crimea.

Е́сли ты зна́ла, почему́ же ты мне не сказа́ла?!

If you knew, why on earth didn't you tell me?

Я пойду́, е́сли он там бу́дет.

I'll go if he'll be there.

Note that both **е́сли** and **ли** can be used with all three tenses.

3. "BY MEANS OF" AND THE INSTRUMENTAL CASE

When used with the preposition **с**, the instrumental means "together with." When used without a preposition, the instrumental case signifies "with, by, by means of." In fact, the case was named after this usage: to state the instrument (by what means), literal or figurative, with which something is done.

Как туда́ дое́хать? —Самолётом и пото́м авто́бусом.

How do I get there? ——By plane and then by bus.

Я предпочита́ю писа́ть ру́чкой, а не карандашо́м.

I prefer to write with a pen rather than a pencil.

Жан-Франсуа́ посыла́ет посы́лку авиапо́чтой.

Jean-Francois is sending the package (by) air mail.

Remember that means of transportation can also be stated in the prepositional case, e.g. **на авто́бусе** (see **Уро́к** 9, Two Verbs of Motion). The instrumental is generally used only for public transportation[1], while the prepositional can be used for any means of transportation.

---

1. Except that it cannot be used with **метро́** and **такси́**, as they are foreign words and do not decline.

4. "SOME-" VERSUS "ANY-" (-TO VERSUS -НИБУДЬ)

These two particles are used to form indefinite pronouns, such as "someone," "anything," "somewhere." They can be attached as suffixes to any question word. The particle -то roughly corresponds to "some-" and -нибудь to "any-." The particle -то conveys definiteness, i.e. it is assumed that what is in question exists, even though its identity may be unknown or unstated. The particle -нибудь, on the other hand, is more open-ended.

someone	кто́-то	кто́-нибудь	anyone
somewhere	где́-то	где́-нибудь	anywhere
(to) somewhere	куда́-то	куда́-нибудь	(to) somewhere
something	что́-то	что́-нибудь	anything
somehow	ка́к-то	ка́к-нибудь	anyhow
sometime	когда́-то	когда́-нибудь	ever
for some reason	почему́-то	почему́-нибудь	for any reason
some kind of	како́й-то	како́й-нибудь	any kind of
someone's	че́й-то	че́й-нибудь	anyone's

Я хочу́ полете́ть на неде́лю в како́е-нибудь краси́вое ме́сто.
I'd like to fly to someplace (lit., any kind of place) beautiful for a week.

Есть ли ещё что-нибудь? —Да, есть ещё что-то.
Is there anything else? —Yes, there is something else.

Ты говори́шь с кем-нибудь? —Нет, я ни с кем не говорю́.
Are you talking with anyone? —No, I'm not talking with anyone.

Ка́ждый год он е́здит куда́-то в го́ры.
Every year he goes somewhere in the mountains.

Notice that the question words continue to decline for case and gender, but -то and -нибудь themselves never change form. Also, note that forms with -то or -нибудь cannot be used to make negative statements.

5. THE FUTURE AND THE PAST WITH IMPERSONAL CONSTRUCTIONS

When using impersonal constructions in the past or future tense, the verb is neuter, just as it is in the present tense. Remember that the subject of expressions with **у меня́, у вас,** etc., is an understood, neuter subject, even though the sentence as a whole refers to a specific person or group.

Не волну́йся, всё бу́дет хорошо́.
Don't worry, everything will be fine.

Ему́ бы́ло всё равно́.
He didn't care. (lit., It was all the same to him.)

У вас не бу́дет доста́точно вре́мени.
You won't have enough time.

У нас никогда́ не́ было пробле́м с э́тим туристи́ческим аге́нством.
We've never had a problem with this travel agency.

Notice that negation with **не** is very common in past and future tense impersonal constructions, e.g. **Не́ было**… (There wasn't . . .), **Не бу́дет**… (There won't be . . .). The verb phrase **не́ было** is accented as one word, with the accent on **не**.

Не обяза́тельно бы́ло смотре́ть переда́чу.
It wasn't necessary to watch the program.

Тебе́ не бу́дет ску́чно про́сто лежа́ть на со́лнце?
You won't be bored (it won't be boring for you) simply lying in the sun?

6. CONJUGATION OF -ОВАТЬ/-ЕВАТЬ VERBS

Verbs ending in **-овать** or **-евать** in the infinitive are very common in Russian. Many of them are Russianized foreign words, and they are considered regular Conjugation I verbs. To conjugate most infinitives ending in **-овать/-евать**, simply replace the **-овать/-евать** ending with **-у** or **-ю** (according to the spelling rules) followed by the regular Conjugation I endings.

рекомендова́ть: to recommend

I recommend	я рекоменду́ю	мы рекоменду́ем	we recommend
you (fam.) recommend	ты рекоменду́ешь	вы рекоменду́ете	you (pl./pol.) recommend
he/she recommends	он/она́ рекоменду́ет	они́ рекоменду́ют	they recommend

stem = рекоменду́+
imperative: Рекоменду́й(те)!

Two common reflexive **-овать** verbs are **интересова́ться** (to be interested in) and **чу́вствовать себя́** (to feel). They are conjugated just like **рекомендо́вать**, but with **-ся or себя́** added back on. **Танцева́ть** (to dance), unlike some other **-евать** verbs which have the soft ending **-ю**, is conjugated just like an **-овать** verb.

Что вы рекоменду́ете? —Я рекоменду́ю Крым.
What do you recommend? —I recommend the Crimea.

Чем ты интересу́ешься?
What are you interested in?

Хорошо́, тогда́ мы всё организу́ем.
Fine, we'll arrange everything then.

Я сего́дня хорошо́ себя́ чу́вствую. —Тогда́ дава́й потанцу́ем!
I feel good today. —Then let's go dancing!

7. "DIFFERENT" VERSUS "ANOTHER"

There are three ways to express "another" or "different:" **ещё оди́н** (another, one more), **друго́й** (another, not this one, different), and **ра́зный** (different, various). Of the three, only **ра́зный** and **друго́й** can be used to express alternatives, but **друго́й** is the best word for this purpose. **Ещё оди́н** is only used when referring to more of the same. Like all modifiers, they agree in case, gender, and number with the nouns they modify.

Есть ли ещё горноль́жный куро́рт в э́том райо́не? —Да, есть ещё оди́н.
Is there another ski resort in that region? —Yes, there's another one.

Восемна́дцатый уро́к

Нет друго́го ви́да тра́нспорта, как наприме́р по́езд?

There's no other way to get there, like the train?

Там есть хоро́шие гости́ницы? —Да, есть неско́лько ра́зных гости́ниц.

Are there any good hotels there? —Yes, there are several different ones.

C. СЛОВАРЬ

аге́нт	agent
вид	means
Вот тепе́рь вы говори́те де́ло!	Now you're talking!
где́-то/где́-нибудь	somewhere/anywhere
гора́	mountain
горнолы́жный куро́рт	ski resort
доста́точно	enough
друго́й	another; not this one; different
е́сли	if; in case; in the event that
ещё оди́н/-на́/-но́/-ни́	another; one more
жильё	accomodation
загора́ть (загора́ю, загора́ешь, загора́ют)	to get a tan
заказа́ть	to order
замеча́тельный	wonderful
Интере́сно ...	I wonder . . .
купа́ться (купа́юсь, купа́ешься, купа́ются)	to swim
лежа́ть (лежу́, лежи́шь, лежа́т)	to lie, lay (II.)
лета́ть (лета́ю, лета́ешь, лета́ют)	to fly (round trip; verb of motion)
лете́ть (лечу́, лети́шь, летя́т)	to fly (in one direction; verb of motion)
ли	if; whether (particle)
мо́ре	sea
наприме́р	for example
организова́ть (организу́ю, организу́ешь, организу́ют)	to arrange, to organize
останови́ться	to stay
отсю́да	from here
пляж	beach
плани́рование	planning
по́сле обе́да	in the afternoon (lit., after lunch)
пого́да	weather
про́сто	simple(ly); just

ра́зный	different; various
рекомендова́ть (рекоменду́ю, рекоменду́ешь, рекоменду́ют)	to recommend
самолёт	airplane
снег	snow
со́лнечный	sunny
со́лнце	sun
тра́нспорт	transportation
тру́дно	difficult
тури́сти́ческое аге́нство	tourist office; travel agency

РУССКАЯ КУЛЬТУРА

Many Russians cannot afford the time or the money to travel during the year. They do, however, sometimes take short trips during the summer to their **да́ча** (summer house, often small and without amenities), or a day- or weekend-long hiking or skiing trip, or they go out to the country for a day **ходи́ть за гриба́ми** (gathering mushrooms), just to get out of the city. The month of August is when most Russians have their yearly vacation (**о́тпуск**), which they might spend at their **да́ча,** at a popular resort destination like **Со́чи** (Sochi) or **Ялта** (Yalta) on the **Чёрное мо́ре** (Black Sea), as well as abroad in Turkey, Greece, Tunisia, or Egypt. If a Russian family can't afford to go away together for vacation, then usually one parent will go with the children, or they will try to send the children to camp in a resort area for a month. Quite a few Russian couples also choose to vacation separately.

As a foreign tourist in Russia in the summer, you may prefer to visit the north where it is not too hot. During the St. Petersburg **Бе́лые но́чи** (White Nights) from June 21 to June 29, the sun never really sets and people are out strolling, singing, and playing guitar all night. In alternate years in Moscow, the International Film Festival takes place in July, with films from all over the world. The summer is also a good time to visit the Baltic states. In the winter, you can go skiing in the **Кавка́з** (the Caucasus), featuring some of the world's most stunning scenery, or visit the northern cities of Moscow and St. Petersburg to experience the beauty of a Russian winter. Keep in mind, though, that January and February are a little too cold for most visitors. Spring and fall are good times to visit Central Asia and the Caucasus, which can be too hot and dusty in the summer. Moscow and central Russia can also get quite hot in the summer. Siberia is best avoided in the depths of winter, but it gets quite warm in summer and has a beautiful, though very short, spring and fall.

УПРАЖНЕНИЯ

A. **Поста́вьте слова́ в ско́бках в предло́жный паде́ж и запо́лните про́пуски.** (Put the words in parentheses into the prepositional case, and fill in the blanks.)

1. Что ты ду́маешь о _____ в _____ ? (национа́льные блю́да, э́ти рестора́ны)
2. Пе́тя мне сказа́л о _____ ! (ва́ши хоро́шие но́вости)
3. Я говори́ла о _____ . (мои́ ру́сские друзья́)
4. Он купа́ется в мо́ре на _____ в Крыму́. (все пля́жи)
5. Я люблю́ ката́ться на _____ . (лы́жи)

B. **Запо́лните про́пуски слова́ми «ли» и́ли «е́сли».** (Fill in the blanks with ли or е́сли.)

1. Интере́сно, лу́чше _____ пое́хать на Кавка́з?
2. Я забы́л, сказа́л _____ мне он.
3. Я не зна́ю, здесь _____ на́ши места́ и́ли там.
4. Скажи́ мне, _____ ты зна́ешь!
5. Ей всё равно́, рабо́таем _____ мы и́ли отдыха́ем.

C. **Переведи́те на англи́йский.** (Translate into English.)

1. Мо́жно туда́ е́хать на метро́?
2. Мо́жно писа́ть ру́чкой?
3. Я не хочу́ туда́ е́хать по́ездом. Я хочу́ туда́ лете́ть самолётом.
4. Мне не нра́вится писа́ть карандашо́м.
5. Она́ увлека́ется те́ннисом.
6. Вы е́здили куда́-нибу́дь ле́том?
7. Ты здесь кого́-нибу́дь зна́ешь?
8. Кни́ги где-то здесь. Я про́сто не зна́ю, где то́чно.
9. Ты когда́-нибу́дь была́ в э́том теа́тре?—Нет, никогда́.
10. Кто-то мне сказа́л, что на Кавка́зе хорошо́ ката́ться на лы́жах.

D. 1. **Поста́вьте предложе́ния в проше́дшее вре́мя.** (Put the sentences into the past tense.)

2. **Поста́вьте предложе́ния в бу́дущее вре́мя. Доба́вьте «ско́ро».** (Put the sentences into the future tense. Add ско́ро.)

1. Ему́ не на́до занима́ться.
2. Ему́ не тру́дно.
3. Де́душке всё равно́.
4. Им ну́жно де́лать переса́дку.
5. Всё поня́тно.

E. **Запо́лните про́пуски пра́вильными оконча́ниями глаго́лов.** (Fill in the blanks with the correct endings of the verbs.)

1. Чем они́ тепе́рь интерес_____ ?
2. Что рекоменд_____ фармаце́вт?
3. Она́ о́чень хорошо́ танц_____ .
4. Как ты сего́дня себя́ чу́вств_____ ?
5. Я чу́вств_____, что ему́ ну́жно отдохну́ть.

F. **Запо́лните про́пуски пра́вильными фо́рмами прилага́тельных «ещё оди́н,» «друго́й» и́ли «ра́зный.»** (Fill in the blanks with the correct forms of the adjectives ещё оди́н, друго́й, or ра́зный.)

1. Есть _____ маршру́т в Ки́ев?
2. Там _____ хоро́шие рестора́ны. Не беспоко́йся!
3. Да́йте, пожа́луйста, _____ ча́шку ко́фе.
4. У вас есть _____ ко́мната?
5. В Москве́ есть _____ ви́ды тра́нспорта.

УРОК 19

БЫТОВЫЕ УСЛУГИ. Domestic services.

А. ДИАЛОГ

В химчи́стке.

ТАММИ: До́брый день. Мне ну́жно почи́стить пла́тье. Кто-то на него́ проли́л вино́, когда́ мы вчера́ у́жинали. Вы не мо́жете вы́вести э́то пятно́?

СЛУЖИТЕЛЬ: Могу́. Что-нибу́дь ещё?

ТАММИ: Да, у меня́ шесть веще́й.

СЛУЖИТЕЛЬ: Так... две блу́зки, па́ра брюк, руба́шка и пла́тье. Но э́то то́лько пять веще́й.

ТАММИ: О, и га́лстук му́жа. А когда́ они́ бу́дут гото́вы?

СЛУЖИТЕЛЬ: Когда́ вам ну́жно?

ТАММИ: В сре́ду, е́сли возмо́жно.

СЛУЖИТЕЛЬ: Хорошо́.

ТАММИ: Спаси́бо большо́е!

СЛУЖИТЕЛЬ: Вот ва́ша квита́нция.

Че́рез четы́ре дня.

ТАММИ: Здра́вствуйте! Муж вчера́ заходи́л за оде́ждой. Он не заме́тил, что э́то не мои́ брю́ки и что не хвата́ет блу́зки с карма́нами.

СЛУЖИТЕЛЬ: Я непра́вильно прочита́л квита́нцию, и отдал блу́зку кому́-то друго́му по оши́бке. Но э́та клие́нтка мне уже́ её принесла́.

ТАММИ: Ох, я ра́да, что она́ у вас есть!

СЛУЖИТЕЛЬ: Да, прошу́ проще́ния за пу́таницу ... Вот она́!

At the dry cleaner's.

TAMMY: Good afternoon. I need this dress cleaned. Someone spilled some wine on it yesterday while we were eating dinner. Can you get this stain out?

CLEANER: I think so. Anything else?

TAMMY: Yes, I have six things.

CLEANER: Let's see . . . two blouses, a pair of pants, a shirt, and a dress. But that's only five pieces.

TAMMY: Oh, and a tie of my husband's. And when will they be ready?

CLEANER: When do you need them?

TAMMY: On Wednesday, if possible.

CLEANER: Fine.

TAMMY: Thanks a lot!

CLEANER: Here's your ticket.

Four days later.

TAMMY: Hello. My husband picked up these clothes yesterday. He didn't notice that these pants weren't mine, and the blouse with the pockets is missing.

CLEANER: I read the ticket wrong and gave it to someone else by mistake. But she already brought it back in.

TAMMY: Oh, I'm glad you have it!

CLEANER: Yes, I'm very sorry for the mix-up . . . Here it is!

B. ГРАММАТИКА И СЛОВОУПОТРЕБЛЕНИЕ

1. THE INSTRUMENTAL PLURAL OF NOUNS

The instrumental plural of nouns is formed by simply replacing the nominative plural ending with the appropriate instrumental plural ending: **-ями** if the nominative ends in **-и** or **-я**, and **-ами** otherwise. Notice that the instrumental plural noun endings are very similar to the dative plural noun endings (**-ам/-ям**).

NOMINATIVE ENDS IN:	INSTRUMENTAL ENDS IN:	EXAMPLE
-ы	-ами	карма́ны » карма́нами
-а	-ами	пи́сьма » пи́сьмами
(г/к/ж/х/ч/ш/щ +) -и	-ами	ю́бки » ю́бками
-и	-ями	неде́ли » неде́лями
-я	-ями	пла́тья » пла́тьями

Не хвата́ет блу́зки с карма́нами.

The blouse with pockets is missing.

Та́мми здесь живёт с друзья́ми.

Tammy's staying here with friends.

Я зайду́ за¹ брю́ками по́сле обе́да.

I'll stop by for the pants in the afternoon.

Some common nouns have the irregular instrumental plural ending **-ьми́**. For example, **лю́ди » людьми́, де́ти » детьми́, до́чери » дочерьми́**. Note that **ма́тери**, unlike **до́чери**, is regular: **матеря́ми**.

Я рабо́таю с дочерьми́? —Нет, я рабо́таю с детьми́!

I'm working with the daughters? —No, I'm working with the children!

2. INTRODUCTION TO VERB ASPECT

You've already learned how to express when an action takes place by using the past, present, and future tenses. In Russian, you can also specify the nature of an action by using aspect. All Russian verbs are either imperfective or perfective, and most have both imperfective and perfective forms. In general, imperfective verbs focus on process, while perfective verbs focus on the end result. If aspect were represented graphically, imperfective aspect would look like this: —————— , and perfective aspect would look like this: •. In other words, imperfective verbs are used to describe habitual or continuous actions, while perfective verbs describe a single, complete action, or a series of such actions. Most

---

1. Notice that the instrumental follows the preposition **за** in this expression.

of the verbs you have learned so far have been imperfective. The perfective form usually consists of the imperfective plus a prefix or minus a suffix.

Я непра́вильно <u>прочита́л</u> квита́нцию. Но обы́чно я их внима́тельно <u>чита́ю</u>.
I didn't read the ticket right. But usually I read them carefully.

Он не <u>заме́тил</u>, что э́то не мои́ брю́ки. —Неуже́ли? Ра́ньше он всё <u>замеча́л</u>!
He didn't notice that these pants aren't mine. —Really? He used to notice everything!

Мне ну́жно <u>почи́стить</u> пла́тье. —О, но здесь не <u>чи́стят</u> пла́тья!
I need this dress cleaned. —Oh, but they don't clean dresses here!

Когда́ мы <u>у́жинали</u>, кто-то проли́л вино́.
While we were eating dinner, someone spilled some wine.

It is important not to think of perfectives and imperfectives as opposites, but merely as a different ways of looking at an activity. As you continue to learn about Russian verb aspect, remember that just as verbs are listed in glossaries by their infinitives, verb aspect pairs are generally listed with the imperfective verb first followed by the perfective verb. From now on, verbs will be listed in such pairs in this manual. If only one verb is given, its aspect will be stated.

3. VERBAL ASPECT IN THE PAST TENSE

In the past tense, the imperfective describes continuous actions, and the perfective describes completed actions. The past tense of perfective verbs is formed the same way as that of imperfective verbs: remove the infinitive ending, and add -л/-ла/-ло/-ли according to the gender and number of the subject. Following are the past imperfective and perfective forms of **чита́ть** (to read).

	IMPERFECTIVE	PERFECTIVE
MASCULINE	чита́л	прочита́л
FEMININE	чита́ла	прочита́ла
NEUTER	чита́ло	прочита́ло
PLURAL	чита́ли	прочита́ли

Я непра́вильно <u>прочита́л</u> квита́нцию, а обы́чно я их внима́тельно <u>чита́ю</u>.

I didn't read (perfective) the ticket right, but I usually read (imperfective) them carefully.

Я <u>пришла́</u> за оде́ждой, кото́рую я вам <u>принесла́</u> позавчера́.

I've come (perfective) for the clothes that I brought (perfective) you the day before yesterday.

Вы <u>сказа́ли</u>, что она́ бу́дет гото́ва сего́дня.

You said (perfective) they'd be ready today.

Aspect can also be used to indicate intentions or point of view. If the speaker believes that an action is likely to be completed or intends to complete it, the perfective is used. If, on the other hand, the speaker is simply indicating that an action is, was, or will be performed, without any reference to its completion, the imperfective is used. Compare:

Я хочу́ стира́ть бельё.

I want to do the laundry. (The speaker is not sure that the action will be completed.)

Я хочу́ выстира́ть бельё.

I want to do the laundry. (The speaker intends to finish the job.)

When describing two actions in the past, the imperfective is used for the background action.

Кто-то <u>проли́л</u> вино́ на него́, когда́ мы <u>у́жинали</u>.

Someone spilled (perf.) some wine on it while we were eating dinner (imp.).

Мы <u>смотре́ли</u> телеви́зор, когда́ она́ <u>позвони́ла</u>.

We were watching (imp.) television when she called (perf.).

Verbs denoting a state of being or an action that cannot have results, e.g. **быть** (to be), **жить** (to live), **знать** (to know), **рабо́тать** (to work), **гуля́ть** (to go for a walk, to stroll), are inherently imperfective by virtue of their meaning. They have no perfective form. The following sentence contrasts imperfective and perfective verbs.

Они́ там жи́ли, когда́ ты роди́лся.

They were living (imp.) there when you were born (perf.).

Мы не́ бы́ли до́ма, когда́ ты позвони́л.

We weren't (imp.) home when you called (perf.).

4. ПО- AS A PERFECTIVE PREFIX

Many perfective infinitives are formed by adding a prefix to an imperfective verb: **чита́ть/прочита́ть** (to read), **писа́ть/написа́ть** (to write), **де́лать/сде́лать** (to do, to make), **смотре́ть/посмотре́ть** (to watch, to look at).

Тсcc! Я не хочу́ сде́лать оши́бку. —Но ты всегда́ де́лаешь оши́бки!

Shhh! I don't want to make a mistake. —But you're always making mistakes!

Он написа́л мне письмо́. —Но он никогда́ не пи́шет пи́сьма!

He wrote me a letter. —But he never writes letters!

Вчера́ ве́чером мы посмотре́ли о́чень хоро́ший фильм.

Last night we saw a really good movie.

One of the most common perfective prefixes is **-по**. It implies the completion of the action. Following are some common perfectives formed with **по-**.

IMPERFECTIVE PERFECTIVE

	IMPERFECTIVE	PERFECTIVE	
to clean	чи́стить	почи́стить	to clean completely
to like	нра́виться	понра́виться	to like
to watch	смотре́ть	посмотре́ть	to watch all of something
to eat breakfast	за́втракать	поза́втракать	to finish eating breakfast
to eat lunch	обе́дать	пообе́дать	to finish eating lunch
to eat supper	у́жинать	поу́жинать	to finish eating supper
to listen	слу́шать	послу́шать	to finish listening
to study	занима́ться	позанима́ться	to finish studying
to call	звони́ть	позвони́ть	to make a call
to try	про́бовать	попро́бовать	to try, to take a taste of

Мне ну́жно почи́стить пла́тье.

I need this dress cleaned.

Мы за́втра бу́дем до́ма. Позвони́!

We'll be home tomorrow. Give us a call!

Хо́чешь попро́бовать мой суп?

Do you want to try my soup?

Verbs that form perfectives by adding a prefix to the imperfective are listed in a special way in the glossary: the imperfective is listed first, then the prefix alone, e.g. **писа́ть/на-**. This indicates that the perfective is conjugated exactly like the imperfective.

5. MORE ON SHORT-FORM ADJECTIVES

Long-form adjectives generally precede the noun. However, they can be used following a noun and a state of being verb to denote an inherent quality of the noun. Short-form adjectives following a state of being verb denote a temporary condition. Compare:

Ой, я сего́дня рассе́яна!

Oh, I'm absentminded today!

Она́ о́чень рассе́янная. Она́ всё забыва́ет.

She's very absentminded (a very absentminded person). She forgets everything.

Он дово́лен отве́том.

He's satisfied with the answer.

Он дово́льный челове́к.

He's a satisfied man.

Many short-form adjectives come in pairs of opposites that are easy to remember.

го́лоден/сыт	hungry/full
здоро́в/бо́лен	healthy/sick
сча́стлив/несча́стен	happy/unhappy
жив/мёртв	alive/dead
прав/непра́в	right/wrong

Та́мми сча́стлива, что химчи́стка не потеря́ла блу́зку.

Tammy's happy that the dry cleaner didn't lose the blouse.

Ра́ньше я была́ так голодна́, а тепе́рь я сли́шком сыта́!
I was so hungry before, and now I'm too full!

C. СЛОВА́РЬ

блу́зка	blouse
бытовы́е услу́ги	domestic services
возмо́жно	possible
вы́вести	to take out, to remove (perf.)
га́лстук	tie
должно́ быть	must (be), undoubtedly
жив/-а́/-о/-ы	alive
зайти́ (зайду́, зайдёшь, зайду́т) (за чем)	to drop by, to pick up (something) (perf.)
замеча́ть (замеча́ю, замеча́ешь, замеча́ют)/ *заме́тить* (заме́чу, заме́тишь, заме́тят)	to notice
здоро́в/-а/-о/-ы	healthy
карма́н	pocket
квита́нция	claim check
костю́м	suit
пролива́ть (пролива́ю, пролива́ешь, пролива́ют)/ *проли́ть* (пролью́, прольёшь, пролью́т)	to spill
мёртв/-а́/-о́/-ы	dead
не хвата́ет (чего́)	(something) is missing
непра́в/-а́/-о/-ы	wrong
несча́стен/-на/-но/-ны	unhappy
обслу́живание	service; tip
оде́жда	clothing
оши́бка	mistake
па́ра брюк	pair of pants
пла́тье	dress
позавчера́	day before yesterday
послеза́втра	day after tomorrow
прийти́	to come (perf.)
принести́	to bring (perf.)
Прошу́ проще́ния!	Forgive me! (lit. I beg forgiveness!)
пу́таница	mix-up, muddle
пятно́	stain

рассе́ян/-а/-о/-ы	absentminded
руба́шка	shirt
сле́дующий	next
сча́стлив/-а/-о/-ы	happy
сыт/-а́/-о/-ы	full (opp. of hungry)
химчи́стка	dry cleaning; dry cleaner's
хоте́ть сказа́ть	to mean, to want to say
чи́стить (чи́щу, чи́стишь, чи́стят)/по-	to clean

РУССКАЯ КУЛЬТУРА

Dry cleaning services in Russia are often too time-consuming for travelers, and they can be rough on clothes. If you are not in a hurry, get a recommendation for a good dry cleaner from a Russian friend. Some dry cleaners are also a **пра́чечная** (laundry) and will on occasion even do mending for you. If you are staying in a hotel, speak to your chambermaid about laundry service and to the porter about dry cleaning. Be sure to tip anyone involved well, possibly in advance, especially if you plan to use the service again. Hotel dry cleaning and laundry can be slow, not always punctual, and hard on your clothes. Therefore, you may choose to do it yourself, or go to an **Америка́нская пра́чечная** (American laundry), which is similar to our laundromats. Most hotels also have a self-service ironing room.

If you are renting an apartment and need any domestic services, such as repairs or cleaning, ask a Russian friend for advice. There are official services to do such things, but you would do better to ask a Russian's help. If you have no one to ask for suggestions, look in a phone book under the item in question first, and then look for the service you need: repair (**ремо́нт**), mending (**поши́в**), or rental (**прока́т**). For instance, if your boots or shoes (**о́бувь**) need repair, look under **Обуви, ремо́нт,** or look for shops that say «**Ремо́нт** (of the item)».

In dealing with anyone who provides services in Russia, it is helpful to remember that the service economy is fairly new. If your request or question is met with a surly or unsmiling face, try to remember that Russians do not smile as a matter of course in public. They tend to have two very different faces: an unsmiling, set face in public, and a warm, expressive one in private, with family and friends.

УПРАЖНЕНИЯ

A. Поста́вьте сушестви́тельные из ско́бок в твори́тельный паде́жи заполните про́пуски.

(Put the nouns in parentheses into the instrumental case, and fill in the blanks.)

1. Я за́втра зайду́ за _____ . (руба́шки)
2. Она́ занима́ется _____ . Она́ меха́ник. (маши́ны)
3. До́чери не должны́ жить с _____ . (ма́тери)
4. Е́сли вы рабо́таете с _____ , вы не должны́ кури́ть. (де́ти)
5. Я познако́милась с _____ из Росси́и. (лю́ди)

B. Како́го ви́да подчёркнутые глаго́лы—соверше́нного и́ли несоверше́нного? (Identify the aspect of the the underlined verbs—perfective or imperfective?)

1. Я весь день <u>смотре́ла</u> телеви́зор.
2. Вчера́ ве́чером я <u>посмотре́ла</u> интере́сную переда́чу по телеви́зору.
3. Она́ обы́чно <u>де́лает</u> уро́ки ве́чером, а сего́дня она́ их <u>сде́лала</u> у́тром.
4. Ты уже́ <u>прочита́л</u> э́тот журна́л? —Нет, я его́ ещё <u>чита́ю</u>.
5. В воскресе́нье я <u>поза́втракала</u> в 11 часо́в и пото́м <u>позвони́ла</u> подру́жке.
6. Он <u>бу́дет писа́ть</u> пи́сьма сего́дня ве́чером.
7. Он <u>написа́л</u> им письмо́ сего́дня ве́чером.
8. Мы здесь <u>живём</u> уже́ де́сять лет.
9. Ле́том мы <u>отдыха́ем</u> на ю́ге.
10. Они́ наве́рно <u>позвони́ли</u>, когда́ мы <u>гуля́ли</u> в па́рке.

C. Образу́йте предложе́ния, испо́льзуя глаго́лы ну́жного ви́да и вре́мени по образцу́. (Form sentences according to the example, using verbs in the appropriate tense and aspect.)

ОБРАЗЕ́Ц: Мы ча́сто про́бовали но́вые блю́да. (сего́дня на обе́д) »
          Сего́дня на обе́д мы попро́бовали но́вое блю́до.

1. Он ча́сто пролива́ет вино́ на меня́. (вчера́)
2. Где вы у́жинали? (вчера́ ве́чером)
3. Они́ ре́дко де́лали оши́бки в химчи́стке. (сего́дня)
4. Она́ хорошо́ почи́стила оде́жду. (всегда́)

5. Она́ обы́чно замеча́ет, кто там сиди́т. (вчера́)
6. Кто живёт в э́том зда́нии? (ра́ньше)
7. Мы слу́шали но́вости по ра́дио. (сего́дня)
8. Я пообе́дал в два часа́. (ка́ждый день)
9. Он всю неде́лю чита́л э́ту кни́гу. (вчера́ наконе́ц)
10. Ему́ о́чень понра́вился э́тот фильм. (ра́ньше)

D. Поста́вьте глаго́лы в ну́жное вре́мя по образцу́ и переведи́те предложе́ния. (Put the verbs into the necessary tense according to the example, and translate the sentences.)

ОБРАЗЕЦ: Вам э́то удо́бно? (послеза́втра) »
Послеза́втра вам бу́дет удо́бно?

1. Оде́жда гото́ва. (за́втра)
2. Они́ о́чень го́лодны. (вчера́)
3. Я больна́. (сего́дня)
4. Химчи́стка закры́та. (за́втра)
5. Он рассе́ян. (позавчера́)

УРОК 20

ОБЩЕСТВЕННЫЙ ТРАНСПОРТ. Public transportation.

А. ДИАЛОГ

В Санкт-Петербу́рге на остано́вке авто́буса.

ДАВИД: *Извини́те, вы не зна́ете, как дое́хать до у́лицы Дзержи́нского?*

БАБУШКА: *Вам ну́жен седьмо́й авто́бус.*

ДАВИД: *Спаси́бо.*

МУЖЧИНА: *Нет-нет, что вы! Это совсе́м непра́вильно! Улица тепе́рь называ́ется Горо́ховая и вам ну́жен пя́тый трамва́й. Вы́йдите на остано́вке «Сенна́я пло́щадь».*

БАБУШКА: *О чём вы говори́те! Я живу́ здесь уже́ шестьдеся́т лет, и коне́чно я лу́чше зна́ю! А заче́м вам нужна́ Горо́ховая? Что там интере́сного? Лу́чше пойди́те в Эрмита́ж.*

ДАВИД: *Мо́жет быть, но на Горо́ховой меня́ ждут мой друзья́.*

БАБУШКА: *Ой, как хорошо́ он говори́т по-ру́сски! А где вы учи́ли ру́сский язы́к?*

ДАВИД: *Спаси́бо. Я учи́л ру́сский в университе́те.* (ти́хо, мужчи́не) *Я прошу́ вас, скажи́те мне, как пройти́ от Сенно́й до Горо́ховой.*

МУЖЧИНА: *Ну, хорошо́. Ся́дьте на пя́тый трамва́й и вы́йдите на Горо́ховой у́лице. А вы зна́ете, как купи́ть биле́т в трамва́е?*

ДАВИД: *Да, я зна́ю. Спаси́бо и до свида́ния!*

МУЖЧИНА: *Пожа́луйста.*

БАБУШКА: *Не забу́дьте об Эрмита́же!*

ДАВИД: *Обяза́тельно! Спаси́бо!*

БАБУШКА: *Ой, како́й ве́жливый молодо́й челове́к!*

In St. Petersburg, at a bus stop.

DAVID: Excuse me, could you tell me how to get to Dzerzhinsky Street?

OLD WOMAN: You need Bus No. 7.

DAVID: Thank you.

MAN: No! No! That's completely wrong! The street is named Gorokhov now, and you need Tram No. 5. Get off at the Sennaya Square station.

OLD WOMAN: What are you talking about?! I've lived here for sixty years, so of course I know better! And what do you want Gorokhov Street for? What's of interest there? You'd be better off going to the Hermitage.

DAVID: Maybe, but my friends are waiting for me on Gorokhov Street.

OLD WOMAN: Oh, how well he speaks Russian! And where did you learn Russian?

DAVID: Thank you. I learned it in college. *(quietly, to the man)* I beg you, tell me how to get from Sennaya to Gorokhov Street.

MAN: Well, okay. Get on Tram No. 5, and get off at Gorokhov Street. Do you know how to buy a ticket on the tram?

DAVID: Yes, I do. Thank you, and goodbye!

MAN: You're welcome.

OLD WOMAN: Don't forget about the Hermitage!

DAVID: Of course! Thank you.

OLD WOMAN: What a polite young man!

B. ГРАММАТИКА И СЛОВОУПОТРЕБЛЕНИЕ

1. EXPRESSING NEED WITH НУЖЕН AND НУЖНО/НАДО

In Russian, there is no verb that directly corresponds to the English verb "to need." Instead, an impersonal construction with **нýжен** or **нáдо/нýжно** is used. It translates literally as "(to someone) something is necessary." The English subject thus becomes an indirect object in Russian and takes the dative case, while the English object functions as the subject in Russian and takes the nominative case. When referring to a need expressed by a noun, ну́жен/нужна́/нужны́/ну́жно is used, and it agrees with the subject (that which is needed) in gender and number.

Вам ну́жен седьмо́й авто́бус.
You need Bus No. 7.

Её джи́нсы о́чень ста́рые. Ей нужны́ но́вые джи́нсы.
Her jeans are very old. She needs new jeans.

Кака́я маши́на вам нужна́?
What kind of car do you need?

Им ну́жно такси́.
They need a taxi.

When the need is represented by a verb, the unchanging forms ну́жно or на́до are used. Note that на́до is somewhat more emphatic.

Ско́лько ну́жно (на́до) плати́ть за кни́жечку биле́тов?
How much do you have to pay for the booklet of tickets?

Уже́ 11 часо́в! Мне на́до (ну́жно) идти́ домо́й.
It's already 11 o'clock! I have to go home.

2. PREFIXES AND VERBS OF MOTION

Following are some of the prefixes[1] which, when added to the verbs of motion идти́ (to go on foot) and е́хать (to go by vehicle), make them perfective.

до-*	as far as, up to, until
про-	through, past
по-*	for a while, a bit, or to start doing something
вы́-	out/out of, off/off of (transportation) (opposite of в(о)-)
в(о)-*	in/into, on/onto (transportation) (opposite of вы́-)
у-*	away (from), departure (opposite of при-)
при-*	towards, arrival (opposite of у-)

1. All of the starred prefixes can also be used as prepositions, but their meaning may then change. For more on prepositions, please refer to the Appendix.

пере-	across, over
за-*	to drop by, pick up (something, someone)
под-*	approaching, right up to
от-*	(away) from a given point

дойти́/дое́хать
    to reach, to get to

пройти́/прое́хать
    to go through, past

пойти́/пое́хать
    to start out (for)

вы́йти/вы́ехать
    to go out of, get off of
    (transportation)

Вы́йдите на остано́вке «Сенна́я пло́щадь».
Get off at the Sennaya Square metro station.

Лу́чше пойди́те в Эрмита́ж.
You'd be better off going to the Hermitage.

Мину́точку! Я сейча́с приду́!
Just a minute! I'm coming!

Note that **идти́** changes to **-йти** when used with a prefix, in order to facilitate pronunciation. Prefixed verbs of motion are often used in conjunction with prepositions. The prepositions determine the case of the following noun.

дое́хать до + чего́ (genitive)
to reach, to get somewhere

пое́хать в/на + что (accusative)
to start out by vehicle for somewhere

вы́йти на + чём (prepositional)
to get off at a station

вы́йти из + чего́ (genitive)
to go out of, get off of (transportation)

пройти́ от + чего́ (genitive) **до + чего́** (genitive)
to go from one place to another

Как дое́хать до Кра́сной пло́щади?
How do I get to Red Square?

Когда́ нам на́до пойти́ в шко́лу?
When do we need to leave for school?

Как мо́жно пройти́ от Кра́сной пло́щади до Большо́го теа́тра?
How can one get from Red Square to the Bolshoi Theater?

Вам ну́жно вы́йти на остано́вке «Большо́й теа́тр».
You need to get out at the Bolshoi Theater.

Я зайду́ за ни́ми по́сле обе́да.
I'll stop by for them in the afternoon.

Since Russian consistently makes a distinction between location and direction, these common prefixes are used to specify the type and direction of the motion.

3. ADJECTIVES USED AS NOUNS

In Russian certain adjectives may be used without the nouns they describe, but they nevertheless retain the gender and number of the omitted noun. These adjectives essentially function as nouns, but they retain adjectival case endings. For example, **столо́вая ко́мната** (dining room) becomes simply **столо́вая** and means "cafeteria." This usage is also very common with the names of places. For example:

Сенна́я пло́щадь (square) = **Сенна́я**

Не́вский проспе́кт (prospect) = **Не́вский**

ста́нция (station) **«Академи́ческая»** = **«Академи́ческая»**

Горо́ховая у́лица (street) = **Горо́ховая**

Как пройти́ от Сенно́й до Горо́ховой?
How do you get from Sennaya (Square) to Gorokhov (Street)?

Я иду́ в столо́вую. (feminine accusative adjective)
I'm going to the cafeteria.

Лю́ся рабо́тает на Не́вском?
Lyusya works on Nevsky (Prospect)?

4. ORDINAL NUMBERS

Ordinal numbers (e.g. first, second) are declined as regular adjectives. These numbers are important because they are used to identify buses, trams, and trolleys, as well as dates. Where English speakers would say "Bus 56," Russians say "the fifty-sixth bus." Following is the nominative case of ordinal numbers 1–20, which should be familiar to you from the chapter numbers at the bottom of each even-numbered page in this text.

1st	пе́рвый	оди́ннадцатый	11th
2nd	второ́й	двена́дцатый	12th
3rd	тре́тий (fem.: тре́тья, neuter: тре́тье)[2]	трина́дцатый	13th
4th	четвёртый	четы́рнадцатый	14th
5th	пя́тый	пятна́дцатый	15th
6th	шесто́й	шестна́дцатый	16th
7th	седьмо́й	семна́дцатый	17th
8th	восьмо́й	восемна́дцатый	18th
9th	девя́тый	девятна́дцатый	19th
10th	деся́тый	двадца́тый	20th

остано́вка двена́дцатого авто́буса
the stop for Bus No. 12

второ́е такси́
the second taxi

пе́рвые дни
(the) first days

Вам ну́жен шестна́дцатый тролле́йбус.
You need Trolley No. 16.

Вы́йдите на четвёртой остано́вке.
Get off at the fourth stop.

2. **Тре́тий** is irregular in all the other cases as well. (In genitive, for example, it's **тре́тьего, тре́тьей.**)

C. СЛОВАРЬ

ве́жливый	polite
вход	entrance
вы́йти	to go out of, get off of (transportation) (perf.)
вы́ход	exit
де́лать переса́дку/пересе́сть	to transfer
забы́ть	to forget (perf.)
заче́м	for what purpose
Как дое́хать до ... ?	How do I get to . . . ?
контролёр	ticket inspector
молодо́й челове́к	young man
ну́жен/*нужна́*/*ну́жно*/*нужны́* (кому́)	needed; is necessary (to someone)
остано́вка	stop (tram, trolley, bus)
переда́ть	to pass (on, down), convey (perf.)
пойти́	to go (on foot) (perf.)
проездно́й	monthly pass
пройти́	to go through, to go past (perf.)
проси́ть (прошу́, про́сишь, про́сят)/по- (кого́)	to request, to beg (of someone)
рассказа́ть (что-кому́)	to tell about (something, to someone)
совсе́м	completely
ста́нция	station (metro, train)
стоя́нка	taxi-stand
Ся́дьте на ... (что)	Sit/Get on . . . (something) (transportation)
тало́н	token; single ride pass
трамва́й	tram
троллейбус	trolley
штраф	fine (noun)

РУССКАЯ КУЛЬТУРА

As many Russians do not own cars, they depend heavily on public transportation: buses, trams, trolleys, and the subway are all still very cheap and a good way to get around. When public transportation stops running for the night, however, there is no alternative other than a taxi (often a private car serving as a taxi).

The public transportation system in most Russian cities is generally easy to use, quite extensive, and the vehicles run fairly often. The only drawback is that all forms of transportation tend to be extremely crowded, especially at peak hours. Cities are served by trolleys, trams, buses, and in some cases, subways. The subways in St. Petersburg and Moscow are still very cheap and efficient, and they have quite comprehensible maps, but they are no longer as immaculate and safe as they once were. To use the subway you must get a token or a pass from a booth where you can pay with rubles. Because buses, trams, and trolleys are frequently very crowded, it is customary, upon entering, to pass down money for a ticket to the little ticket booth inside the vehicle. Though it can seem like too much trouble, it is worthwhile to avoid possible embarrassment by the ticket inspectors!

УПРАЖНЕНИЯ

A. **Заполните пропуски, используя нужен/нужна/нужно/нужны или нужно/надо.** (Fill in the blanks using нужен/нужна/нужно/нужны or нужно/надо.)

1. Зачем им _____ Гороховая?
2. Нам _____ купить молоко.
3. Ей _____ новые джинсы.
4. Сколько тебе _____ платить?
5. Мне _____ шестой трамвай.
6. Ему _____ новое радио.

B. **Составьте предложения по образцу. Добавьте приставки и предлоги, если нужно.** (Form complete sentences according to the example. Add prefixes and prepositions if necessary.)

ОБРАЗЕЦ: мне надо + ехать + работа в девять часов =
Мне надо поехать на работу в девять часов.

1. идти (command form) + Эрмитаж =
2. как + ехать + Невский проспект =
3. идти (command form) + станции «Чёрная речка» =
4. я не знаю как + идти + Невский + Академическая =
5. идти (command form) + станция «Невский проспект» =

C. **Заполните про́пуски по образцу́.** (Fill in the blanks according to the example.)

ОБРАЗЕЦ: Они́ меня́ ждут на <u>Горо́ховой</u>. (Горо́ховая у́лица)

1. Пе́тя живёт на _____ . (Пионе́рская пло́щадь)
2. Ма́ма рабо́тает на _____ . (Не́вский проспе́кт)
3. Они́ иду́т на _____ . (ста́нция «Академи́ческая»)
4. Я не зна́ю как пройти́ от _____ до _____ ?
   (ста́нция «Академи́ческая»/Сенна́я пло́щадь)
5. Как дое́хать до _____ ? (Не́вский проспе́кт)

D. **Замени́те коли́чественные числи́тельные поря́дковыми числи́тельными. По́мните о ро́де, числе́ и падеже́.** (Provide the indicated ordinal number. Remember gender, number, and case.)

1. (7) тролле́йбус идёт в центр?
2. Ся́дьте на (11) трамва́й у па́рка.
3. Вы́йдите на (3) остано́вке.
4. Вы не зна́ете, где остано́вка (10) тролле́йбуса?
5. Сего́дня она́ е́дет в шко́лу на (18) авто́бусе.

A. Восстанови́те диало́г в логи́ческий поря́док. (Put the lines of the dialogue into a logical order.)

HINT: 3. k. (**Да.** is the third line of the dialogue.)

1. Лю́ся:	a. А что вы бу́дете пить?
2. Официа́нтка:	b. А сла́дкое?
3. Лю́ся: k. (Да.)	c. Да, я возьму́ харчо́ и пото́м шашлы́к.
4. Официа́нтка:	d. Спаси́бо, нет. То́лько счёт. Всё бы́ло о́чень
5. Лю́ся:	вку́сно!
6. Ли́нда:	e. Отли́чно, вот свобо́дный стол. Я так хочу́ есть!
7. Официа́нтка:	f. Де́вушка! Принеси́те, пожа́луйста, ча́ю и
8. Лю́ся:	ча́шку ко́фе.
По́сле еды́	g. Я возьму́ ры́бу и на заку́ску чебуре́ки. Ты
9. Лю́ся:	вы́брала, Ли́нда?
10. Официа́нтка:	h. Минера́льную во́ду и одну́ буты́лочку сухо́го
11. Лю́ся:	бе́лого вина́.
	i. Сто́лик на двои́х?
	j. Сади́тесь сюда́, пожа́луйста. Вот меню́... Что
	вы зака́жете?
	k. Да.

B. Подбери́те соотве́тствующие оборо́ты в коло́нке А к коло́нке Б. (Match the phrases in column A to those in column B.)

A	B
1. не́сколько челове́к	a. Bus No. 15
2. чуть-чу́ть ры́бы	b. a lot of people
3. ча́ю и молока́	c. all the bottles
4. все зна́ют	d. a few bottles
5. пятна́дцатый авто́бус	e. one bottle
6. немно́го де́нег	f. a few people
7. мно́го наро́да	g. fifteen buses
8. не́сколько буты́лок	h. few seats
9. пе́рвый год	i. too much money
10. одна́ буты́лка	j. everyone knows
11. се́мьдесять лет	k. everything's OK
12. пятна́дцать авто́бусов	l. some tea and some milk

13. все буты́лки   m. the first year
14. ма́ло мест   n. a little money
15. всё в поря́дке   o. seventy years
                                      p. a little bit of fish

C. **Переведи́те на англи́йский.** (Translate into English.)

   1. Мне бы́ло пло́хо.
   2. Как дела́? —Непло́хо.
   3. Всё бы́ло поня́тно.
   4. Здесь прия́тно.
   5. Не хоти́те ли туда́ пое́хать по́ездом?
   6. Он почему́-то ничего́ не сказа́л.
   7. Ему́ о́чень понра́вилась э́та переда́ча.
   8. Они́ позвони́ли, когда́ мы гуля́ли в па́рке.
   9. Вам ну́жно вы́йти на «Академи́ческой».
  10. Когда́ он уе́хал на Кавка́з?

D. **Переведи́те на ру́сский.** (Translate into Russian.)

   1. Which dish (**блю́до**) do you recommend?
   2. There's no other vegetarian (**вегетариа́нский**) restaurant?
   3. If you work with children, you shouldn't smoke (**кури́ть**).
   4. The government doesn't care.
   5. I wonder whether I should write with a pen (**ру́чка**)?
   6. Everything will be fine.
   7. I didn't sleep all night.
   8. Someone told him something about the news.
   9. I made two mistakes (**оши́бка**) when I was speaking Russian.
  10. How do I get to the Hermitage (**Эрмита́ж**)?

ТЕКСТ ДЛЯ ЧТЕНИЯ (Reading)

ВЫСШЕЕ ОБРАЗОВАНИЕ

Ни́на сейча́с у́чится на шесто́м ку́рсе[1] в медици́нском институ́те, на факульте́те[2] педиатри́и. По́сле пра́ктики[3] и оконча́ния[4] институ́та в ию́не она́ хо́чет поступи́ть в аспиранту́ру. Ни́на собира́ется изуча́ть педиатри́ю по специа́льности[5] кардиоло́гия. Она́ всегда́ хоте́ла быть врачо́м и всегда́ люби́ла дете́й. Её мать то́же вра́ч и её брат хиру́рг.[6] Она́ зна́ет что жизнь у враче́й о́чень тру́дная, но полна́[7] смы́сла.[8] Ни́на представля́ет[9] себе́, как она́ когда́-нибудь бу́дет де́лать докла́д[10] на конгре́ссе враче́й.

Ни́на о́чень хо́чет слу́шать ку́рс[11] ле́кций знамени́того[12] профе́ссора Обло́мовой. Она́ слы́шала, что профе́ссор Обло́мова прекра́сно чита́ет ле́кции.[13] Хотя́[14] Ни́на была́ отли́чницей[15] в университе́те, она́ о́чень волну́ется[16] по по́воду[17] экза́мена в аспиранту́ру. Сли́шком мно́го студе́нтов то́же хотя́т туда́ поступи́ть! Она́ сдава́ла[18] экза́мен неде́лю наза́д[19] и то́лько че́рез ме́сяц узна́ет,[20] сдала́[21] ли она́. Она́ не мо́жет дожда́ться[22] до ле́тних кани́кул[23] — ей ну́жно хорошо́ отдохну́ть![24] Она́ мно́го занима́лась и рабо́тала в э́том уче́бном году́,[25] и, е́сли она́ посту́пит в аспиранту́ру, у неё совсе́м не бу́дет свобо́дного вре́мени. Всё вре́мя бу́дет за́нято ле́кциями и дома́шними зада́ниями. Отдыха́йте хорошо́, Ни́на, и успе́ха вам в аспиранту́ре!

СЛОВА́РЬ

1. **курс**	year in school; course
2. **факульте́т**	academic division
3. **пра́ктика**	internship; practical training
4. **оконча́ние**	graduation
5. **по специа́льности (что)**	with a specialization in (something)
6. **хиру́рг**	surgeon
7. **по́лон/-на/-но/-ны (чего́)**	full (of something)
8. **смысл**	meaning, sense
9. **представля́ть (представля́ю, представля́ешь, представля́ют)/ предста́вить (предста́влю, предста́вишь, предста́вят) (себе́)**	to imagine (oneself)
10. **докла́д**	scholarly paper
11. **слу́шать курс**	to take (lit., to listen to) a course

12. знамени́тый	well-known, famous
13. чита́ть ле́кцию	to give (lit., to read) a course
14. хотя́	although
15. отли́чник/-ница	excellent student
16. волнова́ться (волну́юсь, волну́ешься, волну́ются)	to worry (imp.)
17. по по́воду (чего́/кого́)	regarding, about (someone/thing)
18. сдава́ть (сдаю́, сдаёшь, сдаю́т)	to take (an exam) (imp.)
19. наза́д	ago
20. узнава́ть (узнаю́, узнаёшь, узнаю́т) /узна́ть (узна́ю, узна́ешь, узна́ют)	to recognize (imp.); to find out (perf.)
21. сдать (сдам, сдашь, сдаду́т) экза́мен	to pass (an exam) (perf.)
22. дожда́ться (дожду́сь, дождёшься, дожду́тся) (чего́)	to wait (for/until something)
23. ле́тные кани́кулы	summer vacation
24. отдохну́ть	to rest (perf.)
25. уче́бный год	school year

УРОК 21

ЛЕЧЕНИЕ ЗУБОВ. Dentistry.

А. ДИАЛОГ

В буфете.

ИРА: Ой, мамочка!

ВАЛЕРА: Что с тобой?

ИРА: У меня зуб болит всю неделю. Я ничего не могу есть!

ВАЛЕРА: Ты должна пойти к зубному врачу.

*ИРА: Ты прав, но я боюсь. В прошлый раз мне было очень больно. Ты не
знаешь хорошего зубного врача?*

*ВАЛЕРА: Да, в самом деле, я знаю опытного врача, который работает
очень осторожно.*

ИРА: О, можно взять его номер телефона?

ВАЛЕРА: Да, вот. Она тебе понравится. Она очень симпатичная.

На следующий день у зубного врача.

*ЗУБНОЙ ВРАЧ: Откройте широко рот. Гмм ... Видно, вы плохо чистили
зубы, но дупла у вас нет.*

ИРА: Я не могла их чистить из-за боли.

*ЗУБНОЙ ВРАЧ: Да, у вас выпала пломба. Если я её заменю, болеть
перестанет.*

ИРА: Ох, скорее бы!!

*ЗУБНОЙ ВРАЧ: Я также дам вам зубную нить и щётку и покажу, как ими
правильно пользоваться.*

ИРА: Спасибо большое.

ЗУБНОЙ ВРАЧ: Так. Сейчас будет больно секундочку ...

At a snack-bar.

IRA: Ow!

VALERA: What's the matter?

IRA: My tooth has been hurting all week. I can't eat anything!

VALERA: You should go to a dentist.

IRA: You're right, but I'm afraid. It was very painful last time. Do you know a good dentist?

VALERA: Yes, as a matter of fact, I know a skilled dentist who is also very gentle.

IRA: Oh, can I get his phone number?

VALERA: Sure, here you go. You'll like him. He's very nice.

The next day, at the dentist's.

DENTIST: Open wide, please. Hmm . . . I see you haven't been brushing your teeth very well, but you don't have any cavities.

IRA: I wasn't able to brush because of the pain.

DENTIST: Yes, you've lost a filling. If I replace it, the pain will stop.

IRA: Oh, the sooner the better!!

DENTIST: I'll also give you dental floss and a toothbrush, and I'll show you how to use them properly.

IRA: Thanks a lot.

DENTIST: Okay. Now this will hurt for just a second . . .

B. ГРАММАТИКА И СЛОВОУПОТРЕБЛЕНИЕ

1. PERFECTIVE VERBS IN THE FUTURE TENSE

By definition, a completed action cannot take place in the present, so verbs have no perfective form in the present tense. The perfective future is identical to the imperfective present plus a prefix.

читáть/прочитáть: to read

	PRESENT IMPERFECTIVE	FUTURE PERFECTIVE
я	читáю	прочитáю
ты	читáешь	прочитáешь
он/онá	читáет	прочитáет
мы	читáем	прочитáем
вы	читáете	прочитáете
они́	читáют	прочитáют

The future tense of a perfective verb indicates a one-time, brief action that the speaker intends to complete in the future.

Что ты зáвтра бýдешь дéлать? —Я бýду читáть э́ту кни́гу.
What will you be doing tomorrow? —I'll be reading this book. (I may or may not finish it.)

Когдá ты прочитáешь кни́гу? —Я прочитáю её зáвтра.
When will you read the book? —I'll read it (all the way through) tomorrow.

The perfective verb **смочь** (to be able to) consists of the imperfective **мочь** plus the prefix **с-**.

Вы тепéрь смóжете есть без бóли в зýбе.
Now you'll be able to eat without pain in your tooth.

The perfective verb **зайти́** (to drop/go by) consists of the imperfective **идти́** plus the prefix **за-**.

Я зайдý за ни́ми пóсле обéда.
I'll pick them up (go by for them) in the afternoon.

2. КОТÓРЫЙ (WHICH, THAT, WHO, WHOM)

Котóрый is used to begin an adjective clause, i.e. a clause that describes a noun. **Котóрый** has regular adjective endings and agrees with the noun to which it refers in gender and number.

У вас гнилóй зуб, котóрый нáдо удалúть.
You have an infected tooth that needs to be removed.

Вот дуплó, котóрое нýжно запломбировáть.
Here's the cavity which needs to be filled.

Я там вúдел мнóго людéй, котóрые ждáли дóктора.
I saw many people there who were waiting for the doctor.

Котóрый does *not* agree with the noun in case. Rather, its function in the ad-jective clause determines its case, i.e. if it is the subject of the clause, it will be in the nominative, regardless of the case of the noun to which it refers. Note that a **котóрый** clause never begins a sentence and is always preceded by a comma.

Я знáю óпытного врачá, котóрый рабóтает óчень осторóжно.
I know a skilled dentist who is also very gentle (literally, who works very carefully).

У вас вы́пала плóмба, котóрую нáдо заменúть.
You've lost a filling which needs to be replaced.

Ты былá в химчúстке, о котóрой я тебé сказáла?
Have you been to the dry cleaner that I told you about (about which I told you)?

Вот человéк, котóрого я знáла.
There's the man (whom) I used to know.

3. IRREGULAR VERBS

a. Verbs with irregular conjugations

Few Russian verbs are truly irregular, i.e. with a conjugation that does not fit either the Conjugation I or Conjugation II pattern, but those that are must be memorized. You learned the present tense, imperfective forms of the irreg-ular verbs **хотéть** (to want), and **есть** (to eat) in **Урóк** 6 and 16. The perfec-tives of both **хотéть** (**захотéть**) and **есть** (**съесть**) are also irregular, since they conjugate just like the imperfectives plus a prefix. **Дать** (to give; perfec-tive) is another irregular verb, which conjugates something like **есть**.

дать: to give (perfective)

I will give	я дам	мы дади́м	we will give
you (fam.) will give	ты дашь	вы дади́те	you (pl./pol.) will give
he/she will give	он/она́ даст	они́ даду́т	they will give

stem = да+/дад+ (sing./pl.)
imperative: Да́й(те)!

Я та́кже вам дам зубну́ю ни́ть и щётку.

I'll also give you dental floss and a toothbrush.

Он съест э́ту таре́лку су́па? —Наве́рно нет.

Will he finish (eat up) this plate of soup? —Probably not.

b. Verbs with an irregular past tense

Есть (to eat) and **мочь** (to be able to) have irregular past tense forms: **есть ›› ел/-а/-и; мочь ›› мог/-ла́/-ло́/-ли**. In general, the past tense of infinitives ending in **-есть** or **-чь** are irregular: **печь** (to bake) **›› пёк/-ла́/-ло́/-ли; сесть** (to sit down) **›› се́л/-а/-о/-и.**

Я не могла́ их чи́стить из-за бо́ли.

I wasn't able to brush them because of the pain.

Что вы е́ли? —Я ничего́ не ел.

What were you eating? —I wasn't eating anything.

Он пёк тако́й вку́сный хлеб!

He used to bake such delicious bread!

Мы се́ли обе́дать в два часа́.

We sat down to eat dinner at two o'clock.

Дать and **хоте́ть** have regular past participles: **дал/-а/-о/-и; хоте́л/ -а/-о/-и.**

Зубно́й врач мне дал зубну́ю нить и но́вую щётку.

The dentist gave me dental floss and a new toothbrush.

4. VERBS ENDING IN -ABATЬ

Some common imperfective verbs have an infinitive form ending in -ава́ть, e.g. дава́ть (to give), встава́ть (to get up), узнава́ть (to find out), or перестава́ть (to stop). To conjugate such verbs, simply replace the final -вать with the appropriate Conjugation I ending.

дава́ть: to give (imperfective)

I give	я даю́	мы даём	we give
you (fam.) give	ты даёшь	вы даёте	you (pl./pol.) give
he/she gives	он/она́ даёт	они даю́т	they give

stem = да+
imperative: Дава́й(те)!

Когда́ я хожу́ к зубно́му врачу́, она́ ка́ждый раз мне даёт но́вую щётку.
Every time I go to the dentist, she gives me a new toothbrush.

Боль перестаёт, когда́ я открыва́ю рот.
The pain stops when I open my mouth.

Я обы́чно встаю́ в семь часо́в.
I usually get up at seven o'clock.

Мы ча́сто от него́ узнаём поле́зную информа́цию.
We often find out useful information from him.

5. THE PREPOSITIONS К, ОТ, AND У

The prepositions к (towards, to), от (from, away from), and у (by, at) are used to express motion or location. К is used to express movement towards someone, у is used to express being at someone's house or place of work, and от is used to express movement away from someone or someplace. К takes the dative case, while у and от both take the genitive.

Ты должна́ пойти́ к зубно́му врачу́.
You should go to a dentist.

Я была́ у э́того зубно́го врача́ два го́да наза́д.
I went to (was at) that dentist two years ago.

Отку́да ты идёшь? —От зубно́го врача́.

Where are you coming from? —From the dentist's.

Приезжа́й к нам!

Come visit us!

К чёрту!

Go to hell! (literally, To the devil!)

Отста́нь от меня́!

Leave me alone!

6. INTERJECTIONS

Many of the interjections we use, such as "Hmm … ," "Shh!," and "Oh!," are fairly international and, though pronounced slightly differently in different languages, are easily understandable. Here are some of the most common in Russian.

Ой!	Oh! Ow! Oops!	Уф!	Ugh! Ooh! (fatigue)
Ой-ой-о́й!	Tsk-tsk-tsk!	Фу!	Ooh! Phew! (relief, fatigue, disgust)
Тссс!	Shh!	Оп-пля!	Whoops! Up/down you go!
Ах!	Ah!	Ура́!	Hurray!
Ох!/О!	Oh!	Гмм …	Hmm . . .
Ух!	Ooh! Gosh!	Гм? А?	Huh?
Ага́!	Aha!	Хм! Гм!	Huh! (contempt)

Ой, ма́мочка! Как боли́т э́тот зуб! (Ой, ма́мочка! is stronger than just Ой!)

Oww! This tooth really hurts!

Тссс! Вот дирижёр!

Shh! Here comes the conductor!

C. СЛОВАРЬ

анесте́тик	anesthetic
бо́льно	painful
боя́ться (бою́сь, бои́шься, боя́тся) (чего́/кого́)	to be afraid (of someone/thing) (II.)
боль	f. pain
в са́мом де́ле	as a matter of fact

ви́дно	evident
гнило́й	infected (lit. rotten)
дава́ть (даю́, даёшь, даю́т)	to give
/*дать* (дам, дашь, даст, дади́м, дади́те, даду́т)	
дупло́	cavity
заменя́ть (заменя́ю, заменя́ешь, заменя́ют) /*замени́ть* (заменю́, заме́нишь, заме́нят) (что-чем)	to replace, to substitute (one thing for another)
зуб	tooth
зубно́й врач	dentist
зубна́я па́ста	toothpaste
из-за (кого́/чего́)	because of (someone/thing)
кото́рый	that, which, who(m) (cannot begin sentence)
о́пытный	skillful, experienced
осторо́жно	careful(ly)
Ох, скоре́е бы!	Oh, the sooner the better!
переставáть (перестаю́, перестаёшь, перестаю́т)/ *переста́ть* (переста́ну, переста́нешь, переста́нут)	to stop, to cease
пло́мба	filling
по́льзоваться (по́льзуюсь, по́льзуешься, по́льзуются)	to use (imp.)
про́шлый раз	last time
рот	mouth
теря́ть (теря́ю, теря́ешь, теря́ют)/по-	to lose
чи́стить (чи́щу, чи́стишь, чи́стят)/по- (зу́бы)	to clean; to brush (one's teeth)
широко́	wide(ly)
щётка	brush; toothbrush

РУССКАЯ КУЛЬТУРА

Dentistry in the Former Soviet Union left much to be desired. There was not a great deal of emphasis on preventive care—there was no fluoride in the water and people did not go for regular cleanings. This has changed greatly over the past years. Now there are numerous dental offices all over Moscow and St. Petersburg that offer a first rate service. As a result, people are starting to pay much more attention to their dental health.

In this chapter you may have noticed the expression **К чёрту!** (Go to hell!)
It is important to be able to recognize Russian slang, but avoid using obscenities when you speak. Even when a Russian expletive seems analogous to an English one that is used casually, don't be fooled: the expression is probably much stronger in Russian, and you could get yourself into some serious trouble. Especially avoid any expletives including the word **мать** (mother). As in many other cultures, the strongest insult is one involving someone's mother.

УПРАЖНЕНИЯ

A. **Переведи́те глаго́лы с англи́йского на ру́сский.** (Translate the verbs in English into Russian.)

1. Мне на́до обяза́тельно <u>to read</u> э́ту статью́ до заня́тия.
2. Я люблю́ <u>to read</u> газе́ту у́тром.
3. Он <u>will drop by</u> за́втра у́тром.
4. Боль <u>will stop</u> че́рез мину́ту.
5. Че́рез год вы <u>will be reading</u> по-ру́сски.

B. **Запо́лните про́пуски пра́вильной фо́рмой сло́ва «кото́рый».** (Fill in the blanks with the correct form of **кото́рый.**)

1. Вот америка́нка, _____ здесь живёт.
2. Фильм идёт в теа́тре, _____ нахо́дится недалеко́ от тебя́.
3. Вот фотогра́фия дру́га, о _____ я тебе́ говори́ла.
4. Вот щётки, _____ купи́л Юра.
5. Я пойду́ к зубно́му врачу́, _____ рекомендова́л мне Вале́ра.

C. **Переведи́те предложе́ния на ру́сский.** (Translate the sentences into Russian.)

1. You (familiar) should always brush your teeth after (**по́сле того́ как**) you eat.
2. She used to eat well before, but now (**тепе́рь**) she eats poorly.
3. Ira wasn't able to eat all week. —Tsk-tsk-tsk!
4. You'll give me his telephone number? —I already gave you (familiar) his number!
5. Mom used to bake bread (**хлеб**) for us. Oh, it was delicious!

D. Заполните пра́вильные оконча́ния и переведи́те предложе́ния.
   (Fill in the blanks with the correct endings and translate the sentences.)

   1. Боль переста_____ , когда́ я сплю.
   2. Ба́бушка и де́душка ча́сто да_____ нам пода́рки.
   3. Во ско́лько ты вста_____ ?
   4. Ка́ждое у́тро мы узна_____ отве́ты на вопро́сы.
   5. Зубно́й врач обы́чно да_____ мне но́вую щётку.

E. Заполните про́пуски предло́гами «у», «к» и́ли «от» и подбери́те
   ру́сские предложе́ния, соотве́тствующие англи́йским значе́ниям.
   (Fill in the blanks with the prepositions у, к, or от, and match the sentences
   with their meanings.)

1. Отста́нь _____ меня́!	a. He was at their place yesterday.
2. Приезжа́й _____ мне!	b. Go to hell!
3. Он вчера́ был _____ них.	c. You should go to the dentist.
4. Иди́ _____ чёрту!	d. I was at the dentist's yesterday.
5. Ты до́лжен пойти́ _____ зубно́му врачу́.	e. Leave me alone!
	f. Come visit me!

УРОК 22

ВЫРАЖЕНИЯ БЛАГОДАРНОСТИ И КОМПЛИМЕНТЫ.

Expressions of gratitude and compliments.

А. ДИАЛОГ

В кварти́ре под Но́вый го́д.

РАНДИ: *До́брый ве́чер всем!*

СЕРЁЖА: *Ра́нди пришла́! Входи́, входи́! Ох, спаси́бо за цветы́!*

РАНДИ: *Ха, ха. Для тебя́ я принесла́ шампа́нское! А э́то тебе́* (даёт Ната́ше буке́т).

НАТАША: *Ой, како́й краси́вый буке́т!*

СЕРЁЖА: *И мой люби́мый сорт шампа́нского! Ты бу́дешь винова́та, е́сли я ста́ну пья́ницей!*

РАНДИ: *Я не бою́сь. А где Марк?*

МАРК: *Вот и я! Ра́нди, кака́я ты сего́дня наря́дная!*

РАНДИ: *О, э́то пла́тье мое́й сосе́дки по ко́мнате.*

За столо́м.

НАТАША: *Ра́нди, ещё кусо́чек то́рта?*

РАНДИ: *Да, пожа́луйста. Всё бы́ло о́чень вку́сно!*

НАТАША: (даёт Ра́нди кусо́к то́рта) *Прия́тного аппети́та! Ты тепе́рь говори́шь по-ру́сски почти́ без акце́нта.*

РАНДИ: *То́лько благодаря́ ва́шей по́мощи. Вы мне всё-таки скажи́те, е́сли я сде́лаю оши́бку, хорошо́?*

СЕРЁЖА: *Да, коне́чно, но Ната́шка права́: ты ста́ла намно́го лу́чше говори́ть по-ру́сски.*

МАРК: *Дава́йте вы́пьем за Ра́нди, кото́рая тепе́рь настоя́щая ру́сская!*

РАНДИ: *И за кулина́рный тала́нт Ната́ши!*

ВСЕ: *За Ра́нди и Ната́шу!* (все пьют)

МАРК: *Ребя́та, уже́ почти́ по́лночь! Три, два, оди́н ...*

ВСЕ: *С Но́вым го́дом!* (все целу́ются и обнима́ются)

In an apartment, on New Year's Eve.

RANDY: Good evening, everyone!

SERYOZHA: Randy's here! Come in, come in! Oh, thanks for the flowers!

RANDY: Ha, ha! For you I've brought champagne! And these are for you. *(gives Natasha the flowers)*

NATASHA: Oh! What a beautiful bouquet!

SERYOZHA: And my favorite kind of champagne! It'll be your fault if I become a drunk!

RANDY: I'm not worried. And where's Mark?

MARK: Here I am! Randy, how elegant you are today!

RANDY: Oh, this is my roommate's dress.

At the table.

NATASHA: Randy, another little piece of cake?

RANDY: Yes, please. Everything was delicious!

NATASHA: *(gives Randy a piece of cake)* Bon appetit! You now speak Russian with almost no accent.

RANDY: Only thanks to your help. You'll still tell me if I make a mistake, right?

SERYOZHA: Yes, of course, but Natasha's right: your Russian has improved a lot.

MARK: Let's drink to Randy, who's now a real Russian!

RANDY: And to Natasha's cooking!

EVERYONE: To Randy and Natasha! *(everyone drinks)*

MARK: Guys, it's almost midnight! Three, two, one . . .

EVERYONE: Happy New Year! *(Everyone kisses and hugs each other.)*

B. ГРАММАТИКА И СЛОВОУПОТРЕБЛЕНИЕ

1. ASPECT PAIRS

As you know, many perfective verbs are formed by adding prefixes to an imperfective verb. Less commonly, aspectual pairs are made up of verbs that appear unrelated. Such pairs must simply be memorized.

говори́ть/сказа́ть	to speak/to say, to tell
брать/взять	to take
класть/положи́ть	to put
лови́ть/пойма́ть	to hunt/to catch

Ты те́перь говори́шь по-ру́сски почти́ без акце́нта.
You now speak Russian with almost no accent.

Вы мне всё-таки скажи́те, е́сли я сде́лаю оши́бку, хорошо́?
You'll still tell me if I make a mistake, right?

На заку́ску мы возьмём икру́. —А почему́ ты всегда́ берёшь икру́?
For an appetizer, we'll take caviar. —Why do you always get (take) caviar?

Куда́ ты положи́ла по́чту? —На стол, куда́ я всегда́ её кладу́.
Where did you put the mail? —On the table, where I always put it.

Они́ весь день лови́ли ры́бу, но ничего́ не пойма́ли.
They were fishing all day, but they didn't catch anything.

Notice that although **говори́ть** and **сказа́ть** form an aspectual pair, they translate into English quite differently. In Russian "speaking" is an imperfective action, but "telling" or "saying" is perfective. Similarly, **пойма́ть** means "to catch," while **лови́ть** means "to try to catch."

2. МНОГО VERSUS ОЧЕНЬ

In order not to confuse these two words, it is necessary to avoid thinking in English. When used with adverbs or adjectives, **очень** means "very" or "really."

Всё было очень вкусно!

Everything was very good (tasty)!

When used with verbs, **очень** serves as an intensifier of feeling or action and can be translated as "really" or "very much," depending on context.

Я очень люблю говорить по-русски.

I really love speaking Russian.

Он очень спешит.

He's in a big hurry. (He's really hurrying.)

Я очень хочу познакомиться с ней.

I would very much like to meet her.

When you use "a lot" in English, you should generally use **много** (a lot, much) in Russian.

Она много знает об этом. —Да, слишком много!

She knows a lot about this. —Yes, too much!

Ты стала намного[1] лучше говорить по-русски.

Your Russian has improved a lot.

3. THE PREPOSITION ЗА

The preposition **за** has many different usages and meanings. It is used:

a. to express gratitude for something.

Ох, спасибо за цветы!

Oh, thanks for the flowers!

---

1. Another way of saying **много,** used only in comparative situations.

b. to indicate payment or exchange for something.

Он заплати́л за газе́ту.

He paid (gave money in exchange) for the paper.

c. in toasts.

Дава́й вы́пьем за Ра́нди! —И за кулина́рный тала́нт Ната́ши!

Let's drink to (for) Randy! —And to (for) Natasha's cooking!

За Ра́нди и Ната́шу!

To (for) Randy and Natasha!

Notice that toasts are made "for" rather than "to" someone or something. When **за** is used to mean "for," as it does in these three contexts, it is followed by the accusative case.

4. THE PAST TENSE OF UNIDIRECTIONAL VERBS OF MOTION

The unidirectional verbs of motion **идти́** (to go), **везти́** (to convey), **вести́** (to lead), and **нести́** (to carry) have irregular past tense forms.

	идти́	везти́	вести́	нести́
MASCULINE	шёл	вёз	вёл	нёс
FEMININE	шла	везла́	вела́	несла́
PLURAL	шли	везли́	вели́	несли́

The past tense of unidirectional verbs of motion such as these, and of the verb **éхать**, is most commonly used with prefixes[2] in the perfective aspect.

Ра́нди пришла́!

Randy's here!

Для тебя́ я принесла́ шампа́нское!

For you I've brought champagne!

Мне на́до бы́ло отвезти́ Са́шку к ма́ме.

I had to take Sashka to my mother's.

2. Please see **Уро́к** 20 for a list of common prefixes and their meanings.

Поéхали!

Let's go [by car]! (lit., We went!)

Unprefixed, unidirectional verbs of motion are imperfective and seldom used in the past tense. When they are, they express two simultaneous actions or describe something that can only move in one direction, such as rain.

Кудá ты éхала, когдá я тебя́ ви́дел? —Я éхала в центр.

Where were you going (by vehicle) when I saw you? —I was on my way downtown.

Шёл дождь.

It was raining.

5. ДАВÁЙ(ТЕ) … ! (LET'S … !)

Давáй(те) (Let's) is most often used with the first person plural of perfective verbs to suggest a specific, one–time only, joint action.

Давáй вы́пьем за Рáнди!

Let's drink to Randy!

Давáйте познакóмимся.

Let's get acquainted.

Such suggestions can also be made without **Давáй(те)**, but including it makes them more polite. Verbs of motion are often used without **Давáй(те)** in this manner.

Пойдём!

Let's go [on foot]!

Поéдем вмéсте!

Let's go [ride] together!

Перейдём на ты!

Let's switch to **ты**!

C. СЛОВАРЬ

без акце́нта	without an accent
благода́рность	f. gratitude
благодаря́ (кому́/чему́)	thanks/owing to (someone/thing)
буке́т	bouquet
везти́ (везу́, везёшь, везу́т)	to convey (by vehicle) (unidirectional)
вести́ (веду́, ведёшь, веду́т)	to lead (unidirectional)
води́ть (вожу́, во́дишь, во́дят)	to lead (multidirectional)
вози́ть (вожу́, во́зишь, во́зят)	to convey (by vehicle) (multidirectional)
винова́т/-а/-ы	sorry; guilty; at fault
вку́сно	delicious, tasty
всё-таки	all the same; nevertheless
Входи́!	Come in!
выраже́ние	expression (of an idea)
Дава́й(те)	Let's
Дава́й(те) *вы́пьем за* (кого́/что)!	Let's drink to (someone/thing)!
за столо́м	at the table
класть (кладу́, кладёшь, кладу́т)/*положи́ть* (положу́, поло́жишь, поло́жат) (что-куда́)	to put (lay flat) (something somewhere)
комплиме́нт	compliment
кулина́рный тала́нт	good cooking
кусо́чек	a little piece
лови́ть (ловлю́, ло́вишь, ло́вят)/ *пойма́ть* (пойма́ю, пойма́ешь, пойма́ют)	to hunt (imp.); to catch (perf.)
наря́дный	elegant; well-dressed
настоя́щий	real; present
нести́ (несу́, несёшь, несу́т)	to carry (unidirectional)
Но́вый год	New Year
носи́ть (ношу́, но́сишь, но́сят)	to carry (multidirectional); to wear
обнима́ть (обнима́ю, обнима́ешь, обнима́ют)/ *обня́ть* (обниму́, обни́мешь, обни́мут)	to hug, to embrace
оши́бка	mistake
Прия́тного аппети́та!	Bon appetit!; Enjoy your meal!
по́лдень	noon (lit. half-day)
по́лночь	midnight (lit. half-night)
по́мощь	f. help

пья́ница	drunk (noun)
Рождество́	Christmas
С Но́вым го́дом!	Happy New Year!
сорт	kind, sort
сосе́д(ка) *по ко́мнате*	roommate (lit. neighbor in the room)
станови́ться (становлю́сь, стано́вишься, стано́вятся)/*стать* (ста́ну, ста́нешь, ста́нут) (кем/чем)	to become (someone/thing)
торт	cake
целова́ть (целу́ю, целу́ешь, целу́ют)/по-	to kiss
шампа́нское	champagne

РУССКАЯ КУЛЬТУРА

The Russian **Но́вый год** (New Year) is the equivalent of Christmas, New Year's, Halloween, and Thanksgiving all rolled into one. Although celebrated on December 31, it is considered the Russian sectarian Christmas. It is the best-loved holiday of the year and is celebrated festively with family and friends. Other than birthdays, it is the main gift-giving occasion. There are some well-loved characters associated with it, like our Santa Claus, elves, and reindeer. **Дед Моро́з** (Grandfather Frost), who looks something like Santa Claus, hands out the presents. There is also a **ёлка** (New Year's tree), often decorated with candles, and **Снегу́рочка** (Snow Maiden), who dances and plays games with the children.

As New Year's is the biggest holiday of the year, everyone serves as many delicacies as possible for the festive meal, and guests usually contribute something also. It is customary to serve alcohol, and Russians are particularly fond of toasting everyone and everything repeatedly. There is a tradition of seeing off the old year with a toast. Some groups of friends celebrate together every year and put on skits and charades with fancy costumes. Another tradition is to watch the film "**Иро́ния судьбы́**" (*Irony of Fate*), which takes place on New Year's Eve and illustrates the holiday's significance for Russians.

Но́вый год incorporates elements of the traditional Russian Orthodox Christmas, and it can be somewhat solemn also. People often take stock of their lives at this time, and it is said that the person you spend New Year's Eve with is the one you will be with when the year is out. It is a high point of the year, looked forward to with anticipation, and remembered with nostalgia. Russians prefer to celebrate New Year's Eve at intimate gatherings with close friends and family, at least until midnight and the New Year arrive. Then many people go out onto the streets for the all-night public celebration, which includes skating, sledding, singing, and outdoor performances.

УПРАЖНЕНИЯ

A. Запо́лните пропу́ски соотве́тствующими глаго́лами.
(Match the verbs with the blanks in the sentences.)

1. Он не _____ , что ты сказа́ла.
2. Я за́втра тебе́ _____ , ла́дно?
3. Кто _____ мой журна́л?
4. Кто-то всегда́ _____ мои журна́лы!
5. Я _____ твой ключ на шкаф, ла́дно?

a. положу́
b. говори́ли
c. берёт
d. по́нял
e. взял
f. скажу́

B. Запо́лните про́пуски слова́ми «о́чень», «мно́го».
(Fill in the blanks with the words о́чень or мно́го.)

1. Прости́те, но я _____ спешу́!
2. Ру́сские _____ говоря́т о поли́тике.
3. Ру́сские _____ лю́бят говори́ть о поли́тике.
4. Он _____ пло́хо пи́шет по-англи́йски.
5. Мне _____ нра́вится э́тот торт.

C. Да́йте коро́ткие отве́ты на вопро́сы о диало́ге. (Answer the questions about the dialogue with short answers in Russian.)

1. Како́е бы́ло число́?
2. Чья э́та кварти́ра?
3. Что Ра́нди дала́ Серге́ю?
4. За что Ната́ша сказа́ла Ра́нди спаси́бо?
5. Чьё пла́тье бы́ло на Ра́нди?
6. Что Ра́нди понра́вилось?
7. Как Ната́ша отве́тила на э́тот комплиме́нт?
8. За кого́ они́ вы́пили?
9. За что Ра́нди предложи́ла (proposed) тост?
10. Что они́ де́лали в по́лночь?

D. **Подери́те соотве́тствующие глаго́лы из коло́нки Б к коло́нке А.**
   Употреби́те оди́н отве́т два ра́за. (Match the verbs in column B to those
   in column A. Use one answer twice.)

A   B

1. Марк <u>пришёл</u> по́сле Ра́нди.   a. took
2. Он <u>привёз</u> торт на маши́не.   b. went (by car)
3. Марк и Ра́нди <u>ушли́</u> по́сле полу́ночи. c. came up
4. Когда́ Ра́нди <u>пошла́</u> к Серге́ю и Ната́ше, d. carried (in)
   шёл снег.   f. crossed
5. Марк <u>прое́хал</u> от це́нтра до их дома. e. brought (by vehicle)
6. Марк <u>отвёл</u> Ра́нди домо́й.   g. left
7. Ната́ша <u>внесла́</u> цветы́ в ко́мнату.   h. to leave
8. Они́ <u>перее́хали</u> че́рез мост.   i. arrived
9. Ста́рик <u>подошёл</u> ко мне и зада́л мне вопро́с. j. started for
10. Марк <u>довёз</u> Ра́нди пря́мо до её две́ри.

E. **Переведи́те на ру́сский.** (Translate into Russian.)

   1. Let's dance!/Let's go dancing!
   2. Let's go for a walk (гуля́ть/погуля́ть) in the park.
   3. Let's drink to the New Year!
   4. Let's get acquainted.
   5. Let's go!

УРОК 23

ДОМАШНИЕ ДЕЛА. Domestic activities.

A. ДИАЛОГ

После обеда, на работе.

СОТРУДНИЦА: *Что с тобой сегодня случилось?*

КСЮША: *Ой, сегодня—кошмар! Всю ночь Сашку рвало, так что я проспала. Я обычно встаю в шесть, но сегодня я проснулась только в семь.*

СОТРУДНИЦА: *Ой–ой–ой! Маленкие детки—маленкие бедки.*

КСЮША: *Верно! Потом каждое утро я принимаю душ, пока муж помогает детям одеваться.*

СОТРУДНИЦА: *Хорошо, что он тебе помогает.*

КСЮША: *Да. Но сегодня трубы лопнули, и везде была вода.*

СОТРУДНИЦА: *Какой ужас!*

КСЮША: *Муж пошёл на работу. А затем мне надо было отвезти Сашку к маме и убрать в квартире. К счастью, наш сосед—водопроводчик.*

СОТРУДНИЦА: *Тебе повезло!*

КСЮША: *Да. Но обычно я провожаю детей в школу, а потом ем, одеваюсь, немножко убираю в квартире и читаю газету.*

СОТРУДНИЦА: *Да, твоё личное время.*

КСЮША: *Верно! А сегодня я не приняла душ и не позавтракала. Едва умылась, оделась и побежала на работу!*

СОТРУДНИЦА: *Бедная! Ну и утро!*

After lunch, at work.

COWORKER: What happened with you today?

KSENYA: Oh, today's been a nightmare! Sashka was throwing up all night, so I overslept. I usually get up at six o'clock, but today I didn't even wake up until seven.

COWORKER: Tsk! Tsk! Tsk! Little children are little troubles.

KSENYA: For sure! Then every morning I take a shower while my husband helps the children get dressed.

COWORKER: It's good that he helps you.

KSENYA: Yes. But today the pipes burst, and water was everywhere.

COWORKER: How awful!

KSENYA: My husband left for work. And then I had to take Sashka to my mother's and clean up the apartment. Fortunately, our neighbor is a plumber.

COWORKER: That's lucky!

KSENYA: Yes. But usually I see the kids off to school, and then I eat, get dressed, clean up a little, and read the paper.

COWORKER: Yes, a little time to yourself.

KSENYA: Right! But today, I didn't take a shower or eat breakfast. I barely washed, got dressed, and ran to work!

COWORKER: You poor thing! What a morning!

B. ГРАММАТИКА И СЛОВОУПОТРЕБЛЕНИЕ

1. ASPECT AND VERBS OF MOTION

Aspect with verbs of motion can seem confusing because of the additional factor of whether a verb is uni- or multidirectional. By definition, only unidirectional verbs can be perfective.[1] They are made perfective by adding prefixes, e.g. **принести́, отвезти́, пойти́**. Remember that adding a prefix often changes

---

1. It is impossible to move in more than one direction, or to repeatedly perform an action in a complete, one-time only, perfective way.

a verb's meaning. Here are some common pairs of imperfective verbs of motion with their perfective counterparts, created by adding the prefix по-.

UNIDIRECTIONAL IMPERFECTIVE	MULTIDIRECTIONAL IMPERFECTIVE	PERFECTIVE	
идти́	ходи́ть	пойти́	to go (on foot)
е́хать	е́здить	пое́хать	to go (by vehicle)
бежа́ть	бе́гать	побежа́ть	to run
лете́ть	лета́ть	полете́ть	to fly
нести́	носи́ть	понести́	to carry
вести́	води́ть	повести́	to lead
везти́	вози́ть	повезти́	to convey (by vehicle)

These prefixes can also be added to multidirectional verbs, but in that case they do not make the verb perfective. Rather, a prefix is added to both forms of a verb of motion, causing the uni-/multidirectional distinction to disappear, and creating a normal imperfective/perfective pair. For example, **носи́ть/нести́** means "to carry," round trip or in one direction, but **приноси́ть/принести́** (to bring) is a regular imperfective/perfective pair.

Я едва́ побри́лся и оде́лся и побежа́л на рабо́ту.
I barely shaved and got dressed, and I ran to work.

Муж Ксе́ни пошёл на рабо́ту в во́семь часо́в.
Ksenya's husband left for work at eight o'clock.

Мне на́до бы́ло отвезти́ Са́шку к ма́ме.
I had to take Sashka to my mother's.

Вы́йдите на остано́вке «ста́нция Академи́ческая».
Get off at the Akademicheskaya metro station.

Вы сейча́с выхо́дите? —Нет, проходи́те.
Are you getting out now? —No, go ahead (literally, pass by).

Note that if a prefix is added to the multidirectional verb **е́здить**, it becomes **-езжа́ть**.

Мы всегда́ уезжа́ем на ле́то в ию́не.
We always leave for the summer in June.

2. ASPECT PAIRS WITH DIFFERENT STEMS

Another way to derive a perfective verb from an imperfective verb is to change the stem. Perfectives are often shortened versions of imperfective verbs.

IMPERFECTIVE	PERFECTIVE	
вставáть	встать	to get up
давáть	дать	to give
забывáть	забы́ть	to forget
закрывáть	закры́ть	to close
одевáться	одéться	to get dressed
открывáть	откры́ть	to open
покáзывать	показáть	to show
помогáть	помóчь	to help
принимáть	приня́ть	to take
расскáзывать	рассказáть	to tell about
убирáть	убрáть	to tidy up
умывáться	умы́ться	to wash oneself

Я обы́чно встаю́ в шесть часóв, а сегóдня я встала́ в семь.
I usually get up at six o'clock, but today I got up at seven.

Я обы́чно принимáю душ, а сегóдня я егó не приняла́. Я едвá умы́лась, одéлась и побежáла на рабóту!
Usually I take a shower, but today I didn't. I barely washed, dressed, and ran to work!

Обы́чно я спокóйно одевáюсь и немнóжко убирáю в квартúре, а сегóдня мне нáдо бы́ло убрáть в квартире.
Usually I get dressed calmly and clean up a little, but today I had to clean up the apartment.

Он всегдá забывáет мой день рождéния, а в э́тот раз он егó не забы́л!
He always forgets my birthday, but this time, he didn't forget!

Клúника кáждое ýтро открывáется в семь, а зáвтра онá открóется в дéвять.
The clinic opens every morning at seven, but tomorrow they're opening at nine.

Двáдцать трéтий урóк

A verb can also be made perfective by changing it from a Conjugation I -ать ending to a Conjugation II -ить ending. Of course not all -ать verbs are imperfective, and not all -ить verbs are perfective, but often that is the case, e.g. конча́ть/ко́нчить (to finish), продолжа́ть/продо́лжить (to continue), повторя́ть/повтори́ть (to repeat).

Ну, когда́ ты ко́нчишь писа́ть письмо́? —Я сейча́с конча́ю.
Well, when are you going to be finished writing the letter? —I'm finishing it right now.

Де́душка всегда́ всё повторя́ет. —Да, он сего́дня что-то повтори́л три ра́за!
Grandfather always repeats everything. —Yes, he repeated something three times today!

Often the two verbs in an aspectual pair have different, but related, meanings, e.g. загора́ть/загоре́ть (to sunbathe/to get a tan), реша́ть/реши́ть (to figure out/to decide).

Мои́ роди́тели ско́ро бу́дут загора́ть в Крыму́. Наве́рно, они́ загоря́т.
My parents will be sunbathing in the Crimea soon. They'll probably get a tan.

Я весь день реша́ла, что де́лать, и вдруг реши́ла.
I was figuring out what to do all day, and all of a sudden, I decided.

3. ТОГДА VERSUS ПОТОМ VERSUS ЗАТЕМ

All three of these adverbs can be translated into English as "then," but they are used quite differently. Тогда́ means "at that time; in that case," пото́м means "afterwards, later," and зате́м means "right after/following that, next."

Я проводи́ла му́жа, а зате́м мне на́до бы́ло отвезти́ Са́шку к ма́ме.
I saw my husband off, and then (following that) I had to take Sashka to my mother's.

Обы́чно я провожа́ю дете́й в шко́лу, а пото́м ем и одева́юсь.
Usually I see the kids off to school, and then (sometime later) I eat and get dressed.

Дава́й встре́тимся за́втра в час. —Ла́дно. Тогда́ до за́втра!
Let's meet tomorrow at one. —Alright. Until tomorrow then (in
that case)!

4. WORD ROOTS

One root in Russian can be the basis for adjectives, nouns, verbs and adverbs.
In general, if you think two words have the same basic root, you're probably
right. So, by learning one word, you can often learn a whole group of words.
For example, many common adjectives are formed from nouns, especially
words for furniture, e.g. **пи́сьменный стол** (desk) literally means "letter writing table," and comes from **письмо́** (letter), which comes from **писа́ть** (to
write). The word for "book shelf," **кни́жный шкаф**, comes from **кни́га** (book).
Such connections between words in Russian are common, and as you learn
more Russian, you will see more and more of these correspondences.

Я не просну́лась до семи́.
I didn't wake up until seven.

К сча́стью, наш сосе́д—водопрово́дчик.
Fortunately, our neighbor is a plumber.

А сего́дня я приняла́ душ и не поза́втракала.
But today I didn't take a shower, and I didn't eat breakfast.

Training yourself to look for common roots in Russian words will help you to
guess the meanings of new words, thereby greatly increasing your existing vocabulary.

5. THE VERB ПРОВОДИ́ТЬ

The verb **проводи́ть** has two meanings. It is the perfective form of **провожа́ть**
(to see off, to accompany), and it is also the imperfective form of the verb
провести́, meaning "to spend (time), to lead." In both cases the conjugation
is the same, so context alone reveals the meaning. Compare:

Обычно я провожа́ю дете́й в шко́лу, но вчера́ муж проводи́л их.

Usually I see the kids off to school, but yesterday my husband saw them off.

В ию́ле мы всегда́ прово́дим вре́мя на да́че.

We always spend time at our dacha in July.

Я вчера́ хорошо́ провела́ вре́мя.

I had a great time yesterday.

C. СЛОВАРЬ

бе́гать (бе́гаю, бе́гаешь, бе́гают)	to run (multidirectional)
бе́дный	poor
бежа́ть (бегу́, бежи́шь, бежи́т, бежи́м, бежи́те, бегу́т)/по-	to run (unidirectional) (irregular)
бри́ться (бре́юсь, бре́ешься, бре́ются)/по-	to shave (oneself)
ве́рно	right; true, faithful
везде́	everywhere
вода́	water
водопрово́дчик	plumber
встава́ть (встаю́, встаёшь, встаю́т)/ *встать* (вста́ну, вста́нешь, вста́нут)	to get up
де́ло	task, affair, doing
дома́шний	domestic, done at home
душ	shower
едва́	barely
зате́м	then, after that, next
кошма́р	nightmare
ли́чный	private, personal
ло́паться (лопа́ется, лопа́ются)/ *ло́пнуть* (ло́пнет, ло́пнут)	to burst, to break (it/they)
одева́ться (одева́юсь, одева́ешься, одева́ются) /*оде́ться* (оде́нусь, оде́нешься, оде́нутся)	to get dressed
отвози́ть (отвожу́, отво́зишь, отво́зят) /*отвезти́* (отвезу́, отвезёшь, отвезу́т)	to take away (by vehicle)
повезло́ (кому́)	(someone, in dative) lucked out

провожа́ть (провожа́ю, провожа́ешь, провожа́ют) **/проводи́ть** (провожу́, прово́дишь, прово́дят)	to see off, to accompany
проспа́ть (просплю́, проспи́шь, проспя́т)	to oversleep (perf.) (II.)
просыпа́ться (просыпа́юсь, просыпа́ешься, просыпа́ются)**/просну́ться** (просну́сь, проснёшься, просну́тся)	to wake up
рвать (рвёт, рва́ло + accus. subject)/**вы-**	to throw up; to tear, to rip
реша́ть (реша́ю, реша́ешь, реша́ют), **/реши́ть** (решу́, реши́шь, реша́т)	to figure out (imp.); to decide to solve (perf.)
случа́ться (случа́ется, случа́ются) **/случи́ться** (случи́тся, случа́тся)	to happen[2] (it/they)
сотру́дник/-ница	co-worker
споко́йно	calm(ly), peaceful(ly)
труба́	pipe
у́жас	disaster; terrible thing
умыва́ться (умыва́юсь, умыва́ешься, умыва́ются) **/умы́ться** (умо́юсь, умо́ешься, умо́ются)	to wash (oneself)
убира́ть (убира́ю, убира́ешь, убира́ют)/**убра́ть** (уберу́, уберёшь, уберу́т)	to tidy up, to clear up

РУССКАЯ КУЛЬТУРА

Russian women were encouraged by the officially egalitarian Communist regime to work. In practice, however, they usually held, and still hold, less prestigious and lower-paid positions than men. In addition, they are expected to take primary or full responsibility for the children and for running the household. This alone is much more stressful and demanding a task than in the United States. There are fewer modern conveniences, and most things are done by

2. Cannot be used with an animate subject.

hand. Most foods are not processed, and the space and means for storing perishables are usually limited, requiring almost daily cooking and shopping.

In addition to caring for their children, women must often take care of an elder family member, as nursing homes are rare and of poor quality. Many Russian parents are either unable or unwilling to put their children into daycare, and **ба́бушки** (grandmothers), who provide free childcare for their grandchildren, are what makes this system even remotely workable.

Not surprisingly, many Russian women have expressed that they would prefer to work part-time or not at all. Part-time work is rare, however, and most families cannot live on one person's salary. Many women are single parents. When they hear North American women talk about feminism, Russian women often think, "Who needs it? We already have equality, and it's killing us![3]"

УПРАЖНЕНИЯ

A. **Запо́лните про́пуски глаго́лами в ско́бках в настоя́щем вре́мени.**
(Fill in the blanks with the verbs in parentheses in the present tense.)

1. Он мне _____ приве́т ка́ждую неде́лю. (передава́ть)
2. Де́ти _____ сли́шком мно́го вопро́сов. (задава́ть)
3. Я весь день _____ до́ма потому́, что я больна́. (остава́ться)
4. Ты никогда́ не _____ свою́ бы́вшую сотру́дницу! (узнава́ть)
5. Моя́ тётя _____ кварти́ру америка́нцам. (сдава́ть)

---

3. For a good description of the typical Russian woman's daily routine, read Natalia Baranskaya's short piece, **Неде́ля как неде́ля** (A Week Like Any Other).

B. Подбери́те соотве́тствующие предложе́ния в коло́нке А к глаго́лам в коло́нке Б. (Match the sentences in column A to the verbs in column B.)

A

1. Я ча́сто _____ в па́рке по́сле рабо́ты.
2. Я вчера́ _____ в па́рке по́сле рабо́ты.
3. На́ши америка́нские друзья́ _____ че́рез час.
4. На́ши америка́нские друзья́ ча́сто _____ в Москву́.
5. Во ско́лько ты _____ Са́шку?
6. Вчера́ я проспа́л, и на́до бы́ло _____ на рабо́ту.
7. Она́ всегда́ _____ дете́й куда́-то на маши́не.
8. Вы _____ из Москвы́ ка́ждый уике́нд?
9. Вы _____ из Москвы́ в э́тот уике́нд?
10. Я люблю́ _____ но́чью.

B

a. отвезёшь
b. прилета́ют
c. уе́дете
d. побе́гал
e. уезжа́ете
f. лета́ть
g. бе́гаю
h. во́зит
i. прилетя́т
j. бежа́ть
k. приношу́

C. Запо́лните про́пуски слова́ми «зате́м», «пото́м», «тогда́». (Fill in the blanks with зате́м, пото́м, or тогда́.)

1. Я пло́хо себя́ чу́вствую. —О, _____ ты не должна́ идти́ в шко́лу.
2. Обы́чно я кормлю́ дете́й и провожа́ю их в шко́лу, а _____ я ем и чита́ю газе́ту.
3. Он при́нял душ, побри́лся и _____ оде́лся.
4. Мы до́лго жи́ли в Оде́ссе, а _____ жи́ли в Петербу́рге.
5. Мы _____ не говори́ли по-англи́йски.

D. Подбери́те соотве́тствующие ру́сские несоверше́нные глаго́лы к англи́йским значе́ниям, и дайте их соверше́нный ви́д. (Match the imperfective verbs with their English meanings, and give the perfective counterparts.)

1. провожа́ть
2. помога́ть
3. загора́ть
4. продолжа́ть
5. закрыва́ть
6. пока́зывать

a. to close
b. to figure out
c. to tidy up
d. to spend [time], to lead
e. to see off
f. to get dressed

7. **расска́зывать**
8. **убира́ть**
9. **реша́ть**
10. **проводи́ть**

g. to help
h. to sunbathe
i. to show
j. to tell about
k. to continue

УРОК 24

ЗАПОЛНЕНИЕ АНКЕТ. Filling out forms.

А. ДИАЛОГ

У врача.

БОБ: Здравствуйте. У меня приём у доктора Петрова.

СЕКРЕТАРЬ: Да, вы записаны на два часа. Доктор просил вас заполнить эту анкету. Здесь вопросы о вас и о вашей семье.

БОБ: Хорошо. (читает вслух) Возраст? Сорок лет. Дата рождения? Гмм ... Можно задать вопрос?

СЕКРЕТАРЬ: Да, пожалуйста.

БОБ: Как пишется по-русски дата рождения?

СЕКРЕТАРЬ: Когда вы родились?

БОБ: Восьмого декабря тысяча девятьсот пятьдесят седьмого года.

СЕКРЕТАРЬ: Пишите так: 8/XII/1957.

БОБ: Спасибо. Так. (читает вслух) Женат/замужем? Да. Сколько детей? Двое. Возраст? Два года и восемь лет. Извините, какое сегодня число?

СЕКРЕТАРЬ: Двадцать второе февраля.

БОБ: Спасибо. Так, всё.

СЕКРЕТАРЬ: Ещё вопрос: вы или кто-нибудь в вашей семье лежали в больнице из-за серьёзной болезни?

БОБ: Нет.

СЕКРЕТАРЬ: Вы не знаете, умер ли кто-нибудь в семье от рака или инфаркта?

БОБ: Да, моя бабушка умерла от инфаркта.

СЕКРЕТАРЬ: Садитесь, пожалуйста. Я вас позову, когда доктор сможет вас принять.

At the doctor's.

BOB: Good morning. I have an appointment with Doctor Petrov.

SECRETARY: Yes, I have you down here for 2 p.m. The doctor requested that you fill out this form. It asks about you and your family.

BOB: Fine. *(reading aloud)* Age? Forty. Date of birth? Hmm . . . Can I ask you a question?

SECRETARY: Yes, go ahead.

BOB: How do I write my date of birth in Russian?

SECRETARY: When were you born?

BOB: December 8, 1957.

SECRETARY: Write it like this: 8/XII/1957.

BOB: Thanks. So. *(reading aloud)* Married? Yes. How many children? Two. Their ages? Two and eight. Excuse me, what's today's date?

SECRETARY: February twenty-second.

BOB: Thanks. Okay, that's it.

SECRETARY: One more question: have you or anyone in your family been in the hospital with a serious illness?

BOB: No.

SECRETARY: And has anyone in your family died of cancer or a heart attack?

BOB: Yes, my grandmother died of a heart attack.

SECRETARY: Please have a seat, and I'll call you when the doctor's ready to see you.

B. ГРАММАТИКА И СЛОВОУПОТРЕБЛЕНИЕ

1. THE DATE AND THE YEAR

In **Уро́к** 12 you learned how to state the date, including the day and month. To specify the year as well, the final number of the year must be ordinal and genitive singular (**-ого**), followed by **го́да** ("year" in the genitive singular). The century (**ты́сяча ___сот**) can be omitted if it is clear from context, especially when referring to the current century.[1]

Како́го числа́? —Восьмо́го декабря́ (ты́сяча девятьсо́т) пятьдеся́т седьмо́го го́да.

On what date (when)? —December 8, 1957.

Мы бы́ли в Москве́ в ма́е (ты́сяча девятьсо́т) пятьдеся́т седьмо́го го́да.

We were in Moscow in May, 1957.

в октябре́ (ты́сяча девятьсо́т) шестьдеся́т пя́того го́да

in October of 1965

When simply stating the year in which an event took place (i.e. without the day and month), the year is introduced by the preposition **в,** and the ordinal number at the end is in the prepositional singular (**-ом**), as is **году́** ("year" in the prepositional singular).

В како́м году́? —В (ты́сяча девятьсо́т) пятьдеся́т седьмо́м году́.

In what year? —In 1957.

в ты́сяча восемьсо́т девяно́сто восьмо́м году́

in 1898

Since years are rarely written out as words, the sentence above would be written:

В како́м году́? —В 57-о́м году́.

In what year? —In '57.

---

1. Note that Russians never say the equivalent of "nineteen fifty-seven."

Remember that if the year is a compound number, only the last word in the number ends in **-ого** or **-ом**. If the year ends in 0, it also ends in **-ого** or **-ом**.

в ию́не сорокового го́да
in June (of) 1940

в пятидеся́том году́ и в восьмидеся́том году́
in 1950 and in 1980

Dates are usually abbreviated in writing. Remember that the day always precedes the month. December 8, 1957 can be written as: **8 дек. 1957 г.**, 8.12.57, or 8/XII/1957.

You should be able to understand a year when it is spoken at normal speed (i.e. quickly), to write a given year either in abbreviated form or as numerals, and to pronounce the year of your birth and the years of any other such life-cycle events.

2. COLLECTIVE NUMBERS

Collective numbers are often used when referring to a number of people, usually two, three, or four. "Two" is **дво́е**, "three" is **тро́е**, and "four" is **че́тверо**. They are declined similarly to special modifiers.

NOMINATIVE	дво́е	тро́е	че́тверо
ACCUSATIVE INANIMATE	дво́е	тро́е	че́тверо
ACCUSATIVE ANIMATE	двои́х	трои́х	четверы́х
GENITIVE	двои́х	трои́х	четверы́х
DATIVE	двои́м	трои́м	четверы́м
INSTRUMENTAL	двои́ми	трои́ми	четырьмя́
PREPOSITIONAL	о двои́х	о трои́х	о четверы́х

Ско́лько у вас дете́й? —Дво́е.
How many children do you have? —Two.

Сто́лик на трои́х?
A table for three [people]?

У вас есть ко́мната на четверы́х?
Do you have a room for four [people]?

3. EXPRESSING "TO ASK"

There are three Russian verbs that mean "to ask," but each is used differently.

VERB	FOLLOWED BY	MEANING
спра́шивать/спроси́ть		to ask for information
проси́ть/попроси́ть	что у кого́	to request, ask someone for something
	кого́ + infinitive	to request, ask someone to do something
задава́ть/зада́ть	вопро́с	to ask a question

Note that **спра́шивать** is not followed by an object or an infinitive.

Секрета́рь спра́шивает о семье́ Бо́ба.
The secretary is asking about Bob's family.

Мо́жно зада́ть вопро́с?
Can I ask you a question?

До́ктор проси́л вас запо́лнить э́ту анке́ту.
The doctor requested that you fill out this form.

Они́ про́сят у меня́ де́ньги.
They're asking me for money.

4. THE VERBS РАСТИ́ (TO GROW UP) AND УМИРА́ТЬ (TO DIE)

Both **умира́ть/умере́ть** (to die) and **расти́** (to grow)/**вы́расти** (to grow up) are regular verbs with irregular perfective past tense forms.

	вы́расти	умере́ть
MASCULINE	вы́рос	у́мер
FEMININE	вы́росла	умерла́
NEUTER	вы́росло	у́мерло
PLURAL	вы́росли	у́мерли

Умер ли кто́-нибудь в ва́шей семье́ от ра́ка и́ли инфа́ркта?
Has anyone in your family died of cancer or a heart attack?

Моя тётя умерла́ от ра́ка.

My aunt died of cancer.

Где вы вы́росли? —Я вы́рос в Бо́стоне.

Where did you grow up? —I grew up in Boston.

5. СВОЙ VERSUS МОЙ

As you learned in **Уро́к** 7, **свой** means "one's own." It can be used instead of a specific possessive modifier whenever the possessive refers back to the subject. **Свой** is declined like **мой** or **твой.**

Я забыва́ю во́зраст своего́ сы́на.

I forget my son's age.

Они́ оста́вили свой уче́бники до́ма.

They left their textbooks at home.

In the third person, *only* **свой** can be used to express "one's own." A specific possessive modifier implies "someone else's."

Боб заполня́ет свою́ анке́ту.

Bob is filling out his (own) form.

Боб заполня́ет его́ анке́ту.

Bob is filling out his (someone else's) form.

Note that **свой** *cannot* be used as part of the subject or in the nominative case (except in certain idiomatic expressions). Instead the specific possessive modifier must be used.

Вы и́ли кто́-нибу́дь в ва́шей семье́ неда́вно бы́ли в бо́льнице?

Have you or anyone in your family been in the hospital recently?

Моя́ ба́бушка умерла́ от инфа́ркта.

My grandmother died of a heart attack.

C. СЛОВАРЬ

анке́та	form, questionnaire
больни́ца	hospital
боле́знь	f. illness
В како́м году́?	In what year?
во́зраст	age
врач	general practitioner
вслух	aloud
да́та рожде́ния	date of birth
дво́е	two (of them)
жена́т	married (for men only)
за́мужем	married (for women only)
задава́ть (задаю́, задаёшь, задаю́т)/ *зада́ть* (зада́м, зада́шь, зада́дут) (вопро́с)	to ask (a question)
запи́сан/-а/-ы	to be registered/entered (for something)
заполня́ть (заполня́ю, заполня́ешь, заполня́ют) /*запо́лнить* (запо́лню, запо́лнишь, запо́лнят)	to fill in
звать (зову́, зовёшь, зову́т)/по-	to call, to summon; to name
инфа́ркт	heart attack
Как пи́шется … ?	How is . . . written?
Како́го числа́?	On what date? When?
Како́е сего́дня число́?	What's today's date?
поликли́ника	clinic; health center
приём (у кого́)	appointment (with someone)
проси́ть (прошу́, про́сишь, про́сят)/по-	to request
расти́ (расту́, растёшь, расту́т)/вы-	to grow/to grow up
рожда́ться (рожда́юсь, рожда́ешься, рожда́ются)/ *роди́ться* (рожу́сь, роди́шься, родя́тся)	to be born
свой	one's own
серьёзный	serious
тро́е	three (of them)
умира́ть (умира́ю, умира́ешь, умира́ют) /*умере́ть* (умру́, умрёшь, умру́т)	to die
че́тверо	four (of them)

РУССКАЯ КУЛЬТУРА

For Russians, medical care is free, but it can be difficult to get an appointment with a doctor, and hospitals are often understaffed. Furthermore, good medical care and equipment are generally found only in larger cities. Hospital patients often arrange for family to take care of them, or pay a nurse's aide (**ня́ня**, female; **санита́р**, male) extra to ensure proper care. The majority of Russian doctors are women, although men still tend to hold the highest-ranking positions. Nurses can be male (**медбра́т**) or female (**медсестра́**), though they, too, are overwhelmingly female.

When travelling to Russia, it is a good idea to bring along any medicines that you use, as well as a spare pair of glasses or contact lenses, as these things may be difficult to procure there. In major cities such as Moscow and St. Petersburg, there are special clinics for foreigners and other privately-owned clinics that care for both foreigners and Russians who can afford their care. These have bilingual staff and possibly some Western doctors. In an emergency, dial O3 for a **ско́рая по́мощь** (an ambulance).

УПРАЖНЕНИЯ

A. **Напиши́те ука́занную да́ту и́ли год в слова́х и́ли в чи́слах.** (Write out the requested date or year in words or in numbers as indicated.)

1. Write in numerals: **ты́сяча девятьсо́т девяно́сто седьмо́й год.**
2. Write answer in words: **В како́м году́ вы бы́ли в Петербу́рге?** ('92)
3. Translate: **Я там была́ в пятьдеся́т девя́том году́.**
4. Write answer in words: **Како́го числа́?** (2/XII/1986)
5. Write answer in words: **Когда́ вы роди́лись?** (5.6.63)

B. **Переведи́те на ру́сский.** (Translate into Russian.)

1. three children
2. a table for four
3. a room for two
4. the father of two children
5. story (**расска́з**) about four children

C. Заполните пропуски глаголами «спрашивать/спросить», «просить/попросить» или «задавать/задать», а затем переведите предложения на английский. (Fill in the blanks with the verbs спрашивать/спросить, просить/попросить, or задавать/ задать, and then translate the sentences into English.)

1. Я _____ , где находится поликлиника.
2. Он _____ хорошие вопросы.
3. Они _____ у меня информацию.
4. Они _____ меня, где находится поликлиника.
5. Мы его _____ нам помочь.

D. Переведите слова в скобках на русский и заполните пропуски. (Translate the words in parentheses into Russian, and fill in the blanks.)

1. Кто здесь _____ ? (died)
2. Сталин _____ в Грузии. (grew up)
3. Его бабушка и дедушка _____ в Ленинграде в 1944-ом году. (died)
4. Мама _____ на восточном побережье в США. (grew up)
5. В каком городе вы _____ ? (grew up)

УРОК 25

ПОКУПКИ В УНИВЕРМАГЕ. Shopping in a department store.

A. ДИАЛОГ

В Гости́ном дворе́, в Петербу́рге.

ЭЛЛЕН: *Ты зна́ешь, мне действи́тельно ну́жно купи́ть ша́пку. Я не ожида́ла тако́го моро́за!*

ЛИЗА: *Я спрошу́, где они ... Извини́те, где отде́л головны́х убо́ров?*

ПРОДАВЕЦ: *На второ́м этаже́, ря́дом с же́нской оде́ждой.*

В отде́ле головны́х убо́ров.

ЛИЗА: *Что ты предпочита́ешь: мех и́ли шерсть? По-мо́ему, мех лу́чше.*

ПРОДАВЕЦ: *У нас мно́го мо́дных ша́пок, не́которые из них меховы́е. Меховы́е ша́пки недешёвые, но о́чень тёплые, а зима́ у нас обы́чно холо́дная и ве́треная.*

ЭЛЛЕН: *Ну, ла́дно. Я приме́рю мехову́ю ша́пку. Я ношу́ седьмо́й америка́нский разме́р.*

ПРОДАВЕЦ: *Вот 54 ра́змер. Мне ка́жется, что вам она́ подойдёт.*

ЭЛЛЕН: *(ме́рит ша́пку) Она́ сли́шком больша́я. У вас есть 53?*

ПРОДАВЕЦ: *Да, пожа́луйста.*

ЭЛЛЕН: *Она́ мне о́чень идёт, и она́ така́я краси́вая и удо́бная! Как ты счита́ешь?*

ЛИЗА: *Она́ тебе́ идёт. Ты вы́глядишь, как ру́сская же́нщина в э́той ша́пке.*

ЭЛЛЕН: *Спаси́бо ... Хорошо́, я её беру́. Где плати́ть?*

ПРОДАВЕЦ: *Заплати́те в ка́ссу и принеси́те мне чек, пожа́луйста.*

At Gostiny Dvor, in St. Petersburg.

ELLEN: You know, I really should buy a hat. I didn't expect it to be so cold!

LIZA: I'll ask where they are . . . Excuse me, where is the hat department?

SALESMAN: On the second floor, next to women's apparel.

At the hat department.

LIZA: Which do you prefer: fur or wool? In my opinion, fur is better.

SALESMAN: We have many nice hats, some of them fur. Fur hats aren't cheap, but they are very warm, and our winters are usually cold and windy.

ELLEN: Well, alright. I'll try a fur hat. I wear an American size 7.

SALESMAN: Here's a size 54. I think it will fit you.

ELLEN: *(tries it on)* It's too big. Do you have a 53?

SALESMAN: Yes, here you are.

ELLEN: This fits perfectly, and it's so beautiful and comfortable! What do you think?

LIZA: It looks great on you. You look like a Russian woman in that hat.

ELLEN: Thanks . . . Okay, I'll take it. Where do I pay?

SALESMAN: You pay the cashier, and then bring the receipt back to me, please.

В. ГРАММАТИКА И СЛОВОУПОТРЕБЛЕНИЕ

1. ПО PLUS THE DATIVE CASE

In addition to being a prefix for verbs, e.g. **пойти, по** can also stand on its own as a preposition. When used with the dative case, **по** can mean:

a. "on; in" with time expressions; "on; along"; "on the subject of, in the field of."

Она́ по среда́м рабо́тает по утра́м.
On Wednesdays she works in the mornings.

Шла Са́ша по шоссе́.
Sasha was walking along the highway.

Она́ преподаёт курс по англи́йскому языку́ и америка́нской культу́ре.
She teaches a course on English language and American culture.

b. "by; over"; "by; according to, in accordance with"; "by; in respect to"; "by (reason of); on account of; from."

Я получи́ла по по́чте э́ту запи́ску.
I received this note by mail.

Всё идёт по расписа́нию.
Everything's going according to (by) schedule.

Кто вы по профе́ссии? —Я писа́тель.
What are you by profession? —I'm a writer.

Он сего́дня оста́лся до́ма по боле́зни.
He stayed home today because (by reason of) of illness.

c. "around; about."

Эллен и Ли́за ходи́ли по магази́нам.
Ellen and Liza were going around the stores (shopping).

d. the object of a feeling.

Ты скуча́ешь по до́му?
Are you homesick (do you miss your home)?

As you continue to learn Russian, you will encounter **по** used with other cases.

2. "TO FIT, TO SUIT"

To say that a piece of apparel fits or suits someone, use the verbs подходи́ть/подойти́ or идти́. The person you are talking about is in the dative case, and the article of clothing is in the nominative.

Мне ка́жется, что вам э́то подойдёт.
I think it will fit you.

Э́та ша́пка мне о́чень идёт, и она́ така́я краси́вая и удо́бная!
This hat fits perfectly, and it's so beautiful and comfortable!

Она́ тебе́ о́чень идёт.
It looks great on you (it suits you).

3. EXPRESSING OPINIONS

In Russian, there are two common ways to indicate that an opinion is being expressed. The first is по- plus a possessive modifier in the dative case, e.g. по-ва́шему (in your opinion). Note that with его́, её, and их, the dative noun мне́нию (opinion) must be used, as well.

По-мо́ему, мех лу́чше.
In my opinion, fur is better.

Как по-тво́ему?
What do you (informal) think? (How is it in your opinion?)

По его́ мне́нию, охо́титься гре́шно, и никто́ не до́лжен носи́ть мех.
According to him, hunting is wrong, and no one should wear fur.

Second, you can use the reflexive verb каза́ться/показа́ться (to seem), with the person whose opinion is being expressed in the dative case. Or you can use the verb счита́ть (to consider), with the person whose opinion is being expressed in the nominative.

Мне ка́жется, что вам э́то пойдёт.
I think (it seems to me that) it will fit you.

Как э́то Ли́зе показа́лось? —Ей э́то показа́лось о́чень до́рого.
What did Liza think? —It seemed expensive to her.

Как ты счита́ешь? —Я счита́ю, что э́ти брю́ки тебе́ иду́т.

What do you think? —I think that those pants look good on you.

4. VERBS WITH CONSONANT MUTATIONS/STRESS SHIFTS

Each verb in the vocabulary section is listed by infinitive, followed by its **я**-form, **ты**-form, and **они́**-form.[1] The reason for this is that changes are most likely to occur in the first person singular, and often in the third person plural as well, while the second person singular always reflects the "regular" pattern of the verb, i.e., the stem and the stress pattern of the verb. There are too many different patterns of consonant mutation and stress shift to list, so you must simply rely on your ear and learn them as you go. When you first learn a verb, notice whether the **я** form or both the **я** and the **они́** forms undergo consonant mutations or stress shifts. This will make memorizing conjugations much easier. Following are some common verbs that undergo such changes.

	купи́ть to buy	спроси́ть to ask	ходи́ть to go	смотре́ть to watch	мочь to be able to	сказа́ть to say
я	куплю́	спрошу́	хожу́	смотрю́	могу́	скажу́
ты	ку́пишь	спро́сишь	хо́дишь	смо́тришь	мо́жешь	ска́жешь
он/она́	ку́пит	спро́сит	хо́дит	смо́трит	мо́жет	ска́жет
мы	ку́пим	спро́сим	хо́дим	смо́трим	мо́жем	ска́жем
вы	ку́пите	спро́сите	хо́дите	смо́трите	мо́жете	ска́жете
они́	ку́пят	спро́сят	хо́дят	смо́трят	мо́гут	ска́жут

Я ношу́ седьмо́й америка́нский разме́р.

I wear an American size 7.

Я спрошу́, где отде́л мужско́й оде́жды.

I'll ask where the men's clothing department is.

Ты хорошо́ чи́стишь зу́бы? —Да, я их хорошо́ чи́щу.

Are you brushing your teeth well? —Yes, I'm brushing them well.

Я заплачу́. —Нет, нет, мы запла́тим. Ты наш гость.

I'll pay. —No, no, we'll pay. You're our guest!

---

1. Except for the completely irregular verbs **дать, есть, хоте́ть,** where the entire conjugation is given.

5. EXPRESSING PROXIMITY

There are several different ways to say "next to" in Russian. **Ря́дом с** plus the instrumental means "alongside, side by side with"; **во́зле** plus the genitive means "by, near, past"; and **у** plus the genitive means "by, in the general area of, at."

На второ́м этаже́, ря́дом с же́нской оде́ждой.
On the second floor, alongside (next to) women's apparel.

Он сиди́т ря́дом с ней.
He's sitting side by side with (next to) her.

Стул стоя́л у окна́.
The chair was by (next to) the window.

Ли́за стоя́ла во́зле окна́.
Liza stood near (next to) the window.

С. СЛОВА́РЬ

ве́треный	windy
во́зле (чего́)	by, near, past, next to (something)
го́лый	bare
головно́й убо́р	headgear
гре́шно	wrong (morally)
действи́тельно	really
дешёвый	cheap, inexpensive
же́нский	women's, feminine
каза́ться (кажу́сь, ка́жешься, ка́жутся)/по- (кому́)	to seem (to someone)
ме́рить (ме́рю, ме́ришь, ме́рят)/при-	to try on; to measure
мех	fur
мехово́й	made of fur
мо́дный	stylish
моро́з	bitter cold, frost
мужско́й	men's, masculine
не́который	some (of them); certain
носи́ть (ношу́, но́сишь, но́сят)	to wear; to carry (imp.)
оде́жда	apparel
ожида́ть (ожида́ю, ожида́ешь, ожида́ют)	to expect (imp.)

Два́дцать пя́тый уро́к

отде́л	department
охо́титься (охо́чусь, охо́тишься, охо́тятся)	to hunt (for)
плати́ть (плачу́, пла́тишь, пла́тят)/**за-**	to pay (for)
по-(чьему́)	in (someone's) opinion
подходи́ть (подхожу́, подхо́дишь, подхо́дят) /**подойти́** (подойду́, подойдёшь, подойду́т) (кому́)	to fit, to suit (someone)
покупа́ть (покупа́ю, покупа́ешь, покупа́ют) /**купи́ть** (куплю́, ку́пишь, ку́пят)	to buy
предпочита́ть (предпочита́ю, предпочита́ешь, предпочита́ют)/**предпоче́сть** (предпочту́, предпочтёшь, предпочту́т)	to prefer
продаве́ц/продавщи́ца	salesperson (m./f.)
ря́дом с (кем/чем)	next to, alongside, side by side with
разме́р	size
счита́ть (счита́ю, счита́ешь, счита́ют) /**счесть** (сочту́, сочтёшь, сочту́т)	to consider; to count
те́ло	body
тёплый	warm
универма́г	department store
чек	check, slip, receipt
ша́пка	fur hat
шерсть	f. wool
Это (кому́) **идёт.**	It fits/suits (someone).

РУССКАЯ КУЛЬТУРА

Although there are many smaller stores that specialize in one or a few items, travelers to Russia will most likely shop at a large **универма́г** (department store) or **торго́вый центр** (mall). The most famous and impressive are **ГУМ** (**Госуда́рственный универса́льный магази́н**) and **Охо́тный ряд** in Moscow and **Гости́ный двор** in St. Petersburg. These stores are similar to American department stores, but the layout is more like that of an American mall. They are divided into **отде́лы** (departments), which sell women's, men's, and children's clothing, toys, shoes, Russian **сувени́ры** (souvenirs), handicrafts, and many other things.

Russian clothing items of particular interest to travelers are fine wool shawls, fur[2] hats, and ethnic or national clothing particular to each area. These can often be found in the department stores. When buying clothing in Russia, be sure to try it on, as returning items for exchange or refund is not customary. Getting clothing altered is more common there, but it is usually done by a tailor rather than in a store. Russian clothing sizes, like European sizes, use the metric system.

In stores, items are usually not out on racks or shelves, but behind the sales counter, and you must ask the salesperson to get each one for you. To purchase an item, you must first obtain a sales slip from the salesperson, pay the specified amount at the **касса** (cashier), and then present the receipt to the salesperson in exchange for your purchase. Also, since most stores are arranged into smaller departments, each of which does its own bookkeeping, you must tell the cashier in which department you are making a purchase, and obtain a separate check to give to each salesperson. This three-step **касса** system is used in most stores, including food stores.

УПРАЖНЕНИЯ

A. **Подберите предложения из колонки A, соответствующие значениям по/по- в колонке Б. Употребите один ответ два раза.** (Match the sentences in column A to the meanings of **по/по-** in column B. Use one answer twice.)

A		B	
1. <u>По</u> дороге домой только одна запра́вка (gas station).		a.	According to
		b.	(in the [language] manner)
2. У нас бу́дет экску́рсия <u>по</u> го́роду.		c.	by
3. Я е́хала <u>по</u> у́лице.		d.	for (object of feeling)
4. <u>По-мо́ему</u>, Ра́нди вы́глядит хорошо́.		e.	on
		f.	for a while
5. Она́ почти́ всё вы́учила к экза́мену <u>по</u> фи́зике.		g.	along
		h.	about (on the subject of)

---

2. Fur items are used in Russia for practical reasons: to protect against extreme cold. There has been some recognition of the need to preserve wildlife, especially of species threatened with extinction, but much more needs to be done. The same is true of the environment.

Два́дцать пя́тый уро́к

6. Мы не поéхали <u>по</u> причи́не плохо́й   i. around
погóды.   j. on account of (due to)

7. Эллен скучáет <u>по</u> дóму.

8. Илья́ хóдит в лаборатóрию <u>по</u>
средáм.

9. Ты говори́шь <u>по-рýсски</u>.

10. Они́ <u>погуля́ли</u> в пáрке.

B.   Переведи́те на англи́йский. (Translate into English.)

    1. Ты счита́ешь, что онá сли́шком мáленькая?

    2. Эта шáпка ей пойдёт.

    3. Эта шáпка ей идёт.

    4. Тебé кáжется, что онá сли́шком мáленькая?

    5. Шáпки ей идýт.

C.   Запóлните прóпуски. (Fill in the blanks.)

    1. Какóй размéр ты нóсишь? —Я _____ 52 размéр.

    2. Какóй хлеб ты печёшь? —Я _____ слáдкий хлеб.

    3. Как чáсто ты чи́стишь зýбы? —Я _____ зýбы два рáза в день.

    4. Скóлько ты плáтишь в мéсяц? —Я _____ пятьсóт дóлларов в
мéсяц.

    5. Ты лю́бишь меня́? —Да, я, конéчно, тебя́ _____ !

    6. Что ты кýпишь? —Я _____ тёплую шáпку.

    7. Ты спрóсишь, где егó кабинéт? —Да, я _____ чéрез секýндочку.

    8. Ты чáсто хóдишь в кинó? —Да, я _____ в кинó кáждую
недéлю.

    9. На что ты смóтришь? —Я _____ на э́ти краси́вые плáтья.

    10. Ты мóжешь пойти́ со мной? —Нет, к сожалéнию, не _____ .

D.   Постáвьте словá в скóбках в нýжную фóрму и запóлните прóпуски.
Не забýдьте добáвить предлóги, éсли нýжно. (Put the words in
parentheses into the correct form and fill in the blanks. Remember to add a
preposition if necessary.)

    1. Кто сиди́т ря́дом _____? (бáбушка)

    2. Мужчи́на продаёт билéты вóзле _____ . (вход)

    3. Библиотéка ря́дом _____ , в котóром я рабóтаю. (здáние)

    4. Мать сиди́т у _____ своегó ребёнка. (кровáть)

    5. Они́ живýт в дóме ря́дом _____ . (наш)

ПЯТАЯ ПРОВЕРКА (Fifth Review)

A. **Запо́лните про́пуски глаго́лами в ско́бках и переведи́те предложе́ния.** (Fill in the blanks with the verbs in parentheses, and translate the sentences.)

1. Утром я _____ в семь часо́в, _____ в полвосьмо́го и _____ окно́. (просыпа́ться/просну́ться, встава́ть/встать, закрыва́ть/закры́ть)
2. Зате́м я _____ душ, _____ и _____ . (принима́ть/приня́ть, бри́ться/по-, одева́ться/оде́ться)
3. Пото́м я немно́жко _____ кварти́ру и _____ газе́ту, когда́ я _____ чай и _____ ка́шу. (убира́ть/убра́ть, чита́ть/про-, пить/вы́-, есть/с-)
4. По́сле э́того я _____ зу́бы и _____ на рабо́ту. (чи́стить/почи́стить, ходи́ть/идти́/пойти́)
5. Я всегда́ _____ в буфе́те, где я _____ со свои́м сотру́дником, Петро́м Ива́новичем. (обе́дать/по-, сиде́ть/по-)
6. Когда́ я _____ за обе́д, он всегда́ _____ : «Почему́ вы _____ обе́д? Лу́чше его́ _____ из до́ма!» (плати́ть/за-, спра́шивать/спроси́ть, покупа́ть/купи́ть, приноси́ть/принести́)
7. Ка́ждый день он _____ мне э́тот вопро́с. Он _____ , что я _____ де́ньги. (задава́ть/зада́ть, счита́ть/счесть, теря́ть/по-)
8. Я ка́ждый день _____ ему́, что я _____ покупа́ть обе́д. (говори́ть/сказа́ть, предпочита́ть/предпоче́сть)
9. Но он _____ _____ свой вопро́с. Мне _____ , что он никогда́ не _____ ! (продолжа́ть/продо́лжить, повторя́ть/повтори́ть, каза́ться/по-, перестава́ть/переста́ть)
10. Одна́ко (However), я никогда́ не _____ , как он _____ мне _____ тру́дную пробле́му на рабо́те. (забыва́ть/забы́ть, помога́ть/помо́чь, реша́ть/реши́ть)

B. **Поста́вьте в проше́дшее вре́мя с «вчера́», а пото́м в бу́дущее с «за́втра».** (Put into the past tense with вчера́, and then into the future tense with за́втра.)

1. Во ско́лько он ухо́дит на рабо́ту?
2. Мои́ друзья́ даю́т мне хоро́ший сове́т.
3. Ба́бушка и де́душка привозят нам пода́рки, когда́ они приезжа́ют.
4. Мы мо́жем узна́ть его́ и́мя.
5. Что ты ешь на за́втрак?

C. **Переведи́те на ру́сский.** (Translate into Russian.)

1. She was born in Russia, but her children grew up in America.
2. The hat that she's wearing really suits her.
3. We asked him for a table for two.
4. I've spent a lot of time at my friends' in Moscow.
5. Let's take a stroll (**гуля́ть/по-**) around the park!
6. The bank I go to is next to (alongside) the post office.
7. In that case, let's go (fly) on March twenty-first.
8. He died of cancer in April, 1972.
9. What's her profession (Who is she by profession)? —She became a dentist in 1995.
10. Ugh, I hate filling out forms!

УРОК 26

СВАДЬБА. A wedding.

А. ДИАЛОГ

Джу́ди получа́ет приглаше́ние на сва́дьбу.

ДЖУДИ: *Ната́ша пригласи́ла меня́ на свою́ сва́дьбу в апре́ле!*

ЛЕНА: *Неуже́ли? Где?*

ДЖУДИ: *В це́ркви Свято́го Михаи́ла.*

ЛЕНА: *Здо́рово! Ты бу́дешь го́стьей на правосла́вной сва́дьбе!*

ДЖУДИ: *Как происхо́дит венча́ние?*

ЛЕНА: *Это о́чень торже́ственно. Жени́х и неве́ста несу́т свечи́, над голова́ми у них коро́ны. Ру́ки их свя́заны полоте́нцем.*

ДЖУДИ: *Почти́ как в сре́дние века́! Как они́ оде́ты?*

ЛЕНА: *На ней обы́чно бе́лое пла́тье и фата́, а на нём тёмный костю́м.*

ДЖУДИ: *Кста́ти об оде́жде, скажи́ мне, что я должна́ наде́ть, чего́ нельзя́ де́лать и так да́лее.*

ЛЕНА: *Пре́жде всего́ ты должна́ наде́ть пла́тье и́ли ю́бку и к тому́ же что́-то на го́лову. Кро́ме того́ да́же е́сли ты уста́нешь, нельзя́ сади́ться в це́ркви.*

ДЖУДИ: *Да́же больны́м и пожилы́м?*

ЛЕНА: *Коне́чно, им мо́жно сиде́ть. О, я чуть не забы́ла: ты заме́тила, что ру́сские но́сят обруча́льное кольцо́ на пра́вой руке́?*

ДЖУДИ: *(смо́трит на свою́ пра́вую ру́ку) Ой, вот почему́ все ду́мают, что я заму́жняя!*

———————

Judy receives a wedding invitation.

JUDY: Natasha's invited me to her wedding in April!

LENA: Really? Where?

JUDY: At St. Michael's Church.

LENA: Great! You'll be a guest at a Russian Orthodox weddir

JUDY: What happens during the ceremony?

LENA: It's very solemn. The bride and groom carry candles, and c
over their heads. Their hands are tied together with a towel.

JUDY: It sounds almost medieval. What do they wear?

LENA: She usually wears a white dress and a veil, and he wears a dark

JUDY: Speaking of clothes, tell me what to wear, what not to do, and so fo

LENA: First of all, you should wear a dress or a skirt, as well as something
your head. Besides that, even if you get tired, sitting in church is not allowe

JUDY: Even for sick or elderly people?

LENA: They're allowed to sit, of course. Oh, I almost forgot: did you notice that
Russians wear their wedding ring on their right hand?

JUDY: *(looking at her right hand)* Oh, so *that's* why everyone thinks I'm married!

B. ГРАММАТИКА И СЛОВОУПОТРЕБЛЕНИЕ

1. THE DATIVE CASE OF PLURAL ADJECTIVES AND SPECIAL MODIFIERS

The dative endings for plural adjectives and special modifiers are the same
across all genders. As with nouns, the dative plural forms are derived from the
nominative plural forms. For adjectives, simply replace the final -e with -м, and
for special modifiers, simply add -м. As always, the third person forms его, её
and их do not change.

	NOMINATIVE	DATIVE	EXAMPLE
ADJECTIVES	-ые	-ым	ста́рые » ста́рым
	-ие	-им	други́е » други́м
PECIAL MODIFIERS	-и	-им	мой » мои́м, э́ти » э́тим
	-е	-ем	все » всем

Да́же нельзя́ больны́м и пожилы́м? —Нет, им мо́жно сиде́ть.

It's even forbidden for the sick and elderly? —No, they're allowed to sit.

Всем на́шим ру́сским друзья́м понра́вился э́тот фильм.

All our Russian friends liked this movie.

Переда́й приве́т свои́м!

Say hello to your family (literally, your own)!

Note that the dative plural adjective endings are identical to the instrumental singular adjective endings. They can easily be distinguished by context, however.

2. THE INSTRUMENTAL AFTER СТАНОВИ́ТЬСЯ/СТАТЬ AND БЫТЬ

When a noun or adjective referring to a state of being, condition, or profession follows the verbs **быть** (to be) or **станови́ться/стать** (to become) in the infinitive, future, or imperative form, the noun or adjective must be in the instrumental case.

Здо́рово! Ты бу́дешь го́стьей на правосла́вной сва́дьбе!

Great! You'll be a guest at a Russian Orthodox wedding!

Она́ хо́чет стать инжене́ром.

She wants to become an engineer.

Будь всегда́ до́брым!

Always be nice/kind!

Твой план стано́вится сли́шком сло́жным.

Your plan is getting too complicated.

Два́дцать шесто́й уро́к

In the past tense, the instrumental is generally used only if the profession or condition was temporary. Otherwise, the nominative is used.

Кем был оте́ц неве́сты? —Он был врачо́м. Он сейча́с на пе́нсии.
What did the bride's father do? —He was a doctor. He's retired now.

Семья́ жениха́ была́ бога́той.
The groom's family used to be wealthy.

Кварти́ра ста́ла о́чень гря́зной, когда́ они́ там жи́ли.
The apartment became very dirty when they lived there.

Note that in Russian you say "Who (not what) do you want to be?", and that any profession following **рабо́тать** (to work) must also be in the instrumental case.

3. ASPECT WITH НЕЛЬЗЯ́ AND МО́ЖНО

The imperfective following **нельзя́** and **мо́жно** generally implies permission, while the perfective implies ability. So, **нельзя́** followed by an imperfective infinitive means "forbidden, prohibited, may not," while **нельзя́** followed by a perfective infinitive means "impossible, cannot."

Скажи́ мне, что на́до наде́ть, чего́ нельзя́ де́лать и так да́лее.
Tell me what to wear, what not to do (what is prohibited), and so forth.

В це́ркви да́же е́сли ты уста́нешь, нельзя́ сади́ться.
Even if you get tired in church, you may not sit down.

Нельзя́ войти́.
You can't get in (perhaps the door is broken or locked).

With **мо́жно,** this distinction is not as clear as with **нельзя́,** and the only way to be sure of the meaning is through context.

Мо́жно стоя́ть на коле́нях в це́ркви.
Kneeling in church is allowed.

Где мо́жно купи́ть сва́дебный пода́рок?
Where can I (where is it possible to) buy a wedding present?

Мо́жно входи́ть.

You may go in (it is permissible).

Do not confuse **мочь** (to be able to) with **мо́жно** or **нельзя́. Мочь** is used to express ability, possibility, or the lack thereof, from the standpoint of personal responsibility. **Мо́жно** and **нельзя́**, on the other hand, express possibility or impossibility due to external circumstances.

Э́то сли́шком тру́дно. Я не могу́ э́того сде́лать.

It's too difficult. I can't do it.

Нам о́чень жаль, что мы не могли́ прийти́ на венча́ние.

We're very sorry that we couldn't come to the ceremony.

Возмо́жно (it is possible, perhaps) and **невозмо́жно** (impossible) are similar to **мо́жно** and **нельзя́**, but they cannot be used in the sense of "forbidden" or "permitted."

Возмо́жно, что они́ поже́нятся.

Perhaps they're going to get married.

Э́то возмо́жно.

That's possible (that may be).

Э́то про́сто невозмо́жно.

That's simply impossible.

4. EXPRESSING "ALSO, BESIDES"

There are several different ways to express "also" in Russian:

то́же	also, too, as well
та́кже	also, too, as well
и	too
кро́ме того́	besides that, moreover, in addition to that
к тому́ же	besides, moreover, as well as

То́же and **та́кже** are often confused. **То́же** can only be used when two or more subjects are engaged in the same activity, while **та́кже** is used when one subject is engaged in two or more activities. **Та́кже** is often used after the conjunction **а**, while **то́же** cannot follow **а**.

Невеста надевает белое платье и фату, а также несёт свечу.
The bride wears a white dress and a veil, and carries a candle, too.

Я получила приглашение на свадьбу Наташи! —Я тоже.
I received an invitation to Natasha's wedding! —So did I (Me, too).

The conjunction и (and) can be used to mean "too, also, as well."

У нас принято и подарки дарить.
For us it's customary to also give gifts.

Её муж хорошо говорит по-английски. —Он понимает и по-немецки.
Her husband speaks English well. —He also understands German.

Note that **к тому же** and **кроме того** are quite similar, but not interchangeable. **Кроме того** generally introduces a sentence, and can be translated as "besides that." **К тому же** generally introduces a phrase.

Ты должна надеть платье или юбку и к тому же что-то на голову.
You should wear a dress or a skirt, as well as something on your head.

Кроме того, даже если ты устанешь, нельзя садиться в церкви.
Besides that, even if you get tired, you can't sit down in church.

5. ПОЧТИ VERSUS ЧУТЬ НЕ (ALMOST)

There are two ways to say "almost" in Russian: **почти** (not quite) and **чуть не** (very nearly/barely). **Чуть не** is used with perfective verbs and usually refers to averting an undesirable event, while **почти** can be used with almost any part of speech and in any context.

Звучит почти средневеково.
It sounds almost medieval.

О, я чуть не забыла: кольцо на правой руке значит, что ты замужняя.
Oh, I almost forgot: a ring on your right hand means that you're married.

Сестра невесты чуть не пропустила свадьбу!
The bride's sister almost missed the wedding!

Он говори́т по-ру́сски почти́ без акце́нта.
He speaks Russian almost without an accent.

C. СЛОВА́РЬ

бога́тый	wealthy
брак	marriage
век	century, era
венча́ние	wedding ceremony
гость	guest
дари́ть (дарю́, да́ришь, да́рят)/по- (что–кому́)	to give a present (to someone)
дружки́ жениха́	the groom's attendants
жени́ться (женю́сь, же́нишься, же́нятся)/по-	to get married
жени́х	groom
заму́жняя	married (for women only)
и так да́лее (и т. д.)	and so forth; et cetera (etc.)
к тому́ же	besides, moreover
коро́на	crown
костю́м	suit
кро́ме того́	besides that, moreover
кста́ти	by the way; speaking of
ле́вый	left
неве́ста	bride
обруча́льное кольцо́	wedding ring
па́ра	couple, pair
подру́жка неве́сты	bridesmaids
пожило́й	elderly (noun or adjective)
полоте́нце	towel
почти́	almost, not quite
пра́вый	right
правосла́вный	Orthodox (adjective or noun)
при́нято (+ infinitive)	it's customary (to)
приглаша́ть (приглаша́ю, приглаша́ешь,приглаша́ют)/ **пригласи́ть** (приглашу́, пригласи́шь, приглася́т)	to invite
приглаше́ние	invitation
происходи́ть (происхо́дит, происхо́дят) /**произойти́** (произойдёт, произойду́т)	to be going on (imperfective only); to take place

пропуска́ть (пропуска́ю, пропуска́ешь, пропуска́ют)/ *пропусти́ть* (пропущу́, пропу́стишь, пропу́стят)	to miss, to skip, to let through
рука́	hand; arm
сади́ться (сажу́сь, сади́шься, садя́тся) */сесть* (ся́ду, ся́дешь, ся́дут) (куда́)	to sit down (somewhere)
свято́й	saint; holy, sacred, saintly
сва́дьба	wedding
свеча́	candle
сре́дний	middle, average (soft adjective)
сре́дние века́	the Middle Ages
станови́ться (становлю́сь, стано́вишься, стано́вятся)/ *стать* (ста́ну, ста́нешь, ста́нут)	to become, to grow, to stand, to start
та́кже	also, too, as well
торже́ственный	solemn
устава́ть (устаю́, устаёшь, устаю́т)/ *уста́ть* (уста́ну, уста́нешь, уста́нут)	to get tired, to be tired
фата́	veil
це́рковь	f. church
чуть не	almost, very nearly, barely averted

РУССКАЯ КУЛЬТУРА

Russians were traditionally a very religious people, but the overt practice of religion was restricted under the Soviet regime, except for the elderly. The advent of glasnost and perestroika brought a religious renaissance to the CIS. The buildings themselves—many of which the Soviets had turned into museums or warehouses or simply closed—were reclaimed as places of worship. Russian Orthodoxy regained its traditional status as the ancient religion of the Russians, and it remains the largest and most powerful religious organization in Russia today. Judaism, Islam, Buddhism, and other forms of Orthodoxy are also practiced, though to a significantly lesser degree, and religions new to Russia have also gained converts, among them the Hare Krishnas, the Mormons, the Christian Scientists, and the Baptists.

If you are planning to attend a service at a Russian Orthodox church, be prepared to stand. All Russian Orthodox Church ceremonies or services, including the wedding ceremony, tend to be quite long and solemn. There are no seats or pews in the main section of the church, although there are some seats on the perimeter for the elderly or ill. There is a fair amount of pageantry, and the prayers are generally in Old Church Slavonic, an older form of modern Russian. People generally pray to and light candles for one or more of the saints on the iconostasis, which usually covers the entire rear wall of the church and is often gorgeously decorated with gold leaf. Congregants cross themselves many times during a service, often touching their heads to the floor. Women must wear skirts or dresses and a head-covering, and men must remove their hats.

УПРАЖНЕНИЯ

A. **Запо́лните про́пуски по образцу́.** (Fill in the blanks according to the example.)

ОБРАЗЕ́Ц: <u>Ру́сским</u> нра́вится пить шампа́нское на сва́дьбе. (ру́сские)

1. Переда́й приве́т _____ . (твои́ хоро́шие друзья́)
2. _____ мо́жно, а де́тям нельзя́. (взро́слые)
3. Я помогла́ _____ . (америка́нские тури́сты)
4. _____ повезло́! (э́ти лю́ди)
5. _____ нужны́ их ма́тери. (все неве́сты)

B. **Переведи́те на англи́йский.** (Translate into English.)

1. Пого́да ста́ла сли́шком жа́ркой.
2. Кем ты хо́чешь стать?
3. Что он тепе́рь де́лает? — Он рабо́тает учи́телем.
4. Эта це́рковь ра́ньше была́ краси́вой.
5. В ию́не Илья́ ста́нет зубны́м врачо́м.

C. Подбери́те предложе́ния из коло́нки А, соотве́тствующие коло́нке Б.
(Match the sentences in column A to those in column B.)

A

1. Здесь мо́жно кури́ть?
2. Мо́жно войти́.
3. Мо́жно входи́ть.
4. Это невозмо́жно.
5. Да, возмо́жно.
6. Им нельзя́ здесь сесть.
7. Здесь нельзя́ сади́ться.
8. Нельзя́ есть на рабо́те.
9. Эту по́рцию нельзя́ съесть (to eat, perf.).
10. Мы мо́жем э́то сде́лать.

B

a. Она́ сейча́с не занята́.
b. Да, мо́жет быть в бу́дущем.
c. Здесь нет мест.
d. Нача́льник сказа́л, что нельзя́.
e. Телефо́н не рабо́тал.
f. Она́ сли́шком больша́я.
g. Это не о́чень тру́дно.
h. Коне́чно нет! Это це́рковь!
i. Ты прав. Этого не мо́жет быть.
j. Эти места́ зака́заны для семьи́.
k. Дверь не заперта́ (locked).

D. Переведи́те на ру́сский. (Translate into Russian.)

1. I (masculine) almost forgot to tell you (familiar) that Natasha called.
2. Almost everyone came to the wedding.
3. He's Russian. She's Russian, too.
4. She likes this color. — And this one, too?
5. My head hurts. Besides that, I feel sick (I don't feel well).

УРОК 27

ПОП-КУЛЬТУРА, НАРОДНАЯ МУЗЫКА. Popular culture, folk music.

А. ДИАЛОГ

На вечери́нке.

КОСТЯ: Рик, кто твой люби́мый ру́сский певе́ц?

РИК: Окуджа́ва.

КОСТЯ: Он бард! Ты не слу́шаешь поп-музыку?

РИК: Немно́жко.

ВЕРА: Эй Рик, како́й твой знак зодиа́ка?

РИК: Ове́н.

ВЕРА: Я так и зна́ла! Овны́ лю́бят носи́ть кра́сное.

КОСТЯ: Она́ всегда́ говори́т таку́ю ерунду́! Америка́нцы то́же ве́рят в астроло́гию?

РИК: Кто как.

ВЕРА: Не обраща́й внима́ния на него́. Он типи́чный Теле́ц—упря́мый. Если ты хо́чешь, я соста́влю твой гороско́п.

РИК: Почему́ бы и нет?

ВЕРА: Ла́дно, когда́ ты роди́лся: да́та и час?

РИК: Два́дцать тре́тьего а́вгуста се́мьдесят пя́того го́да в три часа́ утра́.

ВЕРА: А где?

РИК: Я из Гано́вера, кото́рый нахо́дится в двух часа́х к се́веру от Бо́стона, в шта́те Нью Гэ́мпшир.

ВЕРА: Како́е расстоя́ние ме́жду Бо́стоном и Гано́вером?

РИК: Около ста два́дцати миль.

ВЕРА: Отли́чно. Я за́втра расскажу́ тебе́ о твоём гороско́пе, ла́дно?

КОСТЯ: *Достáточно астролóгии. Рик, послýшай эту кассéту. Это Борúс Гребенщикóв ...*

At a party.

KOSTYA: Rick, who's your favorite Russian singer?

RICK: Okudzhava.

KOSTYA: He's a folk singer! Don't you listen to popular music?

RICK: A little.

VERA: Hey, Rick, what's your sign?

RICK: Aries.

VERA: I knew it! Aries love to wear red.

KOSTYA: She's always talking such nonsense! Do Americans believe in astrology, too?

RICK: Some do, some don't.

VERA: Don't pay any attention to him. He's a typical Taurus: stubborn. If you want, I'll do your horoscope.

RICK: Why not?

VERA: Okay, when were you born: the date and time?

RICK: On August 22nd, 1975, at 3 A.M.

VERA: And where?

RICK: I'm from Hanover, which is two hours north of Boston, in the state of New Hampshire.

VERA: What's the distance between Boston and Hanover?

RICK: About one hundred and twenty miles.

VERA: Great. I'll tell you about your horoscope tomorrow, alright?

KOSTYA: Enough astrology. Rick, listen to this cassette. It's Boris Grebenshikov . . .

B. ГРАММАТИКА И СЛОВОУПОТРЕБЛЕНИЕ

1. PREPOSITIONS REQUIRING THE INSTRUMENTAL CASE

The following prepositions usually take the instrumental,[1] though some may take other cases as well. They are prepositions of position, used to locate a noun literally or figuratively in relation to another noun in time or space.

ме́жду	between
под	under; near (a town)
над	over; above
пе́ред	in front of; just before (an event)
за	behind; on the other side of; beyond; for (to fetch)

Како́е расстоя́ние <u>ме́жду</u> Бо́стоном и Гано́вером?
What's the distance between Boston and Hanover?

<u>Над</u> чем ты смеёшься?
What are you laughing at (over)?

<u>Ме́жду</u> на́ми, я не ве́рю в астроло́гию.
Between you and me, I don't believe in astrology.

<u>Пе́ред</u> ва́ми ве́щи царя́ и его́ семьи́.
In front of (before) you are some belongings of the tsar and his family.

Ты душ при́мешь <u>пе́ред</u> у́жином? —Нет, <u>пе́ред</u> сном.
Are you going to take a shower (right) before dinner? — No, (right) before going to bed.

Жени́х и неве́ста несу́т све́чи, <u>над</u> голова́ми у них коро́ны.
The bride and groom carry candles, and crowns are held over their heads.

Но́ра Григо́рьевна рабо́тает <u>над</u> уче́бником.
Nora Grigorievna is working on a textbook.

Кни́га о побе́де <u>над</u> фаши́змом <u>под</u> мое́й сумко́й.
The book about the victory over Fascism is under my bag.

---

1. Except за, which, as you've learned, often takes the accusative.

Мы живём за городом под Москвой.

We live in a suburb near Moscow (literally, under Moscow).

Мы сидели за столом.

We were sitting at the table.

Он живёт за городом, а она живёт за границей.

He lives in the country (literally, beyond the city), and she lives abroad (beyond the border).

Note that, for a woman, the state of being married to someone is expressed with the instrumental, but the act of marrying someone is expressed with the accusative. Compare:

Она замужем за американцем.

She's married to an American.

Она вышла замуж за американца.

She married an American.

2. A SUMMARY OF ASPECT

The following chart summarizes the differences between imperfective and perfective verbs. Compare:

imperfective	perfective
<<————>>	– – – • – – –

imperfective	perfective
•emphasis on process, duration	•emphasis on completion, end result
•activity itself emphasized	•product of action (direct object) emphasized
•used in statements of fact	
•denotes habitual or repeated actions	•denotes one-time, complete actions or a series of actions
•used in past, present, and future tenses	•used in past and future tenses only
•required with adverbs of frequency (e.g. часто, обычно, всегда, редко, никогда)	•not associated with any particular adverbs
•corresponds to English "used to," simple present, or continuous "-ing" (past, present, or future)	•corresponds to English simple past or future
•"base" form of the verb	•imperfective verb + prefix or - suffix

You're already familiar with most of the information in this chart. The only new information is that only perfective actions can result in finished products. The product of such an action is a direct object. Imperfective verbs can also have direct objects, but those objects are not finished products *resulting* from an action. Compare the difference in meaning between the imperfective and perfective verbs below.

Ко́стя пи́шет письмо́.
Kostya is writing a letter.

Ко́стя написа́л письмо́.
Kostya wrote (completed) a letter.

Ве́ра составля́ет гороско́п.
Vera is working on the horoscope.

Ве́ра соста́вила гороско́п.
Vera did (completed) the horoscope.

In general, you should answer a question in the same aspect that it was asked.

О чём вы говори́ли? —Мы говори́ли об астроло́гии.
What were you talking about? — We were talking about astrology.

Что ты сказа́л? —Я сказа́л, что пора́ идти́.
What did you say? —I said that it's time to go.

Почему́ я не могу́ включи́ть ра́дио? —Оно́ не рабо́тает. Его́ нельзя́ включи́ть.
Why can't I turn the radio on? —It's broken. It's impossible to turn it on.

However, to emphasize a distinction between achieving a desired result and not achieving it, you may use a different aspect.[2]

Я весь день ему́ звони́ла. —Хорошо́, я за́втра ему́ позвоню́ на рабо́ту.
I was calling him all day (I didn't reach him). —Okay, I'll get him at work tomorrow.

3. THE PREPOSITIONS ИЗ, ОТ, AND С

When used with the genitive, these prepositions all mean "from," but they are used differently. Also, **из** and **от** can only be used with the genitive, but **с** can

---

2. Of course this only applies to verbs that have both imperfective and perfective forms.

Два́дцать седьмо́й уро́к

be used with either the genitive or the instrumental (see **Уро́к** 12, Instrumental Case of Pronouns).

Preposition	Refers to	Meanings with the Genitive Case
из	source	"from" (a source)
от	origin limits in time or space	(away) from a given point "from" (a time or place) when/where something begins protection from, evasion, riddance of
с	numerical limits in time or space	"from" (a number/date/time) since (a number or date)

Я из Гано́вера.

I'm from Hanover.

Оди́н из нас говори́т по-англи́йски.

One of (from) us speaks English.

Э́то я узна́л из газе́ты.

I learned that from the paper.

Гано́вер нахо́дится недалеко́ от Бо́стона.

Hanover is not far from Boston.

Да́йте, пожа́луйста, лека́рство от ка́шля.

Please give me some cough medicine.

С э́того моме́нта, на рабо́те вы рабо́таете. Ясно?

From this moment on, at work you work. Is that clear?

Ско́лько с меня́?

How much do I owe you (lit., How much from me?)

Although both **с** and **от** can be used with **до** to mean "from . . . to . . . " **с** is commonly used with numbers, and **от** otherwise.

Ско́лько киломе́тров от Москвы́ до Владивосто́ка?

How many kilometers is it from Moscow to Vladivostok?

Как пройти́ от Кра́сной пло́щади до Большо́го теа́тра?

How do you get from Red Square to the Bolshoi Theater?

Twenty-seventh Lesson

Когда́ мо́жно посла́ть телегра́мму? —С 9 (девяти́) часо́в до 5 (пяти́) часо́в.

When can I send a telegram? —From 9 A.M. to 5 P.M.

Он отдыха́ет с тре́тьего января́ до деся́того января́.

He's on vacation from January 3rd to January 10th.

4. VERBS WITH AN ADDED SOFT л

Any Conjugation II verb whose stem ends in the consonants б-, в-, м-, п-, or ф-
will have a soft -л- added before the ending in the first person singular *only*.

	люби́ть to love	соста́вить to form	терпе́ть to be patient	спать to sleep	корми́ть to feed
я	люблю́	соста́влю	терплю́	сплю	кормлю́
ты	лю́бишь	соста́вишь	те́рпишь	спишь	ко́рмишь
он/она́	лю́бит	соста́вит	те́рпит	спит	ко́рмит
мы	лю́бим	соста́вим	те́рпим	спим	ко́рмим
вы	лю́бите	соста́вите	те́рпите	спи́те	ко́рмите
они́	лю́бят	соста́вят	те́рпят	спят	ко́рмят

Каку́ю му́зыку ты лю́бишь? —Я лю<u>блю́</u> му́зыку Юлия Ки́ма.

What kind of music do you love? —I love Yulii Kim's music.

Е́сли ты хо́чешь, я соста́<u>влю</u> твой гороско́п.

If you want, I'll do your horoscope.

5. THE FOUR COMPASS POINTS

While in English we often use "north, south, etc." as adjectives, in Russian the
adjective forms must be used whenever an adjective is needed.

north	се́вер	се́верный	northern
south	юг	ю́жный	southern
east	восто́к	восто́чный	eastern
west	за́пад	за́падный	western

Гано́вер нахо́дится к се́веру от Босто́на.

Hanover is located to the north of Boston.

Два́дцать седьмо́й уро́к

Я живу́ на Да́льнем Восто́ке. А вы? —Я живу́ на восто́чном побере́жье США.

I live in the Far East. And you? —I live on the East(ern) Coast of the United States.

Они́ живу́т за грани́цей в За́падной Евро́пе.

They live abroad, in Western Europe.

6. THE TWELVE SIGNS OF THE ZODIAC

Astrology is popular in Russia, so don't be surprised if you are asked **Како́й твой/ваш знак зодиа́ка?** (What's your sign?) Following are the signs of the zodiac. Note that they are capitalized, just as in English.

Ове́н	Aries	Весы́	Libra
Теле́ц	Taurus	Скорпио́н	Scorpio
Близнецы́	Gemini	Стреле́ц	Sagittarius
Рак	Cancer	Козеро́г	Capricorn
Лев	Leo	Водоле́й	Aquarius
Де́ва	Virgo	Ры́бы	Pisces

Овны́ лю́бят носи́ть кра́сное.

Aries love to wear red.

Он типи́чный Теле́ц: упря́мый.

He's a typical Taurus: stubborn.

Мой знак зодиа́ка Близнецы́. А твой?

My sign is Gemini. What's yours?

C. СЛОВАРЬ

астроло́гия	astrology
ве́рить (ве́рю, ве́ришь, ве́рят)/по-	to believe
вечери́нка	party
вы́йти за́муж (за кого́)	to marry (a man)
гороско́п	horoscope
гру́ппа	group
ерунда́	nonsense
за грани́цей	abroad

за го́родом	in the country; in the suburbs
знак зодиа́ка	zodiac sign
кассе́та	cassette
Кто как.	Some do, some don't.
культу́ра	culture
ме́жду (чем/кем и чем/кем)	between (two things/people)
ме́жду на́ми	between you and me
над	over, above
над голово́й	overhead
о́коло	about, approximately, around
обраща́ть внима́ние (обраща́ю, обраща́ешь, обраща́ют)/ *обрати́ть внима́ние* (обращу́, обрати́шь, обратя́т) (на кого́/что)	to pay attention (to someone/thing)
певе́ц	singer
пе́ред	in front of, (just/right) before
пе́ред сно́м	before going to bed
под under	
расска́зывать (расска́зываю, расска́зываешь, расска́зывают)/*рассказа́ть* (расскажу́, расска́жешь, расска́жут)	to tell about, to recount
расстоя́ние	distance
смея́ться (смею́сь, смеёшься, смею́тся)/за- (над чем/кем)	to laugh (at someone/thing), to smile
составля́ть (составля́ю, составля́ешь, составля́ют)/ *соста́вить* (соста́влю, соста́вишь, соста́вят)	to compose, to form, to construct
типи́чный	typical
упря́мый	stubborn
штат	state
Я так и зна́л(а)!	I knew it!

РУССКАЯ КУЛЬТУРА

Western **джаз** (jazz) and "classic" **рок** (rock) groups, such as the Beatles, have long been popular in Russia. Since Russian society opened up, Russian punk, reggae, blues, heavy metal, and many other kinds of bands have also become commonplace there. There are older Russian rock/pop groups and singers such as **Маши́на Вре́мени, ДДТ, На́утилус-Помпи́лиус, Бори́с Гребенщико́в,** and **Алла Пугачёва,** as well as widely known popular singer-songwriters, such as **Юлий Ким** and **Алекса́ндр Га́лич.** Russia is also the country of the **бард,** a singing poet who sings his own verse. **Була́т Окуджа́ва** is one of Russia's best-loved bards.

Влади́мир Высо́цкий (1938–1980), another **бард,** remains a folk hero for Russians of all ages. He was known as an actor (at the experimental modern drama **Тага́нка** Theater), as a folk-rock poet/musician, and for being one of the few Russian performers who continued to try to change society through his art during the stagnant period of the 1980s. Even before **гла́сность** and **перестро́йка** there was an underground music culture, of which **Высо́цкий** was the best-known performer.

There is also a very rich Russian tradition of folk music, both regional and national. Most Russians know such traditional folk songs as **Кали́нка** and Moscow Nights (part of which is played when Russian radio signs off at night), and many others. Traditional Russian folk instruments include the **гита́ра** (guitar) and the **балала́йка,** a guitar-like stringed instrument with a triangular body.

УПРАЖНЕНИЯ

A. **Запо́лните про́пуски одни́м из э́тих предло́гов: за, перед, ме́жду, над, под и переведи́те предложе́ния.** (Fill in the blanks with one of these prepositions: **за, перед, ме́жду, над,** or **под,** and translate.)

1. Ко́стя смеётся _____ Ве́рой, потому́ что она́ ве́рит в астроло́гию.
2. _____ на́ми, мне не о́чень нра́вится Ко́стя.
3. _____ вечери́нкой я хочу́ убра́ть кварти́ру.
4. Рик к Ве́ре зашёл _____ свои́м гороско́пом.
5. Ве́ра живёт _____ го́родом, _____ Петербу́ргом.

B. **Запо́лните про́пуски в коло́нке А глаго́лами из коло́нки Б и переведи́те предложе́ния.** (Fill in the blanks in column A with the verbs in column B and translate.)

A	B

1. Но я Ове́н, и я не _____ носи́ть кра́сное.
2. Весь ве́чер на вечери́нке Ве́ра Ри́ку _____ вопро́сы.
3. Ве́ра уже́ _____ твой гороско́п? —Нет, она́ ещё _____ .
4. Когда́ ты _____ в институ́т? —Я _____ в январе́.
5. Кому́ ты _____ ? —Я _____ Ри́ку, а его́ не́ту.
6. Что ты за́втра _____ ? —Я _____ не́сколько кассе́т.
7. Я никогда́ не _____ по-ара́бски.
8. Нет, нет, я не _____ уста́лым!
9. Ве́ра за́втра _____ Ри́ку о его́ гороско́пе.
10. Кто где _____ ? —Я _____ здесь, а сёстры спят вон там.

a. расска́жет
b. позвони́ла, звони́ла
c. задава́ла
d. обрати́л
e. говори́л
f. соста́вила, составля́ет
g. спит, сплю
h. люблю́
i. ку́пишь, куплю́
j. посту́пишь, поступлю́
k. стано́влюсь

C. **Переведи́те на ру́сский.** (Translate into Russian.)

1. Rick is from Hanover.
2. One of them understands English.
3. Khabarovsk is 600 kilometers from Vladivostok.
4. How can one get from Kiev to Moscow?
5. We were on vacation from the 1st of May to the 15th of May.

D. **Запо́лните про́пуски по образцу́.** (Fill in the blanks according to the example.)

ОБРАЗЕЦ: Нью-Йорк к <u>восто́ку</u> от Чика́го.

1. Сан-Франци́ско к _____ от Чика́го.
2. Штат Флори́ды к _____ от Бо́стона.
3. Слова́кия нахо́дится в _____ Евро́пе.
4. Кана́да нахо́дится в _____ Аме́рике.
5. Колу́мбия нахо́дится в _____ Аме́рике.

УРОК 28

ПОКУПКА ПРОДУКТОВ. Shopping for food.

A. ДИАЛОГ

Коля и Пат покупают на рынке продукты для ужина по случаю дня рождения.

ПРОДАВЕЦ: *Вишни—самые лучшие на рынке! Налетай—подешевело! Было рубль—стало два!*

КОЛЯ: *Они пахнут хорошо. Можно попробовать?*

ПРОДАВЕЦ: *Конечно, кушайте на здоровье!*

ПАТ: *В самом деле, они вкуснее других.*

КОЛЯ: *Они мне тоже нравится. Ладно, мы возьмём немного вишен.*

ПРОДАВЕЦ: *Кило?*

КОЛЯ: *Нет, это слишком много. Полкило, пожалуйста.*

ПАТ: *Ох, вот арбузы. Я очень люблю арбузы. Что ты скажешь?*

КОЛЯ: *Этот хорош на звук. Девушка, взвесьте вот этот арбуз, пожалуйста.*

ПАТ: *А что ещё? Виноград?*

КОЛЯ: *Нет, для сладкого винограда уже слишком поздно а «зелен виноград» я ненавижу!*

ПАТ: *Вот овощи и зелень. Нам нужно купить полкило солёных огурцов, кило помидоров и полтора кило картошки.*

КОЛЯ: *И банку кислой капусты ... Хорошо, а сейчас пойдём в булочную за булочками и в молочную за творогом.*

ПАТ: *И в мясной за курицей. Лично я не могу дождаться пирога на сладкое!*

КОЛЯ: *Терпи, казак, атаманом будешь. Прежде всего маме надо его приготовить!*

Kolya and Pat shop at the farmers' market for a birthday dinner.

SELLER: Cherries—the best in the market! Hurry, the price just dropped! It was a ruble, now it's two![1]

KOLYA: They smell good. May we try some?

SELLER: Of course, help yourself!

PAT: Actually, they are better than the others.

KOLYA: I like them, too. Alright, we'll take some of these cherries.

SELLER: A kilo?

KOLYA: No, that's too much. A half-kilo, please.

PAT: Oh, here are the watermelons. I really love watermelon. What do you say?

KOLYA: This one sounds good. Miss, please weigh this watermelon for me.

PAT: And what else? Grapes?

KOLYA: No, it's already too late for sweet grapes, and I hate "sour grapes"!

PAT: Here are the vegetables and herbs. We need to get a half kilo of pickles, a kilo of tomatoes, and a kilo and a half of potatoes.

KOLYA: And a jar of pickled cabbage . . . Good, now we'll go to the bakery for the rolls, and the dairy store for the farmer's cheese.

PAT: And don't forget the chicken at the butcher's. Personally, I can't wait for the pie for dessert!

KOLYA: Hold your horses. First, my mother has to make it!

В. ГРАММАТИКА И СЛОВОУПОТРЕБЛЕНИЕ

1. THE GENITIVE AND ACCUSATIVE CASE OF PLURAL ADJECTIVES AND SPECIAL MODIFIERS

The genitive plural endings for adjectives and special modifiers are the same for all genders and are derived from the nominative plural forms. For adjec-

---

1. This is a typical farmers' market joke.

tives, replace -**e** with -**x**. For special modifiers, simply add -x. As always, the third person forms **его, её** and **их** do not change.

	NOMINATIVE/ ACCUSATIVE INANIMATE	ACCUSATIVE ANIMATE/ GENITIVE	EXAMPLE
ADJECTIVES	-ые -ие	-ых -их	ста́рые/ста́рых други́е/други́х
SPECIAL MODIFIERS	-и -е	-их -ех	мой/мои́х, э́ти/э́тих все/всех

Да́йте, пожа́луйста, немно́го э́тих ви́шен.
Please give me some of these cherries.

Нам ну́жно купи́ть полкило́ солёных огурцо́в.
We need to get half a kilo of pickles (literally, salted cucumbers).

В са́мом де́ле, они́ вкусне́е други́х.
Actually, they are better (tastier) than the others.

Я люблю́ ру́сские вечери́нки.
I like Russian parties.

Note that the plural endings are identical in the genitive and prepositional cases. They can easily be distinguished by context, however.

2. THE COMPARATIVE

The comparative degree of adjectives (e.g. bigger, more expensive) is one of the simplest structures you will learn in Russian because it does not change according to case, gender, or number. If the adjective follows the noun, simply replace the ending with -**ee** (the equivalent of the English comparative ending -*er*), **e.g. вку́сный ›› вкусне́е** (tastier). If it precedes the noun, add **бо́лее** (more) before the adjective e.g. **вку́сный хлеб** (delicious bread) **›› бо́лее вку́сный хлеб** (more delicious bread).

Бо́лее вку́сные ви́шни продаю́тся вон там.
The more delicious cherries are sold over there.

Эта говя́дина свеже́е.
This beef is fresher.

Пого́да стано́вится холо́днее.

The weather's getting colder.

Бо́лее can be replaced by **ме́нее** (less) to express a lesser degree.

Это ме́нее дорого́й арбу́з.

This is a less expensive watermelon.

When comparing two nouns in the same case, "than" is expressed by **чем**.

У меня́ бо́лее све́тлые глаза́, чем у тебя́.

I have lighter eyes than you do (than you have).

Пого́да на ю́ге тепле́е, чем на се́вере.

The weather in the south is warmer than (the weather) in the north.

If the first item is in the nominative case, **чем** may be omitted in which case the second item must be in the genitive.

В са́мом де́ле, они́ вкусне́е други́х.

Actually, they are better (tastier) than the others.

Ваш сад краси́вее на́шего.

Your garden is prettier than ours (our garden).

Кни́га интере́снее фи́льма.

The book's more interesting than the movie.

3. UNITS OF FOOD

Following are some of the common units of Russian foods listed with the foods usually bought in those forms or amounts.

паке́т молока́, смета́ны
a package of milk, of sour cream

буты́лка вина́, ма́сла, молока́
a bottle of wine, of oil, of milk

ба́нка майоне́за, горчи́цы, ры́бы, джа́ма
a jar of mayonnaise, of mustard, of fish, of jam

па́чка ча́я, со́ли, ри́са
a packet of tea, of salt, of rice

буха́нка чёрного хле́ба
a loaf of dark bread

бато́н бе́лого хле́ба
a long loaf of white bread

коча́н капу́сты
a head of cabbage

деся́ток яи́ц
ten eggs

коро́бка конфе́т
a box of candy

Remember that numbers ending in 1 are followed by the nominative or the accusative; numbers ending in 2, 3, or 4 are followed by the genitive singular; and numbers ending in 5–9 or 0 are followed by the genitive plural. Thus, you need to know how to decline the units of food as well.

Мне, пожа́луйста ... (Please give me . . .)

1	2, 3, 4	5–9, 0
одно́ ки́ло(грамм)	два ки́ло(грамма)	пять ки́ло(грамм)
оди́н паке́т	два паке́та	пять паке́тов
одну́ па́чку	две па́чки	пять па́чек
одну́ ба́нку	две ба́нки	пять ба́нок
одну́ буты́лку	две буты́лки	пять буты́лок
одну́ коро́бку	две коро́бки	пять коро́бок
одну́ буха́нку	две буха́нки	пять буха́нок
оди́н бато́н	два бато́на	пять бато́нов
оди́н коча́н	два кочана́	пять кочано́в
оди́н деся́ток	два деся́тка	пять деся́тков

Нам ну́жно полкило́ солёных огурцо́в, кило́ помидо́ров, полтора́ кило́ карто́шки и ба́нка ки́слой капу́сты.
We need half a kilo of pickles, a kilo of tomatoes, a kilo and a half of potatoes, and a jar of pickled cabbage.

4. LOVE AND HATE

Люби́ть means "to love" in a general sense, but it is also used to indicate strong feelings for someone or something you've been acquainted with for a while. It is used more often in reference to people, although it can be used with abstract nouns or non-specific things, e.g. **я́блоки** (apples). **Люби́ть** is stronger than the English "to love," which is often used in a more casual way. The best translation for "to love" in the casual sense is **нра́виться** (to be pleased by;

to like). **Нра́виться** is often used in reference to a single experience, such as a movie, or someone you don't know well or at all. Remember that with **нра́виться,** the object or person liked is the subject (in the nominative case), while the person who is pleased is in the dative (see **Уро́к** 11, To Like).

Мне о́чень нра́вится арбу́з.
  I really like watermelon (but have only had it once or a few times).

Тебе́ должны́ понра́виться карти́ны передви́жников.
  You'd love the Wanderers' paintings.

Я люблю́ тебя́.
  I love you.

Мы лю́бим америка́нские фи́льмы.
  We love American movies (and have seen quite a few).

Ненави́деть (to hate, to detest, to loathe) is the opposite of **люби́ть,** and **не нра́виться** (to dislike, to not be pleased by) is the opposite of **нра́виться.**

Уже́ по́здно для сла́дкого виногра́да, а я ненави́жу зелёный виногра́д!
  It's already too late for sweet grapes, and I hate "sour grapes"!

Ему́ не нра́вится ры́нок. Там сли́шком шу́мно.
  He doesn't like the farmers' market. It's too noisy there.

C. СЛОВА́РЬ

апельси́н	orange
арбу́з	watermelon
ба́нка	jar
бато́н	long loaf
бу́лочная	bakery
буха́нка	loaf
взве́шивать (взве́шиваю, взве́шиваешь, взве́шивают)/ *взве́сить* (взве́шу, взве́сишь, взве́сят)	to weigh
ви́шни	cherries

виногра́д	grape(s)
говя́дина	beef
гото́вить (гото́влю, гото́вишь, гото́вят)/при-	to prepare; to cook
грамм	gram
деся́ток яйц	ten eggs
звуча́ть (звучу́, звучи́шь, звуча́т)/про-	to sound; to be heard
зе́лень	f. greens
капу́ста	cabbage
карто́шка	potato
ки́слый	sour
коро́бка	a box
коча́н	head (cabbage, lettuce)
Ку́шай(те) на здоро́вье!	Help yourself!; Eat it in good health!
ли́чно	personally
мясно́й	butcher's (the)/meat (adj.)
ма́сло	butter; oil
моло́чная	dairy store
ненави́деть (ненави́жу, ненави́дишь, ненави́дят)	to hate (imp.) (II.)
огуре́ц	cucumber
па́хнуть (па́хну, па́хнешь, па́хнут) (чем)	to smell (of something) (imp.)
па́чка	packet
паке́т	package
пиро́г	pie; cake
полтора́	one and a half
помидо́р	tomato
проду́кты	food-stuffs
рис	rice
ры́нок	farmers' market
смета́на	sour cream
солёный	pickled, salted
солёный огуре́ц	pickle (lit. pickled cucumber)
соси́ска	sausage
сыр	cheese
творо́г	farmer's cheese; cottage cheese
Терпи́, каза́к, атама́ном бу́дешь.	Hold your horses. (lit., Be patient, Cossack, you'll get to be head of your tribe.)
я́блоко	apple
яйцо́	egg

РУССКАЯ КУЛЬТУРА

Although the farmers' markets can be expensive, there is generally a wider variety and higher quality of food there than in the stores, and bargaining is common. Many people grow vegetables and fruits on small plots at their dachas, but for anything that can't be grown there, the farmer's market is often the answer. Most families cannot afford to buy produce there regularly and shop there only for special occasions. Most cities have at least one farmers' market, and the larger cities often have more than one.

For basic staples people go to regular stores. There are supermarkets, but people usually go to a different store for each type of food. There are bakeries for bread; special bakeries for cakes and sweet baked goods; dairy stores; meat and fish stores; vegetable stores; wine and liquor stores. Fresh food is not always available in these stores, particularly in the winter, but they are generally well-stocked in canned, pickled, salted, or preserved foods. Due to the fact that food can be expensive, people often bring gifts of food or drink when they are invited to someone's home for a meal.

УПРАЖНЕНИЯ

A. **Отве́тьте на вопро́сы по образцу́ и переведи́те отве́ты.** (Answer the questions according to the example and translate the answers.)

ОБРАЗЕЦ: Что вам ну́жно? (солёные огурцы́)
Мне нужны́ солёные огурцы́. I need some pickles.

1. Кто вам позвони́л? (оди́н/из/взро́слые)
2. Како́й ваш люби́мый сала́т? (сала́т/из/све́жие помидо́ры)
3. Для кого́ он купи́л пода́рки? (все свои́ родстве́нники)
4. Кого́ ты не понима́ешь? (ру́сские мужчи́ны)
5. Кого́ вы ждёте? (на́ши хоро́шие друзья́)

B. **Соста́вьте сравни́тельные предложе́ния по образцу́.** (Construct comparative sentences according to the example.)

ОБРАЗЕЦ: У меня́ дли́нные во́лосы. —А у неё? (longer)
У неё длинне́е во́лосы, чем у меня́.

1. Ко́ля купи́л вку́сный арбу́з. —А Пат? (more delicious)
2. Сего́дня пого́да тёплая. —А за́втра? (warmer)
3. Фру́кты на ры́нке све́жие. —А в магази́не? (less fresh)
4. Ехать на маши́не удо́бно. —А на метро́? (more convenient)
5. Моя́ кварти́ра но́вая. —А их? (newer)

C. **Переведи́те на ру́сский по образцу́.** (Translate into Russian according to the example.)

ОБРАЗЕЦ: Мне, пожа́луйста, <u>деся́ток яи́ц</u>. (ten eggs)

Мне, пожа́луйста,

1. 1 bottle of milk.
2. 2 jars of jam.
3. 3 loaves of dark bread.
4. 4 packets of tea.
5. 500 grams of cheese.

D. **Переведи́те на ру́сский.** (Translate into Russian.)

1. Parents should love their children.
2. I love Russian movies.
3. Why don't you (familiar) like the farmers' market?
4. She's married to Maksim, but she loves Victor.
5. I hate working (to work) in the summer.

УРОК 29

НА ДОСУГЕ. At leisure.

А. ДИАЛОГ

На да́че.

ДАН САНДЕРС: Како́й удиви́тельный сад!

ЛЕВ ЛЬВОВИЧ: Спаси́бо. Жена́ лю́бит садово́дство.

ДАН САНДЕРС: Э́то ви́дно. Моя́ то́же. У нас нет да́чи, но до́ма у нас большо́й сад.

ЛЕВ ЛЬВОВИЧ: Кро́ме садово́дства, что вы де́лаете в свобо́дное вре́мя—занима́етесь спо́ртом?

ДАН САНДЕРС: Да, я люблю́ игра́ть в баскетбо́л.

ЛЕВ ЛЬВОВИЧ: А семья́?

ДАН САНДЕРС: Так же как и я, сын лю́бит баскетбо́л. До́чка постоя́нно болта́ет по телефо́ну со все́ми свои́ми подру́жками. Она́ лю́бит ходи́ть по магази́нам ...

ЛЕВ ЛЬВОВИЧ: Ходи́ть по магази́нам для развлече́ния?

ДАН САНДЕРС: Да, э́то америка́нское хо́бби! А вы с семьёй?

ЛЕВ ЛЬВОВИЧ: Ну, нам не́когда ходи́ть по магази́нам ра́ди удово́льствия. Мы игра́ем в ка́рты и́ли сын игра́ет на гита́ре, и мы поём. И мы ча́сто хо́дим в теа́тр.

ДАН САНДЕРС: Хорошо́, когда́ вся семья́ интересу́ется одни́ми и те же веща́ми.

ЛЕВ ЛЬВОВИЧ: Как бы не так! Бо́льше всего́ я люблю́ сиде́ть и разгова́ривать в саду́, как мы сейча́с де́лаем, а де́тям ску́чно.

ДАН САНДЕРС: Де́ти все одина́ковые, не так ли? Чем шумне́е, тем лу́чше!

ЛЕВ ЛЬВОВИЧ: Соверше́нно ве́рно!

At a dacha.

DAN SANDERS: What an amazing garden!

LEV LVOVICH: Thank you. My wife loves gardening.

DAN SANDERS: I can see that. Mine, too. We don't have a summer house, but we have a big garden at home.

LEV LVOVICH: Besides gardening, what do you do in your free time—do you play any sports?

DAN SANDERS: Yes, I love to play basketball.

LEV LVOVICH: And your family?

DAN SANDERS: My son loves basketball just like I do. My daughter is constantly on the telephone with all her girlfriends. They love to go shopping . . .

LEV LVOVICH: Shopping for fun?

DAN SANDERS: Yes, it's an American hobby! And what about you and your family?

LEV LVOVICH: Well, we don't have time to shop for fun. We play cards, or my son plays the guitar and we sing. And we often go to the theater.

DAN SANDERS: It's nice when a family is interested in the same things.

LEV LVOVICH: Nothing of the sort! More than anything, I love to sit out in the garden and chat like we're doing now, but for the kids that's boring.

DAN SANDERS: Kids are all alike, aren't they? The noisier, the better!

LEV LVOVICH: That's for sure!

B. ГРАММАТИКА И СЛОВОУПОТРЕБЛЕНИЕ

1. THE INSTRUMENTAL CASE OF PLURAL ADJECTIVES AND SPECIAL MODIFIERS

The instrumental plural adjective and special modifier endings are the same across all genders. For adjectives, replace the nominative plural ending -e with

-ми. For special modifiers, simply add **-ми** to the nominative plural form. As always, **его, её** and **их** do not change.

	NOMINATIVE	INSTRUMENTAL	EXAMPLE
ADJECTIVES	-ые	-ыми	ста́рые » ста́рыми
	-ие	-ими	други́е » други́ми
SPECIAL MODIFIERS	-и	-ими	мои́ » мои́ми, э́ти » э́тими
	-е	-еми	все » все́ми

До́чка беспреста́нно болта́ет по телефо́ну со все́ми свои́ми подру́жками.
My daughter is constantly on the telephone with all her girlfriends.

Хорошо́, когда́ семья́ интересу́ется одни́ми и те́ми те веща́ми.
It's nice when a family is interested in the same things.

Мы ходи́ли за гриба́ми с на́шими ру́сскими колле́гами.
We went mushroom-hunting with our Russian colleagues.

2. EXPRESSING SIMILARITY

There are different ways to indicate a similarity or likeness. Following are some of the most common:

одина́ковый	same, alike
так же как (и) (noun)	same as/just like (noun)
оди́н/одна́/одно́/одни́	the same; one
как у нас/вас	same as us/you

Де́ти все одина́ковые, не так ли?
Kids are all alike (the same), aren't they?

Так же как и я, сын лю́бит баскетбо́л.
My son loves basketball, just like I do.

Хорошо́, когда́ семья́ интересу́ется одни́ми и те́ми же веща́ми.
It's nice when a family is interested in the same things.

Как и у вас, неве́ста обы́чно надева́ет бе́лое.
Just as in your country (literally, as by you), the bride usually wears white.

3. НЕ- PLUS QUESTION WORDS

Accented **не-** can be used with any question word in order to indicate "there is no … (to)." The resulting words must be followed by **было/будет +** an infinitive, and any noun or pronoun preceding them must be in the dative case. **Нечего and некого** can be declined.

не́чего	there is nothing (to)
не́кого	there is no one (to)
не́когда	there is no time (to)
не́где	there is nowhere (to)
не́куда	there is nowhere (to) (direction)
не́зачем	there is no point (in)

Нам не́когда ходи́ть по магази́нам для развлече́ния.

We don't have time (literally, there is no time for us) to shop for fun.

Мне ску́чно. Не́чего де́лать и не́ с кем говори́ть.

I'm bored. There's nothing to do and no one to talk with.

Де́тям не́куда бы́ло е́хать.

The children had nowhere to go.

Note that **не́кто** (someone) and **не́что** (something) have a different meaning and cannot be used in the above construction.

Дава́й сде́лаем не́что но́вое! Мы всегда́ е́здим на да́чу ле́том.

Let's do something new! We always go to the dacha in the summer.

Там стоя́л не́кто в кра́сной руба́шке.

Someone in a red shirt was standing there.

4. THE VERB ИГРА́ТЬ (TO PLAY)

Just as in English, the Russian verb **игра́ть** (to play) can refer to games or musical instruments. When used with games or sports, it must be followed by **в** and the accusative case; when used with instruments, it is followed by **на** and the prepositional case.

Я люблю́ игра́ть в баскетбо́л.

I love to play basketball.

Мы игра́ем в ка́рты и́ли сын игра́ет на гита́ре, и мы поём.
We play cards, or my son plays the guitar and we sing.

Мы игра́ли в ша́хматы, он игра́л на роя́ле, а они́ игра́ли в футбо́л.
We were playing chess, he was playing the piano, and they were playing soccer.

Note that **занима́ться** rather than **игра́ть** is used to express "to play sports."

Вы занима́етесь спо́ртом?
Do you play any sports?

5. IRREGULAR SHORT-FORM COMPARATIVES

Some adjectives have irregular short-form comparatives. You will need to memorize the most common of these. Following is a partial list.[1]

	ADJECTIVE	COMPARATIVE	
good	хоро́ший	лу́чше	better
bad	плохо́й	ху́же	worse
big	большо́й	бо́льше	bigger, more
small	ма́ленький	ме́ньше	smaller, less
tall	высо́кий	вы́ше	taller
short	коро́ткий	коро́че	shorter
expensive;	дорого́й	доро́же	more expensive;
dear			dearer
cheap	дешёвый	деше́вле	cheaper
quiet	ти́хий	ти́ше	quieter
loud	гро́мкий	гро́мче	louder
near	бли́зкий	бли́же	nearer
easy	лёгкий	ле́гче	easier
young	молодо́й	мла́дше, моло́же	younger
old	ста́рый	ста́рше	older
late	по́здний	по́зже	later

Чем шумне́е, тем лу́чше!
The noisier, the better!

1. Please see the Appendix for a more complete list.

Лу́чше по́здно, чем никогда́!

Better late than never!

Ва́ша систе́ма обще́ственного тра́нспорта деше́вле, чем на́ша.

Your public transportation system is cheaper than ours.

Short-form comparatives are the same for both adjectives and adverbs. How-ever, some short-form comparatives, e.g. **пре́жде** (before, first, formerly), **ра́ньше** (earlier, before, formerly), and **да́льше** (farther), are used mostly as adverbs and not as adjectives.

Бо́льше всего́ я люблю́ сиде́ть и разгова́ривать.

More than anything (most of all), I love to sit and talk.

Говори́те ме́дленнее, пожа́луйста.

Please speak more slowly (slower).

Пре́жде всего́ ма́ме на́до его́ пригото́вить!

First of all, Mom has to prepare it!

Ти́ше е́дешь, да́льше бу́дешь.

Slow and steady wins the race. (literally, The more quietly you ride, the farther you'll be.)

6. MASCULINE NOUNS ENDING IN -ý IN THE PREPOSITIONAL CASE

Some nouns end in -ý rather than -e in the prepositional case, when they fol-low the prepositions **в** or **на** to denote location. Here are some of the most common:

в аэропорту́	in/at the airport	на полу́	on the floor
на берегу́	on/at the shore	во рту́	in the mouth
на верху́	on top	в саду́	in the garden
в глазу́	in the eye	в снегу́	in the snow
в Крыму́	in/at the Crimea	в/на углу́	in/at the corner
в лесу́	in the woods	в шкафу́	in the cupboard
на мосту́	at the bridge		

Бо́льше всего́ я люблю́ сиде́ть в саду́.

More than anything, I love to sit out in the garden.

Он нас подождёт в аэропорту́.
　　He'll wait for us at the airport.

Мы шесть неде́ль жи́ли на берегу́.
　　We lived on the shore for six weeks.

С. СЛОВА́РЬ

бли́же	nearer
бо́льше	more; bigger
бо́льше всего́	more than anything; most of all
болта́ть (болта́ю, болта́ешь, болта́ют)	to chat (imp.)
гро́мче	louder
да́льше	farther (mostly an adverb)
да́ча	summer-house, country house
дешёвле	cheaper, less expensive
для развлече́ния	for fun
доро́же	more expensive, dearer
занима́ться спо́ртом	to play sports
игра́ть в баскетбо́л/футбо́л	to play basketball/soccer
игра́ть в ка́рты/ша́хматы	to play cards/chess
игра́ть на гита́ре	to play the guitar
Как бы не так!	Nothing of the sort!
как ви́дно	as is evident; as can be seen
как у (кого́)	same as (someone)
ле́гче	easier
лу́чше	better
ме́ньше	less; smaller
мла́дше, моло́же	younger
не так ли	aren't they, doesn't it, etc.
не́где	there is nowhere (to)
не́когда	there is no time (to)
не́кого	there is no one (to)
не́куда	there is nowhere (to) (direction)
не́чего	there is nothing (to)
одина́ковый	alike, the same, identical
оди́н/-на́/-но́/-ни́	one; one and the same
петь (пою́, поёшь, пою́т)/с–	to sing (I.)
по́зже	later

постоя́нно	constantly
сад	garden
садово́дство	gardening
свобо́дный	free
ску́чно	boring
Соверше́нно ве́рно!	Exactly!, That's right!
ста́рше	older
так же как и (кто/что)	just like (someone/something)
ти́ше	quieter
удиви́тельный	amazing, surprising
хо́бби	hobby
ходи́ть за гриба́ми	to go mushroom-picking
ху́же	worse
шу́мный	noisy

РУССКАЯ КУЛЬТУРА

Russians love nature and are very social, often spending their leisure time with friends and family in natural settings. Many people have a **да́ча** (country or summer-house) where they garden and enjoy sitting and chatting or sunbathing. Another typical Russian pastime is to spend the day in the woods hunting for mushrooms, and then have a picnic, perhaps around a campfire, with someone playing songs on the guitar while everyone sings. You can see a similar scene in the film *Moscow Doesn't Believe in Tears*.

Summer leisure activities in the city can include a visit to an amusement park, such as **Парк Го́рького** (Gorky Park) in Moscow, or other parks where people love to stroll, rent paddle-boats, have their portraits drawn or caricatured by artists, eat ice cream, or buy little souvenirs. Russians, especially older men, also enjoy playing chess and dominoes outdoors in parks in nice weather. St. Petersburg is known for its beautiful parks, such as **Ле́тний сад** (the Summer Garden), **Петерго́ф** (Peterhof), and **Екатери́нинский дворе́ц** (Catherine's Palace), all remnants from tsarist days. Russians also love to sunbathe whenever possible, along the coast or by a large river, such as the **Нева́** (Neva) in St. Petersburg or the **Во́лга** (Volga) in Volgograd. In the summer, everyone is out on the streets, especially in the evening, strolling up and down the main thoroughfare or around the main square of the city or town.

Other favorite pastimes in the city include going to the circus (for which Russia is justly famous), to a movie, to a museum, out to eat, to an exhibition or market, to a theatrical or musical performance, or to the **ба́ня** (banya)—the communal or private baths where people soak, often with friends while drinking vodka.

УПРАЖНЕНИЯ

A. **Соста́вьте сравни́тельные предложе́ния по образцу́.** (Construct comparative sentences according to the example.)

ОБРАЗЕЦ: Ей два́дцать лет, а мне три́дцать лет. (Я/она́. Она́/я.)
Я ста́рше её. Она́ моло́же меня́.

1. У меня́ большо́й сад. У него́ ма́ленький сад. (Мой сад/его́ сад. Его́ сад/мой сад.)
2. Ша́пка дорога́я, а ю́бка дешёвая. (Ша́пка/ю́бка. Ю́бка/ша́пка.)
3. Ва́ша систе́ма хоро́шая. На́ша систе́ма плоха́я. (Ва́ша систе́ма/на́ша систе́ма. На́ша систе́ма/ва́ша систе́ма.)
4. Говори́ть по-ру́сски тру́дно. Понима́ть по-ру́сски легко́. (Говори́ть по-ру́сски/понима́ть по-ру́сски. Понима́ть по-ру́сски/говори́ть по-ру́сски.)
5. Москва́ бли́зко. Ки́ев далеко́. (Москва́/Ки́ев. Ки́ев/Москва́.)

B. **Запо́лните про́пуски.** (Fill in the blanks.)

1. По́чта нахо́дится за _____ . (э́ти больши́е зда́ния)
2. Ра́ньше она́ увлека́лась _____ . (други́е ве́щи)
3. Мы говори́ли с _____ . (его́ америка́нские друзья́)
4. Он занима́ется _____ . (полити́ческие вопро́сы)
5. Како́е расстоя́ние ме́жду _____ и _____ ? (Кавка́зские го́ры, Ура́льские го́ры)

C. **Переведи́те на англи́йский.** (Translate into English.)

1. Жена́ лю́бит садово́дство, так же как и вы.
2. Нет ра́зницы (difference) ме́жду ни́ми. Они́ одина́ковые.
3. Мы всегда́ еди́м в одно́м рестора́не.
4. Они́ живу́т в одно́м до́ме.
5. И́ре бу́дет всё равно́, како́й фильм мы вы́берем.

D. **Переведи́те на ру́сский.** (Translate into Russian.)

1. They'll have nowhere to go.
2. There was no time to call.
3. She was playing the flute (**фле́йта**) while we were playing chess.
4. Do you play the guitar or the piano?
5. They have a summer-house on the shore in the Crimea.

УРОК 30

В МУЗЕЕ. At a museum.

А. ДИАЛОГ

В Эрмитаже.

ЭКСКУРСОВОД: *Мы с вами стоим в Малахитовом зале. Перед вами некоторые личные вещи царя и его семьй.*

КАРМЕН: *Я бы хотела видеть его сто лет назад.*

ЭДИК: *Да, но тогда здесь были бы только Романовы, а мы были бы крестьянами!*

КАРМЕН: *Слушай, гид идёт слишком быстро, а говорит ещё быстрее. Можно ходить по музею одними?*

ЭДИК: *Я спрошу. (говорит с охранником) Да, но нельзя ничего касаться, хорошо?*

КАРМЕН: *Конечно ... Ой, как красиво!*

ЭДИК: *Да, Фаберже сам сделал это яйцо для царя.*

КАРМЕН: *Представь, сколько оно сегодня стоит ... Видишь, вот импрессионисты!*

ЭДИК: *В Эрмитаже самая лучшая в мире коллекция западно-европейского[1] искусства, если не считать Лувра.*

КАРМЕН: *Это очень красиво, но я хотела бы посмотреть русское искусство. Здесь есть такой музей?*

ЭДИК: *Да, Русский Музей. Тебе должны понравиться картины передвижников и Репина. Он один из наших самых знаменитых художников. Он выражает русский дух.*

At the Hermitage Museum.

GUIDE: We're standing in the Malachite Hall. In front of you are some belongings of the tsar and his family.

---

1. When two words are combined, the resulting compound word has two accents— one for each word.

CARMEN: I would like to have seen it a century ago.

EDIK: Yes, but only the Romanovs would've been here then, and we would've been peasants!

CARMEN: Listen, the guide is going too fast, and talking even faster. Can we walk around the museum by ourselves?

EDIK: I'll ask. *(speaks with the guard)* Yes, but we can't touch anything, alright?

CARMEN: Of course . . . Oh, how beautiful!

EDIK: Yes, Faberge himself made that egg for the tsar.

CARMEN: Imagine how much it's worth today . . . Look, there are the Impressionists!

EDIK: The Hermitage has the best collection of Western European art in the world, not counting the Louvre.

CARMEN: They're very beautiful, but I'd like to see some Russian art. Is there such a museum here?

EDIK: Yes, the Russian Museum. You'd love the Wanderers' paintings and Repin's. He's one of our most famous artists. He expresses the Russian spirit.

В. ГРАММАТИКА И СЛОВОУПОТРЕБЛЕНИЕ

1. THE SUPERLATIVE

The superlative degree of adjectives is formed by simply adding the modifier самый before the adjective in question. Самый has the same endings as the adjective it precedes, and agrees with the noun in number, gender, and case.

В Эрмита́же са́мая лу́чшая в ми́ре колле́кция за́падноевропе́йского иску́сства, е́сли не счита́ть Лу́вра.

The Hermitage has the best collection of Western European art in the world, not counting the Louvre.

Ре́пин оди́н из на́ших са́мых знамени́тых худо́жников.

Repin is one of our most famous artists.

Это самое красивое яйцо, которое я когда-нибудь видела!
This is the most beautiful egg I've ever seen!

Note that **лучший** (best) is used instead of **хороший** to form the superlative.

Вишни— самые лучшие на рынке!
Cherries—the best in the market!

2. THE CONDITIONAL WITH БЫ

The conditional mood is used to express possibility or to depict an "unreal" (hypothetical) situation in the past or future, i.e. "would/could/should (have)." It consists of the particle **бы** and a verb in the past tense. **Бы** usually follows the verb but may also precede it. It is never accented and cannot begin a sentence.

Пойти ещё в Русский Музей было бы невозможно.
It would have been impossible to go to the Russian Museum as well.

Завтра я с удовольствием пошла бы в театр.
I would very much like to go to the theatre tomorrow.

Хорошо было бы провести месяц на море.
It would be good to spend a month at the sea.

Note that it must be determined from context whether the verb refers to the future or the past.

В этом музее хотела бы посмотреть русское искусство.
I'd like to see (would like to have seen) the Russian art in this museum.

Я бы хотела видеть его сто лет назад.
I would like to have seen it a century ago.

In complex sentences, **бы** can appear in both the main and the subordinate clause, or just in one clause.

Тогда здесь были бы только Романовы, а мы были бы крестьянами!
Only Romanovs would've been here then, and we would've been peasants!

Она́ хоте́ла бы сего́дня отдыха́ть, но не мо́жет.
She would like to rest today, but she can't.

Мы хоте́ли бы пойти́ в Эрмита́ж, но не смо́жем.
We would like to go to the Hermitage, but we won't be able to.

Although the Russian conditional is quite simple to use, remember that "would" in English does not necessarily correspond to **бы** in Russian. A future action from the standpoint of the past is expressed simply by using the past and future tenses together.

Эдик сказа́л, что он придёт.
Edik said that he'd come (or: Edik said that he will come.)

"Would" can also be expressed by **до́лжен** followed by an infinitive.

Тебе́ должны́ понра́виться карти́ны передви́жников.
You'd love (you should/will love) the Wanderers' paintings.

3. PLURAL SUBJECTS WITH с

In conversation, two subjects are usually combined into a special plural construction with the preposition **с**. The first subject is a plural pronoun in the nominative (**мы, вы,** or **они́**), followed by **с** and the instrumental case of the second subject. Regardless of whether the first subject is singular or plural, a plural pronoun must be used.

Мы с ва́ми стои́м в Малахи́товом за́ле.
We (literally, we with you, meaning "You and I") are standing in the Malachite Hall.

Карме́н, вы с Э́диком ходи́ли в Эрмита́ж?
Carmen, did you and Edik go to the Hermitage?

Они́ с Э́диком (Карме́н и её друг Э́дик) ходи́ли в Эрмита́ж.
They (literally, they with Edik, meaning Carmen and Edik) went to the Hermitage.

4. DECLENSION AND NUMBER OF SURNAMES

Most Russian surnames were originally possessive adjectives. Therefore, they reflect the gender and number of the person.

Здесь бы́ли бы то́лько Рома́новы. (masc.: Рома́нов, fem.: Рома́нова)
Only Romanovs would've been here then.

Вот Лев Ильи́ч Ка́мкин и его́ жена́, Анна Льво́вна Ка́мкина. (pl.: Ка́мкины)
There's Lev Ilyich Kamkin and his wife, Anna L'vovna Kamkina.
(pl.: the Kamkins)

Some surnames are more clearly adjectives, and they behave like regular adjectives. Non-Russian surnames do not agree with the person to whom they refer. All surnames decline, however, unless they are obviously foreign and do not have a suitable ending.

Я смотрю́ карти́ны Марти́роса Сарья́на.
I'm looking at paintings by Martyros Saryan.

Я люблю́ чита́ть кни́ги Достое́вского.
I love reading Dostoevsky's books.

Мы говори́м о карти́нах Джо́рджи Оки́ф и Ива́на Ши́шкина.
We're talking about the paintings of Georgia O'Keefe and Ivan Shishkin.

5. СТОЯ́ТЬ VERSUS СТО́ИТЬ

The verbs **стоя́ть** (to stand, to be standing) and **сто́ить** (to cost; to be worth) are often confused because they look exactly the same when conjugated, except for the accent. Note, also, that **сто́ить** does not have a perfective form, whereas **стоя́ть** does: **постоя́ть.**

Мы с ва́ми стои́м в Малахи́товом за́ле.
We're standing in the Malachite Hall.

Предста́вь, ско́лько оно́ сего́дня сто́ит ...
Imagine how much it's worth today . . .

Ско́лько сто́ят э́ти репроду́кции?

How much do these reproductions cost?

C. СЛОВАРЬ

бы́стрый	fast; quick
выража́ть (выража́ю, выража́ешь, выража́ют) /**вы́разить** (вы́ражу, вы́разишь, вы́разят)	to express; to convey; to voice
гардеро́б	cloakroom
гид	guide
дух	spirit(s), heart, mind
жи́вопись	f. painting
знамени́тый	famous; celebrated; reknowned
импрессиони́сты	the Impressionists
иску́сство	art
карти́на	painting
каса́ться (каса́юсь, каса́ешься, каса́ются) /**косну́ться** (косну́сь, коснёшься, косну́тся)	to touch (on); to concern
колле́кция	collection
крестья́нин	peasant
лу́чший	best
мир	world; peace
музе́й	museum
мы с ва́ми	we (you and I)
охра́нник	guard
представля́ть (представля́ю, представля́ешь, представля́ют)/ **предста́вить** (предста́влю, предста́вишь, предста́вят)	to present; to represent; to imagine
репроду́кция	reproduction (of a painting)
рисова́ть (рису́ю, рису́ешь, рису́ют)/на-	to draw, to paint, to portray
рису́нок	drawing, illustration, design
са́мый	the most (+ adjective)
сто́ить (сто́ю, сто́ишь, сто́ят)	to be worth; to cost (imp.)
стоя́ть (стою́, стои́шь, стоя́т)/по-	to stand, to be standing
тала́нтливый	talented
худо́жественный	artistic
худо́жник	artist
царе́вич	the tsar's son (heir to the throne)

цари́ца	tsarina
царь	m. tsar
экскурсово́д	guide
Я хоте́л(а) бы . . .	I'd like . . .

РУССКАЯ КУЛЬТУРА

Many Russian painters traveled and painted throughout Europe in the nineteenth and early twentieth century. They developed an artistic tradition influenced by Europe yet uniquely Russian in flavor. There are a number of fine art museums in Russia. In St. Petersburg, the most famous is the Hermitage, the former Winter Palace of the tsars. Among its many exhibits, the Hermitage houses an extensive collection of Western European art, especially of the Impressionists, as well as some of the tsars' treasures. The Russian Museum in St. Petersburg has a wonderful collection of Russian art from ancient icons to modern art. The **Третьяко́вская галере́я** (Tretyakov Gallery) in Moscow houses Pavel Tretyakov's (1832–1898) comprehensive collection of Russian art. Tretyakov did much to collect, preserve, and further Russian art. In virtually every city throughout the CIS, there is a local museum with examples of national and local artists' work as well as a wide variety of traditional handicrafts. These are well worth seeing as they provide a vivid picture of the area's culture and history. **Та́почки** (slipper-like shoe coverings) must be worn in most Russian museums in order to protect the floors. You will generally be outfitted with these upon entering the museum.

Many Russian artists remain virtually unknown elsewhere. A notable exception is **Марк Шага́л** (Marc Chagall) who is better-known outside of Russia than in his own country of birth. Some reknowned Russian artists include **Васи́лий Канди́нский** (Vasilii Kandinsky) and **Казими́р Мале́вич** (Kasimir Malevich), whose styles were modern and abstract, **Ива́н Айвазо́вский** (Ivan Aivazovsky), famous for stormy ocean scenes, and **Илья́ Ре́пин** (Ilya Repin), who is believed to have captured the Russian soul in his work, particularly in his famous painting **Бурлаки́ на Во́лге** (The Volga Boatmen). Many paintings by the Wanderers (**передви́жники**), a school of realist painters active in the second half of the nineteenth century, are also highly regarded.

A. Соста́вьте предложе́ния с превосхо́дной сте́пенью по образцу́.
(Construct sentences in the superlative according to the example.)

ОБРАЗЕ́Ц: Эти худо́жники о́чень тала́нтливые. (в музе́е)
Это са́мые тала́нтливые худо́жники в музе́е.

1. Ре́пин о́чень знамени́тый худо́жник. (в стране́)
2. В Эрмита́же хоро́шая колле́кция за́падноевропе́йского иску́сства.
(в ми́ре)
3. Это краси́вое яйцо́. (в ми́ре)
4. Эта карти́на о́чень стра́нная. (кото́рую я когда́-нибудь ви́дел)
5. Этот зал о́чень большо́й. (в го́роде)

B. Соста́вьте предложе́ния с сослага́тельным наклоне́нием, а зате́м
переведи́те их. (Construct sentences in the conditional, and then translate
them.)

1. Это бы́ло хорошо́.
2. Я хочу́ пойти́ в Эрмита́ж.
3. Тогда́ здесь бы́ли то́лько Рома́новы.
4. Тебе́ бу́дет тру́дно позвони́ть.
5. Я хочу́ посмотре́ть ру́сское иску́сство.

C. Запо́лните про́пуски по образцу́. (Fill in the blanks according to the
example.)

ОБРАЗЕ́Ц: Мы с жено́й лю́бим ходи́ть в музе́и. (я и моя́ жена́)

1. _____ стои́м в Малахи́товом за́ле. (я и вы)
2. Что _____ сего́дня бу́дем де́лать? (я и ты)
3. _____ за́втра уе́дете? (ты и твой сын)
4. _____ хоте́ли бы посмотре́ть я́йца, кото́рые сде́лал Фаберже́. (вы
и они́)
5. _____ ходи́ли по музе́ю? (вы и ваш гид)

D. **Переведи́те на ру́сский.** (Translate into Russian.)

1. The Romanovs used to live here.
2. How much is it?
3. I like Ilya Repin's paintings a lot.
4. I don't know very much about the lives of Anton Chekhov or Maksim Gor'kiy.
5. The guard is standing by the door.

ШЕСТАЯ ПРОВЕРКА (Sixth Review)

A. **Переведи́те на ру́сский.** (Translate into Russian.)

1. Vera likes working as a guide.
2. Kolya wants to become a dentist, just like his father.
3. They almost missed the plane. They were lucky (**повезло́**) that it was also late!
4. Lev L'vovich loves to play chess, but his children hate to play.
5. Can I (is it possible) buy grapes at the market? —Yes, you can (it's possible).
6. Women are forbidden (it's forbidden for women) to wear pants in church.
7. It's impossible to do a horoscope without (**без**) the date of birth.
8. I'd like to hear (to listen to how) you (informal) play the guitar and sing sometime.
9. I imagine that Edik would play (plays) the piano very well.
10. Lena did (painted) two paintings in the Crimea.

B. **Поста́вьте прилага́тельные снача́ла в сравни́тельную сте́пень и пото́м в превосхо́дную сте́пень по образцу́.** (Put the adjectives into the comparative and then into the superlative according to the example.)

ОБРАЗЕЦ: Хлеб дорого́й. (сыр, мя́со) Сыр доро́же хле́ба, но мя́со са́мое дорого́е.
> Bread is expensive. Cheese is more expensive than bread, but meat is the most expensive.

1. Ши́шкин знамени́тый худо́жник. (Ре́пин, Шага́л)
2. Я́блоки хоро́шие. (апельси́ны, ви́шни)
3. Фильм сло́жный. (пье́са (play), кни́га)
4. Моя́ ко́мната ма́ленькая. (его́ ко́мната, их ко́мната)
5. У нас хоро́ший сад. (у них, у него́)

C. **Поста́вьте во мно́жественное число́, употребля́я слова́ в ско́бках, е́сли есть.** (Make the sentences plural, using the words in the parentheses if there are any.)

1. Э́та ру́сская же́нщина за́мужем за америка́нцем.
2. Ско́лько сто́ит <u>одна́</u> больша́я па́чка ча́я? (пять)
3. Не обраща́йте внима́ния на э́того шу́много ребёнка.

4. Джу́ди подари́ла <u>своему́ дру́гу</u> типи́чный наро́дный сувени́р. (все свои́ друзья́)
5. Мы всегда́ приглаша́ем бога́того челове́ка, к тому́ же тала́нтливого молодо́го худо́жника, на на́шу вечери́нку.

D. **Отве́тьте на вопро́сы, одни́м сло́вом, е́сли возмо́жно.** (Answer the questions, in one word if possible.)

1. Что тяжеле́е (тяжёлый, heavy), ба́нка майоне́за и́ли бато́н бе́лого хле́ба?
2. Что не́когда де́лать Льву Льво́вичу и его́ семье́?
3. По мне́нию Джу́ди, правосла́вное сва́дебное венча́ние почти́ как что?
4. По мне́нию Да́на Сандерсона, кто одина́ковый?
5. Что зна́чит «и т. д.» по-англи́йски?

ПРАЗДНИКИ

В любо́й[1] ру́сский пра́здник, мо́жно сказа́ть: «Поздравля́ю/ Поздравля́ем[2] с пра́здником!»[3] Совреме́нные[4] ру́сские пра́здники включа́ют Но́вый год (31 декабря́), Междунаро́дный же́нский день (8 ма́рта), День весны́ (1 ма́я), День побе́ды[5] (9 ма́я), и День Росси́и (12 ию́ня). В Но́вый год Дед Моро́з со Снегу́рочкой да́рят пода́рки де́тям у ёлки и ро́дственники и друзья́ гото́вят вку́сный у́жин, и мно́го едя́т и пьют. Восьмо́го ма́рта (Же́нский день) мужчи́ны да́рят же́нщинам цветы́ и откры́тки. В День весны́ (бы́вший[6] День трудя́щихся[7]) лю́ди гуля́ют в па́рках и́ли рабо́тают на да́чном[8] уча́стке.[9] В День побе́ды лю́ди вспомина́ют[10] поги́бших[11] на войне́.[12] В День Росси́и (День незави́симости[13]) обы́чно быва́ет[14] салю́т[15] и вое́нный[16] пара́д.

Гла́вные правосла́вные пра́здники — Рождество́[17] (7 января́), ма́сленица и Па́сха.[18] Они́ пра́зднуются[19] до сих пор.[20] Ма́сленица — э́то неде́ля карнава́ла до по́ста[21] пе́ред Па́схой, когда́ лю́ди едя́т мно́го блино́в и игра́ют в ра́зные и́гры. Па́сха — о́чень ва́жный пра́здник для ве́рующих.[22] Па́сха всегда́ выпада́ет[23] ме́жду четвёртым апре́ля и восьмы́м ма́я. Ве́рующие хо́дят в це́рковь и едя́т кули́ч (традицио́нный сла́дкий хлеб для Па́схи) и кра́шеные[24] я́йца. Кра́шеные я́йца бы́ли осо́бенно краси́вые на Украи́не.

СЛОВАРЬ

1. любо́й — any
2. поздравля́ть (поздравля́ю, поздравля́ешь, поздравля́ют)/ поздра́вить (поздра́влю, поздра́вишь, поздра́вят) — to congratulate
3. С пра́здником! — Happy Holiday!
4. совреме́нный — contemporary
5. побе́да — victory
6. бы́вший — former
7. трудя́щиеся — workers
8. да́чный — dacha (adjective)
9. уча́сток — plot (of land)

10.	вспомина́ть (вспомина́ю, вспомина́ешь, вспомина́ют)/ вспо́мнить (вспо́мню, вспо́мнишь, вспо́мнят)	to remember, to recall
11.	поги́бшие	those who perished, died
12.	война́	war
13.	независимость	f. independence
14.	быва́ть (быва́ет, быва́ют)	to take place, to happen (with some frequency) (imp.)
15.	салю́т	fireworks
16.	вое́нный	military
17.	Рождество́	Christmas
18.	Па́сха	Easter
19.	пра́здновать (пра́здную, пра́зднуешь, пра́зднуют)/от-	to celebrate
20.	до сих пор	up until now; to the present
21.	пост	fast (вели́кий пост = Lent)
22.	ве́рующий	believer; religious person
23.	выпада́ть (выпада́ю, выпада́ешь, выпада́ют)/ вы́пасть (вы́паду, вы́падешь, вы́падут)	to fall (out), to occur
24.	кра́шеный	colored, painted

УРОК 31

ГОТОВКА. Cooking.

А. ДИАЛОГ

Гали́на Ива́новна, Ко́ля и Пат гото́вят у́жин по слу́чаю дня рожде́ния.

ГАЛИНА ИВАНОВНА: *Так, ку́рица жа́рится в духо́вке и карто́шка ва́рится. Ко́ля, пожа́луйста, наре́жь лу́ка для сала́та.*

КОЛЯ: *Где нож?*

ГАЛИНА ИВАНОВНА: *За тобо́й, виси́т на стене́.*

КОЛЯ: *(пока́зывает ма́ме таре́лку с лу́ком)* **Вот так?**

ГАЛИНА ИВАНОВНА: *Немно́жко поме́льче. А я испеку́ пиро́г!*

ПАТ: *А что я должна́ де́лать?*

ГАЛИНА ИВАНОВНА: *Посиди́ и поговори́ с на́ми, пока́ мы гото́вим у́жин.*

ПАТ: *Ла́дно. Вы всегда́ са́ми де́лаете пиро́г, а не покупа́ете?*

ГАЛИНА ИВАНОВНА: *Покупа́ть пиро́г?! Никогда́! На день рожде́ния мы всегда́ гото́вим я́блочный пиро́г по реце́пту прабабушки.*

КОЛЯ: *Я же тебе́ говори́л! Она́ скоре́е умрёт, чем ку́пит пиро́г! Така́я го́рдая!*

ГАЛИНА ИВАНОВНА: *Веди́ себя́ хорошо́, а то ты у меня́ пирога́ не полу́чишь!*

КОЛЯ: *Ах, прости́ меня́! (он целу́ет её ру́ку и смеётся)*

ГАЛИНА ИВАНОВНА: *Пат, тебе́ нра́вится стря́пать?*

ПАТ: *Не осо́бенно. У меня́ сейча́с почти́ нет посу́ды, но э́то мне не меша́ет. Я предпочита́ю ходи́ть в рестора́н!*

ГАЛИНА ИВАНОВНА: *Вот почему́ ты така́я ху́денькая! К сожале́нию, я люблю́ печь—как сама́ ви́дишь!*

Galina Ivanovna, Kolya, and Pat prepare a birthday dinner.

GALINA IVANOVNA: So, the chicken's roasting in the oven, and the potatoes are boiling. Kolya, please chop the onions for the salad.

KOLYA: Where's the knife?

GALINA IVANOVNA: Behind you, hanging on the wall.

KOLYA: *(showing his mother the plate of onions)* Like this?

GALINA IVANOVNA: A little smaller. And I'll start on the pastry for dessert!

PAT: And what should I do?

GALINA IVANOVNA: Sit and talk with us a bit while we make dinner.

PAT: Alright. Do you always make the cake yourself, rather than buying one?

GALINA IVANOVNA: Buy it? Never! For birthdays we always make my great-grandmother's apple pastry.

KOLYA: What did I tell you? She'd sooner die than buy a cake! Oh, such pride!

GALINA IVANOVNA: Behave yourself, or else you won't get any!

KOLYA: No! No! Forgive me! *(he kisses her hand, laughing)*

GALINA IVANOVNA: Pat, do you like to cook?

PAT: Not especially. I have practically no dishes at my house now, but that doesn't bother me. I prefer to eat out!

GALINA IVANOVNA: That's why you're so thin! Unfortunately, I love to bake, as you can see.

B. ГРАММАТИКА И СЛОВОУПОТРЕБЛЕНИЕ

1. THE COMMAND FORM

To form commands or requests, known as imperatives, drop the third person plural ending of a verb, and replace it with -й (singular) or -йте (plural or polite) if the resulting stem ends in a vowel. If the stems ends in a consonant, there are two options. If the stem ends in a *single* consonant and is not end-stressed throughout conjugation, the endings are **-ь** and **-ьте**. If it is end-stressed, the endings are **-и** and **-ите**.

STEM ENDS IN:	ENDING	EXAMPLE
a vowel	-й/-йте	де́лать ≫ де́лают ≫ де́ла+ й ≫ Де́лай(те)!
a consonant, with shifting or ending stress	-и/-ите	говори́ть ≫ говоря́т ≫ говор+ и ≫ Говори́(те)! смотре́ть ≫ смотрю́, смо́трят ≫ смотр+ и ≫ Смотри́(те)!
single consonant, with stem stressed	-ь/-ьте	быть >> бу́д+ >> бу́д + ь >> Бу́дь(те)!

Слу́шайте, ребя́та! (слу́шать: слу́шают)
Listen, guys!

Смотри́! Кака́я то́нкая рабо́та! (смотре́ть: смотрю́, смо́трят)
Look! What fine workmanship!

Веди́ себя́ хорошо́! —Ах, прости́ меня́! (вести́: веду́т; прости́ть: простя́т)
Behave yourself! —Oh, forgive me!

Ко́ля, пожа́луйста, наре́жь лу́ка для сала́та. (наре́зать: наре́жут)
Kolya, please chop the onions for the salad.

Прове́рьте аккумуля́тор, пожа́луйста. (прове́рить: прове́рят)
Check the battery, please.

Some common verbs have irregular imperatives. Single-syllable infinitives ending in **-ить** take the imperative ending **-ей(те),** infinitives ending in **-ава́ть** take the imperative ending **-ава́й(те),** and prefixed forms of **е́хать,** e.g. **пое́хать, приезжа́ть,** have the imperative ending **-езжа́й(те).** Also, irregular verbs have irregular imperatives: **дать** (and any of its compounds, such as **переда́ть**) has the imperative form **Дай(те)!,** and **есть** has the imperative form **Ешь(те)!**

Пат, переда́й ему́ нож. (переда́ть)
Pat, hand him the knife.

Пожа́луйста, вы́пейте и пое́шьте! (вы́пить, пое́сть)
Please, drink (up) and eat (up)!

Дава́йте потанцу́ем! (дава́ть)
Let's (all) dance!

Ребя́та, встава́йте! (встава́ть)
Get up, guys!

Приезжа́йте ко мне! (прие́хать/приезжа́ть)
Come visit me!

2. СЕБЯ VERSUS САМ

The pronoun **себя́** corresponds to the English pronouns "myself, herself," etc. It always refers to the subject. **Себя́** declines like **тебя́,** except that it does not have a nominative form. It often follows a preposition.

Он принёс проду́кты с собо́й.
He brought the groceries with him (self).

Не тяни́те к себе́, а толка́йте от себя́.
Don't pull it towards you(rself); push it away from you(rself).

Себя́ is also used as a reflexive pronoun, in which case it is invariable. It then functions like the reflexive verb suffix **-ся,** which is an abbreviation of **себя́.**

Веди́ себя́ хорошо́, а то ты у меня́ пирога́ не полу́чишь!
Behave yourself, or else you won't get any cake!

Как вы сего́дня себя́ чу́вствуете?
How do you feel today?

Сам, on the other hand, is used either for emphasis or to note that the action was or will be performed without extraneous help. It usually follows a pronoun and agrees with the subject in gender and number.

Вы всегда́ <u>са́ми</u> де́лаете пиро́г, а не покупа́ете?
Do you always make the cake *yourself,* rather than buying one?

К сожале́нию, мне о́чень нра́вится печь—как <u>сама́</u> ви́дишь!
Unfortunately, I love to bake, as you can see (for *yourself*).

3. THE PREFIX ПО- (A LITTLE BIT, A WHILE)

The prefix **по-** generally conveys the meaning "a little." It can be attached to verbs or to short-form comparatives of adjectives.

Посиди́ и поговори́ с на́ми.
Sit and talk with us a bit.

Вот так? —Нет, немно́жко поме́льче.
Like this? —No, a little finer.

When attached to imperfective verbs, the resulting perfectives can mean "to do something for a little while."

	IMPERFECTIVE	PERFECTIVE	
to speak	говори́ть	поговори́ть	to talk for a while
to think	ду́мать	поду́мать	to think for a while
to go (by vehicle)	е́здить	пое́здить	to drive around for a while
to go (on foot)	ходи́ть	походи́ть	to walk around for a while
to lie, lay	лежа́ть	полежа́ть	to lie/stay in bed for a while
to sit	сиде́ть	посиде́ть	to sit for a while
to sleep	спать	поспа́ть	to sleep for a while
to stand	стоя́ть	постоя́ть	to stand for a while
to dance	танцева́ть	потанцева́ть	to dance for a while

Гмм … на́до поду́мать об э́том.
Hmm … I'll have to think about this a little.

За́втра суббо́та. Я у́тром хочу́ немно́жко полежа́ть.
Tomorrow's Saturday. I want to stay in bed for a while in the morning.

Many imperfective verbs, including the verbs above, can also be made into regular perfectives with the prefix **по-**. You can generally infer the correct meaning from context. Note that with **е́хать** and **идти, по-** does not mean "for a while," but "to start (going)."

Позвони́те попо́зже, ла́дно?

Call me a little later, okay?

Химчи́стка хорошо́ почи́стила оде́жду, как всегда́.

The dry cleaner cleaned the clothes well, as usual.

Она́ пое́хала на рабо́ту в де́вять часо́в.

She left for (started for, by vehicle) work at nine.

Мы пойдём домо́й че́рез час.

We'll go home (start for home, on foot) in an hour.

Following are some common short-form comparative adjectives with the prefix **по-**.

поме́ньше	a little less, a little smaller	**побо́льше**	a little more, a little bigger
повы́ше	a little higher	**пони́же**	a little lower
попо́зже	a little later	**пора́ньше**	a little earlier
поху́же	a little worse	**полу́чше**	a little better
погро́мче	a little louder	**поти́ше**	a little quieter

Как ты чу́вствуешь себя́ сего́дня? —Чуть-чу́ть полу́чше.

How do you feel today? —A little bit better.

Говори́те погро́мче, пожа́луйста. Я вас не слы́шу.

Speak a little louder, please. I can't hear you.

4. EXPRESSING "WHILE"

"While" or "as" can be expressed in two ways in Russian. When describing two simultaneous actions use **пока́**.

Посиди́ и поговори́ с на́ми, пока́ мы гото́вим.

Sit and talk with us a bit while we cook.

Пока́ мы у́жинали, они́ смотре́ли телеви́зор.

While we were eating dinner, they were watching television.

When a single (perfective) action interrupts a continuous or "background" (imperfective) action, use **когда́** (when).

Они́ позвони́ли, когда́ мы у́жинали.
They called while we were eating dinner.

Когда́ я возвраща́лась домо́й, я уви́дела твою́ подру́гу Пат.
While (as) I was returning home, I saw your friend Pat.

C. СЛОВА́РЬ

вари́ть(ся) (варю́, ва́ришь, ва́рят(ся))/с-	to boil; to be boiling (reflexive)
вести́ себя́ (хорошо́, пло́хо)	to behave oneself (well, badly)
висе́ть (вишу́, виси́шь, вися́т)	to be hanging (imp.)
Вот так?	Like this?
го́рдый	proud
гото́вка	cooking
духо́вка	oven
жа́рить(ся) (жа́рю, жа́ришь, жа́рят)/под-	to fry, to roast; to be frying, roasting (reflexive)
лук	onion
меша́ть (меша́ю, меша́ешь, меша́ют)/по- (кому́)	to bother (someone)
мука́	flour
нож	knife
переме́шивать (переме́шиваю, переме́шиваешь, переме́шивают)/**перемеша́ть** (перемеша́ю, перемеша́ешь, перемеша́ют)	to mix (together); to combine
печь(ся) (пеку́, печёшь, пеку́т(ся))/ис-	to bake; to be baking (reflexive)
пиро́г	pie; cake; pastry
поговори́ть	to talk for a while
подава́ть (подаю́, подаёшь, подаю́т) /**пода́ть** (пода́м, пода́шь, пода́ст, подади́м, подади́те, подаду́т[1])	to serve (food)
пока́	while
поме́ньше	a little less; a little smaller
посу́да	dishes
прабабушка	great-grandmother
расто́пленный	melted

---

1. This verb is a compound of **дать** and has the same irregular pattern.

ре́зать (ре́жу, ре́жешь, ре́жут)/на-	to cut, to chop
реце́пт	recipe; prescription
сам/-а́/-и	self; oneself
сковорода́	frying pan
скоре́е	sooner
стена́	wall
стря́пать (стря́паю, стря́паешь, стря́пают)/со-	to cook (old-fashioned)
таре́лка	plate, dish
толка́ть (толка́ю, толка́ешь, толка́ют)/**толкну́ть** (толкну́, толкнёшь, толкну́т)	to push
тяну́ть (тяну́, тя́нешь, тя́нут)/по-	to pull
у меня́	at my house; at my home
ху́денький	thin
худе́ть (худе́ю, худе́ешь, худе́ют)/по-	to get thin
Я же тебе́ говори́л(а)!	What did I tell you!
я́блочный	apple (adjective)

РУССКАЯ КУЛЬТУРА

Birthdays are important in Russia, but less than in the States. In the distant past, people did not even celebrate their day of birth, but instead celebrated the day of the patron saint for whom they were named. Birthdays are sometimes still referred to as **имени́ны** (name days) from the Russian Orthodox custom of naming children after saints. It is customary for the person whose birthday it is to give a celebratory dinner, rather than the other way around.

Russian **за́втрак** (breakfast) is substantial, often with meat and/or **ка́ша** (porridge); **обе́д** (lunch) is the main meal of the day, eaten from twelve to three, and has three courses: soup, a hot dish with meat or fish, usually with a vegetable side dish, and dessert. **Ужин** (dinner) is usually lighter and served at around eight. It generally includes **заку́ски** (appetizers), a hot dish, possibly soup, and dessert. For snacks or after meals, there are baked goods, fruit, or **се́мечки** (sunflower seeds). At every meal there is always a lot of bread and tea with lots of sugar. Coffee is much stronger than ours. Milk is seldom consumed alone; its more common forms are **творо́г** (farmer's cheese) or **кефи́р** (soured yogurt). Tap water, unless it is boiled, is rarely used for drinking; mineral water is preferred.

ЯЗЫК В ДЕЙСТВИИ (Language in Action)

Label your kitchen utensils, appliances, and foods in Russian, and repeat the word when you use the item. This is an easy way to memorize kitchen-related vocabulary. And, try preparing **блины** (thin Russian pancakes), using the following recipe.[2] **Блины** are traditionally filled with jam or caviar, but any sweet or savory filling will do.

Перемешáть э́ти ингредие́нты:
1 ча́шка молока́
200 г. муки́[3]
3 яйца́
6 ст. ло́жек[4] ма́сла (расто́пленное)
Поджа́рить блины́ на сковороде́ с ма́слом. Пода́ть смета́ну. Прия́тного аппети́та!

УПРАЖНЕНИЯ

A. Поста́вьте глаго́лы в повелите́льное наклоне́ние по образцу́.
   (Put the sentences into the imperative according to the example.)

ОБРАЗЕЦ: Боб до́лжен слу́шать э́ту кассе́ту.   Боб, слу́шай э́ту ка́ссету!

1. Ко́ля до́лжен купи́ть проду́кты.
2. Мы должны́ де́лать уро́ки.
3. Я должна́ говори́ть по-ру́сски.
4. Пат должна́ переда́ть Ко́ле нож.
5. Де́ти должны́ хорошо́ вести́ себя́.
6. Вы должны́ прие́хать ко мне.
7. Ребя́та должны́ встава́ть в семь.
8. Он до́лжен прове́рить аккумуля́тор.
9. Ко́ля до́лжен наре́зать лу́к.
10. Вы должны́ быть осторо́жны.

---

2. Please see the chapter glossary for definitions of any unfamiliar words in the recipe.
3. 1 1/2 cups
4. столо́вая ло́жка (tablespoon)

B. **Запо́лните про́пуски слова́ми «себя́» и́ли «сам» и переведи́те на англи́йский.** (Fill in the blanks with **себя́** or **сам**, and translate into English.)

1. Вы _____ пригото́вили еду́? Бы́ло о́чень вку́сно!
2. Как она́ вчера́ чу́вствовала _____ ?
3. Они́ обы́чно веду́т _____ хорошо́ на ры́нке.
4. Он лю́бит говори́ть о _____ . Како́й зану́да (a bore)!
5. Де́душка _____ не по́мнит своего́ во́зраста.

C. **Подбери́те предложе́ния из коло́нки А соотве́тствующие коло́нке Б.** (Match the sentences in column A to those in column B.)

A	B
1. Мне на́до поговори́ть с ним.	a. Sit down for a bit and have a smoke.
2. Дава́й погуля́ем.	b. She cleaned the dress really well.
3. Посиди́ и покури́.	c. Do you want to dance a little?
4. Сего́дня у́тром мы искупа́лись.	d. I need to have a talk with him.
5. Ей сего́дня на́до порабо́тать.	e. They ate lunch at 2 p.m.
6. Я поспала́ по́сле рабо́ты.	f. I'll think about it for a bit, and then tell you.
7. Хо́чешь потанцева́ть?	g. He really liked this movie.
8. Я поду́маю и пото́м тебе́ скажу́.	h. Let's go for a walk.
9. Она́ хорошо́ почи́стила пла́тье.	i. She needs to work for a while today.
10. Ему́ о́чень понра́вился э́тот фильм.	j. I had a nap after work.
	k. We went for a swim this morning.

D. **Запо́лните про́пуски слова́ми «когда́», «пока́» и переведи́те на англи́йский.** (Fill in the blanks with **когда́** or **пока́**, and translate into English.)

1. Она́ отдыха́ла, _____ мы рабо́тали.
2. Он зашёл, _____ мы за́втракали.
3. _____ ты ко́нчил университе́т?
4. Дава́й пригото́вим сала́т, _____ карто́шка ва́рится.
5. Он всегда́ поёт, _____ принима́ет душ.

E. **Переведи́те на ру́сский.** (Translate into Russian.)

1. She brought the cake (or pie) with her.
2. I want to stay in bed for a while tomorrow morning.
3. Chop the tomatoes a little finer.
4. Kolya, be careful!
5. Tell me where you (plural) live.

УРОК 32

МЕДИЦИНА. Medicine.

А. ДИАЛОГ

В поликли́нике.

МЕДСЕСТРА: *Я изме́рю вам температу́ру и давле́ние, а пото́м до́ктор вас посмо́трит. Пожа́луйста, сними́те сви́тер и рассла́бьте ру́ку ...*

ДЕБОРА: *Каки́е у меня́ температу́ра и давле́ние?*

МЕДСЕСТРА: *Давле́ние у вас норма́льное, а температу́ра чуть-чу́ть повы́шена: 37,5. Разде́ньтесь до по́яса и наде́ньте хала́т. До́ктор ско́ро придёт.*

До́ктор вхо́дит.

ДОКТОР: *Здра́вствуйте. Что у вас?*

ДЕБОРА: *Голова́ кру́жится, меня́ тошни́т, и у меня́ боли́т у́хо.*

ДОКТОР: *Поня́тно. Глубоко́ вдохни́те ... И ещё раз ... Хорошо́. (щу́пает её ше́ю) Здесь?*

ДЕБОРА: *Да.*

ДОКТОР: *У вас увеличе́ние в лимфати́ческих узла́х. А тепе́рь у́ши ...*

ДЕБОРА: *Ой, здесь боли́т!*

ДОКТОР: *Я зна́ю, не дви́гайте голово́й ... У вас воспале́ние сре́днего уха.*

ДЕБОРА: *Ой, когда́ у меня́ была́ инфе́кция в го́рле, я должна́ была́ до́лго остава́ться в посте́ли. Мне не́когда сно́ва так боле́ть!*

ДОКТОР: *Вы должны́ бу́дете принима́ть антибио́тики в тече́нии десяти́ дней, но вам не на́до бу́дет лежа́ть в посте́ли. Не уныва́йте, всё бу́дет хорошо́!*

At the health center.

NURSE: I'll check your temperature and blood pressure, and then the doctor will take a look at you. Please take off your sweater, and relax your arm ...

DEBORA: And how are my temperature and blood pressure?

NURSE: Your blood pressure's normal, but you've got a bit of a temperature: 37.5. Undress to the waist, and put on this gown. The doctor will be here shortly.

The doctor comes in.

DOCTOR: Hello. What's wrong?

DEBORA: I'm dizzy, I'm nauseous, and my ear hurts.

DOCTOR: I see. Breathe deeply ... And again ... Good. *(feeling her neck)* Does that hurt?

DEBORA: Yes.

DOCTOR: There's swelling in your lymph nodes. Now the ears ...

DEBORA: Ow, that hurts!

DOCTOR: I know, but don't move your head ... You have a middle ear infection.

DEBORA: Oh, when I had a throat infection I had to stay in bed for a long time. I don't have time to be that sick again!

DOCTOR: You'll have to take antibiotics for ten days, but you won't have to stay in bed. Cheer up, everything will be okay!

B. ГРАММАТИКА И СЛОВОУПОТРЕБЛЕНИЕ

1. PERFECTIVE AND IMPERFECTIVE IMPERATIVES

Perfective imperatives refer to a single, complete, one-time action.

Пожа́луйста, сними́те сви́тер и рассла́бьте ру́ку. (снима́ть/снять; расслабля́ть/рассла́бить)
Please take off your sweater, and relax your arm.

Разде́ньтесь до по́яса и наде́ньте хала́т. (раздева́ться/разде́ться; надева́ть/наде́ть)
Undress to the waist, and put on this gown.

Глубоко́ вдохни́те. (вдыха́ть/вдохну́ть)
Breathe deeply.

Imperfective imperatives are used for:

a. negative commands;

Не уныва́йте, всё бу́дет хорошо́! (уныва́ть)
Cheer up (lit., don't be depressed), you'll be fine!

Рик, не обраща́й внима́ние на него́. (обраща́ть/обрати́ть)
Rick, don't pay any attention to him.

b. urgent commands or requests;

Не дви́гайте голово́й. (дви́гать/дви́нуть)
Don't move your head.

Смотри́, Ле́на, Ната́ша пригласи́ла меня́ на свою́ сва́дьбу! (смотре́ть/посмотре́ть)
Look, Lena, Natasha's invited me to her wedding!

c. invitations, general injunctions, exhortations, or expressions of wishes.

Входи́, входи́! (входи́ть/войти́)
Come in, come in!

Всегда́ слу́шайте свои́х роди́телей. (слу́шать/послу́шать)
Always listen to your parents.

Собира́йте макулату́ру! (собира́ть/собра́ть)
Recycle (lit., Collect recyclable paper)!

Выздора́вливай! (выздора́вливать/вы́здороветь)
Get well soon!

However, perfective imperatives are sometimes used to show politeness or formality where you would normally expect an imperfective.

Извини́те, како́е сего́дня число́? (извиня́ть/извини́ть)
Excuse me, what's today's date?

Где на́до плати́ть? —Заплати́те в ка́ссу, пожа́луйста. (плати́ть/заплати́ть)
Where do I pay? —Please pay at the cash register.

2. "AGAIN"

Ещё раз, опя́ть, and сно́ва can all be translated into English as "again," but they are used differently. Ещё раз means "once more" and refers to a specific, countable action. Сно́ва indicates resumption rather than repetition. Опя́ть indicates a repetition but with possible overtones of irritation at the repetition.

Глубоко́ вдохни́те. И ещё раз.
Breathe deeply. And again (once more).

Мне не́когда сно́ва так боле́ть!
I don't have time to be that sick (all over) again!

Опя́ть идёт дождь! Мне надое́л дождь!
It's raining *again*! I'm fed up with the rain!

3. THE METRIC SYSTEM

In Russia, the metric system is used to express temperature (degrees Celsius), height (meters), weight (grams or kilos), volume (liters), and distance (kilometers). Following are some common measures and their closest American approximations.

10 см (10 cm)	= 4 inches
1 метр (1 meter)	= 1 yard
1 литр (1 liter)	= 1 quart
1 кило́ (1 kilogram)	= 2 pounds
500 гра́мм (500 grams)	= 1 pound
1 киломе́тр (1 kilometer)	= 1.5 miles
0 гра́дусов по Це́льсию (0° Celsius)	= 32° Fahrenheit (freezing point)

Температу́ра у вас чуть-чу́ть повы́шена: 37,5 гра́дусов.

You've got a bit of a temperature: 37.5° (99.5° Fahrenheit).

Он ро́стом в метр во́семьдесят пять, а она́ ро́стом в метр шестьдеся́т.

He's 1.85 meters (1 meter 85 cm., or 6 feet) tall, and she's 1.6 meters (1 m. 60 cm., or 5 ft.) tall.

Како́й у них вес? —Он ве́сит 80 ки́ло, а она́ ве́сит 52 ки́ло.

What do they weigh? ——He weighs 80 kilos (176 lbs.), and she weighs 52 kilos (114 lbs.).

Да́йте, пожа́луйста, две́сти пятьдеся́т грамм сы́ра и ки́ло апельси́нов.

Please give me 250 grams (8.75 oz.) of cheese and a kilo (2.2 lbs.) of oranges.

Со́рок ли́тров 72–о́го, пожа́луйста.

Forty liters (10.4 gallons) of 72 [octane], please.

Я живу́ в Хаба́ровске, шестьсо́т киломе́тров к се́веру от Владивосто́ка.

I live in Khabarovsk, 600 kilometers (372 miles) to the north of Vladivostok.

Normal body temperature is 37° Celsius, and it is generally taken under the arm rather than in the mouth; an outside temperature of 30° Celsius is very hot, and 20° Celsius is about 70° Fahrenheit. Food is measured in grams (100 grams is about a quarter pound serving), as are drinks by the glass (100 grams is also one serving of alcohol); drinks by the bottle are measured in liters. Normal height for a man is 1.75 meters (5 feet, 10 inches), and for a woman is 1.65 meters (5 feet, 6 inches).

4. THE PAST AND FUTURE TENSES WITH ДОЛЖЕН

До́лжен (have to; must) can be used with the past or future tense of the verb **быть** directly following it. Both **до́лжен** and **быть** must agree with the subject in gender and number.

Дебо́ра должна́ была́ до́лго лежа́ть в посте́ли.

Debora had to stay in bed for a long time.

Вы должны́ бу́дете принима́ть антибио́тики, но вы не должны́ бу́дете лежа́ть в посте́ли.

You'll have to take antibiotics, but you won't have to stay in bed.

Он за́втра до́лжен бу́дет о́чень ра́но встать.

He will have to get up very early tomorrow.

5. PARTS OF THE BODY

In Russian, a single word refers to both "leg" and "foot," "arm" and "hand," and "finger" and "toe."

бедро́	hip, thigh	па́лец/па́льцы	finger/fingers;
бок	side		toe/toes
глаз/глаза́	eye/eyes	плечо́/пле́чи	shoulder/
грудь	chest		shoulders
живо́т/желу́док	stomach	по́яс	waist (band)
ко́жа	skin	рот	mouth
коле́но	knee	рука́/ру́ки	arm/arms;
лёгкие	lungs		hand/hands
лицо́	face	се́рдце	heart
нога́/но́ги	leg/legs;	спина́	back
	foot/feet	у́хо/у́ши	ear/ears
нос	nose	ше́я	neck

Разде́ньтесь до по́яса и наде́ньте хала́т.

Undress to the waist, and put on this gown.

Пожа́луйста, сними́те сви́тер и рассла́бьте ру́ку.

Please take off your sweater, and relax your arm.

Голова́ кру́жится, меня́ тошни́т, и у меня́ боли́т у́хо.

I'm dizzy, I'm nauseous, and my ear hurts.

До́ктор щу́пает ей ше́ю.

The doctor feels her neck.

С. СЛОВАРЬ

в тече́ние (чего́)	for (a period of time)
вдыха́ть (вдыха́ю, вдыха́ешь, вдыха́ют) /*вдохну́ть* (вдохну́, вдохнёшь, вдохну́т)	to breathe
ве́сить (вешу, ве́сишь, ве́сят)	to weigh (imp.)
воспале́ние	inflammation
выздора́вливать (выздора́вливаю, выздора́вливаешь, выздора́вливают)/*вы́здороветь* (вы́здоровею, вы́здоровеешь, вы́здоровеют)	to recover
глубо́кий	deep
го́рло	throat
голова́ кру́жится	I'm dizzy (lit. my head is spinning)
давле́ние	blood pressure (lit. pressure)
дви́гать (двига́ю, двига́ешь, двига́ют) /*дви́нуть* (дви́ну, дви́нешь, дви́нут)	to move
до по́яса	to the waist (lit. to the waistband)
инфе́кция	infection
Како́й у вас вес?	What do you weigh?
медсестра́/медбра́т	nurse (female/male)
меня́ тошни́т	I'm nauseous (lit. it sickens me)
опя́ть	again
повы́шен/-а/-о/-ы	a little high
поликли́ника	clinic; health center
раздева́ться (раздева́юсь, раздева́ешься, раздева́ются)/ *разде́ться* (разде́нусь, разде́нешься, разде́нутся)	to get undressed
расслабля́ть (расслабля́ю, расслабля́ешь, расслабля́ют)/ *рассла́бить* (рассла́блю, рассла́бишь, рассла́бят)	to relax (part of the body)
ро́стом	in height
снима́ть (снима́ю, снима́ешь, снима́ют) /*снять* (сниму́, сни́мешь, сни́мут)	to take off; to rent; to photograph
сно́ва	again
сре́днее у́хо	middle ear

Тридцать второ́й уро́к

увеличе́ние	swelling
у́хо (у́ши)	ear (ears)
уныва́ть (уныва́ю, уныва́ешь, уныва́ют)	to be depressed (imp.)
Не уныва́й(те)*!*	Cheer up!
хала́т	dressing gown; hospital smock
Что у вас?	What's wrong?
ше́я	neck
щу́пать (щу́паю, щу́паешь, щу́пают)/по-	to feel (for), touch, probe

РУССКАЯ КУЛЬТУРА

Each Russian city has a system of polyclinics, or health centers, and residents are assigned to the nearest one. There are also children's hospitals, other specialized hospitals, as well as various private clinics. Polyclinics serve primarily as outpatient clinics and referral and information services. Two of their most important functions are providing medical excuses for sick days and performing medical exams when required for employment, e.g., for food workers, or those who work with children. Certified medical leave (signed by a doctor and stamped by the polyclinic) entitles an employee to a set number of sick days, at full or partial pay. Polyclinics also provide a range of physical therapy treatments. In general, the emphasis is on preventive medicine and "rest cures," either in the hospital or at a sanatorium.

УПРАЖНЕНИЯ

A. **Запо́лните про́пуски и переведи́те на англи́йский.** (Fill in the blanks and translate into English.)

1. Заплати́те в ка́ссу, пожа́луйста, а зате́м _____ мне чек. (неси́те/принеси́те)

2. _____ домо́й! (иди́те/пойди́те)

3. Не _____ никому́ об э́том. (говори́те/скажи́те)

4. _____ лека́рство вме́сте с едо́й. (пе́йте/вы́пейте)

5. _____ , _____ и _____ . (встава́й/встань, одева́йся/оде́нься, за́втракай/поза́втракай)

B. Запóлните прóпуски словáми «ещё раз,» «снóва», «опя́ть».
(Fill in the blanks with ещё раз, снóва, or опя́ть.)

1. Я ей позвоню́_____ .
2. Онá _____ живёт в Москвé.
3. Я бою́сь, что у меня́ _____ инфéкция.
4. _____ ты больнá!
5. Я хочу́ _____ прочитáть э́ту кни́гу. Я всё забы́л.

C. Переведи́те на рýсский. (Translate into Russian.)

1. She has a temperature of 39°.
2. How tall are you (formal)? —I'm 1.7 meters tall.
3. How much do you (formal) weigh? —I weigh 60 kilos.
4. We need 300 grams of butter and one liter of wine.
5. What's the distance between the hotel and the center of town?
   —Five kilometers.

D. Постáвьте глагóлы в прошéдшее врéмя и затéм в бýдущее врéмя.
(Put the sentences into the past and then into the future tense.)

1. Дебóра должнá дóлго лежáть в постéли.
2. Вы должны́ принимáть антибиóтики.
3. Дóктор говори́т, что больнóй дóлжен отдыхáть.
4. Дéти должны́ дéлать урóки.
5. В семь часóв мáма должнá пойти́ на рабóту.

УРОК 33

СОБЕСЕДОВАНИЕ ПРИ ПРИЁМЕ НА РАБОТУ. A job interview.

А. ДИАЛОГ

Алекса́ндра Григо́рьевна интервьюи́рует Би́лла.

АЛЕКСАНДРА ГРИГОРЬЕВНА: *Мы и́щем кого́-нибудь, кто о́чень хорошо́ зна́ет и ру́сский, и англи́йский.*

БИЛЛ: *Как ви́дно из моего́ резюме́, я переводи́л для ру́сских делега́ций и рабо́тал в междунаро́дной фи́рме. На обе́их рабо́тах мне на́до бы́ло всё вре́мя говори́ть по-ру́сски.*

АЛЕКСАНДРА ГРИГОРЬЕВНА: *Как и когда́ вы ушли́ из фи́рмы?*

БИЛЛ: *Я ушёл то́лько что, ме́сяц наза́д, потому́ что я хоте́л рабо́тать в Росси́и.*

АЛЕКСАНДРА ГРИГОРЬЕВНА: *Вам не тру́дно бу́дет привы́кнуть здесь жить?*

БИЛЛ: *Я ещё со шко́лы увлека́юсь ру́сской культу́рой, и я мно́го раз быва́л в Росси́и. Мне ка́жется, что мне бы́ло бы прия́тно здесь жить.*

АЛЕКСАНДРА ГРИГОРЬЕВНА: *Хорошо́. Вы когда́-нибу́дь руководи́ли ру́сско-америка́нским прое́ктом?*

БИЛЛ: *Я руководи́л ру́сско-америка́нским коллекти́вом, кото́рый организова́л в Москве́ семина́р по пробле́мам управле́ния. Вот описа́ние прое́кта.*

АЛЕКСАНДРА ГРИГОРЬЕВНА: *Отли́чно. Пожалу́й, вы и́менно тот, кто нам ну́жен! Ну, спаси́бо. Мы всем кандида́там позвони́м че́рез неде́лю.*

БИЛЛ: *Бы́ло очень прия́тно с ва́ми познако́миться, и спаси́бо за то, что вы удели́ли мне вре́мя. До свида́ния.*

Aleksandra Grigorievna is interviewing Bill.

ALEKSANDRA GRIGORIEVNA: We're looking for someone who knows both Russian and English very well.

BILL: As you can see from my resume, I've interpreted for Russian delegations and worked at an international firm. In both jobs I had to speak Russian all the time.

ALEKSANDRA GRIGORIEVNA: Why and when did you leave the firm?

BILL: I just left a month ago because I wanted to work in Russia.

ALEKSANDRA GRIGORIEVNA: Will it be difficult for you to get used to living in Russia?

BILL: Well, I've been fascinated with Russian culture since high school, and I've been to Russia many times. I think I would enjoy living here.

ALEKSANDRA GRIGORIEVNA: Good. Have you ever managed a Russo-American project?

BILL: I was in charge of a U.S.-Russian team that arranged a management seminar in Moscow. Here's an outline of the project.

ALEKSANDRA GRIGORIEVNA: Excellent. You may be just the person we need! Well, thank you. We'll be calling all the candidates in a week.

BILL: It was very nice to meet you, and thank you for your time. Good-bye.

B. ГРАММАТИКА И СЛОВОУПОТРЕБЛЕНИЕ

1. BOTH (ОБА)

In Russian, "both (of)" is expressed by **óба** (masculine/neuter/a mixed group) or **óбе** (feminine). As with the cardinal number **два**, any nouns following **óба** must be in the genitive singular.

Оба места уже заняты.
Both (of the) positions are already filled.

Обе работы были в Нью-Йорке.
Both (of the) jobs were in New York.

Как ветера́ны, мы о́ба здесь получи́ли но́вые кварти́ры по́сле войны́.

As veterans we both received new apartments here after the war.

О́ба also behaves like a special modifier, i.e. if the noun it modifies is declined, it will agree with that noun in case and gender.

	MASCULINE/NEUTER	FEMININE
Nominative	о́ба	о́бе
Accusative	о́ба/обо́их	о́бе
Genitive	обо́их	обе́их
Dative	обо́им	обе́им
Instrumental	обо́ими	обе́ими
Prepositional	обо́их	обе́их

На обе́их рабо́тах мне на́до бы́ло всё вре́мя говори́ть по-ру́сски.

In both (of the) jobs I had to speak Russian all the time.

Билл перево́дит в о́бе сто́роны, с ру́сского на англи́йский и наоборо́т.

Bill interprets both ways, from Russian to English and vice versa.

Мы интересу́емся обо́ими кандида́тами.

We're interested in both (of the) candidates.

2. THE PAST AND FUTURE TENSE WITH IMPERSONAL EXPRESSIONS

The understood subject of sentences with **ну́жно** or **на́до,** or any impersonal constructions, is considered neuter (see **Уро́к** 17). The past or future tense of such expressions, formed with **быть,** must therefore also be neuter (**бы́ло, бу́дет**).

Мне на́до бы́ло мно́го говори́ть по-ру́сски на рабо́те.

I had to speak Russian a great deal at work.

Вам не ну́жно бу́дет лежа́ть в посте́ли.

You won't have to stay in bed.

Ну́жно бы́ло бы́стро к нему́ дозвони́ться.

It was necessary to reach him quickly.

Хорошо́ бы́ло, когда́ мы бы́ли в Петербу́рге.

It was fine while we were in St. Petersburg.

Мне легко́ бу́дет привы́кнуть жи́ть в Росси́и.

It will be easy for me to get used to living in Russia.

It is important to remember that **бу́дет** is part of **ну́жно, на́до,** or the impersonal construction, and is not part of the future imperfective of the following verb.

3. THE ADVERB "JUST"

The adverb "just" has four meanings: "very recently," "exactly," "only," and "simply." In Russian these different meanings are rendered by **то́лько что, и́менно то, то́лько,** and **про́сто,** respectively.

то́лько что	just, very recently
и́менно то	just, exactly
то́лько	just, only
про́сто	just, simply

Я то́лько что ушла́, ме́сяц наза́д.

I just left a month ago.

Он чита́ет письмо́, кото́рое он то́лько что получи́л.

He's reading the letter that he just received.

Пожа́луй, вы и́менно тот, кто нам ну́жен!

You may be just the person we need!

Это и́менно то, что на́до мои́м роди́телям.

It's just the thing for my parents.

Я то́лько хочу́ су́пу.

I just want some soup.

Мы про́сто не зна́ем, что де́лать.

We just don't know what to do.

4. CONJUGATION OF -НУТЬ VERBS

Verbs ending in -**нуть** are Conjugation I verbs and are often perfective.

привы́кнуть: to get used to (perfective) [1]

I'll get used to	я привы́кну	мы привы́кнем	we'll get used to
you'll (fam.) get used to	ты привы́кнешь	вы привы́кнете	you'll (pl./pol.) get used to
he'll/she'll get used to	он/она́ привы́кнет	они́ привы́кнут	they'll get used to

stem = привы́кн+
imperative: Привы́кни(те)!

Вам не тру́дно бу́дет привы́кнуть к жи́зни в Росси́и?
Will it be difficult for you to get used to life in Russia?

Она́ ско́ро привы́кнет встава́ть в шесть.
She'll soon get used to getting up at six.

Other common perfective verbs conjugated like **привы́кнуть** include:

	IMPERFECTIVE	PERFECTIVE
to return	возвраща́ться	верну́ться
to breathe	вдыха́ть	вдохну́ть
to move	дви́гать	дви́нуть
to freeze	замерза́ть	замёрзнуть
to fall asleep	засыпа́ть	засну́ть
to disappear	исчеза́ть	исче́знуть
to touch, concern	каса́ться	косну́ться
to rest, relax	отдыха́ть	отдохну́ть
to wake up	просыпа́ться	просну́ться
to jump	пры́гать	пры́гнуть
to pull	тяну́ть	потяну́ть
to push	толка́ть	толкну́ть

Он продви́нется на рабо́те, когда́ он зако́нчит э́тот прое́кт.
He'll advance (move forward) at work when he finishes this project.

1. imperfective: привыка́ть

Мы отдохнём, а потóм поýжинаем.

We'll rest, and then we'll have dinner.

The following verbs have masculine past tense forms that do not end in **-л**: **замёрзнуть » замёрз, исчéзнуть » исчéз, привы́кнуть » привы́к.** In such cases, simply add **-ла/-ло/-ли** for the feminine, neuter, and plural forms. Most **-нуть** verbs have regular imperatives ending in **-ни(те)** or **-ни(те)сь.**

Зáвтра ты рáно проснёшься? —Да, я привы́кла рáно просыпáться.

Will you wake up early tomorrow? —Yes, I'm used to waking up early.

У меня́ из сýмки исчéз журнал! —Не волнýйся, я егó вы́тащил. Вот он.

The magazine has disappeared from my bag! —Don't worry, I pulled it out. Here it is.

5. "SINCE"

There are several ways to translate "since" in Russian: **с** (since a day or time), **с тех пор (как)** (since an action or event), and **так как** (since; because; seeing as how).

Я ещё со шкóлы увлекáюсь рýсской культýрой.

I've been fascinated with Russian culture ever since high school.

Я там рабóтаю с прóшлого гóда.

I've worked there since last year.

С тех пор, как я переéхал, я бóльше их не ви́жу.

Since I moved I haven't seen them.

Так как ты идёшь, и я пойдý.

Since you're going, I'll go, too.

С. СЛОВАРЬ

быва́ть (быва́ю, быва́ешь, быва́ют)/ ***побыва́ть*** (побыва́ю, побыва́ешь, побыва́ют)	to be (repeatedly), to visit, to happen, (frequently) (imp.) to visit (perf.)

вперёд	forward
всё вре́мя	all the time
делега́ция	delegation
дозвони́ться (к кому́)	to reach (someone) by phone
заполня́ть (заполня́ю, заполня́ешь, заполня́ют)/ **запо́лнить** (запо́лню, запо́лнишь, запо́лнят)	to fill (in)
зарпла́та	salary
засыпа́ть (засыпа́ю, засыпа́ешь, засыпа́ют)/**засну́ть** (засну́, заснёшь, засну́т)	to fall asleep
и наоборо́т	and vice versa (lit. the opposite)
и́менно то (что/кто)	just the, exactly the (someone/ thing)
интервью́	interview
интервью́и́ровать (интервью́и́рую, интервью́и́руешь, интервью́и́руют)	to interview (imp. and perf.)
исчеза́ть (исчеза́ю, исчеза́ешь, исчеза́ют)/**исче́знуть** (исче́зну, исче́знешь, исче́знут)	to disappear
кандида́т	candidate
коллекти́в	team; group
контра́кт	contract
о́ба/о́бе	both
описа́ние	description
организова́ть (организу́ю, организу́ешь, организу́ют)	to organize (imp., perf.)
отноше́ние	relation; attitude
переезжа́ть (переезжа́ю, переезжа́ешь, переезжа́ют)/ **перее́хать** (перее́ду, перее́дешь, перее́дут)	to move (to a new location)
пожа́луй	I suppose; perhaps; it may be
предприя́тие	business, enterprise
привыка́ть (привыка́ю, привыка́ешь, привыка́ют) /**привы́кнуть** (привы́кну, привы́кнешь, привы́кнут) (чем)	to get used to (something)
прое́кт	project
про́сто	just, simply; simple
резюме́	resume

руководи́ть (руковожу́, руководи́шь, руководя́т)	to lead, direct, manage (imperfective)
с тех пор	since then
семина́р	seminar; workshop
си́ла	strength; skill
собесе́дование	interview; conversation, discussion
так как	since; because
то́лько что	just; very recently
управле́ние	management
фи́рма	firm, company

РУССКАЯ КУЛЬТУРА

When applying for a job or doing business in Russia, it will help to remember a few things about the culture. For example, the term **бизнесме́н** (businessman) has been associated with dishonesty, greed, and low morals. Demonstrated concern for and sensitivity to others is more valued than self-reliance, and modesty is valued over confidence, which is often interpreted as arrogance. Talking or laughing loudly in public or in any way drawing attention to yourself will be seen as rude or uncultured.

For an interview or business meeting, Russians tend to dress less formally than Americans. They usually wear something less formal than a dark suit with a white shirt, but more formal than jeans. Women should wear skirts, with neatness being more important than elegance. Be punctual for a job interview or business meeting, and expect firmer and more frequent handshakes than in the United States. If you know your potential employer's or business associate's first name and patronymic and can use them properly, do so. Otherwise, address them in English with "Mr." or "Ms." If asked how you heard of the company, remember that getting positions and information through friends and acquaintances is not only acceptable in Russia, but is the general rule. Business is not usually discussed at meals, but tea, bottled water, and perhaps cookies might accompany a business discussion.

УПРАЖНЕНИЯ

A. Запо́лните про́пуски по образцу́ и переведи́те на англи́йский.
(Fill in the blanks according to the example and translate into English.)

ОБРАЗЕЦ: Он говори́т об <u>обе́их</u> гости́ницах.

1. Я люблю́ _____ бра́тьев.
2. Мы _____ хоти́м рабо́тать в Росси́и.
3. _____ резюме́ от америка́нцев.
4. Она́ поговори́ла с _____ кандида́тами.
5. Мне нра́вятся _____ стра́ны.

B. Поста́вьте глаго́лы в проше́дшее вре́мя и зате́м в бу́дущее вре́мя.
(Put the sentences into the past tense and then into the future tense.)

1. Нам ну́жно купи́ть хле́ба и молока́.
2. Кому́ на́до поговори́ть с Алекса́ндрой Григо́рьевной?
3. Ну́жно хорошо́ говори́ть по-ру́сски.
4. Им ну́жно иска́ть рабо́ту.
5. На́до подожда́ть.

C. Запо́лните про́пуски в коло́нке А глаго́лами из коло́нки Б.
(Match the sentences in column A to the verbs in column B.)

A	B
1. Она́ о́чень уста́ла. Она́ _____ сра́зу по́сле у́жина.	a. замёрзла
2. Утро—его́ люби́мое вре́мя. Он сего́дня _____ в шесть часо́в.	b. исче́з
3. Бы́ло так хо́лодно, что вода́ _____ в тру́бах.	c. па́хнет
4. Пожа́луйста, _____ его́ резюме́. Я хочу́ его́ посмотре́ть.	d. верни́тесь
5. Ива́н Петро́вич был здесь, а зате́м—он _____ !	e. привы́кли
6. Ситуа́ция в Росси́и ско́ро _____ всех из нас.	f. пры́гнули
7. Де́ти _____ от ра́дости (joy), когда́ они́ уви́дели пода́рки.	g. засну́ла
8. _____ ско́ро!	h. принеси́те
9. Мы поговори́м по́сле того́, как вы немно́жко _____ .	i. коснётся
10. Что здесь так пло́хо _____ ?	j. просну́лся
	k. отдохнёте

D. **Переведи́те на ру́сский.** (Translate into Russian.)

1. He just left a minute ago.
2. Bill's been in Moscow since May.
3. She just called five minutes ago.
4. This computer is exactly what we need!
5. The business has grown (**вы́расти**) since we were here two
   years ago.

УРОК 34

ПОКУПКА ПОДАРКОВ И СУВЕНИРОВ.

Shopping for souvenirs and presents.

А. ДИАЛОГ

На Арба́те.

КАТЯ: *Здесь краси́вые куста́рные изде́лия. Хо́чешь посмотре́ть?*

ДЖЕССИКА: *Да, с удово́льствием! Мне ну́жно купи́ть пода́рки для роди́телей, сестры́ и племя́нниц.*

КАТЯ: *Не хо́чешь па́лехскую шкату́лку? Посмотри́, кака́я то́нкая рабо́та!*

ДЖЕССИКА: *И каки́е я́ркие цвета́! Из чего́ сде́лана шкату́лка?*

КАТЯ: *Из де́рева, покры́того эма́лью. Ви́дишь, э́то ска́зка про жа́р-птицу!*

ДЖЕССИКА: *Да, так оно́ и есть! Как замеча́тельно! Это и́менно то, что на́до мои́м роди́телям. Они́ мо́гут поста́вить её на по́лку над ками́ном.*

КАТЯ: *Вот матрёшки. Твои́м племя́нницам они́ о́чень понра́вятся! Эта хоро́шенькая.*

ДЖЕССИКА: *А та смешна́я. Хоро́шая иде́я. Ой, посмотри́ на э́ти се́рьги из янтаря́!*

КАТЯ: *Краси́вые ... и о́чень необы́чные.*

ДЖЕССИКА: *В то́чности во вку́се мое́й сестры́! Они́ ей о́чень пойду́т.*

КАТЯ: *Я ра́да. Зна́чит, у тебя́ есть всё, что ну́жно!*

ДЖЕССИКА: *Ну, вот и прекра́сно—я оста́лась почти́ без де́нег!*

ПРОДАВЕЦ: *Если вы хоти́те, мы всё вам доста́вим.*

ДЖЕССИКА: *Спаси́бо, э́то бы́ло бы отли́чно! Я останови́лась в гости́нице «Золото́е кольцо́».¹*

1. Named after the so-called "Golden Ring" of historic cities ringing Moscow.

On the Arbat.

KATYA: They have beautiful hand-crafted things here. Would you like to take a look?

JESSICA: Yes, I'd love to! I need to buy presents for my parents, my sister, and my nieces.

KATYA: How about a Palekh box? Look, what fine workmanship!

JESSICA: And what bright colors! What is the box made of?

KATYA: Wood, painted with enamel. See, this is the story of the Firebird!

JESSICA: Why, so it is! How wonderful! It's just the thing for my parents. They can put it on the shelf above the fireplace.

KATYA: Here are the nesting dolls. Your nieces would love them! This one's pretty.

JESSICA: And that one's funny. Good idea. Oh, look at these amber earrings!

KATYA: Beautiful . . . and very unusual.

JESSICA: Exactly my sister's taste! They'll suit her perfectly.

KATYA: I'm glad. So, you have everything you need!

JESSICA: It's a good thing, too—I'm almost out of money!

SALESMAN: We'll deliver everything to you if you'd like.

JESSICA: Thanks, that would be great! I'm staying at the Golden Ring[1] Hotel.

В. ГРАММАТИКА И СЛОВОУПОТРЕБЛЕНИЕ

1. TOT (THAT ONE, THOSE ONES)

The demonstrative pronoun **тот/та/то/те** (that one, those ones) agrees with the noun it replaces in gender, number, and case. It declines like **э́тот**.

	MASCULINE	NEUTER	FEMININE	PLURAL
NOMINATIVE	тот	то	та	те
ACCUSATIVE INANIMATE	тот	то	та	те
ACCUSATIVE ANIMATE	того	того	ту	тех
GENITIVE	того	того	той	тех
PREPOSITIONAL	том	том	той	тем
DATIVE	тому	тому	той	тем
INSTRUMENTAL	тем	тем	той	тёми

Тот can be used:

    a. in contrast with **э́тот/э́та/э́то/э́ти.** When contrasted with **тот, э́тот** can be used alone or with a noun.

Эта хоро́шенькая, а та смешна́я.
This one's pretty, and that one's amusing.

Этот самова́р большо́й, а тот бо́льше.
This samovar is big, but that one's bigger.

Это кольцо́ мне нра́вится, а то мне не о́чень нра́вится.
I like this ring, but I don't like that one very much.

    b. to mean "he," "she," or "the latter." **Тот** can replace the name of a person in order to avoid ambiguity: while personal pronouns are used to refer to an aforementioned subject, **тот** is used to refer to an object. Compare:

Ка́тя показа́ла Дже́ссике шка́тулку. <u>Та</u> её купи́ла для роди́телей.
Katya showed Jessica a wooden box. She (Jessica) bought it for her parents.

Ка́тя показа́ла Дже́ссике шка́тулку. <u>Она́</u> её купи́ла для роди́телей.
Katya showed Jessica a wooden box. She (Katya or Jessica) bought it for her parents.

    c. with the relative pronouns **кото́рый** or **кто.** When followed by **кото́рый** and referring to a previously introduced noun, **тот** means "the one."

Вот знамени́тая гости́ница, та, в кото́рой у́мер поэ́т Есе́нин.
There's a famous hotel, the one in which the poet Esenin died.

Тот, кто поко́нчил собо́й, и написа́л э́ти знамени́тые стихи́? —Да, тот са́мый.

The one who killed himself and wrote that famous poem? —Yes, that one.

Я согла́сен с те́ми, кто ду́мает, что гре́шно продава́ть ико́ны.

I agree with those who think it's wrong to sell icons.

d. with **не** to mean "the wrong (one)."

Ой, я купи́ла не ту матрёшку!

Oh, I bought the wrong matryoshka!

Это не тот авто́бус. Нам ну́жен пя́тый авто́бус.

That's the wrong bus. We need bus No. 5.

e. in many set expressions and constructions.

Веди́ себя́ хорошо́, а то ты у меня́ пирога́ не полу́чишь!

Behave yourself, or else you won't get any!

Это и́менно то, что на́до мои́м роди́телям.

It's just the thing for my parents.

Many of these expressions have to do with time: в **то** вре́мя, как/когда́ (while), с **тех** пор (since then), до **тех** пор (until then), по́сле **того́** как (after), до **того́** как (before).

Я жила́ в Петербу́рге в **то** вре́мя, когда́ я учи́лась.

I lived in Petersburg while (during the time that) I was in school.

2. VERBS OF POSITION

To describe the act of placing an object somewhere, different verbs are used depending on the object's position, i.e. whether it is lying flat (**класть/положи́ть**) or standing up (**ста́вить/поста́вить**). In either case, the object being placed is in the accusative, as is its location (**куда́**). Note that the verb **класть** is a somewhat irregular Conjugation I verb. Its past tense forms are **клал/-а/-о/-и**. The remaining verbs are regular Conjugation II verbs.

кла́сть: to put; to lay down (imp.)

I put	я кладу́	мы кладём	we put
you (fam.) put	ты кладёшь	вы кладёте	you (pl./pol.) put
he/she puts	он/она́ кладёт	они́ кладу́т	they put

stem: клад+

imperative: Клади́(те)!

Они́ мо́гут поста́вить её на по́лку над ками́ном.

They can put it on the shelf above the fireplace.

Куда́ он положи́л кни́гу? —Он сейча́с её кладёт на стол.

Where did he put the book? —He's putting it on the table now.

Я поста́влю буты́лки в холоди́льник.

I'll put the bottles into the refrigerator.

If an object is already in place, another set of verbs is used to describe its location: **лежа́ть** (to be lying) and **стоя́ть** (to be standing). Although by nature imperfective, these verbs can take the perfective prefix **по-,** in which case they mean "to be lying/standing for a while." The object of these verbs is in the prepositional (**где**).

Твоя́ кни́га лежи́т на столе́, а где моя́? —Она́ стои́т на по́лке.

Your book is lying on the table, but where's mine? —It's standing on the shelf.

Салфе́тки лежа́ли на столе́, а таре́лки стоя́ли на плите́.

The napkins were lying on the table, and the plates were sitting (standing) on the stove.

Лежа́ть and **стоя́ть** may also be used in reference to people or other animate nouns. In addition, there are special verbs of position that can only refer to people or animate nouns: **встава́ть/встать** (to get up; stand up), **сади́ться/сесть** (to sit down), **сиде́ть** (to be sitting), and **ложи́ться/лечь** (to lie down). Both **сесть** and **лечь** have irregular conjugations. Their past forms are **сел/-а/-о/-и** and **лёг/-ла́/-ло́/-ли́**. Only animate nouns (people and animals) can sit (**сиде́ть**) in Russian.

сесть: to sit down (perf.)

I'll sit down	я ся́ду	мы ся́дем	we'll sit down
you'll (fam.) sit down	ты ся́дешь	вы ся́дете	you'll (pl./pol. sing.) sit down
he'll/she'll sit down	он/она́ ся́дет	они́ ся́дут	they'll sit down

stem: ся́д+

imperative: Ся́дь(те)!

лечь: to lie down (perf.)

I'll lie down	я ля́гу	мы ля́жем	we'll lie down
you'll (fam.) lie down	ты ля́жешь	вы ля́жете	you'll (pl./pol. lie down
he'll/she'll lie down	он/она́ ля́жет	они́ ля́гут	they'll lie down

stem: ля́г+

imperative: Ля́г(те)[2]!

Вста́ньте, де́ти, вста́ньте в круг!

Stand up, children; stand in a circle!

Я обы́чно ложу́сь спать в де́сять часо́в, а вчера́ я лёг спать в два часа́ но́чи.

I usually go to bed (literally, lie down to sleep) at ten, but yesterday I went to bed at two a.m.

Он сейча́с ля́жет, и че́рез два́дцать мину́т он вста́нет.

He'll lie down now, and in twenty minutes he'll get up.

Куда́ ты ся́дешь? —Ну, вчера́ я се́ла вон там, а сего́дня я ся́ду сюда́.

Where will you sit (down)? —Well, yesterday I sat (down) over there, but today I'll sit here.

3. CONVERSATIONAL FILLERS

Conversational stalling devices, fillers, and pause words, such as "um," "well," "so to speak," are an essential part of fluency. They will also help you gain time while you figure out what you want to say.

2. Use **Ся́дь(те)!** and **Ля́г(те)!** only with animals and stubborn children. Otherwise, use **Сади́(те)сь!** and **Ложи́(те)сь!**

ну	well	Как вам сказа́ть?	How should I
ну, вот	well, there you		say it?
	have it	как говори́тся	so to speak
вот	there you have it	ска́жем	let's say
так	so	вы зна́ете (ты	you know
вот так	like this, like so	зна́ешь)	
вот так вот	well, so, there it is	зна́чит	that means, so
так сказа́ть	so to say	допу́стим	let us suppose
в основно́м	on the whole	то есть	that is [to say]
де́ло в том, что	the thing is	в о́бщем	in general
		… , что ли?	… , or what?

Зна́чит, у тебя́ есть всё, что ну́жно!

So, you have everything!

В о́бщем, я боя́лся, что их все уничто́жили.

In general, I was afraid that they might have been destroyed.

Вот так … *(чита́ет письмо́)*

So, then … *(reads the letter)*

4. ОСТАНОВИТЬ(СЯ), ОСТАВАТЬСЯ, AND ОСТАВИТЬ

Остана́вливать/останови́ть means "to stop (someone or something); to stop short, to restrain (someone or something)." Adding the suffix -ся changes the meaning. Остана́вливаться/останови́ться means "to stop (oneself, or a vehicle one is driving), to come to a stop," as well as "to stay (somewhere); to put up (for a period of time), to stop over (somewhere)." Остава́ться/оста́ться also means "to stay," but in the sense of "to remain." Be sure not to confuse it with the similar verb оставля́ть/оста́вить, which means "to leave behind."

Где вы останови́лись? —Я останови́лась в гости́нице «Золото́е кольцо́».

Where are you staying? —I'm staying at the Golden Ring Hotel.

Авто́бус здесь остано́вится? —Нет, авто́бус остана́вливается вон там.

Will the bus stop here? —No, the bus stops over there.

Так как её ребёнок был бо́лен, Ка́тя оста́лась до́ма.

Since her child was sick, Katya stayed home.

Я тебе́ оста́вил её а́дрес. Он на твоём пи́сьменном столе́.

I left her address for you. It's on your desk.

The noun **остано́вка**, formed from the verb "to stop," literally means "stop" for a vehicle (e.g. bus stop) or figuratively means "hold-up; delay."

Мне на́до прое́хать ещё одну́ остано́вку.

I need to go one more stop.

Остано́вка за ви́зами.

There's a hold-up with the visas.

5. THE SUFFIX -ЕНЬК-

The diminutive suffix -**еньк**- can be used with nouns and adjectives to express smallness or approval or tenderness.

Э́та хоро́шенькая.

This one's pretty.

Вот почему́ ты така́я ху́денькая!

That's why you're so thin!

Па́шенька, ку́колки, кото́рые ты подари́л де́тям, о́чень ми́ленькие!

Pasha dear, the little dolls you gave the kids are quite adorable!

Too much use of this suffix, as in the last example, can sound very gushy. Note that **ма́ленький** (small) is formed from **ма́ло** (less, not very much) plus the suffix -**еньк**-.

C. СЛОВАРЬ

а то	or else
без де́нег	out of money; broke
в то́чности	exactly
вкус; во вку́се (кого́)	taste; to the taste (of someone)
Да, так оно́ и есть!	Why, so it is!
де́рево	wood (material); tree
доставля́ть (доставля́ю, доставля́ешь, доставля́ют)/ *доста́вить* (доста́влю, доста́вишь, доста́вят)	to deliver, to convey, to supply, to furnish

замеча́тельный	wonderful; fantastic
зна́чит	(it/that) means
Вот и прекра́сно!	Good thing, too!
иде́я	idea
изде́лия	manufactured goods; wares
ками́н	fireplace
класть (кладу́, кладёшь, кладу́т) /*положи́ть* (положу́, поло́жишь, поло́жат)	to put (lying flat); to lay; to place
ку́кла	doll, puppet
куста́рный	hand-crafted
ложи́ться (ложу́сь, ложи́шься, ложа́тся) /*лечь* (ля́гу, ля́жешь, ля́гут)	to lie down
ложи́ться/лечь спать	to go to bed (lit. to lie down to sleep)
матрёшка	wooden nesting doll
не тот (та/то/те)	the wrong (one)
необы́чный	unusual
остава́ться (остаю́сь, остаёшься, остаю́тся) /*оста́ться* (оста́нусь, оста́нешься, оста́нутся)	to stay; to remain
остана́вливаться (остана́вливаюсь, остана́вливаешься, остана́вливаются)/ *останови́ться* (остановлю́сь, остано́вишься, остано́вятся)	to stop (oneself/vehicle), come to a halt; to stay, stop over
племя́нница	niece
племя́нник	nephew
по́лка	shelf
покры́тый	covered
про (кого́, что)	on the subject of (someone/thing)
ска́зка	story, fairy tale
сде́лан/-а/-о/-ы,	made (of);
Из чего́ они́ сде́ланы?	What are they made of?
се́рьги	earrings
смешно́й	funny; amusing
сувени́р	souvenir
то́нкий	fine; thin; subtle
тот/та/то/те	that/those (one/ones)
хоро́шенький	pretty

шкату́лка	decorative box; case
эма́ль	f. enamel
янта́рь (из янтаря́)	amber (made of amber)
я́ркий	bright

РУССКАЯ КУЛЬТУРА

Certain parts of Russia and the CIS are known for specific handcrafted items. The area of **Па́лех** (Palekh) is famous for fine lacquerware with bright colors and detailed paintings. The typical lacquer objects are pins and boxes, often delicately painted with figures from Russian fairy tales, such as the **жар-пти́ца** (Firebird). In this fable, an orphan girl is turned into a Firebird by a wicked sorcerer because she refuses the riches he offers in favor of sharing the beautiful things she makes with everyone. Most of the samovars, the traditional tea vessels with the teapot on top and an urn of hot water below, are made in **Ту́ла** (Tula). **Матрёшки**, the Russian nesting dolls, are now made in many places, in various sizes and amounts of detail, and they are painted with everything from American baseball stars to former Soviet leaders to the traditional Russian peasant women for whom they are named (**Матрёна**, a typical peasant name). Amber jewelry is also typically Russian, as are delicately crafted birchbark boxes from Siberia and brightly embroidered shirts, though the latter are also typically Ukrainian. Fine woven carpets are made in Central Asia, each region known for a specific style. Amber, Central Asian carpets, Georgian wines, Armenian brandy, and, of course, high-quality vodka, are generally available in most parts of the CIS.

УПРАЖНЕНИЯ

A. **Запо́лните про́пуски ну́жной фо́рмой сло́ва «тот» и переведи́те.**
(Fill in the blanks with the correct form of the word **тот** and translate the sentences.)

1. Эти се́рьги краси́вые, а _____ краси́вее.
2. Билл зна́ет бра́та Ка́ти. _____ живёт в Нью-Йо́рке.
3. Я не понима́ю _____ , кому́ всё равно́, где их де́ти.

4. Они́ мне да́ли не _____ су́мку!

5. Встань, а _____ у тебя́ за́втрака не бу́дет!

B. **Переведи́те на ру́сский.** (Translate into Russian.)

1. She lay down on the sofa.
2. They put (stood) the glasses (стака́ны) on the shelf.
3. She always puts napkins (салфе́тки) on the table.
4. Have a seat, Jessica. —No, thanks. I should go to bed.
5. No, don't get up. I'm standing because my back hurts when I sit for a long time.

C. **Переведи́те на англи́йский.** (Translate into English.)

1. В основно́м, мне нра́вится моя́ рабо́та, то есть э́то инте́ресно.
2. Ой, Са́шенька! Что с тобо́й?
3. Да́йте мне, пожа́луйста, ска́жем, две буты́лки во́дки.
4. Тако́й то́лстенький ребёнок!
5. Де́ло в том, что э́ти самова́ры стоя́т сли́шком до́рого.

D. **Запо́лните про́пуски в коло́нке А глаго́лами из коло́нки Б.**
(Match the verbs in column B to the sentences in column A.)

A	B
1. В Москве́ я всегда́ _____ в «Золото́м Кольце́».	a. оста́нешься
2. Она́ ка́ждое у́тро тебя́ _____ в коридо́ре?	b. останови́л
3. Движе́ние почему́-то _____ .	c. стано́вится
4. Ма́льчик хоте́л убежа́ть, но оте́ц его́ _____ .	d. остава́ться
5. Мне ка́жется, что _____ до́ма о́чень ску́чно.	e. остана́вливался
6. Ты за́втра по́здно _____ на рабо́те?	f. оста́вил
7. Ой, я _____ свои́ часы́ в гости́нице!	g. остана́вливается
8. Ты всегда́ _____ ве́щи в гости́ницах!	h. останови́лось
9. Пого́да _____ холо́днее.	i. ста́ну
10. Я _____ профе́ссором!	j. остана́вливает
	k. оставля́ешь

УРОК 35

ИСТОРИЯ, ПЛАКАТЫ И ГАЗЕТЫ. History, posters, and newspapers.

А. ДИАЛОГ

В библиотеке.

БЕН: *Извините. Я слышал, что у вас есть плакаты и газеты двадцатых и тридцатых годов. Можно их посмотреть?*

БИБЛИОТЕКАРЬ: *(подозрительно) Да, есть, но зачём они вам нужны? Вы журналист?*

БЕН: *Нет, я профессор советской истории из США. Я провожу исследование о политической обстановки при Ленине, и после его смерти, чтобы лучше рассказать о ней студентам.*

БИБЛИОТЕКАРЬ: *(непреклонно) Где ваше разрешение на доступ к архивам?*

БЕН: *Пожалуйста.*

БИБЛИОТЕКАРЬ: *Так... (читает письмо) Ну, хорошо. Следуйте за мной ... Вот они. Отсюда нельзя выносить никаких документов. И будьте осторожны — бумага стала очень хрупкой.*

БЕН: *Обязательно ... Это похожи на плакаты, что я видел везде в восьмидесятых годах: «Слава КПСС!», «Мы придём к победе социалистического труда!», ударники и так далее.*

БИБЛИОТЕКАРЬ: *Да, сейчас у нас всё по-другому.*

БЕН: *Вы знаете, я боялся, что их все уничтожили.*

БИБЛИОТЕКАРЬ: *Почему? Нам нужно их сохранить, чтобы новое поколение знало свою историю!*

БЕН: *Вы правы. Я хочу, чтобы мой студенты их тоже могли бы видеть!*

At the library.

BEN: Excuse me. I heard that you have posters and newspapers from the twenties and thirties here. May I see them?

Тридцать пятый урок

LIBRARIAN: *(suspiciously)* Yes, we do, but what do you need them for? Are you a journalist?

BEN: No, I'm a professor of Soviet history from the United States. I'm doing research on the political climate in the days of Lenin and after his death in order to better teach the students about it.

LIBRARIAN: *(sternly)* Where is your letter of permission to use the archives?

BEN: Here it is.

LIBRARIAN: So . . . *(reading the letter)* Well, alright. Follow me . . . Here they are. They can't be removed from this room, and be careful; the paper's become very fragile.

BEN: I will . . . These are like the posters that I saw everywhere in the 80s: "Glory to the Communist Party!" "Socialist Labor Will Triumph!" shockworkers[1], et cetera.

LIBRARIAN: Yes, now everything's different.

BEN: You know, I was afraid that they might have been destroyed.

LIBRARIAN: Why? We need to keep them so the young know their history!

BEN: You're right. I wish my students could see these, too!

B. ГРАММАТИКА И СЛОВОУПОТРЕБЛЕНИЕ

1. ЗАЧЕМ VERSUS ПОЧЕМУ

Both of these words mean "why." However, **зачём** means "for what purpose?" and refers to the goal or aim of an action, while **почему́** means "for what reason?" and refers to the cause of an action or a state.

Зачём они́ вам нужны́? —Что́бы рассказа́ть студе́нтам об э́том вре́мени.
What do you need them for (for what purpose)? —To tell the students about that period.

Почему́ вы и́ми интересу́етесь? —Я профе́ссор сове́тской исто́рии.
Why are you interested in them (for what reason)? —I'm a professor of Soviet history.

---

1. Workers who greatly exceeded their monthly quota.

Я боя́лся, что их все уничто́жили. —Почему́?

I was afraid that they might have been destroyed. —Why (for what reason)?

Заче́м Бен пошёл в библиоте́ку? —Посмотре́ть ста́рые плака́ты и газе́ты.

Why (for what purpose) did Ben go to the library? —To look at old posters and newspapers.

Почему́ их нельзя́ выноси́ть? —Потому́ что они́ ста́рые и хру́пкие.

Why (for what reason) is it forbidden to take them out? —Because they're old and fragile.

2. THE CONJUNCTION ЧТОБЫ

Что́бы can be translated as "so that" or "in order to." When it connects two clauses with the same subject, it is followed by an infinitive.

Я провожу́ иссле́дование, чтобы лу́чше <u>рассказа́ть</u> студе́нтам.

I'm doing research in order to better teach the students.

Я позвони́л в библиоте́ку, чтобы <u>узна́ть</u> их рабо́чие часы́.

I called the library to find out their operating hours.

If the first clause contains a verb of motion, **что́бы** may be omitted.

Он <u>пришёл</u> (что́бы) поговори́ть.

He came to have a chat.

Она́ <u>пое́дет</u> в Росси́ю познако́миться со свои́ми ру́сскими ро́дственниками.

She's going to Russia to get to know her Russian relatives.

When connecting two clauses with different subjects, **что́бы** must be followed by a verb in the past tense. Note that this past tense verb translates into English as the present tense or as an infinitive.

Нам ну́жно их сохрани́ть, чтобы но́вое поколе́ние <u>зна́ло</u> свою́ исто́рию!

We need to keep them so the young know their history!

Скажи́ ей, чтобы она́ не <u>уходи́ла</u>.

Tell her not to leave.

Remember that **чтобы** follows **хотеть** to introduce the subjunctive, e.g., I want them to know (I want that they should know). In this case, the verb following **чтобы** will always translate into English as an infinitive.

Я <u>хочу</u>, чтобы мои студенты тоже их <u>увидели</u>!
I want my students to see these (I want that my students should see them), too!

Я <u>хотел</u>, чтобы мои студенты тоже их <u>увидели</u>!
I wanted my students to see these, too!

Я <u>захочу</u>, чтобы мои студенты тоже их <u>увидели</u>!
I'll want my students to see these, too!

3. SLOGANS

Because of their widespread use in the Communist era, slogans have also crept into everyday language. Except for their use by politicians, they are generally quoted sarcastically, or slightly changed to create a pun, indicative of the Russian love of wordplay. You should not use them but just be able to understand them.

«Слава КПСС!»
"Glory to the Communist Party!"

«Да здравствует партия Ленина!»
"Long live the Party of Lenin!"

«Мы придём к победе социалистического труда!»
"Socialist Labor Will Triumph!"

«Вперёд к победе коммунизма!»
"Forward to the Victory of Communism!"

«БАМ—комсомолу по зубам!»
"BAM—The Communist Youth League Can Do It!"

«Наша цель[2]—коммунизм!»
"Our Goal is Communism!"

2. **Цель** also means "target," so this slogan was supposedly posted at a firing range as a joke.

4. THE PREPOSITION ПРИ

The preposition **при** is always followed by the prepositional case. One of its many meanings is "in the time of; under; during the reign of."

Я провожу иссле́дование о полити́ческой обстано́вки при Ле́нине.
I'm doing research on the political climate in the days of Lenin.

При сове́тской вла́сти ча́стная со́бственность была́ запрещена́.
Under Soviet rule, private ownership was forbidden.

При жи́зни ба́бушки и де́душки бы́ли две мировы́е во́йны.
There were two world wars in my grandparents' lifetimes.

При also means "in the presence of; in front of."

При свиде́телях он обеща́л верну́ть де́ньги.
In the presence of witnesses, he promised to return the money.

5. DECADES

To talk about a specific decade, use an ordinal number followed by the noun **год** (year). Both should be plural and in the appropriate case.

Я слы́шал, что у вас есть плака́ты двадца́тых го́дов.
I heard that you have posters from the twenties here.

Это те же плака́ты, что я ви́дел везде́ в восьмидеся́тых года́х.
These are just like the posters that I saw everywhere in the 80's.

C. СЛОВАРЬ

архи́в	archive
библиоте́ка	library
библиоте́карь	librarian
боя́ться (бою́сь, бои́шься, боя́тся) (чего́/кого́)	to be afraid (of someone/thing) (imp.)
бума́га	paper (material)
в восьмидеся́тых года́х	in the 80s
везде́	everywhere

власть	f. power
выноси́ть (выношу́, выно́сишь, выно́сят) */вы́нести* (вы́несу, вы́несешь, вы́несут)	to carry out/away; to take out
Да здра́вствует (что/кого́)!	Long live (someone/thing)!
двадца́тых годо́в	of/from the 20s
докуме́нт	document
до́ступ	access; admittance; entrance
журнали́ст	journalist
запрещён/-на́/-но́/-ны́	forbidden (adjective)
зачём	why; for what purpose
иссле́дование	research
исто́рия	history
красть (краду́, крадёшь, краду́т)/у-	to steal
мирово́й	world (adjective)
обеща́ть (обеща́ю, обеща́ешь, обеща́ют)/по-	to promise
обстано́вка	situation, conditions, environment
отсю́да	from here
па́ртия	party (political)
плака́т	poster
по-друго́му	different (lit. in a different manner)
по зуба́м	in one's capacity; a beating (lit. up to one's teeth)
побе́да	victory
подозри́тельно	suspiciously
поколе́ние	generation
полити́ческий	political
при	in the time/presence of; during the reign/administration of
рабо́чие часы́	operating (lit. working) hours
разреше́ние	permission
свиде́тель	witness
сла́ва (чему́/кому́)	glory (to someone/thing)
сле́довать (сле́дую, сле́дуешь, сле́дуют)/по-(за кем)	to follow, go after (someone)
сохраня́ть (сохраня́ю, сохраня́ешь, сохраня́ют)/ *сохрани́ть* (сохраню́, сохрани́шь, сохраня́т)	to preserve, to keep (safe), to retain
социалисти́ческий	socialist (adjective)
стро́гий	stern

уда́рник	worker who exceeds the quota
уничтожа́ть (уничтожа́ю, уничтожа́ешь, уничтожа́ют)/ **уничто́жить** (уничто́жу, уничто́жишь, уничто́жат)	to destroy, to wipe out, to abolish
хру́пкий	fragile, brittle
цель	f. goal; target
чита́тельский биле́т	library card
что́бы	so that; in order to

РУССКАЯ КУЛЬТУРА

During the years of Soviet rule, there were huge, colorful posters in every city, with slogans urging the citizens onward towards a bright communist future. Many of them were bright red, and they usually showed happy workers and the accomplishments of the society. Vladimir Ilyich Lenin was, of course, the subject of many posters, as well as many statues around the country. In the early nineties, however, when the Soviet Union was dissolved, these posters, along with the newspapers that were largely party organs, started to disappear. They gradually became collector's items for visitors from the West and were replaced by large, colorful billboards advertising Western and Russian products, beer brands, and restaurants.

Along with many other changes in the early nineties, for the first time since the Soviets came to power, various archives were opened up to the public. These included some of the archives of the KGB. Westerners and Russians flocked to discover information that had been suppressed for more than seventy years, and there were hot debates in the press about all the information coming to light. At last, the press no longer bore out the old saying about the two main government-run newspapers, **Изве́стия** ("News") and **Пра́вда** ("Truth"): **В «Пра́вде» нет изве́стий, а в «Изве́стиях» нет пра́вды**. (There's no news in "Truth," and there's no truth in "News.").

УПРАЖНЕНИЯ

A. **Запо́лните про́пуски слова́ми «заче́м» и́ли «почему́» и переведи́те.**
(Fill in the blanks with **заче́м** or **почему́,** and translate.)

1. _____ он так поздно проснулся? —Потому что он очень поздно лёг спать.
2. _____ она тебе позвонила? —Она хотела адрес моих друзей в Москве.
3. Я не понимаю, _____ русский такой сложный (complicated) язык!
4. _____ Бену нужны старые плакаты? —Он хочет лучше понять политическую атмосферу при Ленине.
5. _____ Бен интересуется старыми плакатами? —Потому что он профессор советской истории.

B. Ответьте на вопросы по диалогам, используя слова в скобках. Употребите «чтобы». (Answer the questions from the dialogues according to the words in parentheses. Use чтобы.)

1. Зачем он проводил исследование? (лучше рассказать студентам о ...)
2. Зачем нужно было сохранить плакаты и газеты? (новое поколение/знать свою историю)
3. Чего Бен захотел? (Бен/хотеть/студенты/тоже мочь увидеть плакаты)
4. Зачем Джессика вошла в магазин кустарных изделий? (купить подарки)
5. Что, по мнению Кати, должна купить Джессика? (Катя/хотеть/Джессика/купить матрёшки)

C. Переведите на русский. (Translate into Russian.)

1. Someone stole my library card!
2. When are you open (what are your operating hours)?
3. The journalist follows the librarian to the archives.
4. It's forbidden to remove any documents from this room.
5. In the 1950s we were afraid of the world-wide victory of communism.

D. Переведите на английский. (Translate into English.)

1. Они поженились при свидетелях.
2. При коммунизме у всех была работа.
3. Не говори об этом при детях!
4. При советской власти было закрыто много церквей.
5. Европейская архитектура была очень популярна в России при Петре Первом.

A. Поста́вьте глаго́лы в повели́тельный наклоне́ние по образцу́.
   (Put the sentences into the imperative mood according to the example.)

ОБРАЗЕ́Ц: Она́ глубоко́ вдыха́ет.   Глубоко́ вдохни́те.

1. Ребёнок дви́гает па́льцами.
2. Я за́втра буду спать до десяти́.
3. Маши́на остана́вливается.
4. Мы останови́ли маши́ну.
5. Я положу́ карто́шку на таре́лку. (не)
6. Ба́бушка ложи́тся спать.
7. Мы оста́вили а́дрес до́ма. (не)
8. Они́ доставля́ют поку́пки.
9. Наконе́ц ты выздора́вливаешь!
10. Они́ пожима́ют друг дру́гу ру́ки.

B. Поста́вьте глаго́лы в проше́дшее вре́мя. (Put the sentences into the past tense.)

1. Мне о́чень тру́дно испе́чь хоро́шую буха́нку хле́ба.
2. Ко́ля не до́лжен обеща́ть, е́сли он не мо́жет э́то де́лать.
3. Ну́жно свари́ть карто́шку.
4. Нам на́до купи́ть бензи́на.
5. Е́сли у вас голова́ кру́жится, вы должны́ сесть.

C. Отве́тьте на вопро́сы по диало́гам слова́ми в ско́бках.
   (Answer the questions from the dialogues using the words in parentheses.)

1. Заче́м Дебо́ра снима́ет сви́тер? (что́бы медсестра́ …)
2. Почему́ Билл ушёл из фи́рмы? (так как он …)
3. Когда́ он ушёл из фи́рмы? (то́лько что; наза́д)
4. У Дебо́ры боля́т о́ба у́ха? (то́лько)
5. Гали́на Ива́новна покупа́ет пиро́г в магази́не? (сам)
6. Что Гали́на Ива́новна про́сит Пат де́лать? (пока́ они́ гото́вят)
7. Когда́ Билл увлёкся ру́сской культу́рой? (увлека́ется … с …)
8. Что Дебо́ре не́когда де́лать? (сно́ва)
9. Дже́ссике нра́вится па́лехская шкату́лка? (и́менно то)
10. Каки́м вре́менем интересу́ется Бен? (года́ми)

D. **Переведи́те на англи́йский.** (Translate into English.)

1. Это поху́же твоего́, а то полу́чше твоего́.
2. Быва́ет, что вас тошни́т, по́сле того́ как вы принима́ете лека́рство?
3. Ты зна́ешь, того́, кто руководи́т фи́рмой с тех пор, как Давы́дов заболе́л.
4. Са́шенька, ты опя́ть пло́хо вёл себя́ в шко́ле? Что с тобо́й?
5. Когда́ мы интервьюи́ровали кандида́тов, он, так сказа́ть, засну́л. —Опя́ть?!

УРОК 36

ПОЛИТИКА. Politics.

___

А. ДИАЛОГ

Три соседа обсуждают выборы местного мэра.

БОРЯ: *За кого ты голосуешь?*

ДИМА: *За Симонова.*

САША: *Симонов ни рыба, ни мясо. Кроме того он старый коммунист и чиновник!*

ДИМА: *Всё-таки при коммунистах, по крайней мере, мы точно знали, чего от них можно ждать!*

САША: *Да—ничего! Нам нужен кто-нибудь с широким кругозором, как Никитин.*

ДИМА: *Никитин! Он обещает отремонтировать все школы и больницы, но где он возьмёт на это деньги? У нас!*

БОРЯ: *Зачем вы спорите? Все политики одинаковы. Вот почему я не голосую. Они только разговаривают, пока мы голодаем!*

САША: *Если бы все так думали, никогда бы ничего не изменилось!*

ДИМА: *Да не будь таким пессимистом!*

БОРЯ: *Они никак не решают главных проблем—экономика, образование, здравоохранение.*

САША: *Это неправда. Никитин—*

БОРЯ: *Никитин—мечтатель, а Симонов—слабый старик. Всё это просто дурная шутка!*

ДИМА: *Пусть не голосует, если не хочет! По крайней мере, его голос не будет против наших кандидатов!*

___

Three neighbors discuss the election of the local mayor.

BORYA: Who are you voting for?

DIMA: For Simonov.

SASHA: Simonov's wishy-washy. Besides, he's an old communist and a bureaucrat!

DIMA: All the same, in the Communists' time at least we knew exactly what to expect!

SASHA: Yeah—nothing! We need someone with vision, like Nikitin.

DIMA: Nikitin! He promises to renovate all the schools and hospitals, but where's the money going to come from? From us!

BORYA: Why argue? All politicians are the same. That's why I don't vote. They just talk while we go hungry!

SASHA: If everyone thought like that, nothing would ever change!

DIMA: Yes, don't be such a pessimist!

BORYA: They don't do anything about the real problems—the economy, education, health care.

SASHA: That's not true! Nikitin—

BORYA: Nikitin's a dreamer, and Simonov's a weak, old man. What a joke!

DIMA: Let him not vote if he doesn't want to! At least his vote won't count against our candidates!

B. ГРАММАТИКА И СЛОВОУПОТРЕБЛЕНИЕ

1. ЕСЛИ БЫ (THE "UNREAL" CONDITIONAL)

You have already learned the "real conditional" with **éсли**, which is used to indicate a condition (in the **éсли** clause) and its results, if the condition is fulfilled.

Если никто́ не бу́дет голосова́ть, ничего́ не изме́нится.
If no one votes, nothing will change.

You've also learned the "unreal conditional" with **бы,** which is used to indicate a condition that was not fulfilled in the past, or the speaker's uncertainty as to whether it will be fulfilled in the future.

Я хоте́л бы познако́миться с ней.

I would like to get to know her./I would have liked to have gotten to know her.

However, the most common form of the "unreal conditional" is with **е́сли бы,** which denotes a condition that was not fulfilled in the past, or that is unlikely to be fulfilled in the future. In such a sentence the main clause contains the past tense of the verb plus **бы,** and the conditional clause contains **е́сли бы** plus the past tense of the verb. Remember that **бы** may neither begin a sentence, nor follow prepositions or particles, including **не.**

Е́сли бы все так ду́мали, никогда́ бы ничего́ не измени́лось!

If everyone thought like that, nothing would ever change!

Я пошла́ бы, е́сли бы меня́ пригласи́ли.

I would go if they invited me./I would have gone if they had invited me.

The main clause can sometimes be omitted.

Е́сли бы мы зна́ли!

If we had only known!

Е́сли бы мо́лодость зна́ла, е́сли бы ста́рость могла́.

If only youth knew and old age could.

2. ПУСТЬ (THE INDIRECT IMPERATIVE)

The indirect imperative, e.g. "Let/Have him do it," is formed with **пусть,** followed by a present tense or perfective future verb in the third person.

Пусть (он) не голосу́ет, е́сли не хо́чет!

Let him not vote if he doesn't want to!

Пусть она́ завтра́ мне позвони́т, пожа́луйста.

Have her call me tomorrow, please.

Пусть они́ приду́т, е́сли хотя́т.

Let them come if they want.

Три́дцать шесто́й уро́к

3. NEITHER ... NOR ... (НИ ... НИ ...)

The Russian construction for "neither ... nor ... " is **ни ... ни ... Ни** precedes both negated elements. If the sentence contains a verb, it is preceded by **не**.

Симонов ни рыба, ни мясо.
Simonov's wishy-washy (lit., neither fish nor fowl/meat).

Ни пуха ни пера!
Good luck/break a leg (lit., Neither fluff nor feathers!)!

Она не понимает ни по-английски, ни по-русски.
She doesn't understand English or Russian.

Боря не голосует ни за того, ни за другого.
Borya's voting neither for one nor for the other.

Note that **ни** does not affect case in any way.

4. "TO TALK"

There are four verbs that all mean "to talk" but each has a different connotation. **Разговаривать** means simply "to talk (to, with); to converse;" **обсуждать/обсудить** means "to discuss; to consider;" "**рассказывать/рассказать** means "to tell (about); to recount;" and **болтать** means "to chat; to jabber."

Три соседа обсуждают выборы местного мэра.
Three neighbors discuss the election of the local mayor.

Они только разговаривают, пока мы голодаем!
They just talk while we go hungry!

Больше всего я люблю сидеть и болтать в саду, как мы сейчас делаем.
More than anything I love to sit out in the garden and chat, like we're doing now.

Расскажи нам о своём путешествии!
Tell us about your trip!

C. СЛОВАРЬ

всё-таки	nevertheless; all the same
вы́боры	election
гла́вный	main
го́лос	voice; vote
голода́ть (голода́ю, голода́ешь, голода́ют)	to starve, to go without food (imp.)
голосова́ние	voting; poll; hitch-hiking
голосова́ть (голосу́ю, голосу́ешь, голосу́ют) /про– (за кого́, чего́)	to vote (for someone/thing)
дурно́й	bad; evil; nasty
е́сли бы	if (unreal conditional)
здравоохране́ние	health care
избира́ть (избира́ю, избира́ешь, избира́ют) /*избра́ть* (изберу́, избере́шь, изберу́т)	to elect
изменя́ться (изменя́юсь, изменя́ешься, изменя́ются)/ *измени́ться* (изменю́сь, изме́нишься, изме́нятся)	to change (intransitive)
коммуни́ст	Communist
кругозо́р	horizon (fig.); range of interests
ме́стный	local
мечта́тель	m. dreamer
мо́лодость	f. youth
мэр	mayor
ни ры́ба ни мя́со	wishy-washy (lit. neither fish nor meat)
ни ... ни ...	neither . . . nor . . .
Ни пу́ха ни пера́![1]	Good luck!/Break a leg! (lit. Neither fluff nor feathers!)
образова́ние	education
обсужда́ть (обсужда́ю, обсужда́ешь, обсужда́ют)/ *обсуди́ть* (обсужу́, обсу́дишь, обсу́дят)	to discuss
пессими́ст	pessimist
по кра́йней ме́ре	at least
поли́тика	politics

---

1. Originally a good luck wish for someone hunting wild fowl, based on the superstition that openly wishing success would jinx the hunt.

поли́тик	politician
про́тив (чего́/кого́)	against (someone/thing)
Пусть (он/она́/они́) ...	Let/Have (him/her/them) ...
разгова́ривать (разгова́риваю, разгова́риваешь, разгова́ривают) (с кем)	to talk, to converse (with someone) (imp.)
ремонти́ровать (ремонти́рую, ремонти́руешь, ремонти́руют)/от-	to renovate
сла́бый	weak
сосе́д(ка)	neighbor (m./f.)
спо́рить (спо́рю, спо́ришь, спо́рят)/по- (о чём)	to argue (about something)
ста́рость	f. old age
то́чно	exactly
чего́ (от кого́/чего́) *мо́жно ждать*	what to expect (from someone/thing)
чино́вник	bureaucrat
широ́кий	wide
шу́тка	joke
эконо́мика	economy

РУССКАЯ КУЛЬТУРА

The first real elections in Russia took place in the spring of 1993 amid much excitement. Since then, people have become more used to going to the polls, and many have returned to their habitual cynicism about the entire process. However, discussing and arguing are virtually national sports, and politics is certainly a popular subject. During the Communist years, when discussions of politics had to be fairly circumspect, people argued about their favorite sports teams, philosophy, or any other suitable subject. With the advent of glasnost, politics once again became fair game. Political debates tend to be extremely vitriolic with strong views expressed quite emotionally, and they may sound very adversarial to Americans. However, it's generally understood by all that this invective is not personal, but rather part of a game in which the goal is to outshout and out-vilify your opponents and whatever views they are professing. Any non-Russian who does not understand these rules had best not enter the arena!

УПРАЖНЕНИЯ

A. **Поста́вьте предложе́ния в усло́вное наклоне́ние с «е́сли бы» и переведи́те.** (Put the sentences into the unreal conditional with **е́сли бы** and translate.)

1. Си́монов проигра́ет, е́сли Ники́тин полу́чит ещё сто голосо́в.
2. Е́сли Ники́тин ста́нет мэ́ром, он отремонти́рует шко́лы и больни́цы.
3. Бо́ря проголосу́ет за́втра, е́сли он смо́жет.
4. Поли́тики никогда́ не реша́т гла́вных пробле́м, е́сли они́ то́лько бу́дут разгова́ривать!
5. Е́сли Бо́ря бу́дем голосова́ть, за кого́ он проголосу́ет?

B. **Переведи́те на англи́йский.** (Translate into English.)

1. Пусть она́ пора́ньше ложи́тся спать.
2. Е́сли они́ не пи́шут по-ру́сски, пусть они́ напи́шут письмо́ по-англи́йски.
3. Он за Си́монова. —Пусть он голосу́ет за э́того коммуни́ста, е́сли хо́чет!
4. Ей не нра́вится говори́ть ни о поли́тике, ни о спо́рте.
5. Ни Ди́ма, ни Са́ша не по́няли, почему́ Бо́ря не голосу́ет.

C. **Переведи́те на ру́сский.** (Translate into Russian.)

1. Borya's not for Simonov or Nikitin (neither for Simonov nor for Nikitin).
2. They don't like to play (either) baseball or basketball (they like playing neither).
3. She's neither Russian nor American; she's French.
4. Have him come in, please.
5. Irochka wants to buy jeans. What do you think? —Let her buy [them].

D. Запо́лните пропу́ски в коло́нке А глаго́лами из коло́нки Б.
    Измени́те оконча́ния, е́сли ну́жно, и употреби́те два отве́та два ра́за.
    (Match the sentences in column A to column B. Change the endings if
    necessary, and use two answers twice.)

	A		B
1.	Они́ _____ вопро́с, и, наконе́ц, реши́ли что де́лать.	a.	болта́ть
2.	До́чка беспреста́нно _____ по телефо́ну со свои́ми подру́жками.	b.	расска́зывать/рассказа́ть
		c.	разгова́ривать
3.	Мы всю неде́лю_____ вы́боры.	d.	обсужда́ть/обсуди́ть
4.	Она́ нам _____ о вы́борах в Аме́рике.		
5.	Я _____ с нача́льником о своём о́тдыхе.		

УРОК 37

A. ДИАЛОГ

В да́мском сало́не.

СИНТИЯ: *До́брое у́тро. Мо́жно записа́ться на стри́жку на сего́дня?*

ПАРИКМАХЕР: *У нас одна́ клие́нтка отмени́ла визи́т на полдеся́того. Вы не мо́жете подожда́ть пятна́дцать мину́т?*

СИНТИЯ: *Да, могу́.*

ПАРИКМАХЕР: *Хорошо́. Сади́тесь, пожа́луйста.*

Че́рез пятна́дцать мину́т ...

ПАРИКМАХЕР: *Так, вам го́лову мыть?*

СИНТИЯ: *Нет, спаси́бо. Я мо́ю го́лову ка́ждое у́тро.*

ПАРИКМАХЕР: *Во́лосы у вас сухова́ты. Когда́ вы в после́дний раз де́лали зави́вку?*

СИНТИЯ: *Три ме́сяца наза́д. Мне надое́ло.*

ПАРИКМАХЕР: *Поня́тно. Ну, поре́же суши́те го́лову фе́ном, и вот вам увлажня́ющий крем. Втира́йте его́ в во́лосы раз в неде́лю пе́ред тем, как мыть го́лову.*

СИНТИЯ: *Спаси́бо.*

ПАРИКМАХЕР: *А как вас постри́чь?*

СИНТИЯ: *Подстриги́те ко́ротко сбо́ку и сза́ди.*

ПАРИКМАХЕР: *А впереди́?*

СИНТИЯ: *Оста́вьте там немно́жко подлинне́е. И сде́лайте пробо́р посереди́не.*

Че́рез не́которое вре́мя.

ПАРИКМАХЕР: *(даёт ей зе́ркало и повора́чивает стул)* **Ну как?**

СИНТИЯ: Подстригите ещё немножко сверху ... Да, вот так.

ПАРИКМАХЕР: Вам лаком покрыть?

СИНТИЯ: Нет, так хорошо. Спасибо большое.

ПАРИКМАХЕР: Заплатите, пожалуйста, в кассу у выхода.

СИНТИЯ: Хорошо. А это вам. (даёт ему чаевые)

At a beauty salon.

CYNTHIA: Good morning. Can I get a haircut appointment for today?

HAIRDRESSER: One of our clients cancelled for 9:30. Would you be able to wait fifteen minutes?

CYNTHIA: Yes, I could.

HAIRDRESSER: Good. Please have a seat.

Fifteen minutes later . . .

HAIRDRESSER: So, would you like a shampoo?

CYNTHIA: No, thanks. I wash my hair every morning.

HAIRDRESSER: Your hair is a little dry. When did you have your last perm?

CYNTHIA: Three months ago. I got tired of it.

HAIRDRESSER: I see. Well, blow dry your hair less, and here's a moisturizing lotion. Rub it into your hair once a week before washing it.

CYNTHIA: Thanks.

HAIRDRESSER: How would you like your hair cut?

CYNTHIA: Please cut it short on the sides and in the back.

HAIRDRESSER: And in the front?

CYNTHIA: Leave it a little longer there, and make the part in the middle.

A little later.

HAIRDRESSER: (*gives her a mirror and turns the chair around*) Well, how's that?

Thirty-seventh Lesson

CYNTHIA: Could you cut a bit more off on top . . . ? Yes, that's perfect.

HAIRDRESSER: Would you like some hairspray?

CYNTHIA: No, it's fine like that. Thank you very much.

HAIRDRESSER: You're welcome. You can pay on your way out.

CYNTHIA: Alright. And this is for you. *(handing him a tip)*

B. ГРАММАТИКА И СЛОВОУПОТРЕБЛЕНИЕ

1. ADVERBIAL PREPOSITIONS

There is a group of words that function both as adverbs and prepositions and take the genitive. Although **наверху** (above, upstairs), **све́рху** (from above, from the top), and **сбо́ку** (on the side, from the side) appear to belong to this group, they function as adverbs only.

	ADVERB	PREPOSITION
вверху́	above, overhead	on top (of)
внизу́	below, downstairs	on the bottom (of)
впереди́	in front, ahead	in front (of), before
посереди́не	in the middle	in the middle (of)
сза́ди	behind, from the end/rear	behind (a/the)
спе́реди	in front, from the front	in front (of)

Пожа́луйста, подстриги́те ко́ротко сбо́ку и сза́ди. —А впереди́?
Please cut it short on the sides and in the back. —And in front?

Сде́лайте пробо́р посереди́не.
Make the part in the middle.

Подстриги́те ещё немно́жко све́рху.
Could you cut a bit more off on top?

Она́ написа́ла да́ту вверху́ страни́цы.
She wrote the date on top of the page.

2. "BEFORE" AND OTHER TEMPORAL CONJUNCTIONS

In English, the same word often functions as a preposition and a conjunction. For example, the word "before" acts as a preposition in "she called before dinner," and as a conjunction in "she called before they left." In Russian, however, different words are used to reflect the different functions. Prepositions are used to introduce a noun phrase, while conjunctions are used to introduce a clause.

	PREPOSITION	CONJUNCTION	
after dinner	по́сле у́жина	по́сле того́ как мы уе́хали	after we left
since dinner	с у́жина	с тех пор как мы уе́хали	since we left
before dinner	до у́жина	до того́ как/пре́жде чем мы уе́хали	before we left
just before dinner	пе́ред у́жином	пе́ред тем, как мы уе́хали	just before we left

Notice that there are three different conjunctions that mean "before." **Пе́ред тем как** means "just before."

Втира́йте его́ в во́лосы раз в неде́лю пе́ред тем, как мыть го́лову.
Rub it into your hair (right) before washing it.

Она́ позвони́ла пе́ред тем, как мы уе́хали.
She called just before we left.

До того́ как and **пре́жде чем** both mean "before; up to; earlier than; at a previous time."

Мы жи́ли в го́роде до того́, как мы перее́хали за́ город.
We used to live in the city before we moved to the suburbs.

Она́ позвони́ла до того́, как мы уе́хали.
She called (sometime) before we left.

Пре́жде, чем путеше́ствовать за грани́цу, на́до посмотре́ть свою́ страну́.
Before traveling abroad, one should see one's own country.

Ду́майте пре́жде, чем говори́те!
Think before you speak!

3. PREPOSITIONS WITH TIME (SUMMARY)

In this section, we will review the different ways of answering the question Когда́? Note that some expressions do not contain a preposition at all, while in others, the same preposition used with a different case has a different meaning.

в/на + accusative	"at" + time of day, "on" + day of week, (times) per unit of time
в + prepositional	"in" + specific month/year/century про́шлом/э́том/сле́дующем ме́сяце/году́ (last/this/next month/year)
на + prepositional	про́шлой/э́той/сле́дующей неде́ле (last/this/next week)
на + accusative	"for (the)" + a unit of time (day/week/month/year/today/tomorrow/yesterday)
че́рез + accusative	"in" + a unit of time (from now)
accusative + наза́д	a unit of time + "ago"
с + genitive ... до + genitive	"from" + specific hour/day/month/year ..."to" + specific hour/day/month/year
accusative (no preposition)	весь/всю/всё/все (all) + a unit of time (day/morning/evening night/week/month/spring/summer/fall/winter/year) "for" + an amount of time (number of minutes/hours/days/weeks/months/years)
instrumental (no preposition)	"in the" + time of day/season (morning/afternoon/evening/night/spring/summer/fall/winter)

У нас одна́ клие́нтка отмени́ла визи́т на полдеся́того.

One of our clients cancelled for 9:30.

Че́рез пятна́дцать мину́т.

In fifteen minutes.

Когда́ вы реши́ли изба́виться от хи́мии? —В про́шлом ме́сяце.

When did you decide to get rid of your perm? —Last month.

Втира́йте его́ в во́лосы раз в неде́лю пе́ред тем, как мыть го́лову.

Rub it into your hair once a week before washing it.

Мо́жно записа́ться на стри́жку на сего́дня?

Can I get a haircut appointment for today?

Вы не мо́жете подожда́ть пятна́дцать мину́т?

Would you be able to wait (for) fifteen minutes?

Note that any verb used with a time expression that answers the question **Как до́лго?** (For how long?) is by definition imperfective. Remember to use the perfective with expressions indicating a specific moment in time but the imperfective with expressions indicating duration or repetition of an action. Compare:

Она́ прие́дет че́рез час.

She'll arrive in an hour.

Она́ е́хала весь день.

She's been driving all day.

4. CONJUGATION OF -ЫТЬ VERBS

Verbs ending in **-ыть** in the infinitive have irregular conjugations in the present tense, but regular past tense forms, e.g. **мыл/-а/-о/-и**. Following is a sample conjugation:

мы́ть/вы-: to wash

I wash	я мо́ю	мы мо́ем	we wash
you (fam.) wash	ты мо́ешь	вы мо́ете	you (pl./pol.) wash
he/she washes	он/она́ мо́ет	они́ мо́ют	they wash

stem: **мой+**
imperative: **Мо́й(те)(ся/сь)!**

Most **-ыть** verbs are perfective, e.g., **откры́ть** (to open), **закры́ть** (to close), and **покры́ть** (to cover); **мыть**, however, is imperfective.

Вам го́лову мыть? —Нет, спаси́бо. Я мо́ю го́лову ка́ждое у́тро.

Would you like a shampoo? —No, thanks. I wash my hair every morning.

Втира́йте его́ в во́лосы раз в неде́лю пе́ред тем, как мыть го́лову.

Rub it into your hair before washing it.

Вам ла́ком покры́ть?

Would you like some hairspray (literally, to cover your hair with lacquer)?

Если мы откро́ем окно́, они́ его́ закро́ют!

If we open the window, they'll close it!

Remember that **быть**, or any verb that contains **быть**, **e.g. забы́ть** (to forget, perfective), is an exception to the conjugation pattern above. As you know, the stem of **быть** is **буд+**, so the stem of **забы́ть** is **забу́д+**.

Ты за́втра не забу́дешь мне позвони́ть? —Коне́чно, я, не забу́ду!

You won't forget to call me tomorrow? —Of course I won't forget!

С. СЛОВА́РЬ

вверху́	overhead; above (someone/thing)
век	century
визи́т	visit, call, appointment
внизу́	downstairs; below (someone/thing)
впереди́	ahead; in front (of) (someone/thing)
втира́ть (втира́ю, втира́ешь, втира́ют) /*втере́ть* (вотру́, вотрёшь, вотру́т) (в что)	to rub (into something)
да́мский сало́н	beauty salon (lit. women's salon)
до того́ как	before (conjunction)
зави́вка	curling, waving (hair)
запи́сываться (запи́сываюсь, запи́сываешься, запи́сываются)/ *записа́ться* (запишу́сь, запи́шешься, запи́шутся)	to sign up, to make an appointment
зе́ркало	mirror
ко́ротко	short
крем	cream; lotion
лак	hairspray (lit. lacquer)
мыть (мо́ю, мо́ешь, мо́ют)/вы-	to wash
мыть/вы́мыть го́лову	to wash one's hair
наверху́	above, overhead

Три́дцать седьмо́й уро́к

надое́сть (надое́м, надое́шь, надоедя́т) (кому́)	to be tired of, fed up with
отменя́ть (отменя́ю, отменя́ешь, отменя́ют)/**отме́нить** (отменю́, отме́нишь, отме́нят)	to cancel
парикма́хер	hairdresser; barber
парикма́херская	barbershop; hairdresser's
пе́ред тем как	(just) before (conjunction)
по́сле того́ как	after (conjunction)
повора́чивать (повора́чиваю, повора́чиваешь, повора́чивают)/**поверну́ть** (поверну́, повернёшь, поверну́т)	to turn
подлинне́е	a little longer
подстрига́ть (подстрига́ю, подстрига́ешь, подстрига́ют)/**подстри́чь** (подстригу́, подстрижёшь, подстригу́т)	to clip, to trim
покрыва́ть (покрыва́ю, покрыва́ешь, покрыва́ют)/**покры́ть**[1] (покро́ю, покро́ешь, покро́ют)	to cover
поре́же	less often
посереди́не	in the middle (of) (something)
пре́жде чем	before (conjunction)
причёска	hairstyle, hairdo
пробо́р	part (in hair)
сбо́ку	on the side, from the side
све́рху	on the top, from the top
сза́ди (чего́, кого́)	from behind; behind (someone/thing)
спе́реди	in front (of) (from the front)
стри́жка	haircut; haircut appointment
сухова́т/-а/-о/-ы	dry; dried out
суши́ть (сушу́, су́шишь, су́шат)	to dry (imp.)
у вы́хода	by the exit; by the door
увлажня́ющий	moisturizing
фен	blowdryer
хи́мия (пермане́нт)	perm (coll.); chemistry
чаевы́е	tip; gratuity (from the word **чай**, tea)
Э́то вам.	This is for you.

1. **Покры́ть** has another imperfective, **крыть** (кро́ю, кро́ешь, кро́ют), also meaning "to cover."

РУССКАЯ КУЛЬТУРА

Most hotels have their own barber shop and beauty parlor, at which you can generally make an appointment. Elsewhere, it is more common to just walk in and wait for your turn. All of the personal care services that exist in the United States are generally available in Russia, but if you do venture outside your hotel for them, it is advisable to get a recommendation first. Many Russians still rely on friends and family for their haircuts, rather than going to a barbershop or beauty parlor— especially if they cannot afford to go to one of the higher priced and higher quality salons. Also, women should be aware that the hairspray, hair dyes, and chemicals used for permanents may be somewhat harsher, used more liberally, or simply different from what they are used to. Styles as well may be somewhat different, so travelers might prefer to opt for a simple trim rather than experiment with a new cut.

УПРАЖНЕНИЯ

A. **Переведи́те на англи́йский.** (Translate into English.)

1. Оста́вьте подлинне́е сза́ди, пожа́луйста.
2. Же́нщина, кото́рая живёт наверху́ де́лает хоро́шую стри́жку.
3. Подстриги́те ко́ротко све́рху.
4. Де́ти шли впереди́ взро́слых.
5. Сосе́ди, кото́рые живу́т внизу́, ра́но ложа́тся спать.

B. **Запо́лните про́пуски слова́ми «пе́ред тем как», «до того́ как», «пре́жде чем», «перед», «до» и переведи́те на англи́йский.** (Fill in the blanks with **пе́ред тем как, до того́ как, пре́жде чем, пе́ред,** or **до,** and translate.)

1. Нам на́до бу́дет прие́хать _____ семи́.
2. _____ я нашла́ э́того парикма́хера, у меня́ бы́ли ужа́сные стри́жки.
3. _____ учи́ться бе́гать (to run), на́до научи́ться ходи́ть.
4. Всегда́ мо́йте ру́ки _____ едо́й (meal).
5. Всегда́ мо́йте ру́ки _____ есть.

C. **Отве́тьте на вопро́сы по диало́гу.** (Answer the questions about the dialogue.)

1. На како́е вре́ма клие́нтка отмени́ла визи́т в да́мский сало́н?
2. Ско́лько вре́мени Си́нтия ждала́?
3. Как ча́сто Си́нтия мо́ет го́лову?
4. Когда́ Си́нтия в после́дний раз де́лала зави́вку?
5. Когда́ она́ должна́ бу́дет втира́ть крем в во́лосы?

D. **Переведи́те на ру́сский.** (Translate into Russian.)

1. If we don't open the window, it will be too hot (**жа́рко**) in the room.
2. If you wash your hair before going to bed, you'll have a cold (**просту́да**) tomorrow.
3. I need to wash my hair.
4. Sashka will probably forget about his haircut appointment today.
5. Close the door!!

УРОК 38

СПОРТ. Sports.

А. ДИАЛОГ

На стадио́не, к концу́ второ́го та́йма футбо́льного ма́тча.

БОРЯ: *Сего́дня Дина́мо так пло́хо игра́ет. Неуже́ли они́ проигра́ют?*

ДИМА: *Ве́рно, но и Спарта́к то́же пло́хо игра́ет.*

БОРЯ: *Почему́ они́ так ме́дленно бе́гают? Да́же я мог бы дви́гаться быстре́е!*

ДИМА: *Ещё бы! Ведь ты сам хорошо́ игра́ешь в футбо́л.*

БОРЯ: *Что ты! Я то́лько люби́тель. Я не уме́ю пасова́ть.*

ДИМА: *Иногда́, ка́жется, что они́ то́же не уме́ют э́того де́лать! Зна́ешь, и мне иногда́ хо́чется сыгра́ть в футбо́л.*

БОРЯ: *Почему́ же ты не игра́ешь?*

ДИМА: *Я бе́гаю трусцо́й, а ле́том мы с жено́й ката́емся на велосипе́де. Мяч у Миха́йлова!!*

БОЛЕ́ЛЬЩИКИ ДИНА́МО: *Ди-на-мо! Ди-на-мо! … Гол! … Мо-лод-цы́! Мо-лод-цы́!*

ДИМА: *(кричи́т) Ну что же!! Что происхо́дит?!*

БОРЯ: *(кричи́т) Судью́ на мы́ло! Мяч был в воро́тах! Что он слепо́й, что ли?!*

ДИМА: *Ну, вот и всё! Счёт 3–2. Мы проигра́ли! А должна́ была бы быть ничья́!*

БОРЯ: *Како́й у́жас! Как бы мы ни сыгра́ли сле́дующую игру́, мы всё равно́ тепе́рь не попадём в фина́л!*

At the stadium, towards the end of the second half of a soccer game.

BORYA: Dinamo is playing so badly today. I can't believe they're losing!

DIMA: True, but Spartak is playing badly, too.

BORYA: Why are they running so slowly? Even I could move faster!

DIMA: I bet you could! After all, you play pretty well yourself.

BORYA: Come off it! I'm just an amateur. I'm not very good at passing.

DIMA: Sometimes it seems like they don't know how to do it either! You know, sometimes I feel like playing soccer, too.

BORYA: So why *don't* you play?

DIMA: Well, I go jogging, and in the summer my wife and I go biking. Mihailov has the ball!!

DINAMO FANS: Di-na-mo! Di-na-mo! … Goal! … Way to go! Way to go!

DIMA: *(yelling)* What?! What's going on?

BORYA: *(yelling)* Send the ref to the showers! The ball was in the goal! Is he blind, or what?

DIMA: Well, that's it! The score's 3–2. We've lost! And it should've been a tie!

BORYA: What a disaster! However we play the next game, we'll never make the playoffs now!

B. ГРАММАТИКА И СЛОВОУПОТРЕБЛЕНИЕ

1. CAN: МОЧЬ/СМОЧЬ VERSUS УМЕТЬ/СУМЕТЬ

Мочь/смочь (to be able to) is often confused with уме́ть/суме́ть (to know how to, to manage to) because they can both be translated into English as "can." Уме́ть denotes having the knowledge or skill to do something, while мочь refers to having the physical ability, the opportunity, or the permission to do something.

Я не уме́ю пасова́ть. —Иногда́ ка́жется, что они́ то́же не уме́ют э́того де́лать!
    I don't know how to pass. —Sometimes it seems like they can't do it either!

Да́же я мог бы дви́гаться быстре́е!

> Even I could (am physically capable of) move faster!

То́лько по́сле го́да в Росси́и, она́ смогла́ говори́ть по-ру́сски без акце́нта.

> After only a year in Russia, she managed to speak Russian fluently.

Я хочу́, что́бы мои́ студе́нты их то́же могли́ бы ви́деть!

> I wish my students could see them, too!

2. PARTICLES

Russian colloquial speech contains many particles, e.g. **же, ну, не, так, вот, что, да**. Particles add meaning to the words they precede or follow, but they often have no meaning of their own. It is important to understand their grammatical environments, rather than think of them as words.

PARTICLE	EXAMPLE	ENGLISH
бы	Ещё бы!	You bet!; I'll say!
ведь	Ведь	after all; you know; you see; Now, …
вот	Вот и всё!	That's all!
	Вот (noun, in nom.)!	What a … !
да	Да нет!	Of course not!
	Да здра́вствует … !	Long live … !
лишь	лишь бы …	If only …
ну	Ну, хорошо́.	Well, alright.
уж	Тако́й уж … !	What/such/definitely a … !
хоть	Хоть (imperative)!	At least …!
что	Что ты!	Come off it!
	… что ли?	… or what?

Ещё бы! Ведь ты сам хорошо́ игра́ешь. —Что ты! Я то́лько люби́тель.

> I'll say! After all you play pretty well yourself. —Come off it! I'm just an amateur.

Она́ скоре́е умрёт, чем ку́пит торт в магази́не. Тако́й уж хара́ктер!

> She'd rather die than buy a cake at the store. Such a character!

Вот почему́ я не голосу́ю!

> That's why I don't vote!

Лишь бы мы вы́играли э́тот матч!

If only we win this game!

Хоть переоде́нься! Вот неря́ха!

At least change your clothes! What a slob!

Particles often combine to add further nuance to an expression.

Что он слепо́й, **что ли**?!

Is he blind, or what?

Ну, вот и всё! Счёт 3–2. Мы проигра́ли!

Well, that's it! The score's 3–2. We've lost!

Ну что же!! Что происхо́дит?!

What?! What's going on?

3. EXPRESSING "HOWEVER, WHATEVER," ETC.

The Russian equivalent of the English suffix -ever (whatever, whoever, when-ever, etc.) is **бы + ни. Бы** immediately follows a question word (but is not at-tached to it, as in English), and **ни** directly precedes the verb.

<u>Как бы</u> мы <u>ни</u> сыгра́ли сле́дующую игру́, мы всё равно́ тепе́рь не попадём в фина́л!

However we play the next game, we'll never make the playoffs now!

<u>Что бы</u> они́ <u>ни</u> де́лали, они́ не забью́т гол.

Whatever they do, they won't score a goal.

<u>Что бы ни</u> случи́лось, мы уви́димся в сле́дующем году́!

Whatever happens, I'll see you next year!

<u>Ско́лько бы</u> мы <u>ни</u> упражня́лись, мы никогда́ не ста́нем профессиона́лами!

However much we practice, we'll never become pros!

<u>Когда́ бы</u> ты <u>ни</u> пришёл, мы бу́дем ра́ды тебя́ ви́деть.

Whenever you come, we'll be happy to see you.

<u>Какóй бы</u> дорóгой вы <u>ни</u> пошлú, вы успéете.
Whichever way you go, you'll be on time.

<u>Кто бы ни</u> пришёл, бýдет желáнным гóстем.
Whoever comes will be welcome.

<u>Кудá бы</u> мы <u>ни</u> поéхали, лю́ди бы́ли óчень дружелю́бными.
Wherever we went people were very friendly.

4. EXCLAMATIONS

Here are a few colorful expressions for trying moments. Be careful how and when you use them.

Судью́ на мы́ло!!
Send the ref to the showers!!

Пошёл вон!
Go to hell!

(Идúте) К чёрту!
Go to hell (lit., to the devil!)

(Идúте) Прочь!
Go away!/Get out of here!

Ёлки-пáлки!
Darn it! (nonsense word, euphemism for stronger language)

C. СЛОВАРЬ

бéгать трусцóй	to go jogging
болéльщик	fan
ведь	you see; after all
ворóта	goal (sports); gate(s); gateway
Вот (что)*!*	What a (noun)!
Вот и всё!	Well, that's it!; It's over!
гол	goal (sports)
Ещё бы!	I'll say!; You bet!
Ёлки-пáлки!	Darn!

забива́ть (забива́ю, забива́ешь, забива́ют)/*забить* (забью́, забьёшь, забью́т) (забить гол)	to drive in, to hammer in, to seal, to block, (score a goal)
игра́	game
иногда́	sometimes
ката́ться на велосипе́де	to go bike riding
кома́нда	team (sports)
коне́ц	end; finish
крича́ть (кричу́, кричи́шь, крича́т)/за-	to shout
Лишь бы я мог(ла)!	If only I could!
люби́тель	m. amateur
мяч	ball
На мы́ло (кого́)*!*	Send (someone) to the showers!
наверняка́	for sure; certainly; definitely
ничья́	tie (sports)
Ну что же!	What?!
пасова́ть	to pass (sports)
про́игрывать (про́игрываю, про́игрываешь, про́игрывают)/ *проигра́ть* (проигра́ю, проигра́ешь, проигра́ют)	to lose, to be losing
произойти́ (произойду́, произойдёшь, произойду́т)	to happen, to occur, to take place (perf.)
происходи́ть (происхожу́, происхо́дишь, происхо́дят)	to go on, to be going on (imp.)
профессиона́л	professional (noun)
Прочь!	Go away!; Get out of here!
слепо́й	blind
спорт	sports
спортсме́н(ка)	athlete (m./f.)
судья́	judge; referee
тайм	half (sports)
уме́ть (уме́ю, уме́ешь, уме́ют)/с-	can; to know how; to manage (perf.)
упражня́ться (упражня́юсь, упражня́ешься, упражня́ются)	to practice, to train (sports) (imp.)
фина́л	finals, playoffs (sports)
футбо́л	soccer
футбо́льный матч	soccer game
Хоть ... !	At least (imperative verb)!
... что ли?	. . . or what?
Что ты!	Come off it!

РУССКАЯ КУЛЬТУРА

Although the health craze hasn't quite reached Russia, the average Russian is still fairly sturdy as a result of carrying around heavy parcels and walking a fair amount. Some people exercise to television or radio programs in the morning. Volleyball, jogging, and cross-country skiing are very popular, and Russian athletes are well-known for their skill at ice hockey, figure-skating, gymnastics, and basketball. However, of all the sports played and watched in the CIS, soccer (**футбол**) and hockey (**хоккей**) are definitely the most popular.

Soccer is even more important to Russians than baseball is to Americans. The fans take the fortunes of their chosen team very seriously and often come to blows over them. Games between well-known teams are always crowded, and emotions run very high. There is sometimes a ring of policemen around the bottom tier of seats in the stadium to prevent overzealous fans from jumping onto the field. After the game, especially if the score was close or if the game was important, police try to funnel the crowd onto waiting buses in order to avoid a melee. Good soccer players are revered almost as gods, and practically every little boy grows up playing soccer. Almost every town or city has a team named Spartak, Dinamo, or Torpedo, but the best known ones are from Moscow.

УПРАЖНЕНИЯ

A. **Заполните пропуски словами мочь/смочь, уметь/суметь и переведите.** (Fill in the blanks with **мочь/смочь** or **уметь/суметь**, and translate.)

1. Он много играл в футбол, и теперь он _____ очень хорошо пасовать.
2. К сожалению, мы не _____ пойти на матч.
3. Вы _____ читать и писать по-русски?
4. Я хочу, чтобы ты _____ пойти с нами!
5. Я не _____ поверить, что мы выиграли!

B. **Переведи́те на англи́йский.** (Translate into English.)

1. Вот где я живу́.
2. Ну что же!! Что происхо́дит?
3. Он спит, что ли?
4. Мы должны́ пригласи́ть их. Ведь они́ то́же здесь живу́т.
5. Лишь бы они́ уме́ли говори́ть по-ру́сски!

C. **Подбери́те соотве́тствующие предложе́ния в коло́нке А к коло́нке Б. Употреби́те оди́н отве́т два ра́за.** (Match the sentences in column A to column B. Use one answer twice.)

A	B
1. Судью́ на _____ !	a. Вот
2. _____ ты! Я то́лько люби́тель.	b. Хоть
3. Что же он де́лает? _____ дура́к (idiot)!	c. Иди́
4. Пошёл _____ !	d. Ещё бы
5. _____ поза́втракай!	e. ёлки-па́лки
6. _____ и всё! Счёт 2–1. Пора́ идти́ домо́й!	f. мы́ло
7. К _____ !	g. вон
8. _____ ! Я с удово́льствием пойду́ на матч с тобо́й!	h. что ли
9. Иди́те _____ !	i. чёрту
10. Что он слепо́й, _____ ?	j. Что

D. **Переведи́те на ру́сский.** (Translate into Russian.)

1. Whatever you (familiar) do, don't forget to write us!
2. Whenever you (familiar) have time, call me.
3. Whichever day you (formal) want is fine with me (suits me; **мне подоидёт**).
4. However badly they play, Dinamo is still (**всё-таки**) my favorite (**люби́мая**) team!
5. Wherever I look, I see flowers.

УРОК 39

ЗНАКОМСТВО С ГОРОДОМ. Exploring the city.

А. ДИАЛОГ

В па́рке у па́мятника.

ЛОИС: *Извини́те, вы не зна́ете, кому́ э́тот па́мятник? Мне непоня́тно, что там напи́сано.*

РОМАН НИКОЛАЕВИЧ: *Коне́чно зна́ю, де́вушка. На́шим му́жественным защи́тникам во вре́мя Вели́кой оте́чественной войны́.*

ЛОИС: *Вели́кая оте́чественная война́?*

РОМАН НИКОЛАЕВИЧ: *То есть Втора́я мирова́я война́.*

ЛОИС: *Поня́тно. А когда́ был постро́ен па́мятник?*

РОМАН НИКОЛАЕВИЧ: *Я не по́мню то́чно когда́, но э́то бы́ло в одно́ вре́мя с па́рком, приме́рно в шестидеся́том году́.*

ВЛАДИМИР НИКОЛАЕВИЧ: *По́мните, ра́ньше па́рк называ́лся Парк геро́ев? Неда́вно измени́ли назва́ние. Я ника́к не могу́ вспо́мнить но́вое.*

РОМАН НИКОЛАЕВИЧ: *До девяно́сто тре́тьего го́да здесь бы́ли и други́е па́мятники. Они́ стоя́ли вон там.*

ЛОИС: *Что с ни́ми случи́лось?*

ВЛАДИМИР НИКОЛАЕВИЧ: *Они́ бы́ли разру́шены хулига́нами.*

ЛОИС: *Жаль. Вы давно́ живёте в э́том райо́не?*

РОМАН НИКОЛАЕВИЧ: *С са́мой войны́. Пока́ мы не ушли́ на фронт, мы жи́ли в селе́. Пото́м, как ветера́ны, мы получи́ли здесь кварти́ру по́сле войны́.*

ЛОИС: *Ну, спаси́бо за информа́цию, и до свида́ния.*

РОМАН НИКОЛАЕВИЧ: *Не́ за что.*

In a park, by a monument.

LOIS: Excuse me, would you happen to know who this monument is to? I don't understand what's written there.

ROMAN NIKOLAEVICH: Of course I know, young woman. To our brave defenders during the Great Patriotic War.

LOIS: The Great Patriotic War?

ROMAN NIKOLAEVICH: That is, World War II.

LOIS: I see. And when was the monument built?

ROMAN NIKOLAEVICH: I don't recall exactly when, but it was built at the same time as the park, around 1960.

VLADIMIR NIKOLAEVICH: Remember, the park was called Heroes' Park? They changed the name recently. I can't remember the new one.

ROMAN NIKOLAEVICH: Until '93 there were other monuments here, too. They stood over there.

LOIS: What happened to them?

VLADIMIR NIKOLAEVICH: They were destroyed by hooligans!

LOIS: That's a shame. Have you lived in this area for a long time?

ROMAN NIKOLAEVICH: Since the war. We lived in a village until we left for the front. Then, as veterans, we received an apartment here after the war.

LOIS: Well, thanks for the information, and goodbye.

VLADIMIR NIKOLAEVICH: You're welcome.

B. ГРАММАТИКА И СЛОВОУПОТРЕБЛЕНИЕ

1. "TO REMEMBER"

Some of the verbs meaning "to remember, to recall" can be used inter-changeably. The main thing to keep in mind is that the imperfective verb

по́мнить is the root verb from which the other verbs are formed. Since memory is a continuing process, **по́мнить** does not have a perfective form. Therefore, when you use "remember, recall" in a perfective way, you must use one of the other verbs listed below. Note, also, that **по́мнить** is generally not used with **мочь**.

вспомина́ть/вспо́мнить	to recall, to bring back to mind, to recollect
запомина́ть/запо́мнить	to commit to memory, to memorize
напомина́ть/напо́мнить	to remind (someone, dative) (of, accusative), to recall (resemble)
по́мнить (imperfective)	to remember, to recall, to keep/have in mind
припомина́ть/припо́мнить	to remember, to recollect, to recall

Я не по́мню то́чно когда́, но э́то бы́ло приме́рно в шестидеся́том году́.
I don't recall exactly when, but it was around 1960.

По́мните, ра́ньше парк называ́лся Парк геро́ев?
Remember, the park used to be called Heroes' Park?

Я ника́к не могу́ вспо́мнить но́вое назва́ние.
I can't remember the new name.

Два ветера́на сиде́ли и кури́ли, и вспомина́ли войну́.
The two veterans were sitting and smoking and remembering the war.

Она́ напомина́ет мне сестру́.
She reminds me of my sister.

Вы мо́жете припо́мнить, где вы оста́вили су́мку?
Can you recall where you left the bag?

Мы стара́емся запо́мнить слова́ э́того стихотворе́ния.
We're trying to memorize the words to this poem.

2. ПОКА НЕ (UNTIL)

The conjunction **пока́ не** (until) is always followed by a perfective verb.

Пока́ мы не ушли́ на фронт, мы жи́ли в селе́.
We lived in a village until we left for the front.

Подожду́, пока́ ты не ко́нчишь.

I'll wait until you finish.

Не приходи́те, пока́ я вас не позову́.

Don't come until I call you.

The conjunction **до тех пор** also means "until," but it can only be used to refer to a previously specified moment or period of time, i.e. until then, thus far. Unlike **пока́ не,** it is not directly followed by a verb but by a clause, and its usage is more restricted. You should be able to recognize **до тех пор** when you hear it, but use **пока́ не** in your own speech.

Ла́ра мне рассказала́ о блока́де Ленингра́да, но я никогда́ не слы́шала об э́том до тех пор.

Lara told me about the Siege of Leningrad, but until then I had never heard about it.

3. THE PASSIVE VOICE WITH БЫТЬ (SHORT-FORM PAST PASSIVE PARTICIPLES)

In active sentences the subject performs the action of the verb:

Коммуни́сты постро́или па́мятник.

The Communists constructed (built) the monument.

In a passive sentence, however, the subject is the recipient of that action. In other words, the passive form indicates that something is/was/will be done to someone or something.

Па́мятник был постро́ен коммуни́стами.

The monument was constructed by the Communists.

Note that the object in the active sentence (the monument) becomes the subject of the passive sentence, but the meaning of both sentences is the same. In Russian, the passive voice is formed with the appropriate tense of the verb **быть** and the past passive participle of the main verb. Past passive participles function just like short-form adjectives (see **Уро́к** 6 and **Уро́к** 19). They are formed by dropping the infinitive ending of a perfective transitive verb and replacing it with the appropriate short-form adjective ending. The endings are:

-ать/-ять	-н	написа́ть » напи́сан/а/о/ы
-ить	-ен/-ён	постро́ить » постро́ен/а/о/ы
-ыть	-т	откры́ть » откры́т/а/о/ы

Following are some of the most commonly used past passive participles, with the verbs from which they are formed.

to do	сде́лать	сде́лан	done
to found	основа́ть	осно́ван	founded
to lose	потеря́ть	поте́рян	lost
to finish	ко́нчить	ко́нчен	finished
to sell	прода́ть	про́дан	sold
to invite	пригласи́ть	приглашён	invited
to send	посла́ть	по́слан	sent
to cover	покры́ть	покры́т	covered
to close	закры́ть	закры́т	closed
to forget	забы́ть	забы́т	forgotten

А когда́ был постро́ен па́мятник?

And when was the monument built?

Они́ бы́ли располо́жены вон там.

They were (situated) over there.

Мне непоня́тно, что там напи́сано.

I don't understand what's written there.

Note that the participle agrees with the subject of the sentence. If the first person singular ends in a mutated consonant, e.g. **куплю́**, so will the past passive participle; **ку́плен.** Also, some infinitives have irregular participles ending in -т.

to begin	нача́ть	на́чат	begun
to accept	приня́ть	при́нят	accepted
to take	взять	взят	taken
to occupy	заня́ть	за́нят	occupied
to dress	оде́ть	оде́т	dressed
to kill	уби́ть	уби́т	killed

Эти места́ за́няты?

Are these seats taken (literally, occupied)?

The passive voice is often used to avoid specifying the agent of an action or to place emphasis on the passive subject. If the agent of the action is stated, it is in the instrumental case.

Что случи́лось? —Они́ бы́ли разру́шены хулига́нами.

What happened? —They were destroyed by hooligans!

Кем был постро́ен па́мятник? —Он был постро́ен Ивано́вым.

Who was the monument constructed by (by whom)? —It was constructed by Ivanov.

When you learn a new past passive participle, note whether the stress changes from the infinitive to the participle, or within the different gender forms. Finally, remember that the passive voice is sometimes expressed with a present tense verb: either the third person plural form or the third person singular of a reflexive verb, in both cases without a stated subject. This construction is generally used when the English equivalent has an understood "you," "people," or "they" as the subject.

Здесь говоря́т по-ру́сски.

Russian is spoken here (they speak Russian here).

Как пи́шется по-ру́сски да́та рожде́ния?

How is the date of birth written in Russian?

Как говори́тся, о вку́сах не спо́рят.

As they say, to each his own.

4. ДОЛГО VERSUS ДАВНО

Both **до́лго** and **давно́** mean "a long time." **Давно́** means "a long time ago," when used with a past tense verb, or it can be used to describe something that began in the past and continues in the present. **До́лго** means "for a long time" and refers to something that had, has, or will have a beginning and an end in the past or the future. Only **до́лго** can be used with the future tense.

Вы давно́ живёте в э́том райо́не?

Have you lived in this area for a long time (since long ago)?

Они́ познако́мились уже́ давно́.

They met a long time ago.

Мы до́лго разгова́ривали об исто́рии райо́на.

We talked for a long time about the history of the area.

Я бу́ду до́лго рабо́тать в Москве́.

I'll be working in Moscow for a long time.

5. THE GENITIVE CASE WITH PREPOSITIONS OF TIME

The following prepositions take the genitive case: **до** (before, until), **во вре́мя** (during), and **по́сле** (after).

До девяно́сто тре́тьего го́да здесь бы́ли и други́е па́мятники.

Before '93 there were other monuments here, too.

Наши́м му́жественным защи́тникам во вре́мя Вели́кой оте́чественной войны́.

To our brave defenders during the Great Patriotic War.

Как ветера́ны, мы получи́ли здесь кварти́ру по́сле войны́.

As veterans, we received an apartment here after the war.

Be sure not to confuse **во вре́мя,** which means "during" and consists of two separate words, with **во́время,** which means "on time" and is written as a single word.

Я о́чень постара́юсь во́время прие́хать.

I'll really try to get there on time.

C. СЛОВА́РЬ

а́рмия	army
бить (бью, бьёшь, бьют)	to beat (imp.)
в одно́ вре́мя (с чем)	at the same time (as something)

вели́кий	great
ветера́н	veteran
во́время	on time
во вре́мя	during
война́	war
вспомина́ть (вспомина́ю, вспомина́ешь, вспомина́ют)/ *вспо́мнить* (вспо́мню, вспо́мнишь, вспо́мнят)	to recall, to bring back to mind
геро́й	hero
запомина́ть (запомина́ю, запомина́ешь, запомина́ют)/ *запо́мнить* (запо́мню, запо́мнишь, запо́мнят)	to commit to memory, to memorize
защи́тник	defender
изменя́ть (изменя́ю, изменя́ешь, изменя́ют) */измен́ить* (изменю́, изме́нишь, изме́нят)	to change; to betray
му́жественный	brave
назва́ние	name (only for things)
напи́сан/-а/-о/-ы	written
напомина́ть (напомина́ю, напомина́ешь, напомина́ют)/ *напо́мнить* (напо́мню, напо́мнишь, напо́мнят)	to remind (of), to resemble
неда́вно	recently
оде́т/-а/-о/-ы	dressed; clothed
осно́ван/-а/-о/-ы	founded
оте́чественный	patriotic
па́мятник	monument
па́мять	memory
парк	park
по́мнить (по́мню, по́мнишь, по́мнят)	to remember, to keep in mind (imp.)
пока́ не	until (conjunction)
постро́ен/-а/-о/-ы	built, constructed
при́нят/-а/-о/-ы	accepted
при́нято (де́лать что-то)	it's customary (to do something)
приме́рно	approximately
припомина́ть (припомина́ю, припомина́ешь, припомина́ют)/ *припо́мнить* (припо́мню, припо́мнишь, припо́мнят)	to remember, to recollect

про́дан/-а/-о/-ы	sold
разру́шен/-а/-о/-ы	destroyed, demolished, wrecked
райо́н	area; region
располо́жен/-а/-о/-ы	situated; placed
сде́лан/-а/-о/-ы	done
село́	village
солда́т	soldier
убива́ть (убива́ю, убива́ешь, убива́ют) /*уби́ть* (убью́, убьёшь, убью́т)	to kill
уйти́ на фронт	to leave for the front (military)
хулига́н	hooligan

РУССКАЯ КУЛЬТУРА

In Russia, World War II is known as **Вели́кая Оте́чественная война́** (The Great Patriotic War). This gives you some idea of its significance. Russia suffered incredible losses during that war, especially in Stalingrad (now Volgograd), where a decisive battle was fought, and in Leningrad (now St. Petersburg), which was under siege for 900 days. During this siege, many people starved and froze to death, although some relief was obtained through harrowing winter expeditions across the frozen Lake Ladoga to Russian territory in Finland. In Petersburg, monuments, poems, stories, museums, and cemeteries have all been dedicated to the memory of those who suffered and died at that time. All across Russia men were conscripted into the army, and they died by the thousands. Of the generation that fought the war, there are approximately ten women to every man.

Of course such great suffering and loss of life had a tremendous impact on the people, and those who survived were very proud of their endurance and the sacrifices they made for their country. One still gets the feeling that World War II ended only a few years ago. World War II veterans often proudly wear their badges and medals from the war, even though **День побе́ды** (Victory Day, May 9) is no longer celebrated with parades and speeches to commemorate their defense of the **ро́дина** (motherland).

УПРАЖНЕНИЯ

A. **Запо́лните про́пуски глаго́лами: по́мнить, вспомина́ть, запомина́ть, напомина́ть, припомина́ть и переведи́те.** (Fill in the blanks with по́мнить, or the other verbs having to do with memory, and translate.)

1. Я не _____ , в како́м году́ я сюда́ прие́хал.
2. Я не могу́ _____ её и́мя.
3. _____ , он был солда́том и был из То́мска?
4. Вы _____ мне отца́.
5. Я ча́сто _____ свои́х друзе́й в Петербу́рге.

B. **Переведи́те на ру́сский.** (Translate into Russian.)

1. They lived in the village before the war. After the war, they lived in the city.
2. We waited until she called us.
3. This monument is to the brave defenders of the city during the war.
4. I'll stay (remain) here until you come back (return).
5. There used to be (was) a monument there until hooligans destroyed it.

C. **Поста́вьте в действи́тельный зало́г, испо́льзуя слова́ в ско́бках, е́сли есть.** (Put into the active voice using the words in parentheses, if there are any.)

1. Дверь откры́та. (кто-то)
2. Все биле́ты уже́ про́даны. (они́)
3. Университе́т был осно́ван в 1755 Михаи́лом Ломоно́совом.
4. Когда́ но́вые зда́ния бу́дут постро́ены? (они́)
5. Э́ти стихи́ бы́ли напи́саны Анной Ахма́товой.

D. **Запо́лните про́пуски слова́ми «давно́» и́ли «до́лго».**
(Fill in the blanks with давно́ or до́лго.)

1. Как _____ вы бу́дете жить на се́вере?
2. Он _____ здесь рабо́тает.
3. Втора́я мирова́я война́ уже́ _____ ко́нчилась.
4. Мы _____ жи́ли в дере́вне, а тепе́рь мы живём в Москве́.
5. Они́ _____ сиде́ли и кури́ли, и разгова́ривали о поли́тике.

УРОК 40
ЛИТЕРАТУРА. Literature.

А. ПОЭЗИЯ (Poetry)

Ты и Вы

Пусто́е *вы* серде́чным *ты*
Она́, обмо́лвясь, замени́ла,
И все счастли́вые мечты́,
В душе́ влюблённой возбуди́ла.
Пред ней заду́мчиво стою́;
Свести́ оче́й с неё нет си́лы;
И говорю́ ей: как *вы* ми́лы!
И мы́слю: как *тебя́* люблю́!
　　　—Алекса́ндр Пу́шкин, 1828

До свида́нья, друг мой, до свида́нья.
Ми́лый мой, ты у меня́ в груди́.
Предназна́ченное расстава́нье
Обеща́ет встре́чу впереди́.

До свида́нья, друг мой, без руки́, без сло́ва,
Не грусти́ и не печа́ль брове́й, —
В э́той жи́зни умира́ть не но́во,
Но и жить, коне́чно, не нове́й.
　　　　—Серге́й Есе́нин, 1925

Он люби́л три ве́щи на све́те:
За вече́рней пе́нье, бе́лых павли́нов,
И стёртые ка́рты Аме́рики,
Не люби́л, когда́ пла́чут де́ти
Не люби́л ча́я с мали́ной
и же́нской исте́рики.
... А я была́ его́ жено́й.
　　　　—Анна Ахматова[1]

1. Reprinted with permission from *A Treasury of Love Poems,* published by Hippocrene Books, Inc.

Thou and You

She replaced an empty "you"
with a heartfelt "thou"
And stirred up all the happy reveries
In a soul moved by love.
I stand before her lost in thought
Powerless to turn my eyes away
And I say: How kind it is of you!
And I think: How I do love thee!
                    —Alexander Pushkin, 1828

Farewell, my friend, farewell.
Dear one, you are in my heart.
This predestined parting
Holds the promise of a future reunion.

Farewell, my friend, no handshake, no words.
Grieve not and hold no sorrow upon your brow.
In this life, dying is nothing new.
But then, of course, neither is living.
                    —Sergei Yesenin, 1925

He loved three things alone:
White peacocks, evensong,
Old maps of America.
He hated children crying,
And raspberry jam with his tea,
And feminine hysteria.
… And he had married me.
                    —Anna Akhmatova

B. ГРАММАТИКА И СЛОВОУПОТРЕБЛЕНИЕ

The language covered in this lesson is literary and written Russian. Such language is essential for reading but is seldom used in everyday speech.

1. SPOKEN VERSUS WRITTEN RUSSIAN

Following are some guidelines that will help you avoid sounding "bookish" when you speak.

a. то́же versus та́кже

Та́кже sounds stilted in spoken language. Use и (and, too) instead, or change the word order (place the new information first) and use то́же (see Уро́к 26).

Я ходи́л в теа́тр, а та́кже в кино́.
I went to theater and also to the movies.

Я ходи́л в теа́тр и в кино́.
Я ходи́л в теа́тр. В кино́ я то́же ходи́л.
I went to theater and to the movies, too.

b. на́до/ну́жно versus необходи́мо

На́до, ну́жно, and необходи́мо all mean "it is necessary." На́до and ну́жно usually suffice to express need, and they sound more natural in conversation than необходи́мо.

На́до поговори́ть с ме́неджером о счёте.
It's necessary to speak to the manager about an account.

Мне ну́жно купи́ть ша́пку.
I need to buy a hat.

However, необходи́мо can be used in spoken language for added emphasis, to express stronger necessity.

Вам ну́жно—вам про́сто необходи́мо пойти́ к врачу́.
You need to—you simply have to go to the doctor.

2. GERUNDS (VERBAL ADVERBS)

Gerunds are used to describe or qualify the action in the main clause. They answer questions such as Как? and Когда́? and are often used to replace subordinate clauses beginning with these words or with потому́ что or так как.

Когда́ я сиде́л у окна́, я чита́л газе́ту.

While I was sitting at the window, I was reading the paper.

Си́дя у окна́, я чита́л газе́ту.

While sitting at the window, I was reading the paper.

Gerunds act as adverbs, and are therefore invariable. They may refer to the past, present, or future, as determined by the verb in the main clause. The gerund clause is separated from the main clause by a comma, and may precede or follow it.

a. Imperfective Gerunds

Imperfective gerunds express an incomplete action occurring simultaneously with the action of the main clause. Their implied subject is always the same as the subject of the main clause. They generally translate into English as "while" plus an -ing form of a verb. These gerunds are derived from present tense verbs, which are by definition imperfective. To form them, simply drop the **-ут, -ют, -ат,** or **-ят** ending of the third person plural (**они́**) form, and replace it with **-я,** or with **-а** if the stem ends in **-ж, -ч, -ш,** or **-щ,** e.g. **сидя́т »** **си́дя** (while sitting).

Че́стно говоря́, он мне не о́чень нра́вится.

To tell the truth (honestly speaking), I don't like him very much.

Я не люблю́ есть сто́я.

I don't like to eat (while) standing up.

Он чита́л, лёжа на дива́не.

He was reading, while lying on the couch.

For **дава́ть** or verbs ending in **-дава́ть, -знава́ть,** or **-става́ть**, simply replace the infinitive ending **-ть** with **-я,** e.g. **дава́ть »** **дава́я** (while giving). The verb **быть** has a special gerund form: **бу́дучи** (being). As always, reflexive verbs retain their **-ся/-сь** ending, e.g. **ложа́тся »** **ложа́сь** (while lying down).

Встава́я, он вы́ключил ра́дио.

While getting up he turned off the radio.

Бу́дучи уста́лым, я реши́л не идти́.

Being tired, I decided not to go.

Some verbs, including all imperfectives ending in -**нуть**, do not have an imperfective gerund, e.g. бежа́ть, есть, е́хать, ждать, звать, мочь, петь, писа́ть, хоте́ть, каза́ться, па́хнуть.

b. Perfective Gerunds

The perfective gerund is derived from perfective verbs and generally indicates a completed action that occurred prior to the action in the main clause. To form most perfective gerunds, simply replace the past tense ending -**л** with -**в,** or -**лся** with -**вшись**, e.g. написа́л » написа́в, (having written), верну́лся » верну́вшись (having returned).

Она́, обмо́лвясь, замени́ла пусто́е вы серде́чным ты.
She, having made a slip (literally, spoken accidentally), replaced an empty "you" with a heartfelt "thou."

Написа́в письмо́, он встал.
Having written the letter, he got up.

Верну́вшись домо́й, он при́нял душ и лёг спать.
Having returned home, he took a shower and went to bed.

Ко́нчив рабо́ту, она́ се́ла смотре́ть телеви́зор.
Having finished work, she sat down to watch television.

3. ACTIVE PARTICIPLES (VERBAL ADJECTIVES)

Active participles, also called verbal adjectives, can be used to replace **кото́рый** clauses that describe a noun. Like **кото́рый** clauses, they are separated from the main clause by a comma. Like regular adjectives, they agree in gender, number, and case with the noun they modify.

a. Present Active Participles

Present active participles are derived from the present tense and are, therefore, by definition imperfective. They are used to replace **кото́рый** and a verb in the present tense, and they translate into English as the -ing form of a verb. To form a present active participle, simply replace the third person plural (**они́**) ending -**т** with the adjective ending -**щий**,[2] e.g. чита́ют » чита́ющий (who is reading). For reflexive participles, simply add -**ся** to the regular participial endings, e.g. возвраща́ются » возвраща́ющий » возвраща́ющийся (who

---

2. These adjectives agree and decline like хоро́ший (-ая/-ее/-ие).

is returning). Compare the usage of **который** clauses and active participles below.

Смотри́ на всех люде́й, кото́рые чита́ют в метро́!
Look at all the people who are reading on the subway!

Смотри́ на всех люде́й, чита́ющих в метро́!
Look at all the people reading on the subway!

Вот идёт же́нщина, кото́рая преподаёт нам ру́сский язы́к.
Here comes the woman who teaches us Russian.

Вот идёт же́нщина, преподаю́щая нам ру́сский язы́к.
Here comes the woman teaching us Russian.

b. Past Active Participles

Past active participles are similar to present active participles, but they can be either imperfective or perfective, and they replace **кото́рый** and a past tense verb. To form a past active participle, simply replace the past tense ending **-л** with the adjective ending **-вший**,[3] e.g. **прочита́л ›› прочита́вший** (who read). For reflexive verbs, simply add **-ся** to the regular participial endings, e.g. **смея́лся ›› смея́вш›› смея́вшийся** (who was laughing). Verbs whose masculine past tense does not end in **-л** have the participial ending **-ший**, e.g. **нёс ›› нёсший** (who was carrying).

Челове́к, чита́вший (кото́рый чита́л) газе́ту, живёт в на́шем до́ме.
The man, who was reading the paper, lives in our building.

Челове́к, да́вший (кото́рый дал) мне газе́ту, живёт в на́шем до́ме.
The man, who gave me the paper, lives in our building.

There is really no difference in meaning between past active participles and the **кото́рый** clauses they replace, but participles sound awkward in spoken language. However, some active participles have come to be used as regular adjectives, e.g. **настоя́щий** (real, present), **сле́дующий** (next, following), **бу́дущий** (future), **бы́вший** (former), **проше́дший** (past).

Это её бы́вший муж.
That's her former husband.

---

3. Also agrees and declines like **хоро́ший**.

4. LONG-FORM PASSIVE PARTICIPLES OR VERBAL ADJECTIVES

In Уро́к 39 you learned the passive voice with быть and short-form past passive participles. Long form past passive participles (PPPs) replace быть and the short-form participles. They are declined like adjectives. To form long-form PPPs, simply add regular adjective endings to the short-form passive participles in Уро́к 39. For example, оде́т (dressed) **» оде́тый**. For short forms ending in -н, add an extra -н- as well, e.g. постро́ен (built) **» постро́енный**. Compare the following sentences:

Вот цветы́, кото́рые бы́ли ку́плены Вади́мом.
Here are the flowers that were bought by Vadim.

Вот цветы́, ку́пленные Вади́мом.
Here are the flowers bought by Vadim.

The first sentence is more appropriate for spoken language, but long-form PPPs are common in literary and poetic language.

И все счастли́вые мечты́ в душе́ влюблённой возбуди́ла.
And she stirred up all the happy reveries in a soul in love.

Предназна́ченное расстава́нье обеща́ет встре́чу впереди́.
This foreseen parting holds the promise of a future reunion.

Он люби́л ... стёртые ка́рты Аме́рики.
He loved ... old maps of America.

C. СЛОВА́РЬ

бровь	f. eyebrow
бы́вший	former
в груди́	in (my) heart (lit. in the breast, chest)
вече́рний	evening; twilight; dusk (vespers)
влюблённый	in love; loving; tender
возбужда́ть (возбужда́ю, возбуда́ешь, возбуда́ют)/ *возбуди́ть* (возбужу́, возбу́дишь, возбу́дят)	to excite, to rouse, to arouse
грусти́ть (грущу́, грусти́шь, грустя́т)	to mourn, to grieve

душа́	soul; heart; spirit; feeling; inspiration
заду́мчивый	thoughtful; pensive
заменя́ть (заменя́ю, заменя́ешь, заменя́ют) /*замени́ть* (заменю́, заме́нишь, заме́нят) (что/кого́-чем/кем)	to replace, to substitute (someone/thing for someone/ thing)
исте́рика	hysterics
любо́вь	love
мали́на	raspberries
мечта́	dream; daydream
милы́ (ми́лый)	dear, sweet, nice (adjective); dear, darling (noun)
мы́слить (мы́слю, мы́слишь, мы́слят)	to think, to reason (imp.)
но́во/новей	new (poetic)
обмо́лвиться (обмо́лвлюсь, обмо́лвишься, обмо́лвятся)	to say accidentally, to make a slip in speaking (perf.)
о́чи	eyes (archaic, poetic)
павли́н	peacock
пе́нье (пе́ние)	singing; song
печа́ль	f. grief; sorrow
пла́кать (пла́чу, пла́чешь, пла́чут)	to weep, to cry (imp.)
поэ́зия	poetry
поэ́т	poet
пред (пе́ред)	before; in front of (poetic)
предназна́ченный	predestined; destined (for); intended (for)
произведе́ние	works (literary, artistic)
пусто́й	empty; hollow; impersonal
расстава́ние	parting
свет (на све́те)	light; world (in this world)
серде́чный	heartfelt, sincere
си́ла	strength; force
стёртый	worn, effaced
стихи́	verses; poetry
стихотворе́ние	poem
счастли́вый	happy; lucky; fortunate

РУССКАЯ КУЛЬТУРА

Russia has an extremely rich literary tradition. The case system makes Russian a wonderfully flexible language, ideal for poetry. Words can easily be moved around, and each word is extremely rich in meaning and nuance. Therefore, it

Fortieth Lesson

is worth reading Russian poetry in the original. Some of Russia's major poets are: Алекса́ндр Пу́шкин (1799–1837), Михаи́л Ле́рмонтов (1814–41), Алекса́ндр Блок (1880–1921), Андре́й Бе́лый (1880–1934), А́нна Ахма́това (1889–1966), О́сип Мандельшта́м (1891–1938), Мари́на Цвета́ева (1892–1941), Влади́мир Маяко́вский (1893–1930), Серге́й Есе́нин (1895–1925) and Ио́сиф Бро́дский (1940–1996).

Although Pushkin died long ago (in a duel, like Lenskii, a character of his famous poem Евге́ний Оне́гин), he is still revered as the greatest of all Russian poets. He is credited with creating the language of modern Russian literature. Lines from his poems are constantly quoted, and many people learn their favorites by heart. He was a master at bringing to life the Russian soul and Russian landscape. His finest poems are about love and experiencing nature in an intense way, often combining the two. Many Russian poets have written about these subjects, but no one has equalled his brilliance or gift with words.

Anna Akhmatova, whose first husband was shot by a firing squad and whose close friends were incarcerated in Siberian labor camps, wrote some of her most moving poetry about these experiences. The personal and religious tone of her poetry caused problems, and some of her finest work had to be published abroad. Along with Marina Tsvetaeva, Akhmatova is revered by many as the mother of Russian poetry. She wrote evocatively and brilliantly about what it meant to be Russian, especially a Russian woman. In her work, as in Pushkin's, nature is a living creature, a strong presence actively participating in life, love, and grief.

Russia has also produced some of the greatest writers in the world: Фёдор Достое́вский (*The Brothers Karamazov, Crime and Punishment*), Лев Толсто́й (*War and Peace, Anna Karenina*), Никола́й Го́голь (*Dead Souls*), Ива́н Турге́нев (*Fathers and Sons*), Михаи́л Булга́ков (*The Master and Margarita*), Бори́с Пастерна́к (*Doctor Zhivago*), Влади́мир Набо́ков (*Lolita*), who wrote in both English and Russian, and the exiled Алекса́ндр Солжени́цын (*A Day in the Life of Ivan Denisovitch*).

УПРАЖНЕНИЯ

A. **Объедини́те предложе́ния, испо́льзуя «то́же», и́ли замени́те «та́кже» на «то́же».** (Combine the sentences using то́же, or replace та́кже with то́же.)

1. Я хочу́ хле́ба, а та́кже ры́бы.
2. Мне о́чень нра́вятся стихи́ Ахма́товой. Мне о́чень нра́вятся стихи́ Пу́шкина.
3. Я ходи́ла в теа́тр. Пе́тя ходи́л в теа́тр.
4. Мы запо́мнили стихотворе́ние. Эти студе́нты запо́мнили стихотворе́ние.
5. Он лю́бит есть, а та́кже спать.

B. Замени́те дееприча́стия предложе́ниями со слова́ми «когда́» и́ли «так как» (потому́ что) и переведи́те. (Substitute clauses which begin with когда́ or так как/потому́ что for the verbal adverb clauses and translate.)

1. Я чита́ю газе́ту, сидя́ у окна́.
2. Прочита́в кни́гу, он дал её мне.
3. Возвраща́ясь домо́й, он ду́мал о ней.
4. Проведя́ здесь вре́мя о́чень хорошо́, он не хо́чет возвраща́ться домо́й.
5. Не зна́я его́ а́дрес, я не могу́ ему́ написа́ть.

C. Перефрази́руйте предложе́ния, употребля́я «кото́рый» и переведи́те. (Rephrase sentences using кото́рый and translate.)

1. Это моя́ сотру́дница, говоря́щая по-ру́сски.
2. Они́ говори́ли о студе́нтке, рабо́тающей здесь.
3. Уезжа́ющие тури́сты обеща́ют верну́ться че́рез год.
4. Скажи́те смея́вшимся де́тям, чтобы они́ вели́ себя́ хорошо́!
5. Ты зна́ешь челове́ка, заше́дшего к нам вчера́ ве́чером?

D. Замени́те кра́ткие прича́стия по́лными прича́стиями, измени́те предложе́ния е́сли ну́жно и переведи́те. (Replace short-form participles with the long form, make any necessary changes, and translate.)

1. Вы ви́дели цветы́, кото́рые бы́ли ку́плены Анто́ном?
2. Я ищу́ су́мку, кото́рая вчера́ была́ оста́влена жено́й в но́мере.
3. Муж Анны Ахма́товой люби́л америка́нские ка́рты, кото́рые бы́ли стёрты.
4. Пу́шкин, кото́рый был влюблён, написа́л э́ти стихи́ о свое́й любви́.
5. Почему́ Есе́нин ду́мал, что расстава́ние с его́ дру́гом бы́ло предназна́чено?

ВОСЬМАЯ ПРОВЕРКА (Eighth Review)

A. **Переведи́те на ру́сский.** (Translate into Russian.)

1. It is absolutely necessary to know how to pass if you (plural) want to play basketball.
2. Let him cry for a few minutes. It won't kill him. (He won't die.)
3. Close your eyes … now open them.
4. If only we could have discussed the situation!
5. If she had talked (conversed) with him, they would have argued.
6. I'd tell you (familiar) what her name was (how she is called) if I could remember.
7. He reminded me to vote tomorrow
8. She never remembered to (blow) dry her hair before we bought the new blowdryer.
9. For a long time he could only train in the summer during the day (in the daytime).
10. Now he trains whenever he can, all year, from Monday to Saturday.
11. Whoever (with whomever) our team played last year, they always lost.
12. During the war we lived in the countryside and had a good time.
13. Bill Clinton was elected in 1992.
14. Neither Alexander Pushkin nor Mikhail Lermontov lived in this century.
15. Both poets were killed in duels (на дуэ́лях) a long time ago.

B. **Отве́тьте на вопро́сы по диало́гам испо́льзуя слова́ в ско́бках.**
(Answer the questions about the dialogues with the words in parentheses.)

1. По мне́нию Са́ши, что мо́жно бы́ло ждать от коммуни́стов?
2. Что обеща́л Ники́тин?
3. Что Бо́ря хоте́л, что́бы поли́тики де́лали?
4. Как Си́нтия попроси́ла у парикма́хера подстри́чь её? (сбо́ку, сза́ди, впереди́)
5. Что ей надое́ло и когда́? (свой)
6. Где ей на́до бы́ло плати́ть?
7. Что крича́ли боле́льщики по́сле того́, как Дина́мо заби́ло гол?
8. У кого́ был мяч пе́ред тем, как Дина́мо заби́ло гол?
9. В па́рке бы́ли други́е па́мятники? (пока́ не)

10. Когда́ э́ти дво́е мужчи́н жи́ли в селе́, и как давно́ они́ прие́хали в э́тот райо́н?

C. Переведи́те на англи́йский. Если вы не зна́ете сло́во, постара́йтесь догада́ться. (Translate into English. If you don't know a word, try to guess.)

1. Два челове́ка шли вме́сте по доро́ге, и ка́ждый нёс на плеча́х свою́ но́шу.
2. Оди́н челове́к нёс, не снима́я её всю доро́гу, а друго́й ча́сто остана́вливался, снима́л но́шу и сади́лся отдыха́ть.
3. Но он до́лжен был вся́кий (every, each) раз опя́ть поднима́ть (to lift) но́шу на пле́чи.
4. И тот челове́к, кото́рый снима́л но́шу, уста́л бо́льше, чем тот, кото́рый нёс её не снима́я.
5. Сле́дующая рекла́ма (advertisement) из газе́ты «Аргуме́нты и фа́кты», 4 янв., 1996 г.:
6. Моско́вский институ́т иностра́нных языко́в объявля́ет приём (offering) на ку́рсы:
7. Англи́йского, францу́зского, неме́цкого языко́в (для начина́ющих и продолжа́ющих изуче́ние иностра́нного языка́).
8. Ги́дов-перево́дчиков по Москве́.
9. Подготови́тельные ку́рсы.
10. А́дрес: Б. Трёхго́рный переу́лок (alley), д. 11. Тел. 205-72-02, 733-02-58.

ТЕКСТ ДЛЯ ЧТЕНИЯ (Reading)

ЕКАТЕРИНА ВТОРАЯ

Екатери́на II (Екатери́на Вели́кая), урождённая[1] принце́сса Со́фи Анха́льт-Зербст, роди́лась в Герма́нии в 1729 году́. Когда́ ей бы́ло пятна́дцать лет, она́ вы́шла за́муж за бу́дущего царя́ Петра́ Тре́твего. Со́фи приняла́ правосла́вие и получи́ла и́мя Екатери́на. Её муж Пётр, нездоро́вый[2] и инфанти́льный, стал царём в 1761 году́. Петра́ не люби́ли в Росси́и. Наоборо́т, у́мная[3] и очарова́тельная[4] Екатери́на, кото́рая ста́ла совсе́м ру́сской, была́ о́чень популя́рна. В 1762 году́ Пётр был аресто́ван и уби́т офице́рами[5] а́рмии, а она́, с по́мощью[6] свои́х любо́вников[7]—Орло́ва, Потёмкина и други́х—ста́ла цари́цей Екатери́ной Второ́й.

Екатери́на пра́вила[8] Росси́ей приме́рно че́рез со́рок лет по́сле Петра́ Пе́рвого (Пётр Вели́кий), кото́рый постро́ил Санкт-Петербу́рг и основа́л росси́йскую[9] импе́рию. Как и[10] Пётр I, Екатери́на ве́рила в рефо́рмы и модерниза́цию и смотре́ла на За́пад, на Евро́пу. Внача́ле[11] Екатери́на хоте́ла провести́ рефо́рмы, но по́сле револю́ции во Фра́нции и восста́ния[12] крестья́н в Росси́и, она́ ста́ла ме́нее либера́льной. Она́ уси́лила[13] крепостни́чество[14] и дала́ бо́льше привиле́гий дворя́нам.[15] Она́ проводи́ла импе́рскую[16] вне́шнюю поли́тику.[17] Кро́ме того́, Екатери́на была́ покрови́тельницей[18] культу́ры. При ней расцвели́[19] литерату́ра и иску́сство. Она́ основа́ла Эрмита́ж в 1764 году́, перепи́сывалась[20] с Вольте́ром и други́ми францу́зскими филосо́фами, и сама́ писа́ла по́вести, статьи́ и пье́сы. Екатери́на Вели́кая умерла́ в 1796 году́.

СЛОВАРЬ

1. урождённая	née (maiden name)
2. здоро́вый (не-)	healthy (un-)
3. у́мный	intelligent
4. очарова́тельный	charming, fascinating
5. офице́р	officer

6. по́мощь	f. help
7. любо́вник	lover
8. пра́вить (пра́влю, пра́вишь, пра́вят)	to rule (over), to govern (imp.)
9. росси́йский	Russian
10. как и	like
11. внача́ле	at first, in the beginning
12. восста́ние	uprising
13. уси́ливать (уси́лииваю, уси́ливаешь, уси́ливают)/ уси́лить (уси́лю, уси́лишь, уси́лят)	to strengthen, to reinforce
14. крепостни́чество	serfdom
15. дворя́нин	noble
16. импе́рский	imperialistic
17. вне́шняя поли́тика	foreign policy
18. покрови́тель(ница)	patron(ness)
19. расцвета́ть (расцвета́ю, расцвета́ещь, расцвета́ют)/ расцвести́ (расцвету́, расцветёщь, расцвету́т)	to bloom, to flourish
20. перепи́сываться (перепи́сываюсь, перепи́сываешься, перепи́сываются) (с кем)	to correspond (with someone) (imp.)

С БОЛЬШИ́М УСПЕ́ХОМ!

Now that you have completed the course, you'll be able to use this manual as a reference book for expressions, grammar and usage. The appendixes that follow provide even more information for additional study. We also recommend that you review the material, looking carefully at sections that seemed difficult the first time around. Both sets of recordings will be of further use as you study and review at home, in your car, or anywhere you and your tape-player may go . . .

Ни пу́ха ни пера́!

КЛЮЧ К УПРАЖНЕНИЯМ (Answer Key)

УРОК 1:

A. 1. karate 2. zigzag 3. cooperative 4. Tashkent 5. Massachusetts 6. boxer 7. banker
   8. Tokyo 9. Marina 10. Canada

B. 1. This/It is Anya. 2. Here is a/the modem. 3. Jim is a tourist. 4. We are from San Francisco.
   5. This/it is a/the Macintosh? (or: Is this/it a/the Macintosh?)

C. 1. вы 2. ты 3. вы 4. ты 5. вы 6. ты 7. вы 8. вы 9. ты 10. ты

D. 1. f 2. c 3. a 4. e 5. d 6. b

E. 1. А кто э́то? 2. А кто э́то? 3. А что э́то? 4. А кто э́то? 5. А что э́то?

УРОК 2:

A. 1. f 2. a 3. b 4. d 5. g 6. e

B. 1. Fem. 2. Masc. 3. Neut. 4. Masc. 5. Neut. 6. Fem. 7. Fem. 8. Masc. 9. Fem. 10. Masc.

C. 1. ви́зы 2. компью́теры 3. носи́льщики 4. актри́сы 5. места́ 6. дя́ди 7. строи́тели
   8. упражне́ния 9. компа́нии 10. продавщи́цы

D. 1. d 2. e 3. a 4. b 5. c

УРОК 3:

A. 1. -ете/-ю 2. -ют/-ют 3. -ет/-ет 4. -ем/ю 5. -ет

B. 1. де́сять 2. оди́н 3. де́вять 4. шесть 5. ноль

C. 1. паспорта́ 2. учителя́ 3. ключи́ 4. носки́ 5. америка́нцы 6. кафе́ 7. времена́
   8. ви́зы 9. номера́ 10. пирожки́

УРОК 4:

A. 1. Nominative 2. Nominative 3. Prepositional 4. Accusative 5. Prepositional 6. Conjugate

B. 1. собра́нии 2. Москве́ 3. столе́ 4. па́рке 5. чемода́не 6. Пари́же 7. Цинцинна́ти
   8. Санкт-Петербу́рге 9. рабо́те 10. институ́те

C. 1. в 2. на 3. на 4. в 5. в/в/в

D. 1. пробле́ме 2. Анта́рктике 3. Росси́и 4. собра́нии 5. тебе́

УРОК 5:

A. 1. e 2. i 3. b 4. f 5. g 6. a 7. k 8. d 9. j 10. h

B. 1. Ма́шу 2. тетра́дь 3. статью́ 4. му́зыку 5. пи́сьма 6. деклара́цию 7. джаз 8. че́ки
   9. ра́дио 10. валю́ту

C. 1. четве́рг 2. понеде́льник 3. Сего́дня—суббо́та. 4. в сре́ду 5. пя́тница

D. 1. I'm a businessman. And you? 2. That's not Eleanor, it's Anya (but Anya). 3. That/this is a
   computer.—And what's that/this? 4. Yes, that's Putin. And (or but) who's this/that? 5. That's
   not Clinton, it's Bush (but Bush).

E. 1. Ольга Ива́новна 2. Алексе́й 3. Никола́евна 4. Ни́на Никола́евна Петро́ва
   5. Макси́м Алекса́ндрович Ники́тин

ПЕРВАЯ ПРОВЕРКА (First Review):

A. 1. до́ма 2. что 3. там 4. когда́ 5. где 6. вон там 7. кто 8. здесь 9. у́тром 10. как

B. 1. -ют 2. -ет 3. -ет 4. -ет 5. -ете/-ем 6. -ете/-ем 7. -ет/журна́л 8. -у́/тетра́дь 9. -ют/
   му́зыку 10. валю́ту 11. че́ки 12. Анта́рктике 13. деклара́цию 14. статью́, Росси́и
   15. собра́нии 16. Гонолу́лу 17. Санкт-Петербу́рге 18. рабо́те 19. счёте 20. Аню́

C. 1. Olga is walking in the park. 2. Yes, I have a tape recorder. 3. Do you have a car? 4. Where are the cigarettes? 5. Who lives in apartment No. 13? 6. This isn't an office; it's a circus! 7: I read/am reading *Time* magazine. 8. Misha's eating lunch now. 9. Thank God today's Friday! 10. The letter is on the table. 11. Is there a restaurant? 12. Good night! 13. Where's the bank? 14. They work at the institute? 15. She's on a business trip in Paris.

D. 1. Америка́нцы чита́ют журна́лы и газе́ты. 2. У тебя́ есть па́спорт? —Да, есть. 3. Кни́ги в чемода́не. 4. Вот ключи́! 5. Они́ студе́нты? —Нет, они́ не студе́нты.

УРОК 6:

A. 1. плохи́е 2. хоро́шая 3. безопа́сный 4. интере́сное 5. неудо́бные
B. 1. хочу́ 2. хо́чешь 3. хотя́т 4. хоти́м 5. хоти́те
C. 1. 650 2. 30 3. 45 4. 375 5. 90
D. 1. -на/-ен; John: If Marina Aleksandrovna agrees, I agree. 2. no change; Petya's very glad. 3. -а; Is the apartment ready? 4. -о; The window is closed. 5. -ы; They're always busy.

УРОК 7:

A. 1. Его́. 2. Их. 3. Мой. 4. Твой. 5. На́ша. 6. Ваш.
B. 1. како́й/э́той 2. мое́й 3. Да́льнем 4. восто́чном 5. э́том
C. 1. -ите/-у́ 2. -ишь/-лю́ 3. -я́т 4. -ат/-ат 5. -ите/-им
D. 1. похо́жа/вас 2. похо́ж/Серге́я 3. похо́ж/Пе́тю 4. похо́жи/тебя́ 5. лю́бят/учителя́

УРОК 8:

A. 1. Фи́мы 2. Анто́на 3. ме́ста 4. орке́стра 5. ве́щи 6. исполне́ния 7. Со́ни 8. Була́та Окуджа́вы 9. Я́кова Семёновича 10. Серге́я
B. 1. него́ 2. вас 3. них 4. вас/нас 5. кого́/неё
C. 1. Нет, у Со́ни нет ме́лочи. 2. Нет, у Анто́на нет ме́ста. 3. Нет, у меня́ нет симфо́нии Мо́царта. 4. Нет, его́ не́ту (Анто́на нет до́ма). 5. Нет, не у неё.
D. 1. I don't know where Mama is. 2. He thinks that she's at a concert. 3. Would you happen to know when the intermission is? 4. I'm sure that Shostakovich is Russian. 5. They don't know what it is.
E. 1. d 2. f 3. j 4. g 5. c 6. a 7. k 8. e 9. b 10. h

УРОК 9:

A. 1. е́дет 2. идёшь/е́дешь 3. Поезжа́й 4. иди́ 5. идёт
B. 1. h 2. c 3. g 4. i 5. k 6. b 7. e 8. j 9. f 10. a
C. 1. твою́/ста́рую 2. недорого́й 3. наш/но́вый 4. э́ти/класси́ческие/ру́сские 5. моё/ста́рое
D. 1. -ешься 2. -и́мся 3. -ется 4. -йтесь 5. -ется

УРОК 10:

A. 1. жене́, ма́тери 2. до́чери, сы́ну 3. на́шему дру́гу 4. э́той хоро́шей ма́ленькой де́вочке 5. мо́ей ру́сской подру́ге
B. 1. мое́й ма́тери, на́шей жи́зни 2. э́той ве́щи 3. па́рка 4. Владивосто́ка, Москвы́ 5. час 6. выходны́х 7. мину́ту 8. обе́да 9. э́ту часть 10. музе́я, це́нтра
C. 1. h 2. j 3. k 4. a 5. f 6. b 7. c 8. g 9. d 10. i
D. 1. го́да, ме́сяца 2. год, неде́ли 3. дня, часа́ 4. мину́ты, секу́нды 5. рубля́, копе́йки

ВТОРАЯ ПРОВЕРКА (Second Review):

A. 1. -бе/-бе 2. -бе/-ое 3. -ая/-ая 4. -ой/-ий 5. -ы/-ы 6. -ы/-ен 7. -а/-ая/-а/-ю
8. -ьи/-и/-и 9. -бм/-ем 10. -у/-ую/-ому/-ому

B. 1. поменять 2. любят/учить/знаю/учат 3. говорит/люблю/понимаю
4. возвращаешься/возвращаюсь 5. продолжается

C. 1. Дайте/проходите 2. слушай 3. возвращайтесь 4. идёшь/еду 5. идёт/идёт

D. 1. Ira's very happy because the weekend begins tomorrow. 2. We don't know whose seat this
is.—Oh, that's my seat! 3. Petya, please.—You've got the wrong number. 4. We don't accept
this credit card. What would you like to do? 5. Misha and Masha, come here right now!
6. Оля, дай ручку, пожалуйста.—У меня нет ручки. Может быть, у Саши есть ручка.
7. Катя уверена, что папа возвращается туда через 3 часа. 8. Я пишу письмо нашему
новому другу в России. 9. Извините, вы не знаете, где можно взять напрокат машину?
10. У нас большое собрание в первое воскресенье месяца.

УРОК 11:

A. 1. хотела/хотела 2. гуляли 3. отдыхал/слушал 4. делал/читал 5. говорили

B. 1. Парк находился там. 2. О чём он читал вчера? 3. Где они жили? 4. Ты была в этом
кинотеатре? —Нет, никогда. 5. Что вы делали сегодня утром? —Мы отдыхали дома.

C. 1. Ей 2. нам 3. Кому/им 4. тебе 5. Мне

D. 1. i 2. c 3. g 4. j 5. h 6. b 7. e 8. f 9. c 10. a

УРОК 12:

A. 1. c 2. d 3. a 4. e 5. b

B. 1. Первого 2. старого 3. Первое 4. её 5. моей 6. девятого 7. Дальнего 8. этого
прекрасного 9. твоей любимой 10. их

C. 1. мной 2. ними 3. тобой 4. ней 5. ним

D. 1. Со мной? 2. с ним 3. о её 4. к ней 5. обо мне

УРОК 13:

A. 1. Я буду принимать . . . 2. Мама и папа будут ездить . . . 3. Мы будем жить . . . 4. Ты
будешь ходить . . . 5. Вы будете говорить . . .

B. 1. удовольствием 2. другом 3. мужем 4. едой 5. тётей Машей, днём

C. 1. не должна/c 2. должны/e 3. не должны/a 4. должен/b 5. должен/d

D. 1. Мы никуда ни с кем не едем! We're not going anywhere with anyone! 2. Я там никого не
знаю. I don't know anyone there. 3. Я никогда не жила в Москве. I never lived in Moscow.
4. Он ничего не думает об этом! He doesn't think anything about it! 5. Я ни о чём не
говорю. I'm not talking about anything.

УРОК 14:

A. 1. g 2. c 3. e 4. a 5. d

B. 1. a 2. но 3. и, а 4. но 5. а

C. 1. с вашей женой 2. американской историей 3. Каким спортом, Скалолазанием
4. с новым секретарём 5. Чем, Медициной

D. 1. друг друга 2. друг о друге 3. друг друга 4. друг с другом 5. друг с другом

УРОК 15:

A. 1. понедельникам 2. студентам 3. родителям 4. детям 5. воскресеньям

B. 1. g 2. d/f 3. c 4. a 5. h

C. 1. у́чит 2. де́лаю 3. учу́сь 4. изуча́л 5. занима́лся/–ась 6. преподаёт 7. занима́юсь
8. у́чится 9. изуча́ем 10. учи́ть

D. 1. Ча́сто. 2. Давно́. 3. За́втра. 4. Домо́й. 5. Ско́ро.

E. 1. уже́ 2. ещё 3. уже́ 4. ещё 5. уже́

ТРЕТЬЯ ПРОВЕРКА:

A. 1. m 2. h 3. a 4. g 5. j 6. c 7. k 8. f 9. d 10. i 11. b 12. n 13. l 14. e

B. 1. Фильм начина́лся в семь. Фильм бу́дет начина́ться в семь. 2. Они́ бы́ли в Пско́ве.
Они́ бу́дут во Пско́ве. 3. Что вы де́лали ве́чером? Что вы бу́дете де́лать ве́чером?
4. Я ходи́ла в кино́ ка́ждую неде́лю. Я бу́ду ходи́ть в кино́ ка́ждую неде́лю. 5. Как она́
чу́вствовала себя́? Как она́ бу́дет чу́вствовать себя́?

C. 1. Фильм , «Манхэттен», в кинотеа́тре «Росси́я». 2. В шесть и в де́вять. 3. Два часа́.
4. Три биле́та, на ночно́м по́езде, в мя́гком ваго́не. 5. В полвосьмо́го ве́чера, на
второ́е апре́ля. 6. Для касси́рши. 7. Отдыха́ть, пить тёплое питьё и поста́вить ба́нки.
8. Одну́ табле́тку, три ра́за в день. 9. В ию́не. 10. Она́ сво́дит его́ с ума́.

D. 1. Лю́дям обы́чно нра́вится ходи́ть в кино́. 2. Кому́ нра́вится игра́ть в те́ннис? —Ната́ша
увлека́ется те́ннисом. 3. Ско́лько вре́мени? —Сейча́с час.—А когда́ (во ско́лько) тебе́
на́до идти́? —В полдеся́того ве́чера. 4. Како́е сего́дня число́? —Пе́рвое ию́ня.—А когда́
(како́го числа́) бу́дет твой экза́мен? —Четвёртого ию́ня. 5. Како́го цве́та бу́дет цвето́к?
—Жёлтого. 6. С кем вы живёте? —С му́жем и на́шей до́чкой. 7. Мы уже́ е́здили в твоё
люби́мое ме́сто. 8. Они́ пи́шут друг дру́гу, но ре́дко. 9. Как мы друг дру́га узна́ем?
—Я высо́кого ро́ста, у меня́ дли́нные ру́сые во́лосы и очки́, и на мне бу́дет больша́я
ора́нжевая шля́па. 10. С днём рожде́ния! 11. Ой! У меня́ боли́т голова́! 12. Ты ча́сто
у́чишь твоего́ ру́сского дру́га англи́йским слова́м? 13. Она́ не должна́ сего́дня никуда́
идти́. 14. Како́й предме́т она́ преподава́ла в университе́те? —Ру́сскую литерату́ру.

УРОК 16:

A. 1. c 2. g 3. j 4. k, i 5. a 6. b 7. i 8. e 9. d 10. h

B. 1. часо́в 2. раз, ме́сяцев 3. лет 4. неде́ль 5. мину́т 6. о́кон 7. зда́ний 8. рубле́й,
друзе́й 9. пи́сем 10. мест

C. 1. d 2. g 3. k 4. i 5. j 6. a 7. f 8. e 9. h 10. c

D. 1. ка́ши и мёду 2. со́ку 3. ко́фе и са́хару 4. су́пу и хле́ба 5. вина́

E. 1. ем 2. ешь 3. есть 4. еди́м 5. едя́т, ест

УРОК 17:

A. 1. adverb 2. short-form adjective 3. adverb 4. short-form adjective 5. adverb

B. 1. It's time to go. 2. It's clear to us that she doesn't care. 3. There's time. 4. Grandpa doesn't
care. 5. Maksim's hot, but they're cold.

C. 1. Де́душка сказа́л, что сейча́с иду́т вече́рние но́вости. 2. Ди́ктор сказа́л, что э́та
ситуа́ция бу́дет продолжа́ться ещё мно́го лет. 3. Де́душка сказа́л, что он хо́чет пойти́ на
ры́нок. 4. Лю́ся сказа́ла, что всё бы́ло о́чень вку́сно. 5. Внук сказа́л, что он бу́дет
смотре́ть специа́льную переда́чу.

D. 1. всё 2. Все 3. одно́, оди́н 4. всё э́то 5. Все э́ти, одно́й

E. 1. f 2. d 3. e 4. b 5. a

УРОК 18:

A. 1. национа́льных блю́дах, э́тих рестора́нах 2. ва́ших хоро́ших новостя́х 3. мои́х
ру́сских друзья́х 4. всех пля́жах 5. лы́жах

B. 1. ли 2. ли 3. ли 4. е́сли 5. ли

C. 1. Is it possible to/Can I go by metro? 2. Can I write with (by means of) a pen? 3. I don't want to go there by train. I want to fly there. 4. I don't like to write with a pencil. 5. She's fascinated with tennis. 6. Did you go anywhere this summer? 7. Do you know anyone here? 8. The books are here someplace. I just don't know exactly where. 9. Have you ever been to this theater? —No, never. 10. Someone told me that the skiing in the Caucasus is good.

D. 1. Ему́ не на́до было занима́ться. Ско́ро ему́ не на́до бу́дет занима́ться. 2. Ему́ не́ было тру́дно. Ско́ро ему́ не бу́дет тру́дно. 3. Де́душке бы́ло всё равно́. Ско́ро де́душке бу́дет всё равно́. 4. Им ну́жно было де́лать переса́дку. Ско́ро им ну́жно бу́дет де́лать переса́дку. 5. Всё бы́ло поня́тно. Ско́ро всё бу́дет поня́тно.

E. 1. -у́ются 2. -у́ет 3. -у́ет 4. -у́ешь 5. -у́ю

F. 1. друго́й 2. ра́зные 3. ещё одну́ 4. друга́я 5. ра́зные

УРОК 19:

A. 1. руба́шками 2. маши́нами 3. матеря́ми 4. детьми́ 5. людьми́

B. 1. imperfective 2. perfective 3. imperfective, perfective 4. perfective, imperfective 5. perfective, perfective 6. imperfective 7. perfective 8. imperfective 9. imperfective 10. perfective, imperfective

C. 1. Вчера́ он проли́л на меня́ вино́. 2. Где вы поу́жинали вчера́ ве́чером? 3. Сего́дня они́ сде́лали оши́бку в химчи́стке. 4. Она́ всегда́ хорошо́ чи́стила /чи́стит оде́жду. 5. Она́ вчера́ заме́тила, кто там сиди́т. 6. Кто ра́ньше жил в э́том зда́нии? 7. Сего́дня мы послу́шали но́вости по ра́дио. 8. Я ка́ждый день обе́дал в два часа́. 9. Вчера́ он наконе́ц прочита́л э́ту кни́гу. 10. Ему́ ра́ньше о́чень нра́вился э́тот фильм.

D. 1. За́втра оде́жда бу́дет гото́ва. The clothes will be ready tomorrow. 2. Вчера́ они́ бы́ли о́чень го́лодны. Yesterday they were very hungry. 3. Я сего́дня больна́. I'm sick today. 4. За́втра химчи́стка бу́дет закры́та. The drycleaner's will be closed tomorrow. 5. Позавчера́ он был рассе́ян. He was very absentminded the day before yesterday.

УРОК 20:

A. 1. нужна́ 2. ну́жно/на́до 3. нужны́ 4. ну́жно/на́до 5. ну́жен 6. ну́жно

B. 1. Пойди́те в Эрмита́ж. 2. Как дое́хать до Не́вского проспе́кта? 3. Вы́йдите на ста́нции «Чёрная ре́чка». 4. Я не зна́ю, как пройти́ от Не́вского до Академи́ческой. 5. Вы́йдите на ста́нции «Не́вский проспе́кт».

C. 1. Пионе́рской 2. Не́вском 3. Академи́ческую 4. «Академи́ческой», Сенно́й 5. Не́вского

D. 1. Седьмо́й 2. оди́ннадцатый 3. тре́тьей 4. деся́того 5. восемна́дцатом

ЧЕТВЁРТАЯ ПРОВЕРКА:

A. 1. e 2. i 3. k 4. j 5. g 6. c 7. a 8. h 9. f 10. b 11. d

B. 1. f 2. p 3. l 4. j 5. a 6. n 7. b 8. d 9. m 10. e 11. o 12. g 13. c 14. h 15. k

C. 1. I didn't feel well (I felt poorly). 2. How are you? —Not bad. 3. Everything was clear (understandable). 4. It's nice (pleasant) here. 5. Would you/Perhaps you'd like to go there by train? 6. For some reason he didn't say anything. 7. He really liked that program. 8. They called while we were walking in the park. 9. You have to (need to) get out at Akademicheskaya (Station). 10. When did he leave for the Caucasus?

D. 1. Како́е блю́до вы рекоменду́ете? 2. Нет друго́го вегетериа́нского рестора́на? 3. Е́сли вы рабо́таете с детьми́, вы не должны́ кури́ть. 4. Прави́тельству всё равно́. 5. Интере́сно, до́лжен(должна́) ли я писа́ть ру́чкой? 6. Всё бу́дет хорошо́. 7. Я всю ночь не спал(а́). 8. Кто́-то ему́ сказа́л что́-то о новостя́х. 9. Я сде́лал(а) две оши́бки, когда́ я говори́л(а) по-ру́сски. 10. Как дое́хать до Эрмита́жа?

Ключ к упражне́ниям

УРОК 21:

A. 1. прочита́ть 2. чита́ть 3. зайдёт 4. переста́нет 5. бу́дете чита́ть
B. 1. кото́рая 2. кото́рый 3. кото́ром 4. кото́рые 5. кото́рого
C. 1. Ты до́лжен (должна́) всегда́ чи́стить зу́бы по́сле того́, как ты ешь. 2. Ра́ньше она́ хорошо́ е́ла, а тепе́рь она́ пло́хо ест. 3. Ира всю неде́лю не могла́ есть. —Ой-ой-ой! 4. Ты дашь (вы дади́те) мне но́мер его́ телефо́на? —Я уже́ тебе́ дал(а́) его́ но́мер! 5. Ма́ма пекла́ хлеб для нас. Ох э́то бы́ло вку́сно!
D. 1. -ёт; The pain stops when I sleep. 2. -ют; Grandma and Grandpa often give us presents. 3. -ёшь; What time do you get up? 4. -ём; Every morning we find out the answers to the questions. 5. -ёт; The dentist usually gives me a new toothbrush.
E. 1. от; e 2. ко; f 3. у; a 4. к; b 5. к; c

УРОК 22:

A. 1. d 2. f 3. e 4. c 5. a
B. 1. о́чень 2. мно́го 3. о́чень 4. о́чень 5. о́чень
C. 1. Три́дцать пе́рвое декабря́. 2. Серге́я и Ната́ши. 3. Шампа́нское. 4. За цветы́. 5. Её сосе́дки по ко́мнате. 6. торт 7. Прия́тного аппети́та! 8. За Ра́нди и Ната́шу. 9. За кулина́рный тала́нт Ната́ши. 10. Они́ целова́лись и обнима́лись.
D. 1. i 2. e 3. g 4. j 5. b 6. a 7. d 8. f 9. c 10. a
E. 1. Дава́й потанцу́ем! 2. Дава́й погуля́ем в па́рке. 3. Вы́пьем за Но́вый год! 4. Дава́йте познако́мимся. 5. По́йдём!

УРОК 23:

A. 1. передаёт 2. задаю́т 3. остаю́сь 4. узнаёшь 5. сдаёт
B. 1. g 2. d 3. i 4. b 5. a 6. j 7. h 8. e 9. c 10. f
C. 1. тогда́ 2. пото́м 3. зате́м 4. пото́м 5. тогда́
D. 1. e; проводи́ть 2. g; помо́чь 3. h; загоре́ть 4. k; продо́лжить 5. a; закры́ть 6. i; показа́ть 7. j; рассказа́ть 8. c; убра́ть 9. b; реши́ть 10. d; провести́

УРОК 24:

A. 1. 1997 2. В девя́носто второ́м году́. 3. I was there in '59. 4. Второ́го декабря́ ты́сяча девятьсо́т во́семьдесят шесто́го го́да. 5. Пя́того ию́ня ты́сяча девятьсо́т шестьдеся́т тре́тьего го́да.
B. 1. тро́е дете́й 2. сто́лик на четверы́х 3. ко́мната на двои́х 4. оте́ц двои́х дете́й 5. расска́з о четверы́х де́тях
C. 1. спрошу́; I'll ask where the clinic is. 2. задаёт; He asks good questions. 3. попроси́ли; They asked me for information. 4. спроси́ли; They asked me where the clinic is located. 5. про́сим; We asked him to help us.
D. 1. у́мер 2. вы́рос 3. у́мерли 4. вы́росла 5. вы́росли

УРОК 25:

A. 1. g 2. i 3. g 4. a 5. h 6. j 7. d 8. e 9. b 10. f
B. 1. Do you think it's too small? 2. That hat will fit her. 3. That hat fits her. 4. Does it seem too small to you? 5. Hats look great on her.
C. 1. ношу́ 2. пеку́ 3. чи́щу 4. плачу́ 5. люблю́ 6. куплю́ 7. спрошу́ 8. хожу́ 9. смотрю́ 10. могу́
D. 1. с ба́бушкой 2. вхо́да 3. со зда́нием 4. крова́ти 5. с на́шим

ПЯТАЯ ПРОВЕРКА:

A. 1. просыпа́юсь, встаю́, закрыва́ю; In the morning I wake up at 7, get up at 7:30, and close the window. 2. принима́ю, бре́юсь, одева́юсь; Then (next) I take a shower, shave, and get dressed. 3. убира́ю, чита́ю, пью, ем; Then (later) I tidy up a little, and read the paper while I drink tea and eat kasha. 4. чи́щу, иду́; After that I brush my teeth and leave for work. 5. обе́даю, сижу́; I always eat lunch in the snack-bar where I sit with my co-worker, Pyotr Ivanovich. 6. плачу́, спра́шивает, покупа́ете, приноси́ть; When I pay for my lunch, he always asks, "Why do you buy lunch? It's better to bring it from home!" 7. задаёт, счита́ет, теря́ю; Every day he asks me this question. He thinks (considers) that I am losing money. 8. говорю́, предпочита́ю; Every day I tell him that I prefer to buy lunch. 9. продолжа́ет, повторя́ть, ка́жется, переста́нет; But he continues to repeat his question. I don't think he'll ever stop (I think he'll never stop)! 10. забу́ду (ог забыва́ю), помо́г, реши́ть; However, I'll never forget (I've never forgotten) how he helped me to solve a problem at work.

B. 1. Во ско́лько он вчера́ ушёл на рабо́ту? Во ско́лько он за́втра уйдёт на рабо́ту? 2. Мои́ друзья́ вчера́ да́ли мне хоро́ший сове́т. Мои́ друзья́ за́втра даду́т мне хоро́ший сове́т. 3. Ба́бушка и де́душка вчера́ привезли́ нам пода́рки, когда́ они́ прие́хали. Ба́бушка и де́душка за́втра привезу́т нам пода́рки, когда́ они́ прие́дут. 4. Вчера́ мы смогли́ узна́ть его́ и́мя. За́втра мы смо́жем узна́ть его́ и́мя. 5. Что ты вчера́ съе́л(а) на за́втрак? Что ты за́втра съешь на за́втрак?

C. 1. Она́ родила́сь в Росси́и, но её де́ти вы́росли в Аме́рике. 2. Ша́пка, кото́рую она́ но́сит, о́чень ей идёт. 3. Мы попроси́ли у него́ стол на двои́х. 4. Я провожу́ (провёл/-вела́) мно́го вре́мени у свои́х друзе́й в Москве́. 5. Дава́йте погуля́ем по па́рку! 6. Банк, к кото́рому я хожу́, (нахо́дится) ря́дом с по́чтой. 7. Тогда́ дава́й полети́м два́дцать пе́рвого ма́рта. 8. Он у́мер от ра́ка в апре́ле ты́сяча девятьсо́т семдеся́т второ́го го́да. 9. Кто она́ по профе́ссии? —Она́ ста́ла зубны́м врачо́м в ты́сяча девятьсо́т девяно́сто пя́том году́. 10. Уф! Я ненави́жу заполня́ть анке́ты!

УРОК 26:

A. 1. твои́м хоро́шим друзья́м 2. Взро́слым 3. америка́нским тури́стам 4. Э́тим лю́дям 5. Всем неве́стам.

B. 1. The weather became too hot. 2. What do you want to be? 3. What's he doing now? —He's working as a teacher. 4. That church was beautiful before. 5. Ilya will be a dentist in June.

C. 1. h 2. k 3. a 4. i 5. b 6. c 7. j 8. d 9. f 10. g

D. 1. Я чуть не забы́л тебе́ сказа́ть, что позвони́ла Ната́ша. 2. Почти́ все пришли́ на сва́дьбу. 3. Он ру́сский. Она́ то́же ру́сская. 4. Ей нра́вится э́тот цвет. —А та́кже э́тот? 5. У меня́ боли́т голова́. Кро́ме того́, я пло́хо себя́ чу́вствую.

УРОК 27:

A. 1. над; Kostya is laughing at Vera because she believes in astrology. 2. Ме́жду; Between you and me, I don't really like Kostya. 3. Пе́ред; Before the party I want to tidy the apartment. 4. за; Rick dropped by Vera's for his horoscope. 5. за, под; Vera lives in a suburb of St. Petersburg.

B. 1. h; But I'm an Aries, and I don't like (love) to wear red. 2. c; All evening at the party Vera was asking Rick questions. 3. f; Did Vera already do your horoscope? —No, she hasn't done it yet. 4. j; When will you enroll at the institute? —I'll enroll in January. 5. b; Who did you call? —I called (tried to call) Rick, but he wasn't home. 6. i; What will you buy tomorrow? —I'll buy some cassettes. 7. e; I was never able to speak Arabic. 8. k; No, no, I'm not getting tired! 9. a; Vera will tell Rick about his horoscope tomorrow. 10. g; Who sleeps where? —I sleep here, and my sisters sleep over there.

C. 1. Рик из Ганóвера. 2. Одúн из них понимáет по-англúйски. 3. Хабáровск 600 (шестьсóт) киломéтров от Владивостóка. 4. Как доéхать от Кúева до Москвы? 5. Мы отдыхáли с пéрвого мáя до пятнáдцатого мáя.

D. 1. зáпаду 2. ю́гу 3. Востóчной 4. Сéверной 5. Ю́жной

УРОК 28:

A. 1. Одúн из взрóслых мне позвонúл. One of the grownups called me. 2. Я люблю́/Мне нрáвится салáт из свéжих помидóров; I love/like fresh tomato salad (salad of fresh tomatoes). 3. Он купúл подáрки для всех своúх рóдственников.; He bought presents for all his relatives. 4. Я не понимáю рýсских мужчúн. I don't understand Russian men. 5. Мы ждём нáших хорóших друзéй. We're waiting for our good friends.

B. 1. Пат купúл бóлее вкýсный арбýз, чем Кóля. 2. Зáвтра погóда бýдет теплéе, чем сегóдня. 3. Фрýкты в магазúне менéе свéжие, чем на рынке. 4. Ехать на метрó удóбнее, чем (éхать) на машúне. 5. Их квартúра нóвее моéй (... нóвее, чем моя́.)

C. 1. однý бутылку молокá 2. две бáнки джéма 3. три бухáнки чёрного хлéба 4. четыре пáчки чáя 5. пятьсóт грамм сыра.

D. 1. Родúтели должны любúть своúх детéй. 2. Мне óчень нрáвятся (Я люблю́) рýсские фúльмы. 3. Почемý тебé не нрáвится рынок? 4. Онá зáмужем за Максúмом, но онá лю́бит Вúктора. 5. Я ненавúжу рабóтать лéтом.

УРОК 29:

A. 1. Мой сад бóльше, чем егó. Егó сад мéньше, чем мой. 2. Шáпка дорóже ю́бки. Ю́бка дешéвле шáпки. 3. Вáша систéма лýчше, чем нáша. Нáша систéма хýже, чем вáша. 4. Говорúть по-рýсски труднéе, чем понимáть. Понимáть по-рýсски лéгче, чем говорúть. 5. Москвá блúже Кúева. Кúев дáльше Москвы.

B. 1. э́тими большúми здáниями 2. другúми вещáми 3. егó америкáнскими друзья́ми 4. политúческими вопрóсами 5. Кавкáзскими горáми, Урáльскими горáми

C. 1. My wife loves gardening, just like (the same as) you. 2. There's no difference between them. They're the same. 3. We always eat in the same restaurant. 4. They live in the same house. 5. It won't matter to Ira which film we choose.

D. 1. Им нéкуда бýдет éхать. 2. Нéкогда было звонúть. 3. Онá игрáла на флéйте, когдá мы игрáли в шáхматы. 4. Вы игрáете на гитáре úли на роя́ле? 5. У них дáча на берегý Крыма.

УРОК 30:

A. 1. Он сáмый знаменúтый худóжник в странé! 2. В Эрмитáже сáмая лýчшая в мúре коллéкция зáпадноевропéйского искýсства! 3. Это сáмое красúвое яйцó в мúре! 4. Это сáмая стрáнная картúна, котóрую я когдá-нибудь вúдел! 5. Это сáмый большóй зал в гóроде!

B. 1. Это было бы хорошó. That would be/would have been fine. 2. Я бы хотéл(а) пойтú в Эрмитáж. I'd like/would have liked to go to the Hermitage. 3. Тогдá здесь были бы тóлько Ромáновы. Only Romanovs would have been here then. 4. Тебé было бы трýдно звонúть. It would be/would have been hard to call you. 5. Я бы хотéл(а) посмотрéть рýсское искýсство. I'd like/would have liked to see some Russian art.

C. 1. Мы с вáми 2. мы с тобóй 3. Вы с сыном 4. Вы с нúми 5. Вы с гúдом

D. 1. Здесь жúли Ромáновы. 2. Скóлько (это) стóит? 3. Мне óчень нрáвятся картúны Ильú Рéпина. 4. Я мáло знáю о жúзни Антóна Чéхова úли Максúма Гóрького. 5. Охрáнник стоúт у двéри.

ШЕСТАЯ ПРОВЕРКА:

A. 1. Ве́ре нра́вится рабо́тать экскурсово́дом (ги́дом). 2. Ко́ля хо́чет стать зубны́м врачо́м, так же, как и его́ оте́ц. 3. Они́ чуть не опозда́ли на самолёт. Им повезло́, что он то́же опозда́л! 4. Лев Льво́вич лю́бит игра́ть в ша́хматы, но его́ де́ти ненави́дят игра́ть. 5. Мо́жно купи́ть виногра́д на ры́нке? —Да, мо́жно. 6. В це́ркви же́нщинам нельзя́ носи́ть брю́ки. 7. Нельзя́ соста́вить гороско́п без да́ты рожде́ния. 8. Я когда́-нибудь хоте́л(а) бы послу́шать, как ты игра́ешь на гита́ре и поёшь. 9. Я представля́ю, что Э́дик о́чень хорошо́ игра́ет на роя́ле. 10. Ле́на в Крыму́ нарисова́ла две карти́ны.

B. 1. Ре́пин бо́лее знамени́тый худо́жник, чем Ши́шкин, но Шага́л са́мый знамени́тый худо́жник.; Repin is a more famous artist than Shishkin, but Chagall is the most famous. 2. Апельси́ны лу́чше я́блок (чем я́блоки), но ви́шни са́мые лу́чшие.; Oranges are better than apples, but cherries are the best. 3. Пье́са сложне́е фи́льма (чем фильм), но кни́га са́мая сло́жная. The play is more complicated than the film, but the book is the most complicated. 4. Его́ ко́мната ме́ньше мое́й (чем моя́), но их ко́мната са́мая ма́ленькая.; His room is smaller than mine, but their room is the smallest. 5. У них лу́чше (лу́чший) сад, чем у нас, но у него́ са́мый лу́чший сад. They have a better garden than us (than we do), but he has the best garden.

C. 1. Э́ти ру́сские же́нщины за́мужем за америка́нцами. 2. Ско́лько сто́ят пять больши́х па́чек ча́я? 3. Не обраща́йте внима́ния на э́тих шу́мных дете́й. 4. Джу́ди подари́ла всем свои́м друзья́м типи́чные наро́дные сувени́ры. 5. Мы всегда́ приглаша́ем бога́тых люде́й, к тому́ же тала́нтливых молоды́х худо́жников, на на́ши вечери́нки.

D. 1. Ба́нка майоне́за. 2. Ходи́ть по магази́нам ра́ди удово́льствия. 3. Сре́дние века́. 4. Де́ти. 5. and so forth (etc.)

УРОК 31:

A. 1. Ко́ля, купи́ проду́кты. 2. Де́лайте уро́ки! 3. Говори́(те) по-ру́сски! 4. Пат, переда́й ему́ нож. 5. Де́ти, веди́те себя́ хорошо́! 6. Приезжа́йте ко мне! 7. Ребя́та, встава́йте в семь! 8. Прове́рьте, пожа́луйста, аккумуля́тор. 9. Ко́ля, наре́жь лук. 10. Бу́дьте осторо́жны!

B. 1. са́ми; Did you make the food yourself? It was delicious! 2. себя́; How did she feel yesterday? 3. себя́; They usually behave at the farmers' market. 4. себе́; He loves to talk about himself. What a bore! 5. сам; Grandfather himself doesn't know his (own) age.

C. 1. d 2. h 3. a 4. k 5. i 6. j 7. c 8. f 9. b 10. g

D. 1. пока́; She relaxed while we worked. 2. когда́; He dropped by while we were having breakfast. 3. Когда́; When did you graduate from college? 4. пока́; Let's make the salad while the potatoes are cooking. 5. пока́; He always sings while he takes a shower.

E. 1. Она́ принесла́ с собо́й пиро́г. 2. Я за́втра у́тром хочу́ полежа́ть. 3. Наре́жь(те) помидо́ры немно́жко поме́льче. 4. Ко́ля, будь осторо́жен! 5. Скажи́те мне, где вы живёте.

УРОК 32:

A. 1. принеси́те; Please pay the cashier and then bring the check back to me. 2. Иди́те; Go home! 3. говори́; Don't tell anyone about this. 4. Пе́йте; Take (drink) the medicine with food. 5. Встань, оде́нься, поза́втракай; Get up, get dressed, and eat breakfast.

B. 1. ещё раз 2. сно́ва (опя́ть) 3. сно́ва (опя́ть) 4. Опя́ть 5. ещё раз

C. 1. У неё температу́ра 39 (три́дцать де́вять) гра́дусов. 2. Како́го вы ро́ста? —Метр се́мьдесят. 3. Како́й у вас вес? —Мой вес 60 (шестьдеся́т) кило́. 4. Нам ну́жно 300 (три́ста) грамм ма́сла и литр вина́. 5. Како́е расстоя́ние ме́жду гости́ницей и це́нтром го́рода? —Пять киломе́тров.

Ключ к упражне́ниям

D. 1. Дебо́ра должна́ была́ до́лго лежа́ть в посте́ли. Дебо́ра должна́ бу́дет до́лго лежа́ть в
посте́ли. 2. Вы должны́ бы́ли принима́ть антибио́тики. Вы должны́ бу́дете принима́ть
антибио́тики. 3. До́ктор сказа́л, что больно́й до́лжен был отдыха́ть. До́ктор ска́жет, что
больно́й до́лжен бу́дет отдыха́ть. 4. Де́ти должны́ бы́ли де́лать уро́ки. Де́ти должны́
бу́дут де́лать уро́ки. 5. В семь часо́в ма́ма должна́ была́ пойти́ на рабо́ту. В семь часо́в
ма́ма должна́ бу́дет пойти́ на рабо́ту.

УРОК 33:

A. 1. обо́их; I love both (of) my brothers. 2. о́ба (о́бе); We both want to work in Russia. 3. Оба;
Both (of the) resumes are from Americans. 4. обо́ими; She spoke with both (of) candidates.
5. о́бе; I like both (of the) countries.
B. 1. Нам ну́жно бы́ло купи́ть хле́ба и молока́. Нам ну́жно бу́дет купи́ть хле́ба и молока́.
2. Кому́ на́до бы́ло поговори́ть с Алекса́ндрой Григо́рьевной? Кому́ на́до бу́дет
поговори́ть с Алекса́ндрой Григо́рьевной? 3. Ну́жно бы́ло хорошо́ говори́ть по-ру́сски.
Ну́жно бу́дет хорошо́ говори́ть по-ру́сски. 4. Им ну́жно бы́ло иска́ть рабо́ту. Им ну́жно
бу́дет иска́ть рабо́ту. 5. На́до бы́ло подожда́ть. На́до бу́дет подожда́ть.
C. 1. g 2. j 3. a 4. h 5. b 6. i 7. f 8. d 9. k 10. c
D. 1. Он то́лько что ушёл мину́ту наза́д. 2. Билл в Москве́ с ма́я. 3. Она́ то́лько что
позвони́ла, пять мину́т наза́д. 4. Этот компью́тер и́менно то, что нам ну́жно!
5. Предприя́тие вы́росло с тех пор, как мы бы́ли здесь два го́да наза́д.

УРОК 34:

A. 1. те; These earrings are beautiful, but those are even more beautiful. 2. Тот; Bill knows Katya's
brother. He (the brother) lives in New York. 3. тех; I don't understand those who don't care
where their children are. 4. ту; They gave me the wrong bag! 5. то; Get up, or else you won't
have any breakfast!
B. 1. Она́ легла́ на дива́н. 2. Они́ поста́вили стака́ны на по́лку. 3. Она́ всегда́ кладёт
салфе́тки на стол. 4. Сади́(те)сь, Дже́ссика. —Нет, спаси́бо. Я должна́ ложи́ться спать.
5. Нет, не встава́й(те). Я стою́, потому́ что у меня́ боли́т спина́, когда́ я до́лго сижу́.
C. 1. On the whole, I like my work, that is, it's interesting. 2. Oh, Sasha dear! What's the matter?
3. Please give me, let's say, two bottles of vodka. 4. Such a fat little baby (child)! 5. The thing
is, these samovars cost too much.
D. 1. e 2. j 3. h 4. b 5. d 6. a 7. f 8. k 9. c 10. i

УРОК 35:

A. 1. Почему́; Why did he wake up so late? —Because he went to bed very late. 2. Заче́м; What
did she call you for (why did she call you)? —She wanted the address of my friends in Moscow.
3. почему́; I don't understand why Russian is such a complicated language! 4. Заче́м; Why
(for what purpose) is Ben interested in old posters? —He wants to better understand the
political atmosphere in Lenin's time. 5. Почему́; Why (for what reason) is Ben interested in old
posters? —Because he's a professor of Soviet history.
B. 1. Он проводи́л иссле́дование, что́бы лу́чше рассказа́ть студе́нтам о полити́ческой
обстано́вке при Ле́нине. 2. Ну́жно бы́ло сохрани́ть плака́ты и газе́ты, что́бы но́вое
поколе́ние зна́ло свою́ исто́рию. 3. Он (за)хоте́л, что́бы его́ студе́нты то́же могли́ бы
уви́деть плака́ты. 4. Она́ вошла́ в магази́н куста́рных изде́лий, что́бы купи́ть пода́рки.
5. Ка́тя хоте́ла, что́бы Дже́ссика купи́ла матрёшки.
C. 1. Кто-то укра́л мой чита́тельский биле́т! 2. Каки́е у вас рабо́чие часы́? 3. Журнали́ст
сле́дует за библиоте́карем в архи́в. 4. Отсю́да нельзя́ выноси́ть никаки́х докуме́нтов.
5. В пятидеся́тых года́х мы боя́лись всеми́рной побе́ды коммуни́зма.

D. 1. They got married in the presence of witnesses. 2. Under communism everyone had work. 3. Don't talk about that in front of the children! 4. Many churches were closed under Soviet power. 5. During the reign of Peter the First (or Great) European architecture was very popular in Russia.

СЕДЬМАЯ ПРОВЕРКА:

A. 1. Дви́ньте (подви́гайте) па́льцами. 2. Спи́(те) за́втра до десяти́. 3. Останови́тесь! 4. Останови́те маши́ну! 5. Не клади́(те) карто́шку на таре́лку. 6. Ложи́(те)сь спать. 7. Не оставля́йте а́дрес до́ма. 8. Доста́вьте поку́пки. 9. Выздора́вливай! 10. Пожми́те друг дру́гу ру́ки.

B. 1. Мне о́чень тру́дно бы́ло испе́чь хоро́шую буха́нку хле́ба. 2. Ко́ля не до́лжен был обеща́ть, е́сли он не мог э́то де́лать. 3. Ну́жно бы́ло свари́ть карто́шку. 4. Нам на́до бы́ло купи́ть бензи́на. 5. Е́сли у вас голова́ кружи́лась, вы должны́ бы́ли сесть.

C. 1. Она́ снима́ет сви́тер, что́бы медсестра́ могла́ изме́рить ей давле́ние. 2. Он ушёл из фи́рмы, так как он хоте́л рабо́тать в Росси́и. 3. Он то́лько что ушёл, ме́сяц наза́д. 4. Нет, у неё боли́т то́лько одно́ у́хо. 5. Нет, она́ сама́ печёт (гото́вит) пиро́г. 6. Она́ про́сит Пат посиде́ть и поговори́ть с ни́ми, пока́ они́ гото́вят. 7. Он увлека́ется ру́сской культу́рой со шко́лы. 8. Ей не́когда сно́ва так боле́ть. 9. Да, э́то и́менно то, что на́до её роди́телям. 10. Он интересу́ется двадца́тыми года́ми.

D. 1. This one's worse than yours, and (but) that one's better than yours. 2. Does it happen that you feel sick after you take the medicine? 3. You know, the one who's been in charge (leading) of the company since Davidov got sick. 4. Sashenka, you've been behaving badly at school again? What's the matter? 5. While we were interviewing the candidates, he, so to speak, fell asleep. —Again?!

УРОК 36:

A. 1. Си́монов проигра́л бы, е́сли бы Ники́тин получи́л ещё сто голосо́в. Simonov would have lost if Nikitin had received 100 more votes. 2. Е́сли бы Ники́тин стал мэ́ром, он отремонти́ровал бы шко́лы и больни́цы. If Nikitin had won (become mayor), he would have renovated the schools and hospitals. Or: If Nikitin wins (becomes mayor), he would renovate the schools and hospitals. 3. Бо́ря проголосова́л бы за́втра, е́сли бы он смог. Borya would vote tomorrow if he could. 4. Поли́тики никогда́ не реши́ли бы гла́вных пробле́м, е́сли бы они́ то́лько разгова́ривали! The politicians would never have solved the real problems, if they (had) only talked! Or: The politicians would never solve the real problems if they only talked! 5. Е́сли бы Бо́ря голосова́л, за кого́ он проголосова́л бы? If Borya had voted, who would he have voted for? Or: If Borya voted, who would he vote for?

B. 1. Have her go to bed a little earlier. 2. If they don't write in Russian, have them write the letter in English. 3. He's for Simonov. —Let him vote for that Communist if he wants! 4. She doesn't like talking about (either) politics or sports (she likes talking about neither). 5. Neither Dima nor Sasha understood why Borya wasn't (isn't) voting.

C. 1. Бо́ря ни за Си́монова, ни за Ники́тина. 2. Им не нра́вится игра́ть ни в бейсбо́л, ни в баскетбо́л. 3. Она́ ни ру́сская, ни америка́нка—она́ францу́женка. 4. Пусть он войдёт, пожа́луйста. 5. Иро́чка хо́чет купи́ть джи́нсы. Что ты ду́маешь? —Пусть (она́) ку́пит.

D. 1. d; обсуди́ли 2. a; болта́ет 3. d; обсужда́ем 4. b; расска́зывает 5. c; разгова́ривал

УРОК 37:

A. 1. Leave it long in the back, please. 2. The woman who lives above me (overhead) cuts hair very well. 3. Cut it short on (the) top. 4. The children were walking ahead of the adults. 5. The neighbors downstairs (who live downstairs) go to bed early.

B. 1. до; We need to get there (arrive) before 7. 2. До того́ как; Before I found this hairdresser, my haircuts were awful. 3. Пре́жде чем; You (One) need to learn to walk before you (one) can run.

4. пе́ред; Always wash your hands before a meal. 5. пе́ред тем, как; Always wash your hands before eating.

C. 1. Она́ отмени́ла визи́т на полдеся́того. 2. Она́ ждала́ пятна́дцать мину́т. 3. Она́ мо́ет го́лову ка́ждое у́тро. 4. Она́ де́лала зави́вку три ме́сяца наза́д. 5. Она́ должна́ бу́дет втира́ть крем в во́лосы раз в неде́лю пе́ред тем, как мыть го́лову.

D. 1. Е́сли мы не откро́ем окно́, бу́дет сли́шком жа́рко в ко́мнате. 2. Е́сли ты вы́моешь го́лову пе́ред сном, у тебя́ за́втра бу́дет просту́да. 3. Мне на́до вы́мыть го́лову. 4. Са́шка, наве́рно, забу́дет о (его́) стри́жке сего́дня. 5. Закро́й дверь!!

УРОК 38:

A. 1. уме́ет; He's been playing soccer a lot, and now he can (knows how to) pass really well. 2. мо́жем; Unfortunately, we can't go to the game. 3. уме́ете; Can you (do you know how to) read and write in Russian? 4. мог(ла́); I want you to come with us! 5. могу́; I can't believe (that) we won!

B. 1. That's where I live. 2. What?! What's going on? 3. Is he asleep (sleeping) or what? 4. We should invite them. After all, they live here, too. 5. If only they can (know how to) speak Russian!

C. 1. f 2. j 3. a 4. g 5. c 6. a 7. i 8. d 9. g 10. h

D. 1. Что бы ты ни де́лал(а), не забыва́й нам писа́ть! 2. Когда́ бы у тебя́ ни бы́ло вре́мени, позвони́ мне. 3. Како́й бы день вы ни захоте́ли, мне подойдёт. 4. Как бы пло́хо они́ ни игра́ли, Дина́мо всё равно́ моя́ люби́мая кома́нда! 5. Куда́ бы я ни смотре́л(а), я ви́жу цветы́.

УРОК 39:

A. 1. по́мню; I don't remember (recall) what year I came here. 2. вспо́мнить; I can't recall (remember) her name. 3. По́мните; Remember, he was a soldier and was from Tomsk? 4. напомина́ете; You remind me of my father. 5. вспомина́ю; I often remember (think about) my friends in Petersburg.

B. 1. До войны́ они́ жи́ли в селе́. По́сле войны́ они́ жи́ли в го́роде. 2. Мы подожда́ли, пока́ она́ не позвала́ нас. 3. Э́тот па́мятник му́жественным защи́тникам го́рода во вре́мя войны́. 4. Я оста́нусь здесь, пока́ ты не вернёшься. 5. Там был па́мятник, пока́ хулига́ны не разру́шили его́.

C. 1. Кто́-то откры́л дверь. 2. Они́ уже́ про́дали все биле́ты. 3. Михаи́л Ломоно́сов основа́л университе́т в 1755 году́. 4. Когда́ (они́) постро́ят но́вые зда́ния? 5. Э́ти стихи́ написа́ла А́нна Ахма́това.

D. 1. до́лго 2. давно́/до́лго 3. давно́ 4. до́лго 5. до́лго

УРОК 40:

A. 1. Я хочу́ хле́ба. Ры́бы я то́же хочу́. 2. Мне о́чень нра́вятся стихи́ А́нны Ахма́товой. Стихи́ Пу́шкина мне то́же о́чень нра́вятся. 3. Я ходи́ла в теа́тр, и Пе́тя то́же. 4. Мы запо́мнили стихотворе́ние, и э́ти студе́нты то́же. 5. Он лю́бит есть. Спать он то́же лю́бит.

B. 1. Я сижу́ у окна́, когда́ я чита́ю газе́ту. I'm sitting by the window while I read the paper. 2. Когда́ он прочита́л кни́гу, он дал её мне. When he had read the book, he gave it to me. 3. Когда́ он возвраща́лся домо́й, он ду́мал о ней. While he was going home (on his way home) he was thinking about her. 4. Так как он о́чень хорошо́ провёл здесь вре́мя, он не хо́четь возвраща́ться домо́й. Since he's had such a good time here, he doesn't want to go back home. 5. Так как я не зна́ю его́ а́дрес, я не могу́ ему́ написа́ть. I can't write to him since I don't know his address.

C. 1. Э́то моя́ сотру́дница, кото́рая говори́т по-ру́сски. That's my co-worker who speaks Russian. 2. Они́ говори́ли о студе́нтке, кото́рая здесь рабо́тает. They were talking about the student who works here. 3. **Тури́сты, кото́рые уезжа́ют, обеща́ют верну́ться че́рез год.** The tourists who are leaving are promising to return in a year. 4. **Скажи́те де́тям, кото́рые смея́лись, что́бы они́ вели́ себя́ хорошо́!** Tell the kids who were laughing to behave themselves! 5. **Ты зна́ешь челове́ка, кото́рый зашёл к нам вчера́ ве́чером?;** Do you know the man who dropped by our place last night?

D. 1. **Вы ви́дели цветы́, ку́пленные Анто́ном?** Did you see the flowers bought by Anton (which were bought by Anton)? 2. **Я ищу́ су́мку, оста́вленную вчера́ жено́й в но́мере.** I'm looking for a bag which had been (was) left in our room yesterday by my wife. 3. **Муж Анны Ахма́товой люби́л стёртые америка́нские ка́рты.** Anna Akhmatova's husband loved worn-out (old) American maps. 4. **Пу́шкин, влюблённый, написа́л э́ти стихи́ о свое́й любви́.;** Pushkin, in love, wrote this poem about his love. 5. **Почему́ Есе́нин ду́мал, что расстава́ние с его́ дру́гом бы́ло предназна́ченное?** Why did Esenin think that the parting from his friend was predestined?

ВОСЬМАЯ ПРОВЕРКА:

A. 1. Необхо́димо уме́ть пасова́ть, е́сли вы хоти́те игра́ть в баскетбо́л. 2. Пусть он попла́чет не́сколько мину́т. Он не умрёт. 3. Закро́й(те) глаза́ ... сейча́с откро́й(те) их. 4. Лишь бы мы могли́ обсуди́ть ситуа́цию! 5. Е́сли бы она́ разгова́ривала с ним, они́ спо́рили бы. 6. Я тебе́ сказа́л(а) бы, как её зову́т, е́сли бы я мог(ла́) вспо́мнить. 7. Он мне напо́мнил проголосова́ть за́втра. 8. Она́ всегда́ забыва́ла суши́ть фе́ном во́лосы до того́, как (пре́жде чем) мы купи́ли но́вый фен. 9. Он до́лго мог упражня́ться ле́том то́лько днём. 10. Тепе́рь он упражня́ется, когда́ бы он ни мог, весь год, с понеде́льника до суббо́ты. 11. С кем бы на́ша кома́нда ни игра́ла в про́шлом году́, она́ всегда́ прои́грывала. 12. Во вре́мя войны́ мы жи́ли в дере́вне и хорошо́ проводи́ли вре́мя. 13. Билл Кли́нтон был и́збран в 1992-ом году́. 14. Ни Алекса́ндр Пу́шкин, ни Михаи́л Ле́рмонтов не жи́ли в э́том ве́ке. 15. Оба поэ́та да́вно бы́ли уби́ты на дуэ́лях.

B. 1. По мне́нию Са́ши, ничего́. 2. Он обеща́л отремонти́ровать все шко́лы и больни́цы. 3. Он хоте́л что́бы поли́тики реши́ли гла́вные пробле́мы. 4. Она́ попроси́ла у парикма́хера подстри́чь её ко́ротко сбо́ку и сза́ди, и немно́жко подлинне́е впереди́. 5. Ей надое́ла своя́ зави́вка три ме́сяца наза́д. 6. Ей на́до бы́ло плати́ть в ка́ссу у вы́хода. 7. Они́ крича́ли: «Молодцы́! Молодцы́!» 8. Пе́ред тем, как Дина́мо заби́ло гол, мяч был у Миха́йлова. 9. Да, в па́рке бы́ли други́е па́мятники, пока́ хулига́ны их не разру́шили (пока́ они́ не́ бы́ли разру́шены хулига́нами). 10. Они́ жи́ли в селе́ до войны́ и прие́хали в э́тот райо́н по́сле войны́.

C. 1. Two men walked along the road together, and each carried his burden on his shoulders. 2. One man carried it all the way not putting it down (removing it), while the other man stopped often, putting down the burden and sitting down to rest. 3. But he had to lift the burden each time onto his shoulders again. 4. And this man, who kept putting down the burden, became more tired than the one who carried it without putting it down (removing it). 5. The following advertisement is from the newspaper *Arguments and Facts*, January 4, 1996: 6. The Moscow Institute of Foreign Languages announces the offering of courses: 7. 1. English, French, German languages (for beginning and continuing study of a foreign language). 8. 2. For guides/interpreters around Moscow. 9. 3. Preparatory courses. 10. Address: B. Tryokhgorniy (Three Hill) Alley, No. 11. Tel. 205-72-02, 733-02-58.

ПРИЛОЖЕНИЯ
(Appendixes)

A. GRAMMAR SUMMARY

1. SUMMARY OF CASES

NOMINATIVE (N)	subject
ACCUSATIVE (A)	direct object
GENITIVE (G)	1. possession (of)
	2. object of neg. verbs
	3. numbers, quantity
PREPOSITIONAL (P)	only after prepositions (locative/about)
DATIVE (D)	1. indirect object (to)
	2. with impersonal expressions
INSTRUMENTAL (I)	1. "being" verbs
	2. with, by, as

2. DECLENSION OF NOUNS[1]

MASCULINE SINGULAR

	ANSWERS THE QUESTION	BASIC ENDING	HARD REGULAR	HARD UMBRELLA	SOFT -й	SOFT -ь
N	Что? Кто?	zero	стол	ма́льчик	музе́й	портфе́ль
A Inan.	Что?	zero	стол		музе́й	портфе́ль
A Anim.	Кого́?	-а		ма́льчика		
G	Чего́? Кого́?	-а	стола́	ма́льчика	музе́я	портфе́ля
P	О чём? О ком?	-е	столе́	ма́льчике	музе́е	портфе́ле
D	Чему́? Кому́?	-у	столу́	ма́льчику	музе́ю	портфе́лю
I	Чем? Кем?	-ом	столо́м	ма́льчиком	музе́ем	портфе́лем

MASCULINE PLURAL

	ANSWERS THE QUESTION	BASIC ENDING	HARD REGULAR	HARD UMBRELLA	SOFT -й	SOFT -ь
N	Что? Кто?	-ы	столы́	ма́льчики	музе́и	портфе́ли
A Inan.	Что?	-ы	столы́		музе́и	портфе́ли
A Anim.	Кого́?	-ов		ма́льчиков		
G	Чего́? Кого́?	-ов	столо́в	ма́льчиков	музе́ев	портфе́лей
P	О чём? О ком?	-ах	стола́х	ма́льчиках	музе́ях	портфе́лях
D	Чему́? Кому́?	-ам	стола́м	ма́льчикам	музе́ям	портфе́лям
I	Чем? Кем?	-ами	стола́ми	ма́льчиками	музе́ями	портфе́лями

1. Please see **Уро́к** 2 and 3 on the nominative plural of nouns and **Уро́к** 16 on the genitive plural.

FEMININE SINGULAR

	ANSWERS THE QUESTION	BASIC ENDING	HARD REGULAR	HARD UMBRELLA	-й	SOFT -ия	-ь
N	Что? Кто?	-a	газе́та	колле́га	неде́ля	ле́кция	вещь
A	Что? Кого́?	-y	газе́ту	колле́гу	неде́лю	ле́кцию	вещь
G	Чего́? Кого́?	-ы	газе́ты	колле́ги	неде́ли	ле́кции	ве́щи
P	О чём? О ком?	-e	газе́те	колле́ге	неде́ле	ле́кции	ве́щи
D	Чему́? Кому́?	-e	газе́те	колле́ге	неде́ле	ле́кции	ве́щи
I	Чем? Кем?	-ой	газе́той	колле́гой	неде́лей	ле́кцией	ве́щью

FEMININE PLURAL

	ANSWERS THE QUESTION	BASIC ENDING	HARD REGULAR	HARD UMBRELLA	-й	SOFT -ия	-ь
N	Что? Кто?	-ы	газе́ты	колле́ги	неде́ли	ле́кции	ве́щи
A Inan.	Что?	-ы	газе́ты		неде́ли	ле́кции	ве́щи
A Anim.	Кого́?	zero		колле́г			
G	Чего́? Кого́?	zero	газе́т	колле́г	неде́ль	ле́кций	веще́й
P	О чём? О ком?	-ах	газе́тах	колле́гах	неде́лях	ле́кциях	веща́х
D	Чему́? Кому́?	-ам	газе́там	колле́гам	неде́лям	ле́кциям	веща́м
I	Чем? Кем?	-ами	газе́тами	колле́гами	неде́лями	ле́кциями	веща́ми

NEUTER SINGULAR

	ANSWERS	BASIC ENDING	HARD	SOFT -e	-ие
N	Что?	-o	окно́	мо́ре	зда́ние
A	Что?	-o	окно́	мо́ре	зда́ние
G	Чего́?	-a	окна́	мо́ря	зда́ния
P	О чём?	-e	окне́	мо́ре	зда́нии
D	Чему́?	-y	окну́	мо́рю	зда́нию
I	Чем?	-ом	окно́м	мо́рем	зда́нием

NEUTER PLURAL

	ANSWERS	BASIC ENDING	HARD	SOFT -e	-ие
N	Что?	-a	о́кна	моря́	зда́ния
A	Что?	-a	о́кна	моря́	зда́ния
G	Чего́?	zero	о́кон	море́й	зда́ний
P	О чём?	-ах	о́кнах	моря́х	зда́ниях
D	Чему́?	-ам	о́кнам	моря́м	зда́ниям
I	Чем?	-ами	о́кнами	моря́ми	зда́ниями

IRREGULAR NOUNS—SINGULAR

	MASCULINE	FEMININE		NEUTER	
N	путь	мать	дочь	и́мя	вре́мя
A	путь	мать	дочь	и́мя	вре́мя
G	пути́	ма́тери	до́чери	и́мени	вре́мени
P	(о) пути́	(о) ма́тери	(о) до́чери	(об) и́мени	(о) вре́мени
D	пути́	ма́тери	до́чери	и́мени	вре́мени
I	путём	ма́терью	до́черью	и́менем	вре́менем

IRREGULAR NOUNS—PLURAL

N	пути́	ма́тери	до́чери	имена́	времена́
A	пути́	матере́й	дочере́й	имена́	времена́
G	путе́й	матере́й	дочере́й	имён	времён
P	(о) путя́х	(о) матеря́х	(о) дочеря́х	(об) имена́х	(о) времена́х
D	путя́м	матеря́м	дочеря́м	имена́м	времена́м
I	путя́ми	матеря́ми	дочеря́ми (дочерьми́)	имена́ми	времена́ми

REGULAR NOUNS WITH IRREGULAR PLURALS

N sing.	друг	сосе́д	сын	брат	сестра́	ребёнок
N pl.	друзья́	сосе́ди	сыновья́	бра́тья	сёстры	де́ти
A pl.	друзе́й	сосе́дей	сынове́й	бра́тьев	сестёр	дете́й
G pl.	друзе́й	сосе́дей	сынове́й	бра́тьев	сестёр	дете́й
P pl.	(о) друзья́х	(о) сосе́дях	(о) сыновья́х	(о) бра́тьях	(о) сёстрах	(о) де́тях
D pl.	друзья́м	сосе́дям	сыновья́м	бра́тьям	сёстрам	де́тям
I pl.	друзья́ми	сосе́дями	сыновья́ми	бра́тьями	сёстрами	детьми́

3. DECLENSION OF ADJECTIVES

MASCULINE/NEUTER SINGULAR

	ANSWERS QUESTION	BASIC ENDING	REGULAR		END-STRESSED		UMBRELLA	SOFT
N	Како́й?	-ый	но́вый	ру́сский	второ́й	большо́й	хоро́ший	си́ний
	Како́е?	-ое	но́вое	ру́сское	второ́е	большо́е	хоро́шее	си́нее
A Inan.	Како́й?	-ый	но́вый	ру́сский	второ́й	большо́й	хоро́ший	си́ний
	Како́е?	-ое	но́вое	ру́сское	второ́е	большо́е	хоро́шее	си́нее
A Anim.	Како́го?	-ого	но́вого	ру́сского	второ́го	большо́го	хоро́шего	си́него
G	Како́го?	-ого	но́вого	ру́сского	второ́го	большо́го	хоро́шего	си́него
P	О како́м?	-ом	но́вом	ру́сском	второ́м	большо́м	хоро́шем	си́нем
D	Како́му?	-ому	но́вому	ру́сскому	второ́му	большо́му	хоро́шему	си́нему
I	Каки́м?	-ым	но́вым	ру́сским	вторы́м	больши́м	хоро́шим	си́ним

FEMININE SINGULAR

	ANSWERS QUESTION	BASIC ENDING	REGULAR		END-STRESSED		UMBRELLA	SOFT
N	Кака́я?	-ая	но́вая	ру́сская	втора́я	больша́я	хоро́шая	си́няя
A	Каку́ю?	-ую	но́вую	ру́сскую	втору́ю	большу́ю	хоро́шую	си́нюю
G	Како́й?	-ой	но́вой	ру́сской	второ́й	большо́й	хоро́шей	си́ней
P	О како́й?	-ой	но́вой	ру́сской	второ́й	большо́й	хоро́шей	си́ней
D	Како́й?	-ой	но́вой	ру́сской	второ́й	большо́й	хоро́шей	си́ней
I	Како́й?	-ой	но́вой	ру́сской	второ́й	большо́й	хоро́шей	си́ней

PLURAL

	ANSWERS QUESTION	BASIC ENDING	REGULAR		END-STRESSED		UMBRELLA	SOFT
N	Каки́е?	-ые	но́вые	ру́сские	вторы́е	больши́е	хоро́шие	си́ние
A Inan.	Каки́е?	-ые	но́вые	ру́сские	вторы́е	больши́е	хоро́шие	си́ние
A Anim.	Каки́х?	-ых	но́вых	ру́сских	вторы́х	больши́х	хоро́ших	си́них
G	Каки́х?	-ых	но́вых	ру́сских	вторы́х	больши́х	хоро́ших	си́них
P	О каки́х?	-ых	но́вых	ру́сских	вторы́х	больши́х	хоро́ших	си́них
D	Каки́м?	-ым	но́вым	ру́сским	вторы́м	больши́м	хоро́шим	си́ним
I	Каки́ми?	-ыми	но́выми	ру́сскими	вторы́ми	больши́ми	хоро́шими	си́ними

4. DECLENSION OF PRONOUNS

PERSONAL

N	я	ты	он/оно́	она́	мы	вы	они́
A	меня́	тебя́	(н)его́	(н)её	нас	вас	(н)их
G	меня́	тебя́	(н)его́	(н)её	нас	вас	(н)их
P	(обо) мне́	(о) тебе́	(о) нём	(о) ней	(о) нас	(о) вас	(о) них
D	мне	тебе́	(н)ему́	(н)ей	нам	вам	(н)им
I	мной	тобо́й	(н)им	(н)ей	на́ми	ва́ми	(н)и́ми

INTERROGATIVE   REFLEXIVE

N	что	кто	(себя́)
A	что	кто	себя́
G	чего́	кого́	себя́
P	(о) чём	(о) ком	(о) себе́
D	чему́	кому́	себе́
I	чем	кем	собо́й

5. DECLENSION OF SPECIAL MODIFIERS

a. Possessive

The possessive special modifiers **его́, её,** and **их** are not included because they never change.

MASCULINE/NEUTER SINGULAR

N	Чей?	мой	твой	свой	наш	ваш
	Чьё?	моё	твоё	своё	на́ше	ва́ше
A Inan.	Чей?	мой	твой	свой	наш	ваш
	Чьё?	моё	твоё	своё	на́ше	ва́ше
A Anim.	Чьего́?	моего́	твоего́	своего́	на́шего	ва́шего
G	Чьего́?	моего́	твоего́	своего́	на́шего	ва́шего
P	О чьём?	(о) моём	(о) твоём	(о) своём	(о) на́шем	(о) ва́шем
D	Чьему́?	моему́	твоему́	своему́	на́шему	ва́шему
I	Чьим?	мои́м	твои́м	свои́м	на́шим	ва́шим

FEMININE SINGULAR

N	Чья?	моя́	твоя́	своя́	на́ша	ва́ша
A	Чью?	мою́	твою́	свою́	на́шу	ва́шу
G	Чьей?	мое́й	твое́й	свое́й	на́шей	ва́шей
P	О чьей?	(о) мое́й	(о) твое́й	(о) свое́й	(о) на́шей	(о) ва́шей
D	Чьей?	мое́й	твое́й	свое́й	на́шей	ва́шей
I	Чьей?	мое́й	твое́й	свое́й	на́шей	ва́шей

PLURAL

N/A Inan.	Чьи?	мой	твой	свой	на́ши	ва́ши
A Anim.	Чьих?	мои́х	твои́х	свои́х	на́ших	ва́ших
G	Чьих?	мои́х	твои́х	свои́х	на́ших	ва́ших
P	О чьих?	(о) мои́х	(о) твои́х	(о) свои́х	(о) на́ших	(о) ва́ших
D	Чьим?	мои́м	твои́м	свои́м	на́шим	ва́шим
I	Чьи́ми?	мои́ми	твои́ми	свои́ми	на́шими	ва́шими

b. Demonstrative and Quantitative

MASCULINE/NEUTER SINGULAR

N	э́тот	тот	весь	оди́н	тре́тий
	э́то	то	всё	одно́	тре́тье
A Inan.	э́тот	тот	весь	оди́н	тре́тий
	э́то	то	всё	одно́	тре́тье
A Anim.	э́того	того́	всего́	одного́	тре́тьего
G	э́того	того́	всего́	одного́	тре́тьего
P	(об) э́том	(о) том	(обо) всём	(об) одно́м	(о) тре́тьем
D	э́тому	тому́	всему́	одному́	тре́тьему
I	э́тим	тем	всем	одни́м	тре́тьим

FEMININE SINGULAR

N	э́та	та	вся	одна́	тре́тья
A	э́ту	ту	всю	одну́	тре́тью
G	э́той	той	всей	одно́й	тре́тьей
P	(об) э́той	(о) той	(обо) всей	(об) одно́й	(о) тре́тьей
D	э́той	той	всей	одно́й	тре́тьей
I	э́той	той	всей	одно́й	тре́тьей

PLURAL

N/A Inan.	э́ти	те	все	одни́	тре́тьи
A Anim.	э́тих	тех	всех	одни́х	тре́тьих
G	э́тих	тех	всех	одни́х	тре́тьих
P	(об) э́тих	(о) тех	(обо) всех	(об) одни́х	(о) тре́тьих
D	э́тим	тем	всем	одни́м	тре́тьим
I	э́тими	те́ми	все́ми	одни́ми	тре́тьими

THE NUMBERS 2–5

	TWO	THREE	FOUR	FIVE
N/A Inan.	два/две	три	четы́ре	пять
A Anim.	двух	трёх	четырёх	пяти́
G	двух	трёх	четырёх	пяти́
P	(о) двух	(о) трёх	(о) четырёх	(о) пяти́
D	двум	трём	четырём	пяти́
I	двумя́	тремя́	четырьмя́	пятью́

Note: The numbers 6 to 20 follow the same declension pattern as 5.

6. CARDINAL AND ORDINAL NUMBERS

	CARDINAL	ORDINAL		CARDINAL
0	ноль		101	сто оди́н
1	оди́н/одна́/одно́	пе́рвый	200	две́сти
2	два/две	второ́й	300	три́ста
3	три	тре́тий/тре́тья/тре́тье	400	четы́реста
4	четы́ре	четвёртый	500	пятьсо́т
5	пять	пя́тый	600	шестьсо́т
6	шесть	шесто́й	700	семьсо́т
7	семь	седьмо́й	800	восемьсо́т
8	во́семь	восьмо́й	900	девятьсо́т
9	де́вять	девя́тый	1.000	ты́сяча
10	де́сять	деся́тый	1 million	миллио́н
11	оди́ннадцать	оди́ннадцатый	1 billion	миллиа́рд
12	двена́дцать	двена́дцатый		
13	трина́дцать	трина́дцатый		
14	четы́рнадцать	четы́рнадцатый		
15	пятна́дцать	пятна́дцатый		
16	шестна́дцать	шестна́дцатый		
17	семна́дцать	семна́дцатый		
18	восемна́дцать	восемна́дцатый		
19	девятна́дцать	девятна́дцатый		
20	два́дцать	двадца́тый		
21	два́дцать оди́н	два́дцать пе́рвый		
30	три́дцать	тридца́тый		
40	со́рок	сороково́й		
50	пятьдеся́т	пятидеся́тый		
60	шестьдеся́т	шестидеся́тый		
70	се́мьдесят	семидеся́тый		
80	во́семьдесят	восьмидеся́тый		
90	девяно́сто	девяно́стый		
100	сто	со́тый		

7. DECLENSION FOLLOWING NUMBERS

NUMBERS ENDING IN:	REQUIRE THE:	AND ARE OFTEN USED WITH:
1	Nominative singular	оди́н час/год
		одна́ мину́та
2, 3, 4	Genitive singular	четы́ре часа́
		три го́да
		две мину́ты
5–9, 0	Genitive plural	пять часо́в
		де́вять лет
		три́дцать мину́т

8. COMMON IRREGULAR COMPARATIVE ADJECTIVES

	ADJECTIVE	COMPARATIVE	
bad	плохо́й	ху́же	worse
big	большо́й	бо́льше	bigger/more
cheap	дешёвый	деше́вле	cheaper
easy	лёгкий	ле́гче	easier
expensive/dear	дорого́й	доро́же	more expensive/dearer
fat	то́лстый	то́лще	fatter
frequent	ча́стый	ча́ще	more often
good	хоро́ший	лу́чше	better
late	по́здний	по́зже	later
loud	гро́мкий	гро́мче	louder
narrow	у́зкий	у́же	narrower
near	бли́зкий	бли́же	nearer
old	ста́рый	ста́рше	older
quiet	ти́хий	ти́ше	quieter
short	коро́ткий	коро́че	shorter
simple	просто́й	про́ще	simpler
small	ма́ленький	ме́ньше	smaller/less
tall	высо́кий	вы́ше	taller
wide	широ́кий	ши́ре	wider
young	молодо́й	мла́дше, моло́же	younger

9. COMMON VERBS AND THE CASES THEY REQUIRE

INFINITIVE	MEANING	CASE REQUIRED
all verbs of motion		accusative
тре́бовать/по	to demand	genitive
избега́ть/избежа́ть	to avoid	genitive
боя́ться	to be afraid of	genitive
ждать/подожда́ть	to wait (for)	genitive
дава́ть/дать	to give	dative
пока́зывать/показа́ть	to show	dative
помога́ть/помо́чь	to help	dative
отвеча́ть/отве́тить	to answer/reply to	dative
меша́ть/по-	to bother/disturb	dative
зави́довать/по-	to envy	dative
обеща́ть/по-	to promise	dative
сове́товать/по-	to advise	dative
учи́ться/на-	to learn to	dative
нра́виться/по-	to please (like)	dative
по́льзоваться	to make use of	instrumental
занима́ться/по-	to study/be occupied with	instrumental
интересова́ться/за-	to be interested (in)	instrumental
горди́ться	to be proud of	instrumental
увлека́ться/увле́чься	to be fascinated by	instrumental
станови́ться/стать	to become	instrumental
остава́ться/оста́ться	to remain	instrumental

10. CASES AND PREPOSITIONS

CASE	PREPOSITIONS	MEANING
Accusative	в	to, into
	за	for (exchange), behind (direction)
	на	to, onto
	про	about
	че́рез	through, across
Genitive	без	without
	впереди́	to the front of
	для	for (the purpose of)
	до	until, as far as, up to
	из	from (source), out of
	ми́мо	past
	о́коло	near, about
	от	from
	по́сле	after
	про́тив	against
	ра́ди	for the sake of
	с	from
	у	at, by/alongside of, at the home/office of, have
Prepositional	в	in, at, inside of
	на	on, at, on top of
	о	about
	при	in the presence of, during the reign/administration of
Dative	благодаря́	thanks/owing to
	к	to, toward(s)
	по	according to, on (the subject of), around, along, etc.
Instrumental	за	behind (location)
	ме́жду	between
	над	above, over
	пе́ред	in front of, just before
	под	under (location), near (a city)
	с	with

B. VERB CHARTS

1. REGULAR CONJUGATION I AND II VERBS

	CONJUGATION I			CONJUGATION II	
	-ать	-ять	SHIFTING STRESS	-ить	SHIFTING STRESS SOFT л
INFINITIVE	де́лать	гуля́ть	писа́ть	говори́ть	люби́ть
я	де́лаю	гуля́ю	пишу́	говорю́	люблю́
ты	де́лаешь	гуля́ешь	пи́шешь	говори́шь	лю́бишь
он/она́	де́лает	гуля́ет	пи́шет	говори́т	лю́бит
мы	де́лаем	гуля́ем	пи́шем	говори́м	лю́бим
вы	де́лаете	гуля́ете	пи́шете	говори́те	лю́бите
они́	де́лают	гуля́ют	пи́шут	говоря́т	лю́бят
PAST					
Masculine	де́лал	гуля́л	писа́л	говори́л	люби́л
Feminine	де́лала	гуля́ла	писа́ла	говори́ла	люби́ла
Plural	де́лали	гуля́ли	писа́ли	говори́ли	люби́ли
STEM	де́ла+	гуля́+	пиш+	говор+	люб+
IMPERATIVE	де́лай(те)	гуля́й(те)	пиши́(те)	говори́(те)	люби́(те)

2. CONJUGATION I VERBS WITH SPELLING CHANGES

	целова́ть	дава́ть	мыть	па́хнуть	нести́	печь
PRESENT						
я	целу́ю	даю́	мо́ю	па́хну	несу́	пеку́
ты	целу́ешь	даёшь	мо́ешь	па́хнешь	несёшь	печёшь
он/она́	целу́ет	даёт	мо́ет	па́хнет	несёт	печёт
мы	целу́ем	даём	мо́ем	па́хнем	несём	печём
вы	целу́ете	даёте	мо́ете	па́хнете	несёте	гечёте
они́	целу́ют	даю́т	мо́ют	па́хнут	несу́т	пеку́т
PAST						
Masculine	целова́л	дава́л	мыл	па́хнул	нёс	пёк
Feminine	целова́ла	дава́ла	мы́ла	па́хнула	несла́	пекла́
Plural	целова́ли	дава́ли	мы́ли	па́хнули	несли́	пекли́
STEM	целу́+	да+	мо́+	па́хн+	нес+	пек+
IMPERATIVE	целу́й(те)	дава́й(те)	мо́й(те)	па́хни(те)	неси́(те)	пеки́(те)

3. IRREGULAR VERBS

	дать	бежа́ть	есть	хоте́ть	быть
	FUTURE (PERF.)	PRESENT	PRESENT	PRESENT	FUTURE
я	дам	бегу́	ем	хочу́	бу́ду
ты	дашь	бежи́шь	ешь	хо́чешь	бу́дешь
он/она́	даст	бежи́т	ест	хо́чет	бу́дет
мы	дади́м	бежи́м	еди́м	хоти́м	бу́дем
вы	дади́те	бежи́те	еди́те	хоти́те	бу́дете
они́	даду́т	бегу́т	едя́т	хотя́т	бу́дут
PAST					
Masculine	дал	бежа́л	ел	хоте́л	был
Feminine	дала́	бежа́ла	е́ла	хоте́ла	была́
Neuter	да́ло	бежа́ло	е́ло	хоте́ло	бы́ло
Plural	да́ли	бежа́ли	е́ли	хоте́ли	бы́ли
STEM	(дад+)	бег+/беж+	(ед+)	хо́ч+/хот+	бу́д+
IMPERATIVE	да́й(те)	беги́(те)	е́шь(те)	хоти́(те)	бу́дь(те)

4. VERBS OF MOTION[2]

IMPERFECTIVE				
MULTIDIRECTIONAL	UNIDIRECTIONAL	MEANING	PERFECTIVE	MEANING
ходи́ть	идти́	to go/walk	пойти́	to go (set off for) on foot
е́здить	е́хать	to go/ride	пое́хать	to go (set off for) by vehicle
носи́ть	нести́	to carry	понести́	to take (set off for) on foot
вози́ть	везти́	to convey/transport	повезти́	to transport (set off for)
води́ть	вести́	to lead	повести́	to lead (set off for)
бежа́ть	бе́гать	to run	побежа́ть	to run (set off for)
лета́ть	лете́ть	to fly	полете́ть	to fly (set off for)
пла́вать	плыть	to swim/sail	поплы́ть	to swim/sail (set off for)

2. Unidirectional verbs can also be made perfective with any of the other prefixes used with verbs of motion (see Уро́к 20 for a list) just as with идти́ and е́хать. When these prefixes are added to verbs of motion, directionality is no longer an issue, and the verb is a regular imperfective/perfective pair.

C. LETTER WRITING

1. A NOTE ON LETTER WRITING

In both formal and informal writing, the addressee's name, title, and address appear only on the envelope. In formal letters, an institution's name and address often appear at the top of the document, while the date is at the bottom of the page.

Since the break-up of the Soviet Union, the form of address in formal writing has changed. Now Russians write to Mr. or Mrs. (**господи́н, госпожа́**), just as we do in the United States (but there is no term for Ms.). The abbreviated forms are **г-н** or **г.** (Mr.) and **г-жа** (Mrs.). Note that they are not capitalized. In formal writing the use of a title is common, and if one wants to write to editorial offices of newspapers or journals, the phrase "Dear editorial board" (**Уважа́емая реда́кция**) is commonly used. Whether writing formally or informally, the initial greeting is almost always punctuated with an exclamation point, rather than a comma.

The date is written with the day first, followed by the month, and then the year. The abbreviated form differs from the one used in the United States. March 12, 1998, for example, is written as 12–3–98 or as 12/III/98. The order of the address is reversed as well. Russians begin with the country, or with the city (**го́род,** abbreviated **г.**) for domestic mail, and the **и́ндекс** (zip code) on the first line. They then write the street (usually **у́лица,** abbreviated **ул.,** or **проспе́кт,** abbreviated **пр.**) and building number (**дом,** abbreviated **д.**), and perhaps the block number (**ко́рпус,** abbreviated **кор.**), and then the apartment number (**кварти́ра,** abbreviated **кв.**). The company or organization name follows. The name of the addressee in the dative case, with the last name first, appears on the last line. Note also that accents are not marked, and in formal letters, the word **Вы** (and **Ваш, Вас, Вам,** and **Ва́ми**) is capitalized, when used as the polite form of address.

2. BUSINESS LETTERS

г. Москва 157332
ул. Петрова, д. 8
Всероссийское издательство "Наука"
Отдел по международным связям

Уважаемая г-жа Степанова!

Мы получили Ваш заказ на доставку последних номеров журнала «Континент». К сожалению, в связи с повышением почтовых тарифов, мы не смогли отправить заказ вовремя. Доставка журналов предпологается в первых числах ноября.

С уважением
Г. И. Аполлонов,
Директор отдела по международным связям

12 октября 1997
г. Москва

———————

Moscow 157332
8 Petrova Street
All–Russian Publishing House "Science"
Section on Foreign Affairs

Dear Mrs. Stepanova,

We have received your order to deliver the latest issues of the journal *Kontinent*. Unfortunately, due to the increases in postal tariffs, we could not send you your order on time. The delivery of the issues is expected in early November.

Sincerely,
G. I. Apollonov
Director of the Section on Foreign Affairs

October 12, 1997
Moscow

г. Москва 122771
ул. Васнецова, д. 2
Совместное предприятие «Роза»

Уважаемый г. Кожинов!

   Отвечаем на Ваш запрос о возможности установить торговые связи с Германией. К сожалению, в настоящее время мы не в состоянии помочь Вам в этом деле. Наше предприятие не уполномочено действовать в качестве посредника между западными и русскими фирмами.

С уважением
Н. С. Сошников,
Директор предприятия

13/XI/97
г. Москва

Moscow 122771
2 Vasnetsova Street
Joint Venture "Rose"

Dear Mr. Kozhinov,

   This is in response to your inquiry about the possibility of establishing trade contacts with Germany. Unfortunately, we are unable to help you at present. Our business is not authorized to act as a mediator between Western and Russian firms.

Sincerely,
N. S. Soshnikov
Director of the firm

November 13, 1997
Moscow

3. INFORMAL LETTERS

27–10–97

Дорогой Иван!

Наконец, приехал в Псков. С билетами было трудно, но, в конце концов, Ирина достала, и даже на скорый поезд. В общем, могу взяться за работу. Директор нашел неплохую квартиру. Наверное, действительно хотят, чтобы мне было удобно. Жалко, что не успели поговорить в Москве, но в ноябре собираюсь приехать и, конечно, позвоню.

Скучаю по московским друзьям. Не забывай. Пиши!

Твой Сергей.

10–27–97

Dear Ivan,

I have finally arrived in Pskov. There was difficulty with the tickets, but in the end Irina managed to get them and even for an express train. So, I can get down to work. The director found a decent apartment. It seems they really want to make me comfortable. Too bad we didn't have time to talk in Moscow, but I plan to come in November and will call you, of course.

I miss my Moscow friends. Don't forget me. Write!

Yours,
Sergei

17–11–97

Дорогая Наташа!

Давно уже не получаю от тебя писем и очень беспокоюсь о родителях. Как здоровье отца? Собирается мама уходить на пенсию, или опять откладывает? Позвони мне на работу, домашний телефон еще не подключили.

Девочки растут, Марина пошла в первый класс и очень гордится. Таня дает ей советы.

Все у нас хорошо. Миша передает привет. Надеюсь увидеть всех вас на праздники.

Целую,
Ваша Галя

———————

11–17–97

Dear Natasha,

I have not received letters from you in a while and I worry a lot about our parents. How is father's health? Is Mom going to retire or is she delaying again? Call me at work: our home phone hasn't been connected yet.

The girls are growing up. Marina started first grade and is very proud. Tanya gives her advice.

Everything is fine with us. Misha sends his regards. I hope to see you for the holidays.

Love,
Galya

4. FORM OF THE ENVELOPE

a. Letters

Addressee

Sender

г. Москва 332889
ул. Страхова, д. 5, кв. 75
Павлову Ивану Петровичу

г. Псков 32435
ул. Надеждина, д. 4, кв. 1
Сергей Суриков

Moscow 332889
5 Strakhova St, Apt. 75
Pavlov, Ivan Petrovich

Pskov 32435
4 Nadezhdina St., Apt. 1
Sergei Surikov

b. Postcards

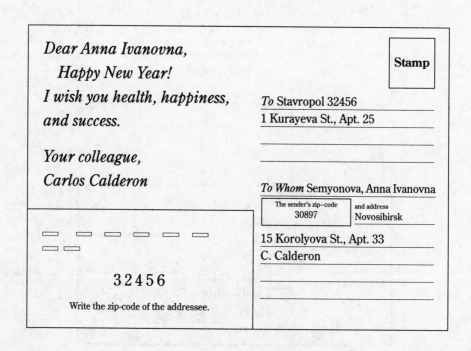

Дорогая Анна Ивановна!

   Поздравляю Вас с Новым годом!

   Желаю Вам здоровья, счастья и успеха.

Ваш коллега Карлос Калдерон

Куда г. Ставрополь 32456
ул. Кураева, д. 1, кв. 25

Кому Семеновой Анне Ивановне

Индекс предприятия связи	и адрес отправителя
30897	г. Новосибирск

ул. Королёва, д. 15, кв. 33
К. Калдерон

▬ ▬ ▬ ▬ ▬ ▬

3 2 4 5 6

Пишите индекс предприятия связи места назначения

Dear Anna Ivanovna,

   Happy New Year!

I wish you health, happiness, and success.

Your colleague,
Carlos Calderon

Stamp

To Stavropol 32456
1 Kurayeva St., Apt. 25

To Whom Semyonova, Anna Ivanovna

The sender's zip–code	and address
30897	Novosibirsk

15 Korolyova St., Apt. 33
C. Calderon

3 2 4 5 6

Write the zip-code of the addressee.

СЛОВАРЬ (Glossary)

ABBREVIATIONS USED IN GLOSSARY

I	Conjugation I	indecl.	indeclinable
II	Conjugation II	intrans.	intransitive
adj.	adjective	irreg.	irregular
adv.	adverb	m.	male/masculine
coll.	colloquial	multi.	multidirectional
conj.	conjunction	perf.	perfective
f.	female/feminine	sing.	singular
fig.	figurative	transport.	transportation
imp.	imperfective	uni.	unidirectional

РУССКО-АНГЛИЙСКИЙ

А

а and, but
 а то or else
а́вгуст August
авиапо́чта airmail
авто́бус bus
автома́т change machine; pay phone
автомоби́ль automobile (m.)
автосе́рвис service station
аге́нт agent
администра́тор manager, clerk
а́дрес address
аллерги́я allergy
Алло́? Hello? (on the telephone)
америка́нец/-ка́нка (m./f.) American
америка́нский (adj.) American
анесте́тик anesthetic
анке́та form, questionnaire
антра́кт intermission
апельси́н orange
апре́ль April
апте́ка pharmacy
арбу́з watermelon
а́рмия army
архи́в archive
аспира́нт(ка) (m./f.) graduate student
аспири́н aspirin
астроло́гия astrology
атмосфе́ра atmosphere; climate (fig.)
аэропо́рт airport

Б

ба́бушка grandmother
бага́ж baggage

бале́т ballet
балла́да ballad
банк bank
ба́нка (ба́нки) jar, can (cupping-glasses)
бар bar
бассе́йн pool
бато́н long loaf of bread
бе́гать to run (multi.)
 бе́гать трусцо́й to go jogging
бе́дный poor
бежа́ть/по– to run (uni.; irreg.)
без (чего́/кого́) without
 без акце́нта without accent
 без де́нег out of money; broke
 без ме́бели unfurnished
безобра́зие outrageous behavior
безопа́сный safe, secure, not dangerous
бе́лый white
бензи́н gasoline (petrol)
бе́рег shore; coast
беспла́тно free of charge
беспоко́иться to worry
беспоря́док mess, disorder
беспреста́нно constantly, incessantly
библиоте́ка library
библиоте́карь librarian (m.)
биле́т ticket
бить to beat (imp.)
благода́рность gratitude (f.)
бли́же nearer
бли́зко near
блины́ thin pancakes
блока́да siege; blockade
блонди́н(ка) (noun; m./f.) blonde
блу́зка blouse
блю́до dish (food)

бог god
    Бо́же мой! My God!
бога́тый wealthy
боле́знь illness (f.)
боле́льщик fan
боле́ть (боли́т, боля́т) to ache, to hurt
    (imp.)
болта́ть to chat
боль pain (f.)
больни́ца hospital
бо́льно painful
больно́й (adj./noun) sick; patient
бо́льше more; bigger
    бо́льше всего́ more than anything;
    most of all
большо́й big
борода́ beard
борщ borshcht (beet soup)
боя́ться (чего́/кого́) to be afraid (of)
    (imp.; II.)
брак marriage
брат brother
брать/взять to take
бри́тва razor
бри́ться/по- to shave (oneself)
бровь eye-brow (f.)
брошю́ра brochure
бу́дущий future
буди́ть/раз- (кого́) to wake (someone)
Бу́дьте добры́ . . . Would you please . . .
буке́т bouquet
бу́лочка bun, roll
бу́лочная bakery
бума́га paper (material)
бутербро́д sandwich
буты́лка bottle
буфе́т buffet; snack-bar
буха́нка loaf
быва́ть to be (repeatedly), to occur
    (frequently) (imp.)
быва́ть/по- to visit
бы́вший former
бы́стро fast; quick(ly)
бытово́й daily
    бытовы́е услу́ги domestic services
быть to be (in future or past)
    быть в гостя́х to be visiting

В

в/во in; at; to
    в двадца́тых года́х in the 20s
    В како́м году́? In what year?
    в командиро́вке on a business trip
    В о́бщем/вообще́ In general; So
    в оди́н коне́ц one-way
    в одно́ вре́мя (с чем) at the same time
    (as)
    в о́тпуске on leave/vacation
    в при́нципе in principle; in general
    в са́мом де́ле as a matter of fact
    в тече́ние (чего́) for the period of
    в то́чности exactly
    в углу́ in the corner
    во вре́мя during
    во вся́ком слу́чае in any case; anyway

Во ско́лько . . . ? —В (time). At what
    time . . . ? —At (time).
во́время on time
ваго́н car (subway, train)
валю́та foreign currency
вам to you (plural/polite sing.)
    Вам на́до . . . (You) need to . . .
ва́нная bathroom
варе́нье preserves
вари́ть(ся)/с- to boil, be boiling
ва́та cotton
ваш/-а/-е/-и your(s) (plural/polite sing.)
вверху́ overhead; above
вдыха́ть/вдохну́ть to breathe
вегетариа́нец (-ка) (noun; m./f.)
    vegetarian
ведь you see; after all
ве́жливый polite
везде́ everywhere
везти́ to convey (by vehicle) (uni.)
век century; era
вели́кий great
велосипе́д bicycle
венча́ние ceremony
ве́рить/по- to believe
ве́рно right; true, faithful
ве́рхний high; higher
весна́ spring
весно́й in the spring
вес weight
ве́сить to weigh (followed by weight)
вести́ to lead (uni.)
    вести́ себя́ (хорошо́, пло́хо) to behave
    oneself (well, badly)
вестибю́ль lobby (f.)
весь/вся/всё/все all
ветера́н veteran
ве́треный windy
ве́чер evening
вечера́ p.m.
вече́рний (soft adj.) evening
ве́чером in the evening
вечери́нка party
вещь thing; piece (artistic) (f.)
взве́шивать/взве́сить to weigh (out)
взро́слый grown-up, adult
взять напрока́т to rent (a car)
вид view, species, type
ви́дно evident
ви́за visa
визи́тка business card
ви́лка fork
вино́ wine
виногра́д grape(s)
винова́т/-а/-ы sorry; guilty; at fault
висе́ть to be hanging (imp.)
ви́шни cherries
включа́ть/включи́ть to include; to turn
    (something) on
вкус taste
    во вку́се (кого́) to the taste (of)
    вку́сно delicious, tasty
власть power (f.)
влюблённый in love; loving; tender
внизу́ downstairs; below

внима́ние attention
внима́тельно attentively
внук grandson
вну́чка granddaughter
внутри́ inside (a container); indoors
вода́ water
водопрово́дчик plumber
води́ть to lead (multi.)
 води́ть маши́ну to drive a car
води́тель driver (m.)
 води́тельские права́ driver's license
во́дка vodka
возбужда́ть/возбуди́ть to excite, to
 rouse
возвраща́ться/верну́ться to return
вози́ть to convey (by vehicle) (multi.)
во́зле (чего́) by; near; past; next to
возмо́жно possible
во́зраст age
война́ war
вокза́л station (train)
волнова́ть(ся) to worry, to become
 agitated
во́лосы hair
вон там over there
воро́та goal (sports); gate(s)
во́семь eight
восьмо́й eighth
воскресе́нье Sunday
воспале́ние inflammation
восто́к east
 восто́чный east; eastern
Вот … Here is/are …
 Вот (что)! What a (noun)!
 Вот и всё! Well, that's it!; It's
 finished/over!
 Вот и прекра́сно! And a good thing,
 too!
 Вот и он! There he is!
 Вот так? Like this?; Like so?
 Вот тепе́рь вы говори́те де́ло! Now
 you're talking!
вперёд forward
впереди́ (чего́/кого́) ahead/in front (of)
врач doctor; general practitioner
вре́мя time
 вре́мя го́да time of year; season
всё everything
 всё вре́мя all the time
 всё равно́ It doesn't matter.
 всё-таки all the same; nevertheless
все all; everyone
 Всего́ наилу́чшего! All the very best!
 Всего́ хоро́шего! All the best!
 Всему́ своё вре́мя. All in good time.
всегда́ always
вслух aloud
вспомина́ть/вспо́мнить to recall, to bring
 back to mind
встава́ть/встать to get up
встре́ча meeting; appointment
встреча́ться/встре́титься to meet
втира́ть/втере́ть (в что) to rub (into
 something)
вто́рник Tuesday

второ́й second
вход entrance
вчера́ yesterday
вы you (plural/polite sing.)
 Вы не зна́ете, … ? You wouldn't happen
 to know … ?
 Вы не туда́ попа́ли. You have the wrong
 number.
выбира́ть/вы́брать to choose, to select
вы́боры election
вы́вести to take out, to remove (perf.)
выздора́вливать/вы́здороветь to
 recover
выи́грывать/вы́играть to win
вы́йти за́муж (за кого́) to marry (a man)
выключа́ть/вы́ключить to turn
 (something) off
Вы́леты Flight Departures
выноси́ть/вы́нести to carry out, away
выража́ть/вы́разить to express, to
 convey
 выраже́ние expression (of an idea)
высо́кий high
 высо́кого ро́ста tall
вы́ставка exhibit; show
вытя́гивать/вы́тянуть to pull out
вы́ход exit
 выходи́ть/вы́йти to exit, to depart, to
 get off (transportation)
 выходно́й (день) day off
 выходны́е (дни) days off, weekend

Г

газе́та newspaper
га́лстук tie
гардеро́б cloakroom
гастроно́м food store
где where (at)
 где́-то somewhere
 где́-нибудь anywhere
герои́ня heroine
геро́й hero
гид guide
гла́вный main; central
глаз(а́) eye(s)
гла́сность openness (f.)
глубо́кий deep, profound
глу́пый stupid, silly
гнило́й rotten, decayed
говори́ть/сказа́ть to speak
говя́дина beef
год year
гол goal (sports)
голова́ head
 Голова́ кру́жится. I'm dizzy.
 головно́й убо́р headgear
голода́ть to starve, to go without food (imp.)
го́лоден/-на́/-но/-ны hungry
го́лос voice; vote
голосова́ние voting; poll; hitch-hiking
голосова́ть/про- (за кого́/чего́) to vote
голубо́й light blue
го́лый bare; naked
гора́ mountain
гора́здо much

го́рдость pride (f.)
го́рло throat
го́род city
гороско́п horoscope
горчи́ца mustard
горя́чий hot (food, liquids)
гости́ница hotel
гость guest (m.)
госуда́рство state/government (the)
  госуда́рственный (adj) state, governmental
гото́вить/при- to prepare, cook
гото́вка cooking
гра́дус degree (temperature)
грамм gram
грани́ца border
гре́шно wrong (morally)
гриб mushroom
грипп flu
гро́мкий loud
гру́ппа group
грусти́ть to mourn, to grieve
гря́зный dirty
гуля́ть/по- to stroll, to walk, to go out

Д
да yes
  Да здра́вствует (что/кого́)! Long live (someone/thing)!
  Да, так оно́ и есть! Why, so it is!
**Дава́йте ... ** Let's ...
  Дава́й(те) вы́пьем за (что/кого́)! Let's drink to (someone/thing)!
дава́ть/дать to give (perf.; irreg.)
  Да́йте, пожа́луйста ... Please give me ...
давле́ние blood pressure
давно́ long ago, long since
далеко́ far away
да́льше (adv.) farther
дари́ть/по- (что-кому) to give a present
да́та date
  да́та рожде́ния date of birth
да́ча country house
два/две two
двадца́тый twentieth
  двадца́тых годо́в of/from the 20s
двена́дцать twelve
дви́гать/дви́нуть to move
  движе́ние traffic, movement
дво́е two (of them)
дворе́ц palace
двушка two-kopeck coin (coll.)
де́вять nine
девя́тый ninth
де́вушка young woman, girl
де́душка grandfather
дежу́рная woman on duty
действи́тельно really, actually
дека́брь December
деклара́ция declaration (customs form)
де́лать/с- to do; to make
  де́лать переса́дку/пересе́сть to transfer
делега́ция delegation

де́ло task, affair, doing
  де́ло в том, что ... the thing is that ...
день day (m.)
де́ньги money
депози́т deposit
  депози́тный счёт savings account
дере́вня village; the countryside
де́рево wood (material); tree
де́сять ten
деся́тый tenth
де́ти children
дешёвый cheap, inexpensive
джаз jazz
дива́н sofa
  дива́н-крова́ть sofa-bed
дирижёр conductor
диссерта́ция dissertation
для (чего́/кого́) for the purpose/sake of
дли́нный long
днём in the afternoon
до (чего́) until; (up) to
  До встре́чи! Until then!
  до по́яса to the waist
  До свида́ния! Good-bye.
  До ско́рого! See you soon!
  до тех пор until/till (then); thus far
  до того́ как before (conj.)
до́брый good; kind
  До́бро пожа́ловать! Welcome!
  До́брое у́тро. Good morning.
  До́брый ве́чер. Good evening. (greeting only, not parting)
  До́брый день. Good afternoon.
дово́лен/-ьна/-ьно/-ьны (чем/кем) satisfied/content (with)
Договори́лись! Agreed!
дождь rain (m.)
дозвони́ться (к кому́) to reach by phone
докуме́нт document
до́лго for a long time
до́лжен/-на́/-ны́ should; must; obligated
  должно́ быть it must be, undoubtedly
до́ллар dollar
дом house; home
  до́ма/домо́й at home/homewards
  дома́шнее зада́ние homework
доро́га road; way
дорого́й (не-) expensive (in-); dear
доста́точно enough
достава́ть/доста́ть to get, to obtain
доставля́ть/доста́вить to deliver, to provide
до́ступ access; admission; entrance
дочь daughter (f.)
  до́чка (little) daughter
друг/друзья́ friend/friends
дру́жба friendship
друг дру́га each other; one another
друго́й another; the other; different
дубли́рованный dubbed; duplicated
ду́мать to think
  Ду́маю, что да. I think so.
дупло́ cavity
дурно́й bad; evil

дух spirit, heart, mind
духи́ perfume
духо́вка oven
душ shower
душа́ soul; spirit
дя́дя uncle

Е

евре́йский Jewish
европе́йский European
его́ his/its; him/it
  Его́ (её/их) не́ту. He's (she's/they're) not here. (coll.)
еда́ food; meal
едва́ barely
её her/hers/its; her/it
е́здить to go by vehicle (multi.)
  е́здить за́ город to go to the countryside
ёлка New Year (Christmas) tree
ёлки-па́лки (adj./adv.) darn
ерунда́ nonsense
е́сли if; in case; in the event that
  е́сли бы if (unreal conditional)
есть there is
есть/съ- to eat (irreg.)
е́хать to go (by vehicle) (uni.)
ещё still; yet; else
  Ещё бы! I'll say!; You bet!
  ещё оди́н/-на́/-но́/-ни another; one more

Ж

жа́ловаться/по- to complain
Жаль. That's too bad.; I'm sorry.
жар fever
жать/по- (ру́ки) to shake hands; to squeeze, to press (I.)
ждать/подожда́ть (чего/кого́) to wait (for)
же emphatic particle
жела́тельно preferably
жела́ть/по- (чего-кому́) to wish, to desire
жёлтый yellow
желу́док stomach
жена́ wife
жена́т married (men only)
жени́ться/по- to get married
жени́х bridegroom
же́нский feminine; women's; female
же́нщина woman
жёсткий ваго́н second class
жив/-а́/-о/-ы alive
жи́вопись painting (f.)
жизнь life (f.)
жильё accommodation
жить to live (I.)
журна́л magazine
  журнали́ст journalist

З

за (что/кого́; чем/кем) for (someone/thing); behind (someone/thing)

за го́родом in the country; in the suburbs
за грани́цей abroad, overseas
за столо́м at the table
забива́ть/заби́ть to hammer in, to seal, to beat
  заби́ть гол to score a goal
заболева́ть/заболе́ть to become ill
забыва́ть/забы́ть to forget
заве́дующий manager
зави́вка waving, curling (hair)
зави́довать/по- to envy
заво́д factory
за́втра tomorrow
за́втрак breakfast
  за́втракать/по- to eat breakfast
загора́ть/загоре́ть to sunbathe, to get a tan
задава́ть/зада́ть (вопро́с) to ask (a question)
зайти́ (за чем) to drop by, to pick (something) up (perf.)
зака́з order, reservation
зака́зывать/заказа́ть to reserve, to order
зака́зан/-а/-о/-ы reserved
заключе́ние conclusion
закрыва́ть/закры́ть to close
заку́ски snacks, appetizers
зал hall, auditorium
заменя́ть/замени́ть (что-чем) to replace, to substitute
замеча́тельно wonderful; fantastic
замеча́ть/заме́тить to notice
за́мужем/за́мужняя married (women only)
занима́ть(ся)/по- (чем) to occupy; to study, to be involved in
  занима́ться спо́ртом to play sports
за́нят/-а/-о/-ы busy; occupied
заня́тия classes; activities
за́пад west
  за́падный western
за́пах odor, smell
запи́сываться/записа́ться to sign up, to make an appointment
запи́сан/-на/-ны to be registered/entered
заполня́ть/запо́лнить to fill in, to complete
запомина́ть/запо́мнить to commit to memory, to memorize
запра́вочная ста́нция gas station
запрещён/-а́/-о́/-ы́ forbidden
зара́нее earlier, in advance
зараба́тывать to earn (imp.)
зарпла́та salary
засыпа́ть/засну́ть to fall asleep
зате́м then, after that, next
заходи́ть/зайти́ to drop by
заче́м why; for what purpose
защи́тник defender
звать/по- (кого́) to call, to summon, to name
звони́ть/по- to call by phone; to ring
  звоно́к (noun) call; ring (sound); bell

звуча́ть/про- to sound, to be heard
зда́ние building
здесь here
здоро́вье health
  здоро́в/-а/-о/-ы healthy
здравоохране́ние health care
здо́рово splendid(ly), magnificent(ly)
Здра́вствуй! Hi! (familiar)
Здра́вствуйте! Hello! (polite)
зелёный green
  зе́лень greens (f.)
земля́ land; Earth
зе́ркало mirror
зима́ winter
  зимо́й in the winter
знак sign, mark, symbol
знако́мить(ся)/по- to acquaint; be/get
    acquainted (ref.)
знамени́тый famous; reknowned
знать to know (imp.)
зна́чит (it/that) means; so, then
золото́й golden
зонт umbrella
зуб tooth
  зубна́я нить dental floss (f.)
  зубна́я па́ста toothpaste
  зубно́й врач dentist

И

и and
  и ... и ... both ... and ...
  и наоборо́т and vice versa
  и так even so
  и так да́лее (и т.д.) and so forth; et
    cetera (etc.)
игра́ game
игра́ть/сыгра́ть в (что) to play (a game; a
    sport)
игра́ть/сыгра́ть на (чём) to play (an
    instrument)
игру́шка toy
иде́я idea
идти́/пойти́ to go (by own power)
из (чего) from, out of
  Из чего они сде́ланы? What are they
    made of?
из-за (кого́/чего́) because of
    (someone/thing)
избира́ть/избра́ть to elect, to choose
извиня́ть/извини́ть to excuse
изде́лие item, article (for sale)
изменя́ть/измени́ть to change, to betray
изменя́ться/измени́ться to change, to
    alter, to vary (intrans.)
изуча́ть/изучи́ть to study in depth
ико́на icon
икра́ caviar
и́ли or
  и́ли ... и́ли ... either ... or ...
име́ть to have (something abstract) (imp.)
и́мя first name
и́мени named after
имени́ны name-day
и́менно то (что/кто) just; exactly the
    (thing/person)

и́ндекс zip code
иногда́ sometimes
иностра́нный foreign
  иностра́нец/-ка foreigner (m./f.)
интервью́ interview
интервьюи́ровать to interview (imp. and
    perf.)
интере́сно interesting; I wonder . . .
интересова́ться/за- (чем) to be interested
    in
инфа́ркт heart attack
инфе́кция infection
информа́ция information
иска́ть/по- to look for, to search
иску́сство art
испо́льзовать to use, to utilize
исполне́ние performance (musical)
иссле́дование research
исте́рика hysteria
исто́рия history
исчеза́ть/исче́знуть to disappear
их their/theirs; them
ию́ль July
ию́нь June

К

к/ко (чему́/кому́) to; toward
    (someone/thing)
  к сожале́нию unfortunately
  к сча́стью fortunately
  к тому́ же besides, moreover
кабине́т office; laboratory; study
ка́ждый (adj.) every; each
каза́ться/по- (кому) to seem
как how
  Как бы не так! Nothing of the sort!
  Как ва́ши дела́? How are you? (polite)
  Как вас зову́т? What is your name?
    (polite)
  как ви́дно as is evident; as can be seen
  как всегда́ as always
  Как вы пожива́ете? How are you?
    (polite)
  Как дела́? How're things? (familiar)
  Как дое́хать до (чего́)? How do I get to
    (someplace)?
  Как пи́шется ... ? How is ... written?
  Как по-(language) _____? How do you
    say _____ in (language)?
  как у (нас) same as (us)
  ка́к-то somehow
  ка́к-нибудь anyhow
како́й which; what kind of
  Како́го ро́ста? How tall is (someone)?
  Како́го цве́та? What color is it?
  Како́го числа́? (Когда́?) On what date?
    (When?)
  Како́е сего́дня число́? What's today's
    date?
  Како́й сего́дня день? What day is
    today?
  Како́й у вас вес? What do you weigh?
  како́й-то some kind of
  како́й-нибудь any kind of
ками́н fireplace

кана́л channel (TV)
кандида́т candidate
капу́ста cabbage
карма́н pocket
ка́рта map
карти́на painting
ка́рточка card
   ка́рточка го́стя hotel pass
   креди́тная ка́рточка credit card
карто́шка potato
каса́ться/косну́ться to touch (on); to concern
ка́сса cash register; ticket window
касси́р(-ша) (m./f.) teller
кассе́та cassette
ката́ться to go (riding); to roll (uni.)
   ката́ться на велосипе́де to go bike riding
   ката́ться на лы́жах to ski; to go skiing
кафе́ cafe
ка́ша kasha, cooked cereal
ка́шель (noun) cough (m.)
   ка́пли от ка́шля cough-drops
кварти́ра apartment
квартпла́та rent (for apartment only)
кефи́р kefir, sour yogurt
ки́слый sour
килогра́мм (кило́) kilogram (kilo)
километр kilometer
кино́ the movies; cinema; movie theater
   кинотеа́тр cinema; movie theater
ки́оск kiosk, stall, stand
класси́ческий classical
класть/положи́ть (что-куда́) to put (lay flat); to place
клуб club
ключ key
кни́га book
   кни́жечка booklet (of tickets)
ковёр carpet
когда́ when
   когда́-то sometime
   когда́-нибудь anytime; ever
колле́га colleague (m.)
колле́кция collection
коллекти́в team; group
кольцо́ ring
кома́нда team (sports)
командиро́вка official business trip, assignment
коммуни́ст Communist
ко́мната room
компа́ния company
комплиме́нт compliment
компози́тор composer
компью́тер computer
   но́тбук компью́тер notebook computer
конве́рт envelope
коне́ц end; finish
коне́чно of course
контра́кт contract
контролёр ticket inspector
конце́рт concert

конча́ть/ко́нчить (что) to finish; to graduate
ко́нчиться to be finished
копе́йка kopeck
коридо́р corridor
корми́ть to feed (imp.)
коро́бка box
коро́ткий short
ко́ротко (adj./adv.) short
костю́м suit
кото́рый that, which, who(m)
ко́фе coffee (indecl.)
кошма́р nightmare
краси́вый beautiful, handsome
кра́сный red
красть/у- to steal
крем cream; lotion
кре́пость fortress; strength (f.)
кре́сло armchair
крестья́нин (крестья́не) peasant (peasants)
крича́ть/за- to shout
крова́ть bed (f.)
кро́ме (как) besides
   кро́ме того́ besides/in addition to that
кроссо́вки sneakers; running shoes
кста́ти (о чём) by the way; speaking of
кто who
   Кто вы по профе́ссии? What is your profession?
   Кто как. Some do, some don't.
   кто́-то someone
   кто́-нибудь anyone
куда́ (to) where
культу́ра culture
купа́ться to swim, to bathe
кури́ть to smoke
ку́рица chicken
куро́рт resort
ку́ртка short jacket
кусо́чек a little piece
куста́рный handcrafted
ку́хня kitchen; cooking; cuisine
ку́шать/по- to eat, snack
   Ку́шай(те) на здоро́вье! Help yourself!; Eat it in good health!

Л

ла́дно okay
лак hairspray; lacquer
ла́мпа lamp
ле́вый left
лёгкий easy; light (opp. of heavy)
легко́ (adj./adv.) easy, easily; light, lightly (opp. of heavy)
лежа́ть to lie, lay (imp.) (ll.)
лека́рство medicine
ле́кция lecture
лес forest, woods
лета́ть to fly (multi.)
лете́ть to fly (uni.)
ле́то summer
ле́том in the summer
лече́ние remedy; cure; treatment

ли if; whether (particle)
лимо́н lemon
литр liter
лифт elevator
лицо́ face
ли́чно personally
ли́чный private, personal
ли́шний spare, extra (soft adj.)
лови́ть/пойма́ть to hunt (imp.), catch (perf.)
ложи́ться/лечь to lie down
   ложи́ться/лечь спать to go to bed
ло́жка spoon
ло́мкий fragile; brittle
ло́паться/ло́пнуть burst, break (it/they)
ло́щадь horse (f.)
лук onion(s)
лу́чше better
лу́чший best
лэпто́п laptop
люби́ть to love; to like
   люби́мый favorite
   люби́тель amateur (m.)
   любо́вь love (f.)
лю́ди people

М

магази́н store
магнитофо́н tape recorder
май May
ма́ленький small
   ма́ленького ро́ста short
ма́ло not much; few; a little
ма́ма mom
ма́рка stamp; make, trade mark
март March
маршру́т route, itinerary
ма́сло butter; oil
матрёшка wooden nesting doll
матч game, match
мать mother (f.)
маши́на car; machine
ме́бель furniture (f.)
меблиро́ванный (не-) furnished (un-)
мёд honey
медици́на medicine (science/study/practice of)
ме́дленно slow(ly)
медбра́т nurse (male)
медсестра́ nurse (female)
ме́жду (чем/кем и чем/кем) between (two things/people)
   ме́жду на́ми between you and me
   ме́жду про́чим by the way
междунаро́дный international
   междунаро́дный ваго́н deluxe class (train)
ме́лко (adj./adv.) fine(ly); into small pieces
ме́лочь change coins (f.)
ме́неджер manager
ме́ньше less; smaller
меню́ menu
меня́ть/по- to exchange (money)
ме́рить/при- to try on; to measure

мёртв/-а́/-о/-ы dead
ме́стный local
ме́сто seat, place
ме́сяц month
метр meter
метро́ subway
мечта́ dream; day-dream
меша́ть/по- (кому́) to bother/disturb (someone); to interfere
мили́ция police
ми́лый dear, nice (adj.); darling (noun)
минера́льная вода́ mineral water
мину́та minute
мир world; peace
мирово́й world (adj.)
мла́дше/моло́же younger
мне to me
   Мне всё равно́. I don't care.; It's all the same to me.
   Мне жаль. I'm sorry.
   Мне хо́чется (+ infinitive) I feel like (verb + -ing)
мно́го much; many; a lot
мо́дный stylish
мо́жет быть maybe
мо́жно it is possible; it is permitted
мой/моя́/моё/мои́ my/mine
Молоде́ц!/Молодцы́! Good for you!; Well done! (sing./plural)
молодо́й young
   молодо́й челове́к young man
   мо́лодость youth (f.)
молоко́ milk
моло́чная dairy store
мо́ре sea
моро́з bitter cold, frost
моро́женое ice cream
мочь/с- to be able to (I.)
муж husband
му́жественный brave
мужско́й men's, masculine
музе́й museum
му́зыка music
музыка́нт musician
мы we
   мы с ва́ми we (you plural and I)
мы́слить to think, reason, conceive
мыть/вы́мыть (го́лову) to wash (one's hair)
мы́ло soap
мэр mayor
мя́гкий soft
   мя́гкий ваго́н first class (trains only)
мя́со meat
мясно́й butcher's
мяч ball

Н

на on; at; to
   на вся́кий слу́чай just in case
   на дворе́ outdoors; outside
   на за́втрак at breakfast
   на и́мя ... under the name of ...
   на мне (бу́дет/бу́дут) ... I'll have on ...
   ... на мы́ло! ... to the showers!

на́ ночь for the night
на пе́нсии retired
на пе́рвое for starters
на ремо́нт for/under repair
На ско́лько вре́мени ... ? For how long
    … ?
на сла́дкое for dessert
наве́рно probably
наверняка́ for sure; certainly
наверху́ above, overhead
над over, above
надева́ть/наде́ть to put on/to have on
    (clothes, etc.)
наде́ятсья/по- (на что-кого́) to hope for,
    to rely on
на́до necessary
надое́сть (кому́) to be tired of, to be fed
    up with
наза́д back(wards); ago
назва́ние name (only for things)
называ́ться to be called (imp.)
найти́ to find
наконе́ц finally
нале́во to/on the left
налива́ть/нали́ть to pour
нам to/for us
Нам пора́ идти́. It's time for us to go.
намно́го much, far (with comparatives)
наоборо́т on the contrary
напи́сан/-а/-о/-ы written
напи́ток beverage, drink
напомина́ть/напо́мнить to remind (of); to
    resemble
напра́во to/on the right
наприме́р for example
нарко́тики narcotics
наро́д people
наро́дный (adj.) folk
наря́дный elegant; well-dressed
наси́лие violence
наско́лько as far as
на́сморк runny nose
настоя́щий real; present
находи́ться to be located (imp.)
национа́льность nationality (f.)
национа́льный national; ethnic
начина́ть(ся)/нача́ть(ся) to begin; to be
    beginning
нача́ло beginning, start
нача́льник boss, chief
наш/-а/-е/-и our/ours
не not
Не́ за что! You're welcome!; Don't
    mention it!
не на до́лго not for long
не совсе́м not entirely
не так the wrong way (direction)
не так ли? aren't they? doesn't it?
не (тот/та/то/те) the wrong (one)
Не уныва́й(те)! Cheer up!
не хвата́ет (чего́) (something) is
    missing
невероя́тно incredible(-ly)
неве́ста bride
невозмо́жно not allowed; impossible

не́где there is no place (to)
неда́вно recently
неде́ля week
не́когда there is no time (to)
не́кого there is no one (to)
не́который some (of them); certain
не́куда there is nowhere (to) (direction)
нельзя́ it is impossible/forbidden
немно́го/немно́жко a little, a few
ненави́деть to hate (imp.) (II.)
необходи́мо (adj./adv.) essential(ly)
необы́чный unusual
непра́в/-а́/-о/-ы wrong, incorrect, untrue
не́сколько (+ gen. plural) several; few
нести́ to carry (uni.)
несча́стен/-на/-но/-ны unhappy
нет no
Нет пробле́м. No problem.
Неуже́ли? Really?
не́чего there is nothing (to)
нея́сно unclearly; unclear
ни ... ни ... neither … nor …
Ни пу́ха ни пера́! Good luck!, Break a
    leg!
ни ры́ба, ни мя́со wishy-washy
нигде́ nowhere
ни́жний low; lower
никако́й no kind of
никогда́ never
никто́ no one
ничего́ nothing; Fine.
Ничего́ осо́бенного. Nothing much.
Ничего́ стра́шного. No big deal.; It's
    nothing.
ничья́ tie
но but
но́вый new
новосе́лье house warming, new
    home
С Но́вым го́дом! Happy New Year!
но́вости news
нож knife
но́мер (№) hotel room; number
но́мер ре́йса flight number
норма́льно O.K.; normal
носи́льщик porter
носи́ть to wear (imp.); to carry (multi.)
ночно́й (adj.) night
ночь night (f.)
но́чью at night
ноя́брь November
нра́виться/по- (кому́) to like (be pleasing
    to)
Ну ... Well …, So …
Ну вот и хорошо́. Well, that's good.
Ну и как? So how is (was) it?
Ну что же! What?!
ну́жно necessary, needed
ну́жен/-на́/-но/-ны (кому́) is
    necessary; is needed

О

о (об, обо) about
о́ба/о́бе both
обе́д lunch

на обе́д for lunch
обе́дать/по- to eat lunch
обеща́ть/по- to promise
о́блачный cloudy
обме́н exchange
обме́н валю́ты foreign currency exchange
обмо́лвиться to say accidentally, to make a slip of the tongue (perf.)
обнима́ть(ся)/обня́ть(ся) to embrace, hug one another
образе́ц example
образова́ние education
обраща́ть/обрати́ть to turn
обраща́ть/обрати́ть внима́ние (на кого́/что) to pay attention to (someone/thing)
обслу́живание service; tip
обстано́вка situation, conditions
обсужда́ть/обсуди́ть to discuss
о́бувь footwear; shoes, boots (f.)
общежи́тие dormitory
о́бщий general, common
объявле́ние announcement; notice
обы́чный usual; ordinary
обы́чная по́чта regular mail
обы́чно usually
обяза́тельно without fail
о́вощи vegetables
огро́мный huge, immense
огуре́ц (солёный) cucumber (pickle)
одева́ться/оде́ться to get dressed
оде́жда clothing, apparel
оде́т/-а/-о/-ы dressed; clothed
оди́н/-на́/-но́/-ни one; one and the same
Одну́ мину́точку. Just a moment.
одина́ковый alike, the same, identical
оди́ннадцатый eleventh
одна́ко however
ожида́ть to expect (imp.)
Ой! Oh! Ow! Oops!
Ой, ма́мочка! (strong physical or emotional distress)
окно́ window
о́коло (чего́) near, about, approximately
окружа́ющая среда́ the environment
октя́брь October
он he
она́ she
они́ they
оно́ it
опа́здывать/опозда́ть to be late
о́пера opera
описа́ние description
о́пухоль swelling (f.)
о́пытный skillful, experienced
опя́ть again
организова́ть to arrange, to organize
о́сень autumn (f.)
о́сенью in the autumn
осно́ван/-а/-о/-ы founded
осо́бенно especially
остава́ться/оста́ться to stay, remain
оставля́ть/оста́вить to leave behind

остана́вливать/останови́ть to halt, stop
остано́вка stop (tram, trolley, bus)
остана́вливаться/останови́ться to come to a halt; to stay (over)
осторо́жно careful(ly)
о́стрый spicy; hot
от (чего́/кого́) from
отвеча́ть/отве́тить to answer
отвози́ть/отвезти́ to take (away) (by vehicle)
отде́л department
отдыха́ть/отдохну́ть to relax, rest
оте́ц father
оте́чественный patriotic
открыва́ть/откры́ть to open
откры́тка postcard
Отку́да вы? Where are you from?
отли́чно excellent, great
отме́на cancellation
отноше́ния impressions, relations, attitudes
отправля́ть/отпра́вить to send
о́тпуск leave, vacation
отсю́да from here
отходи́ть to depart (multi.)
о́тчество patronymic
отъе́зд departure
официа́нт(ка) waiter/waitress
охо́титься to hunt (for)
охра́нник guard
о́чень very
Очень прия́тно. Nice to meet you.
о́чередь line; turn (f.)
о́чи eyes (archaic, poetic)
очки́ glasses
оши́бка mistake

П

павли́н peacock
паке́т package
пальто́ coat
па́мять memory (f.)
па́мятник monument
па́па papa; dad
па́ра pair; couple
па́ра брюк pair of pants
парикма́хер hairdresser, barber
парикма́херская, парикма́херский hairdresser's, barbershop
парк park
па́ртия political party
пасова́ть to pass (sports)
па́спорт passport
пассажи́р passenger
па́хнуть (чем) to smell of (imp.)
па́чка packet, bundle, carton
певе́ц singer
пе́рвый first
переводи́ть/перевести́ to translate
перево́дчик(-чица) (m./f.) interpreter, translator
пе́ред in front of, (just) before

пе́ред сно́м before going to bed
пе́ред те́м как (just) before (conj.)
передава́ть/переда́ть to pass (on), to convey, to transmit
переда́ча broadcast; transmission
переезжа́ть/перее́хать to move (to a new location)
перепу́тывать/перепу́тать to mix up, to confuse
переры́в break, interval
переса́дка transfer (noun; transport.)
перестава́ть/переста́ть to stop, cease
перехо́д pedestrian underpass
пе́рец pepper
пе́сня song
пессими́ст pessimist
петь/с- to sing (I.)
печа́ль grief; sorrow (f.)
печа́тать (на маши́нке) to type
пече́нье biscuit, cookie
печь(ся)/ис- to bake; to be baking
пешко́м on foot
пиро́г pie; cake; pastry
писа́ть/на- to write
письмо́ letter
пи́сьменный стол desk
пить/вы́- to drink
пи́шущая маши́нка typewriter
плака́т poster
пла́кать to weep, to cry (imp.)
план plan; street map
плани́ровать to plan
плати́ть/за- (за что) to pay (for something)
пла́тный for pay; requiring payment
плато́к shawl; kerchief
платфо́рма platform
пла́тье dress
племя́нник nephew
племя́нница niece
плита́ stove
пло́мба dental filling
пло́хо (adj./adv.) poor(ly); bad(ly)
плохо́й bad
пло́щадь square (f.)
пляж beach
по (чему́/кому́) on; by
  по доро́ге on the way (only for people)
  по зуба́м in one's capacity; a beating
  по кра́йней ме́ре at least
  по национа́льности by nationality
  по среда́м on Wednesdays
  по телефо́ну on the telephone
  по Фаренге́йту in Fahrenheit
  по Це́льсию in Celsius
  по-(чьему́) in [someone's] opinion
  по-друго́му different
  по-мо́ему I think; in my opinion
Повтори́те, пожа́луйста ... Please repeat ...
побе́да victory
побо́льше a little more; a little bigger
Повезло́ (Кому́)! (Someone) lucked out!
повора́чивать/поверну́ть to turn
повы́ше a little higher

повы́шен/-на/-но/-ны a little high
поговори́ть to speak/talk for a while
пого́да weather
под under
пода́рок gift
подлинне́е a little longer
подозри́тельно suspiciously
подпи́сывать/подписа́ть to sign
подру́га (подру́жка) female friend; girlfriend
подстрига́ть/подстри́чь to cut, to trim
подходи́ть/подойти́ (кому́) to fit, to suit; to approach
по́езд train
пое́здка trip
Пое́хали! Let's go! (when driving)
пожа́луй I guess/suppose; perhaps; it may be
пожа́луйста please; you're welcome
  Позови́те, пожа́луйста, ... May I speak with ... , please?
пожило́й (noun/adj.) elderly
позавчера́ day before yesterday
по́здно late
по́зже later
пойти́ to go, to start off for (on foot) (perf.)
пока́ while, for the time being
  Пока́! See you!
  пока́ не until (conj.)
пока́зывать/показа́ть (кому́) to show
поколе́ние generation
покрыва́ть/покры́ть to cover
покры́тый covered
покупа́ть/купи́ть to buy
пол floor
по́лдень noon (m.)
по́ле (поля́) field (fields)
поле́зный useful
полежа́ть to lie in bed for a while
поли́тик politician
поли́тика politics
поликли́ника clinic; health center
полити́ческий political
по́лка shelf
по́лночь midnight (f.)
по́лный (adj.) fat; full (not when eating)
полови́на (пол) half
полоте́нце towel
полтора́ one and a half
полу́чше a little better
получа́ть(ся)/получи́ть(ся) to receive, to obtain
полчаса́ half-hour
по́льзоваться to use
поме́ньше a little less; a little smaller
помидо́р tomato
по́мнить to remember, to keep in mind (imp.)
помога́ть/помо́чь (кому́) to help
по́мощь help (f.)
понеде́льник Monday
понима́ть/поня́ть to understand
Поня́тно. I see.; Understood.
  Поня́тия не име́ю. I have no idea.
попро́бовать to try (out)

популя́рный popular
пора́ньше a little earlier
поре́же less (often)
по́рция portion
посереди́не in the middle (of)
по́сле (чего́) after
    по́сле обе́да in the afternoon; after lunch
    по́сле того́ как after (conj.)
после́дний last
после́дствие consequence; after-effect
послеза́втра day after tomorrow
посте́ль bed; bed-clothes (f.)
постро́ен/-а/-о/-ы built; constructed
посу́да dishes
посыла́ть/посла́ть to send
посы́лка package, parcel
пото́м later; then; after that
потому́ что because
похо́д going (process of)
похо́ж/-а/-и similar
похуже a little worse
почему́ why
    почему́-то for some reason
    почему́-нибудь for any reason
по́черк handwriting
по́чта post office; mail
    почтальо́н mail-carrier
    почто́вый я́щик mailbox
почти́ almost, not quite
Пошли́! Let's go!
поэ́т poet
    поэ́зия poetry
поэ́тому therefore
прабабушка great-grandmother
праде́душка great-grandfather
пра́вда truth
    Пра́вда. True./Right.
прав/-а́/-ы right; correct
пра́вильно correctly, properly
пра́вый right, correct
пра́вило rule
прави́тельство government
правосла́вный (noun/adj.) Orthodox (Christian)
пра́здник holiday
пра́чечная laundry (place)
предме́т subject
предназна́ченный predestined; destined (for); intended (for)
предпочита́ть/предпоче́сть to prefer
предприя́тие business, enterprise, works
представля́ть/предста́вить (себе́) to imagine; to present, to represent
пре́жде чем before (conj.)
прейскура́нт price list
прекра́сно wonderful(ly), excellent(ly)
преподава́ть to teach (college/adults)
при in the time/presence of; during the administration of
Приве́т! Hi!
прие́м (у кого́) appointment (with); reception
прие́мная Reception (of a hotel)

при́город suburb
Прилёты Flight Arrivals
при́нят/-а/-о/-ы accepted
    при́нято (де́лать) it's customary (to)
при́нтер printer
привыка́ть/привы́кнуть (к чему́/кому́) to get accustomed, used to
приглаша́ть/пригласи́ть to invite
приглаше́ние invitation
приезжа́ть/прие́хать to arrive, come (by vehicle)
приме́рно approximately
принадлежа́ть (кому́) to belong to
принима́ть/приня́ть to take (medicine; a shower); to accept
приноси́ть/принести́ to bring
    Принеси́те, пожа́луйста, ... Could I please have … ?
припомина́ть/припо́мнить to remember, recollect
приходи́ть/прийти́ to come, arrive
причёска hairdo; hairstyle
причи́на reason
прия́тный nice, pleasant
    Прия́тного аппети́та! Bon appetit!; Enjoy your meal!
про (кого́/что) about; on the subject of
про́бка cork; traffic jam (coll.)
пробле́ма problem
пробо́р part (in hair)
проверя́ть/прове́рить to check, to verify, to test
проводи́ть/провести́ to conduct; to see off
    проводи́ть/провести́ вре́мя хорошо́ to have a good time
провожа́ть/проводи́ть to see off, to accompany
прогно́з forecast
програ́мма program
    программи́ст computer programmer
продава́ть/прода́ть to sell
    про́дан/-а/-о/-ы sold
    продаве́ц/-щи́ца (m./f.) salesperson, clerk
продолжа́ться to continue; to be continuing
проду́кты food-stuffs; groceries; products
проездно́й monthly pass
прое́кт project
прои́грывать/проигра́ть to lose; to be losing
произведе́ние work (literary, artistic)
произойти́ to happen, to occur, (perf.)
происходи́ть to go on, to be happening (imp.)
пролива́ть/проли́ть to spill
про́пуск pass; admission; blank
пропуска́ть/пропусти́ть to miss, to skip, to let pass
проси́ть/по- (что у кого́); (кого́ де́лать) to request, to ask for
проспе́кт avenue
профе́ссия profession

проща́ть/прости́ть to forgive
    Прости́те! Sorry!; Forgive me!
    Прошу́ проще́ния! Forgive me!
про́сто simple(ly); just
просту́да cold (noun)
просыпа́ться/просн́уться to wake up
про́тив (чего́/кого́) against (someone/
    thing)
профессиона́л professional (noun)
прохла́дный cool
проходи́ть/пройти́ to walk along/past, to
    pass
Прочь! Go away!; Get out of here!
про́шлый (раз) past; last (time)
пря́мо straight ahead; directly
пункт point, station, post
пусто́й empty; hollow; impersonal
пуска́ть/пусти́ть to allow
    Пусть (он/она́/они́ ...) Let/Have
    him/her/they (do something)
путеше́ствовать to travel
пыта́ться to attempt, endeavor
пье́са (noun) play
пья́ница drunkard
пять five
пя́тый fifth
пя́тница Friday
пятно́ stain

Р

рабо́та work, labor
рабо́тать to work
    рабо́чие часы́ operating hours
ра́вный same, equal
рад/-а/-ы happy, glad
ра́ди (кого́/чего́) for the sake of
    Ра́ди Бо́га! for God's sake!
    ра́ди удово́льствия for fun('s sake)
радиа́ция radiation
ра́дио radio
раз time (once, twice, etc.); one (counting)
разведён/-на́/-ны́ divorced
разгова́ривать (с кем) to talk, to converse
    (with) (imp.)
разгово́р conversation
раздева́ться/разде́ться to get undressed
разме́р size
ра́зный different; various
разреше́ние permission
разру́шен/-а/-о/-ы destroyed, demolished,
    wrecked
райо́н area; region
рак cancer; crab
ра́но early
ра́ньше before; formerly (adv.)
расписа́ние schedule
располо́жен/-а/-о/-ы situated; placed
рассе́ян/-на/-но/-ны absentminded
расска́зывать/рассказа́ть (кому́) to
    relate, to narrate
расслабля́ть/рассла́бить to relax (part of
    the body)
расстава́ние parting
расстоя́ние distance
расстро́йство желу́дка upset stomach

расти́/вы- to grow, to grow up
рвать (рвёт, рва́ло кого́)/вы-to tear, to
    rip; to vomit
ребёнок child
ребя́та guys, kids
регистра́ция registration; check-in
регистра́тор hotel desk-clerk
ре́дко rarely
режиссёр director (theater, film)
ре́зать/на- to cut, chop
резюме́ resume
рейс flight, voyage
река́ river
рекла́ма advertisement
рекомендова́ть/по- to recommend
рекоменда́ция recommendation
реме́сленный handicraft; trade;
    industrial
ремонти́ровать/от- to renovate
репортёр reporter
репроду́кция reproduction (painting)
рестора́н restaurant
реце́пт recipe; prescription
речь speech (f.)
реша́ть/реши́ть to decide, to solve, to
    resolve
реше́ние decision; solution
рис rice
рисова́ть/на- to draw, to paint, to portray
рису́нок drawing
роди́тели parents
родно́й (adj.) native
ро́дственник relative
рожда́ться/роди́ться to be born
роль role (f.)
ро́зовый pink
рост height
рот mouth
руба́шка shirt
рубль ruble (m.)
рука́ hand, arm
руководи́ть to lead, to direct, to manage
    (imp.)
ру́сский Russian
ры́ба fish
ры́нок market (farmers')
ряд row, series
ря́дом с (кем/чем) next to, alongside

С

с/со (чем/кем); (чего́/кого́) with,
    accompanied by; from
    С больши́м успе́хом! Congratulations!;
    Good job!
    С Но́вым го́дом! Happy New Year!
    С прие́здом! Welcome!
    с сарка́змом sarcastically
    с субти́трами subtitled
    с тех пор since then
    с удово́льствием with pleasure; gladly
    с э́того моме́нта from now on
сад garden
садово́дство gardening
сади́ться/сесть (куда́) (на чём) to sit
    down; to get on (transport.)

сала́т salad
салфе́тка napkin
сало́н salon
   да́мский сало́н beauty salon
сам/-а́-/и self; oneself
самолёт airplane
самообслу́живание self-service
са́мый the most (many other meanings)
сбо́ку on the side, from the side
сва́дьба wedding
све́жий fresh
све́рху on the top, from the top
свет light; world; society
   на све́те in this world
све́тлый light; blonde
светофо́р traffic light
свеча́ candle
свиде́тель witness (m.)
сви́тер sweater
свобо́ден/-на/-но/-ны free; unoccupied
своди́ть (кого́) с ума́ to drive (someone)
   crazy
свой/своя́/своё/свои́ one's own
свято́й saint; holy, sacred, saintly
сдава́ть/сдать экза́мен to take an exam
   (imp.); to pass an exam (perf.)
сдать в наём to rent out
сде́лан/-а/-о/-ы done; made (of)
сеа́нс scheduled showing
себя́ self
се́вер north
се́верный northern
сего́дня today
семь seven
седьмо́й seventh
сейча́с (right) now
секрета́рь/секрета́рша (m./f.) secretary
секу́нда second (1/60th of a minute)
село́ village
семина́р seminar; workshop
семья́ nuclear family
сенна́я лихора́дка hay fever
сентя́брь September
се́рдце heart
   серде́чный heartfelt, sincere
серди́ться/по- to get angry
сере́бряный silver
середи́на (noun) middle
се́рый gray
се́рьги earrings
серьёзный serious
сестра́ sister
сза́ди (чего́/кого́) from behind; behind
си́ла strength; skill; force
си́льно (adj./adv.) strong(ly); extremely
си́льный strong; bad (illness)
синаго́га synagogue
си́ний dark blue (soft adj.)
симпати́чный nice, likeable, attractive
симфо́ния symphony
ситуа́ция situation
сказа́ть (кому́) to say, to tell
ска́зка story, fairy tale
ско́лько how much/many
   Ско́лько (ему́) лет? How old is (he)?

Ско́лько вре́мени? —Сейча́с ... What
   time is it? —It's …
Ско́лько лет, ско́лько зим! Long time
   no see!
ско́ро soon
скоре́е sooner
скуча́ть (по чему́/кому́) to miss, to yearn
   for; to be bored
ску́чно boring
сла́бый weak
сла́ва (чему́/кому́) glory (to)
   Сла́ва Бо́гу сего́дня пя́тница! Thank
   God it's Friday!
сла́дкий sweet (taste)
сле́довать/по- (кому́) to follow, to go
   after
сле́дующий next, following
слепо́й blind
сли́шком too (overly)
слова́рь dictionary (m.)
сло́во word
сло́жно complicated
слу́жащий(-ая) (m./f.) employee; service-
   person
слу́жба service
слу́шать/по- to listen to
   Слу́шаю (вас). Hello?; Yes? (on phone)
случа́ться/случи́ться to happen; to come
   to pass
случа́йно by chance; accidentally
слы́шать/у- to hear
смета́на sour cream
смешно́й funny; amusing
смея́ться/за- (над чем/кем) to laugh (at),
   smile
смотре́ть/по- to watch, look at
снег snow
снима́ть/снять to rent; to occupy; to
   remove; to photograph
   снима́ть/снять кварти́ру to rent/to
   occupy an apartment
сно́ва again, anew, once again
собира́ться to plan to
собра́ние meeting
соверше́нно completely, utterly
   Соверше́нно ве́рно! Exactly!, Absolutely
   right!
сове́товать/по- to advise
сове́тский Soviet
совреме́нный contemporary
совсе́м completely; at all
   совсе́м не not at all
согла́сен/-на/-но/-ны (с кем) to be in
   agreement (with)
сок juice
солда́т soldier
солёный pickled, salted
со́лнце sun
со́лнечный sunny
соль salt (f.)
сорт kind, sort
сосе́д(ка) (m./f.) neighbor
   сосе́д(ка) по ко́мнате (m./f.)
   roommate
соси́ска sausage

составля́ть/соста́вить to compile, to draw up, to form
сотру́дник/-ница (m./f.) co-worker, associate
сохраня́ть/сохрани́ть to preserve, to keep, to retain
социалисти́ческий socialist
спать/про- to sleep, to oversleep (perf.) (II.)
спа́льный ваго́н sleeping car
спа́льня bedroom
спаси́бо thank you
Спаси́бо большо́е! Thank you very much!
спе́реди in front (of); from the front
специа́льный special
спеши́ть to hurry
спи́сок list
спи́чки matches
споко́йно (adj./adv.) calm(ly), peaceful(ly)
Споко́йной но́чи! Good night!
спо́рить/по- (о чём) to argue (about); to dispute (about)
спорт sports
спортсме́н(ка) (m./f.) athlete
спра́шивать/спроси́ть to ask (intrans.)
Спра́вки Information
сра́зу immediately
среда́ Wednesday
сре́дний medium, middle, average (soft adj.)
сре́днего ро́ста of medium height
ста́вить/по- to put (standing)
стадио́н stadium
стака́н glass
станови́ться/стать (кем/чем) to become, to get to be; to stand
ста́нция station (metro, train)
стара́ться/по- to try, to make an effort
ста́рый old
стари́к old man
ста́рость old age (f.)
ста́рше older
статья́ article
стена́ wall
сте́пень degree (f.)
стёртый worn, effaced
стиль style (m.)
стипе́ндия stipend
стихи́ verses; poetry
стихотворе́ние poem
сто one hundred
сто́ить to be worth, to cost (imp.)
стол table
сто́лик на одного́/двои́х/трои́х a table for one/two/three
столо́вая cafeteria
сто́лько (чего́) so much
сторона́ side
стоя́нка taxi-stand
стоя́ть/по- to stand, be standing
страда́ть to suffer (imp.)
страна́ country
страхо́вка insurance

стра́шный terrible, frightful
стри́жка haircut; haircut appointment
стро́гий stern
стро́йный slender; well-built (person)
студе́нт(ка) (m./f.) student
стул (сту́лья) chair (chairs)
стюарде́сса stewardess
суббо́та Saturday
сувени́р souvenir
судья́ judge; referee (m.)
су́мка bag, purse
суп soup
сухо́й dry
сухова́т/-а/-о/-ы dried out
суши́ть to dry (imp.)
сча́стлив/-а/-о/-ы happy; lucky; fortunate
Счастли́вого пути́! Have a good trip!
счёт bill; account
счита́ть/счесть to consider, to count
сын son
сыр cheese
сыт/-а́/-о/-ы full (opp. of hungry)
сюда́ (to) here

Т

табле́тка pill, tablet
тайм period (of a game)
так so
так же как и (кто/что) just like
так как since; because; as
Так себе́. So so.
та́кже also, too, as well
тако́й such (a); so
такси́ taxi (indecl.)
тала́нтливый talented
тало́н token
там there
тамо́женник customs official
тамо́жня customs
танцева́ть/по- to dance
та́почки slippers; slipper-like shoe coverings
таре́лка plate, dish
твой/твоя́/твоё/твои́ your/yours (familiar)
творо́г farmer's/cottage cheese
теа́тр theater
телеви́зор television
телегра́мма telegram
теле́жка baggage cart
телефо́н telephone
те́ло body
тем не ме́нее nevertheless
тёмный dark; brunette
температу́ра temperature
те́ннис tennis
тепе́рь now (opp. of before); nowadays
тёплый warm; hot (for drinks)
теря́ть/по- to lose
тетра́дь notebook (f.)
тётя aunt
те́хника technology
типи́чный typical
ти́хо quiet(ly)
това́ры goods

тогда́ then; in that case; at that time
то́же also
толка́ть/толкну́ть to push
толсте́ть/рас- to get fat
то́лько only
    то́лько что just; very recently
то́нкий fine; thin; subtle
торже́ственный solemn
торт cake; torte
тост toast (to someone); toasted bread
тот/та/то/те that/those (one/ones)
    то есть that is (to say)
то́чно exactly
трамва́й tram
тра́нспорт transportation
тре́тий/тре́тья/тре́тье third
три́ста three hundred
тро́е three (of them)
тролле́йбус trolley
тру́бка pipe; tube; telephone receiver
труд labor; toil
тру́дно difficult, hard
туале́т toilet, rest room
    туале́тная бума́га toilet paper
туда́ (to) there
    туда́ и обра́тно roundtrip
тури́ст(ка) (m./f.) tourist
    туристи́ческое аге́нство tourist office;
    travel agency
ты you (familiar)
ты́сяча one thousand
тяжёлый heavy, serious
тяну́ть/по- to pull

У

у (кого́/чего́) by; at
    У вас есть … ? Do you have … ?
    (plural/polite sing.)
    у вы́хода by the exit; by the door
    у меня́ at my house/home
    У меня́ боли́т голова́. I have a
    headache.
    **У меня́ есть … ** I have …
    У тебя́ есть … ? Do you have … ? (familiar)
убива́ть/уби́ть to kill
убира́ть/убра́ть to tidy up, clear up
уве́рен/-а/-ы sure, positive
увлека́ться (чем) to be fascinated with
удава́ться/уда́ться (кому́) to be
    successful
удиви́тельный amazing, surprising
удо́бно convenient, comfortable
у́жас disaster; horror
уже́ already; yet
у́жин dinner
у́жинать/по- to eat dinner
узнава́ть/узна́ть to recognize, to find out
уи́кенд weekend
у́лица street
уме́ть/с- to know how to; to manage to
    (perf.)
умира́ть/умере́ть to die
умыва́ться/умы́ться to wash (oneself)
универма́г department store
универса́м supermarket

университе́т university
уничтожа́ть/уничто́жить to destroy, to
    wipe out, to abolish
уныва́ть to be depressed (imp.)
упражня́ться to practice, to train (imp.)
упражне́ние (noun) exercise
упря́мый stubborn
у́ровень (noun) level(m.)
услу́ги services
успева́ть/успе́ть to have time
Успе́ха! Good luck (success)!
устава́ть/уста́ть to get tired, to be tired
    уста́л/-а/-ы tired
устра́ивать/устро́ить to arrange, to
    set up
усы́ mustache
у́тро morning
утра́ a.m.
у́тром in the morning
у́хо (у́ши) ear (ears)
уче́бник textbook
учи́ть to study, learn
учи́ться/на- to be studying; to be a
    student; to learn to do smth.
учрежде́ние office (place of work)
ую́тный cozy, comfortable

Ф

факс-мо́дем modem
фами́лия last name
фармаце́вт pharmacist
фата́ veil
февра́ль February
фен dryer; blowdryer
филармо́ния philarmonic society
фильм film; movie
фина́л finals, playoffs
фиоле́товый purple
фи́рма firm, company
    фи́рменные блю́да house specialties
фойе́ foyer
фотоаппара́т camera
фотогра́фия photograph
фотоко́пия photocopy
фру́кты fruit
футбо́л soccer
    футбо́лка jersey
    футбо́льный матч soccer game

Х

хала́т dressing gown; hospital smock
хвата́ть/хвати́ть to be enough, to suffice
    не хвата́ть to be missing
хи́мия (пермане́нт) chemistry; perm
    (hair)
химчи́стка dry cleaning; dry cleaner's
хлеб bread
хо́бби hobby
ходи́ть to go (multi.)
    ходи́ть за гриба́ми to go mushroom-
    picking
    ходи́ть за поку́пками to go shopping
хозя́ин boss; host (etc.)
холо́дный cold
    холоди́льник refrigerator

хоро́ший good
   хоро́шенький pretty
   хорошо́ good; well
хоте́ть/за- to want (irreg.)
   хоте́ть сказа́ть to mean, to want to say
Хоть (+ imperative verb)! At least (verb)! (conj.)
храни́ть/со- to keep (safe), save, retain
хру́пкий fragile, brittle
худе́ть/по- to lose weight
   худо́й skinny
   ху́денький thin
худо́жественный artistic
худо́жник artist
ху́же worse
хулига́н hooligan

Ц

царь tsar (m.)
царе́вич the tsar's son and heir
цари́ца tsarina
цвет color
цвето́к flower
целова́ть/по- to kiss
цель goal; target (f.)
цена́ price
центр center; downtown
центра́льный central
це́рковь church (f.)
цирк circus

Ч

чай tea
чаевы́е tip; gratuity
ча́йник teapot
час hour
часы́ watch, clock
ча́стный private, particular
ча́сто often
часть part (f.)
ча́шка cup
чего́ (от кого́/чего́) мо́жно ждать what to expect (from)
чей/чья/чьё/чьи whose
   чей-то someone's
   че́й-нибудь anyone's
чек check, slip
   че́ковый счёт checking account
челове́к person
чемода́н suitcase
че́рез in (a unit of time); through; across
чёрный black
четве́рг Thursday
четы́ре four
че́тверо four (of them)
четвёртый fourth
че́тверть one quarter (f.)
чино́вник bureaucrat
число́ number, date, day
чи́стить/по- to clean
   чи́стить/по- зу́бы to brush one's teeth
чита́ть/про- to read
   чита́тельский биле́т library card
что what; that
   что ли? or what?

Что но́вого? What's new?
Что тако́е _____ ? What is _____ ?
Что ты! Come off it!
Что у вас? What's wrong?
что́-нибудь anything
что́-то something
Что-что? What? (emphatic)
что́бы so that; in order to
чу́вствовать себя́/по- to feel (in a certain way)
чуть hardly, scarcely
   чуть не almost, practically (barely averted) (conj.)
   чуть-чу́ть a little bit (coll.)

Ш

шампа́нское champagne
шампу́нь shampoo (f.)
ша́пка (шля́па) hat
шерсть wool (f.)
шесто́й sixth
шесть six
ше́я neck
широ́кий wide
широко́ wide(ly) (adj. or adv.)
шкату́лка decorative box
шко́льник/-ница pupil (m./f.)
шоссе́ highway
шофёр driver
штат state
штраф (noun) fine
шум noise
шу́мный noisy
шути́ть/по- to joke
шу́тка joke

Щ

щётка brush; toothbrush, hairbrush
щу́пать/по- to feel (for), to touch, to probe

Э

экза́мен exam
эконо́мика economy
экску́рсия excursion
экскурсово́д guide
электро́нная по́чта e-mail
электропли́тка hot plate
эма́ль enamel (f.)
эне́ргия energy
эта́ж floor, story
э́то this/that/it is
   Это вам. This is for you.
   Это всё. That's all.
   Это говори́т _____ . This is _____ speaking.
   э́то зна́чит that/it means
   Это (кому́) идёт. It fits/suits.
   Это, пожа́луй, всё. I think that's all.
э́тот/э́та/э́то/э́ти this/these

Ю

ю́бка skirt
юг south
ю́жный southern

ю́ность youth (f.)
юри́ст attorney, lawyer

Я

я I
Я возьму́ ... I'll have …
Я же тебе́ говори́л(а)! What did I tell you!
Я наде́юсь, что ... I hope (that) …
Я так и зна́л(а)! I knew it!
Я хоте́л(а) бы ... I'd like …
я́блоко apple
я́блочный (adj.) apple

я́вка appearance; attendance
Я́вка обяза́тельна. Attendance is mandatory.
я́годы berries
язы́к language; tongue
яйцо́ egg
янва́рь January
янта́рь amber (m.)
из янтаря́ made of amber
я́ркий bright
я́рмарка trade fair
я́сно (adj./adv.) clear(ly)

АНГЛО-РУ́ССКИЙ

A

a
a few не́сколько
a little ма́ло; немно́го/немно́жко
a little better полу́чше
a little bigger побо́льше
a little bit чуть-чу́ть
a little earlier пора́ньше
a little high повы́шен/-на/-но/-ны
a little higher повы́ше
a little later попо́зже
a little less поме́ньше
a little longer подлинне́е
a little more побо́льше
a little smaller поме́ньше
a little worse похуже
a long time (ago) давно́
a lot мно́го
a.m. утра́
abolish (to) уничтожа́ть/уничто́жить
about о/об; про (кого́/что)
above над; вверху́; наверху́
abroad за грани́цей
absentminded рассе́ян/-на/-но/-ны
accept (to) принима́ть/приня́ть
accepted при́нят/-а/-о/-ы
access до́ступ
accomodation жильё
accompany (to) провожа́ть/проводи́ть
account счёт
across че́рез
actually действи́тельно
address а́дрес
admission/entrance до́ступ
adult взро́слый
advertisement рекла́ма
advise (to) сове́товать/по-
affair де́ло
affectionate(ly) не́жно
afraid (of) (to be) боя́ться (чего́/кого́)
after по́сле (чего́); по́сле того́ как (conj.)
after all ведь
after that зате́м
after-effect после́дствие
afternoon (in the) днём; по́сле обе́да

again сно́ва; опя́ть
against (someone/thing) про́тив (чего́/кого́)
age во́зраст
agent аге́нт
ago наза́д
agreed (to be) согла́сен/-на/-ны (с кем)
Agreed! Договори́лись!
ahead впереди́ (чего́/кого́)
airmail авиапо́чта
airplane самолёт
airport аэропо́рт
alike одина́ковый
alive жив/-а́/-о/-ы
all весь/вся/всё/все
All in good time. Всему́ своё вре́мя.
All the best! Всего́ хоро́шего!
all the same всё-таки
all the time всё вре́мя
All the very best! Всего́ наилу́чшего!
almost почти́; чуть не (conj.)
alongside ря́дом с (кем/чем)
aloud вслух
already уже́
also то́же; та́кже
always всегда́
amateur люби́тель (m.)
amazing удиви́тельный
amber янта́рь (m.)
and и, а
And a good thing, too! И вот и прекра́сно!
And how is (was) it? Ну и как?
and so forth и так да́лее
and vice versa и наоборо́т
anesthetic анесте́тик
announcement объявле́ние (posted)
another ещё оди́н/-на́/-но́/-ни; друго́й
answer отве́т
answer (to) отвеча́ть/отве́тить
any kind of како́й-нибудь
anyhow ка́к-нибудь
anyone кто́-нибудь
anyone's че́й-нибудь
anything что́-нибудь

anytime когда-нибудь
anyway во всяком случае
anywhere где-нибудь
apartment квартира
apparel одежда
appetizers закуски
apple яблоко; яблочный (adj.)
appointment встреча; приём (у кого)
approach, come up to (to) подходить/
    подойти
approximately примерно; около (чего)
April апрель
archive архив
area район
argue/dispute (to) спорить/по- (о чём)
arm рука
armchair кресло
army армия
around около (чего)
arrange (to) устраивать/устроить;
    организовать
Arrivals (flight) Прилёты
art искусство
article статья
artist художник
artistic художественный
as так как, как
    as a matter of fact в самом деле
    as always как всегда
    as far as насколько
    as is evident/can be seen как видно
    as well также
ask (to) спрашивать/спросить;
    просить/по- (someone for smth;
    someone to do smth.); задавать/задать
    (вопрос) (a question)
aspirin аспирин
astrology астрология
at в, на, у (кого/чего)
    at all совсем
    at breakfast на завтрак
    at home дома
    at least по крайней мере
    at my house/home у меня
    at night ночью
    at that time тогда
    at the same time as в одно время (с
    чем)
    at the table за столом
    At what time ... ? —At (time). Во
    сколько ... ? —В (time).
athlete спортсмен(ка) (m./f.)
atmosphere атмосфера
attempt/endeavor (to) пытаться
attendance явка
    Attendance is mandatory. Явка
    обязательна.
attention внимание
attentively внимательно
attitudes отношения
attorney/lawyer юрист
attractive (likeable) симпатичный
auditorium зал
August август
aunt тётя

automobile автомобиль
avenue проспект
average средний (soft adj.)

B

back(wards) назад
bad плохой, плохо; сильно (illness);
    дурной (evil)
bag сумка
baggage багаж
    baggage cart тележка
bake/be baking (to) печь(ся)/ис- (I.)
bakery булочная
ball мяч
ballads баллады
ballet балет
bank банк
bar бар
barber парикмахер
barbershop парикмахерский
bare голый
barely едва
bathing suit купальник
bathroom ванная; туалет
battery аккумулятор
be (repeatedly) (to) бывать (imp.)
be (to) быть (used only in future or
    past)
beach пляж
beard борода
beat (to) бить (imp.); забивать/забить
beautiful красивый
beauty salon дамский салон
because потому что; так как
    because of из-за (кого/чего)
become/get to be (to)
    становиться/стать (кем/чем)
become sick (to) заболевать/заболеть
bed кровать (f.); постель (f.)
    bed-clothes постель (f.)
bedroom спальня
beef говядина
before раньше (adv.); до того как
    (conj.); прежде чем (conj.)
    before (just) перед (чего, кем); перед
    тем как (conj.)
    before bed перед сном
begin (to) начинаться/начаться
beginning/start начало
behave (to) вести себя
behind сзади (чего/кого)
believe (to) верить/по-
belong (to) принадлежать (кому)
berries ягоды
besides к тому же; кроме как
    besides that кроме того
best лучший
betray (to) изменять/изменить
better лучше
between между (чем/кем и чем/кем)
    between you and me между нами
beverage напиток
bicycle велосипед
bigger больше
bill счёт

birthday день рожде́ния (date of birth);
    имени́ны (name-day)
black чёрный
blank про́пуск (noun)
blind слепо́й
blockade блока́да
blonde блонди́н(ка) (noun; m./f.);
    све́тлый (adj.)
blood pressure давле́ние
blouse блу́зка
blowdryer фен
blue голубо́й (light); си́ний (dark; soft adj.)
board (to) сесть на (чём) (transport.)
body те́ло
boil/be boiling (to) ва́рить(ся)/с-
Bon appetit! Прия́тного аппети́та!
book кни́га
booklet кни́жечка
border грани́ца
bored (to be) скуча́ть
boring ску́чно
born (to be) рожда́ться/роди́ться
boss нача́льник; хозя́ин
both о́ба/о́бе
    both … and … и … и …
bother (someone) (to) меша́ть/по- (кому́)
bottle буты́лка
bouquet буке́т
box коро́бка
brand ма́рка
brave му́жественный
bread хлеб
    bread roll бу́лочка
break/interval переры́в
breakfast за́втрак
breathe (to) вдыха́ть/вдохну́ть
bride неве́ста
bridegroom жени́х
bright я́ркий
bring (to) приноси́ть/принести́
brittle хру́пкий; ло́мкий
broadcast переда́ча
brochure брошю́ра
broke без де́нег
brother брат
brunette тёмный, брюне́т(ка) (m./f.)
brush щётка
brush one's teeth (to) чи́стить/по- зу́бы
building зда́ние
built/constructed постро́ен/-а/-о/-ы
bureaucrat чино́вник
burst/break (to) ло́паться/ло́пнуть
bus авто́бус
business предприя́тие
    business card визи́тка
    business hours рабо́чие часы́
    business trip/assignment (official)
        командиро́вка
    on a business trip в командиро́вке
    business person бизнесме́н(ка)
        (m./f.)
busy за́нят/-а/-ы
but но, а
butcher's мясна́я ла́вка
butter ма́сло

buy (to) покупа́ть/купи́ть
by во́зле/у (чего́/кого́)
    by accident случа́йно
    by chance случа́йно
    by the way кста́ти; ме́жду про́чим
    by nationality по национа́льности

C

cabbage капу́ста
cafe кафе́
cafeteria столо́вая
cake пиро́г; торт
call by phone (to) звони́ть/по-
call (to) звать/по- (кого́)
called (to be) называ́ться (things only)
calm(ly) споко́йно
camera фотоаппара́т
can уме́ть/с- (know how to); мочь/с- (be
    able to)
can ба́нка (noun)
cancellation отме́на
cancer рак
candidate кандида́т
candle свеча́
car маши́на
car (train/subway) ваго́н
card ка́рточка; откры́тка
    credit card креди́тная ка́рточка
careful(ly) осторо́жно
carpet ковёр
carry (to) нести́; носи́ть
    carry/take out, away (to)
        выноси́ть/вы́нести
carton па́чка
cash register ка́сса
cassette кассе́та
catch (to) пойма́ть (perf.)
caviar икра́
cavity дупло́
cease (to) перестава́ть/переста́ть
Celsius по Це́льсию
center центр
central центра́льный, гла́вный
century век
ceremony венча́ние
certain/some не́который
certainly наверняка́
champagne шампа́нское
change (money) ме́лочь (noun) (f.)
change (to) изменя́ть/измени́ть;
    изменя́ться/измени́ться (intrans.)
channel кана́л
chat (to) болта́ть
cheap дешёвый
check чек
    checking account че́ковый счёт
    Check-in Регистра́ция
check/verify/test (to) проверя́ть/
    прове́рить
Cheer up! Не уныва́й(те)!
cheese сыр
chemistry хи́мия
cherries ви́шни
chicken ку́рица
child ребёнок

children де́ти
choose (to) выбира́ть/вы́брать
chop (to) ре́зать/на-
church це́рковь (f.)
cinema кино́ (кинотеатр)
circus цирк
city го́род
claim check квита́нция
classes заня́тия
classical класси́ческий
clean (to) чи́стить/по-; убира́ть/убра́ть
    (tidy)
clear(ly) я́сно
climate кли́мат; атмосфе́ра (fig.)
clinic поликли́ника
cloakroom гардеро́б
clock часы́
close (to) закрыва́ть/закры́ть
clothed оде́т/-а/-о/-ы
clothing оде́жда
cloudy о́блачный
co-worker/associate сотру́дник/-ница
    (m./f.)
coat пальто́
coffee ко́фе
cold холо́дный (adj.); просту́да (noun)
colleague колле́га (m.)
collection колле́кция
color цвет
    What color is it? Како́го цве́та?
come (to) приходи́ть/прийти́,
    приезжа́ть/прие́хать
    Come off it! Что ты!
comfortable(-ly) удо́бно
communist коммуни́ст (noun)
company фи́рма; компа́ния
compile (to) составля́ть/соста́вить
complain (to) жа́ловаться/по-
complete (to) заполня́ть/запо́лнить
completely соверше́нно; совсе́м
complicated сло́жно
compliment комплиме́нт
composer компози́тор
computer компью́тер
conceive (an idea) (to) мы́слить
concert конце́рт
conclusion заключе́ние
conductor дирижёр
consequence после́дствие
consider (to) счита́ть/счесть
consist (to) составля́ть/соста́вить
constantly беспреста́нно
contemporary совреме́нный
continue/be continuing (to)
    продолжа́ться (imp.)
contract контра́кт
convenient(ly) удо́бно
conversation разгово́р
convey (to) везти́, вози́ть (by vehicle);
    передава́ть/переда́ть, доставля́ть/
    доста́вить (message, thing);
    выража́ть/вы́разить (idea,
    impression)
cook (to) гото́вить/при-
cooking гото́вка

cookie пече́нье
cool прохла́дный
cordial серде́чный
corner (in/on the) в углу́
correct(ly)/proper(ly) пра́вильно
corridor коридо́р
cost (to) сто́ить (imp.)
cozy/comfortable ую́тный
cotton ва́та; хло́пок (fabric)
couch дива́н
cough ка́шель (m. noun)
    cough-drops ка́пли от ка́шля
Could I please have ... ? Принеси́те,
    пожа́луйста, ...
count (to) счита́ть/счесть
country (nation) страна́
    country house да́ча
countryside дере́вня; за го́родом (in the)
couple па́ра
cover (to) покрыва́ть/покры́ть
    covered покры́тый
cream крем (lotion); сли́вки (dairy)
cry/weep (to) пла́кать (imp.)
cucumber огуре́ц
cuisine ку́хня
culture культу́ра
cup ча́шка
current events теку́щие собы́тия
customary to... (it's) при́нято (де́лать
    что-то)
customs тамо́жня
    customs official тамо́женник
cut (to) ре́зать/на- (chop);
    подстрига́ть/подстри́чь (clip)

D

daily бытово́й
dairy store моло́чная
dance (to) танцева́ть/по-
dangerous опа́сный, опа́сно
dark тёмный
darling ми́лый (noun, adj.)
darn ёлки-па́лки (adj.)
date число́; да́та
    date of birth да́та рожде́ния
    What's today's date? Како́е сего́дня
    число́?
daughter дочь (f.), до́чка
day день (m.)
    day after tomorrow послеза́втра
    day before yesterday позавчера́
    day off выходно́й день
    day-dream мечта́
    days off выходны́е дни
    What day is today? Како́й сего́дня
    день?
dead мёртв/-а́/-о/-ы
dear ми́лый
December дека́брь
decide (to) реша́ть/реши́ть
    decision реше́ние
declaration (customs) деклара́ция
deep глубо́кий
defender защи́тник
definitely наверняка́

degree сте́пень (f.); гра́дус (temperature)
delegation делега́ция
delicious вку́сно
deliver (to) доставля́ть/доста́вить
demolished разру́шен/-а/-о/-ы
dental floss зубна́я нить
dentist зубно́й врач
depart (to) отходи́ть/отойти́
department отде́л
   department store универма́г
departure отъе́зд
   Departures (flight) Вы́леты
deposit депози́т, зада́ток **(advance)**
depressed (to be) уныва́ть (imp.)
description описа́ние
desk пи́сьменный стол
destroy (to) уничтожа́ть/уничто́жить
destroyed разру́шен/-а/-о/-ы
dictionary слова́рь (m.)
die (to) умира́ть/умере́ть
different ра́зный, друго́й; по-друго́му
difficult тру́дно
dinner у́жин
direct руководи́ть (imp.)
director (theater, film) режиссёр
dirty гря́зный
disappear (to) исчеза́ть/исче́знуть
disaster у́жас
discuss (to) обсужда́ть/обсуди́ть
dish таре́лка; блю́до (food)
   dishes посу́да
disorder беспоря́док
dissertation диссерта́ция
distance расстоя́ние
dizzy (I'm) голова́ кру́жится
do (to) де́лать/с–
doctor врач (g. p.); до́ктор
document докуме́нт
domestic services бытовы́е услу́ги
done сде́лан/-а/-о/-ы
door дверь (f.)
   by the door у вы́хода
dormitory общежи́тие
downstairs внизу́
downtown центр
draw (to) рисова́ть/на–
   drawing рису́нок
dream мечта́ (noun)
   dreamer мечта́тель (m.)
dress пла́тье
dressed оде́т/-а/-о/-ы
   dressing gown хала́т
drink питьё (noun)
   drink (to) пить/вы–
drive (to) води́ть маши́ну
   drive (someone) crazy (to) своди́ть
      (кого́) с ума́
   driver води́тель (m.); шофёр
   driver's license води́тельские права́
drop by (to) заходи́ть/зайти́ (за чем)
drunkard пья́ница
dry сухо́й, сухова́т/а/о/ы (dried out)
dry (to) суши́ть (imp.)
   dry cleaning/dry cleaner's
      химчи́стка

dubbed дубли́рованный
duplicated дубли́рованный
during во вре́мя
   during the reign of при (ком)

E

each other друг дру́га
each ка́ждый (adj.)
ear (ears) у́хо (у́ши)
earlier зара́нее
early ра́но
earn (to) зараба́тывать (imp.)
earrings се́рьги
Earth земля́
easier ле́гче
east восто́к
   eastern восто́чный
easy легко́/лёгкий
eat (to) есть (ем, ешь, ест, еди́м, еди́те,
      едя́т)/съ– (irreg.)
   eat breakfast (to) за́втракать/по–
   eat dinner (to) у́жинать/по–
   Eat it in good health! Ку́шай(те) на
      здоро́вье!
   eat lunch (to) обе́дать/по–
   eat/snack (to) ку́шать/по–
economy эконо́мика
education образова́ние
effaced стёртый
egg яйцо́
eight во́семь
eighth восьмо́й
either … or … и́ли … и́ли …
elderly пожило́й (noun/adj.)
elect (to) избира́ть/избра́ть
election вы́боры
e-mail электро́нная по́чта
elegant наря́дный
elevator лифт
eleventh оди́ннадцатый
eliminate (to) уничтожа́ть/уничто́жить
else ещё
employee слу́жащий
empty пусто́й
enamel эма́ль (f.)
end коне́ц
energy эне́ргия
enough доста́точно
   be enough (to) хвата́ть/хвати́ть
enterprise предприя́тие
entrance вход
envelope конве́рт
environment (the) окружа́ющая
     среда́
envy (to) зави́довать/по–
equal ра́вный
especially осо́бенно
essential(ly) необходи́мо
et cetera (etc.) и так да́лее (и т.д.)
ethnic национа́льный
European европе́йский
even so и так
evening ве́чер; вече́рний (soft adj.)
   in the evening ве́чером
ever когда́-то, когда́-нибудь

every ка́ждый
  everyone все
  everything всё
  everywhere везде́
evident ви́дно
exactly в то́чности; то́чно
  exactly right ве́рно
  Exactly! Соверше́нно ве́рно!
exam экза́мен
example образе́ц
excellent(ly) отли́чно
exchange (to) меня́ть/по-
excite (to) возбужда́ть/возбуди́ть
excursion экску́рсия
excuse (to) извиня́ть/извини́ть
exercise упражне́ние
  exercise (to) упражня́ться (imp.)
exhibit вы́ставка
exit вы́ход
  exit (by the) у вы́хода
  exit (to) выходи́ть/вы́йти (transport.)
expect (to) ожида́ть (imp.)
expensive (in-) дорого́й (не-)
experienced о́пытный
express (to) выража́ть/вы́разить
expression выраже́ние (of idea)
extra ли́шний
eye(s) глаз(а́); о́чи (archaic, poetic)
  eyebrow бровь (f.)

F

face лицо́
factory заво́д; фа́брика
Fahrenheit по Фаренге́йту
fairy tale ска́зка
faithful ве́рно
fall о́сень
  in the fall о́сенью
fall asleep (to) засыпа́ть/засну́ть
fall ill (to) заболева́ть/заболе́ть
family семья́ (spouse/children only)
famous знамени́тый
fan боле́льщик
fantastic замеча́тельно
far away далеко́
farther да́льше
fascinated with (to be) увлека́ться (чем)
fast бы́стрый
father оте́ц; па́па (dad)
favorite люби́мый
February февра́ль
feed (to) корми́ть (imp.)
feel (to) чу́вствовать себя́/по-
  to feel for щу́пать/по-
  feeling чу́вство; душа́
female же́нский
feminine же́нский
fever жар
few не́сколько (чего́)
field по́ле
fifth пя́тый
figure out (to) реша́ть/реши́ть
fill in (to) заполня́ть/запо́лнить
filling пло́мба
film (camera) плёнка

finally наконе́ц
finals фина́л (sports)
find (to) найти́ (perf.)
  find out (to) узнава́ть/узна́ть
fine хорошо́ (good); ме́лко (small pieces); то́нкий (thin)
finger(s) па́лец/па́льцы
finish коне́ц
  finished (to be) ко́нчиться
  It's finished! Вот и всё!
fireplace ками́н
first пе́рвый
  first class мя́гкий ваго́н (train)
  first name и́мя
fish ры́ба
fit/suit (to) подходи́ть/подойти́ (кому́)
  It fits/suits (someone). Это (кому́) идёт.
five пять
flight рейс
floor пол; эта́ж(story)
flower цвето́к
fluently свобо́дно говори́ть по-(language)
follow (to) сле́довать/по- (за кем)
food еда́
  food store гастроно́м
  food-stuffs проду́кты
for за
  for fun ра́ди удово́льствия
  for God's sake! ра́ди Бо́га!
  For how long … ? На ско́лько вре́мени … ?
  for lunch на обе́д
  for pay/requiring payment пла́тный
  for sure наверняка́
  for the night на́ ночь
  for the period of в тече́ни (чего́)
  for the purpose/sake of для
  for what purpose заче́м
forbidden запрещён/-а́/-о́/-ы́ (adj.)
  it is forbidden нельзя́
force си́ла
forecast прогно́з
foreign иностра́нный
  foreign currency валю́та
  foreign currency exchange bank обме́н валю́ты
foreigner иностра́нец/-ка (m./f.)
forest/woods лес
forgive (to) проща́ть/прости́ть
  Forgive me! Прости́те!; Прошу́ проще́ние!
form анке́та
form (to) составля́ть/соста́вить
former бы́вший
fortress кре́пость (f.)
fortunate счастли́вый
  fortunately к сча́стью
forward вперёд
founded осно́ван/-а/-о/-ы
four че́тыре
  four (of them) че́тверо
fourth четвёртый
foyer фойе́
fragile хру́пкий; ло́мкий

free свобо́дный
  free of charge беспла́тно
fresh све́жий
Friday пя́тница
friend друг/подру́га, подру́жка (m./f.)
frightful стра́шный
from из/от/с (чего́/кого́)
  from behind сза́ди (чего́/кого́)
  from here отсю́да
  from now on с э́того моме́нта
  from the front спе́реди
frost моро́з
fruit фру́кты
funny смешно́й
fur мех
furnished меблиро́ванний
furniture ме́бель (f.)
future бу́дущий

G

game игра́
garden сад
gardening садово́дство
gas бензи́н (petrol)
  gas station запра́вочная ста́нция
gate(s) воро́та
general о́бщий
  general practitioner врач
generation поколе́ние
get (to) достава́ть/доста́ть
  get angry (to) серди́ться/по-
  get dressed (to) одева́ться/оде́ться
  get fat (to) толсте́ть/рас-
  get married (to) жени́ться/по-
  get thin (to) худе́ть/по-
  get tired/be tired (to) устава́ть/уста́ть
  get undressed (to)
    раздева́ться/разде́ться
  get up (to) встава́ть/встать
gift пода́рок
girl (young woman) де́вушка
give (to) дава́ть/дать (дам, дашь, даст,
  дади́м, дади́те, даду́т) (irreg.)
  give a present (to) дари́ть/по-
    (что-кому́)
glass стака́н
glasses очки́
glory (to) сла́ва (чему́/кому́)
go (to) идти́/по-; ходи́ть (by own power)
  Go away!/Get out of here! Прочь!
  go bike riding (to) ката́ться на
    велосипе́де
  go by vehicle (to) е́хать/по-; е́здить
  go jogging (to) бе́гать трусцо́й
  go mushroom-picking (to) ходи́ть за
    гриба́ми
  go on/be going on (to) происходи́ть
    (imp.)
  go shopping (to) ходи́ть за поку́пками
  go to bed (to) ложи́ться/лечь спать
  go to school (to) учи́ться/на-
  go to the countryside (to) е́здить за́
    город
  go without food (to) голода́ть (imp.)
goal цель (f.); гол, воро́та (sports)

going on (to be) происходи́ть (imp.)
golden золото́й
good хорошо́; хоро́ший; до́брый (kind)
  Good afternoon. До́брый день.
  good cooking кулина́рный тала́нт
  Good evening. До́брый ве́чер.
  Good for you!/Great! Молоде́ц!/
    Молодцы́!
  Good luck! Успе́ха!
  Good luck/break a leg! Ни пу́ха ни
    пера́!
  Good morning. До́брое у́тро.
  Good night! Споко́йной но́чи!
  Good-bye. До свида́ния!
goods това́ры
government прави́тельство
governmental госуда́рственный
graduate (to) конча́ть/ко́нчить (что)
gram грамм
grandchild внук/вну́чка (m./f.)
grandfather де́душка
grandmother ба́бушка
grant грант
grape(s) виногра́д
gratitude благода́рность (f.)
gray се́рый; седо́й (hair)
great вели́кий
great-grandfather прадеду́шка
great-grandmother прабаба́ушка
Great. Отли́чно.
green зелёный
greens зе́лень (f.)
grief печа́ль (f.)
group гру́ппа
grow (to) расти́/вы-
  grow up (to) расти́/вы-
  grown-up взро́слый
guard охра́нник
guest гость (m.)
guide гид; экскурсово́д
guilty винова́т/-а/-ы
guys ребя́та

H

hair во́лосы
hairbrush щётка
haircut стри́жка
hairdresser парикма́хер
hairdresser's парикма́херский
hairspray лак
hairstyle/hairdo причёска
half полови́на (пол)
  half-hour полчаса́
hall зал
hand рука́
hand crafted куста́рный
handsome краси́вый
handwriting по́черк
hanging (to be) висе́ть (imp.)
happen (to) случа́ться/случи́ться;
  быва́ть (imp.); произойти́ (perf.)
happy сча́стлив/-а-о/-ы; рад/-а/-ы
  Happy Birthday! С днём рожде́ния!
  Happy New Year! С Но́вым го́дом!
hat ша́пка; шля́па

hate (to) ненави́деть (imp.)
have/has (I, you, he, etc.) у
    меня́/вас/него́ (есть)
have (to) име́ть (abstract only) (imp.)
have a good time (to)
    проводи́ть/провести́ вре́мя хорошо́
Have a good trip! Счастли́вого пути́!
Have him (her/them) call me. Пусть
    он (она́) мне позвони́т. (они́ мне
    позвоня́т).
have time to (to) успева́ть/успе́ть
he он
He's (she's/they're) not here. Его́
    (её/их) не́ту. (coll.)
head голова́; коча́н (cabbage, lettuce)
    headache (I have a) У меня́ боли́т
    голова́.
health здоро́вье
    health care здравоохране́ние
    health center поликли́ника
    healthy здоро́в/-а/-о/-ы
hear (to) слы́шать/у–
heart се́рдце; дух (soul); душа́ (spirit)
    heart attack инфа́ркт
    heartfelt серде́чный
height рост
    of medium height сре́днего ро́ста
Hello! Здра́вствуйте! (polite);
    Здра́вствуй! (familiar)
Hello? (on the telephone) Алло́?;
    Слу́шаю (вас). (Yes?)
help по́мощь (noun) (f.)
help (to) помога́ть/помо́чь (кому)
    Help yourself! Ку́шай(те) на здоро́вье!
her её
here здесь
    to here сюда́
    Here is/are ... Вот ...
hero геро́й
heroine герои́ня
Hi! Приве́т!; Здра́вствуй!
high высо́кий
high(er) ве́рхний
highway шоссе́
hike/walk похо́д (noun)
him его́
his его́
history исто́рия
hobby хо́бби
holiday пра́здник
hollow пусто́й
holy/sacred свято́й
home дом
    at home до́ма
homeward домо́й
homework дома́шнее зада́ние
honey мёд
hooligan хулига́н
hope наде́жда (noun)
    hope (that) ... (I) Я наде́юсь, что ...
horoscope гороско́п
horror у́жас
horse ло́шадь (f.)
hospital больни́ца
    hospital gown хала́т

host хозя́ин (many other meanings)
hot горя́чий (food, liquids); тёплый
    (drinks); жа́ркий (weather)
    hot plate электропли́тка
hotel гости́ница
    hotel desk-clerk регистра́тор
    hotel pass ка́рточка го́стя
    hotel reception desk сто́йка
    регистра́ции
hour час
house дом
    housewarming новосе́лье
how как
    How are things? —Fine. Как дела́?
    —Ничего́. (familiar)
    How are you? Как вы поживаете?
    (polite)
    How do I get (somewhere)? Как
    дое́хать до (чего)?
    How do you say _____ in (language)?
    Как по-(language) _____ ?
    How is ... written? Как пи́шется ... ?
    how much/many ско́лько (+ gen.
    plural)
    How old is (he)? Ско́лько (ему́) лет?
    How tall (is someone)? Како́го ро́ста?
however одна́ко
hug one another (to) обнима́ться/
    обня́ться
huge огро́мный
hungry го́лоден/-на́/-но/-ны
hunt (to) охо́титься (for); лови́ть (imp.)
hurry (to) спеши́ть
hurt/ache (to) боли́т, боля́т (imp.)
hysteria исте́рика

I

I я
    I don't care. Мне всё равно́.
    I feel like ... Мне хо́чется (+ infinitive)
    I guess/suppose пожа́луй
    I have no idea. Поня́тия не име́ю.
    I knew it! Я так и знал(а)!
    I see. Поня́тно.
    I wonder ... Интере́сно, ...
    I'd like ... Я хоте́л(а) бы ...
    I'll say! Ещё бы!
icon ико́на
idea иде́я
identical одина́ковый
if е́сли, ли; е́сли бы (unreal)
    If only I can! Лишь бы я мог(ла́)!
    If you please, ... Бу́дьте добры́, ...
ill (to be) боле́ть/за-
illness боле́знь (f.)
imagine (to) представля́ть/предста́вить
    себя́
immediately сра́зу
impersonal пусто́й
impossible (it is) нельзя́
impression впечатле́ние
improve (to) улучша́ть/улу́чшить
in в
    in (a unit of time) че́рез
    in (my) heart в груди́

in addition/besides кро́ме того́; к тому́ же
in advance зара́нее
in any case во вся́ком слу́чае
in case е́сли
in front (of) пе́ред; впереди́; спереди́
in general в о́бщем/вообще́; в при́нципе
in my opinion по-мо́ему
in order to что́бы
in principle в при́нципе
in that case тогда́
In what year? В како́м году́?
incessantly беспреста́нно
include (to) включа́ть/включи́ть
incredible(ly) невероя́тно
inexpensive дешёвый
infection инфе́кция
infected гнило́й
inflammation воспале́ние
information информа́ция; спра́вки (booth)
inside внутри́
indoors внутри́; в ко́мнате
inspiration вдохнове́ние
insurance страхо́вка
intended предназна́ченный
interested in (to be) интересова́ться/за-(чем)
interesting интере́сно
interfere (to) меша́ть/по-(кому)
intermission антра́кт
international междунаро́дный
interpreter перево́дчик/-чица (m./f.)
interview интервью́
interview (to) интервьюи́ровать (imp./perf.)
invite (to) приглаша́ть/пригласи́ть
invitation приглаше́ние
involved with (to be) занима́ться/по-(чем)
it оно́ (он, она́)
It doesn't matter./It's all the same to me. Мне всё равно́.
item/article (for sale) изде́лие
its его́/её

J

jam варе́нье (preserves); джем
January янва́рь
jar ба́нка
jazz джаз
jersey футбо́лка
Jewish евре́йский
joke шу́тка
joke (to) шути́ть
journalist журнали́ст
judge судья́ (m.)
juice сок
July ию́ль
June ию́нь
just про́сто (simply); то́лько что (very recently)
Just a moment. Одну́ мину́точку.
just in case на вся́кий слу́чай

just like так же как и (кто/что)
It's just what we need! Это и́менно то, что на́до!

K

kasha/cooked cereal ка́ша
keep (safe) (to) сохраня́ть/сохрани́ть
key ключ
kill (to) убива́ть/уби́ть
kilogram (kilo) килогра́мм (кило́)
kilometer киломе́тр
kind до́брый (good); сорт (sort)
kiosk кио́ск
kiss (to) целова́ть/по-
kitchen ку́хня
knife нож
know (to) знать
know how (to) уме́ть/с-

L

labor труд
lamp ла́мпа
land земля́
language язы́к
laptop лэпто́п/лапто́п
last после́дний (final) (soft adj.); про́шлый (preceding)
last name фами́лия
last time про́шлый раз
late по́здно
late (to be) опа́здывать/опозда́ть
later по́зже; пото́м (afterwards)
laugh (at) (to) смея́ться/за-(над чем/кем)
laundry пра́чечная (establishment); бельё (clothes)
lawyer адвока́т, юри́ст
lay flat (to) класть/положи́ть
lead (to) руководи́ть (supervise) (imp.); вести́, води́ть (conduct)
learn (to) учи́ть
learn to do smth. (to) учи́ться/на-
leave/vacation о́тпуск (noun)
on leave/vacation в о́тпуске
leave (to) (у-/от-)йти́/ходи́ть; (у-/от-)(ъ)е́хать/езжа́ть
leave behind (to) оставля́ть/оста́вить
lecture ле́кция
left ле́вый (adj.)
on/from the left сле́ва
on/to the left нале́во
lemon лимо́н (noun); лимо́нный (adj.)
less ме́ньше
less often поре́же
Let him (her/them) wait. Пусть он (она́) ждёт. (они́ ждут).
let pass/through (to) пропуска́ть/пропусти́ть
Let's ... Дава́й(те) ...
Let's drink to (friendship)! Дава́й(те) вы́пьем за (дру́жбу)!
Let's go! Пошли́!; Пое́хали! (driving)
letter письмо́; бу́ква (alphabet)
level у́ровень (noun) (f.)

library библиотека
  librarian библиотекарь (m.)
  library card читательский билет
lie/lay (to) лежать (imp.)
  lie down (to) ложиться/лечь
  lie in bed for a while (to) полежать
life жизнь (f.)
light свет (noun); светлый (adj.); лёгкий
  (opp. of heavy)
  light blue голубой
like/as как
  Like so? Вот так?
like (to) нравиться/по-(кому)
likeable симпатичный
line очередь (queue) (f.)
list список
listen to (to) слушать/по-(что/кого)
liter литр
live (to) жить
loaf буханка; батон (long)
lobby вестибюль (f.)
local местный
located (to be) находиться (imp.)
long длинный
  long ago давно
  Long live (someone/thing)! Да
    здравствует (что, кого)!
  long time (for a) давно
  Long time no see! Сколько лет,
    сколько зим!
look at (to) смотреть/по-
look for (to) искать/по-
lose (to) проигрывать/проиграть
  (defeat); терять/по-(misplace)
lotion крем
lovable милый
love любовь (noun) (f.)
  in love влюблённый
love (to) любить; нравиться (like)
loving влюблённый
low(er) нижний
luck счастье; удача
lucky счастливый (person); удачный
  (event)
  You lucked out! Тебе повезло!
lunch обед
  to eat lunch обедать/по-

M

machine машина
made (of) сделан/-а/-о/-ы (чего)
magazine журнал
mail почта
  mail-carrier почтальон
  mailbox почтовый ящик
main/central главный
  Main Post Office Главпочтамт
make (to) делать/с–
  make an appointment (to)
    записываться/записаться
  make an effort (to) стараться/по-
manage (to) руководить (imp.)
  manage to (to) суметь (perf.);
    успевать/успеть (have time to)
  management управление

manager заведующий;
  администратор; менеджер
many много
map карта
March март
market (farmers') рынок
married женат (m.); замужем, замужняя
  (f.)
  marriage брак
  married (to get) жениться/по-(m./f.);
    выйти замуж (за кого) (f.)
masculine мужской
matches спички
May май (month)
maybe может быть
  it may be пожалуй
mayor мэр
me меня
meal еда
mean (to) хотеть сказать (want to say);
  значить (signify) (imp.)
means (noun) вид
measure (to) мерить/по-
meat мясо
medicine лекарство (medication);
  медицина (science)
meet (to) встречаться/встретиться
meeting собрание; встреча
memorize (to) запоминать/запомнить
  memory память (f.)
menu меню
mess беспорядок
meter метр
middle середина (noun); средний (soft
  adj.)
  in the middle (of) посередине
midnight полночь (f.)
mind дух
mineral water минеральная вода
minute минута
mirror зеркало
miss (to) пропускать/пропустить (skip);
  скучать (yearn for)
missing (be) не хватает (чего)
mistake ошибка
mix up (to) перепутывать/перепутать
mix-up путаница
modem факс-модем
Monday понедельник
money деньги
month месяц
  monthly pass проездной
monument памятник
more больше
  more than anything больше всего
morning утро
  in the morning утром
most (of all) больше всего
  the most самый (+ adj.)
mother мать; мама (mom)
mountain гора
mourn (to) грустить
mouth рот
move (to) двигать/двинуть;
  переезжать/переехать (relocate)

movement движе́ние
movie фильм
   movie theater кино́ (киноте́атр)
much мно́го; гора́здо
museum музе́й
music му́зыка
musician музыка́нт
must до́лжен/-на́/-ны́
mustache усы́
mustard горчи́ца
my мой/моя́/моё/мои́
   My God! Бо́же мой!

N

name и́мя (person); назва́ние (thing)
   What's your name? —My name is ...
   Как вас (тебя́) зову́т? —Меня́
   зову́т (кого́).
name (to) звать/по-
   named after и́мени
napkin салфе́тка
narcotics нарко́тики
national национа́льный
   nationality национа́льность (f.)
native родно́й (adj.)
nauseous (I'm) меня́ тошни́т
near бли́зко; во́зле (чего́)
   nearly о́коло (чего́)
necessary (is/are) на́до/ну́жно (кому́);
   ну́жен/-на́/-но́/-ны́ (кому́)
neck ше́я
need на́до/ну́жно (кому́);
   ну́жен/-на́/-но́/-ны́ (кому́)
neighbor сосе́д(ка) (m./f.)
neither ... nor ... ни ... ни ...
nephew племя́нник
never никогда́
nevertheless всё-таки; тем не ме́нее
new но́вый
   Happy New Year! С Но́вым го́дом!
   Christmas (New Year) tree ёлка
   on New Year's Eve под Но́вый год
   What's new? Что но́вого?
news но́вости
   newspaper газе́та
   newsstand кио́ск
next зате́м (then; adv.); сле́дующий
   (following; adj.)
next to ря́дом с (кем/чем); во́зле (чего́)
nice симпати́чный; прия́тный
   Nice to meet you. Очень прия́тно.
niece племя́нница
night ночь (noun) (f.); ночно́й (adj.)
   nightmare кошма́р
nine де́вять
ninth девя́тый
no нет
   No big deal. Ничего́ стра́шного.
   no kind of никако́й
   no one никто́
   No problem. Нет пробле́м.
noise шум
   noisy шу́мный
nonsense ерунда́
noon по́лдень (m.)

normal норма́льно
north се́вер
   northern се́верный
not не
   not at all совсе́м не
   not for long не надо́лго
   not much ма́ло
   not possible/allowed невозмо́жно
   not quite не совсе́м
notebook тетра́дь (f.)
notebook computer компью́тер-блокно́т
nothing ничего́
   It's nothing! Не́ за что!
   Nothing much. Ничего́ осо́бенного.
   Nothing of the sort! Как бы не так!
notice объявле́ние (posted)
   notice (to) замеча́ть/заме́тить
November ноя́брь
now тепе́рь (opp. of before; nowadays);
   сейча́с (right now)
   Now you're talking! Вот тепе́рь вы
   говори́те де́ло!
nowhere нигде́
number № (но́мер); число́
   flight number но́мер ре́йса
nurse медбра́т (m.); медсестра́ (f.)

O

okay ла́дно; норма́льно
occupy (to) снима́ть/снять
   occupied (to be) занима́ть/заня́ть
occur (to) происходи́ть/произойти́;
   быва́ть (frequently) (imp.)
October октя́брь
odor/smell за́пах
of course коне́чно
office кабине́т; о́фис; учрежде́ние
   (place of work)
often ча́сто
oil ма́сло
old ста́рый
   old age ста́рость (f.)
   old man стари́к
older ста́рше
on на
   on foot пешко́м
   on the contrary наоборо́т
   on the subject of о/об; про (кого́, что)
   on the way (people only) по доро́ге
   on time во́время
   On what date? Како́го числа́?
   on (Mondays) по (понеде́льникам)
one оди́н/одна́/одно́; раз (for counting)
   one and a half полтора́
   one more ещё оди́н/-на́/-но́/-ни́
   one's own свой/своя́/своё/свои́
   one-way в оди́н коне́ц
   one and the same оди́н/-на́/-но́/-ни́
   (и тот же)
oneself сам/-а́/-и
onion(s) лук
only то́лько
open (to) открыва́ть/откры́ть
opera о́пера
or и́ли

or else а то
or what? что ли?
orange апельси́н (noun); ора́нжевый (adj.)
order (to) зака́зывать/заказа́ть
organize (to) организова́ть
other (the) друго́й
our/ours наш/-а/-е/-и
outdoors/outside на дворе́, на у́лице
oven духо́вка
over над
over there вон там
overhead вверху́; наверху́
oversleep (to) проспа́ть (perf.)

P

p.m. вечера́
package паке́т
packet па́чка
pain боль (f.)
painful бо́льно
paint (to) рисова́ть/на-
painting жи́вопись (f.) (action); карти́на
(object)
pair па́ра
pair of pants па́ра брюк
palace дворе́ц
pancakes блины́
paper бума́га (material)
parcel посы́лка; свёрток
parents роди́тели
park парк
part часть (f.) (portion); пробо́р (hair)
parting расстава́ние
party вечери́нка (event); па́ртия (political)
pass (to) проходи́ть/пройти́ (by/along);
передава́ть/переда́ть (convey);
пасова́ть (sports)
pass an exam (to) сдать экза́мен
pass/admission про́пуск (noun)
passenger пассажи́р
passport па́спорт
past про́шлый (last); во́зле (чего́) (adv.)
pastry пиро́г; пиро́жное (noun)
patient больно́й (noun); терпели́вый (adj.)
patriotic оте́чественный
patronymic о́тчество
pay (for) (to) плати́ть/за- (за что)
pay attention to (to) обраща́ть/обрати́ть
(внима́ние на кого́/что)
pay-phone телефо́н-автома́т
peace мир
peaceful(ly) споко́йно
peacock павли́н
peasant крестья́нин
people наро́д
pepper пе́рец
performance исполне́ние
perfume духи́
perhaps пожа́луй
period тайм (sports); пери́од (of time);
ме́сячные (monthly)
permanent зави́вка (wave), хи́мия
(coll.); постоя́нный (adj.)
permission разреше́ние
it is permitted мо́жно

person челове́к
personally ли́чно
pessimist пессими́ст
pharmacy апте́ка
pharmacist фармаце́вт
photocopy фотоко́пия
photograph фотогра́фия
photograph (to) снима́ть/снять
pickled/salted солёный
pie пиро́г
piece кусо́к
little piece кусо́чек
pill табле́тка
pink ро́зовый
pipe труба́
place ме́сто
placed располо́жен/-а/-о/-ы
plan план (noun)
plan (to) плани́ровать/за-
plan to (to) собира́ться (imp.)
plate таре́лка
platform платфо́рма
play пье́са
play (to) игра́ть/сыгра́ть в (гто;
game), на (чём; instrument)
play sports (to) занима́ться спо́ртом
pleasant прия́тный
please пожа́луйста
Please give me … Да́йте, пожа́луйста, …
Please repeat. Повтори́те,
пожа́луйста, …
plumber водопрово́дчик
pocket карма́н
poet поэ́т
poem стихотворе́ние
poetry поэ́зия; стихи́
point пункт (fig.)
polite ве́жливый
politics поли́тика
political полити́ческий
politician поли́тик
poll голосова́ние
poor бе́дный
poor(ly) пло́хо
popular популя́рный
porter носи́льщик
portion по́рция
possible возмо́жно
it is possible мо́жно
post office по́чта
postcard откры́тка
poster плака́т
potato карто́шка, карто́фель (m.)
pour (to) налива́ть/нали́ть
power власть (f.)
practice (to) упражня́ться (imp.)
predestined предназна́ченный
prefer (to) предпочита́ть/предпоче́сть
preferably жела́тельно
prepare (to) гото́вить/при-
prescription реце́пт
present пода́рок (noun); настоя́щий (adj.)
present (to) представля́ть/предста́вить
preserve (to) храни́ть/со-
press (to) жать/по-

pretty хоро́шенький
price цена́
   price list прейскура́нт
pride го́рдость (f.)
printer при́нтер
private ча́стный (individual); ли́чный (personal)
probably наве́рно
probe (to) щу́пать/по-
problem пробле́ма
product проду́кт
profession профе́ссия
   What is your profession? Кто вы по профе́ссии?
professional профессиона́л (noun); профессиона́льный (adj.)
program програ́мма; переда́ча (broadcast)
   programmer программи́ст
project прое́кт
promise (to) обеща́ть/по-
provide (to) доставля́ть/доста́вить
pull (to) тяну́ть/по-
   pull out (to) вытя́гивать/вы́тянуть
purple фиоле́товый
purse су́мка
push (to) толка́ть/толкну́ть
put (to) класть/положи́ть (что-куда́) (lying flat); ста́вить/по- (что-куда́) (standing)
   put on (clothes, etc.) (to) надева́ть/наде́ть

Q

quarter (a) че́тверть (f.)
question вопро́с
   questionnaire/form анке́та
quick(ly) бы́стро
quiet(ly) ти́хо

R

radiation радиа́ция
radio ра́дио
rain дождь (m.)
rarely ре́дко
razor бри́тва
read (to) чита́ть/про-
real настоя́щий
really действи́тельно
   Really? Неуже́ли?
reason причи́на
recall (to) вспомина́ть/вспо́мнить
receive (to) получа́ть(ся)/получи́ть(ся)
recently неда́вно
reception приём
recipe реце́пт
recognize (to) узнава́ть/узна́ть
recollect (to) припомина́ть/припо́мнить
recommend (to) рекомендова́ть/по-
   recommendation рекоменда́ция
recover (to) выздора́вливать/вы́здороветь
red кра́сный
referee судья́
refrigerator холоди́льник

region райо́н
registered запи́сан/-на/-ны
   registration регистра́ция
reknowned знамени́тый
relate (to) расска́зывать/рассказа́ть
   relations отноше́ния
relative ро́дственник
relax (to) отдыха́ть/отдохну́ть (rest); расслабля́ть/рассла́бить (part of body)
remedy лече́ние
remember (to) по́мнить (imp.)
remind of (to) напомина́ть/напо́мнить
remove (to) вы́вести
renovate (to) ремонти́ровать/от-
rent квартпла́та (for apartment)
   rent (to) снима́ть/снять; взять в наём
   rent a car (to) взять напрока́т маши́ну
   rent an apartment (to) снима́ть кварти́ру
   rent out (to) сдать в наём
repair (for) на ремо́нт
repeat (to) повторя́ть/повтори́ть
replace (to) заменя́ть/замени́ть (что/кого чем/кем)
reply (to) отвеча́ть/отве́тить
reporter репортёр
represent (to) представля́ть/предста́вить
reproduction репроду́кция (painting)
request (to) проси́ть/по- (что у кого) (smth. of someone)
request (to) проси́ть/по- (кого де́лать) (someone do smth.)
research иссле́дование
reservation зака́з
   reserve (to) зака́зывать/заказа́ть
   reserved зака́зан/-а/-о/-ы
restaurant рестора́н
resume резюме́
retain (to) сохраня́ть/сохрани́ть
retired на пе́нсии
return (to) возвраща́ться/верну́ться
rice рис
right пра́вый; прав/-а́/-ы
   on/from the right спра́ва
   on/to the right напра́во
ring кольцо́; звоно́к (bell)
river река́
road доро́га
role роль (f.)
room ко́мната; но́мер (hotel)
   roommate сосе́д(ка) по ко́мнате (m./f.)
round trip туда́ и обра́тно
rouse (to) возбужда́ть/возбуди́ть
route маршру́т
row ряд
rub (to) втира́ть/втере́ть
ruble рубль (m.)
rule пра́вило
run (to) бе́гать; бежа́ть/по- (irreg.)
Russian Orthodox правосла́вный (noun/adj.)

S

safe безопа́сный (adj.)
saint свято́й

salary зарпла́та
salesperson продаве́ц/-щи́ца (m./f.)
salt соль (f.)
same ра́вный
  same (the) одина́ковый
sandwich бутербро́д
satisfied (with) дово́лен/-ьна/-ьны (чем/кем)
Saturday суббо́та
sausage соси́ска
save (to) эконо́мить/с- (money, time)
  savings account депози́тный счёт
say/tell (to) сказа́ть (кому́)
say accidentally (to) обмо́лвиться (perf.)
schedule расписа́ние
  scheduled showing сеа́нс
schoolchild шко́льник/-ница (m./f.)
sea мо́ре
search (to) иска́ть/по-
season вре́мя го́да
seat/place ме́сто
second секу́нда (noun); второ́й (adj.)
  second class жёсткий ваго́н (trains)
secretary секрета́рь/секрета́рша (m./f.)
see (to) ви́деть/у- (II.)
  see off (to) провожа́ть/проводи́ть
  See you soon! До ско́рого!
  See you! Пока́!
  seeing as how так как
seem (to) каза́ться/по- (кому́)
self себя́; сам/á/и
  self-service самообслу́живание
sell (to) продава́ть/прода́ть
seminar семина́р
send (to) посыла́ть/посла́ть; отправля́ть/отпра́вить
September сентя́брь
serious серьёзный; тяжёлый
service обслу́живание; слу́жба
service station автосе́рвис
service-person слу́жащий/-ая (m./f.)
services услу́ги; слу́жба (religious)
set up (to) устра́ивать/устро́ить
seven семь
  seventh седьмо́й
several не́сколько (чего́)
shake hands (to) жать/по- (I.) ру́ки
shampoo шампу́нь (f.)
shave oneself (to) бри́ться/по-
shawl плато́к
she она́
shelf по́лка
shirt руба́шка
shoes о́бувь (sg.)
shopping (to go) ходи́ть за поку́пками
shore бе́рег
short ма́ленького ро́ста (height); коро́ткий (length)
  short(ly) ко́ротко (adj./adv.)
  short jacket ку́ртка
should до́лжен/-на́/-ны́
shout (to) крича́ть/за-
show (to) пока́зывать/показа́ть (кому́)
shower душ
sick больно́й

side сторона́
  side by side with ря́дом с (кем/чем)
  on/from the side сбо́ку
siege блока́да
sign знак (noun; fig.)
  sign (to) подпи́сывать/подписа́ть
  sign up (to) запи́сываться/записа́ться
silly/stupid глу́пый
silver сере́бряный
similar похо́ж/-а/-и
simple(ly) про́сто
since так как (because); с
  since then с тех пор
sincere серде́чный
sing (to) петь/с- (I.)
  singer певе́ц
  song пе́сня
sister сестра́
sit down (to) сади́ться/сесть (куда́)
situated располо́жен/-а/-о/-ы
situation ситуа́ция; обстано́вка (conditions)
six шесть
  sixth шесто́й
size разме́р
ski (to) ката́ться на лы́жах
  ski resort горнолы́жный куро́рт
skill уме́ние (competence); ло́вкость (f.) (dexterity)
skillful о́пытный
skinny худо́й
skirt ю́бка
sleep (to) спать (II.)
  sleeping car спа́льный ваго́н
slender стро́йный
slippers та́почки
slow(ly) ме́дленно (adj./adv.)
small ма́ленький
  smaller ме́ньше
smell (of) (to) па́хнуть (чем) (imp.)
smile (to) смея́ться/за-
smoke (to) кури́ть
snacks заку́ски
  snack-bar буфе́т
sneakers кроссо́вки
snow снег
so так
  So, … В о́бщем; зна́чит
  so far as наско́лько
  so much сто́лько (чего́)
  so so Так себе́.
  so that что́бы
soap мы́ло
soccer футбо́л
  soccer game футбо́льный матч
socialist социалисти́ческий
sofa дива́н
  sofa-bed дива́н-крова́ть
sold про́дан/-а/-о/-ы
soldier солда́т
solemn торже́ственный
solve (to) реша́ть/реши́ть
some (of them) не́который
  Some do, some don't. Кто как.
  some kind of како́й-то

somehow как-то
someone кто-то
someone's чей-то
something что-то
sometime когда-то
sometimes иногда
somewhere где-то
son сын
soon скоро
sorry виноват/-а/-ы
Sorry! Простите!
   I'm sorry. Мне жаль.
sort сорт
soul душа
sound (to) звучать/про-
soup суп
sour кислый
   sour cream сметана
south юг
   southern южный
souvenir сувенир
Soviet советский
speak (to) говорить/сказать
   speak for a while (to) поговорить
   speaking of кстати (о чём)
special специальный
   specialties фирменные блюда
   (restaurant)
speech речь (f.)
spicy острый
spill (to) проливать/пролить
spirit дух
spoon ложка
sports спорт
spring весна
   in the spring весной
squeeze (to) жать/по- (l.)
stadium стадион
stain пятно
stall/stand киоск
stand (to) становиться/стать
   be standing (to) стоять/по-
start (to) становиться/стать
starve (to) голодать (imp.)
state штат (noun); государственный
   (governmental)
station станция (metro); вокзал (train)
stay (to) останавливаться/остановиться
   (stop); оставаться /остаться (remain)
steal (to) красть/у-
stern строгий
still ещё
stipend стипендия
stomach желудок
stop остановка (noun; transport)
stop (to) останавливать/остановить
   (halt); переставать /перестать (cease)
store магазин
story сказка
street улица
   street map план
strength сила; крепость (f.)
stroll (to) гулять/по-
strong сильный
   strong(ly) сильно

stubborn упрямый
student студент(ка) (m./f.)
   graduate student аспирант(ка) (m./f.)
study (to) заниматься/по- (чем); изучать/
   изучить (in depth)
style стиль (m.)
stylish модный
subject предмет
substitute (to) заменять/заменить (что-
   чем)
subtitled с субтитрами
subtle тонкий
suburb пригород
subway метро
   subway car вагон
success успех
successful (to be) удаваться/удаться
   (кому)
such (a) такой
suffer (to) страдать; терпеть/по-
suit костюм (noun)
   suit (to) подходить/подойти (кому)
suitcase чемодан
summer лето
   in the summer летом
sun солнце
   sunbathe (to) загорать
   sunny солнечный
Sunday воскресенье
supper ужин
supply (to) доставлять/доставить
sure уверен/-а/-ы
surprising удивительный
suspiciously подозрительно
sweater свитер
sweet сладкий (taste); милый (nice)
swelling опухоль (f.)
swim (to) купаться/по-
   swimming pool бассейн
synagogue синагога

T

table стол
   table for one/two/three столик на
   одного/двоих/троих
tablet таблетка
take (to) брать/взять;
   принимать/принять (medicine;
   shower)
   take (away) (to) отвозить/отвезти (by
   vehicle)
   take an exam (to) сдавать экзамен
   take off outer wear (to)
   раздеваться/раздеться
   take off (to) снимать/снять
   take out (to) вывести
   take place (to) происходить/
   произойти
talented талантливый
talk (with) (to) разговаривать (с кем)
   (imp.)
tall высокого роста
tan (to get a) загореть
tape recorder магнитофон
task дело

taste вкус
  tasty вку́сно
  to (someone's) taste во вку́се (кого)
taxi такси́
taxi-stand стоя́нка
tea чай
  teapot ча́йник
teach (to) учи́ть; преподава́ть
  (college/adults) (imp.)
team (sports) кома́нда (sports);
  коллекти́в (group)
tear (to) рвать/вы-
technology те́хника
telephone телефо́н
  on the telephone по телефо́ну
  telephone receiver тру́бка
television телеви́зор
tell about (to)
  расска́зывать/рассказа́ть (кому)
teller касси́р/-ша (m./f.)
temperature температу́ра
ten де́сять
  tenth деся́тый
tender(ly) не́жно
tennis те́ннис
terrible стра́шный
textbook уче́бник
thank (to) благодари́ть/от-
  Thank God! Сла́ва Бо́гу!
  thank you спаси́бо
  thanks to/owing to благодаря́
  (кому/чему)
that кото́рый (can't begin sentence);
  тот/та/то (one)
  that is, … то есть, …
  That's all. Это всё.
  That's good. Ну вот и хорошо́.
  That's right! Соверше́нно ве́рно!
  That's too bad. Жаль.
  that means э́то зна́чит
the thing is that … де́ло в том, что …
theater теа́тр
their/theirs их
then тогда́ (so; at that time); пото́м
  (later); зате́м (next)
there там
  there is есть
  there is no one (to) не́кого
  there is no time (to) не́когда
  there is nothing (to) не́чего
  there is nowhere (to) не́где
  there is nowhere (to) (direction)
    не́куда
  to there туда́
therefore поэ́тому
they они́
thin ху́денький; то́нкий
thing вещь (f.)
think (to) ду́мать; мы́слить (reason)
  I think по-мо́ему
  I think so. Ду́маю, что да.
  I think that's all. Это, пожа́луй, всё.
this/these э́тот/э́та/э́то/э́ти
  this/that/it is э́то
  This is for you. Это вам.

This is _____ speaking. Это
  говори́т _____ .
those (ones) те
thousand ты́сяча
three три
  third тре́тий/тре́тья/тре́тье
  three hundred три́ста
  three (of them) тро́е
throat го́рло
through че́рез
throw up (to) рвать (рвёт, рва́ло
  кого)/вы-
Thursday четве́рг
thus far до сих пор
ticket биле́т
  ticket booklet кни́жечка
  ticket inspector контролёр
  ticket window ка́сса
tidy up (to) убира́ть/убра́ть
tie га́лстук (clothing); ничья́ (sports)
time вре́мя; раз (once, twice, etc.)
  It's time for us to go. Нам пора́ идти́.
  time of year вре́мя го́да
  What time is it? —It's … . Ско́лько
  вре́мени? —Сейча́с ….
tip чаевы́е
tired уста́л/-а/-ы
  tired (to get) устава́ть/уста́ть
  tired of (to be) надое́сть (кому)
to в; на
toast тост
today сего́дня
  What day is today? Како́й сего́дня
  день?
  What's today's date? Како́е сего́дня
  число́?
toilet туале́т; ва́нная
  toilet paper туале́тная бума́га
token тало́н
tomato помидо́р
tomorrow за́втра
tongue язы́к
too та́кже (also); сли́шком (overly)
tooth зуб
  toothbrush щётка
  toothpaste зубна́я па́ста
top (on/from the) све́рху
touch (to) щу́пать/по-
touch on (to) каса́ться/косну́ться
tourist тури́ст/-ка (m./f.)
  tourist office тури́стическое аге́нство
towel полоте́нце
traffic движе́ние
  traffic jam про́бка (coll.)
  traffic light светофо́р
train по́езд
  train station вокза́л
train (oneself) (to) упражня́ться (imp.)
tram трамва́й
transfer переса́дка (noun; transport.)
transfer (to) де́лать переса́дку/
  пересе́сть (transport.)
translate (to) переводи́ть/перевести́
transmission переда́ча
transmit (to) передава́ть/переда́ть

transportation тра́нспорт
travel (to) путеше́ствовать (imp.)
   travel agency туристи́ческое аге́нство
tree де́рево
trim (to) подстрига́ть/подстри́чь
trip пое́здка
trolley тролле́йбус
true ве́рно
   True. Пра́вда.
truth пра́вда
try (to) стара́ться/по-; пыта́ться
   (attempt)
   try on (to) ме́рить/по-
   try (out) (to) попро́бовать
tsar царь (m.)
   tsar's son/heir царе́вич
tsarina цари́ца
tube тру́бка
Tuesday вто́рник
turn о́чередь (noun) (f.)
   turn (to) повора́чивать/поверну́ть
   turn off (to) выключа́ть/вы́ключить
   turn on (to) включа́ть/включи́ть
twelve двена́дцать
twenty два́дцать
   twentieth двадца́тый
   in the 20s в двадца́тых года́х
twilight ве́черний (soft adj.)
two два/две
   two (of them) дво́е
   two-kopeck coin дву́шка (coll.)
type (to) печа́тать (на маши́нке)
typewriter пи́шущая маши́нка
typical типи́чный

U

umbrella зонт
uncle дя́дя
unclear(ly) нея́сно (adj./adv.)
under под
   under repair на ремо́нт
   under the name of … на и́мя …
understand (to) понима́ть/поня́ть
understood поня́тно
undoubtedly должно́ быть
unfortunately к сожале́нию
unfurnished немеблиро́ванный
unhappy несча́стен/-на/-но/-ны
university университе́т
unoccupied свобо́ден/-на/-но/-ны;
   свобо́дный
until до (чего́) (up to); пока́ не (conj.)
   Until then! До встре́чи!
   until then до тех пор (conj.)
unusual необы́чный
upset stomach расстро́йство желу́дка
use (to) употребля́ть/употреби́ть (make
   use of); по́льзоваться (чем) (utilize)
useful поле́зный
usually обы́чно

V

vacation о́тпуск (work); кани́кулы (school)
   on vacation в о́тпуске
various ра́зный

vary (to) изменя́ться/измени́ться
   (intrans.)
vegetables о́вощи
   vegetarian вегетариа́нец/вегетариа́нка
   (noun) (m./f.)
veil фата́
verses стихи́
very о́чень
veteran ветера́н
victory побе́да
view вид
village село́; дере́вня
violence наси́лие
visa ви́за
vision кругозо́р
visit (to) быва́ть/по-; быва́ть в гостя́х
   visiting (to be) быть в гостя́х
voice го́лос
vote го́лос (noun)
   vote (to) голосова́ть/про- (за кого́/
   чего́)
   voting голосова́ние
voyage рейс

W

waist (to the) до по́яса
wait (for) (to) ждать/подожда́ть
   (чего́/кого́)
waiter официа́нт
waitress официа́нтка
wake (to) буди́ть/раз-
   wake up (to) просыпа́ться/просну́ться
walk (to) проходи́ть/пройти́ (along, past)
wall стена́
want (to) хоте́ть/за- (irreg.)
war война́
wares изде́лия
warm тёплый
wash oneself (to) умыва́ться/умы́ться
   wash (one's hair) (to) мыть/вы́-
   (го́лову)
watch часы́
watch (to) смотре́ть/по-
water вода́
watermelon арбу́з
we мы; мы с ва́ми (you and I)
weak сла́бый
wealthy бога́тый
wear (to) носи́ть (imp.)
weather пого́да
   weather forecast прогно́з пого́ды
wedding сва́дьба
Wednesday среда́
week неде́ля
weekend выходны́е дни; уике́нд
weight вес (noun)
weigh (to) ве́сить (have weight);
   взве́шивать/взве́сить (measure)
   What do you weigh? Како́й у вас вес?
Welcome! Добро́ пожа́ловать!; С
   прие́здом! (on arrival from another
   city/country)
well хорошо́ (adv.)
   Well, … Ну, …
   Well, that's it! Вот и всё!

well-built (person) стро́йный
well-dressed наря́дный
west за́пад
western за́падный
what что
    What a (noun)! Вот (что)!
    What a nightmare! Ой, кошма́р!
    What are they made of? Из чего́ они́ сде́ланы?
    What color is it? Како́го цвета́?
    What day is today? Како́й сего́дня день?
    What did I tell you! Я же тебе́ говори́л(а)!
    What is your name? Как вас (тебя́) зову́т?
    What is your profession? Кто вы по профе́ссии?
    What is ____ ? Что тако́е ____ ?
    what kind of како́й
    What time is it? —It's .... Ско́лько вре́мени? —Сейча́с ....
    What's new? Что но́вого?
    What's today's date? Како́е сего́дня число́?
    What's wrong? Что у вас?
    What? Что-что?
    What?! Ну что же!
when когда́
    When (On what date)? Како́го числа́?
where где
    where (to) куда́
    Where are you from? Отку́да вы?
whether ли
which како́й; кото́рый (can't begin sentence)
while пока́
white бе́лый
who кто; кото́рый (can't begin sentence)
whole це́лый
why заче́м (for what purpose); почему́ (for what reason)
wide(ly) широко́ (adj./adv.); широ́кий
wife жена́
win (to) выи́грывать/вы́играть
window окно́
windy ве́треный
wine вино́
winter зима́
    in the winter зимо́й
wipe out (to) уничтожа́ть/уничто́жить
wish (to) жела́ть/по- (чего́-кому)
    wishy-washy ни ры́ба ни мя́со
with с/со (чем/кем)
    with pleasure с удово́льствием
    with sarcasm с сарка́змом

without без (чего́/кого́)
    without accent без акце́нта
    without fail обяза́тельно
witness свиде́тель (noun) (m.)
woman же́нщина
    woman on duty дежу́рная
women's же́нский
wonderful замеча́тельно; прекра́сно; здо́рово
wood де́рево (material)
wool шерсть (f.)
work рабо́та (job); труд (labor); произведе́ние (of art)
work (to) рабо́тать
workshop семина́р
world мир, свет (noun); мирово́й (adj.)
worn стёртый
worry (to) волнова́ть(ся) (imp.)
worse ху́же
worth (to be) сто́ить (imp.)
wrecked разру́шен/-а/-о/-ы
write (to) писа́ть/на-
written напи́сан/-а/-о/-ы
wrong непра́в/-а́/-о/-ы (incorrect/untrue); гре́шно (morally)
    wrong one (the) не (тот/та/то/те)
    What's wrong? Что у вас?

Y

year год
yellow жёлтый
yes да
yesterday вчера́
yet ещё, уже́
you ты/тебя́ (familiar); вы/вас (plural/polite sing.)
    You bet! Ещё бы!
    You have the wrong number. Вы не туда́ попа́ли.
    you see ведь
    You wouldn't happen to know ... ? Вы не зна́ете, ... ?
    You're welcome! Пожа́луйста.; Не́ за что!
young молодо́й
    young man молодо́й челове́к
    young woman де́вушка
younger мла́дше, моло́же
your/yours твой/твоя́/твоё/твои́ (fam.); ваш/-а/-е/-и (pl./polite)
youth мо́лодость; ю́ность (f.)

Z

zip code и́ндекс
zodiac sign знак зодиа́ка
zoo зоопа́рк

INDEX

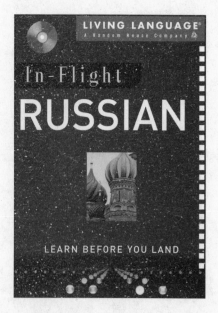